THE SHAAR PRESS

THE JUDAICA IMPRINT
FOR THOUGHTFUL PEOPLE

GATEWAY TO JUDAISM

The What, How, and Why of Jewish Life

Rabbi Mordechai Becher

A SHAAR PRESS PUBLICATION

Photographs by Menachem Adelman

Table of Contents

CALENDAR

PLACE

SELF

ACTION

THOUGHT

GATEWAY
TO JUDAISM

Introduction

The Purpose of This Book

*I*n my position as a lecturer on Judaism to very diverse audiences with many degrees of knowledge, people often ask me for just one book that will give them a picture of the beliefs and practices of Judaism. Until now there was nothing that I felt filled that need. I pray that this book will fulfill the task of providing the reader with an understanding and love for Judaism. The purpose of this book is, first of all, to present a broad view of Jewish belief, practice, law and lifestyle. I have also tried to demonstrate some of the ways in which Judaism is relevant in the 21st century; how it can positively impact our lives and the world; and how we can apply Judaism in our daily lives.

I have tried to paint a picture that will enable someone unfamiliar with Judaism to visualize what a traditional Jewish life looks like. What does an observant Jewish family do on the Sabbath? How do they prepare for Passover? What are their practices regarding charity and communal work? What role does the synagogue play in their life? The introduction of a fictional family, the Levys, will help to answer these questions.

This book is not, however, designed only for the neophyte; I hope that the more knowledgeable reader will also gain new insight into the meaning and philosophy of the commandments and customs that make up Jewish life; to see how the philosophy and beliefs of Judaism are inherent in its laws, practices and customs; and how even the minutiae of Jewish law have incredible significance. Finally, through the footnotes and sources, I have endeavored to provide a basis for further study, to show the origins and sources of Jewish belief, practice and custom, and to make these sources available to teachers who would like to prepare classes on these topics.

Structure

The book is organized around four elements.

1. Each chapter begins with an overview and philosophical introduction to the topic, including the Biblical and Rabbinic sources.
2. Practical laws and instructions are included in each chapter, sometimes incorporated into the body of the text, but most often in a separate section at the end of the chapter.
3. Whenever appropriate, I have also included a segment about the Levy family (see below), to illustrate a realistic view of contemporary Jewish life based on Torah.
4. Almost every idea in the book is referenced in the footnotes and I fervently hope that the reader will study the sources further and arrive at his or her own understanding.

Sources

I have relied extensively on Rabbi Samson Raphael Hirsch's classic guide to Jewish philosophy and law, *Horeb* (written in Germany in the 19th century), both as a frequently quoted source and as a model for my book. Rabbi Hirsch is one of the few writers to have integrated Jewish law and philosophy in a single volume. My revered teacher, Rabbi Moshe Shapiro of Jerusalem, once told me that *Horeb* was the best book to use to teach Jewish law, because it shows the absolute unity of Torah.

The primary sources for this work include: the Torah, Prophets and Writings, the Mishnah, Talmud, Zohar and Midrashim. In addition, I have cited from Maimonides' classic text, the *Mishneh Torah,* Rabbi Yosef Karo's *Code of Jewish Law,* and from the works of the Maharal of Prague on Jewish philosophy and mysticism.

Last, but certainly not least, much of what I have written is based on ideas that I have heard over the years from Rabbi Shapiro. It was he who provided me with the tools of analysis and the methodology for approaching and understanding the depths of our beautiful and holy Torah.

Meet the Levy Family!

Mr. Michael Levy is in his mid 40's; he is a financial analyst who also earned Rabbinic ordination through his many years of Torah study, though he does not practice as a rabbi. Leah Levy, his wife, teaches psychology and English literature part-time, and is a mother full-time (and a half!). Shlomo, their oldest son, is 19 and currently studies at a yeshivah out of state, where he dorms. He is bright, has a great voice and ear for music, and has a passion for learning Torah (and for rock climbing.) Tova, who is 16, is still in high school but is already a talented artist and a budding chef. Eli, who will soon become bar mitzvah is, of course, 12. His hero is Shlomo, who taught him to read the Torah portion for his Bar Mitzvah celebration (and the finer points of rock climbing). He has a great memory, and is a Judo fanatic. Esther, at 3, is much younger than her siblings, and thanks to her brothers and sisters is very articulate and precocious. She is a bit of a terror, though, and to say the least, has a strong personality.

The Levys live in a predominantly Jewish suburb, within walking distance of their synagogue. The children all attend Jewish day schools and Mr. and Mrs. Levy are heavily involved in the Jewish communal life of their city. A few of the Levys' relatives live nearby, but most of their extended family is in Israel or Australia. Shlomo and Tova often talk of moving to Israel, and will probably spend at least a year or two studying there in a post-high school yeshivah and women's seminary, respectively. The family has visited Israel several times to tour and spend time with their relatives.

Any resemblance between the Levy family and any real family is not pure coincidence. The Levys are a conglomerate of many of my friends and family who are observant Jews. I have clearly idealized them a little (O.K., a lot) so that what stands out about them is not their sibling rivalry, daily challenges or petty concerns, but the way Judaism is completely integrated into their lives.

In the following chapters, we invite you to join the Levys and get a sense of what life is like in a typical observant home. The particular style in which different families and communities celebrate the festivals and fulfill the commandments does, of *course, vary widely. What always remains the same, however, is the basic structure and tempo of Jewish life. We hope that the Levy family helps you to become more familiar with this traditional Jewish lifestyle and begin to feel at home.*

Acknowledgments

I feel endless gratitude to the Creator for granting me the privilege and merit to learn and to teach His holy Torah. May this book be a source of honor to Him and the Torah, and may only goodness come from it.

My feelings of gratitude to my teacher, Rabbi Moshe Shapiro of Jerusalem, are overwhelming. I have been blessed with the opportunity to have learned Torah from him for over twenty years and yet know that I have not even scratched the surface of his depths. I pray that God grant him health and length of days to continue inspiring and teaching the Jewish people.

Rabbi Dovid Refson befriended me, gave me my first teaching post, and has continued to guide and encourage me every step of the way in my life. I have been the recipient of his kindness and wisdom for twenty years, including the *shidduch* between ArtScroll and myself — my debt to him is beyond words.

Rabbi Meir Zlotowitz and Rabbi Nosson Sherman of ArtScroll had the vision to begin this project and see it through to publication. In addition to their professionalism, generosity and confidence, they also exhibited patience of Biblical proportions. My sincere gratitude extends to them and their entire staff, especially Art Director Eli Kroen and graphic designer Tzini Fruchthandler. My deep appreciation goes to Ben Gasner of Jerusalem for his cover design, and to Menacham Adelman for photography. Special thanks to my editor at ArtScroll, Charlotte Friedland, for her clarifications, corrections, insights, questions and constructive criticism. Her editing has made this book more readable, consistent and user-friendly. All mistakes are, of course, ultimately my own responsibility.

"I learned much Torah from my teachers, more from my friends and most of all from my students." Thanks to all my students and colleagues at the various institution at which I have taught — Ohr Somayach, Darchei Binah, Ner LeElef and Neve Yerushalayim. To the Gateways Organization, my profound gratitude. Under the leadership of Rabbi Mordechai Suchard, together with his incredible staff, Rabbi Jordan, Dr. Fischer and all the others, Gateways has enabled me to "reach out and teach" thousands of Jews all over North America at our seminars, lectures and classes. I give thanks to God every day for giving me an ideal job, ideal employer and ideal co-workers. Much of the material in this book was developed and refined for my Gateways' lectures.

My dear friends — Rabbi Reuven Lauffer, Rabbi Moshe Newman, Rabbi Menachem Zupnick, Rabbi Yehoshua Karsh, Rabbi Jonathan Rietti and Rabbi David Merkin — all gave me advice, encouragement and shoulders on which to lean throughout the writing of this book. May God grant them strength to continue teaching His Torah.

My parents, Sol and Trudy Becher, were my first and are still my foremost examples of love for God, Torah, the Jewish people and Israel. They will always be my most precious role models of what good Jews and good human beings should be. Their hospitality, kindness and passion for Judaism have always shone brightly. May they live long and healthy lives full of joy and blessing from all their children and grandchildren.

My mother-in-law, Mrs. Reba Borck, always amazes me with her wisdom and has been a source of strength for all of us. My brother-in-law and sister, Dr. Lawrence and Sylvia Cher, and my sister-in-law, Liba Borck, have all helped us in more ways than they realize, with love, support and encouragement. A special thanks to my brother-in-law, Ben Borck, who supplied me with all of my computer needs as well as expert help with all my computer problems. The "parchment and quill" of this book are due to him. May God fulfill all the desires of your hearts for the good and grant you all blessings and joy.

Our dear children — Avraham Shimon, Pinchas Eliyahu, Shmuel Yehoshua, Miriam Devorah, Aryeh Leib and Raphael Zvi — are our pride and joy. Their questions, comments, insights and laughter have all been essential in my teaching and writing. They are a continuous source of happiness (and a blessed font of stories for my lectures). May God bless them with health and happiness, and may they continue to bring joy and pleasure to our family, the Jewish people and to God.

As for my dear wife, soul mate and closest friend, Chavaleah, anything I say will be completely inadequate. Chavy edited, rewrote entire sections and critiqued the book. She was instrumental in this book seeing the light of day, as she is in everything that I do. Chavy has tolerated all our moves, my absences and insane schedule with tireless devotion — fueled by her understanding of the importance of Torah. I can honestly say what Rabbi Akiva said to his students about his wife, "What is mine and what is yours is all hers." May God bless her with health, happiness and strength and may we merit much *nachas* and happiness from our children.

Mordechai Becher

Cheshvan 5766

Two Become One

Dating, the wedding ceremony, marriage and divorce

1 + 1 = 1

The Torah's description of the creation of human beings provides us with a fundamental insight into the nature of human relationships. Genesis 1:27 tells us, "And God created the human in His image, in the image of God He created *him*, male and female he created *them*." This verse appears to contradict itself. First it states that God created one human, but then it refers to two, male and female. The Talmud[1] explains that the original human being was androgynous, a unity of both male and female. Only later was the human divided into male and female halves. We learn from this sequence of events that the ideal, complete human being includes both male and female components, as God originally created Adam.[2]

Knowing that He would later divide the one human being, God created the original state of oneness to enable the two halves to achieve complete unity, to return to their pre-existing condition. For this reason, Jewish law regards a husband and wife as the reunification of a single unit, almost literally, one body,[3] as implied by the verse in Genesis, "Therefore a man shall leave his father and his mother and cling to his wife and they will become one flesh."[4]

Being a Giver

Clearly the Torah considers it crucial that men and women go through this process of reunification. What is the deeper significance of this process? Jewish tradition maintains that the purpose of life is for human beings to develop a relationship with the Creator and through that relationship to experience ultimate joy and happiness. Such a relationship can only be created, however, when the partners are compatible. Compatibility, in turn, requires some basic similarity between the two sides. In order to achieve this similarity, God directed humanity to "walk in His ways."[5] Maimonides explains:

> Just as God is merciful, we should be merciful, just as He is gracious, we should be gracious, just as He is holy, we should be holy... Therefore the prophets described God as slow to anger, abundant in kindness, righteous and upright... to teach us that these are good and upright paths that a person is obligated to follow and to imitate to the best of his ability.[6]

God's creation of the world was an act of perfectly altruistic giving: He created in order to give.[7] If we wish to emulate God, we must also become "givers." It is through a relationship of love between a man and woman that this characteristic can best be developed.

In Jewish thought, being a "giver" is one of the highest ideals to which we aspire. Love is expressed by the desire to *give* to the other person. In contrast, lust, which is based only on the physical aspects of a relationship, originates in the desire to *take* pleasure from the other person.[8] Rabbi Eliyahu Dessler[9] pointed out that when we say "I love fish" we are not really declaring our love for the fish, for immediately afterwards, we will kill, skin, gut, fry and eat it — hardly activities appropriate to a fish-lover. If one really loved the fish, he would throw it back into the river. What people actually mean is "I love myself, and the sensation I experience in eating charred fish is pleasurable to me." Unfortunately, when people say, "I love him/her," all too often they mean that they love themselves, and enjoy the physical, emotional or economic benefits which they derive from their relationship with the other person. Erich Fromm[10] describes "falling in love" in the following terms:

For the man an attractive girl, and for the woman, an attractive man, are the prizes they are after. "Attractive" usually means a nice package of qualities which are popular and sought after on the personality market. I am out for a bargain; the object should be desirable from the standpoint of its social value, and at the same time should want me, considering my overt and hidden assets and potentialities. Two persons thus fall in love when they feel they have found the best object available on the market, considering the limitations of their own exchange values.

This description of the dating and marriage scene is realistic and very tragic. Each person is focusing on what he or she can take from the other; giving is only a means to get, and love really refers to love of self and love of pleasure.

The Jewish view of love stands in stark contrast to this. The two middle letters of the Hebrew word for love, *ahavah*, spell the word *hav*, which means, "give."[11] This expresses the idea that loving is achieved through giving, and that the essence of love is the desire to give, not to take. Remembering that in Jewish thought words with the same numerical value are related in meaning, we note that the numerical value of the word, a*havah*, is thirteen, which is the same as the numerical value of the Hebrew word for one, *echad*. This teaches us that through giving love, two people will become one.[12]

Judaism views marriage as a means of achieving the highest level of spirituality, wholeness and happiness. The Talmud says, "Any man who lives without a wife lives without happiness, without blessing and without goodness."[13] For this reason, the marriage ceremony, which marks the beginning of this new endeavor, is not just a civil contract, but a religious rite that provides an inspiring, spiritual start to the *mitzvah* of marriage.

Oppositional Help

After Adam's creation and prior to the creation of Eve (Hebrew: Chavah), the first woman, the Torah tells us that Adam realized he was incomplete and searched for "an opposing helper."[14] The expression "opposing helper" appears very odd at first glance, since "opposing" and "helping" are contradictory activities. One explanation of this difficulty can be found by considering the human thumb. The human thumb is elongated and can rotate freely, but its main advantage is that it is fully opposable to the other fingers — that is, it grips from the opposite direction of the other fingers. These features make the human hand a perfectly designed instrument for manipulation and grasping. It is precisely because the thumb grips from the direction opposite to the other fingers that the human hand can manipulate objects so well.[15]

In the same way, men and woman have different, and sometimes opposing perspectives on life, and different ways of absorbing, processing and reacting to information — but these opposites can be united.[16] For a complete human view of life and the world, we need help which is opposing and complementary. The combined opposing perspectives of men and women provide the couple with a more complete and true perception of reality than they would achieve alone. A view of life that is solely male or solely female is necessarily incomplete; the only complete way to view life is male and female combined.

Being Fruitful

God gave us the ability to be creators ourselves, and also commanded us to have children and to populate the earth. The very first *mitzvah* to appear in the Torah is the commandment to have children: *God blessed them and God said to them, "Be fruitful and multiply, fill the earth and subdue it ... "*[17]

This verse teaches us that God commanded Adam[18] to have children. According to Jewish law, a couple has not fulfilled this obligation until they have had two children (preferably a son and daughter). Based on the following verse in the book of Isaiah, it is considered appropriate to have more children, if possible:[19]

> *For thus said God, the Creator of the heavens; He is the God, the One Who fashioned the earth, and its Maker; He has established it; He did not create it for emptiness; He fashioned it to be inhabited ...*[20]

The most obvious reason for this commandment is God's desire that we populate the world and create people who can observe the Torah and fulfill the purpose of Creation.[21] Having children also helps the individual achieve his purpose in creation, by improving his character. Nurturing, caring for and educating children encourages the development of sympathy, mercy and sensitivity to others.[22] The Hebrew word for cruel, *achzar*, is composed of the two words, *ach* — "however," and *zar* — "stranger."[23] People allow themselves to behave cruelly primarily because they do not identify with the suffering of another. This is precisely the concept contained in the Hebrew word *achzar*, "but he is [only] a stranger." A child helps us extend compassion outside of ourselves by acting as a bridge between ourselves and others. The child for whom we care so much is similar to the parent, almost part of the parent, yet stands as an independent being, an "other."

Having a child is also one of the ways in which we can emulate the kind of altruistic giving that God demonstrated when He gave us life.[24] Just as God created a world for the purpose of giving, just as He sustains and cares for the world, so a parent creates a child, gives to the child, sustains it and cares for it. The act of creating a child is thus analogous to God's creation of the world.[25]

The Jewish Wedding

The first component of a marriage ceremony is called *Kiddushin,*[26] which means "sanctification" or "dedication." This word precisely reflects our view of what marriage is all about. Sanctification indicates that we are not simply making a social arrangement or contractual agreement; rather, we are creating a spiritual bond and fulfilling a *mitzvah,* a Divine commandment.[27] Dedication indicates that the two individuals will now have an exclusive relationship that involves total dedication of the husband and wife to each other,[28] to the extent of becoming "one soul in two bodies."[29] Let's look at the steps leading to this momentous occasion.

Matchmaker, Matchmaker

Traditionally, the first stage leading to Jewish marriage is the *shidduch,*[30] or matchmaking. Contrary to popular opinion, this does not mean that everything is arranged without taking into account the wishes of the prospective bride and groom. In reality, matches are very often made without the services of a matchmaker; friends and relatives are intermediaries for a prospective couple. Someone who knows a young man and woman and feels that they are compatible may suggest that they date. There is certainly no legal requirement that marriage be arranged, and some Orthodox couples today first meet at social gatherings, a friend's house or the synagogue. The custom of matchmaking has remained strong, however, because Judaism considers choosing a partner for life too important to be done haphazardly. In any case, the final decision rests entirely with the couple.[31] According to Jewish law neither a man nor a woman may be married without consent.[32]

Assume that a *shidduch* has been suggested and the couple (often the couple's parents as well) determines that the prospective match appears reasonable. They arrange to meet. Subsequent dates help them determine if they are indeed compatible. Such meetings provide an opportunity both for casual conversation that enables the couple to become better acquainted and for discussion of issues important to marriage. For these reasons, the dates usually do not involve going to a concert or any place that does not allow for conversation. Personal meetings also allow the couple to determine whether or not the vital ingredient of physical attraction exists between them.[33] If the couple remains interested in each other after the first few dates, they continue meeting until they can determine if marriage is right for them.

One of the features that marks the dating of observant Jews is that physical contact between a man and a woman is prohibited until they are married.[34] According to Jewish law they are also not permitted to be alone together in a closed room or secluded area.[35] These restrictions are made because human nature is such that close contact often leads to sexual intimacy. In addition, they also help ensure that a marriage partner will be chosen for his or her personality, intellect and emotional compatibility and not because of physical desire alone. The absence of any prior physical relationship also enhances the joy of intimacy[36] when the couple marries, and contributes to the stability of the marriage.[37]

L'chaim!

When two people feel that they have found the "right" one, the man proposes marriage (although there is nothing wrong with the woman proposing).[38] Once he has proposed and she has accepted, the families meet and announce the engagement with a small reception, known as a *l'chaim* (presumably because the traditional blessing *"l'chaim"* — *"to life!"*— is usually offered on this occasion).[39] Some families sign a contract, the *tenaim,* meaning engagement conditions that delineate the obligations of each side regarding the wedding expenses, and sets a date for the wedding.[40] This signing is sometimes accompanied by a formal meal to which relatives and close friends are invited.

Because the *tenaim* is a binding contract with strong obligations, many people choose to sign the *tenaim* at the wedding reception an hour or so before the marriage ceremony.[41] During the engagement period the bride and groom get to know each others' families and continue to meet. Even though the couple is engaged, the same restrictions regarding touching[42] and being alone together[43] still apply. In addition, they are forbidden to sleep in the same house.[44] There is a common custom among Ashkenazic Jews for the bride and groom to stop seeing each other one week before the wedding, in order to enhance the joy of meeting at their wedding after a time of separation.[45]

On the Shabbat before the wedding, the groom is given the honor of an *aliyah*: he is called up to recite a blessing during the Torah reading at his synagogue[46] and is showered with nuts and candies thrown by the congregants.[47] This event is called an *aufruf* in Yiddish. After services a special celebration is held, and the rabbi usually makes a short speech.[48]

In Sephardic communities, the groom is called to the Torah on the Shabbat following the wedding. Close friends of the bride usually spend the Shabbat before the wedding with her (called the *Shabbat Kallah,* Shabbat of the Bride) and have an informal party.

It is customary for the bride and groom to fast on the day of the wedding.[49] One reason for this practice is that the bride and groom are considered like new beings when they get married. The day of the wedding therefore becomes a personal Yom Kippur, a Day of Atonement — a time for fasting and repentance, giving them the opportunity to begin their new life with a clean slate.[50]

Mazal Tov! It's a Contract!

During the early stages of the wedding, the first order of business is the completion, signing and witnessing of the *ketubah,* or marriage contract. This contract is required by Rabbinic law[51] and, according to some authorities, dates back to Biblical times.[52] The *ketubah,* which is written in Aramaic, details the husband's obligations to his wife, including food, clothing, dwelling and intimacy. The contract also creates a lien on all his property to pay her a sum of money for support should he divorce her, or predecease her. The document is signed by two witnesses, and has the standing of a legally binding agreement in Jewish law, which in some countries is also enforceable by civil law.[53] The *ketubah* is the wife's possession, and it remains in her care. Because the *ketubah* is the tangible evidence of this momentous occasion in their new life together, it is sometimes decorated or written as an illuminated manuscript. Some couples frame it and display it in their home as a work of art.[54]

An artistic ketubah *with the traditional text. A translation appears on page 32.*

To the Chuppah

While the *ketubah* is being completed and signed, the guests partake of light refreshments, including alcoholic beverages if they wish, for the traditional *l'chaim*.[55] The groom then performs the *bedekin,* or "veiling." Accompanied by his father and future father-in-law, musicians and the male guests, he walks to the room where the bride is receiving her guests. She sits like a queen on a thronelike chair, surrounded by her family and friends. The groom, who has not seen her for a week, covers her face with a veil,[56] just as the Biblical Rebecca covered her face when she first saw her future husband, Isaac.[57] The bride and groom then go to separate rooms where they prepare for the *chuppah.*

The next stage is known as the *chuppah,* or canopy. The *chuppah* is a piece of cloth suspended like a roof over the heads of the bride and groom as a symbolic home for the new couple.[58] When possible, the ceremony is performed under the stars[59] to call to mind the blessings given by God to the patriarch Abraham, that his children shall be as numerous "as the stars of the heavens."[60] Sometimes the ceremony is held outdoors. More often, the *chuppah* is set up under an open skylight inside the wedding hall to comply with this custom. The groom is accompanied by his parents (or his father and father-in-law, depending on custom) to the *chuppah.* He often wears a white robe, known as a *kittel,* indicating that the bride and groom are starting a new life with a clean white slate. They are uniting to become a new entity, without any previous sins. Then the bride, escorted by her parents (or her mother and mother-in-law), walks to the *chuppah.* As the groom and bride respectively walk to the *chuppah* a cantor or friend sings liturgical poems in praise of God and asking for His blessings for the couple. The groom, waiting under the *chuppah*, and the bride, as she approaches, can utilize this holy time to pray for the success of the marriage, for health, children and financial sustenance. In fact, numerous couples take the opportunity of this moment of concentrated sanctity to pray for other matters close to their hearts — for their unmarried friends to find their true partners in life, for the benefit of all Jews in Israel and the Diaspora, and for the health of sick people whom they know or whose names have been submitted to them.

Seven Circles, Seven Blessings

When the bride arrives at the *chuppah* she walks around the groom seven times with her mother and future mother-in-law.[61] This encircling reflects the woman's capacity to create a protective, surrounding light around the household, one that will illuminate it with understanding and love from within and protect it from harm from without. The number seven also corresponds to the seven days of creation, and symbolizes the fact that the bride and groom are about to create their own new world together.[62]

The bride then stands beside the groom, and an honored rabbi or family member recites a blessing over wine, followed by a blessing that praises and thanks God for giving us the laws of sexual morality which preserve the sanctity of family life and the Jewish people. The bride and groom then drink from the wine. The blessings are recited over wine as they are in many other Jewish ceremonies.[63] Wine, as the verse states, "makes man rejoice,"[64] hence it is used at occasions of joy. It may be said also that wine symbolizes the cycle of life. It begins as grape-juice, goes through fermentation, when it is sour and useless, but eventually turns into something much better than the original. In life, we begin as children, experience struggles, but ultimately through these challenges become better people. The full cup of wine also symbolizes the overflowing of God's blessings, which we wish for the couple, as the verse in Psalms states, "My cup runs over."[65]

The groom takes a plain gold ring and places it on the index finger of the bride, then recites in the presence of the two witnesses, "Behold you are sanctified to me with this ring, according to the Law of Moses and Israel."[66] The ring symbolizes the concept of the groom encircling, protecting and providing for his wife. Transferring the ring to the bride fulfills the technical requirement of giving the bride something of value to effect and formalize her change in status from single to married.[67] The shape of the ring, an endless circle, is a way of expressing the hope that the love between these two people should be endless.[68] It also symbolizes the endless love of God — depicted in Jewish thought as the "Groom" of His beloved "Bride," the Jewish people. The *ketubah* is now read aloud, usually by another honoree, after which it is handed to the bride. The bride then gives the *ketubah* to her mother or to a friend for safekeeping for the duration of the wedding, after which it stays in her possession for as long as they are married.

Seven blessings, *Sheva Berachot,* are now recited, either by one rabbi or by several people whom the families have chosen to honor. The one who recites the blessings holds a full cup of wine. They begin by praising God for His creation in general, and for the creation of human beings, and continue with praise for the creation of the human as a "two-part creature," woman and man. The blessings contain prayers that the new couple will rejoice together forever as though they were the original couple, Adam and Eve, before the sin in the Garden of Eden. They conclude with a prayer that Jerusalem be fully rebuilt and restored with the Temple in its midst and the Jewish people within her gates.[69]

If I Forget Thee ...

At this point, the couple sips from the cup of wine, and the groom breaks a glass by stomping on it.[70] This custom dates back to Talmudic times,[71] and is intended to remind us of Jerusalem and Israel even at times of great joy.[72] Just as the Holy Temple in Jerusalem is in a state of destruction, so we break a glass to show that we identify with the Temple, the Land of Israel and the state of exile of the Jewish people. Many also recite the verse, "If I forget thee, O Jerusalem, let my right hand forget its cunning; if I do not raise thee over my own joy, let my tongue cleave to the roof of my mouth."[73] With the breaking of the glass, the band strikes up a lively tune, and everyone wishes the couple "*Mazal tov!*"

Alone at Last

The wedding ceremony completed, the couple is ushered by dancing guests to the door of the *cheder yichud,* "the private room." They are now permitted to be alone with each other in a closed room, an intimacy reserved only for a married couple. According to many Ashkenazic authorities, being alone together in a locked room is a necessary element in legalizing the marriage,[74] therefore their entry into the room must be witnessed by two people, usually the ones who had earlier acted as witnesses to the marriage. The witnesses remain outside the locked room for a few minutes, to ensure that no one disturbs the couple.[75]

Sing, Dance and Juggle

While the bride and groom spend some time with each other in the *yichud* room (there is usually a table for two set with various foods for them, since they have been fasting all day), the guests sit down to a festive meal. The meal is preceded by ritual washing of hands and the blessing over bread. When the couple is ready to make their entrance at the reception, the band begins a lively song and announces their arrival. Everyone joins in dancing around the bride and groom. For reasons of modesty, Jewish law requires that men and women dance separately; usually a *mechitzah* (partition) separates the two groups of dancers.[76] Guests dance in large circles around the "king and queen" because the main focus of the dancing is to entertain and enhance the joy of the newlyweds. It is not unusual to see rabbis, friends and relatives juggling, "eating" fire, doing acrobatics and dancing ecstatically in front of the bride and groom.[77]

Their merrymaking is not solely for the new couple, however. The joy at a Jewish wedding goes beyond the specific individuals, for the marriage is an event that brings a new household into the Jewish nation. Every new couple has the potential to build a home faithful to Jewish heritage and ideals. As such, it is cause for celebration on a deeper level.

The meal ends with the *Birkat Hamazon*, Grace After Meals, and recitation of the *Sheva Berachot*. The seven blessings that were said under the *chuppah* are repeated by several honorees over a cup of wine. The wine is then shared by the bride and groom.

Married Life

The First Week

For a week following the wedding, the bride and groom are invited to festive meals, called *Sheva Berachot*, at the homes of friends and relatives.[78] In addition to close friends and family, people who were not at the wedding are specifically included.[79] Speeches explaining Torah thoughts about marriage are given, and praise is lavished on the bride and groom to further endear them to each other. After each meal, the seven wedding blessings are recited by an honoree as he holds a cup of wine.[80] If the bride and groom come from different locales, the wedding itself is usually held in the city where the bride's parents live.[81] It is common custom for some of the *Sheva Berachot* to be arranged in the city where the groom's parents live. This way, people who were not able to attend the wedding have an opportunity to rejoice with the newlyweds.

The First Year

Jewish law states that a husband should always "honor his wife more than himself and love her as himself. And if he has money he should spend as much as possible for her benefit. He should not demand excessive respect, he should always speak with her politely and he should never act depressed or relate to her with anger."[82]

In the first year of marriage, there is an additional obligation to "rejoice with his bride."

He shall not enter military service or be assigned to any associated duty. He must remain free for his family for one year.[83]

This obligation manifests itself in the directive that he should not travel out of town without her permission,[84] that he should attempt to give her as much joy and pleasure as possible and to fulfill her every wish to the best of his ability.[85] During this first year the bride and groom get to know each other well, become acquainted with each other's likes and dislikes and set the tone for a lifetime of giving to each other.

Intimacy

Judaism views sexuality as holy and pure, something that has the potential of bringing the man and woman to the highest levels of spirituality. Nachmanides, one of our greatest Biblical commentators and Kabbalists, who lived in 13th-century Spain, expressed this idea in the following way:

> Marital relations are holy, pure and clean, when done in the proper manner, at the proper time, and with the proper intentions. Whoever thinks that there is something disgraceful or ugly about these matters is seriously mistaken ... All believers in the Torah believe that God created everything in His great wisdom and that He did not create anything that is disgraceful ... God is pure of spirit and nothing comes from Him that is intrinsically evil, and it was He Who created man and woman in every detail.[86]

A fundamental element of marriage is the reuniting of male and female as one, as discussed above. Sexual intimacy is one of the prime means of achieving this oneness. By giving pleasure to each other, the man and woman truly become one unit.[87] Intimacy must be an expression of love which grows out of the desire to give to one's spouse, not only to take. This is one reason that intimacy is forbidden in situations where the husband has decided to divorce his wife, when either of them is drunk, or if there is coercion.[88] In each of these cases, the intimacy is primarily an act of *taking* pleasure, not of giving. Judaism prohibits intimacy outside of marriage[89] for the same reason. It is only when a man and woman are prepared to publicly, formally and legally commit themselves to each other that their physical relationship will be one of giving, not of taking.[90] The Hebrew word for sexual immorality, *znut*, is related to the word, *zan*, which means "to satiate."[91] The idea is that sexual immorality is generally motivated by a desire for self-gratification; each person thinks only of his or her own satisfaction. In the case of a husband and wife, who love each other and are committed to each other, the main focus is not fulfillment of the self, but the giving of pleasure to the other. The Bible itself obligates the husband to give his wife sexual pleasure, independent of the *mitzvah* of procreation.[92]

Family Purity

Honeymoon Again

The laws of family purity have been observed by the Jewish people for thousands of years, sometimes with incredible self-sacrifice. They have formed the basis of a harmonious married life, have introduced holiness into the physical world, and have taught millions of Jews that the art of self-discipline is a vital key to pleasure and happiness.[93]

The Torah prohibits any physical intimacy between husband and wife for approximately twelve days each month, from the onset of the woman's menstrual period until she has immersed in a *mikveh* (ritual pool)[94] seven days after her period ends.[95] The laws of purity and impurity reflect spiritual realities that are beyond human comprehension.[96] They do, however, confer physical benefits as well.

The Sages of the Talmud[97] discuss some of the effects of the family purity laws in direct, pragmatic terms. Thousands of years ago, they commented on factors in human nature that are only now being confirmed by social scientists. A number of recent studies[98] have found that one of the most common problems experienced by married couples is that of boredom, a lack of novelty in their intimate life. The desire for new and exciting experiences is a major factor in infidelity. The Sages explained that the laws of family purity are designed to provide a solution to this problem. The period of abstinence during and after the wife's menstrual period makes the time that the couple is together again seem like a honeymoon. The joy, newness and desire that existed at the beginning of the marriage are re-experienced every month after the wife has immersed in the *mikveh* and returned to her husband.

The period of separation also creates a situation in which the husband and wife cannot use physical means to communicate. Because they are forced to interact emotionally and intellectually without any physical contact, their relationship is deepened and strengthened. The common complaint of feminists that men treat their wives like "objects" finds no basis in a Jewish marriage where husband and wife interact on multiple levels.

Confusion and Clarity

We can gain some insight into the spiritual significance of the family purity laws if we consider the meaning of the concepts of purity and impurity in the Torah. The Hebrew word for impurity is *tumah,* which is related

*A modern mikveh. A hallmark of every religious
Jewish community, the mikveh is kept clean, warm and inviting.*

*The waiting area of a mikveh
provides a pleasant atmosphere and a comfortable environment.*

to the word *timtum,* confusion.[99] Every time a person has an experience that appears to demonstrate that we are controlled by physical forces, and that we are not essentially spiritually beings, our souls are in a state of confusion[100] and therefore "impure," *tameh.*

Death is the ultimate illusion that a human being is purely physical and lacks moral freedom, because all we see of the corpse is the mortal body, without a hint of the immortal soul.[101] This is why purity is always associated with life and impurity with death. In the case of the family purity laws, it is the loss of potential life (the egg that could have become a new life) indicated by the menstrual cycle that creates a state of impurity. A *mikveh* is always connected to a natural source of water (e.g., rainwater or a spring), which is as close to God's original creation as we can get. Immersion in the *mikveh* symbolically reconnects one to the infinite and reminds us of our essential moral freedom and transcendent spiritual nature. It is an act of rebirth into the natural state of purity and clarity.[102]

Divorce

An Unfortunate Necessity

The Torah recognizes that people make mistakes and may discover too late that they are incompatible or experience conflicts they cannot resolve.[103] Therefore, the possibility of divorce and remarriage was legislated in the Torah.[104] Divorce is a necessity because human beings are fallible, but the Talmud states that "even the altar in the Temple cries when a man divorces his first wife."[105] The commentaries explain that the altar in the Temple in Jerusalem is the point of contact between God and the Jewish people, who are "married" to each other through the Covenant of the Torah. God designed men and women to be united, and their harmony is a metaphor for the unity of God and the Jewish people. When such a union is torn apart by divorce, the altar sheds tears in sympathy.[106]

Just as marriage is created in a specific manner legislated by Biblical and Rabbinic law, so, too, it must be terminated in a manner that conforms to the requirements of Jewish law.[107] A marriage created by *Kiddushin* can only be dissolved by death or divorce.[108] The divorce itself involves writing, signing, witnessing and handing over a divorce document (in Hebrew, *get*) to the wife. The husband must divorce of his own free will,[109] and the wife must accept the divorce willingly.[110] The laws of divorce are extremely complex and carry serious consequences, therefore, the divorce proceed-

A get is written by a scribe with the names of the divorcing couple included. In Jewish law, the couple is married until a get is given and accepted.

ings must always be carried out under the auspices of a Jewish court, a *beit din*.[111] Jewish divorce does not preclude civil divorce; but civil divorce is not sufficient to free a married couple from each other in Jewish law.[112]

Divorce is a painful and stressful process, which can deteriorate quickly into vicious personal attacks. Even under such trying circumstances, the Torah insists that both parties keep in mind that divorce does not exempt either one from their obligations toward each other as human beings. They must continue to treat each other with respect, and not engage in slander or gossip about the other. The obligations of parents toward their children are still operative after divorce, whether or not that parent has custody of the child.[113] Similarly, children in the care of one parent are obligated to honor the other parent as well[114] and also to honor the spouses of their parents.[115]

The Last Word

The legendary warmth, joy and stability of Jewish marriage and family life are well documented.[116] Our success in this area of life originates in the laws and philosophy of the Torah which have formed the basis of Jewish life for thousands of years.[117] In addition to its pragmatic benefits, we have seen that the Jewish marriage is a model for our love relationship with God and serves as a training ground for that relationship.[118] Furthermore, marriage enables us to fulfill our role as partners with God in creation.[119] A couple that approaches marriage with a true understanding of its significance and a desire to emulate the Torah ideal can achieve the promise of the Seven Blessings, "pleasure, delight, love, brotherhood, peace and companionship."[120]

Supplemental Material

The Seven Blessings

From *The Complete ArtScroll Siddur, Ashkenaz*, pages 206 – 207.

1. Blessed are You, Hashem [a name of God], our God, King of the universe, Who has created everything for His glory.

2. Blessed are You, Hashem, our God, King of the universe, Who fashioned Adam.

3. Blessed are You, Hashem, our God, King of the universe, Who fashioned Adam in His image, in the image of His likeness and prepared for him — from himself — a building for eternity. Blessed are You, Hashem, Who fashioned Adam.

4. Bring intense joy and exultation to the barren one through the ingathering of her children amidst her in gladness. Blessed are You, Hashem, Who gladdens Zion through her children.

5. Gladden the beloved companions as You gladdened Your creatures in the Garden of Eden from aforetime. Blessed are You, Hashem, Who gladdens groom and bride.

6. Blessed are You, Hashem, our God, King of the universe, Who created joy and gladness, groom and bride, mirth, glad song, pleasure, delight, love, brotherhood, peace and companionship. Hashem, our God, let there soon be heard in the cities of Judah and the streets of Jerusalem the sound of joy and the sound of gladness, the voice of the groom and the voice of the bride, the sound of the grooms' jubilance from their canopies and of youths from their song-filled feasts. Blessed are You, Who gladdens the groom with bride.

7. Blessed are You, Hashem, our God, King of the universe, Who creates the fruit of the vine.

The Ketubah

Following is a translation of parts of the text
of the standard marriage contract, the Ketubah:

On the ____ day of the week, the ____ day of the month of ____, in the year five thousand seven hundred and ____, since the creation of the world, the era according to that which we are accustomed to reckoning here in the city of ____ how (name of bridegroom) son of (name of bridegroom's father), [of the family (surname)], said to, (name of bride), daughter of (name of bride's father), [of the family (surname)]:

"Be my wife according to the Law of Moses and Israel, and I will cherish, honor, support and maintain you in accordance with the custom of Jewish husbands who cherish, honor, support and maintain their wives in truth. And I herewith make for you this settlement... which belongs to you, according to the Law of Moses and Israel; and I will also give you your food, clothing and necessities,[121] and live with you as husband and wife, according to universal custom." And (name of bride) consented...

And thus said, (name of bridegroom): "The responsibility of this marriage contract... I take upon myself and my heirs after me, so that they shall be paid from the best part of my property and possessions that I have beneath the heavens, which I now possess and or may hereafter acquire. All my property, real and personal, even the cloak on my shoulders, shall be mortgaged to secure the payment of this marriage contract... during my lifetime and after my death, from the present day and forever."[122]

For Further Reading

- *A Hedge of Roses* by Rabbi Norman Lamm (Feldheim, 1987)
- *Doesn't Anyone Blush Anymore?* by Rabbi Manis Friedman (Harper Collins, 1990)
- *Made in Heaven* by Rabbi Aryeh Kaplan (Moznaim, 1983)
- *The Jewish Way in Love and Marriage* by Rabbi Maurice Lamm (Jonathan David, 1991)
- *The Magic Touch: A Jewish Approach to Relationships* by Gila Manolson (Feldheim, 1992)
- *The Sacred Trust: Love, Dating and Marriage — The Jewish View* by Rabbi Pinchas Stolper (OU/NCSY, 1999)
- *Waters of Eden* (about mikveh) by Rabbi Aryeh Kaplan (OU/NCSY, 1993)

NOTES

References to books of the Talmud refer to the Babylonian Talmud unless otherwise noted.

1. *Ketuvot* 8a; *Yevamot* 63a.
2. *Yevamot* 63a.
3. *Berachot* 24a; *Ketuvot* 66a.
4. Genesis 2:24.
5. Deuteronomy 28:9.
6. Maimonides, *Mishneh Torah*, Laws of Character 1:6.
7. Psalms 89:3; Rabbi Moshe Chaim Luzzatto, *The Way of God*, Chaps. 2-4.
8. Rabbi Aryeh Kaplan, *Made in Heaven*, Moznaim Publishing Corporation, NY, 1983, p. 8.
9. 20th-century Jewish ethicist and philosopher. As heard from Rabbi Asher Rubenstein.
10. Erich Fromm, *The Art of Loving*, Harper and Row, NY, 1956, p. 3.
11. In Genesis 30:1 the word *havah* means "give"; See also Proverbs 30:15, *hav, hav* means "give, give."
12. See Rabbi Eliyahu Dessler, *Michtav M'Eliyahu*, vol. I, *Kuntres Hachesed*; Lisa Aiken, *Beyond Bashert: A Guide to Enriching Your Marriage*, Jason Aronson, NY, 1996.
13. *Yevamot* 63a.
14. Genesis 2:20. Some translate *kenegdo* as "parallel" — see Targum Onkelos, ad loc.; *The ArtScroll Stone Edition Chumash* translates this term as "corresponding helper."
15. Michael J. Denton, *Nature's Destiny*, Free Press, NY, 1998, p. 241.
16. Maharal, *Gur Aryeh*, Commentary on Rashi, Genesis 2:20.
17. Genesis 1:28.
18. Only men are obligated; for women, procreation is voluntary. Mishnah *Yevamot* 65b; *Code of Jewish Law*, *Even Haezer* 1:1. One reason for the differing obligations is that since there is tremendous pain and risk in childbirth, the Torah does not deem it appropriate to legally obligate women. Rabbi Meir Simchah, *Meshech Chochmah* on Genesis 9:7.
19. *Yevamot* 61b; Maimonides, *Mishneh Torah*, Laws of Marriage 15:4; *Code of Jewish Law, Even Haezer* 1:5.
20. Isaiah 45:18.
21. *Sefer Hachinuch* Mitzvah 1; Rabbi Menachem Recanati, *Taamei Ha-mitzvot*, Mitzvot Asei, 1.
22. *Sanhedrin* 36b, Rashi ad loc., *"zaken;"* Maimonides, *Mishneh Torah*, Laws of Sanhedrin 2:3, Radvaz ad loc.
23. Rabbi Samson Raphael Hirsch, Commentary on Deuteronomy 32:33.
24. Rav Eliyahu Dessler, *Michtav M'Eliyahu*, vol. I, *Kuntres Hachesed*.
25. *Midrash Tanchuma, Parshat Pekudei* 3; *Otzar Hamidrashim, "olam katan,"* para. 1-2; *Orchot Tzadikim*, Shaar 28, *Yirat Shamayim*.
26. The Talmudic tractate that deals with marriage is called *Kiddushin*.
27. For extensive halachic sources on the Jewish wedding ceremony see Binyamin Adler, *Sefer Hanisuim Kehilchatam*, Hamesorah Publishing, Jerusalem, 1985, vols. I and II.
28. Tosafot, *Kiddushin* 2b, *"d'assar lah."*
29. Rabbi Yishayahu Horowitz, *Shnei Lu-chot Habrit*, Shaar Ha'otiyot, *Emek Berachah* 80.
30. A traditional, professional matchmaker is known as a *shadchan*.
31. *Yoreh Deah* 240:25, Ramah.
32. *Kiddushin* 2a; *Code of Jewish Law, Even Haezer* 42:1. They should, nevertheless, consult with their parents — Rabbi Yehudah Hechasid, *Sefer Chassidim* 562.
33. *Kiddushin* 41a.
34. Maimonides, *Sefer Hamitzvot*, Ne-gative 353; Nachmanides, ad loc.; *Mishneh Torah*, Laws of Prohibited Relationships 21:1; *Code of Jewish Law, Even Haezer* 21:7; *Siftei Cohen* on *Yoreh Deah* 157:10.

35. Mishnah, *Kiddushin* 80b; *Sanhedrin* 21b; *Avodah Zarah* 36b; ibid., Even Haezer 22.

36. Pinchas Stolper, *Jewish Alternatives in Love, Dating and Marriage,* University Press of America, 1984; Gila Manolson, *The Magic Touch,* Har Nof Publications, 1992.

37. Women who cohabited with their future spouse before marriage are 80% more likely to have their marriage dissolve than women who did not cohabit before marriage. Neil Bennett, et al., "Commitment and the Modern Union: Assessing the Link Between Premarital Cohabitation and Subsequent Marital Stability," *American Sociological Review* 53 (1988): 127-138.

38. *Kiddushin* 12b *"Rav mangid"*; Maimonides, *Mishneh Torah,* Laws of Forbidden Relationships 21:14; *Code of Jewish Law, Even Haezer* 26:4.

39. *Tosafot, Nedarim* 27b *"vehilcheta"*; *Turei Zahav, Even Haezer* 50:11-12; *Beit Shmuel,* ad loc. 15.

40. *Nachalat Shivah,* Chaps. 8-9.

41. This practice avoids certain potential legal complications, should the engagement be broken. Binyamin Adler*, Sefer Hanisuim Kehilchatam,* Hamesorah Publishing, Jerusalem, 1985, Chap. 3, para. 184-185.

42. *Be'er Hagolah, Yoreh Deah* 192:7.

43. *Code of Jewish Law, Even Haezer,* 22:2; *Knesset Hagedolah* 66:9:1.

44. Ibid. Ramah 55:1.

45. *Sefer Haminhagim* (Lubavitch) p.79*;* Kaplan*, Made in Heaven,* p.67.

46. *Levush, Magen Avraham, Orach Chaim* 282; *Biur Halachah* 136.

47. *Sefer Taamei Haminhagim,* Inyanei Ishut 940.

48. Rashba, *Mishmeret Habayit* 167; Rabbi Yair Chaim Bachrach, *Responsa Chavot Yair* 70.

49. *Even Haezer,* Ramah 61:1; *Orach Chaim* 573:1.

50. *Yevamot* 63b; *Tashbetz* 465; *Responsa Maharam Mintz* 109.

51. *Ketuvot* 10a; *Chelkat Mechokek, Even Haezer* 66:26; *Beit Shmuel,* ibid., 66:14.

52. *Ketuvot* 10a, 56b, 110b.

53. Irving A. Breitowitz, *Between Civil and Religious Law,* Greenwood Publishing Group, 1993.

54. See p. 32 for translation of the *ketubah.*

55. *Sefer Kol Bo,* Hilchot Birkat Hamazon 25.

56. *Even Haezer,* Ramah, 31:2. Some authorities maintain that this is the legal act of marriage. *Tosafot, Yoma* 13b *"ulechada"*; Ramah, 55:1.

57. Genesis 24:65; Maharil, Hilchot Nissuin.

58. Levush, *Even Haezer* 54:1; Gaon of Vilna, ibid., 55:9; *Aruch Hashulchan, Even Haezer* 55:18.

59. Ramah, ibid. 61:1.

60. Genesis 22:17; 26:4.

61. *Kitzur Shulchan Aruch* 147:5; Sephardim do not have this custom.

62. *Sefer Taamei Haminhagim* 967.

63. Circumcision, *Kiddush* on Shabbat and festivals, Redemption of the First Born, the Passover Seder.

64. Psalms 104:15.

65. Ibid. 23:5.

66. *Sefer Hamanhig,* Hilchot Eirusin; *Tanya Rabati* 89; *Responsa Maharam Mintz* 109.

67. "Kinyan" does not only refer to purchases, but also to formalizing and concluding any contractual arrangement.

68. Kaplan, *Made in Heaven,* Chap. 6.

69. For the text of the wedding service, see *The Complete ArtScroll Siddur, Ashkenaz,* pp. 202-207; see Appendix I for the text of the Seven Blessings.

70. Some break the glass in the middle of the ceremony, some at the end. Adler, ibid.

71. *Berachot* 30b and 31a, *Tosafot* ad loc., *"eisu."*

72. *Code of Jewish Law, Orach Chaim* 560:2, Ramah; ibid. *Even Haezer* 65:3.

73. Psalms 137:5-6.

74. Maimonides, *Mishneh Torah,* Laws of Marriage 10:1; *Code of Jewish Law, Even Haezer* 55:1, *Chelkat Mechokek* 9, *Beit Shmuel* 5; *Bayit Chadash* on Tur, *Even Haezer* 61.

75. Adler, vol. I, pp. 382-383. See footnote 234 ad loc.

76. Rabbi Yisrael Meir Hacohen, *Biur Halachah, Orach Chaim* 339, *"lehakel bakol."*

77. See, for example, Talmud *Ketuvot* 17a.

78. *Code of Jewish Law, Even Haezer* 64:1; Maimonides, *Mishneh Torah,* Laws of Relationships 10:12, Laws of Mourning 5:1; See also Genesis 29:27, commentary of Nachmanides ad loc.

79. *Ketuvot* 7b-8a; ibid. *Even Haezer* 62:7-8.

80. Ibid. 7b; *Code of Jewish Law,* Even Haezer 62.

81. *Beit Shmuel, Even Haezer* 50:20; *Siftei Cohen, Yoreh Deah* 323:43.

82. Maimonides, *Mishneh Torah,* Laws of Relationships 15:19-20.

83. Deuteronomy 24:5.

84. *Sefer Hachinuch* 581-582; *Chochmat Adam* 129:19; *Code of Jewish Law* 149:13.

85. *Aruch Hashulchan, Even Haezer* 64:4; *Sefer Yereim* 190 (228).

86. Nachmanides, *Igeret Hakodesh, Kitvei HaRamban,* vol II, Edited by Rabbi Chaim Dov Chavel, Mossad Harav Kook, Jerusalem, 1985, Chap. II.

87. Nachmanides, ibid.; Rashi, *Sanhedrin* 58a, *"vedavak";* Rabbi Avraham of Sochatchov, Introduction to *Eglei Tal.*

88. *Nedarim* 20b; *Code of Jewish Law, Even Haezer* 25:2-8; 83:1-2.

89. Maimonides, *Mishneh Torah,* Laws of Relationships 1:4.

90. See Edward O. Laumann, et al., *The Social Organization of Sexuality: Sexual Practices in the United States,* University of Chicago Press, Chicago, 1994, p. 364, table 10.5.

91. Heard from my teacher, Rabbi Moshe Shapiro.

92. Exodus 21:10, Rashi ad loc.; *Ketuvot* 47b, 61b, 62b; *Avodah Zarah* 5a; *Code of Jewish Law, Orach Chaim,* 231:1; ibid., *Even Haezer* 76, 154.

93. For more detailed discussions of the laws and philosophy of family purity, see Rabbi Binyomin Forst, *The Laws of Niddah,* and *A Woman's Guide to the Laws of Niddah,* ArtScroll/Mesorah Publications, New York; Rivkah Slonim, *Total Immersion; A Mikvah Anthology,* Jason Aronson, New York, 1997.

94. The *mikveh* is a specially constructed pool specifically used for the act of purification. For a complete explanation of the concept of *mikveh,* see Aryeh Kaplan, *Waters of Eden,* Orthodox Union/NCSY Publications.

95. Leviticus 15:24, 18:19-20, 20:18; Maimonides, *Sefer Hamitzvot,* Negative Commandment 346.

96. Maimonides, *Mishneh Torah,* Laws of Mikveh 11:12.

97. *Niddah* 31b.

98. Kinsey, Pomeroy and Martin, *Sexual Behavior in the Human Male,* Indiana University Press, 1998.

99. *Yoma* 39b; Rabbi Moshe Chaim Luzzatto, *Path of the Just,* Chap. 11.

100. Rabbi Yehudah Halevy, *Kuzari,* Ma'amar 2:60.

101. *Commentary on the Pentateuch,* Leviticus 15:33, Judaica Press, Gateshead, 1982.

102. Aryeh Kaplan, *Waters of Eden,* Orthodox Union/NCSY Publications.

103. Maimonides, *Guide for the Perplexed,* 3:49.

104. Deuteronomy 24:1-3.

105. *Gittin* 90b; *Sanhedrin* 22a.

106. Maharal, *Chidushei Aggadot, Sanhedrin* ibid.

107. Maimonides, *Mishneh Torah,* Laws of Divorce 1:1-2.

108. Mishnah, *Kiddushin* 2a.

109. Ibid.

110. *Responsa of Rabbeinu Asher* 42:1.

111. Maimonides, *Mishneh Torah,* ibid.; *Kiddushin* 6a; *Code of Jewish Law,*

Even Haezer 49:3; Ibid., *Seder Haget,* "*amar hamagiah.*"

112. For contemporary legal issues in divorce, see Irving A. Breitowitz, *Between Civil and Religious Law,* Greenwood Publishing Group, 1993.

113. Maimonides, *Mishneh Torah,* Laws of Marriage 21:17; *Magid Mishneh* ad loc.; *Even Haezer* 82, *Pitchei Teshuvah* 4.

114. This is obvious; the only possible exception to the obligation to honor a parent is when a parent is a deliberate evildoer — and even in that case some authorities say that the child is obligated to honor the parent. *Code of Jewish Law, Yoreh Deah* 240:18.

115. Ibid. 240:21.

116. See Lawrence Kelemen, *Permission to Receive,* Targum/Feldheim, 1996, pp. 127-132; Marshall Sklare, *America's Jews,* Random House, New York, 1971, p. 95.

117. Telushkin and Prager, *Why the Jews?,* Simon and Schuster, New York, 1983, Chap. 4.

118. Maimonides, *Mishneh Torah,* Laws of Repentance 10:3.

119. *Shabbat* 10a, 119b.

120. Appendix I.

121. Based on Exodus 21:10.

122. Version based on *Kitzur Nachalat Shivah,* Chap. 10.

Zero to Thirteen

Birth, naming, circumcision, Pidyon Haben, Bar and Bat Mitzvah

"Fill the Earth"

*G*od blessed His creations with the ability to be creators themselves: human beings are commanded to have children and populate the earth. The commandment to procreate is actually the very first *mitzvah* to appear in the Torah.

> God blessed them and God said to them, "Be fruitful and multiply, fill the land and subdue it ..."
> God blessed Noah and his sons, and He said to them, "Be fruitful and multiply and fill the earth."[1]

These verses refer to an individual's obligation to have children. In the book of Isaiah, the prophet also teaches us that that God desires us to have children in order to "inhabit the land."[2]

Throughout our history the Sages have emphasized the importance of this *mitzvah*, seeing in it the primary means of fulfilling our national purpose, propagating Torah values and transmitting the message of monotheism to the rest of world. The great Italian Kabbalist, Rabbi Menachem Recanati, explains that this *mitzvah* is vital on an individual level as well, because it is a way of actually imitating God, creating human beings in His image:

> *The reason for this mitzvah is to demonstrate that the existence of the world is dependent on the fulfillment of the Torah; that a person should leave descendants who will fulfill the Torah and the mitzvot in his place, and who will acknowledge that there is an omnipotent Creator Who directs the world … He also becomes a partner with God in creation. When he has children he has created the image of God,[3] and when his children are good people he has created the likeness[4] of God.[5]*

At the simplest level, the *Sefer Hachinuch* (the classic encyclopedia of all the *mitzvot* and their rationale) explains that it is this *mitzvah* that enables all other *mitzvot* to be fulfilled. Without human beings there would be no one to freely choose to do God's will.[6]

As each generation makes these choices and progresses in its spiritual development, it transmits these achievements to those who follow and advances the progress of humanity's "spiritual evolution." In the words of Rabbi Samson Raphael Hirsch:

> *Whatever progress you have made in the fear of God, in the love of God, in trust in God, and in filling your life with God, transmit it to the younger generation and perpetuate it in your children and thereby in yourselves… There can be no higher activity than to contribute to the presence on earth of human beings, in order to train them for the perfection of humanity, and there is no greater blessing than to succeed in this endeavor.[7]*

Who Is Commanded?

Interestingly, the Torah only obligates men to have children; for women, this *mitzvah* is voluntary[8] (although many commentaries maintain that a woman is obligated in the directive of the prophets to "inhabit the world."[9]). A number of explanations have been suggested for this exemption. Since childbirth entails great pain as well as a degree of risk (even more so in earlier generations), God did not deem it appropriate to place a legal obligation on women to have children. Consistent with Jewish law's concern for life, the Torah did not want to declare that a woman who did not want to go through this danger and pain was in any way doing something wrong and so it left this as a voluntary act.

It is also possible that a woman has a natural desire to create and nurture and therefore does not have to be commanded to do so. On the other hand, for a man this desire is not built in and he needs the added stimulus of a commandment to have children.

Some point out that since it is the woman who actually bears the child, this is the primary way in which she imitates God as Creator. To obligate her in this matter would therefore undermine the entire objective. Just as God's creation of the world was an act of pure, altruistic giving and goodness on His part, so too, when a woman has a child, it is an act of altruistic giving.[10]

How Many?

Jewish law states that a couple should have at least one son and one daughter — mirroring the original creation of Adam and Eve. Based on the verse in Isaiah however, Rabbinic law states that under general circumstances one should not limit the size of his family.[11]

This imperative to have many children must always be weighed, however, against possible risks to the mother. There is no question that both the mother's physical and mental health is paramount, and therefore Jewish law does allow — and in some cases, requires — family planning.[12] Clearly, each situation has its own unique considerations; family planning should not be undertaken without Rabbinic guidance.

Human life is endowed with sanctity because we are the "image of God." Every life, even that of a fetus, is precious in the eyes of the Torah and therefore, Judaism forbids aborting a fetus[13] and obligates us to try to save the life of an unborn baby[14] with the same urgency that would apply to any other person.[15] The fetus has a soul which is of infinite spiritual value and any interference with it must be approached with an awareness of its identity as a unique, spiritual soul. If, however, the mother's life is threatened by giving birth to or carrying the baby, or if the pregnancy presents a severe threat to the mother's physical or mental health, Jewish law permits,[16] and even requires, an abortion to be performed[17] just as it permits someone to defend his or her life against an attacker by killing the attacker. Since these are questions of life and death, and involve the very definition of where life itself begins, a competent Jewish legal authority must be consulted in every case.

Too Many Jews?

The Jewish people have always been small in number compared to other nations, and therefore, every single Jew is important to the Jewish people.

And you will remain few in number among the nations to which God shall lead you. It is not because you have greater

*numbers than all the other nations that God embraced you and
chose you; for you are among the smallest of all the nations.*[18]

The Talmud states that a minimum number of souls must be present
in the world for the Divine Presence to rest on the Jewish people[19] and
that the Messiah will not come until all souls destined to be born have
arrived in the world.[20] Every child is therefore an incredible blessing, not
just for the parents, but for the entire Jewish people and the entire world.

Happy Birthday!

The birth of a child is an occasion of great joy, but also of great stress.
As we would expect, Judaism has guidelines for dealing with all aspects
of this event. The health of the mother and child are our primary concern
and first priority: prospective parents must make all arrangements, medical and otherwise, to the best of their ability. It is expressly forbidden to
wrap oneself in a cloak of false piety and say, "God will help us." Rather,
we are obligated to act with responsibility and not to rely on miracles.[21]

The husband, wife and all concerned parties should be aware that,
according to Jewish law, a women is considered to be as medically
vulnerable as one who is "dangerously ill" from the onset of labor until
three days after parturition. Even the Sabbath may be "desecrated"[22] for
her needs.[23] The three-day post-partum period applies to every healthy
woman, but if complications arise beyond these three days, her needs
continue to override the Sabbath. This is true even if the mother feels that
she has a specific need unconfirmed by medical opinion.[24]

Mazal Tov! It's a Baby!

The birth of a girl is celebrated with a reception, usually held at
the synagogue, but sometimes at home, on a Sabbath around the time
of her birth. Since the reception is held immediately after services on
Sabbath morning and *Kiddush*[25] is recited then, the reception is known as
a "*Kiddush*." In many Sephardic communities,[26] it is customary to have
an evening celebration called a *Zeved Bat,* "Gift of the Daughter." Special
prayers for the health of the mother and baby and the spiritual growth of
the child are recited at this time.

A baby girl is named in the synagogue (she does not have to be present) when her father is called up to the Torah,[27] usually on the Shabbat following her birth. The following blessing is recited by the *gabbai* (sexton)
or, in some synagogues, the rabbi:

"He Who blessed our forefathers Abraham, Isaac and Jacob — may He bless the woman who has given birth (*mother's Hebrew name*) daughter of (*Hebrew name* of *mother's father*) with her daughter who has been born at an auspicious time, and may her name be called in Israel (*baby's Hebrew name*) daughter of (*baby's father's Hebrew name*) — for her husband, the infant's father, will contribute to charity on their behalf. In reward for this, may they raise her to [the fulfillment of] Torah, marriage and good deeds. Now let us respond: Amen."[28]

A prayer is then recited for the complete recovery of the mother and the health of the child.

In Ashkenazic[29] communities, the celebration of a boy's birth is held on the first Friday night after his birth and is known as a *Shalom Zachor,* "Welcoming the Boy." Its origins date back over 1,500 years, to the Talmudic era.[30] Spiritually, it is a prelude to the circumcision[31] which will be held on the eighth day after his birth, because the child's soul must experience a Shabbat before the circumcision.[32] The gathering also serves to comfort the child's soul upon leaving the purely spiritual world with its unlimited perception of Torah, and entering the physical world of confusion and conflict.[33] The words of Torah and songs of joy and prayer on this night provide reassurance that the spiritual can be found here as well.

The boy is circumcised on the eighth day (health permitting) and is named immediately after the circumcision, just as our Patriarch Abraham received a new name after his circumcision.[34] Usually a rabbi, but sometimes a relative or friend, is honored with reciting the naming prayer. The father whispers the baby's name at the appropriate place in the prayer, and the name is repeated aloud by the person naming him:

"Our God and the God of our forefathers preserve this child for his father and mother, and may his name be called in Israel (*baby's Hebrew name*) son of (*father's Hebrew name*). May his father rejoice in the issue of his loins and may his mother exult in the fruit of her womb, as it is written; 'May your father and mother rejoice and may she who gave birth to you exult'[35]... May this little one (*baby's Hebrew name*) son of (*father's Hebrew name*) become great. Just as he has entered the Covenant so may he enter into the Torah, the marriage canopy and good deeds."[36]

As with a baby girl, a blessing is recited at this point for the complete recovery of the mother and for the health of the baby.

What's in a Name?

From the very beginnings of history, names have held great significance. On the sixth day of Creation, Adam gave names to all the creatures on earth. The Torah implies that due to the highly sensitive spiritual perceptions given to Adam, these names were expressions of the very essence of each being:[37] *"And whatever Adam called each living creature, that remained its name."*[38]

When God made a covenant with Abraham and Sarah and their descendants He changed their names from *Avram* to *Avraham*, and from *Sarai* to *Sarah*. He added the Hebrew letter *"heh,"* a component of the Divine Name, to each of their names, which also changed the meanings to denote "ancestors of many nations."[39] Throughout hundreds of years of slavery and oppression in Egypt, the Jewish people, to their great merit, managed to preserve their national identity.[40] Jewish sources relate that they were able to remain distinct from the Egyptians and avoid assimilation because they did not change their names, their traditional clothing or their language.[41]

Tradition tells us that today one of the last remnants of prophecy we retain is a measure of Divine inspiration when giving a child his/her Hebrew name![42] The Sages maintain that a person's name can have a strong impact on his or her development.[43] They cautioned us, therefore, to choose thoughtfully, and select a name that is associated with righteousness and good.[44] Naming a child after a righteous individual may also serve as an inspiration to emulate his or her ways.

Ashkenazic Jews generally name children after deceased relatives,[45] while most Sephardic Jews name children after living relatives.[46] It is the practice among all groups to name children after righteous people in the Bible and Talmud or with a name associated with the time of year when the child was born. Some examples of seasonal names would be Mordechai or Esther for a child born close to the festival of Purim,[47] Avivah (spring) for a girl born in the spring, and Nachum or Nechamah (comfort) for a child born on or around the mournful Ninth of Av.[48] Sometimes names may also be an expression of prayer, such as, Chaim (life) for a boy, or Bracha (blessing) for a girl.

Due to the pressures of anti-Semitism, government bureaucracy and difficulty of pronunciation, many Jews throughout history have also given their children names in languages other than Hebrew. Sometimes, these names are translations or transliterations of the Hebrew; sometimes they are just similar sounding, though often they bear no relationship at all to the Hebrew name. There is no objection in Jewish law to using someone's non-Hebrew name,[49] and even many great Sages were known by vernacular names.[50] In our multicultural society, however, using one's Hebrew name is considerably more acceptable than it was in the past. Today, many observant Jews use their Hebrew name exclusively.

One's Hebrew name reflects a person's essential, primary identity. At any major life event, such as marriage, or for any religious purpose, such as being called up to the Torah, it is the Hebrew name that is always used.

Circumcision – Engraving an Eternal Covenant

When God made a Covenant to establish a special relationship with Abraham and his descendants, He decreed that a sign of the Covenant should be indelibly marked on the bodies of all Abraham and Sarah's male descendants. Circumcision, *brit milah* or *bris*, is the sign of that Covenant between God and the Jewish people.

> *God spoke to Abraham saying, "...This is My Covenant which you shall keep between Me and you and your descendants after you — every male child among you shall be circumcised."*[51]

Brit milah has tremendous significance, therefore, because it is both a *mitzvah* and a sign of the eternal Covenant between God and the Jewish people.[52] It is the way in which the Jewish people demonstrate their willingness to be joined in partnership with God. So too, a Gentile who converts to Judaism enters into the Covenant through *brit milah*.[53]

The *Sefer Hachinuch*[54] explains that this particular *mitzvah* was designated for the Covenant because "God wanted a permanent sign engraved on the nation that He has chosen, to separate them from other nations in the nature of their physical body, as they are separate from the nations in the nature of their soul..." and He also wanted us to understand that just as the perfection of the body is done by a conscious human action, so too the perfection of the soul is left up to the human's free will.

Other commentaries[55] maintain that circumcision reminds a Jew that he must be in control of his passions and desires, not be controlled by them. The only way for the Jewish people to continue as God's chosen nation, to maintain their allegiance to the Torah through all the vicissitudes of history, is for them to be disciplined masters of self-control. Since sexual urges are among the most powerful of human forces, the sign of Jewish "chosenness" was placed on the reproductive organ. This sign also reminds us to distance ourselves from any type of sexual immorality and to maintain the purity and holiness of the family and marital relations.[56] This is one reason that this sign is only placed on men, who are more inclined to promiscuity and licentiousness than women.

Why the Eighth Day? It's Out of This World!

The Torah specifies that the circumcision must be performed on the eighth day after birth,[57] even if this is a Sabbath.[58] It is not a coincidence that the eighth commandment God gave to humanity was that of circumcision.[59] Numbers are of great consequence in Judaism and they are often used as a code or to hint at certain concepts. When a number forms an integral part of a *mitzvah,* it is certainly not arbitrary. What then is the meaning of the number eight?

The significance of a number can be understood by the way it is used in the Torah, especially the first time that it occurs in the Biblical text. The number 6, which appears first as the six days of Creation, symbolizes the expansion and creation of the physical world. Sabbath, which is the spiritual dimension that forms the focus of the physical world, is the seventh day. The physical world expands to the north, south, east, west, up and down. Six has no center, it has three points on one side and three on the other (*** ***). The seventh day, the Sabbath, is the spiritual center point around which the physical world revolves. It is the Godliness within the world, the point around which the six days of physical creation are arrayed (*** Sabbath ***).[60]

Eight symbolizes going *beyond* the natural world, beyond the seven days of Creation, into the realm of the supernatural.[61] Circumcision is an act which changes and improves on nature, which demonstrates the human ability to go beyond nature into the realm of the supernatural. That is the metaphysical reason why circumcision, the eighth commandment, must always be on the eighth day.

On a pragmatic note, Maimonides, who was a physician in addition to being a great Torah scholar, explained that on the eighth day, but not before, the child is strong enough to be circumcised.[62] In fact, current medical research regarding blood coagulation suggests that the eighth day is the earliest advisable time to perform circumcision.[63]

What Is Circumcision?

Circumcision involves three acts — *chituch* (excision), *priah* (uncovering) and *metzitzah* (drawing out). *Chituch* is the excision of the entire foreskin covering the glans (head of the penis). The foreskin is removed so that the entire glans is visible. *Priah* is peeling back from the glans the thin membrane that usually adheres to it and folding it back so that it remains behind the corona. *Metzitzah* involves extracting blood from the wound, primarily for therapeutic reasons.[64]

Since the act of circumcision is not merely a medical procedure, but the means of joining God's Covenant with Abraham, it must be performed by one who is part of that Covenant, a member of the Jewish people.[65] The person who performs the circumcision is known as a *mohel*. He may be a doctor, but is not necessarily so. Every *mohel*, however, must undergo intense training in order to be certified. An expert *mohel* can be found in most Jewish communities. In places where there is no local *mohel,* one will come to perform the *brit* even if staying over Shabbat is necessary.

The Ceremony:
A Holy Moment ... (Then Back to Mommy!)

The circumcision should be held as soon as possible on the morning of the eighth day, usually right after the morning service.[66] Traditionally, a number of people are honored to play key roles in the ceremony. The child is placed on a special decorated pillow and brought from the mother by another married woman. She hands the baby to her husband, who then gives him to the father. This honored couple is known as the *kvatters* (a Yiddish contraction of the German word for godfather).[67] The father holds the child, recites *Shema Yisrael* and several additional prayers. Someone is then honored to take the child and place him on a chair designated as the Chair of Elijah, the prophet who exhorted the Jewish people to keep the covenant of circumcision. The baby is then placed on the knees of the *sandak,* the person whose privilege it is to hold him during the circumcision. Ideally, the father is supposed to perform the circumcision himself. For most people, this is impossible due to their lack of training and/or nervousness, so at this point the father officially appoints the *mohel* as his agent in this task. The *mohel* then recites a blessing and performs the circumcision:

> *Blessed are You, God, our God, King of the universe, Who has sanctified us with His commandments, and has commanded us regarding circumcision.*[68]

The father immediately continues:

> *Blessed are You, God, our God, King of the universe, Who has sanctified us with His commandments, and has commanded us to bring him into the covenant of Abraham, our forefather.*[69]

All present then respond:

> *Just as he has entered into the covenant, so may he enter into the [study of] Torah, the marriage ceremony, and [the performance of] good deeds.*[70]

After the circumcision, which usually takes only a few moments, the child is held by another honoree while someone else raises a cup of wine and recites several blessings, along with a special prayer for naming the child. The infant is then taken back to his mother by the *kvatters.* The *mohel* usually makes one or two follow-up home visits to check the healing process and change the dressing. In most cases, the baby is healed in about a week.

Redemption of the Firstborn – Pidyon Haben

The final plague that God brought upon the Egyptians prior to the Exodus was the sudden deaths of all first-born Egyptians.[71] Why was this punishment directed specifically against the firstborn? Some scholars[72] explain that the firstborn were generally the leaders of each family, as well as the priests of the Egyptian religion. Since they were the moral and cultural role models and leaders of Egypt, they were most responsible for the evils that were perpetrated against the Jews.

Shortly after describing this plague, the Torah commands the Jewish people to sanctify their own first-born sons.[73] These firstborn were designated to be the antithesis of the Egyptian firstborn, i.e., to lead the Jewish people, and by their example the entire world, toward moral and spiritual excellence. The text goes on to explain that at the moment that God killed the Egyptian firstborn, He acquired the firstborn of the Jews as His own.[74]

Initially, all first-born Jewish males were intended to serve as priests in God's Holy Temple. After the terrible transgression of the Jewish people in worshipping the Golden Calf, however, the first-born sons no longer deserved to fulfill this role. Only the tribe of Levi, who had not participated in this sin, was worthy to serve in the Sanctuary. (The Sanctuary, or *Mishkan*, was the house of worship in the desert following the Exodus and in the early years of the Hebrews' settlement in the Land of Israel. Later, the Holy Temple in Jerusalem served this purpose.) The Levites who descended from Aaron, brother of Moses, became the priests, the *Kohanim* of the Jewish people. From that time on, it became an obligation to carry out an exchange, called *Pidyon Haben*, in which the first-born is, so to speak, redeemed from his obligation to serve as a priest and leader when his parents give the *Kohen* five silver coins.[75]

It is a *mitzvah* for every Jewish male (who is not a *Kohen* or a Levite) to redeem his first-born son, born to a Jewish mother (who is not the daughter of a *Kohen* or Levite), when the child is thirty-one days old.[76] The redemption is performed by the father giving to the *Kohen* 105 grams, or 3.7 ounces, of silver or its equivalent in five coins that have the same value.[77] At current prices, that is worth about $18 - $20 US each. (If a father did not redeem his first-born son, the grown son is obligated to redeem himself from a *Kohen*.[78])

In his commentary on the Torah,[79] Rabbi Samson Raphael Hirsch explains that the *Pidyon Haben* frees the firstborn from his position as a priest in the Sanctuary in order for him to assume the duties of moral leadership in his family and in society.

The Pidyon Haben Ceremony:
Life on a Silver Platter

The *Kohen* is presented with the child, who has been placed on a large silver tray to enhance and honor the *mitzvah*. In order to give the maximum number of people an opportunity to participate in some way in this *mitzvah*, it is customary to place small packages of sugar and garlic around the child. These items can be taken home and used to flavor foods, thereby giving many people a "taste" of the *mitzvah*.[80] It is also customary to adorn the tray with jewelry to beautify the *mitzvah*. Immediately before giving the *Kohen* the silver coins, the father recites two blessings:

> *Blessed are You, God, Our God, King of the universe, Who has sanctified us with His commandments and has commanded us regarding the "Redemption of the Son."*
> *Blessed are You, God, Our God, King of the universe, Who has kept us alive, sustained us, and brought us to this season.*[81]

As with many *mitzvot*, the fulfillment of *Pidyon Haben* is celebrated with a festive meal of bread, meat and wine, during which traditional songs are sung and inspirational words of Torah are shared.[82]

The First Haircut:
A Snip in Time

The custom of letting a little boy's hair grow until he is 3 years old originated with the early Kabbalists in Israel and was popularized by the Chassidic movement in the 18th century. The custom went out of favor in the American Jewish community for several decades, but has now become quite widespread once again.

By the age of three, it is presumed that the child understands enough to begin learning about the commandments[83] and it is customary to begin a more "formal" level of education about the *mitzvot*. He usually begins wearing a *yarmulke* and *tzitzit* (see Chapter 18) and starts to learn the letters of the Hebrew alphabet. It became customary to give a boy his first haircut at this time as a vivid way of teaching him in the commandment of "*payot*"(sideburns)[84] — the prohibition against completely removing the hair on the sides of the head. This first haircut is known as "*Upsherin*" from the Yiddish *upfsherin*, which means "cutting off."

Some commentaries suggest that this custom is based on the commandment of *orlah*:[85] The Torah prohibits the use of all fruits that grow during the first three years after a tree is planted. The Torah is referred to as the Tree of Life.[86] Just as the fruits of a tree cannot be enjoyed in its first three years, so too, the Torah is not really accessible to a child until age three, due to his intellectual limitations. By the time he is 3, the child has developed sufficiently for his parents to start teaching him the Torah and for him to begin performing some of the commandments. He finally gets to taste the sweet fruit of the "Tree of Life."

Some families hold a small celebration on the occasion of this first haircut, to express thanks to God for the opportunity to transmit the Torah to the next generation. It also serves to teach the young child the importance of *mitzvot* and demonstrates how precious the *mitzvot* are to his family. It is customary, if possible, to honor a Torah scholar with snipping the first bit of hair. Some people even weigh the cut hair and give the equivalent weight in gold or silver to charity.[87]

Bat Mitzvah and Bar Mitzvah: Is the Party Over, or Just Beginning?

The greatest milestone in the life of a young boy or girl is becoming a *bar/bat mitzvah*, reaching adulthood. According to Jewish law, a girl becomes an adult at 12 years and a day, when she enters her thirteenth year, and a boy at 13 years and a day, when he enters his fourteenth year.[88] The literal translation of *bar* (masculine) and *bat* (feminine) *mitzvah* conveys the real significance of becoming a Jewish adult. The term means one who is obligated to perform the commandments.[89]

Up to this point, the parents are obligated to educate their child in moral behavior and observance of the commandments. It is the parents who are responsible for their child's behavior.[90] Once the child reaches age twelve, for a girl, and thirteen, for a boy, Jewish law considers them adults and the responsibility becomes their own.[91] They may now enter into legal contracts, incur legal obligations and are obligated to observe all commandments applicable to them. (Of course, the education of the child in Jewish values continues to rest with the parents until the child is an independent adult.)

The Metaphysical Side – Welcoming the Soul

Jewish tradition describes different stages in the development of the soul-body relationship. The soul first descends into the world when the child is still a fetus in its mother's womb. At this stage, the fetus has a completely pure soul without any desire for evil at all. According to tradition, an angel teaches it the entire Torah during this time. One understanding of this angelic tutorial is as a metaphor for the untainted, pure perception of the truth that the soul has before entering this world. Therefore the Torah is actually inherent in the Jewish soul and is its natural status quo.[92] The child must, however, be born into this world of concealment and illusion in order to achieve moral success through its own free will and its own struggle. At birth, the "evil inclination" enters a person, i.e., he or she loses that incredible clarity that they possessed before entering this world. The soul's desires are overshadowed by the physicality of the body and its yearning for spiritual fulfillment is muted by ego, selfishness and materialism. Childhood is a time when the physical world and all its overwhelming desires rule over the human being, and the soul and its aspirations are largely dormant. It is for this reason that a child is not held legally responsible for his/her actions.[93]

Toward the end of childhood — during a girl's twelfth or a boy's thirteenth year — the soul begins to awaken and manifests itself more overtly.[94] When the child reaches adulthood, the soul has reached its full level of activity and therefore this person now has complete free will. He or she is able to choose between good and evil, the spiritual and the material, between egotism and humility, to engage in a full range of moral decisions. Since they now have both a "good inclination" and an "evil inclination" and the ability to choose between the two, they are fully accountable for their actions.[95]

Is This Something to Celebrate?

In the Western world, reaching legal adulthood usually means that one now has certain rights that he or she did not have before. The "new" adult now has the right to drive, to vote, to buy cigarettes and alcohol, to get a credit card and so on. It is a time to enjoy doing many things that were previously not allowed, a celebration of rights and the loosening of restrictions. This view is in stark contrast to the significance of reaching *bar/bat mitzvah.* We celebrate the fact that the child has matured sufficiently to become obligated in the *mitzvot,* to enter a community and join the historical chain that began with Abraham and Sarah.

The occasion of becoming obligated in the commandments is a time of joy and happiness because we understand that the *mitzvot* are not only obligations but also gifts from God, opportunities to become better people. Just as we celebrate the festival of Shavuot when God gave us the Torah on Mt. Sinai — transforming a group of ex-slaves into the Chosen People — so too we celebrate reaching the age of *mitzvot* as our own personal encounter at Sinai.[96] Furthermore, now that the person is obligated in the commandments, he or she can now actually earn greater reward because the *mitzvah* is done through a free-will decision.[97]

The Bar Mitzvah celebration is traditionally celebrated with a festive meal[98] for family, friends, rabbis and teachers.[99] Ideally, this celebration should be held on the actual day that the child becomes a *bar mitzvah*.[100] Speeches on Torah subjects are traditional at the meal. Torah thoughts are expressed to inspire the *bar mitzvah* in his new stage in life.[101] Many communities hold a similar celebration for a *bat mitzvah*. In some circles, a *Kiddush* (a celebratory reception) is held at the synagogue on the Shabbat closest to a girl's *bat mitzvah* birthday in lieu of a larger public reception.

There is clearly no obligation to have a reception worthy of a coronation, to rent a luxury hotel for the weekend or to pay for a Cordon Bleu meal for 800 of your closest friends, complete with a symphony orchestra and the Cirque du Soleil. The excesses of the modern Bar/Bat Mitzvah celebration are a departure from the ancient customs —and they actually send a message to the boy or girl that is the antithesis of this holy occasion. Extravagant spending, silly speeches, embarrassing childhood photographs, Hollywood-themed events (and worse) are not likely to inspire the *bar/bat mitzvah* to spiritual and moral growth. Regarding this problem, Rabbi Moshe Feinstein, the greatest 20th-century halachic authority, said:

> *If I had the power, I would abolish the entire Bar Mitzvah ceremony that is the custom in this country [the United States]. For as it is known, it has not brought even one person closer to the Torah and the mitzvot, let alone the bar mitzvah boy, not even for a short time. On the contrary, in many places it has led to transgression of the Torah ...*[102]

Role Call

One of the most obvious consequences of a boy reaching the age of *bar mitzvah* is that he participates in the synagogue service as an adult. He may now be counted as part of a *minyan* and may also be called up to the Torah and read it for the congregation.[103] To mark this change in status, it is customary for the boy to be called up to the Torah at the earliest possible opportunity. If he becomes a *bar mitzvah* on a day when there is Torah reading (Monday, Thursday, Shabbat and special occasions) he is called up that day. If there is no Torah reading on that day, he is called up on the next occasion at which the Torah is read.[104] In many communities, it is the common practice for a boy to read the portion of the week on the Shabbat immediately following or coinciding with his *bar mitzvah* day. In other communities, the boy is called up to the Torah, reads only the last section of the weekly portion, the *Maftir*, and then reads the *Haftarah,* the section of the Prophets that is read after the last section of the Torah reading.[105] The idea behind these customs is to impress upon the *bar mitzvah* boy the significance of this day and of the new responsibilities which rest upon him.

The blessings that the boy recites before and after the Torah reading are the same ones recited every time a person is called up to the Torah. On this day, however, they bear special significance for him.

> *Blessed are You, God, our God, King of the universe, Who selected us from all the peoples and gave us His Torah. Blessed are You, God, Giver of the Torah.*
>
> *Blessed are You, God, our God, King of the universe, Who gave us the Torah of truth and implanted eternal life within us. Blessed are You, God, Giver of the Torah.*[106]

After the boy recites the second blessing, his father continues with a most unusual blessing: "Blessed is the One Who has freed me from the punishment for this boy."[107] Rabbi Samson Raphael Hirsch explains the significance of these practices.

> *In the public community… of which he [the bar mitzvah boy] has now become a member… he makes a declaration over the Torah, to the fulfillment of which his life is from now on dedicated. For the first time, he declares the comprehensive resolve concerning the Torah in its presence: that he dedicates himself to the service of Him Who has chosen Israel for a special task in life, and has given them His Torah for its fulfillment. He promises to be loyal in the service of Him Who has given us the Torah of truth, thereby planting eternal life in our midst. On the same day, the father also declares his resolve to fulfill the task set him by this new relationship with his son … From this day, it is the son who now independently bears the blame, as well as the merit, for his own life.*[108]

Jewish Wrap

Parents train their children to perform *mitzvot* long before they are obligated to do so. They encourage them to anticipate adulthood by accepting certain responsibilities before their Bar/Bat Mitzvah. The *mitzvah* of *tefillin*, however, is approached very differently. Wearing *tefillin* requires physical cleanliness, purity of thought and the ability to focus on the *tefillin* as long as they are being worn. Because of the sanctity of *tefillin* and the maturity necessary to properly fulfill the obligations upon one who wears them, a boy does not begin wearing *tefillin* until shortly before his *bar mitzvah* day. In some communities, he begins practicing putting them on two or three months before the *bar mitzvah* day. Most commonly, the boy begins one month before, while in other communities he first puts on *tefillin* on the day he becomes a true *bar mitzvah*.[109] If the boy begins wearing *tefillin* before his *bar mitzvah* day, it is customary to arrange a small festive breakfast at the synagogue or at his school on the morning that he first puts on *tefillin*.

It's Eli Levy's Bar Mitzvah Day!

Eli Levy started preparing for his Bar Mitzvah from the day he was born. His parents, family, teachers, rabbis and friends provided a community that warmly nurtured his gradual progress toward increasing study of Torah and observance of its commandments. In the Levy family, saying a blessing before eating, praying every day, studying Torah, giving charity and doing acts of kindness are as normal as apple pie and baseball (which they also enjoy regularly). Eli's preparation for the actual day he would become a bar mitzvah started about two years earlier.

When Eli turned 11, he decided that he would like to learn a specific tractate of the Talmud[110] and complete it in time for his Bar Mitzvah celebration. This was not unusual at his school; in fact, many of the boys in his class were engaged in extracurricular study in order to complete a tractate, or in some cases the entire Mishnah,[111] in time for their Bar Mitzvah. The completion of a tractate or section of the Talmud is an occasion for a celebration in itself. It is called a siyum. At a siyum, certain prayers are said and a seudat mitzvah, festive meal, is eaten. Of course, the Bar Mitzvah meal in itself is a seudat mitzvah, but Eli and his parents felt that it would be greatly enhanced by the completion of a Torah-learning project.[112] Eli also intends to base his drashah [Torah speech] on something that he studied in the tractate. Mr. Levy set aside an hour, two or three times a week, as well as some time on Shabbat, to study with Eli. He will also help Eli prepare his drashah as the day of the Bar Mitzvah approaches.

In the Levy family, it has always been customary for the boys to read the Torah portion, the parshah, in the synagogue. Shlomo, Eli's older brother, is an expert ba'al koreh, Torah reader, so he began teaching Eli how to read the Torah about a year before the Bar Mitzvah. This is not so simple, even for someone like Eli, whose Hebrew is excellent.

The Torah is read from a scroll that has no punctuation and no vowel signs. (In Hebrew, the vowels are separate characters distinct from the consonant letters, and are necessary to know how to pronounce a word.) In addition, the ba'al koreh must sing the Torah portion using the traditional cantillation, with each sentence and phrase having its own unique combination of musical modulations. In essence, the bar mitzvah boy has to know his entire portion, sometimes up to 150 verses, virtually by heart, with precise pronunciation and chant. There is also the discomforting fact that the congregation will correct the ba'al koreh if he makes a mistake, since no inaccuracy is allowed or overlooked when reading the Torah.

Shlomo is a patient teacher; nevertheless Eli feels the pressure as the time of his Bar Mitzvah approaches. He has reviewed his parshah so often that his sisters, Tova and Esther, know parts of it as well as he does. Mr. and Mrs. Levy offered Eli the option of not reading the Torah portion, but a combination of pride, stubbornness and a desire to have the skill of a ba'al koreh made Eli decide to persevere.

The Levys are planning a Kiddush (festive reception) at the synagogue after prayers on Shabbat so the entire congregation can participate in the celebration. Eli's thirteenth birthday (on the Jewish calendar) is actually on a Thursday, so he will read a small part of his Torah portion and be called up that morning. The celebratory meal is planned for the night before his birthday (which in the Jewish calendar is already the day of his Bar Mitzvah) and will take place at the synagogue's reception hall. The Levys' immediate and extended family (living within a reasonable distance) number about 75. With Eli's class of 20, close family, friends, rabbis and teachers, there will be about 150 people at the Bar Mitzvah. A tasty, but not elaborate, three-course meal is planned. A local yeshivah student will provide lively entertainment playing the keyboard; and short speeches will be given by Eli, Mr. Levy, the rabbi of the synagogue and Eli's grandfather.

As the date approaches, Eli goes with his mother to buy a new suit, shirt and tie for his Bar Mitzvah. His father orders tefillin from a sofer, a scribe that he knows in Jerusalem, who has supplied the Levy family with all their tefillin. Eli's sister Tova, who is artistic and computer savvy, prints up invitations on postcards and addresses them using the database of contacts from her Bat Mitzvah and Shlomo's Bar Mitzvah.

The Monday before his Bar Mitzvah, Eli's grandparents fly in from Australia and his grandfather fine-tunes Eli's Torah reading (which by now Eli knows as well as his phone number). Mrs. Levy has been baking delicacies for the Kiddush for the past month: the freezer is full and the neighbors are storing much of the food for the

Shabbat meals. Quite a few relatives are coming for Shabbat and the Levys have arranged places for all of them to stay in the community. They will be having 35 relatives for all the Shabbat meals — a bit of a squeeze, but a lot of fun — especially for all the cousins who rarely see each other.

On Wednesday night the whole family goes to the reception hall early to make sure that everything is ready. A table of cakes and drinks has been set up for the early arrivals. The meal starts, accompanied by music on the keyboard. Between courses, the boys from Eli's class get up and start dancing in a circle and singing to the lively music. Many of the adults join the dancing as well, with the rabbi, Mr. Levy, the grandfathers and Eli's teachers all taking turns to dance with Eli in the middle of the circle of dancers.

After the main course is served, Eli gets up to give his speech. About one minute into the speech, the boys in his class start singing and interrupting him. They do this a few times, but Eli insists on carrying on with his well-prepared drashah and the siyum. The custom of singing and interrupting the bar mitzvah boy's speech actually gives an opportunity to a boy, who really does not want to continue, to stop without embarrassment.[113] The evening finishes with a few more speeches, more dancing and singing, and taking pictures to remember the occasion. Most of the presents Eli receives are Jewish books, and he is thrilled to receive them. Generally a child begins to build his or her own library of Torah works at bar/bat mitzvah age.

Thursday morning arrives, and Eli and his family go to the synagogue for the 7 a.m. morning service. Eli reads the Torah beautifully and is called up to the Torah to say the blessings. When his father finishes his blessing, everyone in the synagogue sings and shouts "Mazal Tov!" After the service, Mr. Levy puts out some liquor, pastries and orange juice, the traditional midweek celebration breakfast at their synagogue.

On Friday, the Levys put up extra tables in the dining room to accommodate all the relatives staying in the neighborhood and eating with them. The whole family pitches in to prepare the meals and set the table. The children go by bike to deliver small gifts to each of the families hosting someone for Shabbat. On Shabbat itself, everyone joins in the singing at the meals and children and adults take turns to explain a brief idea about the parshah. Shabbat morning services begin at 8:30 a.m., and Eli has some hot tea with honey, at the insistence of his grandfather, before he goes to the synagogue.

The reading of the Torah begins at about 9:30. The shul is packed with relatives and friends. Eli begins his reading with a hint of nervousness in his voice, but as he continues he becomes more confident, chanting louder and faster. Shlomo stands near him on the bimah (the platform from which the Torah is read) to encourage, correct and help him if necessary. After he finishes, everyone sings and people crowd around Eli and his parents, wishing them "Mazal Tov, Mazal Tov!"

Eli's main emotion now is relief that he performed well and that the public "show" is over. He knows however, that becoming a bar mitzvah is actually the beginning of a new era for him. He understands that he is now responsible for his own actions and has joined the Jewish people as a full participant in its national goals and purpose. It's a great day for him and for all of his fellow Jews!

NOTES

References to books of the Talmud refer to the Babylonian Talmud unless otherwise noted.

For Further Reading

▶ *Bris Milah* by Rabbi Paysach J. Krohn (ArtScroll/Mesorah, 1986)

▶ *Positive Parenting: Developing Your Child's Potential* by Rabbi Abraham J. Twerski, M.D. and Ursula Schwartz, Ph.D. (ArtScroll/Mesorah, 1999)

▶ *The Bat Mitzvah Treasury* by Rabbi Yonah Weinrib (Judaica Illuminations/Mesorah, 2004)

▶ *To Kindle a Soul* by Rabbi Lawrence Keleman (Targum/Feldheim, 2001)

▶ *To Raise a Jewish Child* by Haim Halevy Donin (Basic Books, 1991)

NOTES

References to books of the Talmud refer to the Babylonian Talmud unless otherwise noted.

1. Genesis 1:28; 9:1.
2. Isaiah 45:18.
3. Genesis 1:27.
4. Ibid. 5:1.
5. Rabbi Menachem Recanati, *Sefer Taamei Hamitzvot*, Mitzvah 1.
6. Rabbi Aaron Halevi of Barcelona, *Sefer Hachinuch*, Mitzvah 1.
7. Rabbi Samson Raphael Hirsch, *Horeb*, Section V, Mitzvoth, Chap. 80, para. 523.
8. *Yevamot* 65b; *Code of Jewish Law, Even Haezer* 1:1.
9. *Beit Shmuel, Even Haezer* 1:2; Rabbeinu Nissim, Responsa 32.
10. First reason is from Rabbi Meir Simchah of Dvinsk, *Meshech Chochmah, Parshat Bereshit*. Latter reason as heard from my teacher, Rabbi Moshe Shapiro.
11. *Yevamot* 61b, 62a, 62b.
12. *Yevamot* 12b,65b; Rabbi Isaiah Karelitz, *Chazon Ish*, Quoted in *Assia (Journal of Jewish Medical Ethics)* Vol. 4, p. 175; Rabbi Moshe Feinstein, *Igrot Moshe, Even Haezer* 3:24, 4:74.
13. Genesis 9:6, *Sanhedrin* 57b.
14. Novellae of Rabbi Chaim Soloveitchik on Maimonides' *Mishneh Torah*, Laws of Homicide.
15. *Arachin* 7a.
16. Mishnah, *Oholot* 7:6.
17. Maimonides, *Mishneh Torah*, Laws of Homicide 1:9.
18. Deuteronomy 4:27, 7:7.
19. *Midrash Rabbah*, Genesis, 74:41; Rashi, Numbers 11:36.
20. *Yevamot* 62a.
21. *Shabbat* 32a, *Bava Kamma* 91b; Maimonides, *Mishneh Torah,* Laws of Intellect 4:1, Laws of Homicide 11:5.
22. "Desecrated" is in quotes because this is not really desecration of Sabbath, since the Torah permits, indeed obligates, one to save a life even if it involves doing normally forbidden activities on Sabbath.
23. *Code of Jewish Law, Orach Chaim,* 330:1.
24. Ibid. 330:4.
25. See chapter on Shabbat.
26. Jews of Spanish-Portuguese, Middle Eastern and North African origin.
27. See chapter on Prayer.
28. *The Complete ArtScroll Siddur, Ashkenaz*, New York, 1984, pp. 442-443.
29. Jews of Eastern European origin.
30. *Bava Kamma* 80a, *Tosafot* ad loc. "*Lebey yeshuah haben.*"
31. *Code of Jewish Law, Yoreh Deah,* 265:12, Ramah.
32. *Midrash Rabbah*, Leviticus, 27:10.
33. *Code of Jewish Law*, ibid., *Turei Zahav* ad loc.13.
34. Genesis 17:4-5.
35. Proverbs 23:25.
36. *The Complete ArtScroll Siddur, Ashkenaz*, pp. 212-213.
37. Rabbeinu Bachya, Commentary on Genesis, 2:19.
38. Genesis 2:19.
39. Genesis 17:4-5.
40. Maharal, *Gevurot Hashem*, Chap. 43.
41. *Midrash Rabbah*, Leviticus 32:5.
42. Rabbi Isaac Luria, the "AriZal."
43. *Berachot* 7b.
44. *Midrash Tanchuma,* Ha'azinu, 7.
45. Rabbi Yehudah Hechasid, *Sefer Chassidim,* No. 460.
46. Rabbi Moshe ben Nachman, *Collected Writing of Nachmanides*, Letter of Nachmanides to his son Rabbi Shlomo. Edited by Charles B. Chavel, Mossad Harav Kook, Jerusalem 1986.
47. See chapters on Chanukah and Purim.
48. See chapter on Fast Days.

49. Rabbi Moshe Feinstein, *Igrot Moshe*, Orach Chaim 4:66.

50. For example, Maimonides' father who had the Spanish name Maimon.

51. Genesis 17:12.

52. Mishnah *Nedarim* 3:11; Babylonian Talmud *Nedarim* 31b-32a.

53. *Keritut* 9a.

54. Rabbi Aaron Halevi of Barcelona, *Sefer Hachinuch,* Mitzvah 3, *Parshat Lech Lecha*; Rabbi Menachem Re-canati, *Taamei Hamitzvot,* Mitzvat Asei 75.

55. Rabbi Samson Raphael Hirsch, *Horeb,* II Edoth, chap. 36, para. 263-265; Maimonides, *Guide for the Perplexed,* 3:49.

56. *Horeb,* ibid.

57. Leviticus 12:3.

58. *Shabbat* 132a.

59. Maimonides, *Mishneh Torah,* Laws of Kings, 9:3.

60. Wednesday-> Thursday-> Friday-> SHABBAT <-Sunday <-Monday <-Tuesday

61. Maharal, *Chidushei Aggadot, Shabbat* 21b.

62. Maimonides, *Guide for the Perplexed,* 3:49.

63. Rabbi Paysach J. Krohn, *Bris Milah,* ArtScroll Mesorah Publications, NY, 1985 pp. 53-54.

64. Ibid., pg. 99, para. 63-66.

65. *Code of Jewish Law, Yoreh Deah,* 264:1, Ramah ad loc.

66. Ibid. 262:1, Ramah.

67. Ibid. 265:11.

68. *The Complete ArtScroll Siddur, Ashkenaz,* pp. 210-211.

69. Ibid.

70. Ibid.

71. Exodus Chaps. 11-12.

72. Meir Leibush Malbim, *Commentary on Exodus* 11:5.

73. Exodus 13:2.

74. Numbers 3:13.

75. Numbers 3:44-51; 8:15-18; 18:15-16.

76. *Code of Jewish Law, Yoreh Deah* 305:1.

77. Ibid. 305; *Responsa Melamed Leho'il, Yoreh Deah* 100.

78. *Code of Jewish Law, Yoreh Deah* 305:15.

79. Rabbi Samson Raphael Hirsch, *Commentary on the Pentateuch,* Numbers 18:15.

80. Heard from Rabbi Dovid Kaplan, a rabbi and *Kohen* in Jerusalem, with the experience of many Pidyon ceremonies.

81. Ibid. 305:10, Ramah ad loc.

82. *The Complete ArtScroll Siddur, Ashkenaz,* pp. 218-221.

83. *Code of Jewish Law, Orach Chaim,* 17:2, *Shaarei Teshuvah,* ad loc.

84. Leviticus 19:27.

85. See chapter on the Land of Israel.

86. Proverbs 3:18.

87. From the Ohr Somayach, "Ask the Rabbi" at www.ohr.edu. Based on *Responsa Arugat Habosem, Meam Loez* on Deuteronomy 11:19, *Sefer Hachinuch LeYisrael* p. 239. See also *Sefer Taamei Haminhagim, Inyanei Hilula DeRashbi* 6.

88. Mishnah, *Avot* [Ethics of the Fathers], 5:21; Mishnah, *Niddah* 5:6, 6:11; Talmud, *Nazir* 29b, Rashi ad loc. "*VeReb Yosi*" — The age of *bar/bat mitzvah* are of Biblical origin.; *Code of Jewish Law, Orach Chaim,* 55:9; 616:2, *Even Haezer* 167:3, *Choshen Mishpat* 35:1; *Mishnah Berurah,* 53:33, 55:42; *Kaf Hachaim,* 53:48.

89. *Midrash Tanchuma, Parshat Bo,* 14: *Code of Jewish Law, Orach Chaim,* 55:10.

90. Mishnah, *Kiddushin* 1:7; Rashi, *Chagigah* 2a "*Eizehu katan*"; *Nazir* 29b.

91. Mishnah, *Terumot* 1:3; Mishnah, *Niddah* 6:11; Rashi, *Yoma* 82a "*mechanchin.*"

92. *Niddah* 30b; Maharal, *Chidushei Aggadot,* ad loc.; *Midrash Tanchuma, Parshat Pekudei,* 3; Rabbi Moshe Chaninah Neiman, *Shaarei Bar Mitzvah,* p. 9, Bnei Brak, 1996.

93. *Sanhedrin* 91b; *Piskei Tosafot, Nedarim* 62; *Avot D'Rebbi Natan,* 16:12.

94. *Nazir,* 62a-b; *Zohar* Vol. 1, p. 78b, *Sitrei Torah;* Rabbi Elijah, the Gaon of Vilna, *Yahel Ohr,* ad loc.

95. *Zohar* ibid.; *Shaarei Bar Mitzvah,* pp. 16-17.

96. *Shaarei Bar Mitzvah,* p. 29, footnotes.

97. Rabbi Shlomo Luria, *Yam Shel Shlomoh, Bava Kamma,* Chap. 7, para. 37.

98. *Yam Shel Shlomoh,* ibid.; *Mishnah Berurah,* 225:6; *Bava Kamma* 87a.

99. Rabbi Yosef Chaim of Baghdad, *Ben Ish Chai, Shana Rishonah, Parshat Re'eh,* 17.

100. *Mishnah Berurah,* 225:6.

101. Rabbi Yair Chaim Bachrach, *Responsa Chavot Yair,* 123.

102. Rabbi Moshe Feinstein, *Igrot Moshe, Orach Chaim* 1:104.

103. See chapter on Prayer.

104. *Shaarei Ephraim,* Shaar 4:25; *Chayei Adam,* 65:3; *Kitzur Shulchan Aruch* 61:8; *Aruch Hashulchan* 225:4.

105. See chapter on Prayer.

106. *The Complete ArtScroll Siddur, Ashkenaz,* pp. 142-143.

107. *Midrash Rabbah,* Genesis, 63:10; *Code of Jewish Law, Orach Chaim* 225:2 Ramah; *The Complete ArtScroll Siddur, Ashkenaz,* pp. 144-145.

108. Rabbi Samson Raphael Hirsch, *Horeb,* VI, Avodah, Chap. 111, para. 681.

109. *Code of Jewish Law, Orach Chaim,* 37:3, Ramah; *Mishnah Berurah* 12, *Biur Halachah* ad loc.; *Magen Avraham,* Orach Chaim, 37:14; *Aruch Hashulchan* 37:4; *Kaf Hachaim,* 37:14.

110. The Babylonian Talmud is the 21-volume edited version of the comments, discussion and arguments of the great Torah academies of Babylon over a period of approximately 200 years of study of the Mishnah. [See note 111.] There are 63 tractates, or subsections of the Talmud, called *masechtot* in Hebrew (singular, *masechet*). It was completed c.500 CE. It is written in Aramaic, and is also referred to as Gemara.

111. The Mishnah is the 6-volume summary of the Oral Tradition, edited c. 200 CE by Judah the Prince. It has 523 chapters. It is written in Hebrew and forms the basis of the Talmud.

112. Rabbi Moshe Feinstein, *Igrot Moshe, Orach Chaim* 4:23.

113. *Shaarei Bar Mitzvah,* p. 65.

A Time to Cry...

Death, burial, mourning, life after death, Kaddish

Heart and Soul: The Human Essence

The Jewish view of the human being encompasses both physical and spiritual entities. The spiritual aspect is the essence of a person, while the body is like clothing that surrounds and conceals that essence.[1] This spiritual core, the soul, is called *neshamah* in Hebrew. The word *neshamah* is related to *neshimah*, breath, alluding to the verse in Genesis in which God gave life to the first human being, Adam: "[and God] blew into his nostrils the soul of life."[2] This teaches us that the eternal and infinite "breath of God" is that which invests a person with life, and therefore the soul shares many characteristics with the Creator. Just as God Himself is unseen and unlimited by time and space, so too, the human soul[3] is "a portion of God from Above,"[4] not limited in its existence to this temporary, physical world. When we view a human being's life in this world we can see only a small segment of the total existence of his essence, his eternal *neshamah*.

The soul by itself, however, is not a person. It is the unique combination of the soul and the material body that constitutes the human being.[5] In order to achieve moral and spiritual growth, the soul cannot remain in the realm of the purely spiritual, it must descend to the physical world and reside in a material body.[6] Only here is there free will — and therefore only here is there a possibility of achieving moral and spiritual development. Growth can only be achieved through struggle: that struggle is founded on choice. When something is granted as a gift, it does not reflect the recipient's stature; rather it demonstrates the greatness of the one who bestowed this gift.[7] Therefore it is only in *this* world, in the world of deeds where free choice exists, that a human can improve himself or herself. The fruit of these efforts is enjoyed in the "World to Come," i.e. the spiritual world to which the soul returns after the death of the body.[8]

The human body is the interface between spiritual soul and physical world. The soul without the body cannot interact with the world and so cannot fulfill its task. The body without the soul is simply matter, lacking free will and spirituality. Therefore, we value life in this world, recognizing it as the only place where we can perfect ourselves.[9] At the same time, we understand also that the world experienced with our senses does not constitute the totality of our existence or of spiritual reality. Even when the body becomes lifeless and returns to the soil, the soul, which contains the person's true identity, continues to exist.

Death: End or Transition?

The great Biblical commentator, Nachmanides, writes that understanding the concept of the soul's eternity should moderate our reaction to death. Commenting on the Biblical[10] prohibition against mutilation[11] (once a common act of grief), Nachmanides states: *The Torah is saying that since you are a holy people and God's treasure, He did not create you and plan you and your soul in vain, and He will not let it be lost; therefore it is not appropriate to cut yourselves or pull out your hair even for someone who died in his youth.*[12]

The Torah does not prohibit mourning; on the contrary, mourning in an appropriate fashion is a *mitzvah*. What the Torah does prohibit is creating *permanent* signs of mourning on one's body, because doing this is essentially a statement that the soul is gone forever and the loss is permanent. Since the soul continues to exist after it has departed this world, it is certainly inappropriate to mourn excessively[13] or maintain a lifelong state of grief. We mourn our loss, and cry for the soul that can accomplish nothing further in this world, but we are comforted knowing that the soul lives on. My revered teacher, Rabbi Moshe Shapiro, always refers to a deceased scholar with the phrase "who no longer lives with us." The message is clear; he no longer lives *with us*, but he certainly still lives.

There is another reason why our reaction to death should not be excessive. In reality, the beginning of life should be a time of fear and trepidation, much more so than the end. At life's beginning, everything is uncertain: We do not know if the soul will succeed in realizing its potential or fall short. At the end of a good life we know that the soul has gone back to its Creator — that it has achieved a tremendous amount while on this earth — but has now returned to the place it truly desires to be.[14]

The Sages compare life to a ship that is going out to sea. When the ship leaves port for the first time people throw streamers, a band plays and a bottle of champagne is broken on the ship's bow. When the ship returns to port, there is no band and no streamers; only passport control and customs officers await it. In fact, it would be more appropriate to pray when a ship embarks because we do not know what will happen to it on its journey. The time to celebrate is when it returns in peace. Human emotion being what it is, we do not see life and death as a journey. We celebrate a new life and new potential and cry for our loss when a loved one dies. When, however, we consider all the good that the person achieved in his or her lifetime, our mourning is tempered by the knowledge that the ship has returned safely to its homeport.[15]

The Grave: Gateway to Another World

Death is a transition from one type of existence to another. In the Mishnah[16] and Talmud[17] the same word (*kever*) is used to mean both "womb" and "grave."[18] This teaches us that just as the womb is the portal from a limited level of existence to another plane of much greater potential, so too, the grave is a portal from our limited physical existence to a spiritual existence that is not bounded by time, space or matter.[19] This idea, that death precedes another type of life, is clearly alluded to in the verse in Deuteronomy: "See now that I, I am He — and no god is with Me. *I put to death, and I bring life*; I strike down and I will heal …"[20] Note that in the above passage God first brings about death, followed by new life.

The purely spiritual state of being of the soul is known in Hebrew as *Olam Haba*,[21] literally, "the world that comes" or, as it is more commonly known, "the World to Come." We use physical terms to describe *Olam Haba*, saying, for example, that the soul is "there" because we relate to these concepts most easily. In reality, the soul exists in a purely spiritual state, to which the terms "here, there and when" are inapplicable. "The world that comes" is a very precise description of this realm. The condition of the soul's existence in *Olam Haba*, its degree of closeness and connection to God, is directly determined by its previous activities in the physical world; it is the "the world that comes" — the state that results directly from what happens in this world.[22]

The idea of *Olam Haba* is suggested by the various expressions the Torah uses for death.

And Abraham expired and died at a good old age, mature and content, and he was gathered to his people. His sons Isaac and Ishmael buried him in the cave of the Machpelah ...

And Isaac expired and died, and he was gathered to his people, old and fulfilled of days; his sons Esau and Jacob buried him. [23]

"He lay down with his fathers" [24] and "he was gathered to his people," [25] both indicate the continued existence of the soul beyond this world. It also implies that the soul is somehow reunited with ancestors.

Another allusion to *Olam Haba* is the punishment described in the Torah as *karet,* which means "cutting off." This refers to the cutting off of the soul from its eternal existence. The verse states "that soul will be cut off from his people... that soul will be utterly cut off; his sin will remain upon him." [26] The phrase "his sin will remain upon him" seems to indicate the continued existence of the soul. [27]

A verse in Ecclesiastes succinctly describes the different fates of the body and the soul: "Thus the dust returns to the ground, as it was, and the spirit returns to God Who gave it. [28]

The concept of life after death is mentioned in other books of the Bible [29] as well, and it is written about extensively in Rabbinic literature. [30]

Reward and Punishment

The full consequence of an individual's deeds in the physical world, ultimate reward and punishment, are found in the World to Come. [31] Reward and punishment are not arbitrary: they are natural spiritual consequences of a person's actions.

How does this process work? Whatever good a person chooses to do in this world increases the soul's similarity to and compatibility with God, so that it becomes "closer" to Him in the World to Come. Alternatively, one can act in a way that distances his soul from the Creator. [32] The World to Come is a place of absolute truth where excuses and rationalizations evaporate: the soul is fully aware of its failings and its flaws; it will vividly experience the pain of regret and humiliation for a wasted life. Its anguish is profound, as every negative action and event is relived over and over again. However, a soul that accomplished good in this world, one that elevated itself and others, experiences the overwhelming joy of fulfillment in the realization of its potential. It feels the deepest pleasure of closeness to God, the Source of all that is good. These two states of being are the reward and punishment of the World to Come. Thus, the soul creates both its own reward and its own punishment, because the pleasure and pain of the World to Come is the pleasure and pain formed by its actions in this world. [33]

Where On Earth Is the World to Come?

Interestingly, the concept of life after death is never explicitly mentioned in the Five Books of Moses. The commentaries suggest a number of reasons for this omission:[34]

1. The Torah wants us to act righteously and avoid evil for altruistic reasons. Rather than focusing continuously on reward and punishment, we should evaluate the good or evil of a deed, the truth or falsehood inherent in every action. The Torah teaches us this idea by its deliberate silence on the subject of our ultimate reward, as if to say, "Ignore the reward, do this because it is good and true."[35]

2. The World to Come is purely spiritual, but it is impossible for us to describe it without resorting to metaphors from the physical world. These metaphors easily take on the character of reality in people's minds, so that the more *Olam Haba* is described the further it is diminished by our finite imagination.[36] You can see the disastrous results of oversimplification and metaphors by observing the popular western notions of Heaven and Hell with their respective scenes of angels strumming harps and devils with pitchforks!

3. The Torah promises rewards and foretells punishments *that take place in this world*, and are therefore open to observation. Predictions about life in this world, however, are open to refutation or verification, and offer significant testimony[37] to the truth of the Torah. In contrast, predictions about life after death cannot be tested, verified or refuted, therefore they cannot attest to the truth of their Author.[38]

The Holy Body

The human body is the vehicle that God has provided for the soul to fulfill its task of perfecting itself while in the physical world. As body and soul are partners in this task, the body is also holy and sanctified. Just as a worn-out Torah scroll is still treated with respect because it was a container for holiness (the text of the Torah),[39] so a dead body must be treated with respect because it was also once a container for holiness — the soul.[40] For this reason, Jewish law does not allow autopsy or cremation. They are desecrations of the body.

Impurity, Death and Illusion

Paradoxically, once the body loses its life force, the soul, it becomes the ultimate[41] source of impurity, *tumah*. A dead body imparts spiritual impurity through contact and even through its presence being under the same roof.[42] The Torah is teaching us that when the material world is totally devoid of spirituality it is dangerous and polluting, therefore, the empty vessel of the body, now without the soul, becomes impure.[43]

This impurity is also related to the confusion and illusion surrounding death.[44] The Sages relate the word *tumah* (impurity) to the word *timtum* (confusion).[45] A spiritually sensitive person experiences confusion and a feeling of impurity when he or she comes into contact with or even close to a dead body.[46] We know that a human being, in essence, is free willed, spiritual in nature, and has the power to master the physical world. When we see a corpse, we confront physical forces overpowering the spiritual; we can perceive only the material side of the human being, and we become confused and depressed. That which we thought was lofty and eternal seems to be merely decaying flesh. In reality, the essence of the deceased person lives on, but the impression formed by our senses is so overwhelming that we momentarily forget this truth and focus instead on death as the ultimate end, the final victory of "earth" over "heaven."[47] This confusion lies at the heart of the concept of impurity, *tumah*.

In the times of the Holy Temple in Jerusalem, exposure to this type of *tumah* had certain practical consequences. Today, these no longer apply to most people[48] with the exception of *Kohanim*[49] (singular, *Kohen*), who were dedicated for service in the Temple. (Just for the record: One does not "become" a *Kohen* except through heredity. A man is a *Kohen* if his father was a *Kohen*, going back all the way to Moses' brother Aaron, the first *Kohen*. And the rule is "Once a *Kohen*, always a *Kohen*." One cannot denounce his privileges or obligations as a *Kohen*.)

Kohanim, even today, are commanded in particular to stay away from *tumah*.[50] The reason for this restriction on *Kohanim* is that the *Kohen* stands as a representative of the Jewish people.[51] Just as the Jewish people are eternal — a nation that will never die[52] — he too must distance himself from death as much as possible. The *Kohen* also acts as God's representative on earth, a model of human connection to a higher spiritual reality. Since God is eternal and the source of life,[53] His representatives were given stringent regulations about staying away from the impurity of death. The Torah does not expect the *Kohen* to be superhuman, however. He is not expected to suppress his natural emotions; therefore, he is allowed — in fact, obligated — to bury and mourn for his closest relatives.[54]

Although the Temple no longer stands, there is still a prohibition for *Kohanim*[55] to become impure through contact with the dead. Being under the same roof as a corpse is prohibited as well.[56] In practical terms, this means that a *Kohen* should not enter a cemetery, funeral parlor or any building in which there is a dead body. A *Kohen* must, however, attend and participate in the funerals and burial of close relatives for whom he is obligated to mourn (with some exceptions).[57]

The Mitzvah of Burial:
Honoring a Deceased Person

The earliest mention of burial is found in Genesis: "By the sweat of your brow shall you eat bread until you return to the ground, from which you were taken: For you are dust, and to dust shall you return."[58] Just as the soul returns to its spiritual source, so the body is returned to its origins in the earth.

From the moment of death until this process is complete, the body must be treated with the utmost respect. Even regarding a criminal who has been executed, the Torah commands us:

> *You shall not leave his body overnight on the gallows, rather*
> *you shall surely bury him on that day, for a hanging person is*
> *a curse of God, and you shall not contaminate your land, which*
> *God, your God, gives you as an inheritance.*[59]

The commentaries explain that since a human being is created in the "image of God"[60] and is the only being similar to God, treating his corpse with disrespect is a disgrace to God Himself.[61] The above verse teaches us the type of respect due every corpse. It obligates us to bury the body ("you shall surely bury him") promptly ("you shall not leave him overnight") and to treat the body with total respect ("for a hanging person is a curse of God").[62]

Based on this verse, the Talmud rules that one may only delay the burial if it will enhance the honor of the deceased.[63] If, for example, the delay was necessary to obtain something important for the funeral, or to enable close relatives to attend the funeral, delay is permissible.[64] In addition, it is prohibited to desecrate the body[65] or to use the body for any purpose.[66] The body must be kept intact for burial and the entire body must be buried; therefore, cremation,[67] embalming[68] and autopsies[69] are all forbidden by Jewish law. Some exceptions apply, in accordance with the principle that saving a life overrides almost all other commandments.[70] Therefore, in a situation where a life may be saved by performing an autopsy, if a contagious disease is suspected, for example, or to obtain an organ for a specific patient who is dying, a rabbi should be consulted.

Consistent with this attitude of respect, the body is washed in a specific way known as *taharah* (purification).[71] It is never left alone, from the moment of death until the burial (*shmirah,* guarding).[72] After the *taharah,* the body is wrapped in plain, white cloth shrouds (*tachrichin*)[73] or in a *tallit,* prayer shawl. (The *tallit* is rendered unsuitable for fulfillment of a *mitzvah*[74] as an indication that the deceased is no longer obligated in the *mitzvot.*[75])

Jewish tradition requires that the body be buried in such a way that it can decompose and "return to the earth"[76] as quickly as possible. A plain wooden coffin is most often used; coffins made of metal, concrete or impervious materials are prohibited.[77] In Israel, it is customary to bury the deceased without any coffin at all.[78] Outside of Israel, it is the widespread custom to place some soil from the Land of Israel inside the coffin.[79] The deceased should be buried in ground that is consecrated for the sake of burial, in a place where fellow Jews are also buried.[80] It is also customary for people attending the funeral to take turns placing some soil in the grave, to personally honor the deceased by fulfilling the *mitzvah* of burial.[81]

Psalms and *Kaddish* (see below) are recited at the burial accompanied by the beautiful *El Malei Rachamim* prayer:

> *O God, full of mercy, Who dwells on high, grant proper rest on the wings of the Divine Presence — in the lofty levels of the holy and pure ones, who shine like the glow of the firmament — for the soul of (name of the deceased) son or daughter of (name of the deceased's father). May his/her resting place be in the Garden of Eden. Therefore may the Master of Mercy shelter him/her in the shelter of His wings for eternity; and may He bind his/her soul in the Bond of Life. God is his/her heritage; and may he/she repose in peace on his/her resting place. Now let us respond: Amen.*[82]

Eulogy – A Time for Tears

It is appropriate for a rabbi or a relative to eulogize the deceased before the burial. The primary reasons for the eulogy (*hesped*) is to honor the deceased[83] by expressing our admiration, love and the depth of our loss by extolling the virtues of the deceased and to inspire others to emulate his/her good deeds. The eulogy is meant to move people to tears; the "stiff upper lip" advocated by western culture is considered cold and artificial at a Jewish funeral. Since the main reason for the eulogy is to honor the person who died, if he or she requested that there be no eulogy, this wish should be respected.[84] In addition to its obvious focus on the one who died, the eulogy also honors the family of the deceased.[85] The Code of Jewish Law writes:

> *It is a great mitzvah to appropriately eulogize the deceased. It is correct to raise one's voice, say things that will break people's hearts in order to increase the weeping and to speak in praise of the deceased. One should not, however, exaggerate the praise excessively; rather, one should mention the positive characteristics of the deceased and embellish them slightly.*[86]

The "Holy Society" – Boundless Caring and Love

Throughout our history, in Jewish communities around the world, people have always volunteered to take responsibility for the care and burial of the deceased. These groups are known as a *Chevra Kadisha*,[87] Holy Society, or *Chessed Shel Emet*, Society of True Kindness. The men and women who participate in these societies demonstrate true altruistic kindness. When our Patriarch Jacob requested that his son Joseph bury him in Israel, he referred to this act as "kindness and truth."[88] Rashi, the great 11th-century Bible commentator, explains: *The kindness which one shows toward the deceased is kindness of truth* [a true kindness], *because one does not expect any repayment.*[89]

The *Chevra Kadisha* members give of their time and energy to ensure that proper dignity and honor are accorded to the deceased. They take great pains to meticulously fulfill all the precepts of Jewish law and custom regarding the preparation and burial of the body. In many communities the *Chevra Kadisha* is composed of volunteers. In small communities, where the number of members is insufficient for rotations, the individuals who make up the *Chevra Kadisha* take a tremendous responsibility upon themselves and fulfill this great *mitzvah* with devotion and self-sacrifice.

The custom of volunteering to take care of the deceased has its origins in the Bible: Moses himself takes Joseph's remains out of Egypt in order to bury him in Israel.[90] The Talmud describes how some of the greatest Sages would engage in burying the dead,[91] and notes that in every city in ancient Israel there were people who volunteered to care for the deceased.[92] One of the greatest deeds a person can perform is take responsibility for a deceased person who has no one else to care for him.[93] Such a person is known as a *"met mitzvah,"* "a deceased [entailing a] *mitzvah*," and the obligation of providing for his burial overrides virtually all other obligations.[94]

Responding to Tragedy

When, God forbid, a person hears of the death of a close relative, or of anyone whose passing causes him great distress, he should say "Blessed are You, God, Our God, King of the universe, the True Judge."[95] On the surface, this seems like a strange declaration at such a painful moment. But there is great wisdom in this practice: it is an opportunity to reaffirm our faith that God is just and righteous. Even though the death causes us anguish, we affirm our belief in God as the "True Judge" — the only One Who knows what is best for every individual He created. We accept His judgment.

The Talmud[96] points out that this affirmation of belief in times of sorrow is alluded to in various locations of the Bible: *The pains of death encircled me; the confines of the grave have found me; distress and grief I would find. Then would I invoke the Name of God* ...[97] *God has given, and God has taken away, blessed be the Name of God* ...[98]

It is not easy to bless God at a time of shock and sorrow, but ultimately, it is our belief and trust in God that enable us to cope with tragedy. One who looks at events as random happenings, who does not believe in a Divine Plan or Divine Providence, may feel completely abandoned and vulnerable in the face of great loss. One who believes, however, that the soul is now reunited with its Creator, that death is not a random event, but part of a larger plan, is able to take comfort in that knowledge. Trust in God does not mean believing that the "good" (by *our* definition) will necessarily come about as hoped. Rather, trust is built on understanding deeply that God is in control. According to the Chazon Ish, a great twentieth-century Torah scholar: "Trust is the practical side of belief in God. It does not mean that a person should believe that everything will 'turn out for the best' from his or her own limited perspective. Rather, the meaning of trust in God is that one should believe that *no matter what happens, it is ultimately in the hands of God.*"[99]

Despite this trust, Judaism recognizes that the mourner needs to express pain, grief and even anger. Therefore, when a close relative dies, the mourner tears his garment (*kriah*). This dramatic, symbolic act is performed only for immediate relatives: one's father, mother, son, daughter, brother, sister or spouse.[100] This practice is mentioned in the Bible in numerous places.[101] The Talmud[102] cites Job as an example of one who tore his clothing upon hearing tragic news.

> *It happened one day, when his sons and daughters were eating and drinking wine in the home of their eldest brother, that a messenger came to Job and said* .... *"... behold a great wind came from across the desert. It struck the four corners of the house; it collapsed upon the young people and killed them. Only I, by myself, escaped to tell you!" Job stood up and ripped his shirt* ...[103]

Tearing one's clothing symbolizes the annulment of personal dignity, disregard for adornment and pleasure, and rejection of this worldly existence. It dramatically expresses our recognition that the body, which is the clothing of the soul, has been torn from our loved one. It is an expression of grief and pain that must not be restrained.

Today, this ritual is generally carried out at the funeral. The ripping of cloth has a searing affect, one that helps the mourner express true grief and later recover from the loss. Unfortunately, this poignant practice has been replaced in some circles by the donning of a torn black ribbon, which has no Jewish significance and does nothing to help one cope with grief.

The Stages of Mourning

Judaism recognizes that it is dangerous to completely suppress emotion, but that excesses of grief can be paralyzing and destructive. Through the specific directives that govern the nature and duration of the mourning process (*aveilut*), the Torah seeks to avoid both of these dangers. Torah laws help the mourner find comfort and return to normal life.[104] The mourner (*aveil*) progresses through the following stages of mourning when he or she has lost a father, mother, son, daughter, brother, sister or spouse:

1. *Onen*[105] — One Who Is in Intense Mourning

From the moment of death until the deceased has been buried, the close relatives are overwhelmed, feeling as if part of themselves has been torn away. They may experience shock, and be "outraged by the sense of loss."[106] During this period, the *onen* may not eat meat, drink wine or eat sitting at a table in a regular fashion. The mind of the *onen* is preoccupied with the responsibility of burial and is still reeling from the shock of the death. The Torah does not expect such a person to be able to pray or perform any commandments that require him to focus on an action or words. Therefore, the *onen* is exempt from all positive commandments and therefore does not pray, study Torah or even recite blessings (with the exception of "the True Judge" discussed earlier).[107] His primary responsibility, the burial of the deceased, exempts him from other responsibilities as well.[108] Once the burial is complete, the sense of closure allows the mourner to move past this intensity of pain and begin mourning.

2. *Shivah* — Seven (*Shivah*) Days

Seven days are devoted exclusively to mourning, beginning after the burial[109] and ending on the morning of the seventh day, after the visitors have left.[110] Although the mourner's deepest self is still in a state of anguish, the pain is now experienced as more emotional than physical.[111] During the period called "sitting *shivah*" the mourner stays at home and does not work, remaining totally immersed in bereavement. Mirrors in the mourner's home are covered. The mourner neglects external appearance: S/he wears the clothing that s/he tore previously, does not shave or groom him/herself (or put on cosmetics) and bathes only as necessary for hygienic purposes.[112] During the *shivah*, the mourner does not wear leather shoes and sits on a low chair, as attention is focused on the deceased and on the mourning. As Torah study is a pleasurable and distracting experience, the mourner is permitted to study only those sections of the

Torah that relate to mourning, either individual or national.[113] On Shabbat and festivals, all public expressions of mourning are prohibited and only those components of mourning that are not obvious are observed.[114]

During the *shivah,* friends and relatives visit the mourner, pray at the "*shivah* house"[115] and express their sympathy, love and friendship. The mourner should not greet people, but should accept visitors who have come to offer comfort.[116]

The purpose of the "*shivah* call" is *not* to distract the mourner from his or her loss. A common mistake made by visitors is that they engage in small talk, discuss news events, even tell jokes, thinking that their job is to take the mourner's mind off the deceased. The time should be used to talk about the deceased and to listen to others relate their experiences with this person. This is true comforting. (See the section below, "Comfort, Comfort My People," for the do's and don'ts of being a *shivah* visitor.)

The Talmud states "the community never dies."[117] When people come to express their love and concern, it fulfills in some measure the mourner's deep need to feel part of a larger, eternal reality. Although the individual is terribly hurt, he or she can begin to take the first steps toward healing by connecting to the community, the Jewish nation that will live forever.

3. *Shloshim* — Thirty (*Shloshim*) Days[118]

A less intense period of mourning is observed for thirty days, from the conclusion of the *shivah* and until the morning of the thirtieth day.[119] Once the pain during *shivah* begins to subside, the mourner starts the process of returning to his former self. He must once again become independent, regain his self-confidence and become concerned with his own dignity.[120] During these thirty days, the mourner still does not shave or take a haircut, nor does s/he attend any festivities. Numerous other restrictions apply during the *shloshim*, mostly concerned with avoiding situations that will lead to great joy. The mourner does, however, dress normally, converse normally and go to work. At the conclusion of the thirty days, formal mourning ceases for relatives other than parents.

4. *Hakamat Matzeivah* — Erecting the Monument

Depending upon custom, a monument is erected one month or one year after the conclusion of *shivah.* Usually, the ceremony consists of gathering a *minyan* (ten Jewish men) to recite Psalms at the gravesite, after which *Kaddish* (see below) and the memorial prayer *El Malei Rachamim* are recited.[121] The monument is unveiled, and often a family member or friend will speak about the deceased.

5. Twelve Months

The general principle of gratitude,[122] as well as the specific commandment, "Honor your father and mother,"[123] obligate a child to honor his or her parents. These obligations extend even beyond the parent's death,[124] so the laws pertaining to mourning for parents have certain components that continue for a year from the end of *shivah.*[125] For these twelve months, the mourner should not attend festive events or social gatherings,[126] unless it is a *seudat mitzvah* (a meal celebrating a *mitzvah*, at which a Torah message is presented).[127] During this year, he or she should not go on pleasure trips or listen to music.[128] *Kaddish* is said in the presence of a *minyan*[129] for eleven months, from the beginning of *shivah.* A male mourner should make a special effort to lead prayers in the synagogue, if he is able.[130]

6. *Yahrzeit*

Yiddish: *Yahr* (Year) + *Zeit* (Time)

On the anniversary of the death of a parent one should mark the date by devoting part or all of the day to the performance of extra *mitzvot*[131] to "merit" the deceased. The concept of living descendants bringing "merit" to the dead is not as mysterious as it first may seem. We need to understand a little about "the World to Come" in which the soul of the deceased resides.

In this spiritual dimension, the soul is enjoying closeness to God in accordance with his or her own previous activities on earth. It has earned its particular place, and the soul is no longer capable of further perfection or elevation to a higher plane on its own. If, however, that soul served to inspire someone in the human world of action to do good things, then through that person's earthly deeds the soul can posthumously acquire the "merit" of those actions. The result is that the soul moves into a closer relationship with God, an experience called *aliyah* (ascending).[132] We try, therefore, on the anniversary of death, to do positive things in this world in the merit of the deceased.

It is customary to visit the grave of the deceased on this day, as well as to light a candle that will burn for 24 hours, from evening until evening.[133] For relatives other than parents, the *yahrzeit* observance is customary, but not obligatory. Some fast on that day,[134] others give extra charity or study Torah. It is also a common custom to bring light refreshments to the synagogue on the day of the *yahrzeit* and for people to drink a "*L'chaim*,"[135] to celebrate the soul's ascension to a higher realm. The male heirs should say *Kaddish* on that day and also lead the communal prayers, if possible. We commonly address the person observing the *yahrzeit* by saying, "The *neshamah* (soul) should have an *aliyah* (elevation)." This phrase encapsulates the essence of a *yahrzeit*.

During the morning service on certain festival days, a special memorial prayer is recited known as *Yizkor* ("Remember").[136] The underlying concept is similar to that of *yahrzeit* — it is an opportunity to give the soul of a loved one added spiritual pleasure — therefore it is customary to pledge money to charity just before reciting *Yizkor.*

Kaddish

Kaddish, the best-known prayer that is recited by a mourner,[137] was instituted almost 2,000 years ago and is mentioned in numerous places in the Mishnah and Talmud.[138] *Kaddish* is written in Aramaic,[139] the spoken language of the Jews in Israel and Babylon when the Mishnah[140] and Talmud[141] were written. *Kaddish* literally means "sanctification"; the theme of this prayer is the sanctification and praise of God. When we look at the words of the *Kaddish* prayer, we note that there is no hint of sadness or mourning, nor does it mention the deceased in any way!

> *May His great Name grow exalted and sanctified (Congregation — Amen) in the world that He created as He willed. May He give reign to His Kingship in your lifetimes and in your days, and in the lifetimes of the entire Family of Israel, swiftly and soon. Now we respond, Amen.*
>
> *(Cong. — Amen. May His great Name be blessed forever and ever.)*
>
> *May His great Name be blessed forever and ever. Blessed, praised, glorified, exalted, extolled, mighty, upraised, and lauded be the Name of the Holy One, Blessed is He (Cong. — Blessed is He), beyond any blessings and song, praise and consolation that are uttered in the world. Now let us respond: Amen.*
>
> *(Cong. — Amen.)*
>
> *May there be abundant peace from Heaven, and life upon us and upon all Israel. Now let us respond: Amen. (Cong. — Amen.)*
>
> *He Who makes peace in His heights, may He make peace upon us and upon all Israel. Now respond: Amen. (Cong. — Amen.)*[142]

Why is this a prayer recited by mourners and those observing a *yahr-zeit*? By publicly calling upon the congregation to praise and acknowledge God, *Kaddish* bestows merit on the deceased and atones for wrongs that he or she may have done.[143] It is a way for the mourner to counteract any act of the deceased that may have brought dishonor to God's Name or reduced people's awareness of God. It is also a form of acceptance of God's judgment by affirming belief in the greatness of God and recognizing Him as King.[144]

That *Kaddish* does not mention death or the deceased individual at all allows it to focus entirely on the greatness of the Creator. Perhaps this is an attempt to comfort the mourner by helping him realize that although the physical world is transitory, a greater, infinite reality exists beyond the reach of our senses. As one Jewish writer expressed it: "*Kaddish* is total identification with the *ultimate* when the immediate seems to collapse before our eyes."[145]

Kaddish is only recited when a *minyan* is present and it is always recited while standing.[146] Saying *Kaddish* takes faith and courage, and certainly, soon after the death of a loved one, can be a very difficult thing to do. At the same time, saying *Kaddish* is also an act of healing and comfort, which may explain why many Jews who are very distant from formal observance nevertheless say *Kaddish*. At times, when we seem very far from eternity, there is comfort in being part of a historic tradition going back thousands of years, in being part of a community connected to God, the Eternal One.

Comfort, Comfort My People[147]

The primary responsibility of the mourner is toward the deceased; the community's primary responsibility is toward the mourner. The Torah commands us to "walk in His ways,"[148] to imitate God[149] by behaving with kindness toward those in need, burying the dead, attending the funeral and comforting the mourners.[150] It is easy to rejoice together with a friend, but to mourn with someone is the truer test of kindness and friendship and the more difficult thing to do well.

Mourners are usually so involved in their loss that they may be temporarily incapable of caring for their family. A friend or community member's first obligation is to care for the physical and practical needs of the mourner and his or her family. All observant communities have volunteers who arrange meals, childcare and provide for any other needs of the mourners.

It is a great *mitzvah* and true kindness to visit during the *shivah* period,[151] but the visitor must be extremely sensitive to the state of mind of the mourner. Even if the visitor merely sits and does not utter a word the entire time, he has nevertheless helped to comfort the mourner.[152] By his very presence the visitor conveys sympathy, concern and love.[153] In addition, a certain level of communication that is beyond words connects heart to heart and soul to soul and can certainly be felt by the mourner; "As water reflects a face back to a face, so one's heart is reflected back to him by another."[154] If the visitor feels however, that the mourner would prefer to be alone, he should, of course, leave.[155]

Every person reacts differently to tragedy and is comforted in different ways. For this reason, Jewish law does not allow a visitor to initiate conversation in the house of mourning unless it is clear that the mourner would like to talk.[156] When they do talk, the visitor should keep in mind that the occasion is not a social event; the visitors and mourner should not, for example, even greet each other.[157] Ideally, visitors should talk about the goodness of the deceased and offer words of comfort and encouragement.[158] One should not attempt to "explain" the tragedy or to offer an intellectual perspective on death. The mourner's need is emotional, not intellectual; our response should be on an emotional level as well. Just before leaving, one should offer the traditional words of comfort:[159]

"May the Omnipresent[160] One console you among the other mourners for Zion and Jerusalem."[161] ("*HaMakom yenachem etchem betoch sh'ar aveilei Tzion viYerushalayim.*")

This expression joins the personal tragedy with the mourning of the entire Jewish nation over the destruction of the Holy Temple and the exile of the Jewish people from our homeland. It also describes God as being everywhere at all times, conveying the reassurance that God is with the mourner here in his distress, as well.[162]

The Levy Family Faces a Death in the Family

Mr. Levy's father had been sick for a number of years. One Sunday morning, Mr. Levy received a phone call to come to the hospital immediately, as his father's condition had worsened. Mr. and Mrs. Levy, his brother and sister-in-law gathered at his father's bedside, where they spoke together quietly for a few moments. Mr. Levy then suggested that his father say certain prayers together with him. He explained that although these prayers are recited just before a person's death, nevertheless many people have said the prayers and lived afterward, but many had died without saying them.[163] It was clear from his father's eyes that he was well aware of his situation as he recited the Viduy, "Confession":

I acknowledge before You, God, my God and the God of my forefathers, that my recovery and death are in Your hand. May it be Your will that You heal me with total recovery, but, if I die, may my death be an atonement for all the errors, iniquities, and willful sins that I have erred, sinned and transgressed before You. May You grant my share in the Garden of Eden, and let me merit the World to Come that is concealed for the righteous.[164]

The family listened tearfully, then said Shema together with him as he closed his eyes for the last time and passed away. Everyone in the room immediately tore their outer clothing[165] and stood together crying. As soon as she was able, Mrs. Levy called the rest of family to tell them the sad news. It was hardest to tell her children; they had been so close to their Zeida. As much as she had tried to prepare them for his death, she knew it would be their first brush with death and a terrible shock.

She then called the Chevra Kadisha[166] who would take care of the body and prepare it for burial. Since the Levys' father had already purchased a plot in the Jewish cemetery next to his wife's grave and had deposited money with the cemetery committee for his burial,[167] the arrangements were greatly simplified.

Volunteers from the Chevra Kadisha arrived quickly. Once the death certificate was signed and the hospital released the body, the Chevra Kadisha volunteers transferred it to the Jewish funeral home. There the body would be guarded, washed and wrapped in shrouds in preparation for burial.[168]

The Levys set the time of the funeral for late that afternoon, to give time for relatives to drive in and for the Levys' synagogue telephone committee to inform the community of the funeral and shivah arrangements. Care was taken not to delay the burial more than absolutely necessary.[169]

Rabbi Blum, a close personal friend of Mr. Levy, gave a moving eulogy, recounting his personal recollection of the sacrifices the deceased had made in order to be observant and raise his children as committed Jews. Mr. Levy's brother spoke of his father's love of Torah and his great reverence for Torah scholars. He admitted that he doubted that the family could ever measure up to the example his father had set. It was clear to everyone at the funeral that the family, in fact the entire community, would try to live as uprightly as old Mr. Levy had in his lifetime. At the cemetery, Rabbi Blum conducted the funeral service. Mr. Levy and his brother recited Kaddish, tore their garments again and returned home to sit shivah.

The first meal that the mourners ate after the burial, known as the "Seudat Havraah"[170] — "the meal of comfort"[171] was cooked and served by a member of the community.[172]

Friends, relatives and neighbors came to pray with the Levy family in their home every day during the week of shivah.[173] Mr. Levy had set a goal of having all six sections of the Mishnah[174] studied within the next thirty days, to benefit his father's soul through Torah study. Many visitors offered to participate in this undertaking, promising to study Mishnah in the merit of the deceased.[175]

Over the course of the week, hundreds of people came to the Levy home to comfort the mourners. Many people related stories about the deceased while other just listened as the mourners talked. Receptacles labeled with the names of various charity organizations were placed where visitors could contribute to them, again as a merit for the departed. Many people placed coins and small bills into these. In addition, Mr. Levy had decided to establish *a charity fund in memory of his father and to sponsor a public lecture every year on his yahrzeit, at the synagogue where he used to pray.*

The mourning is heartfelt, but the Levys take comfort in the fact that their father lived a long life, was proud of his children and grandchildren, and passed away surrounded by loved ones. They know that his soul still lives, and that he rejoined his wife in the World to Come. They know too that even beyond his life in this world, his soul will continue to be elevated through the mitzvot he had lovingly taught and inspired them to do.[176]

Laws of Mourning

Since the laws of death, burial and mourning are extremely complex and require tremendous sensitivity toward the mourners, a rabbi and/or Chevra Kadisha should be consulted to guide and assist the family through the difficult process. We will not, therefore, elaborate on the laws of death or mourning beyond what has already been discussed above.

For Further Reading

▸ *If You Were God* by Rabbi Aryeh Kaplan (OU/NCSY, 1993)

▸ *Kaddish* by Rabbi Nosson Scherman (ArtScroll/Mesorah, 1980)

▸ *Making Sense of Suffering* by Yonason Rosenblum and Jeremy Kagan (ArtScroll/Mesorah, 2002)

▸ *Mourning in Halachah: The Laws and Customs of the Year of Mourning* by Rabbi Chaim Binyamin Goldberg (ArtScroll/Mesorah, 1991)

▸ *Out of the Whirlwind* by Rabbi Joseph Soloveitchik (Ktav, 2003)

▸ *The Jewish Way in Death and Mourning* by Rabbi Maurice Lamm (Jonathan David, 2000)

NOTES

References to books of the Talmud refer to the Babylonian Talmud unless otherwise noted.

1. Rabbi Isaac Luria, *Shaar Hagilgulim*, First Introduction.
2. Genesis 2:7.
3. *Midrash Rabbah*, Leviticus, *Parsha* 4:8; *Berachot* 10a.
4. Rabbi Chaim ibn Attar, *Ohr Hachaim* on Genesis 1:1 (Par. 20), Exodus 20:20 and 32:4 based on Job 31:2.
5. Rabbi Moshe Chaim Luzzatto, *The Way of God*, Part 1 Chap. 3:2, Sifriati, Bnei Brak, 1989.
6. *Eruvin* 22a; *Avodah Zarah* 3a; Rabbi Moshe Chaim Luzzatto, *Path of the Just*, Chap. 1, Machon Ofek, Jerusalem, 1995.
7. Rabbi Moshe Chaim Luzzatto, *The Way of God*, Part 1 Chap. 2:2, Chap. 3:1.
8. Maharal of Prague, *Tiferet Yisrael*, Chap. 60.
9. Mishnah, Ethics of the Fathers, 4:17.
10. Deuteronomy 14:1-2.
11. This practice still exists today in some cultures.
12. Nachmanides, *Commentary on the Torah*, Deuteronomy 14:1-2; *Ohr Hachaim* ad loc.
13. Nachmanides, ibid.; *Moed Katan* 27b.
14. *Zohar, Parshat Vayeira* 98a.
15. Rabbi Yechiel Michel Tukichinski, *Gesher Hachaim,* Vol. 3, Jerusalem, 1960.
16. Central text of Jewish law, edited by Judah the Prince in 170-200 C.E., Northern Israel.
17. Commentary and expansion of the Mishnah, edited by Ravina and Rav Ashi in 500 C.E., Babylon.
18. *"Kever"* — Mishnah *Ohalot* 7:4; Talmud, *Shabbat* 129a.
19. Heard from Rabbi Moshe Shapiro.
20. Deuteronomy 32:39.
21. Mishnah *Sanhedrin*, 10:1.
22. Heard from Rabbi Moshe Shapiro; Rabbi Chaim of Volozhin, *Ruach Chaim* 1:1; Rabbi Yosef Albo, *Sefer Haikrim*, 4:39-40.
23. Genesis 25:8-9, 35:29.
24. Ibid. 47:30; Deuteronomy 31:16; I Kings 14:20.
25. Ibid. 25:8; 25:17; 35:29; 49:29; 49:33; Numbers 27:13; 31:2; Deuteronomy 32:50.
26. Numbers 15:30-31. *Sanhedrin* 64b.
27. *Sanhedrin* 90b.
28. Ecclesiastes 12:7.
29. See I Samuel Chaps. 25 and 28; Daniel Chap. 12; Ecclesiastes 12; Psalm 16.
30. Mishnah *Sanhedrin* Chap. 11, *Perek Chelek.*
31. Maimonides, *Commentary on the Mishnah Sanhedrin* Chap. 11.
32. Rabbi Moshe Chaim Luzzatto, *The Way of God,* Part 1, Chap. 4:9.
33. Rabbi Chaim of Volozhin, *Nefesh Hachaim,* Shaar 1, Chap. 6, 12; *Ruach Chaim* on Ethics of the Fathers, Introduction.
34. For a summary of a number of approaches to this question, see Commentaries of *Don Isaac Abarbanel* and *Kli Yakar* on Leviticus 26:12.
35. Maimonides, *Mishneh Torah*, Laws of Repentance, Chaps. 8-10.
36. Avraham Ibn Ezra, Commentary on Deuteronomy 32:39; Maharal of Prague, *Tiferet Yisrael,* Chaps. 57-60.
37. Rabbi Yehudah Halevy, *Sefer HaKuzari*, 1:105-109, Gnizi Edition, Bnei Brak, 1979; Rabeinu Nissim, *Drashot HaRan*, End of Drush 1, Machon Shalem, Jerusalem 1977.
38. Rabbi Yehudah Halevy, *Sefer HaKuzari*, 1:105-109; See also *Stanford Encyclopedia of Philosophy*, Article on Sir Karl Popper, The Metaphysics Research Lab, Stanford University, 2004.

39. *Megillah* 26b.

40. *Moed Katan* 25a.

41. Rashi, Commentary on Numbers 19:22.

42. Numbers 19:13-17.

43. Rabbi Aaron Halevi of Barcelona, *Sefer Hachinuch,* Meirav, Jerusalem.

44. Rabbi Samson Raphael Hirsch, Commentary on Numbers Chap. 19.

45. *Yoma* 39a.

46. Rabbi Yehudah Halevy, *Sefer HaKuzari* 2:60.

47. Rabbi Hirsch, ibid.

48. Jewish males who are descended on their fathers' side from Aaron the High Priest, brother of Moses.

49. The main ramifications of *tumah* are prohibitions against entering the Temple and against eating certain offerings, neither of which exist today.

50. Leviticus 21:1.

51. *Yoma* 18b-19a.

52. *Temurah* 15b; Maimonides, *Mishneh Torah,* Laws of Invalid Holy Offerings 4:1.

53. Rabbi Samson Raphael Hirsch, Commentary on Leviticus Chap. 21.

54. Hirsch, ibid.

55. Code of Jewish Law, *Yoreh Deah* 373:1-2.

56. Ibid. 369:1, 371:1.

57. Ibid. 373:3-4.

58. Genesis 3:19.

59. Deuteronomy 21:23.

60. Genesis 1:27.

61. Rashi, Deuteronomy ad loc.

62. Sifri, Deuteronomy ad loc.

63. *Sanhedrin* 46a.

64. *Code of Jewish Law, Yoreh Deah,* 357:1.

65. *Chullin* 11b.

66. *Code of Jewish Law, Yoreh Deah,* 349:1.

67. Rabbi Yekutiel Yehudah Greenwald, *Kol Bo Al Aveilut,* pp. 53-55, Feldheim Publishing, NY.

68. Ibid. p. 51. Some forms of embalming may be permitted in extenuating circumstances.

69. *Chullin* 11b.

70. Talmud, ibid. Rabbi Yechezkel Landau, *Responsa Noda BeYehudah* II, *Yoreh Deah* 210; Rabbi Moshe Sofer, *Responsa Chatam Sofer, Yoreh Deah* 336; Rabbi Moshe Feinstein, *Responsa Igrot Moshe, Yoreh Deah,* 2:17.

71. *Code of Jewish Law, Yoreh Deah,* 352:4, Ramah.

72. *Berachot* 18a.

73. *Code of Jewish Law, Yoreh Deah* 352:1-2

74. Ibid. 351:2, Ramah. Usually, one of the four *tzitzit* (fringes) is cut off.

75. *Shabbat* 30a.

76. Genesis ibid.

77. *Code of Jewish Law, Yoreh Deah,* 362:1, *Siftei Cohen* ad loc. 1.

78. Tur, *Yoreh Deah,* 362.

79. Ibid. 363:1 Ramah; ibid. 362, *Be'er Heitev* 1.

80. Rabbi Yitzchak Elchonon Spektor, *Responsa Ein Yitzchak, Yoreh Deah* 34.

81. *Kol Bo Al Aveilut,* pp. 181-183.

82. *The Complete ArtScroll Siddur, Ashkenaz,* pp. 814-815.

83. *Sanhedrin* 46b.

84. *Code of Jewish Law, Yoreh Deah* 344:10; *Siftei Cohen* 8.

85. Talmud, ibid.

86. *Code of Jewish Law, Yoreh Deah* 344:1.

87. An Aramaic expression; in Hebrew the words are *Chavurah Kedoshah.*

88. Genesis 47:29.

89. Genesis ibid. Rashi ad loc.

90. Exodus 13:19.

91. *Niddah* 24b; Jerusalem Talmud, *Pesachim* 3:7.

92. *Ketuvot* 8b, Rashi "*keneged chazanei ha'ir.*"

93. *Code of Jewish Law, Yoreh Deah* 374:3.

94. *Megillah* 3b; *Code of Jewish Law, Yoreh Deah* 374:1.

95. *Code of Jewish Law, Orach Chaim* 222:2; *Mishnah Berurah* ad loc. 3; ibid. 223:2, *Mishnah Berurah* 8; *The Complete ArtScroll Siddur, Ashkenaz,* pp. 230-231.

96. *Berachot* 60b.

97. Psalms 116:3-4.

98. Job 1:21.

99. Rabbi Isaiah Karelitz, *Chazon Ish, Belief and Trust,* Chap. 1.

100. *Code of Jewish Law, Yoreh Deah* 340:1.

101. For example — Genesis 36:29, 37:34; II Samuel 13:31; II Kings, 6:30.

102. *Moed Katan* 20b.

103. Job 1:13, 18-20.

104. Rabbi Samson Raphael Hirsch, *Horeb,* II Edoth, Chapter 43, The Soncino Press, London, 1981.

105. Deuteronomy 26:14.

106. *Horeb,* ibid. para. 311.

107. *Code of Jewish Law, Yoreh Deah* 341:1.

108. *Berachot* 17b-18a.

109. *Code of Jewish Law, Yoreh Deah* 375:1.

110. Ibid. 395:1.

111. *Horeb,* ibid.

112. Code of Jewish Law, *Yoreh Deah* 381:1.

113. *Code of Jewish Law,* ibid. 384:1- 4.

114. *Code of Jewish Law,* ibid. 400:1.

115. Colloquial expression for observance of the seven days of mourning.

116. Ibid. 380 –391.

117. *Temurah* 15b; Maimonides, *Mishneh Torah,* Laws of Invalid Holy Offerings 4:1.

118. *Code of Jewish Law, Yoreh Deah* 391-392.

119. Ibid. 395:1.

120. *Horeb,* ibid.

121. *Kol Bo Al Aveilut,* Chap. 5.

122. *Bava Metzia* 33a.

123. Exodus 20:12; Deuteronomy 5:16.

124. *Code of Jewish Law, Yoreh Deah* 240:9.

125. Ibid. 395:3.

126. *Moed Katan* 22b.

127. *Pri Megadim* on *Code of Jewish Law, Orach Chaim* 444, *Mishbetzot Zahav* 9.

128. *Code of Jewish Law, Yoreh Deah* 391:2; *Kol Bo Al Aveilut,* pp. 358-362.

129. Ibid. 376:5, *Pitchei Teshuvah* 3.

130. Ibid. *Yoreh Deah* 376:5 Ramah.

131. Ibid. 376:4, Ramah and 402:12, Ramah.

132. *Gesher Hachaim,* vol. 1, Chap. 32.

133. *Kol Bo Al Aveilut,* Chap. 5.

134. Ibid.

135. The traditional toast on drinking wine or liquor, meaning, "To life."

136. *The Complete ArtScroll Siddur, Ashkenaz,* pp. 810-815.

137. Mishnah *Sofrim* 19:12.

138. Ibid. 10:7; *Berachot* 3a; *Shabbat* 119b; *Sotah* 49a.

139. *Berachot* 3a, *Tosafot* ad loc. "*VeOnin.*"

140. Circa 200 C.E.

141. Circa 500 C.E.

142. *The Complete ArtScroll Siddur, Ashkenaz,* pp. 56-57; Transliteration p. 1048.

143. *Tur, Yoreh Deah* 376 — Story of Rabbi Akiva.

144. *Gesher Hachaim,* vol. 1, p.316.

145. Zvi Kolitz, *Survival for What?* p. 144, Philosophical Library, NY, 1969. Thanks to my neighbor, Rabbi Dovid Merkin, for bringing this quote to my attention.

146. *Code of Jewish Law, Orach Chaim* 9.

147. Isaiah 40:1.

148. Deuteronomy 28:9.

149. Maimonides, *Mishneh Torah,* Laws of Character, 1:5-6.

150. *Sotah* 14a.

151. *Gesher Hachaim,* vol. 1, 30:5.

152. *Berachot* 6b.

153. Rabbi Samson Raphael Hirsch, *Horeb,* II Edoth Chap. 43, para. 319.

154. Proverbs 27:19.

155. *Berachot* 27b; *Gesher Hachaim*, vol. 1, 20:5.

156. *Moed Katan* 28b; *Code of Jewish Law, Yoreh Deah* 376:1.

157. *Code of Jewish Law, Yoreh Deah* 385:1.

158. *Gesher Hachaim*, vol. 1, 20:5.

159. *Gesher Hachaim*, ibid.

160. God, Who permeates all of time and space. Literally "The Place" — a Name of God based on the idea that God is the ultimate framework of reality of everything in existence, the ultimate "place." *Pesikta Rabati* 21:5; Rabbi Chaim of Volozhin, *Nefesh Hachaim,* 3:1,2.

161. *The Complete ArtScroll Siddur, Ashkenaz,* pp. 800-801. See *Ketuvot* 8b.

162. Psalms 91:15.

163. *Code of Jewish Law, Yoreh Deah* 338:1.

164. *Code of Jewish Law,* ibid, 338:2; *The Complete ArtScroll Siddur, Ashkenaz,* pp. 796-797.

165. *Code of Jewish Law,* ibid, 340:5.

166. Burial society, see above.

167. *Kol Bo Al Aveilut*, p. 174, paras. 3-4.

168. See above: The Mitzvah of Burial: Honoring a Deceased Person.

169. *Code of Jewish Law,* ibid, 357:1.

170. II Samuel 3:35.

171. *Kol Bo Al Aveilut*, pp. 272-273.

172. *Moed Katan* 27b; *Code of Jewish Law, Yoreh Deah,* 378:1.

173. Ibid. 376:3, Ramah; 393:3, Ramah; *Pitchei Teshuvah* 2.

174. The main collection of the Oral Law, written down by Judah the Prince in Israel c. 200 C.E.

175. This is a common custom.

176. *Berachot* 64a.

The Jewish Calendar

The lunar calendar: history, philosophy and structure

The Sun, the Moon and the Seasons

*M*easuring and marking the passage of time is a universal human preoccupation. At least 40 different calendars are in use around the world today. The most widely used systems are the solar calendar, based on the cycle of the sun, and the lunar calendar, based on the cycle of the moon. Because of its orbit around the earth, the side of the moon facing the earth, alternates between being fully illuminated by sunlight (full moon) and not illuminated at all by sunlight (no moon — "a moonless night"). A lunar month is defined as the time required for the moon to go from a given phase (e.g. new moon, slim crescent) back to that phase again, a period of about 29½ days.[1] In a lunar calendar, the month begins with the sighting of the new moon; the middle of the month coincides with the full moon and the end of the month with the gradual disappearance of the moon. The lunar year consists of 12 lunar months, about 354 days,[2] while the solar year is 365¼ days long,[3] a difference of about 11 days.

The seasons of the year are dependent upon the earth's rotation around the sun, its tilted orbit and its distance from the sun. If the lunar calendar is not adjusted to the seasons of the sun at all, then a particular lunar date will "drift," until over the course of 33 years, it occurs in each of the four seasons.[4] Most of the Western world uses the Gregorian calendar, which is solar.[5] In a solar calendar, the months are not coordinated with the cycles of the moon, and the year is based only on the seasons. Specific dates consistently occur in the same seasons, but with no relationship to the natural cycle of the moon at all (e.g., the first of the month may coincide with a full moon, "no moon" or a quarter moon).

The Jewish calendar is a luni-solar system, combining elements of both the lunar and solar calendars. The Jewish calendar scrupulously follows the phases of the moon,[6] but it also incorporates features that ensure that the festivals always occur in the same seasons.[7] Passover, for example, always falls in the spring and Sukkot is always in autumn. In contrast to the solar calendar, the first day of the Jewish month coincides with the first appearance of the new moon. Complex formulae[8] regulate the periodic adjustment of the calendar to coordinate the cycle of the moon with the cycle of the seasons. Seven times in the course of 19 years, an extra month is added to compensate for the 11-day difference between the solar and lunar years.[9] A Jewish leap year, therefore, has 13 months.[10] The rules and astronomical measurements used to formulate the calendar are part of the Oral tradition as received on Mount Sinai and passed on from one generation to the next.[11] (Owning a current Jewish calendar is a must if you want to know when each Jewish holiday will fall!)

In the Torah (as well as in modern Hebrew), the days of the week are designated by number: i.e., "first day," "second day." Only the seventh day, Shabbat, has a name. The first chapter of Genesis speaks of "evening and morning" when describing the creation of the world, indicating that a day is calculated from nightfall to nightfall, so day one begins at nightfall on Saturday and ends at night on Sunday.[12] Originally, months were also designated only by number rather than by name — beginning with the month in which the Exodus took place.[13] During the Babylonian exile, which followed the destruction of the First Temple, the Jews began using Babylonian names for the months. These names are still in use today.[14]

The Moon in Court

In the following section — and throughout this book — I use the abbreviations B.C.E. and C.E. to denote secular dates. They stand for Before the Common Era, and Common Era. I use these instead of the more common B.C. and A.D. since the classic B.C. and A.D. are direct references to Christian messianic beliefs, whereas B.C.E. and C.E. are more neutral expressions.

In the times of the Holy Temple in Jerusalem (from circa 832 B.C.E. until 70 C.E.), the highest Jewish court in Israel, the Sanhedrin, would determine when a new month began.[15] The beginning of each month was (and still is) marked by a semiholiday known as Rosh Chodesh. Eyewitness reports that a new moon had been sighted were critical in declaring a Rosh Chodesh,[16] but astronomical calculations,[17] as well as agricultural, economic and religious considerations,[18] were also taken into account. The process of determining the beginning of the new month is called *Kiddush Hachodesh,* the Sanctification of the New Moon. Setting Rosh Chodesh ahead or back a day determines when the upcoming festivals will begin; therefore, *Kiddush Hachodesh* creates the holiness of the festival days.

Every member of the Sanhedrin had authority (called *semichah* in Hebrew) conferred upon him by someone else who had authority conferred upon him, in an unbroken chain all the way back to Moses, who had given authority to Joshua.[19] During the period of persecution by the Roman Empire, the Sanhedrin lost much of its power. Early Roman decrees made it illegal to grant or to receive this authority,[20] and when the Roman Empire became Christian under Constantine,[21] the Sanhedrin was forbidden to convene.[22] Since Rosh Chodesh can be declared only by the meeting of a Sanhedrin whose members have *semichah,*[23] it became increasingly difficult and dangerous to sanctify the new moon each month. By about 360 C.E. the Rabbis realized that the situation was only getting worse and the time would come when a Sanhedrin with *semichah* would no longer exist. Hillel II[24] and his court therefore decided at this time to establish a fixed calendar. He calculated, sanctified and declared all subsequent months and years. The calendar that we use today is based on these calculations and sanctifications.[25]

What Year Is It?

Jewish chronology begins with the creation of the first human, Adam.[26] We calculate our current year by adding up the intervals from Adam's age when his son Seth[27] was born, until the age when that son had his first son, and so on, as recounted in Genesis.[28] According to Jewish calculation, Abraham was born in the year 1948 from the creation of Adam (1812 B.C.E.).[29] According to Jewish-year calculations from creation, then, Columbus "sailed the oceans blue" in the year 5252 (1492 on the civil calendar), and the State of Israel was established in 5708 (1948). To convert a particular civil (Gregorian) year to the corresponding Jewish year, one adds 3760 to the civil year.[30]

Diaspora Doubts

In the times of the Temple, the Sanhedrin would decide when to sanctify a new month primarily on the basis of eyewitness reports. Two people would come to the court and testify that they had seen the new moon.[31] If the court accepted the testimony (based on specific criteria), Rosh Chodesh would be immediately declared, making the previous month 29 days long. The Sanhedrin could delay the declaration of the new month until the next day for economic or social considerations, or if they rejected the testimony because it was ambiguous or incorrect. The previous month would then be 30 days long, since a lunar month must be either 29 or 30 days.[32] The declaration of Rosh Chodesh would determine when the festivals would begin, "moving" them either ahead or back by a day.

It was therefore necessary for the Sanhedrin to inform the dispersed Jewish communities of the declaration of the new month as soon as possible, so that Jews in far-flung areas could observe the festivals at the correct times. The court would send messengers out to inform as many people as possible of the new month before the onset of the next festival.[33] The communities outside of Israel, however, were often too far away for the messengers to reach in time, and would remain in doubt about the day on which the festival would begin.[34] These communities, known as the Diaspora,[35] therefore observed the "holy days" of each festival for two days instead of one[36] to account for the two possible days on which Rosh Chodesh may have occurred. The only exception to this is Rosh Hashanah, which is the only festival that begins on the first of the month. Therefore, it was (and is) always observed for two days even in Israel since the messengers were clearly unable to tell people in time when Rosh Chodesh had been declared.[37] Diaspora communities observe the Day of Atonement, Yom Kippur, for only one day, since it is a twenty-five-hour fast, and there is a health risk involved in fasting for two whole days.[38]

Diaspora Doubles – Two-day Festivals

Once Hillel II established the set calendar, there was no longer any doubt about the day on which any given festival was to be celebrated. Nevertheless, the Sages decreed that the Diaspora custom of keeping two-day festivals should remain in force, and they required the Jews of the Diaspora to "keep the custom of their fathers."[39] The Talmud explains that this was done in order to guard against the possibility that the calendar system might collapse in a time of persecution. Should this occur, we would once again be in doubt about when to observe the festivals.[40]

Some commentaries explain that because of the intensity of the spirituality in the Land of Israel, one day is sufficient to absorb the lessons of the festivals, while outside of Israel two are required to achieve the same spiritual fulfillment.[41] Others suggest that we retain this custom as a way of experiencing the idea expressed in the verse in Isaiah,[42] "For from Zion shall come forth the law and the word of God from Jerusalem." Even though we have a fixed calendar today, we remember and hope for a return to the time when we looked to the Sanhedrin in Jerusalem to hear "the word of God."[43]

Jews Are from the Moon, Egyptians Are from the Sun

The first commandment that God gave to the Jewish people in Egypt before the Exodus was to establish the calendar.[44] In order to understand the importance attached to this commandment, we must understand the type of society that the Jews lived in during their exile in Egypt. The Egyptians, along with the rest of the world at that time, worshipped many different gods — each believed to have its own sphere of influence. But all Egyptians revered Ra, their sun god, chief of cosmic deities from whom early Egyptian kings claimed to be descended.[45]

The sun does not exhibit any obvious cycles; it remains a constant presence in the sky, year in, year out. In contrast, the moon waxes and wanes, appearing, disappearing and appearing again, cycling between "non-existence" and "existence" every month. Jewish philosophers have explained that the pagan focus on the sun was based on the belief that life too is constant and unchanging — there is no free will, and no possibility of change.[46] The sun symbolizes an unchanging, permanent reality,[47] which for the pagan was a reflection of the deterministic world without moral freedom; life, like the sun, was predetermined and set.

Judaism, however, is predicated on the belief that human beings are morally free and have the ability to choose between good and evil. Life is not predetermined and we are not controlled by our past.[48] The Jewish calendar is therefore focused on the moon, so that the renewal of the moon will act as a reminder of individual renewal through free will. Rabbi Samson Raphael Hirsch explains the insights that the we are supposed to draw from the Jewish calendar:

> The truth the calendar teaches forms the foundation stone of our Jewishness, and it is this that differentiates it most sharply from all paganism. The pagan knows no newness, not in the world, not in humanity, not in his gods, nor in the powers he places above men and the world. To him, everything is bound by cast-iron necessity. To him, all todays are evolved

from yesterdays, and every tomorrow must with absolute certainty follow from today. Just as he denies creatio ex nihilo,[49] the free creation by the free will of a Creator, so for him there is also no ex nihilo [creativity] in the moral nature of Man,[50] no ex nihilo in the fate of Man.[51] Guilt and evil must forever bring about only guilt and evil. For him, nothing of the god-like freedom dwells in the heart of man, for him no free God reigns in and over the world, everything swims down the stream of blind unalterable necessity, all freedom is but an illusion, everything new is only that which existed in the old![52]

These ideas are implicit in the Hebrew expressions used for the lunar month and for the solar year. The Hebrew word for month is *chodesh,* which is related to the word *chadash*, new.[53] The Hebrew word for year, on the other hand, *shanah,* is related to the words *shinun*, repetition, and *sheni*, second (in other words, *not* first, *not* new).[54]

Spirals and Cycles

Jewish tradition views time as a spiral, not as a linear progression. Every year represents another loop in the spiral, but any given point contains the same spiritual energy every time it recurs. Rather than moving continually onward away from any given point in history, we return again and again to the same spiritual "place" in time. Inherent in the season of Passover, for example, is the spiritual energy of freedom and redemption. These qualities existed even before the Exodus occurred, and can be re-experienced every year at this time. We travel around the spiral, following the path of previous generations, as we return again and again to the same "places in time."[55] Observance of the festivals and the commandments related to them enables us to recapture the spiritual sparks which are integral components of that time.[56] The Biblical commentator Nachmanides notes that the Hebrew word *chag*, festival, is related to the word *chug*, circle.[57] Our observance of the festivals marks our arrival at the same place in the circle of time.

It is commonly believed that the month of Nissan, in which Passover falls, came to be the month of redemption because the Exodus occurred then; in other words, that the designation of the month commemorates the historic event. In fact, exactly the opposite is true! The reason the Exodus occurred then, in the month of Nissan, is because redemption and freedom are intrinsic properties of that time of year.[58]

The spiritual component of the redemption is reflected not only in history, but in the natural events of that season as well. Spring is the time when animals give birth, plants flower and the weather becomes warmer.[59] Thus history, nature, agriculture and spirituality all come together in the cycle and flow of the Jewish year. This idea is beautifully expressed in the following verses from the Song of Songs, the poetic allegory that describes the bond of affection between God and the Jewish people:

> My beloved lifted His voice and said to me: "Arise, My love, My fair one, and go forth. For behold, the winter is passed, the rain is over and gone. The blossoms have appeared in the land, the time of singing has come, and the voice of the turtledove is heard in our land."[60]

The Sages interpreted these verses as a call from God to the Jewish people to prepare for the Exodus, because "the month of spring [Nissan] has arrived and the time of redemption is near."[61] This interpretation demonstrates that time has an intrinsic spiritual dimension which existed prior to the events of history. Moreover, that spiritual dimension manifests itself in the seasons of the year and the events of nature. It is for these reasons that Judaism attaches such importance to celebrating the festivals in the same season and on the same date that the events originally occurred.[62]

Remember the Exodus!

The Exodus from Egypt was the event that created the Jewish nation as a physical entity.[63] The experiences of being freed from slavery, witnessing the Ten Plagues and crossing the Red Sea transformed the Jewish people from a downtrodden family of slaves, steeped in pagan culture, to a proud nation of monotheists.[64] The miracles of the Exodus teach us all the most fundamental components of Jewish faith — belief in God, denial of idolatry, belief in Divine providence, reward and punishment, prophecy, and the concept of the Chosen People.[65] It is for these reasons that the Torah commands us to remember the Exodus from Egypt every day[66] and to transmit its message to our children.[67]

The Jewish calendar itself is a testimony to the Exodus. As mentioned earlier, in the Torah the months are designated only by number; they have no names. The first month of the year is the month in which the Jewish people came out of Egypt; all other months are identified with reference to this event. Seventy years after the destruction of the First Temple[68] and the exile to Babylon,[69] many Jews returned to Israel and rebuilt the Temple.[70] As a reminder of that second "Exodus" the Jewish people began using the Babylonian names for the months. Nachmanides explains the reason for this change in the following way:

"This month shall be for you the first of months"[71] — This is the first commandment that God gave to the Jewish people through Moses ... We are commanded to count this as the first of months, and all the months shall be counted... from this month until the completion of the twelve months of the year... so that any time we mention the month we will be reminded of the great miracle of the Exodus. Therefore the months have no names in the Torah, rather, it says "in the third month"... Just as we remember the Shabbat when we count the days of the week as the first day of Shabbat, the second and so forth, we also remember our redemption from Egypt when we count from this month ... However, when we came out of Babylon and the verse in Jeremiah[72] was fulfilled: "It will not be said, 'God lives! Who took us out of the land of Egypt,' rather — 'God lives! Who brought us from the northern land [Babylon].'" Then we began to call the months by the names that they were called in Babylon, to remember that we were also redeemed from there. For these names, Nissan and Iyar and the others, are all Persian names ... Now we mention the names of the months to remember the second redemption, just as we used to remember the first redemption.[73]

Nachmanides is not saying that the return from Babylon supplanted the Exodus from Egypt in national importance, but rather that this second redemption is commemorated by the use of Persian names for the months. These names are a reminder that the living God can and will redeem His people from the Exile in any generation.

The New Moon – A Festive Reminder

The concepts and lessons contained in the Jewish calendar are so central to our belief that it is necessary to teach and emphasize them regularly. One of the ways in which Jewish tradition makes us aware of the cycle of the calendar and brings home its messages is by celebrating every new moon, Rosh Chodesh, as a minor festival.[74] On the Shabbat immediately preceding the new month, special prayers are recited in the synagogue to announce its arrival and to pray that the coming month will be blessed with success, happiness and righteousness.[75] Before these prayers are begun, the exact astronomical moment that the new moon will appear over Jerusalem is announced. The cantor takes the Torah scroll and, together with the community, recites the following prayers:[76]

May it be Your will, our God and God of our forefathers, that You inaugurate this month upon us for goodness and for bless-

*ing. May You give us long life — a life of peace, a life of good-
ness, a life of blessing, a life of sustenance, a life of physical
health, a life in which there is fear of heaven and fear of sin, a
life in which there is no shame or humiliation, a life of wealth
and honor, a life in which we will have love of Torah and fear
of heaven, a life in which our heartfelt requests will be fulfilled
for the good. Amen.*

(Here the precise time of the appearance of the new moon over
Jerusalem [known as the *molad,* the birth] is announced.)

*He Who has performed miracles for our forefathers and
redeemed them from slavery to freedom — may He redeem us
soon and gather in our dispersed from the four corners of the
earth; all Israel are friends. Now let us respond: Amen.*

*The new month (name of the month) will be on (day of the
week) which is coming to us and to all Israel for goodness.*

*May the Holy One, Blessed is He, renew it upon us and upon
all His people, the Family of Israel, for life and for peace, for
joy and for gladness, for salvation and for consolation. Now let
us respond: Amen.*

On Rosh Chodesh itself prayers are recited that express our joy and
gratitude to God for the life that He has granted us and for His blessings.[77]
We also pray that the coming month will be a fulfilling, good and happy
month and a month in which God will give a positive answer to our prayers
and bring the Final Redemption.[78] An additional prayer called *Mussaf*[79] is
added (which corresponds to the Rosh Chodesh service in the ancient
Holy Temple), as well as a special reading[80] from the Torah scroll. It is customary to eat a more festive meal than usual,[81] and a paragraph is added
in the Grace After Meals.[82]

Although there is no prohibition of work on Rosh Chodesh, it is customary for women to celebrate the day by refraining from certain types
of work.[83] The reason for this is that soon after the giving of the Torah
at Mount Sinai, the Jewish people — fearful that Moses had died on the
mountain — built a golden calf and worshipped it as an idol. The men contributed their gold jewelry for the construction of the idol, but the women
refused to participate.[84] Because of their refusal to give even tacit approval
to this rebellion against God, it became customary for Rosh Chodesh to be
celebrated as a "women's festival."[85]

On Saturday night soon after Rosh Chodesh, sanctification of the new
moon, known as *Kiddush Levanah,*[86] is recited. This prayer focuses on
another aspect of the moon's symbolic meaning concerning the Jewish
people[87] and the monarchy of King David.[88] The phases of the moon symbolize the phases of Jewish history; we pray that just as the moon becomes

full after completely disappearing, so too the Jewish people should merit being a "full moon," fulfilled by the coming of the Messiah.

Supplemental Material

Table of the Months and Events of the Jewish Year

HEBREW MONTH (approximate civil equivalents)	EVENT	EVENT	EVENT
1. NISSAN APRIL/MAY	15TH-22ND – Pesach/Passover. Exodus from Eygpt, creation of the Jewish people.		
2. IYAR MAY/JUNE	18TH – Lag B'Omer. Minor Festival, commemorating the end of the 33-day plague that killed thousands of Rabbi Akiva's students.	18TH – Revelation of mystical teachings of the *Zohar* by Rabbi Shimon bar Yochai and anniversary of his death.	
3. SIVAN JUNE/JULY	7TH – Shavuot. Giving of the Torah and Revelation on Mt. Sinai.		
4. TAMUZ JULY/AUGUST	17TH – Fast. Breach of the walls of Jerusalem before the destruction of the First Temple.	Beginning of the three weeks of mourning for the destruction of the Temples, ending with the 9th of Av.	
5. AV AUGUST/ SEPTEMBER	9TH – Fast. Destruction of First and Second Temples.	15TH – Minor Festival.	
6. ELUL SEPTEMBER/ OCTOBER	Special Selichot prayers recited early in the morning as preparation for Rosh Hashanah. Days of Repentance.		

HEBREW MONTH (approximate civil equivalents)	EVENT	EVENT	EVENT
7. TISHREI SEPTEMBER/ OCTOBER	1ST-2ND – Rosh Hashanah/New Year. Creation of man and judgment of the whole world. 3RD – Fast of Gedaliah. Commemorating assasination of Gedaliah, governor of Israel, following the destruction of the First Temple.	10TH – Yom Kippur/ Day of Atonement. Giving of the second Tablets, forgiveness for the Golden Calf, time of repentance.	15TH-23RD – Sukkot, Shemini Atzeret, Simchat Torah. Commemoration of the physical and spiritual survival of the Jews in the desert and in Exile.
8. CHESHVAN OCTOBER/ NOVEMBER	7TH – Prayers for rain in Israel begin.		
9. KISLEV NOVEMBER/ DECEMBER	25TH THROUGH 2ND TEVET – Chanukah. Victory of the Maccabees over the Greeks, miracle of the Menorah.		
10. TEVET DECEMBER/ JANUARY	8TH – Minor Fast Day. Translation of Torah into Greek at time of Ptolemy, considered a tragedy.	9TH – Minor Fast Day. Death of Ezra the Scribe.	10TH – Fast Day Siege of First Temple by Babylonians.
11. SHEVAT JANUARY/ FEBRUARY	15TH – New Year of Trees.		
12. ADAR I IN A LEAP YEAR FEBRUARY/ MARCH		13TH – Fast of Esther.	14TH-15TH – Purim. Salvation of the Jewish people from destruction during Persian exile.
13. ADAR II MARCH/APRIL	7TH – Anniversary of the birth and death of Moses. In a leap year, Purim is in Adar II.		

For Further Reading

▸ *The Book of Our Heritage* by Rabbi Eliyahu Kitov (Feldheim, 1979)

▸ *The Jewish Calendar: Its Structure and Laws* by Rabbi David Feinstein (ArtScroll/Mesorah, 2004)

▸ www.HebCal.com

NOTES

References to books of the Talmud refer to the Babylonian Talmud unless otherwise noted.

1. *Rosh Hashanah* 25a; The Jewish calendar uses a mean value for the lunar month of 29 days, 12 hours, 793 parts or 29 days, 12 hours, 44 minutes, 3 ⅓ seconds. (In Jewish tradition the hour is 1080 *chalakim*, parts, each part is thus equal to 3⅓ seconds.) For a full description of the way the Jewish calendar works, see Arthur Spier, *The Comprehensive Hebrew Calendar*, Behrman House, Inc. NY, 1952; Leo Levi, *Jewish Chrononomy*, Gur Aryeh Institute, NY, 1967; Schamroth, *A Glimpse of Light*, Targum-Feldheim, Jerusalem, 1998; W.M. Feldman, *Rabbinical Mathematics and Astronomy*, Sepher-Hermon Press, NY, 1978; J. David Bleich, *Bircas Hachamah*, Artscroll/Mesorah Publications, New York, 1980, Introduction.

2. *Arachin* 9b; more precisely — 354.36707 days.

3. Ibid.; more precisely — 365.24219 days.

4. The Moslems use a lunar calendar that does not take into account the discrepancy between the lengths of the lunar and solar years. Therefore, Moslem festivals do not regularly coincide with any particular season. Over the course of about 33 years, a given festival will fall in every season. (33 yrs. x 11-days difference = 363 days, approximately one year.) *Qur'an*, Sura 9:36-37; Huston Smith, *The World's Religions*, Harper San Francisco, 1991, p. 247.

5. Daniel J. Boorstin, *The Discoverers*, Vintage Books, NY, 1985, Book One; Time. The Gregorian calendar replaced the Julian calendar, which was promulgated in the year 45 B.C.E. by Julius Caesar. He inserted 90 days to bring the months of the Roman calendar back to their traditional place with respect to the seasons. The Gregorian calendar is based on Pope Gregory's papal bull "Inter Gravissimus," signed on February 24, 1582. Gregory deleted ten days from the calendar, so that October 4, 1582 was followed by October 15, 1582, thereby causing the vernal equinox of 1583 and subsequent years to occur about March 21.

6. Exodus 12:2, Commentary of Rashi ad loc.; Maimonides, *Book of the Mitzvot*, Positive Commandment 153; *Mishneh Torah*, Laws of Sanctification of the New Moon, 1:1.

7. Deuteronomy 16:1; *Sefer Hachinuch*, Mitzvah 4 — "The foundation of this commandment is in order to have all the festivals in their correct seasons and at their correct times"; Maimonides, ibid.

8. Maimonides, *Mishneh Torah*, Laws of Sanctification of the New Moon; Tur and *Shulchan Aruch, Orach Chaim*, end of 428; *Luchot Ha'ibbur*, Spier, pp. 217-227; Levi, pp. 6-10.

9. 19 yrs. x 11-days difference = 209 days over 19 years. 209 days divided by 30 = 6.97-months difference every 19 years. The duration of 19 solar years is equal to 235 lunar months (12

months x 19 years) + 7 (added leap months) = 235 months; Spier, p. 218.

10. Maimonides, ibid. 1:2.

11. Rabbi Yehudah Halevy, *Kuzari*, 2:64.

12. *Berachot* 2a.

13. Exodus 12:2.

14. *Midrash Rabbah*, Genesis 48:9; *Rosh Hashanah* 6a; Nachmanides, Exodus 12:1.

15. *Sanhedrin* 10b; Maimonides, ibid. 5:1.

16. *Rosh Hashanah* 20a.

17. Maimonides, ibid. 1:6.

18. *Sanhedrin* 20a-20b; Maimonides, ibid., 4:2-5.

19. Numbers 27:23; *Avodah Zarah* 8b. This was known as *semichah*, ordination. Modern-day ordination means that the ordained rabbi passed a series of exams in advanced study of Jewish law.

20. *Sanhedrin* 14a, 41a.

21. Emperor of Rome from 306 C.E. to 337 C.E., also known as Constantine the Great, who converted to Christianity and adopted it as the official religion of the Roman Empire.

22. Regarding increased persecution under the Holy Roman Empire, see Paul Johnson, *A History of the Jews*, Harper and Row, NY, 1987, p.164; *From Yavneh to Pumbeditha*, ArtScroll/Mesorah.

23. Nachmanides, *Critique of Sefer Hamitzvot*, Mitzvat Asei 153.

24. Talmudic Sage, descendant of Rabbi Judah the Prince and of Hillel the Elder, also known as Hillel I; Maimonides, ibid. 5:3; Rabbi Yechiel Halperin, *Seder Hadorot*, Elef Hachamishi, 118.

25. Maimonides, ibid. 5:3-5, 13.

26. Rabbi Yehudah Halevy, *Kuzari*, 1:47.

27. Genesis 5:4. His first-born son, Cain, murdered his brother Abel before Abel had any children, so the calculation uses Seth, his first righteous son to have had children. See Nachmanides, Sforno and Ohr Hachaim, ad loc.

28. Genesis Chaps. 5 and 11; *Seder Olam Rabah* 1.

29. *Avodah Zarah* 9a; Rashi ad loc. "*hachi garsinan.*"

30. This is not always precise, since the Jewish year begins around September, whereas the civil year begins in January.

31. Maimonides, ibid. 1:7.

32. Ibid. 1:3-6.

33. Ibid. 3:9.

34. *Rosh Hashanah* 21a; ibid. Maimonides 3:11-12.

35. The Hebrew term is *golah*, which means, "exile." Diaspora means, "the dispersion," from the Greek *speiro*, scatter.

36. Maimonides ibid. 5:4; Sukkot and Passover begin and end with a "holy day," separated by six intermediate days; Shavuot consists of only one day in Israel and two days in the Diaspora.

37. Ibid. 5:7-8.

38. *Shulchan Aruch*, Orach Chaim, 624:5, Rama; It is observed on the day that it would fall in the majority of years assuming the previous month, Elul, to be 29 days.

39. *Beitzah* 4b; *Eruvin* 3:9; ibid. 5:5-6; *Shulchan Aruch,* Orach Chaim, 496.

40. *Beitzah,* ibid.

41. This may be the explanation of the *Midrash Rabbah*, Song of Songs, Parshah 1:42 and the Jerusalem Talmud in *Eruvin*, ibid.

42. Isaiah 2:3; also in Micah 4:2.

43. See *Meshech Chochmah, Parshat Bo*, "*ubazeh*" which alludes to this idea; also Rabbi Yosef Engel, *Gilyonei Hashas, Beitzah* ad loc. See Rabbi Eliyahu Dessler, *Michtav M'Eliyahu*, vol. 2, p. 75 — Every Rabbinic decree has hidden reasons in addition to the reason that is mentioned explicitly in the Talmud.

44. Exodus 12:1-2; Rashi, Commentary on Genesis 1:1; Nachmanides, Commentary on Exodus 12:2.

45. Beginning with the Middle Kingdom (2134-1668 B.C.E.), Ra worship acquired the status of a state religion, and the god was gradually fused with Amon during the Theban dynasties, becoming the supreme god Amon-Ra. "Egyptian Mythology," *Microsoft*®

Encarta® 98 Encyclopedia.© 1993-1997 Microsoft Corporation. See also James K. Hoffmeier, *Israel in Egypt*, Oxford University Press, N.Y., 1996, p. 151.

46. Rabbi Samson Raphael Hirsch, Commentary on Exodus 12:2, English translation by Isaac Levy, Judaica Press Ltd., Gateshead, 1982; See also *Sukkah* 29a, in which the Gentile nations are compared to the sun.

47. Maharal, *Netzach Yisrael*, Chap. 46.

48. *Ethics of the Fathers* 3:15; *Berachot* 33b; Maimonides, *Mishneh Torah*, Laws of Repentance, 5:1-3.

49. Latin for "creation from nothing." See Nachmanides, Commentary on Genesis 1:26, 2:3; Maimonides, *Guide for the Perplexed,* 2:25-27.

50. In other words, "no free will."

51. In other words, "all is predetermined."

52. Rabbi Hirsch, ibid.

53. Rabbi Hirsch, ibid.; Rabbi David Kimchi, *Sefer Hashorashim*, "*chadash*"; Commentary of Rabbi Meir Leibush Malbim on Exodus 12:2.

54. Rabbi Hirsch, ibid.; Kimchi, ibid. "*shanah*"; Maharal, *Sefer Gevurot Hashem*, Chap. 51.

55. Rabbi Eliyahu Dessler, *Michtav M'Eliyahu*, vol. 1, p. 103, vol. 2, p. 21.

56. Rabbi Shlomo Eliashiv, *Leshem Shvo Ve'achlamah*, Sefer Hadeah, 2, Drush 4, 24:8; Ibid. Drush Miut Hayareach, 6.

57. Nachmanides, Commentary on Leviticus 23:40; Hirsch, Commentary on Exodus 5:1, Leviticus 23:6, Psalms 107:27.

58. Rabbi Yitzchak Ze'ev Soloveitchik, *Chidushei Hagriz al HaTorah*, no. 131.

59. For extensive discussion of the relationship between nature and the Jewish calendar, see Nosson Slifkin, *Seasons of Life*, Targum Press, Jerusalem, 1998.

60. Song of Songs 2:10. This is the literal translation. For the allegorical translation see *The Stone Edition of the Tanach*, ArtScroll/Mesorah Publications, NY, 1998, p. 1687; see also *Rosh Hashanah* 11a.

61. *Midrash Rabbah* ad loc.; See Rashi, ad loc.

62. Dessler, ibid.; Chinuch, ibid.

63. Rabbi Samson Raphael Hirsch, *Horeb*, II Edoth, Chap. 23, par. 165.

64. Maimonides, *Mishneh Torah*, Laws of Idolatry, 1:3; Hirsch, ibid.

65. Nachmanides, Commentary on Exodus 13:16.

66. Deuteronomy 16:3.

67. Exodus 13:8.

68. On the 9th of Av in the year 3338 from Adam, or 423 B.C.E.

69. Approximately where Iraq is located today.

70. See Books of Ezra and Nehemiah. The Second Temple was completed in the year 3408, or 353 B.C.E.

71. Exodus 12:2.

72. Jeremiah 16:14-15.

73. Commentary of Nachmanides, Exodus 12:2.

74. *Shulchan Aruch, Orach Chaim*, 418:1, 419:1.

75. Ibid. *Mishnah Berurah* ad loc., 418:1.

76. *The Complete ArtScroll Siddur, Ashkenaz*, p. 453.

77. *Shulchan Aruch, Orach Chaim*, 422:2; "*Hallel*" ibid., pp. 632-643.

78. Ibid. 422:1; "*Yaaleh veyavo*" ibid., pp. 110-111.

79. Ibid. 423:3; ibid. pp. 644-653.

80. Ibid. 423:1-2; ibid. p. 948.

81. Ibid. 419:1.

82. *The Complete ArtScroll Siddur, Ashkenaz*, pp. 190-191.

83. Such as laundering or sewing — *Code of Jewish Law, Orach Chaim*, 417:1.

84. Exodus 32:3; *Midrash Rabbah*, Numbers, 21:10; *Midrash Tanchuma*, Ki Tisa, 19, Pinchas, 7; *Pirkei D'Rabbi Eliezer*, 44.

85. *Levush Haorah*, ibid.; *Mishnah Berurah*, 417:3.

86. Ibid. 426:1-4; *The Complete ArtScroll Siddur, Ashkenaz*, pp. 612-617.

87. *Midrash Rabbah*, Exodus 15:26.

88. Liturgy, *Siddur* ad loc.

Who Invented
the Weekend Anyway?

The meaning and practice of Shabbat

The Sabbath

*T*he Sabbath (*Shabbos* or *Shabbat* in Hebrew) is one of the most
prominent and central features of Jewish life.[1] To one who is unfamiliar with its laws and philosophy, many aspects of the observance of the Sabbath may appear illogical and even bizarre.

I once spent Shabbat at the Holiday Inn in Kowloon, Hong Kong,
where I was given a room on the 11th floor of the hotel. I did not use
the elevator because of the Shabbat restriction against turning electric
circuits on or off (to be explained later), so instead I used the staircase
designated for the staff. Wheezing and staggering up the 10th flight of
stairs I encountered a waiter at the hotel, who asked me why I was not
using the elevator. I replied, "Because it is the Sabbath, our day of rest."
We looked at each other for a moment; he nervously smiled and sped
away before I could explain how climbing 11 flights of stairs is considered "rest."

In this chapter we will try to explain the meaning of Shabbat and
demonstrate the unity of its law and philosophy. The Torah emphasizes
the importance of the Shabbat in numerous places. It is, in fact, the

fourth of the Ten Commandments. In Jewish tradition, we consider the Ten Commandments to be principles from which all the 613 commandments can be derived.[2] Since Shabbat is one of these "root commandments," it is logical to assume that Shabbat must include within it many other commandments, ideas and principles. The idea that a human should not be a slave to the physical world, that our power comes with obligation, and that it is possible to achieve harmony in life, are all concepts that are embodied within the commandment of Shabbat, as we shall explain.

Shabbat and Creation

The Talmud points out that observance of Shabbat is testimony to belief in God, belief in Creation and belief in Divine Providence.[3] The first chapter of Genesis relates the successive stages of the creation of the world. From a state of absolute nothingness, God created time, space and the entire physical world. This process of creation took six days, and on the seventh day God "rested" and created the Shabbat. Because of the centrality of our belief that God created the world from nothing and continues to be involved in its ongoing existence, it is customary to recite the section in the Torah describing this process[4] during the synagogue services on Friday night.[5] The verses are recited aloud, while standing, just as testimony must be given by witnesses in a Jewish court of law.[6]

The Impact of Shabbat

Shabbat also has a tremendous sociological and psychological impact on the Jewish people. No matter what is going on in the outside world, no matter how hard a person works during the week, on Shabbat everyone feels like royalty — everyone dresses in his or her best clothing, candles are lit, festive meals are eaten. No one engages in work, business is not discussed, and an atmosphere of relaxation and serenity is created. Once the usual weekday distractions are removed, we are able to devote ourselves to more spiritual pursuits. One can pray without rushing to get to work, spend extra time studying Torah and focus on personal growth and relationships.

Shabbat creates a sanctuary in time in which we are forced to suspend our normal activities and re-evaluate the importance of our daily concerns. We are offered the opportunity to turn our attention to those areas of life that are too often neglected. Shabbat is the one time that the entire family can get together without the pressure of school or work and without the intrusion of the phone or television.[7] A common expression, coined by the Zionist writer, Achad Ha'Am, attests, "More than the Jews kept the Shabbat, the Shabbat has kept the Jews."

What Is Work? What Is Rest?

The Torah describes Shabbat as a day of rest,[8] or as a day when work is forbidden. Yet many of the laws seem inconsistent with this description. In order to understand Shabbat, we must understand the meaning of "work." For scientific purposes, work is defined as W=FD (Work equals Force times Displacement). For taxation purposes, work is defined as an activity that produces income. Some define work as whatever one does for a living during the week. According to this definition, a comedian would not be allowed to tell a joke on Shabbat, a cantor would not be allowed to pray and someone who works in a think tank would not be allowed to think for the entire day. Others think of work as physical exertion, which means one wouldn't be allowed to walk a distance to the synagogue. Obviously none of these scenarios are consistent with the Torah's concept of Shabbat. We must examine the sources more carefully in order to understand what the Torah means by "work" with regard to Shabbat.

The Torah's Hebrew word for work that is prohibited on Shabbat is *melachah*. The verse states, "You shall do no manner of *melachah*."[9] There is another Hebrew word for work that means toil (or labor) — *avodah*. The word *avodah* is used in the context of the slavery of the Egyptian exile.[10] *Melachah,* on the other hand, is never used to refer to mere physical exertion. It is clear that what is prohibited on Shabbat is not blood, sweat and tears, but rather specific types of activities.

The Oral Tradition[11] lists 39 categories of *melachot* (plural of *malachah)* that are prohibited on Shabbat. Some examples of *melachot* and their definitions follow:

▸ Planting: anything that encourages the growth of a plant. For instance, it is prohibited to water a plant or move it into sunlight.

▸ Cooking: using heat to effect a change of state. This prohibits any type of boiling, frying, or baking.

▸ Sewing: any permanent bonding of two materials.

▸ Building: construction of dwellings, vessels or implements.

Two noted Jewish philosophers[12] describe the common principles underlying these divergent activities. In all cases, the activities improve the usefulness of the object on which they are performed.[13] This improvement demonstrates human mastery of the world through the constructive use of our intelligence.[14] *Melachah,* then, does not denote physical effort, but rather creative activity.

Who Is the Real Master?

In order to understand the importance of abstaining from the above activities we must look at the sources of these prohibitions. The Torah describes the observance of Shabbat as *imitatio dei,* the imitation of God, Who "rested" (so to speak) after six days of creating the world, as we mentioned above. The Torah states:

> *Remember the Sabbath day to sanctify it. Six days shall you toil and accomplish all your work. But the seventh day is Sabbath to God, your God; you shall not do any work — you, your son, your daughter, your slave, your maidservant, your animal and your convert within your gates — for in six days God made the heavens and the earth, the seas and all that is in them, and He rested on the seventh day. Therefore, God blessed the Sabbath day and sanctified it.*[15]

We are commanded to rest on the Shabbat as testimony to the idea that the world is God's creation and belongs to Him. When we refrain from our own acts of creativity, acts that show our mastery of the world, we acknowledge that we are not the true masters of the world. (Consider a simple analogy: Rockefeller Plaza, once owned by the Rockefeller family, is open to pedestrian traffic virtually all the time. The law requires that the plaza be closed at least one day a year to show that it is privately owned; otherwise the area would revert to public ownership. Similarly, we make a similar statement about God's ownership of the world through our observance of Shabbat.)

During the week, if a fly annoys us, we kill it; if a flower looks attractive, we pluck it; if we want to eat something, we cook it. However, on Shabbat we do not kill, pluck, cook or otherwise effect changes in the world. It is a day when every element of the world is recognized as being a creation of God, when we consciously acknowledge that He is the proprietor of the universe and we exist only by His will. Observing Shabbat helps to combat the view that the world is the possession and slave of the human race.

Fire: Power with Responsibility

The prohibition against igniting fire is a good example of this idea. Without fire, no science or technology would be possible.[16] The development of metal tools and glass, the production of chemical reaction, semiconductors, plastic, refined petroleum and the computer all require the ability to harness the forces of nature, especially fire. The Sages of the Talmud state that the human being was first inspired to make a fire on the first Saturday night of creation, immediately after Shabbat.[17] Why specifically *after* Shabbat? Because fire, inasmuch as it is a means to achieve almost all acts of mastery and creativity,[18] is a symbol of the power of the human being. We are the only creature able to light, control and use fire.[19] Shabbat, however, teaches the human that he is not the ultimate master of the world, rather, that he too is a creation of God — and hence must act with responsibility. That is why fire was given to humans only after the lesson of responsibility was learned on Shabbat. This is why we say a blessing over a newly lit flame during a ritual called *Havdalah* at the conclusion of the Shabbat: fire is symbolic of the difference between Shabbat and the weekdays.[20]

To return to my oxygen-deprived encounter in the stairwell in Hong Kong — while climbing 11 flights of stairs is certainly hard work, it is hardly an example of human mastery over creation. Most animals could accomplish this task faster and with less exertion than the average human. Pressing a button, however, which closes an electric circuit that starts electron flow through the wires, operates a system of motors, computerized switches, weight sensors and lights in the elevator, is a wonderful example of the human mastery of the forces of creation (as surely as laying brick upon brick) and is therefore prohibited on Shabbat.[21]

Taking the Jew Out of Egypt, Taking Egypt Out of the Jew

The centrality of Shabbat also derives from its function as a reminder of our release from slavery in Egypt. The Torah states:

> *Safeguard the Sabbath day to sanctify it, as...your God, commanded you... And you shall remember that you were a slave in the land of Egypt, and... your God, has taken you out from there with a strong hand and an outstretched arm; therefore God, your God, has commanded you to make the Sabbath day.*[22]

Although the Exodus occurred 3,500 years ago, it is the ultimate example of God's involvement in history. It teaches us that He did not create the world and then abandon it to blind chance.[23] Rather, God has a plan and purpose in creation and takes an active role in world events.

The Egyptian Exile is a metaphor for any enslavement — be it physical or spiritual.[24] By ceasing our work, we show that we are not enslaved by the physical world. When a person is incapable of refraining from work, then he is indeed a slave. If he cannot walk past the computer without checking his e-mail, even though it's 3 o'clock in the morning, he is a slave. If he cannot go a day without checking the Dow-Jones, Nikkei or Nasdaq, he is a slave. Slaves used to wear some symbol of their slavery, to show that they were "at work" 24 hours a day, seven days a week. They still do, only now the symbols are pagers, cellular phones and palmtop computers. By prohibiting our involvement with these things for 24 hours, Shabbat prevents us from becoming slaves to the material world and its development.

Shabbat teaches us that human beings should not be engaged exclusively in the struggle for survival. We are designed for much more than merely propagating the species.[25] We remind ourselves of what our real goals should be on Shabbat when we reorder our priorities to allow for Torah study,[26] for enjoying our family,[27] and allotting time for other spiritual[28] and physical pleasures.[29]

Sanctifying Shabbat

Aside from the prohibition against work on Shabbat, there are "positive" commandments to engage in, activities designed to make us aware of the ideas behind Shabbat. What does the Torah mean when it states "Remember the Sabbath day to sanctify it"?[30]

The Oral Tradition tells us that this is the commandment to verbally sanctify the Shabbat[31] over a cup of wine.[32] This practice is known as *Kiddush,* when one holds a cup of wine and recites a paragraph from the Bible about Shabbat, then a blessing over wine, and finally a blessing about Shabbat.[33] In a family setting, it is usually the father who says *Kiddush,* although any Jewish adult can do so. He drinks the wine and distributes some to everyone at the table. The purpose of this practice is to reinforce in our minds the origin and lessons of Shabbat, and to do so in a state of happiness enhanced by the wine.[34]

The prayers that sanctify the Shabbat are very different from the weekday prayers. Supplications are not made for physical matters; no prayers of repentance are recited.[35]

Reciting Kiddush over wine using a silver goblet

The focus is on appreciating the gift of Shabbat.

Shabbat is also sanctified with increased Torah study. The weekly portion of the Torah, as well as a reading from the Prophets, are publicly read in the synagogue.[36] Classes are given on Torah topics, and people of all ages get together to study Torah with each other.[37]

Creating the Palace

Jewish law recognizes that physical environment has a powerful impact on a person's psychological state. Therefore, we go to great effort to create a special atmosphere in the home on Shabbat. On Friday, we honor the upcoming Shabbat by cleaning the house,[38] and grooming ourselves.[39] We prepare special clothing[40] and set the table for a formal dinner.[41] We usher in the Shabbat by lighting candles,[42] which enhance the enjoyment of the meal,[43] and we do our best to create a festive atmosphere appropriate for the visit of a royal guest. Before the advent of electric lights, the candles also prevented stumbling around in the dark.[44]

Even a person who is unfamiliar with Shabbat and with its philosophy cannot help but be drawn into the beautiful, dignified and enjoyable atmosphere that comes from adherence to these Jewish laws.

In 1815 an American sailor, Captain James Riley, was shipwrecked near the coast of Morocco. Members of the Jewish community there invited the captain to spend Shabbat with them. He was surprised by the sumptuousness of the Shabbat feast and presumed that he had stumbled upon a community of noblemen. He describes the Shabbat meal in detail:

> ... their [the Jews'] principal and standing Sunday [Sabbath] dinner, is called skanah or s'hina: it is made of [chick] peas baked in an oven for nearly twenty-four hours, with a quantity of Beeves [oxen's] marrow-bones broken to pieces over them; it is a very luscious and fattening dish, and by no means a bad one: this, with a few vegetables, and sometimes a plumpudding, a good bread, and Jews' brandy distilled from figs and aniseed, and bittered with wormwood, makes up the rest of the repast of the Jews who call themselves rich.[45]

Shabbat of Peace

People greet each other on Shabbat wishing one another "Shabbat Shalom"[46] meaning, "a peaceful Shabbat." The Yiddish term "Gut Shabbos," or "Good Shabbos," is more commonly used in some communities. The

Sages state that Shabbat is a time associated with peace in the home,[47] and peace in the world.[48]

How does Shabbat create peace? The Hebrew word for peace, *shalom,* is related to the word *shalem,*[49] which means whole or complete. The reason for this is that peace is a state in which things that were separated are united, and things that were at odds are now in a state of harmony. During much of the week, we live in a state of tension and lack of harmony, produced by three main areas of conflict:

▸ Between the human being and the rest of the natural world — because of our need to battle natural forces in order to survive, as well as our often unnecessary interference in and destruction of nature.[50]

▸ Between one person and another in society — because of the struggle for survival, and competition in the pursuit of a livelihood.[51]

▸ Between body and soul — because the needs of the body and soul are different, and often are at odds with each other.[52] Fulfillment of physical desires without any other considerations rarely advances one's intellectual and spiritual growth.

Observance of Shabbat enables us to transcend these areas of tension and create a harmonious and peaceful state of being. By refraining from acts of mastering and molding the world, we eliminate the tension between man and nature. We do not engage in commerce, talk about business, or even think about monetary matters on Shabbat. The Shabbat is the only day of the week that we are not in competition with anyone or anything. Finally, by combining the physical pleasures of Shabbat with its spiritual pleasures, and by engaging in pursuits of the mind and soul in a relaxed, dignified atmosphere, we create a situation where both the body and the soul rejoice together.

The Levys Chill Out

Preparations for the Shabbat begin on Thursday at the Levy home with the laundering of clothes for Shabbat.[53] One of the first items on the "to-do" list is determining how many people will be in the Levy house for Shabbat. The Levys have four children, about average for a religious family, but they do not know how many guests there will be. Their oldest son, Shlomo, is studying at a yeshivah in a different city, but he is able to come home for Shabbat from time to time. The other children, Tova, Eli and Esther, often invite friends for a meal or just to play afterward. It is common to have other families over for a Shabbat meal, to invite students who are in dormitories away from their homes, or guests who are visiting from out of town.[54] As it happens, the synagogue's hospitality committee has asked the Levys to host a young man from a nearby college. Once the numbers are known, the shopping begins. Food has to be purchased for two festive meat meals and one dairy meal, as well as treats for the children.[55]

Mrs. Levy generally does most of the cooking on Thursday night; however, she prepares dough for the special braided loaves of bread called challah in the afternoon, so that the younger children can participate. They enjoy punching and pounding the dough, and making their own miniloaves. The preparations themselves are a fulfillment of the Biblical commandment to remember the Shabbat.[56]

On Fridays, all the Levy children have special classes at school about the weekly Torah reading, called Parshat Hashavuah. In kindergarten, Esther hears stories about the Torah portion and learns lesson relevant to her life that is derived from that week's section. She often learns a short song that is related to the parshah, which she sings at the Shabbat table. The older children study the Hebrew text with commentaries and also prepare, with the help of their teacher, short oral explanations known as divrei Torah about a subject in the parshah. They will present these during family discussion at the meals. Most schools also send home a review sheet, so that the parents can review with their children the Torah studies that they learned that week in school. Parents also study the weekly portion.[57]

The Levys prepare all food for the Shabbat meals before Shabbat begins, since cooking is one of the forbidden creative labors. They place the dishes on a warming tray that will keep the evening and lunch meals hot.[58] An electric urn is filled with water for hot drinks on Shabbat, and the electric lights are set on a timer so that they will go on and off automatically at the desired times. (It should be remembered that the prohibition on using electricity on Shabbat is not meant to make life difficult or to deprive anyone of the benefits of electricity. It is perfectly acceptable, and totally within the spirit of Shabbat, to have the benefits of electricity through pre-set timers. The idea is that the specific prohibited malachah is not performed.)

Tova and Eli set the table with a special tablecloth, a tray and decorative cover for the challah, glasses for the Kiddush wine and a silver goblet for Kiddush.[59] All preparations must be finished by about 20 minutes before sunset, which is when Shabbat begins.[60] Of course, this rule makes Friday the most rushed day of the week, enhancing the contrast with the calm and slow pace of Shabbat.

Mrs. Levy lights the Shabbat candles, covers her eyes and recites a blessing: "Blessed are You, Hashem, our God, King of the universe, Who sanctified us with His commandments, and has commanded us to kindle the light of the Sabbath."[61] As is the custom of Jewish women for generations, she takes the opportunity to use this moment of sanctity to pray for the well-being of loved ones as well as for the sick or needy. According to Jewish law, at least two candles must be lit, each corresponding to a different aspect of Shabbat as expressed in the two Torah verses "Remember the Sabbath day," and "Guard the Sabbath day."[62] It is the custom in the Levy family, as in many others, to light one candle for each member of the family,[63] — two parents and four children, making a total of six candles.

After candle lighting, Mr. Levy and the children walk to the synagogue for Friday-night prayers, called Kabbalat Shabbat. The service lasts about 45 minutes and includes the song Lecha Dodi, a poem written in the 16th century by a Kabbalist of the holy city of Safed in the Land of Israel.[64] For the younger children, this is the highlight of the service, aside from getting candy from the synagogue "candy man." (An unofficial feature of many synagogues is an elderly man who gives out candy to the children in exchange for a handshake and sometimes the correct answer to a question about the parshah. In the worst-case scenario, the sweet is accompanied by a pinch on the cheek from the candy man.)

After the service, they return home and welcome the Shabbat with the song Shalom Aleichem, which describes "angels of peace" coming into the house and blessing the family.[65]

Next they sing Chapter 31 of Proverbs, which praises the "woman of valor." This poem describes the virtues of the Jewish wife and mother, but at a deeper level is an allegory for the relationship between the Jewish people and the Torah.[66] The parents then bless the children in age order, after which Mr. Levy says Kiddush. He holds a full cup of wine or grape juice, recites the blessing for Shabbat and the blessing over the wine.[67]

After everyone has sipped a little wine, they all wash their hands in preparation for eating the meal. The Sages instituted the practice of washing before eating bread, not solely out of concern for personal hygiene. It is also intended to cultivate an awareness of purity and sanctity in our eating habits.[68] Everyone is silent until Mr. Levy says the blessing[69] over two challahs (challot, in Hebrew), which commemorate the double portion of manna that fell in the desert on Fridays for the Children of Israel after the Exodus.[70] He distributes pieces to everyone.

Since the Levy family is of European (Ashkenazic) origin, a typical Friday-night menu includes gefilte fish,[71] chicken soup, roast chicken, potato kugel,[72] fresh salad, fruit and cake. During the meal, they sing Shabbat songs (Zemirot), talk about the Torah reading of the week, and listen to the children's divrei Torah (insights on the weekly Torah reading taught to them in school). Their conversation *also includes topics of general interest, but business matters and plans for the workweek are avoided.[73] (Despite its high spiritual value, baseball is not considered a particularly appropriate topic either.)*

After Bircat Hamazon (Grace After Meals) Esther and Eli go to bed, if they haven't already collapsed on chairs or the couch, as is often the case, especially on late Friday nights in the summer. Esther, in particular, loves to fall asleep on the couch as the sweet sound of the family singing Zemirot fills the room. The older children and parents read, study Torah or play quiet games, a welcome change from the incessant beeps and buzzing of electronic games heard throughout the rest of the week.

On Shabbat morning, there is no formal breakfast. Most of the older Levys have coffee or juice,[74] and the younger children have a Danish or some cereal before going to synagogue for the morning service. The prayers last about two and a half hours and include the reading aloud of the weekly portion from the Torah scroll.

Shabbat lunch, the main meal of the day, is very similar to Friday night, including Kiddush, washing the hands, blessing on the two challot, singing and discussion of the weekly Torah portion. The menu varies somewhat, but most often includes some form of cholent, a Shabbat dish found in almost every Jewish community, though known by different names — cholent, hamin, orisa, or schalet. The ingredients also vary widely: For Jews of European origin, the cholent is a stew typically made of beans, potatoes, meat, barley, onions and dumplings; in Morocco it consists of cracked wheat, beef, garlic and spices, and in Calcutta it is a chicken and rice curry. The common feature of all versions of cholent is its purpose. Cooking is prohibited on Shabbat, but the commandment to enjoy and honor Shabbat includes eating delicious foods. In order to fulfill both of these directives, Jews all over the world invented dishes that could be cooked prior to Shabbat, placed on a covered fire on Friday afternoon and simmer unattended all night until served hot at lunchtime.[75]

This week, the Levys' Shabbat guest has never tasted cholent before. When he asks about its origin, Mr. Levy explains that cholent is a protest food! A Jewish sect known as the Karaites[76] flourished in the eighth century, creating a serious schism by their rejection of the Oral Tradition. Reading the Torah verses literally, they believed that it was forbidden to have a fire in the house on Shabbat. They would sit in the dark and eat only cold food. Eating cholent was one way in which the mainstream Jewish community distanced itself from the Karaites and declared its belief in the Oral Tradition as the word of God given to Moses at Mount Sinai. Pulling out a Hebrew reference book from a nearby bookshelf, Mr. Levy quotes a great sage of the 13th century who wrote the following about cholent:

> And some say that it is an enactment of the Sages to enjoy the Shabbat with hamin [hot foods], and anyone who does not eat hamin requires investigation [is suspected of being a Karaite]:…[One who] prepares and cooks, and keeps the food warm, to enjoy the Shabbat by eating hamin — he is a believer and will merit seeing the dawning of the Messianic morning.[77]

Impressed, everyone takes another helping. After lunch, Mr. and Mrs. Levy and their children engage in a variety of activities: reading, studying Torah, playing games, going for walks or to the park, visiting friends or attending Torah classes. They all enjoy this opportunity to spend time together without constantly thinking about their long lists of things they "must do" on a normal weekday.

Late in the afternoon, Mr. Levy and the boys return to the synagogue for the brief Minchah service, followed by the third Shabbat meal, called Shalosh Seudot.[78] This meal, consisting of light vegetarian or dairy dishes, can be eaten at home, though the synagogue often provides it. It is accompanied by inspirational songs that are of a more meditative nature than those of the other meals.

After nightfall and the recitation of the evening prayers, Maariv,

A Havdalah set consisting of a cup, spice box, special multiwicked candle and candle holder.

the Levys gather at home to hear Havdalah, the sanctification of Shabbat at its conclusion.[79] The word Havdalah means separation: This ceremony marks the end of the holy Shabbat and beginning of the mundane workweek. The children bring to the table a silver cup, a special candle made of several wicks twisted together and a decorative box containing fragrant spices. Mr. Levy fills the cup to overflowing, symbolizing the blessings of Shabbat overflowing into the week. He recites the Havdalah blessings, and everyone smells the spices and raises their hands to the flame to enjoy its light.[80] The children take turns from week to week holding the candle for Havdalah. (They consider it a major milestone in life when they are old enough to hold the candle.) The

Levys then wish each other and their guest "Shavua Tov" — "a good week."

Since one may not prepare on Shabbat for the weekday, the majority of the clean-up from the meals happens immediately after Shabbat. After cleaning up from the day's meals and activities, the family enjoys a light meal called Melaveh Malkah, which means to "accompany the queen."[81] This meal is eaten as a way of "seeing out" the Shabbat Queen and easing into the weekday gradually.

Supplemental Material

The Categories of Prohibited Shabbat Work

Following is a list of the major categories of forbidden activities on the Shabbat. What is interesting is that the basic prohibition extends to include derivative actions, given below as examples. It is important to keep in mind that they all share the common quality of creative activity in which the usefulness of an object is improved (as explained above in the section "What Is Work? What Is Rest?") The list is based on the Mishnah in Tractate *Shabbat*, Chapter 7:

1. Sowing: Anything that promotes the growth of a plant — for example, irrigation, pruning, or moving a potted plant into the sunlight.

2. Plowing: Improving soil for agricultural purposes, either by making furrows, softening the soil, or putting fertilizer on the soil.

3. Harvesting: Removing a product from its place of growth — for example, plucking a flower, picking a fruit, or pulling a branch or leaf off a tree.

4. Making sheaves: Gathering agricultural produce from its place of growth into bundles or containers — for example, collecting fallen fruit around a tree into a basket.

5. Threshing: Extracting a food from its husk — for example, squeezing fruit to extract its juice, or milking an animal.

6. Winnowing: Separating "food" from "husks" using the wind —for example, letting the wind blow away chaff while leaving the kernels of grain.

7. Selecting: Removing "waste" from "food." "Waste" is defined as that which is not wanted, and "food" is defined as that which is wanted —

for example, removing rotten grapes from a bunch or taking out the peanuts that are not wanted from a mixture of nuts. Removing the grapes that are edible in order to eat them right away is, however, permitted.

8. Grinding: Making large particles into small particles by grinding or chopping — for example, finely chopping an onion or using a pepper mill.

9. Sifting: Separating fine and coarse particles using a sieve or filter.

10. Kneading: Combining separate solid particles into one mass using a liquid — for example, making dough.

11. Baking: Using heat to effect a change of state in any substance — for example, frying, boiling or grilling foods, melting wax, heating up metal to a molten state.

12. Shearing: Removing fur or hair from a live animal. This includes cutting human hair or pulling it out.

13. Washing: Laundering or any cleaning of absorbent materials.

14. Combing: Separating tangled fibers.

15. Dyeing: Permanent coloring of materials that are usually dyed.

16. Spinning: Twisting of individual fibers into one thread.

17. Setting up a loom.

18. Threading the loom.

19. Weaving — such as basket weaving.

20. Unraveling woven threads.

21. Tying: tying a permanent or craftsman's knot — for example, macramé.

22. Untying one of the aforementioned knots.

23. Sewing: any permanent bonding of two materials — including gluing or taping.

24. Tearing: tearing permanently bonded materials for a constructive purpose.

25. Hunting: capturing or trapping of any animal — for example, trapping a fly.

26. Slaughtering: killing or wounding any living creature — for example, killing a fly, stepping on ants.

27. Flaying: stripping skin off a carcass.

28. Salting: preserving or hardening a substance using chemicals — for example, pickling foods.

29. Tanning: softening and preparing leather — for example, rubbing leather conditioner into a baseball glove.

30. Scraping: smoothing out a surface by scraping.

31. Cutting: cutting materials to a specific size or shape — for example, whittling.

32. Writing: writing, drawing or marking.

33. Erasing in order to write.

34. Building: construction of dwellings or implements — for example, mounting a door on its hinges, putting together a tool.

35. Demolishing in order to build.

36. Extinguishing: putting out or otherwise diminishing a fire for a positive purpose — for example, making charcoal.

37. Burning: igniting or otherwise increasing a fire.

38. Finishing touches: finishing off or touching up an object — for example, removing stitches that seal the pockets of new clothing.

39. Carrying: carrying any item from private to public property and vice versa or carrying in the public domain.[82]

Kiddush for Shabbat Evening

The following prayer is taken from
The Complete ArtScroll Siddur, Ashkenaz, p. 361.
It begin with excerpts from the Bible.

(Recite silently)
And there was evening and there was morning,
(Full voice) the sixth day. Thus the heavens and earth were finished, and all their array. On the seventh day God completed His work which He had done. God blessed the seventh day and hallowed it, because on it He abstained from all His work which God created to make.
Blessed are You, Hashem,[83] our God, King of the universe, Who creates the fruit of the vine.
(All present respond "Amen.")
Blessed are You, Hashem, our God, King of the universe, Who sanctified us with His commandments, took pleasure in us, and with love and favor gave us His holy Sabbath as a heritage, a remembrance of creation. For that day is the prologue to the holy festivals, a memorial to the Exodus from Egypt. For us did You choose and us did You sanctify from all the

nations. And Your holy Sabbath, with love and favor did You give us as a heritage. Blessed are You, Hashem, Who sanctifies the Sabbath.

(All present respond "Amen.")

Kiddush for Shabbat Morning

The following prayer is taken from
The Complete ArtScroll Siddur, Ashkenaz, p. 493.
It begin with excerpts from the Bible.

And the Children of Israel observed the Sabbath, to make the Sabbath for their generations an eternal Covenant. Between Me and the Children of Israel, it is a sign forever, that in six days did Hashem make the heaven and the earth, and on the seventh day He rested and was refreshed.

Remember the Sabbath day to sanctify it. Six days shall you work and accomplish all your work. But the seventh day is Sabbath to Hashem, your God; you shall not do any work — you, your son, your daughter, your slave, your maidservant, your animal and your convert within your gates — for in six days Hashem made the heavens and the earth, the seas and all that is in them, and He rested on the seventh day.

Therefore, Hashem blessed the Sabbath day and sanctified it.

Blessed are You, Hashem, our God, King of the universe, Who creates the fruit of the vine.

(All present respond "Amen.")

For Further Reading

▶ "On the Concept of Sabbath Work," Dr. Azriel Rosenfield, *Proceedings of the Association of Orthodox Jewish Scientists*, Vol. 1 (1966)

▶ "On the Use of Electrical Equipment on Shabbat and Yom Tov," Dr. Leo Levi, *Proceedings of the Association of Orthodox Jewish Scientists*, Vol. 1 (1966)

▶ *Shabbat: Day of Eternity* by Rabbi Aryeh Kaplan (OU/NCSY, 1983)

▶ *Shemirath Shabbath* (English edition) by Rabbi Yehoshua Neuwirth (Feldheim, 1989)

▶ *The Magic of Shabbos* by Rabbi Mordechai Rhine (Judaica Press, 1998)

▶ *The Sabbath* by Rabbi Isadore Grunfield (Feldheim, 1959)

▶ *The Radiance of Shabbos* by Rabbi Simcha Bunim Cohen (ArtScroll/Mesorah, 1986)

▶ *The Sanctity of Shabbos* by Rabbi Simcha Bunim Cohen (ArtScroll/Mesorah, 1988)

▶ *The Shabbos Kitchen* by Rabbi Simcha Bunim Cohen (ArtScroll/Mesorah, 1991)

▶ *The Shabbos Home* by Rabbi Simcha Bunim Cohen (ArtScroll/Mesorah, 1992)

▶ *Muktzeh* by Rabbi Simcha Bunim Cohen (ArtScroll/Mesorah, 1999)

NOTES

References to books of the Talmud refer to the Babylonian Talmud unless otherwise noted.

1. Maimonides, *Mishneh Torah*, Laws of Shabbat 30:15.
2. *Zohar, Parshat Yitro* 55b; *Kitvei HaRamban*, vol. II, p. 521, "*Taryag mitzvot hayotzot me'aseret hadibrot*," Mossad Harav Kook, Jerusalem, 1986.
3. *Chullin* 5a, Rashi ad loc. "*Eilah luv.*"
4. Genesis 2:1-4.
5. *Code of Jewish Law, Orach Chaim*, 268:7, *Mishnah Berurah* 19; *The Complete ArtScroll Siddur*, p. 346.
6. Ibid. *Code of Jewish Law.*
7. *Kuzari* 3:10.
8. Exodus 23:12; Deuteronomy 5:14.
9. Exodus 20:10; Deuteronomy 5:14; Exodus 31 and 35; Leviticus 19, 26.
10. Exodus 1:13,14.
11. Mishnah *Shabbat* 7:2. See Appendix I.
12. Rabbi Samson Raphael Hirsch and Dayan I. Grunfield.
13. Dayan I. Grunfield, *The Shabbos*, Feldheim Publishers, NY, 1959, p. 19.
14. Rabbi Samson Raphael Hirsch, *Horeb*, II Edoth, Chap. 21, para. 144.
15. Exodus 20:8-11.

16. Michael Denton, *Nature's Destiny*, The Free Press, NY, 1998, p. 242.

17. *Pesachim* 54a; *Genesis Rabbah* 11:2, 12:6; *Midrash Tehillim* 92:4; *Midrash Ruth* 8:3; *Code of Jewish Law*, Orach Chaim, 298:1, *Mishnah Berurah* 1.

18. Exodus 35:3, Sforno ad loc.; *Philo, On the Life of Moses* II, para. 219.

19. Ibid. Denton, p. 243.

20. *Genesis Rabbah* 11:2, 12:6; *Midrash Tehillim* 92:4; *Midrash Ruth* 8:3; *The Complete ArtScroll Siddur, Ashkenaz*, pp. 618-621.

21. Rabbi Isaiah Karelitz, *Chazon Ish*, *Orach Chaim*, 50:9, "*od yesh.*"

22. Deuteronomy 5:12-15.

23. Nachmanides, Commentary on Exodus 13:16.

24. Maharal, *Gevurot Hashem*, Chaps. 41-42.

25. Mishnah *Kiddushin* 4:14; Talmud *Sanhedrin* 99b; Rabbi Moshe Chaim Luzzatto, *Path of the Just,* chap. 1.

26. *Tanna Dvei Eliyahu Rabbah* 1; *Yalkut Shimoni*, Vayakhel 408; *Pesikta Rabati* 23.

27. *Yalkut Shimoni*, Psalms 488; Rabbi Yoel Schwartz, *Shabbat Hamalkah*, pp. 55-58.

28. *Beitzah* 16a, Meiri ad loc.; Rabbi Yehudah Halevy, *Kuzari* 3:2-4.

29. *Code of Jewish Law, Orach Chaim,* 242:1, 280:1, 289:1.

30. Exodus 20:8.

31. Maimonides, *Mishneh Torah*, Laws of Shabbat 29:1.

32. *Mechilta Yitro,* Parshah 7; *Pesachim* 106a.

33. See Appendix II for the complete text of *Kiddush.*

34. *Sefer Hachinuch,* Mitzvah 26.

35. *Code of Jewish Law, Orach Chaim,* 602:1.

36. Ibid. 282:1, 284:1.

37. Ibid. 290:2, Ramah.

38. Ibid. 250, *Mishnah Berurah* 3; ibid. 262:1. Because of the Shabbat laws, all preparations must be completed before Shabbat begins.

39. Ibid. *Code of Jewish Law,* 260:1.

40. *Shabbat* 113a; *Code of Jewish Law,* ibid. 262:2, *Mishnah Berurah* 5.

41. *Code of Jewish Law*, 262:1, Rama ad loc.; *Mishnah Berurah* 4.

42. *Shabbat* 25b; Maimonides, *Mishneh Torah*, Laws of Shabbat 5:1.

43. Ibid. Maimonides.

44. *Shabbat* 23b.

45. *Narrative of the Loss of the American Brig Commerce wrecked on the Western coast of Africa in the month of August 1815 with ... observations historical, geographical & C.* (Published by the Author), Captain James Riley, 1817. Quoted in John Cooper, *Eat and Be Satisfied,* Jason Aronson Inc.,1993, p. 105.

46. Rabbi Chaim Ibn Attar, *Ohr Hachaim* on Leviticus 19:3, "*ulederech zeh*"; *Code of Jewish Law, Orach Chaim*, 307, *Be'er Heitev* 2.

47. *Shabbat* 25b.

48. *Zohar,* Numbers 3, p. 176b.

49. *Kiddushin* 66b; *Keritut* 5b; Maharal, *Netivot Olam,* Netiv Hashalom, Chap. 1.

50. Genesis 1:28 "*vekivshuha.*"

51. Rashi, Genesis 3:5; *Midrash Rabbah*, Genesis 19:4; *Midrash Rabbah*, Leviticus 9:9; Maimonides, *Guide for the Perplexed,* 3:30.

52. Rabbi Moshe Chaim Luzzatto, *The Way of God,* 4:2.

53. *Code of Jewish Law, Orach Chaim,* 242:1, *Mishnah Berurah* 5. There is an ancient decree of Ezra the Scribe (circa 400 B.C.E.) to do laundry for Shabbat on Thursday so at to leave Friday free for other preparations.

54. Lawrence Keleman, *Permission to Receive*, Targum/Feldheim, 1996, pp. 148-157.

55. Ibid. *Code of Jewish Law*, 250:2.

56. Ibid. 250.

57. Ibid. 285:1-6.

58. Ibid. 253:1-2, *Biur Halachah*, "*venahagu lehakel.*"

59. Ibid. 262:1.

60. Ibid. 261:2; *Mishnah Berurah* 22.

61. *The Complete ArtScroll Siddur, Ashkenaz*, pp. 296-297.

62. Ibid. 263:1, Ramah.

63. *Responsa Mishneh Halachot* 7:35.

64. Rabbi Shlomoh Alkabetz, see *Siddur Otzar Hatefillot*, Iyun Tefillah on *Lecha Dodi*.

65. *The Complete ArtScroll Siddur, Ashkenaz*, pp. 354-355.

66. See Eitz Yosef in *Siddur Otzar Hatefillot*. However, Rabbi Yaacov Emden, in *Siddur Beit Ya'acov,* says that it refers to the *Shechinah,* the Divine Presence; See also commentary of Gaon of Vilna on Proverbs 31.

67. Appendix II.

68. *Chullin* 106a; *Tosafot* ad loc., *"mitzvah lishmoa."*

69. *The Complete ArtScroll Siddur, Ashkenaz*, pp. 224-225.

70. *Shabbat* 117b; *Code of Jewish Law, Orach Chaim*, 274:1-2; 289:1.

71. *Gefilte fish* is made of boneless minced fish, onions and spices boiled in a vegetable broth.

72. Potato *kugel* is a baked loaf of grated potatoes, onions, eggs and spices.

73. *Code of Jewish Law, Orach Chaim*, 307:1.

74. *Code of Jewish Law, Orach Chaim*, 89:3-4, *Mishnah Berurah* ad loc. 22.

75. For a complete history of *cholent* and other Jewish foods, see John Cooper, *Eat and Be Satisfied,* Jason Aronson Inc., 1993, p. 101.

76. A sect founded by Anan ben David, in 763 C.E. The Aramaic name *Karaim* is related to the word for verse, since they were literalists who rejected anything but what they thought was the literal meaning of the verse.

77. Rabbeinu Zerachiah Halevy, *Hamaor Hakatan*, Tractate *Shabbat*, Chap. 3, p. 16b (*Dapei HaRif*).

78. *Shabbat* 117b; *Code of Jewish Law, Orach Chaim*, 291:1.

79. Maimonides, *Mishneh Torah*, Laws of Shabbat 29:1.

80. *The Complete ArtScroll Siddur, Ashkenaz*, pp. 618-620.

81. *Code of Jewish Law, Orach Chaim*, 300:1.

82. According to Biblical law, one may not carry in a place defined as public property (*Shabbat* 97b). However, many authorities maintain that most neighborhoods are not classic public property, either because the streets are not wide enough, there are not enough people passing through (*Code of Jewish Law, Orach Chaim*, 345:7, *Biur Halachah* ad loc.) or because the buildings and fences form barriers around the city, thus making it an enclosed, "private property" (Chazon Ish, *Orach Chaim/Moed*, 43:7).

Rabbinic law decrees that one may not carry in these areas anyway, because they are so similar to public property. However, Rabbinic law does allow one to carry in areas if a minimum fence is erected around the area, consisting of upright poles with wire or rope stretched between them — this is called a *tzurat hapetach*, or an *eruv* (*Code of Jewish Law, Orach Chaim*, 362). Because the legal requirements are complex, an *eruv* should be constructed only by a competent authority.

In addition, the supervising rabbi takes some food (usually a box of matzah), and makes everyone in town a partner in the food, hence uniting the community as one family in one property — this is called an *eruv chatzerot* (ibid. 387).

This is why you will sometimes see Orthodox Jews carrying on the Sabbath: They have an *eruv* around their community (*Responsa Chatam Sofer, Orach Chaim*, 99: Tashbetz 2:37). To avoid error, it is important for each member of the community to know the boundaries of the *eruv;* and there must be a means of informing everyone should the *eruv* be broken, thereby invalidating it until it is fixed.

83. When reciting the *Kiddush*, even in English, one should say *Ado-noi* instead of *Hashem*.

The Jewish New Year

Rosh Hashanah, shofar and Divine judgment

Two New Years

The first month of the Jewish year is Nissan, the month in which the Jewish people were redeemed from Egypt, the month in which we celebrate Passover.[1] The Torah designates the months by number only, not by name: This month is called the "first of months."[2] Nissan marks the beginning of Jewish history because the Exodus transformed the Jewish people from a family into a nation.[3] This new year is therefore exclusive to the Jewish people.

The universal new year, the anniversary of the creation of all human beings, is Rosh Hashanah, which means, "Beginning of the Year." It does not fall in the first month of the Jewish calendar but in the seventh month, Tishrei. The Biblical source for this holiday is found in Leviticus:

> God spoke to Moses, saying: "Speak to the Children of Israel,
> saying: 'In the seventh month, on the first of the month, there
> shall be a rest day for you, a remembrance with shofar[4] blasts
> — a holy convocation.[5] You shall not do any manner of labori-
> ous work...'"[6]

Although in our prayers on Rosh Hashanah we describe this day as the anniversary of creation,[7] Talmudic commentaries point out that it is more precisely the anniversary of the pinnacle and goal of all creation, the human, Adam.[8] The Mishnah[9] states that, "On Rosh Hashanah, all the inhabitants of the world pass before God like sheep ..."[10] The Talmud explains this expression to mean that every individual is judged.[11]

Because this is the anniversary of our creation, it is the day on which we are evaluated and judged whether we are worthy to have been created and if we merit continued existence. The Jewish new year is therefore not celebrated by parties, fireworks, champagne and midnight dances; it is rather a day of contemplation, prayer and commitment. There is certainly an element of happiness on this day,[12] as it is a celebration of our relationship with God as His children and His creations; however, the mood is more solemn than on other Jewish festivals.[13]

To Be or not to Be?

According to Jewish tradition, before God created the first human being, a debate took place in the heavenly court.

> When the Holy One, Blessed is He, came to create man, the ministering angels formed into groups, some saying that man should be created, some saying that he should not be created... [the angel of] Kindness voted to create man, because people would perform acts of kindness, [the angel of] Peace voted not to create man, because people would argue and fight, [the angel of] Truth voted not to create man because he would be full of falsehood ...[14]

No such discussion took place prior to the creation of the rest of the world. Only the creation of the human was open to debate, because the human being alone has free will; only his actions can be good or evil. All other creatures merely do what they are programmed to do by instinct, and are therefore morally neutral. As Mark Twain once said, "Man is the only animal that blushes. Or needs to."[15]

Adam is never neutral: he must justify his existence by his actions. We can be judged because we have free will, because we were created not merely to be part of the ecosystem, but to use our free will for moral and spiritual achievements. In the words of a contemporary sage, "We are judged because we were created, and we were created because we are judged."[16]

We have the ability to achieve the greatest heights of morality and altruism or to be the most depraved, evil creatures in existence; the choice is in our own hands. This unique capacity of the human being to be good or evil is marked by the festival of Rosh Hashanah. We celebrate our incredible potential to become similar to our Creator, but at the same time, we tremble before our awesome responsibility and the judgment that awaits us.[17]

Judaism does not view time as a linear progression but rather as a circular path. The specific spiritual energies of each part of the very first year in history returns every year at the same point in time. (See the chapter on the Jewish Calendar for a more detailed explanation of this idea.) As the anniversary of the creation of the first human being[18] is Rosh Hashanah, the "angelic debate" is renewed every year at this time, "Does man deserve to exist? Has he justified his existence?" We stand in prayer before our Creator on Rosh Hashanah and declare our commitment to act in such a way that we will be deemed worthy to exist.

Setting the Alarm

As noted in the passage from Leviticus quoted above, the central commandment of Rosh Hashanah, and the defining feature of this festival in the Torah, is the sounding of the *shofar.*

A hollowed-out ram's horn is blown on Rosh Hashanah to produce sounds known as *tekiah, shevarim* and *truah* — a long blast, three shorter blasts and a number of very short blasts. The most obvious idea behind this commandment is that the *shofar* sounds a piercing wake-up call for us to begin an accounting of our lives, to become aware of our responsibilities and to make positive commitments for the future. Maimonides writes:

> *Even though the blowing of the shofar is a decree of the Torah, there is nevertheless a hint within it. That is, "Wake up… from your sleep… Search through your actions, return in repentance and remember your Creator… Look into your souls, improve your ways… and abandon evil…"*[19]

In light of this explanation, we can understand why there is a custom to begin sounding the *shofar* in the synagogue a month before Rosh Hashanah.[20] We have to start the process of change well before Rosh Hashanah to avoid a last-minute, panicked rush. During the month before Rosh Hashanah, known as Elul, the *shofar* is blown every day after the weekday morning services in order to wake us up from our apathy gradually, in the hope that we will not press the "snooze" button.

The Ram's Horn

Abraham, the ancestor of the Jewish people, was subjected to one of the most severe tests imaginable. God asked him to take his beloved son,

Isaac, and bring him as a sacrifice on Mount Moriah. Even though this request contradicted everything that Abraham had known and believed until that moment, he maintained his total trust in God; he took Isaac, put him on the altar and held the knife to his throat.[21]

At the last second, an angel of God told him not to harm the lad.[22] God then showed Abraham a ram whose horns were entangled in a bush nearby and Abraham brought that ram as an offering to God instead of his son. Blowing the horn of a ram reminds us of this event — known forevermore as "The Binding of Isaac" — and of Abraham and Isaac's tremendous devotion to God. (It should be noted that Isaac's willing submission, despite the fact that he had no direct commandment from God as his father had, possibly showed at least equal devotion to God.) The sound of the ram's horn challenges us to dedicate ourselves totally to God, with the same faith, trust and devotion as Abraham and Isaac. If we are sincere in this dedication, God considers it as though we actually performed the same act as Abraham.[23]

The Liberty Horn

In ancient times, the *shofar* was blown on occasions other than Rosh Hashanah as well. The famous verse from Leviticus is inscribed in part on the Liberty Bell in Philadelphia:

[... blow the *shofar* throughout your land...] *Proclaim freedom throughout the land for all its inhabitants* ...[24]

The Biblical context of this verse is the release of indentured servants every jubilee (50th) year, which was proclaimed by the blowing of a *shofar*. The Sages of the Mishnah explained that the primary significance of the *shofar,* including the *shofar* of Rosh Hashanah, is a proclamation of freedom.[25]

The freedom proclaimed by the *shofar* is within our power to achieve. It is the freedom from our past, from our sins and failings. It is the freedom to change ourselves and the entire world through the power of free will and repentance. The *shofar* reminds us that we are always free to choose what is right and good, and that our lives are not predetermined, no matter how many obstacles appear to stand in our way. We believe that when people take this lesson to heart and really change for the better, we will merit the ultimate *shofar* of freedom that will herald the time of the Messiah.[26]

> *It shall be on that day that a great shofar will be blown and those who are lost in the land of Assyria and those cast away in the land of Egypt[27] will come [together], and they will bow down before God on the holy mountain in Jerusalem.*[28]

Rosh Hashanah Prayers

The Rosh Hashanah prayers are found in the Rosh Hashanah *machzor* (festival prayer book). They are divided into three main sections, each focusing on one of the primary themes of the day. As we progress through the prayers, these meditations help us achieve a mental and spiritual state conducive to real change and self-improvement. One of the central themes of the Rosh Hashanah prayers is the emphasis on recognizing God as the King.[29] Since "There cannot be a King without a people"[30] and God created man, His "nation," on Rosh Hashanah, it is on that day that He was, so to speak, crowned as King. A famous poem that has become part of the daily liturgy, *Adon Olam*,[31] expresses this idea in the following words:

Master of the universe, Who reigned
Before any form was created,
At the time when His Will brought all into being —
Then as "King" was His name proclaimed.[32]

In order to impress upon ourselves on this Divine "coronation day" the fact that God is King, with all attendant rights and privileges, we repeatedly refer to Him as King in our prayers. This is the message of the section of prayers known as *Malchiyot*, Kingship,[33] which consists of a description of God as King, along with verses from the Torah, the Prophets and the Writings about God's Kingship.[34]

God's knowledge of human events, thoughts and actions is the second theme of the Rosh Hashanah prayers. This section, called *Zichronot*, "memories," describes God as the One Who "remembers the Covenant" that He made with the Patriarchs. He is the One Who "remembered Noah" in the midst of the flood, the One Who "knows all the deeds of humanity." Verses from the Torah, the Prophets and the Writings that describe God remembering and knowing everything are included.[35]

The third major section of the Rosh Hashanah prayers is called *Shofrot* (plural of *shofar*). This refers to the sound of the *shofar* that was heard when God gave the Torah to the Jewish people at Mt. Sinai, and to the *shofar* blast that will herald the ingathering of the exiles and the coming of the Messiah.[36] These ideas remind us, respectively, of our obligations to other people, to God and ourselves (the Torah), and of our ultimate destiny (the Messianic Era). They encourage us to reassess our priorities and strive to become better people in the coming year.[37]

Probably the most moving prayer of the year is *Unetaneh Tokef*. Written by Rabbi Amnon of Mainz, Germany, about one thousand years ago, the heartrending story behind this prayer sheds light on its significance and lasting relevance.

The bishop of Mainz approached his friend and advisor, Rabbi Amnon, a great Torah scholar, and insisted that he convert to Christianity. In order to buy time, Rabbi Amnon asked for three days' grace to consider the offer. Upon returning home, Rabbi Amnon was distraught that he may have given the impression that he was even considering betraying God by converting. He spent the three days in solitude, fasting and praying to be forgiven for his sin, and did not return to the bishop. Finally, the bishop had him brought to the palace and demanded an answer.

Rabbi Amnon replied that his tongue should be cut out for the sin of saying that he would consider the matter. Furious, the bishop answered that the sin was not in his tongue for what he said, but his legs for not coming back as he had promised. He ordered that Rabbi Amnon's feet be amputated joint by joint, then did the same to his hands. After each amputation, Rabbi Amnon was asked if he would convert, and each time he refused. He was carried home in his broken state, on the verge of death.

Rosh Hashanah arrived a few days later and Rabbi Amnon asked to be carried to the synagogue, where he was placed before the Ark.[38] With his last strength, Rabbi Amnon cried out the words of *Unetaneh Tokef*, a testimony to God's absolute righteousness, His control over all that happens in the universe and man's ability to change God's decree through repentance and good deeds. With this, Rabbi Amnon died. Three days later, he appeared in a dream to Rabbi Klonimos ben Meshullam, a great Talmudic and Kabbalistic scholar of Mainz. Rabbi Amnon taught him *Unetaneh Tokef* and asked him to send the prayer to all Jewish communities to be included in their liturgy. Rabbi Amnon's wish was carried out, and the prayer became an integral part of the Rosh Hashanah and Yom Kippur services.[39] *Unetaneh Tokef* is recited by the cantor and the congregation while the Ark is open. It is worth quoting the text of this searing prayer in its entirety:

"Let us now relate the power of this day's holiness, for it is awesome and frightening. On it Your Kingship will be exalted; Your throne will be established with kindness and You will sit upon it in truth. It is true that You alone are the One Who judges, proves, knows and bears witness; Who writes and seals, counts and calculates; Who remembers all that was forgotten. You will open the Book of Chronicles — it will read itself, and everyone's signature is in it. The great *shofar* will be sounded and a still, slight sound will be heard. Angels will hasten, a trembling and terror will seize them — and they will say, 'Behold, it is the Day of Judgment, to muster the heavenly host for judgment!'— for [even] they cannot be vindicated in Your eyes in judgment.

"All mankind will pass before You like members of the flock. Like a shepherd inspecting his flock, making sheep pass under his staff, so shall You cause to pass, count, calculate and consider the soul of all the living; and You shall allocate the needs of all Your creatures and inscribe their verdicts.

"On Rosh Hashanah will be inscribed, and on Yom Kippur will be sealed, how many will pass from the earth and how many will be created; who will live and who will die; who will die at his predestined time and who before his time; who by water and who by fire, who by sword, who by beast, who by famine, who by thirst, who by storm, who by plague, who by strangulation and who by stoning. Who will rest and who will wander, who will live in harmony and who will be harried, who will be tranquil and who will suffer, who will be poor and who will be rich, who will be degraded and who will be exalted.

"But Repentance, Prayer and Charity remove the evil of the decree!

"For Your Name signifies Your praise: hard to anger and easy to appease, for You do not wish the death of the condemned, but that he repent from his way and live. Until the day of his death You await him; if he repents, You will accept him immediately.

"It is true that You are their Creator and You know their inclination, for they are flesh and blood. A man's origin is from dust and his destiny is back to dust, at risk of his life he earns his bread; he is likened to a broken shard, withering grass, a fading flower, a passing shade, a dissipating cloud, a blowing wind, flying dust and a fleeting dream.

"But You are the King, the Living and Enduring God."[40]

Our Father, Our King

Another prayer central to the Rosh Hashanah liturgy is *Avinu Malkeinu*, "Our Father, Our King." This prayer is first mentioned in the Talmud[41] and therefore dates back at least to 70 C.E. and probably earlier. The Talmud relates that during a time of drought and famine, Rabbi Eliezer led the community in a special prayer that had been formulated to ask for rain in times of drought, yet no rain fell. Rabbi Akiva then began to pray using the formula "Our Father, our King, we have no King but You. Our Father, our King, have mercy upon us for Your sake." Within moments, rain began to fall and thereafter this prayer was adopted by the Sages for use on fast days and during The Ten Days of Repentance — the ten days from Rosh Hashanah through Yom Kippur.[42] *Avinu Malkeinu* consists of 44 stanzas beseeching God, both as our compassionate, loving Father, and as our Ruler and King to act favorably toward us in all aspects of our lives, even if we are undeserving.[43]

Have a Happy, Sweet New Year!

In addition to being a day of prayer and contemplation, Rosh Hashanah is also a festival and a time of celebration. Although the joy is somewhat muted because this is the Day of Judgment,[44] Rosh Hashanah nevertheless has a definite festive component. The *Code of Jewish Law* rules: "[One should] eat, drink and be joyous; and it is forbidden to fast on Rosh Hashanah."[45]

On each day of Rosh Hashanah, we are required to eat two festive meals that include *Kiddush*[46] over a cup of wine, a blessing over bread, good food and song. It is customary to eat specific sweet foods on Rosh Hashanah to symbolize our wishes for a sweet new year and to help put us in an optimistic mood. Many people dip their *challah*[47] in honey instead of (or in addition to) the salt that is normally used. A custom going back to Talmudic times prescribes eating foods whose names evoke ideas of blessing and hint to prayers for good things.[48] For example, *rubia* in Aramaic means increase, so we eat a vegetable called *rubia* (black-eyed peas) and say a prayer asking God to increase our merits.[49] Many people eat a bit from the head of a fish and ask God that we be "as the head and not as the tail." Some people eschew foods that are sour tasting in order to avoid the idea of a sour new year. Probably the most famous Rosh Hashanah food is apple dipped in honey,[50] which is eaten after saying: "May it be Your will, Hashem, our God and the God of our forefathers, that You renew for us a good and sweet year."[51]

As with all Shabbat and festival meals, we eat fine foods, drink wine, sing and discuss Torah ideas about the festival. It is proper to invite guests, especially the needy, to these meals and to ensure that everyone has somewhere to dine on Rosh Hashanah.[52]

Why Are We Happy on Rosh Hashanah?

One would expect that a person on trial for his or her life, God forbid, would not be eating, drinking and singing. It is possible that our happiness is rooted in the following two realizations:

▸ The One Who judges us is not only perfectly just, but also loves us as a parent loves his children — so we clearly have cause to be happy.

▸ In addition, we are confident that God, in His kindness, will judge us favorably[53] and will ultimately fulfill His promise to our forefathers to preserve the Jewish people and redeem us from Exile.

The prophets Ezra and Nehemiah were adamant in delivering this message to the Jewish people, telling them to rejoice on Rosh Hashanah and not be depressed or mournful. The prophets taught that it is more important to fulfill the commands of God in joy and happiness than to mourn over past sins and failures:

Today is sacred to the Lord your God; don't mourn and don't weep…. Go, eat rich foods and drink sweet beverages, and send portions to those who have nothing prepared, for today is sacred to our Lord. Do not be sad; delighting in God is your strength.[54]

The Ten Days of Repentance

Rosh Hashanah begins a ten-day period known as The Ten Days of Repentance, *Aseret Yemei Teshuvah,* which includes and culminates with Yom Kippur, the Day of Atonement. These days are a time of introspection, renewal of commitment and intensified prayers.[55] Changes in the daily prayers were instituted by the Sages for these days to help us focus on these goals. "King" is substituted for the other names of God in some blessings, and prayers requesting God to give us life are inserted in the Silent Prayer, the *Amidah.*[56]

During this time it is customary to be especially scrupulous in every area of Jewish law.[57] Many people have their *mezuzot*[58] and *tefillin*[59] checked (for errors and wear) by a scribe at this time, a custom which serves also to remind us to inspect our most precious "holy object," our own soul.[60] We make every effort to ask forgiveness from anyone whom we may have hurt or offended. This is a prerequisite to full atonement on Yom Kippur because Yom Kippur only atones for sins against God, not those committed against our fellow human beings, unless they have forgiven us.[61] One must also pay compensation for any damages caused to the other person as a condition of forgiveness.[62]

Rosh Hashanah at the Levys – How Sweet It Is!

The Levys begin their preparations for Rosh Hashanah a full month before the Yom Tov[63] of Rosh Hashanah. The shofar is blown in the synagogue every day after the morning service, and because the Levys live next door to a synagogue, the whole family hears the haunting shofar blasts every morning. They seem to be saying, "Rosh Hashanah is coming! Repent now!" (a wonderful way to start their day).

Mr. Levy's custom is to study the classic work, The Gates of Repentance[64] with his chavruta[65] (study partner) every day from the beginning of the Hebrew month of Elul until Yom Kippur. They do this for about fifteen minutes before beginning their study of the daily page of Talmud.[66]

Shlomo Levy, who attends a yeshivah[67] out of town, is experiencing the intensity of the pre-High Holy Days semester. Sessions on ethics and repentance are held, the daily prayers are much more focused and emotional, and many of the students study texts related to Rosh Hashanah and Yom Kippur. Shlomo has decided to study the tractate dealing with Rosh Hashanah in the Talmud, and hopes to complete it before the festival begins.

During Elul, Mrs. Levy has attended a weekly lecture focusing on an in-depth analysis of the holiday prayers. She has also been doing some early cooking and baking of items that can be easily frozen in preparation for the upcoming season of festivals.

It is the custom for women in her family to recite the entire book of Psalms, Tehillim, every week during the month preceding Rosh Hashanah, and up until Yom Kippur. Mrs. Levy recites them from the book that her grandmother used in Europe before the Holocaust. Just holding this book of Tehillim is an emotional experience, its tear-soaked pages containing generations of prayers and hopes.

In addition to learning about Rosh Hashanah in class, the younger Levy children enjoyed a shofar-making and blowing demonstration provided by a man who has blown the shofar at their local shul[68] for the past thirty years.

As Rosh Hashanah approaches, Mr. Levy dusts off the special prayer books, the machzorim, and makes sure that everyone in the family has the one that he or she prefers.

On the Saturday night before Rosh Hashanah, the older members of the family go to the shul shortly before midnight, to say special prayers for forgiveness, Selichot, which are recited early every morning until Yom Kippur. The first Selichot service takes place at midnight, but subsequent services begin a half-hour before the regularly scheduled morning service every day, except Shabbat.

Everyone in the Levy household gets at least one new item of clothing for Rosh Hashanah, which they wear on the second night of the festival. When their father says the blessing of Shehecheyanu that evening (the blessing said on something new[69]), he has in mind the day of Rosh Hashanah itself and the new year, but everyone also keeps in mind that it is referring to their new clothing as well.[70]

The night before Rosh Hashanah, the Levy house is filled with the aroma of the delicious food cooking. Mrs. Levy always bakes sweet, round challahs for Rosh Hashanah — sweet for a sweet new year, and round to symbolize the cycle of time and life. She has also prepared the special foods for the first night known as simanim, (literally, signs or indicators). These are the foods that are eaten to symbolize a happy, healthy, blessed new year. There is apple dipped in honey, a pomegranate ("May our merits be as many as its seeds"), fish ('May we increase in number like fish"), beets, black-eyed peas, leeks, dates and a fish head (which only Mr. Levy is brave enough to eat).

In order to support the people of Israel and also because there is a special sanctity to the produce of the Land of Israel, the Levys make a point of buying something from Israel for every holiday. For Rosh Hashanah, they have chosen a few bottles of sparkling wine from the Golan Heights.

Mrs. Levy plans her guest list weeks before Rosh Hashanah and as the invitations are accepted, she notes on a wall calendar the guests who are coming for each meal. She also makes notes of what she plans to serve at each meal, keeping in mind certain of the guests' dietary restrictions (and preferences!).

This year, they are having a number of single young adults and are hoping that some of the introductions they make may develop further (a major mitzvah!). They are also inviting a young, recently married couple that has just moved into the community.

Prayers are lengthy on Rosh Hashanah. At the Levys' synagogue, they begin at 7:30 a.m. and finish the service at about 2 o'clock in the afternoon. Even the little children are anxious to be in shul for part of the time, so that they do not miss the special mitzvah of hearing the sound of the shofar.

After a leisurely lunch accompanied by singing, words of Torah and conversation, the rest of the afternoon is spent in conversation, reading, Torah study and games for the children. In the afternoon (on the second day, if the first day is on Shabbat) the family walks with other members of the shul to a nearby duck pond and river, where they symbolically cast their sins into the water in a ceremony called Tashlich.[71]

Rosh Hashanah is intense and quite tiring, as much of the day is spent in the synagogue, praying. During the meals, the family relaxes and recharges their energies as they exchange ideas about Rosh Hashanah and their hopes for the new year. Rosh Hashanah ends with the Havdalah prayer,[72] and soon afterward everyone pitches in to help clean up.

Selected Laws and Customs of Rosh Hashanah

1. The Hebrew month preceding Rosh Hashanah, Elul, is a time of preparation for Rosh Hashanah. Every morning, except for Shabbat, the *shofar* is blown after the morning service and Psalm 27 is recited. This psalm is recited again after the evening service, or in some communities, after the afternoon service.[73]

2. Special prayers of supplication, repentance and confession of sin, *Selichot,* are said during this time. *Sephardim*[74] begin saying *Selichot* early in the morning, from the beginning of Elul until the day preceding Yom Kippur. *Ashkenazim*[75] begin reciting *Selichot* on the Saturday night preceding Rosh Hashanah.[76]

3. On the day before Rosh Hashanah it is customary to recite *Hatarat Nedarim,* "Release from Vows," in the presence of three men, who act as a religious court. If a person made a vow but cannot fulfill it, a court must release him from this obligation. In this way the vow is removed from the "record" before the Day of Judgment.[77]

4. Rosh Hashanah begins just before sundown on the last day of the month of Elul. It is a two-day festival and continues until after nightfall on the 1st of Tishrei. (This is usually in September.) Candles are lit (usually by the lady of the house) just before Rosh Hashanah begins on the first night and after the onset of the second night. Two blessings are recited before lighting the candles: "Blessed are You, our God, King of the universe, Who has sanctified us with His commandments and commanded us to kindle the light of the festival"; and (*Shehecheyanu*) "Blessed are You, our God, King of the universe, Who has kept us alive, sustained us and brought us to this season."[78]

5. As on all other Yamim Tovim (Festive Days, pl.) it is prohibited to do any work on Rosh Hashanah, with the exception of activities directly related to the preparation of food and which cannot be done in advance. (For example, one may place something on a fire to cook, but not light the fire. For further details regarding this prohibition refer to the chapter on the Festivals.)[79]

6. One should honor and enjoy the Yom Tov. We honor the day by getting a haircut and/or shaving, bathing and putting on nice clothing in preparation for the festival. Ensuring that our home is clean and the table elegantly set is also part of the honor of the festival. It is also customary for men to immerse in the *mikveh* (ritual pool) on the day before Rosh Hashanah begins.[80]

7. The definition of "enjoying" Yom Tov includes eating two festive meals each day,[81] each beginning with *Kiddush* over wine and a blessing over two loaves of *challah.* One should eat meat and drink wine (unless one does not enjoy them) in celebration of the festival.[82]

8. A husband should buy new clothing or jewelry for his wife. Parents give sweet treats and presents to their children.[83]

9. It is customary to eat specific foods known as *simanim*, symbols, at the evening meals of Rosh Hashanah. These are foods whose names have a double meaning that signify blessing. With each food we recite a prayer that God should bestow upon us the particular blessing symbolized by the food.[84] *Simanim* include fish, carrots, pomegranates, dates and of course, the most famous Rosh Hashanah food, apples dipped in honey.[85]

10. The appropriate greeting on Rosh Hashanah is "May you be inscribed and sealed for a good year." In Hebrew, this blessing is slightly different for men or for women, due to grammatical distinctions. Addressing men, we say — "*Leshanah tovah tikateiv ve'techateim,*" and to women, we say — "*Leshanah tovah tikateivi ve'techateimi.*" (Both phrases have the same meaning.) We also greet each other with "*Shanah tovah,*" "Good year."[86]

11. The prayers of Rosh Hashanah are very different from other festival prayers. It is customary and most practical, therefore to pray from a *machzor*, a prayer book designed specifically for Rosh Hashanah.

12. Just before the Additional Service (*Mussaf*) on Rosh Hashanah, we fulfill the Biblical commandment to hear the blowing of the *shofar* (which is divided into "sets" of 30 sounds). Before blowing the *shofar*, the person who will blow recites two blessings, while the congregation listens and then answers "amen." We stand for the blessings and the blowing of the *shofar*. There must be silence from the moment the blessings are begun until the end of this set of sounds. One should have in mind that one is fulfilling a commandment of God by listening to the *shofar*. One should hear a minimum of 30 sounds of the *shofar* to fulfill the *mitzvah*; however, it is customary to hear 100 blasts.[87]

13. One should invite guests to the Rosh Hashanah meals, especially those who are destitute or lonely; and one should give charity to poor families before the festival to enable them to celebrate it appropriately.[88]

14. On the afternoon of the first day of Rosh Hashanah (on the second day if the first day is Shabbat), it is customary to go to a body of water and symbolically "cast our sins into the depths."[89] This ceremony is known as *Tashlich*, "casting."[90] Prayers are recited at this

time citing God's attributes of mercy and asking God to cast our sins into a place where they "will not be remembered or counted forever."[91]

15. At the end of Rosh Hashanah, after nightfall, *Havdalah*[92] is recited over a full cup of wine.[93]

16. The day after Rosh Hashanah is a fast day known as The Fast of Gedaliah.[94]

For Further Reading

▸ *Days of Awe — Sfas Emes* by Rabbi Yosef Stern (ArtScroll/Mesorah, 1996)

▸ *Living Jewish* by Rabbi Berel Wein (ArtScroll/Mesorah, 2002)

▸ *Rosh Hashanah: Its Significance, Laws, and Prayers* (ArtScroll/Mesorah, 1989)

▸ *Rosh Hashanah/Yom Kippur Survival Kit* by Shimon Apisdorf (Leviathan Press, 1993)

▸ *Tashlich* by Rabbi Avrohom Chaim Feuer (ArtScroll/Mesorah, 1979)

NOTES

References to books of the Talmud refer to the Babylonian Talmud unless otherwise noted.

1. See Chapter 4, The Jewish Calendar.
2. Exodus 12:2.
3. Rabbi Samson Raphael Hirsch, Com-mentary on the Pentateuch, Leviticus 23:9, Judaica Press.
4. A *shofar* is a ram's horn that has been hollowed out to make a musical instrument.
5. Alternative translation: "a day declared holy."
6. Leviticus 23:23-25.
7. *Machzor* for Rosh Hashanah, "*Hayom harat olam.*"
8. *Rosh Hashanah* 8a, *Tosafot*, "*Litekufot K'Rebbi Eliezer.*"
9. Central compilation of Jewish Oral Tradition, edited by Judah the Prince, circa 170 C.E.
10. Mishnah, *Rosh Hashanah* 15a.
11. Babylonian Talmud, ad loc. gives three explanations for the Hebrew "*bnei meron*" — like sheep, like people going one by one up a narrow, steep path or like soldiers being inspected individually.
12. *Code of Jewish Law, Orach Chaim,* 597:1.
13. Ibid. 1-3.
14. *Midrash Rabbah,* Genesis 8:5.
15. Mark Twain, *Following the Equator,* Chap. 27, "*Pudd'nhead Wilson's New Calendar*" (1897).
16. Rabbi Moshe Shapiro.
17. *Rosh Hashanah* 32b.
18. *Rosh Hashanah* 8a.
19. Maimonides, *Mishneh Torah,* Laws of Repentance 3:4.
20. *Code of Jewish Law, Orach Chaim,* 581:1, Ramah.
21. Obviously, this is a topic that requires much more in-depth analysis. See Appendix for suggested readings on this subject.
22. Genesis 22:1-19.
23. *Rosh Hashanah* 16a.
24. Leviticus 25:9-10.
25. *Sifri, Beha'alotcha, Piska* 19.
26. See chapter on Belief, Principle 12.
27. These phrases refer to the Jewish people who have been exiled from the Land of Israel. The "holy mountain" is Mount Moriah, the location of the Temples.
28. Isaiah 27:13.
29. *Code of Jewish Law, Orach Chaim,* 582:1.
30. Maharal of Prague, *Tiferet Yisrael,* Chap. 21.
31. Attributed to Rabbi Solomon ibn Gevirol, Spanish-Jewish poet and scholar, circa 1050 C.E.
32. *The Complete ArtScroll Siddur, Ashkenaz,* pp. 12-13.
33. *Rosh Hashanah* 16a.
34. *The Complete ArtScroll Machzor, Ashkenaz,* Rosh Hashanah, pp. 454-459.
35. Ibid. pp. 458-463.
36. See chapter on Belief, Principle 12.
37. *Machzor* ibid., pp. 462-465.
38. Containing the Torah scrolls.
39. From *The Complete ArtScroll Machzor, Ashkenaz,* Rosh Hashanah, pp. 480-481, footnote on *Unetaneh Tokef.* Based on the *Or Zarua.*
40. Ibid. pp. 480-485.
41. *Ta'anit* 25b.
42. *Code of Jewish Law, Orach Chaim,* 602:1.
43. *Machzor* ibid. pp. 384-389.
44. *Rosh Hashanah* 32b.
45. *Code of Jewish Law,* ibid. 597:1. Some authorities, however, are of the opinion that one may fast. Ibid. 597:2-3.
46. Sanctification — a blessing about the significance of the festival that includes a blessing over the wine.
47. Bread used on Shabbat and festivals.

48. *Horayot* 12a.

49. *Code of Jewish Law,* ibid. 583:1.

50. Ibid. 583:1 Ramah.

51. *The Complete ArtScroll Siddur, Ashkenaz,* pp. 768-769.

52. Nehemiah 8:10.

53. *Code of Jewish Law,* ibid. 581, *Mishnah Berurah* 25.

54. Nehemiah 8:9-10.

55. *Code of Jewish Law,* ibid. Ramah ad loc.

56. *Code of Jewish Law,* ibid. 582:1. See chapter on Prayer.

57. *Code of Jewish Law,* ibid. 603:1.

58. See Chapter 18 on Material Witnesses.

59. See Chapter 24 on Prayer.

60. Rabbi Avraham Danzig, *Chayei Adam,* Section 143.

61. *Yoma* 85b. *Code of Jewish Law,* ibid. 606:1.

62. *Code of Jewish Law,* ibid.; *Mishnah Berurah* ad loc. 1; *Chayei Adam,* Chap. 143.

63. Literally, "Good day," a term for the festivals of the Jewish calendar.

64. Written by Rabbeinu Yonah of Gerondi, circa 1250, known in Hebrew as *Shaarei Teshuvah.*

65. See Chapter 23 on Torah Study.

66. Ibid.

67. Ibid.

68. Synagogue.

69. "Blessed are You, God, our God, King of the universe, Who has kept us alive, sustained us and brought us to this time." See chapter on Blessings.

70. *Code of Jewish Law, Orach Chaim,* 500:2.

71. *The Complete ArtScroll Siddur, Ashkenaz,* pp. 770-772.

72. See Chapter 5 about Shabbat.

73. *Code of Jewish Law,* ibid. 581:1, Ramah; *Mishnah Berurah* ad loc. 2.

74. Literally, "Spaniards" — Jews of North African and Middle Eastern ancestry.

75. Literally, "Germans" — Jews of European ancestry.

76. *Code of Jewish Law, Orach Chaim,* 581:1, *Mishnah Berurah* ad loc.

77. Ibid. 581; *Shaarei Teshuvah* 1.

78. *The Complete ArtScroll Siddur, Ashkenaz,* pp. 296-297.

79. Leviticus 23:24-25.

80. *Code of Jewish Law,* ibid. 581:4 and Ramah ad loc.

81. Ibid. 597:1.

82. Ibid. 529:1.

83. Ibid. 529:1-2.

84. *The Complete ArtScroll Machzor, Ashkenaz,* Rosh Hashanah, pp. 96-99.

85. *Code of Jewish Law,* ibid. 583:1.

86. Ibid. 582:9, Ramah; *Mishnah Berurah* ad loc.

87. Ibid. 585-590.

88. Ibid. 529:2.

89. Micah 7:19.

90. *Code of Jewish Law,* 583:2, Ramah ad loc.

91. *The Complete ArtScroll Siddur, Ashkenaz,* p. 770.

92. For a discussion of *Havdalah,* see Chapter 5 on Shabbat.

93. *Machzor* ibid. pp. 670-671.

94. See Chapter 13 on The Fast Days.

The Day of Atonement

Yom Kippur, fasting and forgiveness

Yom Kippur: The Sabbath of Sabbaths

The Torah designates the tenth day of the seventh month (*Tishrei*)[1] as the Sabbath of Sabbaths. It is a day of atonement from sins, a holy day, that we now call Yom Kippur, the Day of Atonement.

In the seventh month on the tenth of the month you shall afflict yourselves and you shall not do any work, neither the native-born Jew nor the convert who dwells among you. For on this day He shall provide atonement for you to purify you; from all your sins before God you shall be purified.[2]... It is a Sabbath of Sabbaths to you and you shall afflict your souls on the ninth of the month in the evening, from evening to evening you shall observe the Sabbath.[3]

We see from the above Biblical passages that Yom Kippur is described as the holiest day of the year because it combines the Sabbath prohibition against work, atonement from sin and the obligation to fast, described in the Bible as "affliction." We ignore our physical needs and desires on this day and relate to God as if we were completely spiritual beings. On this day, God gives us the opportunity to be cleansed of our sins and to correct the past.

Contrary to most people's perception of the day as very sad, the Sages describe Yom Kippur as one of the happiest days of the year.[4] In a beautiful passage in the Talmud, Rabbi Akiva states:

> *Happy are you, Israel* [i.e. the Jewish people]*! Before Whom are you purified and Who purifies you? Your Father in heaven! As it says, "And I will cast upon you waters of purity and you will be purified."[5] And it says, "God is the hope (mikveh) of Israel."[6] Just as a mikveh purifies the impure, so the Holy One, Blessed is He, purifies Israel.[7]*

Although Yom Kippur is certainly a solemn day of self-reflection, it is also a day of happiness. This is the time when we can become free of the shackles of our past, when God gives us a special opportunity and ability to repent and change ourselves for the better.[8] While on Rosh Hashanah we look forward to and pray for a good new year and commit ourselves to being better people, Yom Kippur focuses us on our past and gives us a chance to "turn back the clock," to actually change our past. This process is called *teshuvah,* repentance, or literally, return, as we will explain in greater detail further on in this chapter.

Second Tablets, Second Chance

The greatest event in history was, without doubt, God's Revelation to the entire Jewish people on Mount Sinai. Very soon afterward, however, mistakenly thinking that Moses had disappeared, the Jewish people built a Golden Calf. Many of the people worshipped the calf as an idol, although most regarded it a replacement for Moses, not God.[9] This act, which our Sages likened to a bride committing adultery at her wedding, damaged the relationship between the Jewish people and God; the effect reverberated throughout history.[10]

When Moses came down from Mount Sinai and saw the Jews dancing around the Golden Calf, he broke the Tablets of the Ten Commandments God had just given him. Moses then turned to God and pleaded with Him for 40 days not to destroy the Jewish people. Finally, on the first day of the Hebrew month of Elul,[11] God told Moses to ascend Mount Sinai once again. There, Moses prayed for 40 days more until God completely forgave the people, renewed His Covenant with them and gave Moses a second set of Tablets.[12] It was on Yom Kippur that these second Tablets were given because atonement and forgiveness are forever imprinted on the spiritual nature of this day.[13] God decreed that this moment in time should be observed every year as the second giving of the Torah, a day which will always provide an opportunity for us to heal the rifts in our relationship with God.

Fasting

One of the best-known features of Yom Kippur — sometimes the only thing people know about this day — is the fact that we are forbidden to eat and drink.[14] What is the meaning and purpose of these prohibitions on Yom Kippur?

An anthropologist visiting a synagogue on Yom Kippur might think that since no one is eating or drinking for an entire 24-hour period, the congregants are all suffering terribly. He would probably conclude that the purpose of the fast is solely to induce suffering for the sake of atonement. These observations would completely miss the mark. It is true that on Yom Kippur there is an obligation to refrain from eating, drinking, washing for pleasure, using lotions or engaging in intimacy. A person observing these prohibitions its not necessarily suffering, however. When I was a child I used to be an avid reader. I would become so engrossed in a book that I would not hear my mother calling me for supper and would be unaware of any hunger or thirst. (In Divine retribution, I now call my own children when they are reading and they too are unable to hear me.) As soon as I had finished the book, however, I would be ravenously hungry and thirsty because my mind was no longer focused on reading.

A similar phenomenon occurs for many people on Yom Kippur. They are focused on their prayers and repentance, on repairing, renewing and improving their relationship with God. When they are engrossed in the spiritual components of the day, they do not experience the sensations of hunger and thirst, just as a reader might not realize that he is hungry or thirsty until he finishes the book.[15]

If the purpose of fasting is not physical suffering, what is it intended to achieve? The simplest explanation seems to be that fasting is a way of ignoring our physical needs and focusing entirely on our spiritual side. This is in marked contrast to how we often act during the rest of the year, when we tend to our physical needs, often neglecting (and sometimes even damaging) our spiritual selves. Recognizing that we have frequently indulged in such behavior, fasting impresses upon us that enjoying the physical world is a privilege we may not deserve. Rabbi Samson Raphael Hirsch explains:

> Yom Kippur also teaches us that in consequence of our sins, we have, from the standpoint of strict justice, no further right to continue our existence and the gratification of our senses.

We… therefore show ourselves on Yom Kippur for what we really are: spiritually poor. And in order to express this fact, on this day we… avoid any gratification of the senses…. For… by gratifying his senses on Yom Kippur, a Jew would be taken to indicate that he thinks he need render no account of his life and that he owes his existence to no one. Theoretically speaking, only a Jew who is perfect and has never sinned — and therefore has not jeopardized his right to life — would not need Yom Kippur. But then, where is there such a righteous person?[16]

Another aspect of fasting is the removal of distractions and temptations in order to focus the individual on the essence of life and the service of God. In addition, fasting contributes to a feeling of humility, appropriate to one who is begging for forgiveness and is in the process of being judged. As the *Sefer Hachinuch*[17] writes:

One of the kindnesses of God toward His creatures was to set one day a year to atone for sin through repentance… And therefore we were commanded to fast on this day, because food, drink and other pleasures of the senses arouse the material [side of man] to follow his desires and can lead to sin. And they will overpower the pure soul whose desire is only to search for truth, which is the service of God, His ethics and His goodness that are the sweetest pleasures for one of wisdom…

In addition, it is not appropriate that on the day that he comes for judgment before his Creator, that he should stand with a soul full of its own importance and somewhat confused by eating, drinking and thoughts of physical pleasures …[18]

Fasting can certainly be difficult, but it remains a primary obligation of the day, even if one does not think of or achieve any of the goals or ideals that we have just discussed. Still, it is important to keep in mind that the ultimate goal of the fast is, in fact, *teshuvah,* repentance.

What's Wrong with Shoes?

The reasons behind the various prohibitions of Yom Kippur become clear in light of what we have explained above. They are the means by which we actively subjugate the physical side of ourselves and the world. Only the prohibition against leather shoes does not seem to fit this pattern. It is possible, Rabbi Hirsch suggests, that this too is a denial of comfort and physical pleasure that expresses our humility and contrition.

Why did God specifically forbid leather shoes (rather than ban sitting in a comfortable chair, for example)?

For a deeper insight into the meaning of this prohibition, we must examine what shoes symbolize in the Torah. The first place they are mentioned in the Torah is at the beginning of Moses' prophecy:

> *Moses was shepherding the sheep… and he came to the mountain of God, Horeb.* [The name of the mountain was Horeb.] *An angel of God appeared to him in a flame from a bush, and behold, the bush was burning with fire but was not consumed… God called to him and said, "Moses, Moses," and he answered, "Here I am." God said, "Do not come any closer, **take your shoes off your feet** because the place where you are standing is holy ground."*[19]

Similarly, when Joshua is confronted by an angel, he is told to take off his shoe.[20] Jewish law forbids wearing shoes in the Temple in Jerusalem.[21] A mourner may also not wear leather shoes[22] during the first and most intense period of mourning.[23] What do these instances have in common?

Some commentaries suggest that the shoe is a metaphor for the human body and physicality.[24] Just as the shoe encloses that part of the body which comes in contact with the earth and enables it to walk in and interact with the world, so too the body encases the component of the soul which interfaces this world and allows it to interact with finite physicality. As our bodies are covered by our skin, so too, shoes are made of animal skin, leather. When God wants us to ignore our physical elements and try to relate to Him only on a spiritual level, He commands us to remove our leather shoes. This is the reason that both Moses and Joshua were told to remove their shoes during prophecy, while on holy ground. This was an experience of the soul, not the body. One does not visit the Temple to enhance his physical well-being but rather to connect to the spiritual dimension. The mourner may take comfort from knowing that although a beloved person is gone from this world, nevertheless, his or her soul still exists, albeit without its "shoe," the body.

So too on Yom Kippur, when we focus entirely on the soul and ignore the body completely, it is appropriate that we avoid wearing that which most symbolizes the body — the leather shoe.[25]

Teshuvah: Being Truly Sorry

The "*mitzvah* of the day" of Yom Kippur is *teshuvah*, repentance. There is no question that at any time when a person has done something wrong, he or she must correct this behavior and change for the better. In that sense, the commandment of *teshuvah* applies year round. On Yom

Kippur, however, there is a special obligation to take advantage of the unique spiritual quality of the day to "do *teshuvah*." Jewish tradition tells us that God is particularly close to us during this time and awaits our smallest step toward Him.[26] As Maimonides explains:

> *Even though repentance and crying out [in prayer] are always beautiful ... during the ten days from Rosh Hashanah to Yom Kippur, they are especially beautiful and are accepted immediately... The day of Yom Kippur is the time of repentance for all, individuals and communities, and it is the final time for forgiveness and pardon for the Jewish people. Therefore everyone is obligated to repent and confess on Yom Kippur.*[27]

Teshuvah, literally translated, means, "return." We believe that the soul is intrinsically pure and began its sojourn on this world in a state of purity.[28] Sins and transgressions are departures from the essential nature of the human soul. Therefore, when a person has done something wrong, the process of *teshuvah* is really that of going back to his or her true essence.

Jewish law describes three essential components of *teshuvah* pertaining to the three dimensions of past, present and future. First the sinner must recognize that he has done something wrong and regret having done it, i.e., feeling remorse for the past. In the present, he must confess his sin to God and pray for forgiveness. The final element is commitment to the future, never to repeat this transgression.[29] If a person sincerely regrets, confesses and resolves to do better, not only is he completely forgiven, his former sins may now be considered merits[30] because, ultimately, they were stepping stones to further growth.[31]

The Book of Jonah is read in the synagogue as part of the Yom Kippur afternoon service, to provide us with a striking example of the power of repentance. The Book of Jonah relates that the city of Nineveh was so evil that God had determined to destroy it. Before carrying out this judgment, however, He sent the (reluctant) prophet Jonah to warn the city of its impending destruction and give them one last chance to redeem themselves. The people of Nineveh listened to the prophet's warning and reacted immediately:

> *The people of Nineveh believed in God, so they proclaimed a fast and donned sackcloth ... The matter reached the king of Nineveh; he rose from his throne, removed his robe ... covered himself with sackcloth and sat on the ashes, and had it ... declared in Nineveh ... "Man and animal ... shall not taste anything; ... every man shall turn back from his evil way, and the robbery that is in his hands. He who knows shall repent and God will relent ..." And God saw their deeds — that they repented from their evil ways — and God relented ...*[32]

The Talmud[33] notes that the verse does not say that God "saw their sackcloth and ashes" but rather, "God saw their deeds — that they repented." The purpose of the sackcloth, ashes and fasting was to help them repent, but what saved the city from destruction was the fact that they had really changed their actions. The people of Nineveh brought no sacrifices[34] and did not build any monuments — they achieved forgiveness entirely through *teshuvah*.

Even Yom Kippur Can't Help

Teshuvah and Yom Kippur help to atone and gain forgiveness for sins committed against God and oneself. But sins committed against a fellow human being only can be forgiven by the injured party. The Talmud makes this distinction between sins committed against God and those against fellow human beings quite clearly:

> *Rabbi Elazar ben Azariah explained: The verse states, "From all your sins **before God** you shall be cleansed."[35] Sins between the person and God, Yom Kippur atones for; sins between one person and another, Yom Kippur does not atone for until he seeks forgiveness from his friend.[36]*

In other words, one must first compensate the harmed person and ask for his forgiveness. Only then can one begin the process of *teshuvah* and be forgiven by God.

In the *Code of Jewish Law*,[37] the section immediately preceding the laws of Yom Kippur is entitled, "One Should Seek Conciliation with One's Friend on the Eve of Yom Kippur." It discusses the obligation to ask for forgiveness from someone whom we have hurt, the laws governing the process of conciliation and the obligation to be forgiving. This section precedes the detailed laws of the fast, because without gaining forgiveness from our fellow human beings, Yom Kippur will not atone for these sins.

Prayer – What to Do While You're Fasting

The prayers of Yom Kippur are an integral part of the day's observance. One of the reasons that we are commanded to fast is to remove all distractions so that we can focus on our connection with God. We create and maintain that connection through prayer. The central theme of many of the prayers is, of course, asking for forgiveness.[38] As part of the *teshuvah* process, we also formally confess our sins in the standardized prayer called *Viduy*. It includes virtually every area of transgression. *Viduy* is recited individually during each of the silent prayers of Yom Kippur, as well as communally along with the cantor during the repetition of the silent prayer.

Another powerful prayer vehicle is known as the Thirteen Attributes of (Divine) Mercy. Taught to Moses by God Himself as a means of breaking through to His mercy when dire threats arise, Moses utilized the Thirteen Attributes when he begged God to forgive the Jews for the sin of the Golden Calf. The Thirteen Attributes list various facets of God's mercy in His relationship to man:

> *Lord, Lord, God, Compassionate and Gracious, Slow to Anger, and Abundant in Kindness and Truth. Preserver of Kindness for thousands of generations, Forgiver of iniquity, willful sin, and error, and Who cleanses.*[39]

This description of God is meant to be contemplated and internalized by the one seeking forgiveness. By focusing on these benevolent attributes of God, one forges a positive connection with Him, worthy of arousing mercy.

Eventually, after Moses used the prayer of the Thirteen Attributes, God did forgive the Jewish people on Yom Kippur and gave them a second set of tablets, replacing the broken first set. Fittingly, the Thirteen Attributes describing God's mercy are recited many times during the Yom Kippur prayers.

Three prayers, which are unique to Yom Kippur, capture the special significance of the day. Yom Kippur begins with the *Kol Nidrei*[40] prayer, recited by the cantor and the congregation. In this prayer, we solemnly ask God to release us from any vows that we may have forgotten,[41] made inappropriately, or been unable to fulfill in the previous year.[42] It is essential to begin Yom Kippur this way because the sin of violating an oath is so serious that it may prevent one from achieving atonement. *Kol Nidrei* also symbolizes the idea of Yom Kippur as an opportunity to free ourselves from our past. The text of *Kol Nidrei* and the haunting tune with which it is chanted are both of great antiquity, but unknown authorship. The poignant melody and the inspiring words set the tone for the rest of Yom Kippur.

The *Mussaf* (Additional Service) of Yom Kippur morning describes the drama and significance of the High Priest's service in the Jerusalem Temple on Yom Kippur. The High Priest (a direct descendant of Aaron, brother of Moses) would enter the Holy of Holies, the innermost sanctum of the Temple only once a year, on Yom Kippur. There he would pray for the Jewish people's forgiveness and bring special offerings and incense. *Mussaf* describes the details of this service and the fervent prayers that the High Priest and the people recited while it was performed. Additional liturgical poems, called *piyutim*, movingly contrast the glory of the Temple in Jerusalem with its destruction and the exile of the Jewish people.[43]

Yom Kippur ends with the third special prayer, *Ne'ilah,* which means "closing of the gates."[44] It is the culmination of a day devoted to repentance, intense concentration and prayer. *Ne'ilah* offers the last chance to seize the moment of Yom Kippur and to tap into the closeness with God that is so accessible on this holy day. *Ne'ilah* is said just before sundown, just before the metaphorical "closing of the Heavenly Gates." The Holy Ark containing the Torah remains open for the entire *Ne'ilah* service, which begins with the silent prayer of Yom Kippur. Instead of saying, "*inscribe* us in the book of life," as we have since Rosh Hashanah, we now say "*seal* us in the book of life." *Ne'ilah* is the time when the Heavenly judgment on each person is "signed and sealed," not merely inscribed. *Ne'ilah* continues with the repetition of the silent prayer, and the congregation joins in reciting the Thirteen Attributes of Mercy along with other prayers in which we literally beg for life and forgiveness.

The service ends with the entire congregation gathering its last reserves of concentration and emotion, and crying out *Shema Yisrael,* "Hear, O Israel: The Lord is our God, the Lord is One,"[45] followed by "Blessed is the Name of His glorious kingdom for all eternity." This is said three times, after which "The Lord — Only He is God!"[46] is repeated seven times.[47] The cantor then recites *Kaddish,*[48] the *shofar* is sounded, and the entire congregation says aloud and in unison, "Next year in Jerusalem!"[49] In many communities, the congregation repeats this phrase many times while dancing with joy. The solemnity of Yom Kippur is transformed into happiness and optimism, an expression of our belief that God will indeed forgive us and bring the redemption for which we have been praying and hoping.

Selected Laws and Customs of Yom Kippur

1. Yom Kippur occurs on the tenth of the Hebrew month of Tishrei, starting just before sunset on the ninth and ending when it is definitely night on the eleventh — when three medium-size stars can be seen.[50]

2. It is obligatory to eat on the day preceding Yom Kippur.[51] It is customary to have a festive meal as the last meal before the fast on the afternoon preceding Yom Kippur; however, one should take care to finish the meal well before sundown.[52]

3. One is obligated to honor the festival by being clean and well groomed, and by wearing special festive clothing. It is customary (but not obligatory) for men to wear a plain, white robe, known as a *kittel,* during the prayers. The house should be clean and orderly for the festival.[53]

4. Candles are lit as before Sabbath and other festivals. In addition, it is customary to light a 24-hour *Yahrzeit*[54] candle.[55]

5. Yom Kippur only atones for sins between man and God; however, sins against other people require forgiveness from the offended party in addition to Divine forgiveness. The offender must therefore ask for forgiveness before Yom Kippur.[56] It is also the obligation of the offended party to be easygoing and forgiving, whenever possible.[57]

6. Prohibitions:

   ▶ Work is forbidden on Yom Kippur. The definition of "work" is the same as on Shabbat.[58]

   ▶ Eating and drinking are prohibited, even minute amounts.[59]

   ▶ Washing and bathing are prohibited, except for the minimum required to maintain personal hygiene.[60]

   ▶ Applying creams, oils and lotions is forbidden.[61]

   ▶ One may not wear leather or leather-covered shoes.[62]

   ▶ A husband and wife may not be intimate on Yom Kippur.[63]

7. As with all festivals and the Shabbat, the saving of life (in Hebrew, *pikuach nefesh*) overrides the prohibitions. A doctor and a rabbi should be consulted ahead of time if there is even a doubt that fasting would endanger one's life due to a medical condition (such as diabetes, for example).[64]

8. The prayers have the same additions and changes as used on Rosh Hashanah, including the use of the appellation "King" in reference to God and the addition of prayers for life in the silent prayer.[65] Numerous prayers relating to repentance and forgiveness are recited. In addition to the evening, morning, additional festive *Mussaf* and afternoon prayers, a fifth prayer, *Ne'ilah*, is added after the afternoon service before nightfall.[66] As on all Sabbaths and festivals, the Torah scroll is removed from the Ark and sections of the Torah pertaining to Yom Kippur are read publicly.

9. It is obligatory to confess one's sins to God on Yom Kippur as part of the process of repentance.[67] This is known as *Viduy*. *Viduy* is recited —

   ▶ while standing[68]

   ▶ with a bowed posture[69]

- ▸ while lightly tapping the heart with the fist as each sin is mentioned[70]
- ▸ with sincerity[71]

Saying Viduy.
The man is wearing a
white kittel and a tallit.

10. The *shofar* is blown after the *Ne'ilah* service. The weekday evening service is then said, followed by *Havdalah*, the prayer for the end of Sabbaths and festivals.[72]

11. *Havdalah* is recited while holding a full cup of wine. A blessing is said for wine, then a blessing for light while holding the hands in front of a candle (ideally a candle that has been alight since just before Yom Kippur began). The prayer concludes with the blessing of separation (literally, *havdalah* in Hebrew) between the holy and the profane.[73] The person reciting *Havdalah* drinks the wine, and the fast is then broken with a festive meal.[74]

12. It is customary to begin building one's *sukkah*[75] for the upcoming holiday of Sukkot immediately after Yom Kippur, in order to proceed immediately from one *mitzvah* to the next.[76]

For Further Reading

▸ *Days of Awe — Sfas Emes* by Rabbi Yosef Stern (ArtScroll/Mesorah, 1996)

▸ *Living Beyond Time: The Mystery and Meaning of the Jewish Festivals* by Rabbi Pinchas Stolper (Shaar Press, 2003)

▸ *Rosh Hashanah/Yom Kippur Survival Kit* by Shimon Apisdorf (Leviathan Press, 1993)

▸ *Viduy/Confession* by Rabbi Nosson Scherman (ArtScroll/Mesorah, 1986)

▸ *Yom Kippur: Its Significance, Laws, and Prayers* (ArtScroll/Mesorah, 1989)

▸ *Yonah/The Book of Jonah* by Rabbi Meir Zlotowitz (ArtScroll/Mesorah, 1978)

NOTES

References to books of the Talmud refer to the Babylonian Talmud unless otherwise noted.

1. Months are counted from Nissan, the month of the Exodus. See chapter on the Jewish calendar.

2. Leviticus 16:29-30.

3. Leviticus 23:27, 31.

4. *Ta'anit* 26b.

5. Ezekiel 36:25.

6. Jeremiah 17:13. The word *mikvah* means "hope" and also means the ritual pool for purification. See chapter on Marriage.

7. *Yoma* 85b.

8. Maimonides, *Mishneh Torah*, Laws of Repentance 1:3, 2:7.

9. Exodus, Chap. 32; Rabbi Yehudah Halevy, *Kuzari*, 1:97.

10. Exodus 32:34; *Sanhedrin* 102a.

11. The month preceding Tishrei. Rosh Hashanah occurs on the 1st and 2nd of Tishrei and Yom Kippur on the 10th of Tishrei.

12. Exodus, Chap. 33-34.

13. See chapter on the Jewish calendar.

14. Maimonides, *Mishneh Torah*, Law of Yom Kippur 1:4-5.

15. This analysis was heard from Rabbi Dr. Dovid Gottlieb.

16. Rabbi Samson Raphael Hirsch, *Horeb II* Edot, Chap. 22 par. 156.

17. *Sefer Hachinuch, The Book of Education*, published anonymously, but believed to be by Rabbi Aaron Halevi of Barcelona, 1233-1300.

18. Ibid. *Parshat Emor*, Mitzvah 313. Mossad Harav Kook, Jerusalem, 1984.

19. Exodus 3:1-5.
20. Joshua 5:13-15.
21. *Berachot* 62b.
22. Ezekiel 26:23.
23. Known as *shivah*, seven, referring to the first seven days after the burial. See Chapter 3.
24. Maharal of Prague, *Netivot Olam, Netiv Ha'Avodah*, Chap. 6; *Chidushei Aggadot, Sanhedrin* 49a.
25. Rabbi Chaim of Volozhin, *Ruach Chaim* on *Pirkei Avot*, Chap. 1, Mishnah 1.
26. *Rosh Hashanah* 18a based on Isaiah 55:6.
27. Maimonides, *Mishneh Torah*, Laws of Repentance 2:6-7.
28. *The Complete ArtScroll Siddur, Ashkenaz*, pp. 18-19 "...The soul that You placed within me is pure."
29. Maimonides, *Mishneh Torah*, Laws of Repentance 2:2.
30. *Yoma* 86b.
31. Rabbi Yitzchak Hutner, *Pachad Yitzchak*, Rosh Hashanah, Ma'amar 5.
32. Jonah 3:5-10.
33. *Ta'anit* 15a.
34. The Book of Jonah stands in stark contrast to the Christian belief that atonement requires a blood sacrifice.
35. Leviticus 16:30.
36. *Yoma* 85b.
37. *Code of Jewish Law, Orach Chaim*, 606.
38. Rabbeinu Yonah of Geronda, *Gates of Repentance*, 1:41, The Fifteenth Principle of Teshuvah.
39. Exodus 34:6-7.
40. *The Complete ArtScroll Machzor*, Yom Kippur, pp. 58-61.
41. Not from vows imposed by a court, Jewish or non-Jewish.
42. *The Complete ArtScroll Machzor*, Yom Kippur, Introduction, pp. 52-55. According to Rabbeinu Tam, *Kol Nidrei* refers to future vows, not past vows.
43. *The Complete ArtScroll Machzor*, Yom Kippur, pp. 486-625.
44. Ibid. pp. 706-765.
45. Deuteronomy 6:4.
46. I Kings 18:39.
47. Ibid. *Machzor*, pp. 762-765.
48. See chapter on Prayer.
49. *Code of Jewish Law, Orach Chaim*, 623; *Mishnah Berurah* 13.
50. Leviticus 23:27, 31.
51. *Yoma* 81b; *Code of Jewish Law, Orach Chaim*, 604:1.
52. *Code of Jewish Law, Orach Chaim*, 608:1.
53. Ibid. 610:4, Ramah.
54. A Yiddish word that literally means "time of year." The term refers to the anniversary of a death, when it is customary to leave a candle burning for 24 hours. These candles are known as *Yarhzeit* candles.
55. Ibid. 610:1-4.
56. Ibid. 606.
57. Ibid. 606:1, Ramah.
58. *Code of Jewish Law*, ibid. 611:2. See chapter on Shabbat, Laws of Shabbat.
59. Ibid. 612.
60. Ibid. 613.
61. Ibid. 614:1.
62. Ibid. 614:2.
63. Ibid. 615:1.
64. Ibid. 618:1-2.
65. Ibid. 582:1-9.
66. Ibid. 623:1-2.
67. Maimonides, *Mishneh Torah*, Laws of Repentance, 2:7.
68. *Code of Jewish Law*, 607:3.
69. Ibid. *Mishnah Berurah* ad loc., 10.
70. Ibid. ad loc., 11.
71. Maimonides, *Mishneh Torah*, Laws of Repentance, 2:3.
72. *Code of Jewish Law, Orach Chaim*, 623:6.
73. Ibid. 624:1-4.
74. Ibid. 624:5, Ramah.
75. See chapter on Sukkot.
76. Ibid.

Jews in Booths: Sukkot

The Sukkah, lulav and etrog, Intermediate Days, Simchat Torah

Festival of Gathering

ive days after the solemnity and intensity of Yom Kippur, Sukkot, the festival of joy and happiness, begins. This festival lasts eight days in Israel and nine everywhere else. The Torah describes the festival as follows:

> ...On the fifteenth day of this seventh month is the Festival of Sukkot, a seven-day period for God: On the first day shall be a sacred holy day when you shall not do any laborious work:[1]... On the fifteenth day of the seventh month, when you gather in the harvest of the land, you shall celebrate God's festival for a seven-day period; the first day is a rest day and the eighth day is a rest day...[2]

This festival is also known in the Torah as *Chag HeAsif*, the Festival of Gathering, because it is celebrated at the time of year when the harvested produce is brought from the fields into storehouses and homes. When a person gathers in the bounty of his land, he is naturally filled with tremendous joy and happiness. This happiness could easily turn into self-aggrandizement; it could make a person full of himself and his accomplishments, distancing him from God.[3]

We might think that the appropriate antidote would be a period of fasting and repentance; however, that would directly contradict the person's natural inclinations. Judaism does not deny or suppress human nature and instinct; rather, it seeks to utilize them in positive ways. The Torah wants us to celebrate and be happy, but to channel that joy toward our relationship with the Creator and with other human beings.[4] We should use this opportunity to appreciate God's benevolence as well as to share our good fortune with others. As we will discuss shortly, the Torah directs us to use the products of the harvest in the fulfillment of *mitzvot*. Thus we neither deny the physical world nor wallow in it; rather, we elevate it toward a higher purpose.[5]

We Did It!

Gathering in the harvest also takes on a spiritual dimension. The Jewish people have just been through an intense period of introspection, repentance and prayer: the Hebrew month of repentance, Elul, followed by the Day of Judgment, Rosh Hashanah and the Day of Atonement, Yom Kippur. During this time we labor in the fields of spiritual growth. On Sukkot, we harvest the inspiration, the joy and the closeness to God that is produced by this period of repentance. The intense feeling of joy on Sukkot is the feeling of one who hears good news (forgiveness) when he was expecting the worst (punishment); of one who has been given a fresh start in life after making many serious mistakes.

In this way, Sukkot reflects the joy of completing a difficult job, celebrating both the conclusion of the physical harvest and more importantly, the culmination of the spiritual harvest. Traditionally, Sukkot is associated with happiness more than any other festival. In our prayers, it is called "the time of our happiness," while in the Mishnah, it is referred to simply as "the festival."[6] On Passover, when we were taken out of Egypt, we were chosen to do a job. On Shavuot, when we were given the Torah, we were told what that task would involve. On Sukkot we, so to speak, come back to God and say, "We have accomplished our task; we have brought in the [spiritual] harvest from the fields."[7]

The Water Dance

In ancient times, a celebration took place in Jerusalem's Holy Temple on Sukkot called the *Simchat Beit Hashoevah,* "the joy of the house of (water) drawing."[8] "Water drawing" refers to the water that the *Kohanim* ("priests") would pour on the altar during the Sukkot service that beseeches God for rain during the upcoming winter.[9] On the evenings of the intermediate days of the festival, people would gather at the Temple. Torches were lit, music played, and the great sages, the elders, would dance and sing, while thousands joyously watched.[10]

The water that gives its name to these festivities refers to rain, but it is primarily understood as a metaphor for the outpouring of Divine inspiration[11] that can only be achieved when one is in a state of happiness.[12] The intensity of the joy experienced during this celebration was such that the Mishnah[13] states that, "One who has not seen the joy of the *Simchat Beit Hashoevah* has not seen joy in his life."

In the course of Maimonides' discussion of the laws of Sukkot and of the *Simchat Beit Hashoevah,* he affirms that, "the happiness that one experiences in performance of a *mitzvah* and in the love of God Who commanded them is a great duty."[14] One of the commentaries on Maimonides' writings explains that joy is a fundamental component in fulfilling all the commandments of the Torah:

> *The idea is that one should not fulfill the mitzvot because they are obligatory and because he is forced to do them. Rather he must do them and rejoice in performing them, and should do that which is good because it is good. He should choose the truth because it is true. The effort should be trivial in his eyes, and he should understand that it is for this that he was created. When he fulfills the purpose of his creation he will be happy. For happiness due to anything else is dependent on things that are temporary and finite, but the happiness of doing a mitzvah and of learning Torah and wisdom is true happiness.*[15]

Today, Sukkot is still a time of tremendous rejoicing. Synagogues and yeshivot around the world, and especially in Israel, celebrate their own "*Simchat Beit Hashoevah,*" with music, dancing, food and discussions of Torah insights.

Booths and Clouds

The most distinctive feature of this festival, and the *mitzvah* from which it derives its name, is the *Sukkah*, the "booth." The Torah writes,

> *You shall dwell in booths for a seven-day period; everyone included in Israel shall dwell in booths: So that your future generations will know that I caused the Children of Israel to dwell in booths when I took them from the land of Egypt; I am the Lord your God.*[16]

We think of a "booth" today as a place that is quite small and confining. In actuality, a *sukkah* can be enormous. It is not the size that makes it a *sukkah*, but the structure's lack of permanence. The Oral Tradition defines this "booth" as a dwelling place consisting of at least three walls (made of any material) and having a roof made of unprocessed, agricultural products, such as branches and leaves. It is an obligation to live in the *sukkah* during the festival of Sukkot. Ideally, one should eat, sleep, relax and socialize in the *sukkah* just as one would in his/her home.

The significance of this *mitzvah,* on the simplest level, is to remind us that God protected and preserved the Jewish people in the desert after He took them out of Egypt. By living in the *sukkah*, we reenact this experience.

A broader historical perspective offers us a deeper insight into the meaning of this observance. Passover celebrates the Exodus, which was the *physical creation* of the Jewish people. Shavuot celebrates the giving of the Torah, our *spiritual creation*. Sukkot celebrates the remarkable *physical survival* and *continuity* of the Jewish people, the result of ongoing and all-encompassing Divine Providence.[17]

Considering Sukkot in this light, some Sages of the Talmud explain that the booths represent not the Jews' physical dwellings in the desert, but rather, God's "Clouds of Glory"[18] that surrounded and protected the Jewish people from the time of the Exodus until they reached the Land of Israel.[19]

In this light, Sukkot is understood not simply as a reminder of a specific historical period, but rather as an experience that renews our awareness of God's relationship to the Jewish people throughout history. The desert symbolizes our exile and wandering, while the clouds represent God's unceasing protection and care.

The central text of the *Kabbalah* (Jewish mysticism), the *Zohar*, refers to the *sukkah* as "the shade of faith."[20] Sitting in the shade of the *sukkah*, the Jewish people understand that they must not place their faith in the walls and roofs of their houses, or in any physical protection they might construct. We have learned through many years of bitter exile that our efforts only offer protection when they are accompanied by God's Divine Providence protecting us.

Rabbi Eliyahu, known as the Gaon of Vilna,[21] notes that the Clouds of Glory left the Jewish people when they sinned at Mt. Sinai by worshipping the Golden Calf. The Clouds did not return until after the Jews repented and were forgiven on Yom Kippur. The Clouds of Glory once again encircled the nation on the 15th day of the month of Tishrei, the first day of Sukkot,[22] which is why Sukkot is celebrated right after Yom Kippur — even though it is related to the Exodus and might be expected to occur soon after Passover. Sukkot demonstrates that God's love for the Jewish people is just as strong after we sin as it was before. The Clouds of Glory were returned to us, even though our own actions had caused them to be removed: the bond between God and the Jewish people is eternal.[23]

Life Is a Sukkah

Jewish law describes the *sukkah* as a temporary dwelling,[24] a status which informs many of the legal specifications for the *sukkah*'s construction.[25] Leaving our permanent houses with solid walls and roofs to live in a flimsy booth with a roof of branches[26] is a dramatic and unequivocal statement that the material world is not what life is all about. By living in the *sukkah*, we are declaring that the entire physical world is really temporary, and that the only things we truly possess forever are the soul and its spiritual accomplishments.

It was certainly within God's power to build five-star hotels and spas for the Jews in the Sinai Desert. Why then did He put them in thatched huts? Because He wanted them, and us, to understand that there is no permanence to the physical world, and that focusing all aspirations and hopes on material attainments — a house, a car, another house, another car — is pointless. By living in the *sukkah*, we are bringing this message home to ourselves, not just as intellectual knowledge, but as an understanding that will impact our lives.[27]

Origin of the Species

Sukkot features one of the most unusual and picturesque *mitzvot,* known as the *Arba Minim*, the "Four Species." The Torah tells us:

> You shall take for yourselves on the first day [of Sukkot], the fruit of a beautiful tree, the branches of date palms, branches of the thick tree, and brook willows; and you shall rejoice before God, your God, for a seven-day period...[28]

Based on the Talmud's Oral Tradition,[29] Maimonides explains which species of plants are referred to in the Torah verses:

- ▸ "Date palms" are the branches of the palm tree that grow before the leaves separate to either side. It has the appearance of a staff, and is called in Hebrew a *lulav*.[30]

- ▸ The "fruit of a beautiful tree" is the *etrog* (citron).

- ▸ The "branches of the thick tree" are the myrtle, whose leaves cover its branches. They are called *hadassim*.

- ▸ "Brook willows" are a specific type of willow that is called "willows of the brook." They are called *aravot*.[31]

Before Sukkot, the most beautiful specimens of a *lulav*, three *hadassim*, two branches of *aravot* and an *etrog* are obtained. Synagogues and Judaica stores usually sell these items, which are often imported from Israel. The branches are tied together with palm leaves. The *Arba Minim*, the Four Species, will be used in the morning service on Sukkot.

It is customary for every family to acquire its own set of *Arba Minim*, and in some families even children are given their own set. During the morning service, the synagogue is awash in shades of green and yellow as everyone stands with his *lulav* and *etrog*.

Immediately after the silent prayer, a blessing is recited, the *etrog* is taken in the left hand, the other three species, often referred to collectively as the *lulav*, are held in the right hand. Together, they are gently shaken in six directions, east, south, west, north, up and down.[32] The *lulav* is also held and shaken at specific points in the *Hallel* prayer.[33] (*Hallel*,[34] "Praise," consists of selections from Psalms that are recited and sung on festivals and joyous occasions.) Afterwards, a Torah scroll is taken out of the Ark and held by someone on the *bimah* (platform),[35] in the center of the synagogue. The congregation then walks around the *bimah*, holding their *lulavim* (pl.) and reciting prayers known as *Hoshanot*.[36]

What the Species Say

In addition to fulfilling a commandment of the Torah with the *Arba Minim*, the action, drama and pageantry of the *mitzvah* also convey important messages. Maimonides understands the Four Species as an expression of our gratitude to God for the Land of Israel. He writes: *The Species represent the bounty of the Land of Israel; with them we express our gratitude to God for taking us from Egypt and blessing us with the beautiful and rich Land of Israel.*[37]

Others understand the Four Species in a broader sense. Rabbi Samson Raphael Hirsch suggests that they represent four different ways that we benefit from the natural world. He begins with an observation made by the Sages of the *Midrash*[38] that the *etrog* can be eaten and has a pleasant smell. The *lulav*, from a date palm, has no aroma but does provide food. The myrtle has a pleasant aroma, but cannot be eaten. The willow offers neither food nor aroma — it is just wood. Rabbi Hirsch explains that these are parallel to different elements found in nature.

Some things — such as air, light, beauty and pleasant aromas — are of benefit to us without requiring any human touch. The myrtle has a pleasant aroma, and the willow offers shade.

Other things, such as most foods, are inherently beneficial to humanity but need some human involvement for the benefit to be extracted. For example, an *etrog*, like all fruit, must be picked from a tree, and to enjoy the benefits of the date palm one must harvest the dates.

Sometimes, extracting a valuable product from raw materials is entirely dependent on human effort. The willow tree provides wood but that must be processed to be useful.

Understanding this hidden meaning in the Four Species will impact on our relationship to the world created by God — for our benefit — and results in a more sublime relationship with our Creator. In Rabbi Hirsch's words:

> *Take these Four [Species] as standing for all that God offers you as gifts of nature; take them as your very own before the Lord, your God; acknowledge and acclaim that it is God Who gives to you all that is good in life. Cling to them only as the means of living in the presence of God according to His will; rejoice in them before your God as the means of fulfilling your duties.*[39]

Another beautiful explanation is found in a source dating back to the times of the Mishnah (170 – 200 C.E.). According to this explanation, taste symbolizes actions and scent symbolizes learning:

The *etrog*, which has scent and taste, symbolizes a Jew who actively performs *mitzvot* as well as studies Torah.

The *lulav* represents a Jew who studies but does not fulfill *mitzvot*.

The myrtle (*hadassim*) symbolizes one who does *mitzvot* but does not study.

The willow (*aravot*) represents a Jew who neither does *mitzvot* nor studies Torah.

When we recite the blessing, all four plants, representing the four types of Jews, are bound and held together, an action that expresses the inherent unity of the Jewish people, and the importance of every individual. Every single Jew contributes toward the achievement of our nation's goals, even if he or she appears to have no merit at all.[40]

All Shook Up![41]

What is the significance of shaking (or pointing) the *lulav* in six directions? If we understand the *mitzvah* as an expression of gratitude, the six directions indicate that God's benevolence and power are found wherever we turn, whether it is the four points of the compass, the heavens or the earth.[42] Pointing the *lulav* in all directions demonstrates our belief that God's presence is everywhere and that He is in control of all of existence.[43] It is interesting to note that the *lulav* is held still when we recite God's Name and is only moved when reciting the other words of the prayer:[44]

Perhaps this is meant to remind us that God should be at the center of everything we do and everywhere we turn.

Another understanding of the shaking is based on a verse in Chronicles:

> The heavens will be glad and the earth will rejoice; let them declare among the peoples, "God reigns!" The sea and its fullness will roar; the field and everything in it will exult: Then all the trees of the forest will sing with joy — before God, for He will have come to judge the earth.[45]

The verse states that the "trees of the forest ... sing with joy" in the presence of God. Nature is a servant of God, in a sense part of a beautiful symphony of praise to its Creator. When we shake the *lulav* during *Hallel*, we are imitating the swaying of branches and the rustling of leaves in the forest, which is also a song to God.[46]

Interfest – Chol Hamoed and Hoshana Rabbah

The festival of Sukkot, like Passover, is one week long. The first two and last two days are full festival days, with Shabbatlike prohibitions against work. Each of the interim days, however, has its own unique character. These days are known as Chol Hamoed, the "weekday of the festival." This means that compared to the first and last days (of the festival) they are like weekdays, but compared to actual weekdays they are holy. During these days we still live in the *sukkah*, bless the Four Species every morning and recite special festival prayers. We honor the festival by wearing nicer clothing and eating better food than usual on weekdays, and by dedicating more time to the study of Torah.[47]

The prohibition against work during these days is much more lenient than on Yom Tov and Shabbat. The Torah recognizes that observing the stricter prohibitions for an entire week would be a tremendous hardship and would not allow enjoyment of the festival. Therefore, the laws of Chol Hamoed cause us to refrain from any great physical effort and limit our concern with material gain, while at the same time allowing us to fully enjoy these intermediate days as a holiday.[48] Generally, activities that do not contribute directly to the enjoyment and fulfillment of the festival are forbidden on the intermediate days.[49] Skilled labor and very strenuous activities, for example, are prohibited, but driving a car is permitted. Similarly, using electricity and all food preparations are permitted. Practically speaking, Chol Hamoed is very similar to a vacation — but in this case a themed vacation, in which we experience, celebrate and learn about the festival.

The last day of the Chol Hamoed of Sukkot is called Hoshana Rabbah, which means "the great salvation." This is a reference to prayers that are recited every day of Sukkot, as the congregation walks around the *bimah* holding their *lulavim* (as described earlier). The constant refrain of these prayers is *Hoshana*, literally meaning, "Please save." We plead with God to save us from the sufferings and tribulations of exile (from the Holy Land). On the last day of Chol Hamoed, the congregation goes around the *bimah* seven times[50] while additional *Hoshana* prayers are recited,[51] as a sign of the great holiness of this day.[52] In the times of the Holy Temple in Jerusalem, the people held willow branches, *aravot*, as they walked around the altar once on all the other days of Sukkot, but seven times on Hoshanah Rabbah.

After completing these prayers, we take five *aravah* branches and, in accordance with a custom that dates back to the prophets, we strike them on the floor five times.[53] One possible reason for this custom is that it is a demonstration of our rejection of a completely materialistic life. We first walk around the Torah, showing that it is the center of our lives, and then take a symbol of the physical world and show how insignificant it is to us in comparison to the Torah.[54]

Shemini Atzeret

> On the fifteenth day of this seventh month is the Festival of Sukkot, a seven-day period for God. On the first day shall be a sacred holiday when you shall not do any laborious work... **The eighth day is a sacred holiday to you... it is a time of assembly**[55] when you may do no laborious work.[56]

Technically, the festival of Sukkot ends after seven days, as indicated in the verses above. It is, however, immediately followed by the festival of Shemini Atzeret, which is considered the eighth day of Sukkot (outside of Israel — the eighth and ninth days). The Hebrew words *Shemini Atzeret* mean the Eighth [day] of Assembly. The commandments of Sukkot, the *sukkah* and the *lulav* do not apply to this day, because it is an independent festival.[57]

Shemini Atzeret is understood by some commentaries as a festival on which we try to "hold on" to the sanctity and inspiration of Sukkot.[58] Other sources suggest that it is a time when God's chosen people spend an extra day (or two) with Him, after the pomp and circumstance of Sukkot. The Sages explain this idea using the metaphor of a king who made a feast for all the citizens of his country. After the week of feasting was over, he asked his closest friends to stay with him an extra day for a simpler, more intimate gathering. In the days of the Temple, 70 special offerings were brought on Sukkot representing the Jewish people's prayers for all the 70 nations of the world.[59] On Shemini Atzeret, however, a single special offering was brought, symbolizing the Jewish people and their unique relationship with God.[60]

Simchat Torah

Over the years, Jewish custom attached a second significance to Shemini Atzeret. Originally, different customs existed regarding the reading of the Torah on Shabbat. In Israel, the Torah was read in a three-year cycle, while in Babylon the custom was a yearly cycle. Eventually, the Babylonian custom became universally accepted,[61] and to this day Jews throughout the world publicly read the entire Five Books of Moses (the complete Torah scroll) in the course of every year.[62] The reading of the Torah is both completed and begun again on Shemini Atzeret (in Israel on the eighth day, and in the Diaspora on the ninth day). This occasion became known as Simchat Torah, the "Joy of the Torah."[63] The *Midrash*[64] traces the concept of rejoicing upon finishing the Torah back to the celebration made by King Solomon when God granted his request for wisdom.[65]

Simchat Torah is a day of tremendous happiness. Completing the reading of the Torah and beginning it again is an occasion marked by dancing, singing, feasting and many beautiful customs. Both in the evening and during the day, all the Torah scrolls are taken out of the Ark and the community dances with them around the *bimah*, while reciting prayers and singing songs that thank God for the precious gift of the Torah. This ceremony is known as *Hakafot*, literally, circuits. In the morning, the *Hakafot* are repeated, and the last section of the Torah is read. On a regular Shabbat or festival, only a few men are called up to the Torah, but on Simchat Torah, every man in the synagogue is called up. (The expression is "given an *aliyah.*")[66] In many synagogues even children are called to the Torah. After reading the final portion as many times as necessary for everyone to have a turn, one honoree, the *Chatan Torah*, "Groom of the Torah," is called up for the privilege of saying the blessings on the last verses of Deuteronomy. Immediately afterward, another honoree, the *Chatan Bereshit*, the "Groom of Genesis," is called up to say the blessings on the first verses of the Torah reading.

An atmosphere of intense joy fills the synagogue, and in many places the dancing continues for hours. Children often carry miniature, toy Torah scrolls and dance with flags inscribed with phrases about the Torah. Refreshments are usually made available in the synagogue during the celebration.

The incredible joy that is felt on Simchat Torah is a testimony to the love that the Jewish people have for the Torah. A great Chassidic rabbi[67] pointed out that greater joy is expressed on Simchat Torah than on Shavuot, even though Shavuot is the festival that marks the giving of the Torah on Mount Sinai. He explained that on Shavuot we were passive recipients of God's gift of the Torah, but on Simchat Torah, we celebrate the fact that we are active partners with God in the Torah. We read and study the Torah, and through the wisdom of our Sages, and the customs of our communities, implement it in our daily lives. Simchat Torah reflects the Jewish peoples' love for the Torah, their involvement in the Torah and their devotion to God, Giver of the Torah.

Rabbi Samson Raphael Hirsch links Shemini Atzeret and Simchat Torah to the yearly pattern of all the festivals. He notes that Passover, celebrating the *physical creation* of the Jewish people, is followed by and linked to Shavuot, when the Torah was given — i.e., the *spiritual creation* of the Jewish people. Sukkot celebrates the *physical preservation* of the Jewish people through Divine Providence. Sukkot in turn is followed by and linked to Shemini Atzeret and Simchat Torah, the festivals celebrating the *spiritual preservation* of the Jewish people, through their attachment to the Torah.[68]

It is significant that immediately after completing one cycle, by reading the end of Deuteronomy, we begin the new cycle by reading from Genesis. There is no interruption in our communal study of Torah; we start again as soon as we have finished because the Torah has infinite depth — one can never really finish studying Torah. When we complete one cycle, we understand one more level of Torah and are now more capable of understanding the next level, and the next, and the next …. What we celebrate on completing the Torah, is the renewed and improved opportunity that we now have to learn Torah even better.[69]

The Levys Camp Out

The Levy family starts building their sukkah immediately after Yom Kippur. The first step is taking the wood boards and bamboo s'chach out of the basement and stacking them in the back yard, which they do at night, soon after breaking the fast. The next morning, Mr. Levy and the older children begin the assembly and the younger children start making decorations. The sukkah materials were chosen by Mr. Levy and Shlomo about five years earlier when they moved into their new home and have been used every year since. The walls are eight-by-four-foot plywood panels with two-by-fours screwed on as a frame. There are holes predrilled in the frame and special long screws with butterfly nuts so that the sukkah can be easily assembled. Each panel is numbered,[70] so all they have to do is line up the numbers, put in the screws and tighten them. The s'chach consists of thin bamboo poles lightly woven together with reeds. This is supported by long two-by-fours that rest in slots cut into the tops of the walls.

The assembly process usually takes about three hours, after which a waterproof light fixture is hung in the middle of the sukkah. Since it often rains at this time of year, the Levys wait until the day before Sukkot to hang decorations and bring in tables and chairs. Each year, they try to innovate some new convenience in the sukkah — a shelf attached to the walls for the candles, another for books as well as hooks for hanging coats. This year, Shlomo has built a frame that is attached over the s'chach at an angle and has a rolled up tarpaulin at its higher end. When it rains, a rope can be pulled and the tarpaulin will unroll down the sloping frame to cover the sukkah. This device, known in Yiddish as a shlock, prevents the s'chach from retaining water that can drip onto the family when they reenter the sukkah after the rain. The shlock must be removed, however, when the sukkah is in use.

The Levys laminate many of the decorations and keep them from year to year. By now, the walls of their sukkah are almost completely covered by pictures of Israel, children's artwork and cards with the blessings and prayers said in the sukkah. They also decorate the sukkah with samples of the seven types of plants with which the Land of Israel is blessed, as recounted in the Torah — wheat, barley, grapes, figs, pomegranates, olives and dates.[71] Weather permitting, Mr. Levy and Shlomo usually sleep in the sukkah on folding cots.

After building the sukkah, Mr. Levy and several of the children go to their synagogue to buy the Four Species, the Arba Minim. The rabbi is available to help people with their choices, but Mr. Levy is an old hand at this and can handle making the selection himself. In fact, he uses the opportunity to train his older children in how to choose each plant in accordance with Jewish law. The younger children love going along too — they learn how to make koshiklach, the woven palm leaf holders for the Four Species, how to tie rings for the lulav, and they even get a lollipop from the rabbi. Well taught by his father, Shlomo likes to shop for his own Arba Minim, so he usually spends a day in Brooklyn with some friends, scouting the hundreds of sellers for the perfect etrog.

Sukkot is one of the Levy family's favorite festivals. The experience of eating in the sukkah is much more than just a meal outside: The beauty of the sukkah, the simple "roof" with the stars shining through, gives one a feeling of being a guest of God in

His house. They love singing the special Sukkot songs and enjoy reciting the Ushpizin (Aramaic for "guests") each night.[72] This is a short prayer based on a Kabbalistic concept that seven great Jewish personalities come to visit the sukkot of the Jewish people, one on each night of Sukkot. With this prayer, we invite them to join us as our guests.[73] The Ushpizin are Abraham, Isaac, Jacob, Joseph, Moses, Aaron and David.[74]

The idea of the Ushpizin is that each night God allows some of the spiritual "light" and ideals of each of these great people to be more accessible to us as we sit in the sukkah. Through our prayers and the contemplation of their specific attributes, we can gain a deeper understanding of their teachings.[75] In some communities, children with the name of one of the Ushpizin invite their friends to their sukkah for a party on the night of their namesake.

Chol Hamoed is a festival for the family in every sense of the word. Everyone is off from school and work, and there is a feeling of relaxation and happiness just being together in the sukkah. Mr. and Mrs. Levy have the luxury of not being hurried or harried as they often are during the year and are able to spend some quality time with the family. The children look forward to special breakfasts that they normally do not have during the hectic weekdays all year. Scones, pancakes and French toast almost have the status of ancient custom in the Levy sukkah. After breakfast, each of the children takes a turn to study Chumash, Mishnah or Gemara with Mr. Levy in the sukkah. Like many families, the Levys arrange several outings during Chol Hamoed: They go to the zoo or a museum, for hikes in a forest, or to an amusement park. They visit relatives and friends and sometimes join them for a meal in their sukkah. Because Chol Hamoed has the status of a holiday, everyone wears clothing that is nicer than usual weekday dress and the meals during Chol Hamoed are fancier than regular weekday meals.[76]

The children's schools and neighborhood synagogues host celebrations on the nights of Sukkot for the whole community. These celebrations, called Simchat Beit Hashoevah (see above), are reminders of the celebrations held in Jerusalem's Holy Temple in ancient times. At the Simchat Beit Hashoevah, there is usually a band playing Jewish music, people dance and sing, and the rabbi or a guest speaker presents an inspirational address about Sukkot.

The climax of joy is reached on Simchat Torah, the ninth and last day of the festival. Jewish festivals are celebrated at night and the next day. At both of these Simchat Torah services the children bring miniature Torah scrolls and flags to the synagogue. The whole community sings and dances around the bimah for hours.

In the Levys' shul, a lavish luncheon is sponsored by the honorees, the Chatan Torah *and* Chatan Bereshit, *to which the entire community is invited. The lunch ends late, everyone is exhausted, the children are on sugar highs, and a bittersweet feeling is in the air as the festival of Sukkot draws to a close.*

After Maariv, the evening service,[77] the Havdalah[78] blessing over a cup of wine is recited by Mr. Levy and the family bids farewell to Sukkot. The next day, they take down the sukkah, put it back into storage in the basement and pack the decorations in a box for next year. The Four Species (by now, a bit dry) are not just thrown away, as they have been used for a sacred purpose and forevermore carry a hint of holiness. The Levys keep them for half a year until Passover, when they burn them as they bake matzah[79] for for the holiday:[80] This establishes continuity from one mitzvah to the next, linking Sukkot with Passover.

The end of Sukkot marks the completion of an intense and eventful season that began with Rosh Hashanah and Yom Kippur. Now, with the onset of winter, it is a time for quiet and tranquility, for the integration of the lessons of the holiday season into everyday life.[81]

Selected Laws of the Sukkah

1. One should begin building the *sukkah* as soon as possible after Yom Kippur ends. It is also correct to be personally involved in building the *sukkah.*[82]

2. One should eat, drink, sleep and, in general, live in the *sukkah*, in the same way that one lives in his house during the year. One should refrain however, from doing any activity in the *sukkah* that is not appropriate to its holiness.[83]

3. Women are exempt from dwelling in the *sukkah*, but they may fulfill the *mitzvah* voluntarily and recite the blessing.[84]

4. A boy should be educated to fulfill the *mitzvah* from the time he is about 5 or 6 years old.[85]

5. One who is sick, and those who are caring for the sick, are exempt from the *mitzvah* of living in the *sukkah.*[86]

6. If one suffers from being in the *sukkah*, he is exempt from the *mitzvah.* If, for example, it is very cold, extremely hot, infested

with insects or has a bad smell, one is exempt. In general, in any situation where the suffering would cause a person to leave his house or the room, he may also leave the *sukkah*.[87] (See note 8 below.)

7. On the first night of Sukkot one should make *Kiddush* in the *sukkah* and eat a minimum amount of bread in the *sukkah*, even if it is raining. The remainder of the meal, however, may be eaten in the house.[88] The minimum amount of bread to be eaten is about .9 to 1.6 oz. (25. – 50 cc.) or about half a regular slice of bread.[89]

8. One who is suffering in the *sukkah* should leave, and not attempt to stay despite the suffering.[90]

9. If one eats bread or any food made of wheat, rye, barley, spelt or oats, he must eat it in the *sukkah*. Other foods, such as, meat, fish, eggs, fruits or vegetables, may be eaten outside the *sukkah*, although it is praiseworthy to eat all food in the *sukkah*.[91]

10. One should sleep in the *sukkah* if it is possible to do so without discomfort. In Europe and North America and countries where it is cold during Sukkot, it is not common to sleep in the *sukkah*.[92]

11. When a person eats bread or food made from any of the grains mentioned above, he should first recite the blessing over the food then say the blessing, "Blessed are You, God, Our God, King of the universe, Who has sanctified us with His commandments and commanded us to dwell in the *sukkah*."[93] On the first two days and the last two days, as well as on Shabbat during Sukkot, the blessing is said during the *Kiddush*.[94]

12. If you are constructing a *sukkah* for the first time, you would be wise to ask a rabbinic authority for guidance. The general rules for building a *sukkah* are as follows: The *sukkah* should have at least three proper walls[95] (ideally four, for privacy and for shelter).[96] The walls may be constructed of any material that can withstand strong weather conditions. They should not be higher than 30.84 feet (9.4 m). The size of the *sukkah* should be at least 2.3 by 2.3 feet (70 X 70 cm).[97]

13. The roof of the *sukkah*, called *s'chach*, should be made of any agricultural product that is not attached to the ground and has not been formed into a vessel or utensil.[98]

14. The *s'chach* should be thick enough to provide more shade than sunlight in the *sukkah*, but sparse enough that the stars can still

be seen. Some maintain that the *s'chach* can be thick enough to block out the stars, but at the very least, it should not be so thick that rain cannot penetrate.[99]

15. The *s'chach* should be the only covering of the *sukkah*, therefore one may not build a *sukkah* under a tree, roof, balcony, etc.[100] If only part of the *sukkah* is covered by a tree, a rabbi should be consulted.

16. The *s'chach* cannot be nailed or tied down nor directly supported by metal supports.[101] If the walls are not made of wood, wooden beams can be placed over a metal frame and the *s'chach* may rest on that.

17. All the materials for the *sukkah* must be legally purchased. One cannot rely on assumptions about trees or branches being "available" or "not missed by the owner." A *sukkah* should not be built on another person's property without consent, nor should it be built on public property.[102]

18. It is customary to decorate the *sukkah* and to hang decorations from the *s'chach*.[103]

19. In Israel, we do not eat in the *sukkah* on the eighth day, because it is really not Sukkot. In the Diaspora, however, since we observe two days of every festival, it is appropriate to eat in the *sukkah* on the eighth day, but without saying a blessing. (There are different customs regarding this practice.) On the ninth day (Simchat Torah), one does not eat in the *sukkah* at all.[104]

20. Many additional laws apply to the construction of the *sukkah*, to unusual circumstances and to the details of the *s'chach*. As can be seen from the above summary of laws, the rules are quite specific. One should consult a rabbi regarding any questions.

Selected Laws of the Four Species (Arba Minim)

1. One should buy the Fours Species and pay for them before Sukkot.[105] According to Biblical law, one must actually own them in order to fulfill the *mitzvah* on the first day. On the other days, it is permitted to borrow a set to fulfill the *mitzvah*.[106]

2. It is correct to try to buy the most beautiful, complete and fresh set of species possible.[107]

3. It is customary to show the Four Species to a rabbi who has expertise in this area to confirm that they are fitting to be used for the *mitzvah* and are also beautiful examples of the species.

4. The *etrog* should not come from a grafted tree, but should have a pure "pedigree." Therefore, it is customary to buy *etrogim* (pl.) that come from an orchard that has a long tradition of being authentic and nongrafted. (These orchards are found in Israel, Morocco and Italy and are known to reliable wholesale purchasers.) It should also be as free of blemishes and cuts as possible, and with the stem of the bud, called *pitom,* intact (if it grew with one).[108] Since blemishes on some parts of an *etrog* are more of a problem than on other parts, ascertain from the seller (if he is knowledgeable) or a rabbi if the *etrog* in question is fit for use.

5. The palm branch, *lulav,* must be from a date palm. Branches of a Canary Palm, a type of palm tree that does not produce dates, should not be used for the *mitzvah.* The *lulav* should be straight, and the uppermost leaves should not be split.[109]

6. Ideally, the leaves of the myrtle, *hadas* (pl. *hadassim*), should grow in groups of three. They should grow from the same place on the stem and should overlap the leaves above, so that the stem is totally surrounded and covered by leaves.[110]

7. The stem of the willow, the *aravah* (pl. *aravot*), should have a reddish tinge; the edges of the leaves should be smooth (not serrated), and the top of the branch should not be cut off.[111]

8. One should take one *lulav,* three *hadassim* and two *aravot* and tie them together with leaves from a palm tree. With the spine of the *lulav* facing the person, the *hadassim* are placed on the right and the *aravot* on the left, with the *hadassim* slightly higher than the *aravot.* A holder woven from palm leaves fits tightly around the three species. Three rings are made from small strips of palm leaves and tied around the *lulav.*[112] The rings may not be made on Yom Tov. (Don't worry! The person selling the Four Species usually does this for you.)

9. The *lulav* is shaken after saying the blessing on this *mitzvah,* usually just before *Hallel.* At various times during *Hallel* (depending on the custom of the synagogue), the *lulav* is shaken again. There are different customs about exactly how to shake the Four Species.[113] The most common custom among Ashkenazim[114] is to hold all the species together and, facing east, shake them in

six directions, east (straight ahead), south (right), west (behind), north (left), up and down. The Four Species are held chest-high, extended in the appropriate direction, shaken so that the leaves of the *lulav* rustle, then brought back to the chest. This procedure is repeated three times.[115]

10. The species should be held in the same direction in which they grow (i.e., not upside down or sideways).[116]

11. The first time that one performs the *mitzvah* on Sukkot he or she should make two blessings — 1) "Blessed are You, Hashem, Our God, King of the universe, Who has sanctified us with His commandments and commanded us concerning the taking of the *lulav*," followed by 2) "*Shehecheyanu*" — "Blessed are You, Hashem, Our God, King of the universe, Who has kept us alive, sustained us, and brought us to this season." Each time the *mitzvah* is performed after the first time, only the first blessing is said.[117]

12. One should say the blessing before fulfilling the *mitzvah*. Therefore, the *etrog* is held upside down (stem up, since it grows stem down) while making the blessing, and then turned the right way up after the blessing.[118]

13. The *mitzvah* of *lulav* is not done on Shabbat.[119]

14. The identification of the Four Species and the details of the laws pertaining to them are complex and require expert knowledge. A rabbi should be consulted regarding any questions.

For Further Reading

▶ *Living Beyond Time: The Mystery and Meaning of the Jewish Festivals* by Rabbi Pinchas Stolper (Shaar Press, 2003)

▶ *Succos: Its Significance, Laws, and Prayers* (ArtScroll/Mesorah, 1982)

NOTES

References to books of the Talmud refer to the Babylonian Talmud unless otherwise noted.

1. Leviticus 23:34-35.

2. Leviticus 23:39.

3. Deuteronomy 8:12-18.

4. Maharal of Prague, *Gur Aryeh*, Genesis 45:29.

5. Rabbi Samson Raphael Hirsch, *Horeb*, II Edoth, Chap. 31, para. 223.

6. Mishnah, *Rosh Hashanah* 1:2.

7. Rabbi Yitzchak Hutner, *Pachad Yitzchak*, Rosh Hashanah (*Hemshech Tishrei*), 9.

8. Mishnah, *Sukkah* 5:1.

9. Rosh Hashanah 16a.

10. Maimonides, *Mishneh Torah*, Laws of Lulav, 8:12-15.

11. *Midrash Rabbah*, Genesis 70:8.

12. Shabbat 30b.

13. Mishnah *Sukkah* 5:1.

14. Maimonides, *Mishneh Torah*, Laws of Lulav, 8:15.

15. Commentary of Rabbi David ben Zimrah (RaDvaZ) ad loc.

16. Leviticus 23:42.

17. Hirsch, *Horeb*, II Edoth, Chap. 23, para. 169-170.

18. Exodus 13:21-22.

19. *Sukkah* 11b.

20. *Zohar, Emor*, 103a.

21. Rabbi Eliyahu Kramer, the 18th-century genius of Vilna, universally referred to as the "Gaon of Vilna."

22. Rabbi Eliyahu Kramer, Commentary of the Gaon of Vilna on Song of Songs, 1:2.

23. Rabbi Yitzchak Hutner, *Pachad Yitzchak*, Rosh Hashanah (*Hemshech Tishrei*), 10:8.

24. *Sukkah* 23a.

25. Ibid. 2a, 21b.

26. *Sukkah* 2a.

27. Rabbi Eliyahu Dessler, *Michtav M'Eliyahu*, vol. 2, p. 106.

28. Leviticus 23:40.

29. *Sukkah* 32a-34b.

30. Since the *lulav* is the most prominent of the group, they are referred to collectively as the *lulav*.

31. Maimonides, *Mishneh Torah*, Laws of Lulav 7:1-3.

32. The order of the directions varies according to custom.

33. *Code of Jewish Law, Orach Chaim*, 651:1-10.

34. *The Complete ArtScroll Siddur, Ashkenaz*, pp. 632-643.

35. See Chapter 14 on the synagogue, "The Torah and Its Home."

36. Ibid. *Code of Jewish Law* 660:1-2.

37. Maimonides, *Guide for the Perplexed*, 3:43.

38. *Midrash Rabbah*, Leviticus 30:14.

39. Hirsch, *Horeb*, Chap. 31.

40. *Pesiktah D'Rav Kahana, Piskah* 27:10.

41. My apologies to Elvis.

42. Hirsch, *Horeb*, chap. 31, para. 224 (e).

43. *Sukkah* 37b.

44. *Code of Jewish Law, Orach Chaim* 651; *Mishnah Berurah* 37.

45. I Chronicles 16:31-33.

46. *Tosafot, Sukkah* 37b, "Behodu leHashem."

47. *Code of Jewish Law, Orach Chaim* 530; *Mishnah Berurah* 1-2.

48. Hirsch, *Horeb*, II Edoth, para. 184.

49. *Code of Jewish Law*, ibid. 530:1.

50. Ibid. 664:1.

51. *The Complete ArtScroll Siddur, Ashkenaz*, pp. 726-757.

52. Ibid. 664; *Mishnah Berurah* 11.

53. *Code of Jewish Law*, Ibid. 664:4; *Sukkah* 45a; *Zohar*, Tzav 31b.

54. Hirsch, *Horeb*, Edoth II, para. 225.

55. *Atzeret* in Hebrew. Literally, "stopping." Some translate as "assembly," others as "holding back," others as "retreat." Aryeh Kaplan, *The Living Torah*, Moznaim Publishing, NY, 1981.

56. Leviticus 23:34-36.

57. *Rosh Hashanah* 4b.

58. Commentary of *Rashi* and *Ibn Ezra* on Leviticus ibid.

59. A figure derived from the count of nations in Genesis Chaps. 10-11.

60. *Midrash Rabbah*, Numbers 21:24; *Sukkah* 55b; *Tolaat Yaakov* p.74.

61. Maimonides, *Mishneh Torah*, Laws of Prayer 13:1.

62. See Chapter 24, "Getting Up on the Right Side of Bed: Prayer."

63. *Tosafot* on *Beitzah* 30b and *Ta'anit* 28b; *Code of Jewish Law, Orach Chaim* 669:1, Ramah.

64. *Midrash Rabbah*, Song of Songs, 1:9; *Midrash Rabbah* Ecclesiastes 1:1.

65. I Kings 3:15.

66. For a complete discussion of the Torah reading and calling up to the Torah see chapter on Prayer, under the subheading "Back to the Mountain."

67. Rabbi Menachem Mendel Schneerson.

68. Hirsch, *Horeb*, II Edoth, Chap. 23, para. 169-170.

69. Heard from my teacher, Rabbi Avraham Gurevitz of Jerusalem.

70. *Code of Jewish Law*, ibid. 630; *Be'er Heitev* 6.

71. Deuteronomy 8:5.

72. *The Complete ArtScroll Siddur, Ashkenaz*, pp. 720-723.

73. *Zohar*, Leviticus Section 3, pp. 103b-104a.

74. The order of the guests varies slightly according to customs of different communities. See *The Complete ArtScroll Siddur, Ashkenaz,* ibid.

75. Dessler, *Michtav M'Eliyahu*, vol. II p. 110; Rabbi Yeshaya Halevi Horowitz, *Shnei Luchot Habrit,* Masechet *Sukkah*, Ner Mitzvah 5.

76. *Code of Jewish Law*, ibid. 530; *Mishnah Berurah* 1.

77. See Chapter 24.

78. See Chapter 5.

79. Unleavened bread.

80. *Code of Jewish Law,* ibid. 664:9 Ramah. See Chapter 11 on Passover.

78. Hirsch, *Collected Writings*, vol. II, The Month of Cheshvan, p. 147, Feldheim Publishing, NY — Jerusalem, 1985.

79. *Code of Jewish Law, Orach Chaim* 625:1 Ramah.

80. Ibid. 639:1-2; *Mishnah Berurah* 28.

81. Ibid. 640:1; *Mishnah Berurah* 1.

82. Ibid. 640:2.

83. Ibid. 640:3.

84. Ibid. 640:4.

85. Ibid. 640:3, 5 Ramah.

86. Measurements are from Rabbi Eliyahu Weissfish, *Arba'at Haminim Hashalem,* Jerusalem, 1974.

87. Ibid. 639:7 Ramah.

88. Ibid. 639:2.

89. Ibid.

90. *The Complete ArtScroll Siddur, Ashkenaz*, pp. 360-361 (Shabbat), 722-724 (Festivals).

91. *Code of Jewish Law,* ibid. 630:5 Ramah.

92. *Code of Jewish Law, Orach Chaim,* 630:1, 2.

93. Ibid. 633:1; Weissfish, ibid.

94. *Code of Jewish Law,* ibid. 634:1; Weissfish, ibid.

95. 86. *Code of Jewish Law*, ibid. 629:1-2.

96. Ibid. 631:1-3; *Mishnah Berurah* 4.

100. Ibid. 626:1.

101. Ibid. 629; *Mishnah Berurah* 22.

102. Ibid. 637:3, Ramah; *Mishnah Berurah* 10-14.

103. Ibid. 638:2; *Mishnah Berurah* 11.

104. See Chapter 4, The Jewish Calendar, for a full explanation.

105. *Code of Jewish Law*, ibid. 668:1.

106. Ibid. 698; *Mishnah Berurah* 10.

107. Ibid. 649:1-2.

108. Ibid. 656:1.

109. Ibid. 648.

110. Ibid. 645.

111. Ibid. 646.

112. Ibid. 647.

113. Ibid. 651:1.

114. Jews of European origin.

115. *Code of Jewish Law,* ibid. 651:9 Ramah; *The Complete ArtScroll Siddur, Ashkenaz*, p. 631.

116. *Code of Jewish Law*, ibid. 651:2.

117. *The Complete ArtScroll Siddur, Ashkenaz*, pp. 630-631.

118. *Code of Jewish Law*, ibid. 651:5.

119. *Code of Jewish Law*, ibid. 658:2.

Spritual Survival: Chanukah

*The history and meaning of Chanukah,
the menorah, latkes and dreidels*

Setting the Scene

srael: Approximately 200 years before the events of Chanukah, hundreds of thousands of Jews returned from the Babylonian exile to the Land of Israel. In time, they rebuilt the Temple in Jerusalem and established an independent Jewish monarchy.

Greece: After the death of Alexander the Great[1] in 323 B.C.E., the Greek-Macedonian Empire split into several smaller kingdoms: the Greek Empire based in Greece; the Seleucid Empire based in Syria; and the Ptolemaic Empire based in Egypt.

A Greek Tragedy

The Land of Israel was situated precisely between the Ptolemaic and Seleucid kingdoms, both of which were Greek in language and culture. In the struggle for regional domination between the Ptolemaic and Seleucid

Empires, control of the trade routes and seaports of the Land of Israel became critical. Under Emperor Antiochus IV[2] of Syria, the Seleucids invaded Israel. Although they did not physically exile the Jewish people, they created a state of virtual exile in the Land of Israel.[3] The Jews were subject to Greek rule and Judaism came under attack from every side.

The Hellenist Seleucids wanted to swallow the Jews culturally and turn Israel into a Greek vassal state. Although they did not destroy the Temple, they defiled it and turned it into a pagan Greek temple.[4] Rather than merely disposing of the olive oil used to light the Temple Menorah (a seven-branched candelabrum), they dedicated it to their pagan gods.[5] The Greeks were not interested in physically destroying the Jewish people; they wanted to destroy them spiritually. Therefore, instead of destroying the Jewish buildings they tried to obliterate the holiness of the sites. They issued decrees designed to undermine the most essential aspects of Jewish life: banning circumcision, the observance of Shabbat, the Jewish calendar[6] and the study of Torah.[7] Jewish brides were required to submit to the local Greek governor on their wedding night.[8] The decrees against circumcision, Shabbat and the calendar were intended to break down the barriers between Jews and Gentiles. By banning Torah study and corrupting the Temple service they tried to sever the connection between the Jews and God. The decree concerning Jewish brides was an attempt to insinuate themselves into the most intimate and holy aspects of Jewish life, to destroy the genealogical chain of Judaism and the purity of Jewish family life and morality.[9]

The Revolt

The Greeks were very successful in their campaign against Judaism. Many Jews were quite content to be Greeks. They adopted Greek clothing, hairstyles and names. There were entire cities in Israel populated by Jews, which to all appearances were Greek cities.[10] To these Jewish Hellenists, the Greeks represented all that was modern, new and scientific, while Judaism was antiquated and out of fashion. They accepted the Greek gods and participated in Greek festivals and athletic events. Many Jewish men who competed in these events, in which the athletes were naked, actually underwent operations in order to look uncircumcised.[11]

Many Jews did remain loyal to Judaism, however, and continued to live as Jews, despite the pressure to assimilate and the great risks involved. A small group of these loyalists felt that they were morally obligated to fight the Greeks and to expel them from Israel. They believed that the Jewish people would only be free to live a full Jewish life if they were independent. The kernel of this group was a family of *Kohanim*, "Priests":[12] Mattathias (Matityahu) son of Yochanan the High Priest (*Kohen*

Gadol) and his five sons. Known as the Hasmoneans[13] (*Chashmonaim*), they were led by their brother Judah (Yehudah) "the Maccabee."[14] Although from a military perspective their cause seemed hopeless, this small army began a guerilla war against the powerful and massive Greek occupying army.[15]

The Lights of Victory

Miraculously, their campaign was successful. The Maccabees defeated the Greek army and entered the Holy Temple in Jerusalem, which had been defiled and tainted by idolatry. They wanted to light the Menorah and rededicate the Temple to God, but the Greeks had systematically broken the seals and desecrated every amphora of pure oil. They finally found a single jar of oil that still bore the seal of the High Priest, indicating its purity. It contained just enough oil to light the Menorah for one day, but miraculously the oil lasted for eight days. The miracle of the oil was understood as a sign from Heaven that the military victory was indeed brought about by Divine intervention, that the Maccabees had acted in accordance with God's wishes, and that the Jewish people would survive and continue to bring the light of Torah to the world.

The following year, the Sanhedrin declared a new festival of gratitude and praise[16] to God for the miracle of Jewish spiritual survival. Beginning on the 25th of Kislev, and lasting eight days, they called it Chanukah, meaning "dedication" (of the Temple). This festival commemorates the miracles of Chanukah for all time.

The Spiritual Battle

The underlying theme of the conflict between the Jews and the Greeks is the clash between two diametrically opposed worldviews. In the Jewish view of reality, everything in the physical world is a reflection of the spiritual. A physical conflict is a superficial manifestation of a deeper spiritual conflict. There are, of course, many points of contention between Jewish tradition and Greek philosophy. The spiritual essence of the Judeo-Greek conflict however, revolves around a single idea — the definition of reality. Nachmanides, one of the greatest Biblical commentators, encapsulates the difference as follows:

> [Our belief is unlike] *that Greek [Aristotle] who denied every-thing that he could not sense. He and his students were arrogant enough to think that anything that they did not arrive at with their own reasoning was not true.*[17]

The essence of Jewish belief is that the senses perceive only the surface of an entity. Beneath this plane of physical perception lies a vast spiritual reality. For Jews, truth is not defined by the human being, but by God. Our system of ethics originates in the Revelation at Mt. Sinai, not in a social contract or human convenience. Rabbi Samson Raphael Hirsch once commented that there is no such thing as Jewish theology — for theology is the opinion of humans about God, but Judaism is God's opinions about humanity: "Not what man thinks of God is of primary importance, but what God thinks of man and wants him to do."[18]

The Greeks believed that their perception defined reality, ethics and truth. The most elegant, beautiful concept constitutes the truth. The Greek ideal of beauty, for example, was something that depended on very specific measurements in the facial structure of a person. The more acute the angle formed by the nose and forehead, the more ugly the individual; the more obtuse the angle, the more beautiful.[19] Western society, the successor of Greek culture, exhibits this attitude in its language as well.

The English word "face" has its origins in the Latin "facies" which is related to "facade," "surface" and "superficial." In contrast, the Hebrew word for face is *panim*, which means "inside." The most beautiful face is one that reveals inner beauty and meaning, not one with idealized angles and texture.[20]

Maimonides points out another theme in the conflict. He maintains that the greatest mistake of Greek philosophy was the belief that matter is eternal and not created.[21] Since in the Greek view God is within nature and not above it, He could not intervene to change nature. This view precludes the possibility of miracles, revelation and Divine Providence. It denies any ultimate purpose in existence. The events of Chanukah provided a dramatic refutation of this Greek worldview.

The Greek Melting Pot

The idea that any one people could be "chosen" or have a Divine revelation was completely contrary to Greek belief. Therefore, the Greek campaign against Judaism and the Jews attempted to eradicate the Jews as a special people. One example of this effort was the Emperor Ptolemy's translation of the Torah into Greek. The Talmud[22] relates that Ptolemy gathered 72 Sages, placed them in 72 separate cubicles and commanded them to translate the Five Books of Moses into Greek. Miraculously, they all translated the Torah in exactly the same way, and they all made the same thirteen changes from a literal translation in order to prevent the Greeks from misinterpreting the Torah.[23] Although this would appear to be a positive event, perhaps as a step toward disseminating the ideas of monotheism and morality, the Jewish Sages looked upon it as a disaster.[24]

They knew that the Torah never could be captured in translation. No language other than Hebrew can convey its depth, beauty, infinite layers and nuances.[25] Another tragic aspect of this event was that the Greeks would now present the Torah, the essence of the bond between the Jews and God, as public property to be accessed by anyone. They would argue that the Jewish people no longer had any claim to a "special relationship" with God, since anyone could take Judaism 101 at Athens U. and know Torah just as well. In truth, in order to properly understand Torah, one must have the Oral Torah[26] — which the Greeks did not have. The true Covenant between God and the Jewish people was manifested in the intimate and personal relationship of the Oral Tradition, even more than in the publicly available and accessible Written Torah.[27]

Celebrate!

After millennia of attempts to assimilate us into our host cultures, whether through force or persuasion, we are still here. But it is not mere physical survival that we celebrate. After all, the genes of other ancient nations have also physically survived. The miracle of Jewish survival is that we have survived with our spiritual heritage intact.[28] When we light the Chanukah candles today we are extensions of the Maccabees, lighting the Menorah in the rededicated Second Temple. In effect, we are continuing the lighting of the Menorah by the Priests in the First and Second Temples. Ultimately, we are even continuing the lighting of the first Menorah in the Sinai Tabernacle by Aaron the High Priest, brother of Moses.[29]

The lights of Chanukah are also a potent reminder that physical might and numbers do not necessarily prevail. As the prophet Zechariah stated, "Not by might, not by power, but by My spirit, said the Lord of Hosts."[30] The miracle of Chanukah was the victory in which God delivered "... the powerful into the hands of the weak, the many into the hands of the few, the impure into the hands of the pure, the evil into the hands of the righteous and the violent into the hands of the those who are devoted to the Torah."[31]

Oh Dreidel, Dreidel, Dreidel!

A traditional pastime on Chanukah is playing with a *dreidel*, a four-sided spinning top with a Hebrew letter on each side. The Hebrew letters *nun, gimmel, heh* and *shin* begin the words in the Hebrew sentence "A great miracle happened there." (In Israel, the letter *peh* is inscribed instead of a *shin* to correspond to the sentence, "A great miracle happened *here.*") Children play a game in which candies or coins are won or lost depending upon which letter is up after the dreidel has stopped spinning and falls.

Playing *dreidel* is more than just a bit of holiday fun, however. It teaches us a profound lesson about Jewish history. It symbolizes the four major exiles that the Jews have experienced: Babylon, Persia, Greece and Rome.[32] Just like a spinning *dreidel*, each of these empires has its moment in the sun but will eventually fall. In history, as with the *dreidel*, only two things remain constant: the point on which it revolves and the handle above. The point around which the *dreidel* revolves symbolizes the eternal Jewish people, while the "hand" from above which spins the *dreidel* of history is the Divine Providence of God.[33]

As in almost all Jewish festivals, food plays a role in the celebration. On Chanukah it is customary to eat dairy foods to remind us of the heroism of Judith (Yehudit), daughter of Yochanan the High Priest. When she was taken to be defiled by the Greek ruler Holofernes, she served him cheese, to make him thirsty, and wine, to quench his thirst. After getting Holofernes completely drunk, she decapitated him. (This was illegal in Greece at the time.)

This was one of the events that sparked the Maccabean uprising.[34] The other, and perhaps more well-known, event occurred in Modi'in, home of the Maccabees. A Jewish Hellenist attempted to publicly offer a pig as a sacrifice to a pagan idol. When Mattathias attacked him, Greek troops intervened, thus starting a battle between the Maccabees and the Greeks.

Food fried in oil is also eaten to commemorate the miracle of the Menorah. Latkes, which are fried pancakes made of grated potato, grated onion and eggs are usually eaten with applesauce (or sour cream, for the brave of heart). In Israel, deep-fried jelly donuts, called *sufganiyot*, are the quintessential Chanukah delicacies.

The Levy Family Lights Up

On the day before Chanukah, Mr. Levy sets up a sturdy shelf near the front window that will be big enough to accommodate all the family's menorahs. The largest menorah is an heirloom, inherited from Mrs. Levy's grandfather. It is sterling silver and has oil containers in the shape of lions with wicks coming out of their mouths. The lions are lined up in front of a wall that is made to look like the Western Wall in Jerusalem. It has a small pitcher to fill the cups with olive oil and a silver holder for the shamash, the candle used to light the menorah. Some of the children have simple oil-burning menorahs. Those who are too young for oil menorahs have a menorah that uses candles. Mr. and Mrs. Levy help the smaller children light, and it is always a big event for the child to graduate to lighting by himself or herself. Eventually each receives his or her very own oil menorah.

As soon as Mr. Levy arrives home from the evening service, the family gathers at the window to light the Chanukah candles. First Mr. Levy recites the blessings and lights the large family menorah, then each of the children lights his or her own menorah. After the lighting, the family sings the traditional song, Maoz Tzur. Mrs. Levy always prepares a dairy treat for Chanukah (a favorite is fudge), which she gives out to the children after the candle lighting. The children then play dreidel until suppertime. Mr. Levy usually studies some Torah with each of the children while the candles are burning, and treats them to his specialty, latkes and applesauce, afterward.

The Levys give their children Chanukah gelt (money) every night of Chanukah. One of the reasons for this custom is based on the law that everyone, no matter how poor, must light Chanukah candles, even if it means begging.[35] Since there were often people begging for charity on Chanukah, it became a custom to give gifts of money on Chanukah so that the poor and needy would not be embarrassed.[36]

Shlomo is away at yeshivah for Chanukah, and he lights his own menorah in the dining room of the yeshivah. From the street, one can see about 150 menorahs crowded together on tables near the windows of the yeshivah. On any given night of Chanukah, the students will be attending parties at the homes of their teachers. Like most students, Shlomo will go home for the Shabbat of Chanukah.

On one night of Chanukah, the Levys always get together with cousins and grandparents for a special evening of conversation, songs and games. They try to plan a few family outings on Chanukah as well. This year, the highlighted trip is to the new aquarium, followed by dinner at a kosher restaurant. The community is organizing a concert of Jewish music on Chanukah, and the local Jewish bookstore has a sale. The synagogue that the Levys attend always brings in a famous rabbi to give a lecture for the community one night of Chanukah, and hires a storyteller to entertain the children during the lecture. Although every holiday is special, the Levy children look forward all year to the special activities and relaxed pace of Chanukah.

Selected Laws of Chanukah

1. Chanukah begins on the evening of the 25th of Kislev (usually December) and continues for eight days.[37]

2. Because of the fact that the dedication of the Temple and Altar took place during Chanukah,[38] it is customary to celebrate by eating special meals, although there is no obligation to do so. During the meal we sing Jewish songs and speak about Torah, in order to make it a *seudat mitzvah*, a meal of religious significance.[39] One should not fast during Chanukah, even on the occasion of a parent's *yahrzeit* (anniversary of death, when there is a custom to fast).[40]

3. There is no prohibition of work on Chanukah. It is customary, however, for women not to work for the first half-hour, at least, after lighting the candles. Some have the custom not to work as long as the candles are still burning. The prohibition includes activities such as sewing and laundry, but cooking is permitted.[41]

4. Every household should light at least one candle each night of Chanukah. The universal custom, however, is to follow the preferred method of adding an additional candle each night. Thus, on the first night one candle is lit, two on the second night and so on. Some families have a *chanukiah* (also popularly known as a menorah) for every adult in the house[42] and many people have one for every child (of appropriate age) to light.

5. Any type of oil is acceptable for use in the menorah; however, it is best to use olive oil as was done in the Temple.[43] Wax candles are also acceptable. Since the menorah should be similar to the Menorah in the Temple, electric lights are not acceptable.[44] It is appropriate to use a beautiful menorah.[45]

6. Note that because the purpose of lighting Chanukah candles is to publicize the miracles of Chanukah, many of the laws related to this *mitzvah* are meant to maximize this effect. Ideally, the menorah should be placed outside the house to the left of the entrance. Since anti-Semitism was so common throughout Jewish history, it became customary among many communities to place the menorah inside the house, near the entrance. It is common practice to place the menorah in a window facing the public, especially where many people share one entrance (e.g., apartment buildings).[46]

7. The menorah should be easily visible; therefore it should be no lower than 10.5 inches (27cm) and no higher than 35.5 ft (10.8m) from ground level. Ideally, it should be placed at a height of about 35 inches (90cm).[47]

8. One should not "benefit" from the light of the menorah (e.g., use it as a light source for reading or other activities), just as it was forbidden to derive benefit from the Menorah in the Temple. This also demonstrates that the purpose of the menorah is to fulfill a *mitzvah*, not merely for illumination.[48]

9. All the candles or wicks on the menorah should be on the same level, none higher or lower than the others. A separate candle known as the *shamash* is used to light the rest of the candles. The *shamash* should be placed in a way that shows that it is not one of the Chanukah candles (e.g., on the side, above or below the others).[49]

10. On the first night of Chanukah a single candle is lit on the extreme right of the menorah. On the second night, a second candle is added immediately to the left of the first, and so on. The newest candle is lit first each night, continuing on to the right.[50]

11. There are different customs regarding the time of candle lighting. Some communities light at sunset, some light about 10 minutes after sunset and some light about a half-hour after sunset (at nightfall). Others light immediately after the evening service (*Maariv*) is recited. Ideally a person should follow the custom of his father's family. If this is not known or is inapplicable for any reason, one should follow the custom of the local community.[51]

12. If one forgot or was not able to light at the correct time, one may light, with a blessing, as long as people are still awake in the house.[52]

13. One should place enough oil or a large enough candle in the menorah to last at least a half-hour after nightfall (i.e., until the appearance of three stars).[53]

14. On the first night, three blessings (*berachot*) are recited: "*Lehadlik ner shel Chanukah*," "*She'asah nissim*" and "*Shehecheyanu*." On the other nights, only the first two blessings are recited. One should not speak between recitation of the blessings and the completion of candle lighting. After lighting, "*Hanerot Hallalu*" and "*Maoz Tzur*" are sung. For the full text and translation of the

blessings and these hymns, see *The Complete ArtScroll Siddur, Ashkenaz*, pp. 782-785.[54]

15. On Friday night, the Chanukah candles should be lit before the Shabbat candles, since once Shabbat has been accepted it is forbidden to light Chanukah candles. The afternoon service, *Minchah*, should be recited, if possible, before lighting.[55] After Shabbat, one should first recite *Havdalah*,[56] and then light the Chanukah candles. One should not use the menorah as the candle for *Havdalah*.[57]

16. One must put in more oil or use larger candles on Friday, so that they burn until a half-hour after nightfall. The menorah is lit just before the Shabbat candles, taking care not to delay lighting the Shabbat candles beyond the appropriate time.[58]

17. During morning prayers, *Shacharit*, the full *Hallel* is recited every day of Chanukah.[59]

18. *Al Hanissim*, a special paragraph of prayers for Chanukah, is added in the silent prayer (*Shemoneh Esreh*) and also in Grace After Meals. If one forgot to say *Al Hanissim*, one should not repeat either *Shemoneh Esreh* or Grace After Meals.[60]

For Further Reading

▶ *Chanukah: Its History, Observance, and Significance* (ArtScroll/ Mesorah, 1986)

▶ *Living Beyond Time: The Mystery and Meaning of the Jewish Festivals* by Rabbi Pinchas Stolper (Shaar Press, 2003)

▶ *The Jewish Self* by Rabbi Jeremy Kagan (Feldheim, 1998)

NOTES

References to books of the Talmud refer to the Babylonian Talmud unless otherwise noted.

1. Also known as Alexander of Macedon.
2. Also known as Antiochus Epiphanes ("The Illustrious"), circa 215-164 B.C.E.
3. *Midrash Rabbah,* Genesis 2:4.
4. Ibid. *Shabbat* 21b; *Avodah Zarah* 52b.
5. Ibid. *Shabbat.*
6. *Otzar Midrashim*, Chanukah, 4:10.
7. *Midrash Tanchuma*, Deuteronomy, *Ki Tavo* 2.
8. *Ketuvot* 3b.
9. Maharal of Prague, *Ner Mitzvah* — Introduction.
10. Josephus Flavius, Antiquities, from *The Complete Works of Josephus Flavius,* Bigelow, Brown and Co., NY.
11. Ibid. Josephus; Jerusalem Talmud, *Yevamot* 8:1 (45a).
12. *Kohanim*, descendants of Aaron the High Priest, brother of Moses.
13. The word means "important." *Siddur Otzar Hatefillot, Eitz Yosef* and *Iyun Tefillah,* commentary on "Al Hanissim."
14. **Maccabee** is a Hebrew acronym for the verse in Exodus 15:11: "Who is like You among the heavenly powers, God!"
15. General Sir Richard Gale, *Great Battles of Biblical History*, Hutchinson, London, 1968, Chaps. 15 and 16.
16. Ibid. *Shabbat.*
17. Nachmanides, *Commentary on the Torah*, Leviticus 16:8 (end of paragraph).
18. Cited by Dayan I. Grunfield, Introduction to *Horeb*, Soncino Press, London, 1962, p. xxxviii.
19. Stephen Jay Gould, *Bully for Brontosaurus*, Norton Paperback, NY, 1992, Chap. 15.
20. Quoted from Rabbi Yitzchak Hutner.
21. Maimonides, *Guide for the Perplexed*, 2:25.
22. *Megillah* 9a.
23. Mishnah *Sofrim* 1:8.
24. Ibid. 1:7.
25. Ibid.
26. See the chapter on The Oral Torah.
27. *Gittin* 60b; *Responsa Beit Halevi,* Drush 18.
28. Rabbi Samson Raphael Hirsch, *Horeb,* II Edoth, Chap. 34, par. 247.
29. Nachmanides, Commentary on Numbers 8:2.
30. Zechariah 4:6.
31. Liturgy — Prayer inserted into Silent Prayer on Chanukah, *The Complete ArtScroll Siddur, Ashkenaz,* pp. 118-119.
32. *Midrash Rabbah*, Genesis 1.
33. *Bnei Yisasschar*, Kislev/Tevet, Essay 2:25.
34. *Otzar Midrashim,* Chanukah, par. 18; *Code of Jewish Law, Orach Chaim,* 670:2, Ramah.
35. *Code of Jewish Law, Orach Chaim,* 671:1.
36. Heard from Rabbi David Cohen.
37. *Code of Jewish Law, Orach Chaim,* 670:1.
38. Ibid. *Mishnah Berurah* ad loc.
39. Ibid. 670:2, Ramah.
40. Ibid.
41. Ibid. 670:1, *Mishnah Berurah.*
42. Ibid. 671:1.
43. Ibid. 671:2.
44. *Kaf Hachaim*, Hilchot Chanukah 673:19; *Levushei Mordechai, Orach Chaim*, 59; *Meorai Aish,* 5:2; *Responsa Beit Yitzchak, Yoreh Deah* 1:120:5; *Responsa Har Zvi, Orach Chaim*, 2:114:2; *Yabia Omer* 3:35.
45. *Code of Jewish Law, Orach Chaim,* 673:1.
46. Ibid. 671:5-7.
47. Ibid.
48. Ibid.

49. Ibid. 673:1.
50. Ibid. 676:5.
51. Ibid. 672.
52. Ibid.
53. Ibid.
54. Ibid. 676.
55. Ibid. 679:1.

56. Prayer signifying the termination of Shabbat. See chapter on Shabbat.
57. Ibid. 681:1-2.
58. Ibid.
59. *The Complete ArtScroll Siddur, Ashkenaz,* pp. 632-643.
60. Ibid. pp. 114-115.

Physical Survival: Purim

The history and meaning of Purim, the Scroll of Esther, celebration

The Miracle of Jewish Survival

The Purim story begins about 900 years after the Exodus from Egypt. The Jews had been living in Israel continually, since they first entered with Joshua. For 410 years, King Solomon's Temple in Jerusalem had been the focal point of Jewish spiritual and national life in Israel. The first major tragedy that the Jews of this era experienced was the division of the country into the northern kingdom of Israel and the southern kingdom of Judea. The northern kingdom was populated by ten of the twelve tribes. It was eventually invaded by the Assyrians under Sennacherib, who exiled the Jews. Sennacherib's policy of forced exile and assimilation directly caused the loss of the ten tribes to the Jewish people.

Less than a hundred years later, the Jews were dealt another terrible blow. This time, the Babylonian Empire under the rule of Nebuchadnezzar invaded Israel, destroyed the Temple[1] and exiled almost all the remaining tribes (Judah, Benjamin, the Priests and the Levites) to Babylon (modern-day Iraq — two weeks by camel, seven minutes by Scud).

Jeremiah the prophet had warned the Jewish people that there would be destruction and exile,[2] but he also predicted that the Jews would return to Israel and rebuild the Temple and their homeland. Jeremiah even put a date on the return, declaring that the Temple would be rebuilt 70 years after its destruction.[3] Nevertheless, there were many who did not believe that they would ever return to Israel, and felt that this exile signified the end of the special relationship between God and the Jewish people.[4] The Jews quickly became acclimated to the condition of exile and built a well-organized Jewish community in Babylon and neighboring Persia (modern-day Iran).

Persian Nights

The Persian Empire eventually took over Babylon, and a military leader by the name of Achashverosh[5] usurped the throne and became the supreme ruler of the Persian Empire.[6] Based on a miscalculation, he believed that the 70-year deadline of Jeremiah's prediction had already passed, and that the Jews must therefore be doomed to remain in exile.[7] Since the Jews had outlived all previous empires (Egyptians, Canaanites, Assyrians and Babylonians) except his own, he became convinced that his was the eternal empire. In his mind, the permanent exile of the Jews was an indication of his empire's immortality.[8]

To celebrate this permanent victory, he threw a colossal party in classic sultanate style, using the holy vessels that Nebuchadnezzar had looted from the Temple in Jerusalem.[9] Even more tragic than the party itself, was the fact that the Jews in the capital city, Shushan, also participated in Achashverosh's celebration, over the strong objections of their religious leadership. The Talmud states that it was this sin that caused the subsequent, nearly fatal, threat to the Jewish people.[10]

Haman's Final Solution

One of the most ancient and persistent enemies of the Jewish people was the nation of Amalek,[11] the first enemy to attack the Jews after the Exodus from Egypt. A descendant of the Amalekites, Haman, had ascended to the position of "prime minister" of the Persian Empire.[12] This rabid anti-Semite planned an empire-wide pogrom to eliminate the Jewish people. He chose the date for this mass murder by casting lots. In Persian, the word for lot is *pur*. The plural form is *Purim,* hence the name of the holiday.

The heroine of the Purim story is Esther, a devout Jewish woman who was forcibly taken as a wife for Achashverosh. She and her uncle Mordechai, one of the religious leaders of that generation, were instrumental in saving the Jewish people from annihilation. After uniting the Jewish nation in repentance and prayer, they set about exposing Haman's plot to the king. Haman and his equally wicked sons were executed when Achashverosh learned that he had planned to kill Queen Esther's nation. The Jews were permitted to defend themselves against their enemies on the appointed day for annihilation, and were totally victorious. Mordechai and Esther recorded the events of Purim in the prophetically inspired *Megillat Esther* (literally, Scroll of Esther).[13] The Megillah is read publicly on the night and day of the Purim festival.

Three years after the events of Purim, King Darius, the son of Esther and Achashverosh, allowed the Jewish people to return to Israel and rebuild the Temple.[14] The Temple was rebuilt exactly 70 years after its destruction, as predicted by Jeremiah.

The Hidden Hand

Although it became part of the Bible, known in English as the Book of Esther, the account never mentions the name of God, though there are veiled allusions. This surprising omission actually reflects a central theme of this holiday. On Purim we celebrate the fact that the hand of God guides us, even at times when we do not see open miracles or obvious Divine intervention. When we read the Megillah, we are not awestruck by dramatic changes in the laws of nature, but by a series of seemingly disconnected events that ultimately resulted in the salvation of the Jewish people. Achashverosh executed his first wife and chose the beautiful Esther as his new queen. These are not miracles, but behavior to be expected from a despotic king. Nor was it a miracle that Mordechai once saved the king from an assassination plot, thereby earning his gratitude. Each event, in and of itself, was not miraculous or even exceptional. When seen in retrospect however, the series of events is seen as engineered from Above for the purpose of evoking repentance from the Jewish people and then saving them from danger.

This theme of allusion may also be the reason behind the custom of wearing costumes on Purim.[15] The masks and costumes show that truth always lies beneath the surface, that the physical world conceals the true spiritual reality.

Anyone who is familiar with Jewish history can see the Purim pattern repeated over and over again. The fact that Judaism and the Jewish people have survived for 3,300 years is, in and of itself, not miraculous. More significantly, our survival was not merely physical, but cultural as well. We still use the Hebrew language, we read and study the Torah, we immerse in the same type of *mikveh* (ritual pool), as that used at Masada

2,000 years ago.[16] We put on the same type of *tefillin* (phylacteries) that were worn in Qumran 1,700 years ago.[17]

Anti-Semites have attempted to eradicate us physically and culturally, missionaries have tried to convert us, while others have tried to tempt us into assimilation, but we still exist as a distinct group. We do not look different from the surrounding populations and we have not been geographically isolated, yet we stand apart. Twice in history, we were brutally exiled from our Land and we returned twice: once after the Babylonian Exile and once in contemporary times with the establishment of the State of Israel and the incredible ingathering of Jews from all over the world to our Land.

If all this is not sufficient evidence of Divine Providence, consider the fact that all of these events were predicted by the Torah over 3,000 years ago: The destruction of Israel and the return to Israel, the worldwide exile, anti-Semitism and the eternity of the Torah are described in the following passages.

> ... *I will make the land desolate; and your foes who dwell upon it will be desolate.*[18]
> ... *I will scatter you among the nations, I will unsheath the sword after you; your land will be desolate and your cities will be in ruin.*
> ... *You will call forth amazement, reproach and scorn from all the nations to which God leads you.*[19]
> ... *Indeed it is a nation that dwells alone, and is not counted among the nations.*[20]
> ... *And the Lord your God shall return you from your captivity and have compassion upon you; and He shall return and gather you from among all the nations to which the Lord your God has scattered you. ... And the Lord your God shall bring you into the Land that your fathers inherited.*[21]
> ... *And it shall come to pass, when many evils and troubles have befallen them, that this song [the Torah] shall testify against them as a witness; for it shall not be forgotten in the mouths of their children.*[22]

Purim, therefore, is the prototype for Jewish survival during exile. The Divine Providence hidden in apparently random events has ensured that we have survived, and even thrived, in the face of continual threats to our existence. Purim demonstrates the fulfillment of God's promise to the Jewish people that:

> ... *despite all this, while they will be in the land of their enemies, I will not despise them nor will I reject them to obliterate them, to annul My Covenant with them — for I am the Lord, their God.*[23]

Eat, Drink and Be Merry – We Almost Died

While the events of Chanukah were principally a threat to our spiritual survival, Purim recalls a threat to the physical existence of the Jewish people. Haman attempted to physically destroy every Jewish man, woman and child. We celebrate our deliverance from this threat with *mitzvot* that focus on the physical.[24] We give money to the poor and gifts of food to our friends; we eat a festive meal and drink wine.[25]

Giving gifts to one another also promotes unity among the Jewish people. When first proposing his evil plot to Achashverosh, Haman described the Jewish people as a "scattered and dispersed nation."[26] He did not mean only that we were geographically dispersed, but that we were not unified, and thus would be easy prey for our enemies.[27] (On a spiritual level, we also understand this to mean that when the Jewish people are disunited, God does not protect them fully. National unity brings about spiritual wholeness and closeness to God.) To counteract this situation, the Sages decreed that we must be concerned with the welfare and friendship of our fellow Jews. We strengthen Jewish unity by giving gifts to the poor, food to our friends, and by celebrating together with festive meals.[28]

Celebrating Under the Influence

One of the most peculiar laws of Purim is the obligation to drink wine, and even become intoxicated. As the Talmud states, "A person is obligated to become inebriated on Purim, until he does not know the difference between 'Blessed is Mordechai and cursed is Haman.'"[29] Excessive drinking is frowned upon by Jewish law,[30] yet here it appears that the law specifically advocates drinking! Clearly, a person may not become so drunk that he loses control of himself and acts or speaks inappropriately;[31] nevertheless, he is obligated to become slightly intoxicated.[32] Some commentaries explain that the purpose of the drinking is to remind us that the Purim miracles happened as a result of intoxication — Achashverosh became drunk at the feast, which resulted in the execution of Vashti, his queen. Esther invited Achashverosh and Haman to a drinking party, which resulted in the hanging of Haman and the salvation of the Jewish people.[33] Since drinking also has the effect of dulling the intellectual and emphasizing the physical aspects of an individual, it is a fitting way to show that the physical component — rather than the intellectual or spiritual — of the Jewish nation was threatened by its enemies on Purim.[34]

Consuming alcohol mirrors the events of Purim in another way as well. Drinking lowers one's inhibitions and amplifies emotions. Intoxication causes a person to reveal elements of his inner self that are usually hidden.[35] What transpired on Purim revealed the love of God for the Jewish people and His Divine Providence, both of which had been concealed during the time of the Persian Exile.

Yom Kippur – A Day Like Purim?

One of the greatest of Jewish mystics, Rabbi Yitzchak Luria,[36] points out that the Biblical term for the Day of Atonement, *Yom Kipurim*,[37] can also be read as *Yom KePurim*, meaning "a day like Purim." On the surface this seems illogical — there are no two days that appear less similar than the solemn fast of Yom Kippur and the boisterous, joyful celebrations of Purim! Moreover, the implication of this statement is that Purim is the greater of the two days. Yom Kippur is compared to Purim, as if Yom Kippur were but a lesser example of the Purim archetype.[38]

A deeper look at the purpose of these two holidays will help us understand their relationship to each other. There are two ways to become close to God: the path of awe and fear, and the path of love and joy. Both are necessary and both play important roles in Judaism. Generally, the various prohibitions in the Torah reflect the relationship of awe and reticence, while the positive obligations reflect the relationship of love and reaching out to God.[39]

Yom Kippur, with its prohibitions against eating, drinking and other physical pleasures, represents the path of awe and fear of God.[40] An individual stops his life, completely ignores the physical side of his being and focuses only on the spiritual. One can achieve clarity of perception on Yom Kippur by subduing the interference and static of the physical world.

Purim, on the other hand, provides a path to God through love and joy. Purim teaches us that one can achieve an even higher level of connection to God and clarity of perception through the feelings of love than through feelings of fear and awe. Thus, Yom Kippur is like Purim, but not quite Purim, because the love of God is more powerful than the fear of God.[41]

Purim! Live at the Levys!

Two months before Purim, Shlomo, the oldest Levy boy, starts practicing the reading of Megillat Esther. He has a beautiful voice and has been reading the Megillah at the local synagogue for the past several years. He must know the pronunciation and the musical notes — cantillation — by heart, since the scroll has neither vowels nor notes. The younger children start thinking about costumes to wear for Purim about a month before the festival. Mrs. Levy takes the "Purim box" out of the attic. The children love rummaging through the costumes accumulated over the years, including a cache of toy guns and swords (not allowed in the Levy house during the rest of the year.)

Before Purim, Mr. and Mrs. Levy make sure that they give a significant amount of money to the local rabbi so he can distribute it to needy families on the day of Purim itself.

Mrs. Levy and the children prepare Mishloach Manot (gifts of food) to send to all their friends. Since they spend more money on the gifts to the poor than on the gifts to friends, the family always tries to think of Mishloach Manot that are not elaborate but still will be enjoyed by the recipients. This year Mrs. Levy is preparing a variety of muffins, accompanied by her exclusive (and famous) ginger-apricot jam. The children make gifts of their own for their friends using lollipops, dried fruit and bags of popcorn. All the gifts are accompanied by the standard Levy family Purim greeting — "Happy Levy! From the Purim Family."

In addition to the gifts, Mrs. Levy is preparing a festive Seudat Purim (Purim meal) to which they have invited two newly married couples and some boys from the local yeshivah.[42] The dessert will be traditional Purim hamantashen, triangular pockets of sweet dough filled with poppy seeds and honey. The Yiddish word for poppy seeds is mohn and tashen means pockets. Mohntashen later evolved into the word **haman**tashen because of the association of the Purim food with Haman.[43] The poppy seeds may also allude to the heroism of the Jewish youths brought to the Persian court after the Temple's destruction. Although tempted by the delicious, but nonkosher food of the king, they subsisted on seeds and water.[44]

Mr. Levy also does some shopping and purchases a variety of wines to please all palates, since even those who normally do not drink will have some wine on Purim.

The Levys all dress in their Shabbat clothes for the reading of the Megillah, and the children bring whistles, a tambourine and a wooden grogger with them, so they can drown out the name of Haman. After the evening service, Shlomo goes to the bimah, (lectern) and reads Megillat Esther. The scroll is folded rather than simply rolled, in order to look like the letters of royal decrees that were sent out to the provinces by King Achashverosh.[45]

The local Jewish high school always puts on a hilarious Purim play at night, sometimes poking fun at their school, always incorporating some aspect of Purim in the plot. Mr. Levy takes the children to see the play, and they stay afterward to sing and dance with the students.

Purim morning begins with the prayers and the second reading of the Megillah in the synagogue. There is usually a later reading for mothers with small children who could not attend the first service. After a healthy breakfast, insisted upon by Mrs. Levy (since the children will be eating candies and "junk" food all day), the family begins the distribution of Mishloach Manot.

The older children go around the neighborhood on roller blades and bikes and Mr. Levy takes the younger children, now in costume, in the car to distribute gifts further away. They usually prepare a number of Mishloach Manot to take to a nearby old-age home as well. Eli and Esther are dressed as a bunch of grapes and a Kiddush cup, and elicit smiles wherever they go. Shlomo is dressed as a giant hamantashen but looks more like a UFO than an article of food. All during the day, people visit the Levy home and bring gifts, which are immediately reciprocated. People collecting for charities stop by the house all day as well, and Mrs. Levy gives each person some money that had been set aside for this purpose.

The festive meal begins in the afternoon and continues well into the night. Everyone has insights and divrei Torah (words of Torah) to share during the meal. These are accompanied by songs, many cries of "L'chaim!" and the firing of cap-guns by the younger boys. As the wine flows more and more freely, the words of Torah become a little more confused, the songs a lot louder, Mr. Levy more emotional. Everyone joins the singing of Grace After Meals. Those who are steady enough help clear the table, and the children fall asleep in their costumes, surrounded by beautifully decorated food baskets, bags of candy and echoes of the Purim songs.

Selected Laws and Customs of Purim

1. Purim is preceded by the Fast of Esther on the 13th of the Hebrew month of Adar (usually corresponding to late February or early March). The fast begins at dawn and ends at night. It commemorates the fact that Queen Esther and the Jews of her city fasted before she entered the king's chambers to ask him for clemency for the Jewish people.[46] The fast also teaches us that the appropriate national or personal response to trouble is repentance and prayer.[47] It is held on the day in which the Jews fought and successfully defended themselves against their enemies.[48] Significantly, the celebration is not held on the day of the battle but rather on the day after the battle. The focus of our celebration is Jewish survival rather than the downfall of our enemies.[49]

2. Purim begins on the night of the 14th of Adar and continues until the next night.[50] In ancient walled cities, like Jerusalem, Purim is celebrated on the 15th of Adar and is called Shushan Purim.[51] This marks the fact that the Jews in Shushan, the Persian capital and a walled city, continued the battle for an additional day. Thus they still fought on the 14th of Adar, and celebrated on the 15th of Adar.[52]

3. The Scroll of Esther (*Megillat Esther*) is read publicly from a parchment scroll[53] at night and in the morning.[54] The blessings that are recited before and after the reading of the Megillah[55] can be found in *The Complete ArtScroll Siddur, Ashkenaz*, pp. 786 – 789.

4. Although one should listen in silence to the reading of the Megillah, it is customary to make noise when the name of Haman is mentioned.[56] This is done in symbolic fulfillment of the Torah's commandment to erase the memory of Amalek (Haman's nation).[57] It is common practice to come to synagogue equipped with noisemaking devices (*groggers*) for this purpose, although some synagogues distribute them to the children.

5. The prayer *Al Hanissim* is added in the silent prayers (*Shemoneh Esreh*) of Purim and in Grace After Meals.[58] See *The Complete ArtScroll Siddur, Ashkenaz*, pp. 114-116 and pp. 186-187. If one forgot to say *Al Hanissim*, one does not repeat the prayer.[59]

6. A special portion of the Torah is read on Purim (Exodus 17:8-16).[60]

7. Specific prayers that are omitted on happy occasions are also omitted on this day.[61]

8. *Mishloach Manot*, a gift of food, should be given to at least one friend, but the more the merrier. The gift should contain at least two, ready-to-eat items of (kosher!) food.[62]

9. Gifts to the poor, *Matanot La'evyonim*, are also distributed on Purim. One should give to at least two poor people, but the more the better. Ideally, one should spend more on gifts to the poor than on gifts to friends. One should give the poor person at least enough money to cover one decent meal.[63] On Purim, we are indiscriminate in giving out charity — one should give to anyone who asks.[64] In many communities, the synagogue collects and distributes money for this *mitzvah*.

10. A festive meal is eaten on Purim afternoon. As with all traditional Jewish meals, it should start with the blessing over bread. One should ensure that there is wine in abundance and, obviously, special foods. We invite guests, exchange insights about Purim and sing traditional Purim songs.[65]

11. Although there is no prohibition against working on Purim, there is a universal custom not to engage in work or business on this day.[66]

12. It is customary for children, and many adults, to dress up in costumes.[67] It is also common for communities to stage a *Purim shpiel*, an entertaining play on the Purim theme.

For Further Reading

▶ *Living Beyond Time: The Mystery and Meaning of the Jewish Festivals* by Rabbi Pinchas Stolper (Shaar Press, 2003)

▶ *Purim: Its Observance and Significance* (ArtScroll/Mesorah, 1991)

▶ *The Megillah/Esther* (ArtScroll/Mesorah, 1976)

▶ *Turnabout* by Rabbi Mendel Weinbach (Feldheim, 1976)

For Children:

▶ *The ArtScroll Children's Megillah* (ArtScroll/Mesorah, 2005)

▶ *ArtScroll Youth Megillah* (ArtScroll/Mesorah, 1988)

NOTES

References to books of the Talmud refer to the Babylonian Talmud unless otherwise noted.

1. Circa 422 B.C.E. or 3338 in the Jewish calendar.
2. Jeremiah 7:32-34, Chaps. 8-9.
3. Ibid. 25:11-13; 29:10.
4. Isaiah 49:14; 50:1.
5. Achashverosh II was king of Media and Persia. He became emperor after the death of Cyrus, although he was not of royal descent.
6. Rashi, Book of Esther, 1:1.
7. *Megillah* 11b.
8. Ibid. 19a.
9. Ibid.
10. Ibid. 12a.
11. Exodus 17:8-16; Deuteronomy 25:17-19.
12. Book of Esther 3:1.
13. *Megillah* 7a.
14. Ibid. 12a.
15. *Code of Jewish Law, Orach Chaim* 696:8, Ramah.
16. Yigal Yadin, *Masada*, Weidenfeld and Nicolson, London, 1966, pp. 164-167.
17. Shrine of the Book, Israel Museum, Jerusalem.
18. Leviticus 26:32 -33.
19. Deuteronomy 28:37.
20. Numbers 23:9.
21. Deuteronomy 30:3-5.
22. Ibid. 31:21; Rashi ad loc.; *Shabbat* 138b.
23. Leviticus 26:44; *Megillah* 11a.
24. *Levush Malchut, Orach Chaim*, 670.
25. Book of Esther 9:22.
26. Ibid. 3:8.
27. *Midrash Rabbah*, Vayikra 26:2; *Midrash Tanchuma*, Bamidbar, Parshat Chukat 4.
28. Rabbi Isaiah Horowitz, *Shnei Luchot Habrit*, Parshat Tetzaveh, Drush 4.
29. *Megillah* 7b.
30. Nachmanides, Commentary on the Torah, Leviticus 19:2; Deuteronomy 21:18-21; *Sanhedrin* 70a, 71b, 72a.
31. *Code of Jewish Law, Orach Chaim*, 695:2, *Biur Halachah* ad loc.
32. Ibid. Ramah and *Mishnah Berurah* ad loc.
33. Ibid.
34. Maharal, *Ohr Chadash*, Introduction.
35. *Eruvin* 65a; *Sanhedrin* 38a; *Eruvin* 65b.
36. Known as the AriZal. Lived in Safed, Israel, in the 17th century.
37. Leviticus 23:28.
38. *Ta'anit* 7a.
39. Nachmanides, Commentary on the Torah, Exodus 20:8.
40. Rabbi Yeshaya Horowitz, *Shnei Luchot Habrit*, Masechet *Rosh Hashanah*, Torah Ohr (14).
41. Rabbi Eliyahu Dessler, *Michtav M'Eliyahu*, vol. 2 pp. 123-125; Nachmanides, ibid.
42. Jewish institute of higher learning. See chapter on Torah Study.
43. John Cooper, *Eat and Be Satisfied*, Jason Aronson Inc., NJ, 1993, p. 193.
44. Daniel 1:5-16.
45. *Code of Jewish Law, Orach Chaim*, 690:17.
46. Book of Esther 4:16.
47. *Code of Jewish Law, Orach Chaim*, 686, *Mishnah Berurah* 2.
48. Ibid. 9:1-18.
49. Proverbs 24:17.
50. Book of Esther 9:15-19.
51. *Code of Jewish Law,* ibid. 688:1.
52. Ibid.
53. Ibid. 891:1.
54. *Code of Jewish Law,* ibid. 687:1.
55. Ibid. 692:1.
56. Ibid. 690:17, Ramah.
57. Deuteronomy 25:19.
58. *Code of Jewish Law,* ibid. 693:2.
59. Ibid.
60. Ibid. 692:4.
61. Ibid. 692:3.

62. Ibid. 695:4.
63. Ibid. 694:1-4.
64. Ibid. 694:3.

65. Ibid. 695:1-3.
66. Ibid. 696:1.
67. Ibid. 696:8, Ramah.

Passover — Free at Last

Exodus, Passover Seder, matzah

Egypt: Boot Camp for the Jewish Experience

*P*assover celebrates a historic event — the freeing of the Jewish people from slavery in Egypt 3,316 years ago.[1] The Torah recounts how God intervened in history, punished the Egyptian slave-masters and took His people — known then as the Hebrews or the Children of Israel — out of Egypt with miracles and wonders.[2] The term Exodus denotes the specific departure of the Hebrews from Egypt. At this time, God created the physical entity known as the Jewish people and paved the way for their transformation into a spiritual entity when they later received the Torah at Mount Sinai.[3] For all of this, we celebrate Passover, give thanks to God, and contemplate the ideas of freedom, Divine intervention and Jewish nationhood.

It is the Eisodus (entry into Egypt) perhaps more than the Exodus that requires explanation. Why were the Jews sent into exile in the first place? When God foretold to Abraham that his children would be exiled, the Jewish nation did not yet exist. Some commentaries suggest that the years in Egypt were not a punishment for any sin. Rather, they were part of an extremely difficult, but necessary, process of purification.

The Patriarchs and Matriarchs were to be the foundation of the Jewish people; therefore it was crucial that the slightest flaws in their personalities be rectified, since even a small defect in the foundation can compromise the integrity of the entire structure. Abraham had asked God to give him a sign that he would eventually inherit the Land of Israel (after God had already promised that this would occur), indicating a lack of perfect faith in God.

Joseph's brothers exhibited hatred and jealousy toward him, symptomatic of a lack of unity at the very core of the Jewish people, which continued in Egypt. These and other deficiencies were also present in their descendants and had to be corrected during the course of the exile in and redemption from Egypt. The miraculous redemption awakened their faith in God and their experiences united them as a people.[4]

Some commentators suggest that beyond correcting any inherent flaws, the fledgling nation had to undergo experiences that would enable them to develop the characteristics of a people capable of carrying out God's mission throughout the centuries. The hardships in Egypt were a training ground for our future; they taught us how to be sensitive to strangers because we were "strangers in Egypt"; how to be considerate of workers and the downtrodden, because we were slaves.[5] The Bible conveys this idea very clearly in the Book of Exodus: "And you shall not oppress the stranger because you know the soul of the stranger, for you were strangers in the Land of Egypt."[6]

Egypt was thus the crucible in which the Jewish people were refined so that they would be able to fulfill their role, to improve and perfect themselves and the world.[7]

Moreover, we learned that there are parallels between the world as a whole and our experiences in Egypt.[8] Just as we were enslaved in Egypt all human beings are, in a sense, enslaved to the physical realities of the world. We lose sight of the spiritual world — the realities of our own souls — in the harsh glare of what appear to be tangible physical desires. In that sense, slavery is still within us.

It is our task to create harmony between this physical realm and the spiritual (using the Torah as our guide). We experience "Egypt" also in that people are continually at odds with each other in their struggle for survival. The Egyptian Exile helped us to understand that it should not be this way; that we must create harmony between one person and another.

Another metaphor understood from our Egyptian experience is that in Egypt the Jewish people lived for generations as strangers in a foreign environment: likewise the soul feels estranged in the environment of the physical world. Once we recognize this feeling and understand its source, we can begin to create a world in which the soul is not a stranger; a world in which holiness and God's presence can be perceived.[9]

Live It!

Merely remembering the pivotal events of Jewish history or reading about them occasionally is not sufficient to imbue ourselves with these messages. God established Passover and the other festivals as interludes in time designed to focus our attention and pick up on specific ideas and values that the ordinary activities of life usually prevent us from contemplating. They are times when we are totally immersed in a specific concept basic to Judaism. We study the concept, experience it through the observances of the festival, talk about it in our prayers and try to internalize its meaning.[10]

The very name of the holiday conveys an important concept in Jewish thought. Passover is the English translation of the Hebrew word *pesach,* which means to skip over. It is derived from the last of the Ten Plagues, in which God struck the Egyptian firstborn in every house, but "skipped over" the houses of the Jews. This skipping over was a clear demonstration of God's Divine Providence, His omniscience and His power over existence itself.

Passover is the classic example of a festival in which we eat, drink and live the ideas that it represents. We modify our home environment by removing all leavened products, we change our diet to eat *matzah* and avoid all leavened foods. Our prayers are different for this entire week; we refrain from working, and we transform a festive meal into a high-impact, super-charged educational experience — the Seder.

There is no doubt that had the Torah merely commanded us to simply *think* about the Exodus for one week a year, no one today would have heard of the Exodus from Egypt. The Torah took the Exodus — the story, the history, the philosophy and the significance — and crystallized it into a multitude of actions, words, foods, songs and prayers. Making the festival experiential, not merely conceptual, ensured the transmission of this vital story from generation to generation and embedded these ideas within the very essence of the Jewish people.[11]

Springtime Is Pesach-time

Passover is always observed in the spring,[12] on the fifteenth day of the Hebrew month of Nissan (around March or April). The Torah describes the month in which Passover falls as the first month, and emphasizes several times that Pesach occurs in the springtime. In terms of the creation of the Jewish people as a nation, it is counted as the first month of the year:

> *God said to Moses and Aaron in the land of Egypt, saying: This*
> *month shall be for you the beginning of the months; it shall*

be for you the first of the months of the year ...[13] *... You shall observe the Festival of Matzot; seven days shall you eat matzot, as I have commanded you, at the appointed time of the month of springtime, for in it you left Egypt...*[14]

We explained previously[15] that Jewish festivals are not mere commemorations of past events. They enable us to access the spirituality inherent in a particular time of year. From the time of Creation, the month of Nissan was designated as a time of beginning, birth and renewal.

The physical manifestation of that spiritual energy is springtime, when the ice and snow thaw, when trees and flowers blossom and when many animals give birth to their young. The historical manifestation of that energy was the Jewish people's Exodus and redemption from Egypt, their entry into the Land of Israel in the time of Joshua[16] and their return to Israel after 70 years in the Babylonian Exile.[17]

That energy is manifested in the Torah through the festival of Pesach. When we observe the festival in its appropriate time and fulfill its commandments we are actually tapping into the spiritual energy beneath the surface of the physical world.[18]

A unique blessing, which is said during the month of Nissan when one sees a blossoming fruit tree, offers us another way of getting "in-sync" with springtime and recognizing God's handiwork in nature.[19] Through all these observances we are able to recapture that revelation of Godliness which our ancestors experienced at this time of year, thousands of years ago.

Passover is associated with spring also because it is the time of the physical birth of the Jewish nation. Just as the soil produces a new crop in the spring and the first buds blossom on the trees, so too, the Jewish nation was born in the spring. The Jews were slaves, considered by society as subhuman, and continually engaged in hard manual labor. They were under constant pressure, and even their time was not their own. In this sense, the Jews as a people were in a state of nonexistence in Egypt. Pesach celebrates our redemption from that state, our physical coming into being as a nation. (This was followed closely by the beginning of our spiritual nationhood, when we accepted the Torah at Mount Sinai on Shavuot.) Pesach therefore occurs in the spring, the time of birth and creation in nature.

These ideas are alluded to in the Song of Songs, in a beautiful verse:

My beloved spoke up and said to me: "Arise, my beloved, my fair one, and come away. For behold, the winter has passed, the rain is over and has gone away. The blossoms have appeared in the land, the time of singing has arrived, and the voice of the turtledove is heard in our land."[20]

The Sages explain this passage as a call from God to the Jewish people in Egypt:

> The Holy One, Blessed is He, said to the Jewish people in Egypt: "Arise, My beloved, the month of spring is here, and the time of redemption has arrived."[21]

Spring Break

The first two and last two days of Pesach are observed as festivals (in Israel, only the first and last days) as the verse in Exodus states: "The first day shall be a sacred holiday[22] and the seventh day shall be a sacred holiday for you, no work may be done on them ..."[23]

On these first and last days, work is prohibited, and we sanctify the day with prayer and *Kiddush*,[24] and enjoy the festival by eating special meals. The intermediate days are also part of the festival, but with many fewer prohibitions. These days, known as Chol Hamoed, "the weekdays of the festival," are a time to study Torah,[25] to relax with the family, visit friends and have a joyful vacation infused with the spirit of Pesach.[26] A more detailed discussion of Chol Hamoed appears in the chapter on Sukkot.

Passover celebrates not only our historic emancipation from slavery, but also our freedom from slavery to the material world. It reminds us of God's guarantee that we have the ability for all time to achieve the moral and spiritual freedom necessary to devote ourselves to God.[27] The prohibitions against physical labor during Pesach symbolize the idea that we are no longer bound to "hard work with mortar and with bricks"[28] as we were in Egypt. We have the ability now to stop working and focus our attention on being servants of God rather than of Pharaoh,[29] the stock exchange or the mortgage company.

In a Crunch

Passover is most often referred to in the Torah as *Chag HaMatzot*, literally, the Festival of Matzahs[30] (unleavened bread).[30] Clearly, the eating of *matzah* and the prohibition against leavened bread (in Hebrew, *chametz*) are defining features of the festival.

> Seven days you shall eat unleavened bread [matzah]... you shall observe the Festival of Matzot; for on this same day I brought you out of the land of Egypt; therefore, you shall observe this day throughout all your generations as a statute forever. In the first month, on the fourteenth day of the month

in the evening, you shall eat unleavened bread, until the twenty-first day of the month in the evening.[31]

... They baked the dough that they took out of Egypt into unleavened cakes, for they could not be leavened, for they were driven from Egypt for they could not delay, nor had they made any provisions for themselves.[32]

It is clear from the above Biblical verses that the obligation to eat *matzah* and the prohibition against eating *chametz* are central to the observances of Pesach. In order to understand the symbolism of *chametz* and *matzah* we must first understand what they are. Both *chametz* and *matzah* are the products of mixing flour made of wheat, rye, barley, oats or spelt, with water.[33] If the dough is left alone, a chemical reaction known as leavening will take place. Enzymes[34] in the flour convert starch into fermentable sugars, which in turn produce carbon dioxide gas[35] as a product of their fermentation. This gas causes the dough to rise. When the risen dough is baked, it becomes regular leavened bread, classic *chametz*.

Matzah is also produced by mixing flour and water together, but rather than leaving the mixture alone, it is continuously and vigorously kneaded so that the gas can escape. The dough is rolled out flat, and holes are made all over it to release steam during baking. It is then placed very quickly into an oven where the intense heat stops the leavening process and bakes the bread. "Bread" produced this way is "unleavened" and is known as *matzah*.[36]

Food of Slavery, Food of Liberation

On the simplest level, the only difference between a loaf of bread and *matzah* is that the bread is inflated and *matzah* is flat. *Matzah* is the food of a humble slave, who does not have time to let the bread rise, and who eats foods that will leave him feeling full for hours afterward.[37] For this reason, *matzah* is also called *lechem oni*, the bread of affliction or poverty.[38] *Matzah* commemorates the bread of slavery that the Jewish people ate in Egypt, prepared in haste, without the luxury of time to let it rise.

The fact that the Jewish people also ate *matzah*, slave food, at the moment of their redemption indicates that the Jews were powerless to save themselves. They were slaves up to the last moment, and only through God's miraculous intervention did they go free. Rabbi Samson Raphael Hirsch explains that Jews ate *matzah* on the eve of the Exodus:

... so that in the great hour of liberation it would be impressed deeply on their minds that they had contributed nothing to their liberation, that in the very hour of liberation they were still

slaves eating the bread of affliction until the word of God cre-
ated anew the freedom which had been wrested from man ...
Thus did unleavened bread become an everlasting memo-
rial throughout the generations to the redemption from Egypt
brought about by God alone.[39]

The *matzah*, therefore, teaches us that the Jews did not leave Egypt through a successful slave revolt. It symbolizes that the Jews were not liberated through outstanding human leadership, bravery or military cunning. Understanding the Exodus inspires us with humility and gratitude to God.

Just in Time

Eating *matzah* also reminds us of another reason for gratitude. The Jews were in Egypt for 210 years[40] and suffered slavery under a brutal and oppressive regime. In addition to physical servitude, the Jewish people suffered spiritually: They abandoned the pure monotheism of Abraham[41] and began to worship Egyptian gods. Many Jews lost hope of ever leaving Egypt or becoming free: Over time, they began to consider themselves Egyptians. According to some sources, as many as four-fifths of the Jewish people died in Egypt before the Exodus.[42] Some suggest that they may not actually have died, but rather ceased to exist as Jews and remained in Egypt.[43]

Kabbalists[44] describe the spiritual state of the Jewish people in Egypt as having descended to the 49th level of impurity. Had they stayed in Egypt even one moment longer and reached the 50th, last level, they would have assimilated entirely into Egyptian culture and been lost forever.[45] God took the Jews out with haste because they were at the brink of oblivion. The departure was so hasty that the Jews did not even prepare food for the trip, and did not even have time to bake regular bread[46] — they ate *matzah* because they got out "just in time." So another reason we eat *matzah* is in recognition of God's kindness in getting us out at the right moment.[47]

Slaves to the Clock

The significance of time in the events of Passover is evident on a number of other levels as well. Time is a critical factor in the difference between *chametz* and *matzah*. Leavened bread is dough that has clearly been affected by time, while *matzah* is dough that has not been affected by time. When it is left alone, the passage of time has an impact on the dough, since it enables the processes of fermentation and rising. Only by kneading the dough continuously and baking it quickly are the effects of time avoided. One of the greatest taskmasters of a human being is time; therefore *matzah* is the ultimate food of liberation. It is bread that was liberated from the effects of time.[48]

Matzah also reminds us of another aspect of the haste with which the Jewish people left Egypt: "... for seven days you shall eat *matzot* ... for you departed from Egypt in haste ..."[49] The transformation from exile to redemption and from slavery to freedom occurred almost instantaneously. This was only possible because it was a miraculous process, outside the normal evolutionary progress of time.[50] The speed with which the redemption took place was therefore a sign of its Divine origin, as the ancient Hebrew saying tells us, "The salvation of God is like the blinking of an eye."[51]

Matzah reminds us that that we "just made it," that we were eating slave food up until the last moment. It is both an acknowledgment of God's kindness in the past as well as a statement of hope for the future. If the dire situation in Egypt could be changed in an instant — in the blink of an eye — from slavery to freedom, from darkness to light and from exile to redemption, then our present state of exile from God and homeland can be reversed just as swiftly.[52]

Burn, Bagel, Burn!

In addition to eating *matzah,* the Torah obligates us to remove all *chametz* from our property before Pesach.[53] We are prohibited from eating, gaining benefit from, or even possessing *chametz* on Pesach.[54]

> For seven days, leaven may not be found in your houses, for anyone who eats leavening — that soul shall be cut off from the assembly of Israel ... You shall not eat any leavening; in all your dwellings shall you eat matzot.[55]

Any *chametz* we do not dispose of (such as expensive liquors), we give away or sell to a non-Jew.[56] (This is done by a rabbi on behalf of the members of his community because there are complex laws involved.) On the morning before Pesach, we take a few pieces of *chametz* outside and burn it, and we recite a declaration relinquishing ownership of any *chametz.*[57]

The commandment concerning ridding ourselves of *chametz* is unusual, in that it is prohibited in just about every way possible. In addition, *chametz*, as opposed to most nonkosher foods, is considered significant even in the smallest concentration.[58] (The only laws in the Torah comparable to the laws governing *chametz* are those concerning idolatry.

One may not possess an idol, gain benefit from idolatry or eat anything associated with idolatry.[59])

The idea behind the severity of the *chametz* laws is that on Passover *chametz* is a symbol of evil desires,[60] egocentricity[61] and idolatry[62] — all of which we must root out and destroy absolutely. For one week each year, the Torah graphically reminds us of the importance of counteracting these influences by prohibiting *chametz* with the same stringency it legislates for idolatry.

The desire to do evil — known in classic Jewish literature as "the evil inclination" — is represented by *chametz* because it thrives on laziness, always seeking the path of least resistance.[63] To create *matzah*, the opposite of *chametz*, it is essential to work with enthusiasm and speed. If these are absent for even a short time, the dough will automatically become *chametz*.

Chametz also symbolizes egocentricity and self-aggrandizement. Like a person impressed with his own magnificence, *chametz* is inflated, full of itself, even though it is made of the same ingredients as the humble *matzah*. This idea also explains the relationship between *chametz* and idolatry as well as the identification of idolatry with egocentricity. *Chametz* is basically inflated *matzah*. The essence of both idolatry and egocentricity is that they take something insignificant and inflate its importance out of all proportion to its true value. Whether a person looks at a force of nature and proclaims it god, takes a piece of wood and calls it the creator,[64] or considers *himself* the ultimate reality, independent of God[65] — it is all idolatry.

As we engage in thoroughly cleaning the house to remove all *chametz*, shop for special *chametz*-free, Passover products and prepare the kitchen for Pesach, we should think of removing any traces of egocentricity, cleaning out "idolatry" in all its forms and becoming *chametz*-free zones ourselves.[66] Enthusiastic and meticulous cleaning of the house before Pesach has been a hallmark of Jewish life for centuries, and may be one of the origins of spring cleaning, but more importantly it is a process that bears within it a vital and eternal message.

Miracles, Signs and Wonders

The Pesach prayers and the narrative that we discuss at the Seder emphasize the miraculous nature of the Exodus from Egypt. To name just a few — Moses' staff became a snake, ten terrifying plagues punished the Egyptians and the Red Sea split for the Jews, but drowned Pharaoh's army.[67] But why were all of these miracles necessary to expedite the redemption? Couldn't God could have ended the slavery and taken the

Jews out of Egypt with fewer miracles? He could have punished the Egyptians with one major plague and "beamed" the Jews out of Egypt into the Sinai desert.

Of course, any number of miracles presents no difficulty for God. In general, though, we find that He chooses not to contravene the laws of nature that He created and therefore does not perform obvious miracles unless they are absolutely necessary.[68] What then was the purpose of all the miracles that we commemorate, relive and describe in our prayers on Pesach?

Nachmanides, the 12th-century Biblical commentator, explains that the plagues and other miracles were really high-impact educational experiences for the Jews as much as for the Egyptians. Nachmanides explains:

> From the time that there was idolatry in the world ... belief started to deteriorate ... Some people denied the existence of God; some denied His knowledge of events in the world ... Some admitted to His knowledge but denied reward and punishment.
>
> When, however, God chooses a community or an individual and performs miracles for them that change the normal running and nature of the world, then the refutation of all the above is apparent. Because a miracle shows that there is a God Who created the world; God Who knows, Who cares and Who is omnipotent.
>
> And when that miracle is first decreed by a prophet, then it also demonstrates the truth of prophecy... Therefore, the Torah states regarding these miracles, "so that you will know that I am God in the midst of the land" ... "so that you will know that the world is God's" ... "so that you will know that there is none like Me in all the world"[69]...
>
> Since God does not perform signs and miracles in every generation in front of every evil person or nonbeliever, He commanded us with eternal reminders and signs of what our eyes witnessed. That we should pass these down to our children, and their children to their children until the last generation ...
>
> And the many commandments that commemorate the Exodus from Egypt are all faithful witnesses to the future generations of these miracles so that they will never be forgotten ...[70]

The Seder – A Judaism Seminar in a Meal!

The central event of Passover is, without question, the Seder (Hebrew for "the order"). The festive meals of the first two nights of Pesach are not merely meals; they are multimedia interactive educational seminars. We eat foods that symbolize slavery and redemption, and drink wine as an expression of our joy and freedom. The special "Seder plate" is adorned with foods that correspond to the *mitzvot* of Pesach. The story of the Exodus is told by one generation to the next. It is discussed and dissected at length. Prayers of praise and gratitude to God are recited and sung, and even our posture at the table (leaning to the side) represents freedom. The Seder is structured around the fulfillment of a number of Biblical and Rabbinic commandments. In a nutshell, these are:

1. **The paschal lamb**

On the night before their departure from Egypt, the Jewish people were commanded to broil a whole lamb on a spit over an open fire and eat it as part of a special meal.[71] (This later became a commandment to be carried out in the Holy Temple in Jerusalem on the first evening of Pesach.) The lamb was a symbol of Egyptian idolatry,[72] specifically representing the ram god Khnum who, according to Egyptian mythology, presided over the annual flooding of the Nile.[73] There could be no greater denial of Khnum and the Egyptian deities than the slaughter, broiling and eating of a lamb by the former slaves.[74] Through this offering, the Jews broke free of their psychological and ideological slavery to the Egyptians and separated themselves completely from idolatry.[75] Today, in the absence of the Temple, we can no longer fulfill this commandment. To remind us of this offering however, we place a piece of broiled meat on the Seder plate[76] and eat an extra portion of *matzah*, the *Afikomen*, at the end of meal, just as we would have eaten *matzah* together with the lamb during Temple times.[77]

2. **The *Mitzvah* of Eating *Matzah* and *Marror* (Bitter Herbs)**

We are commanded to eat *matzah* on the first night of Pesach. Along with the *matzah,* the Torah requires us to eat bitter herbs at the Seder in order to experience a reminder of the bitterness of slavery.[78]

3. **The *Mitzvah* of *Haggadah* — Relating the Story of the Exile and Redemption**

The Torah commands us numerous times to tell the story of the Exodus and to convey to future generations the miracles that God performed for us at that time.[79] We must relate the entire story from the very beginning of exile to the last detail of the redemption, to each child at his or her level of understanding.[80] An integral part of this commandment is the obligation to try to create for each participant the feeling that he or she was personally taken out of Egypt.[81] The *mitzvah* of *Haggadah* is therefore an experiential as well as educational commandment. The word Haggadah has also come to refer to the book that contains the service, prayers and instructions for the Seder.

4. Hallel — Praise

We recite selected chapters of Psalms, known as *Hallel*,[82] to demonstrate our deep gratitude for every miracle that God performed for the Jewish people and each individual act of redemption. Though the impulse to thank God for his goodness to us is a natural feeling, we are actually obligated by Jewish law to thank God and praise Him.[83] This obligation is fulfilled by the *Hallel* and other Psalms that are recited during the Seder, some before and others after the meal.

5. Four Cups of Wine

The *mitzvot* of *Haggadah* and *Hallel* are accompanied by four cups of wine,[84] which we drink as a sign of freedom and joy.[85] This *mitzvah* is Rabbinic, i.e., it is not commanded in the Torah directly, but instituted by the Sages of Mishnaic times.

6. Curiosity Creators

Ideally, the Haggadah should be conveyed in a way that is relevant, interesting and engaging. Jewish law requires, therefore, that the story be told using a question and answer format. The Sages also enacted certain unusual practices at the Seder that are intended to keep the children awake, spark their interest and encourage them to ask questions.[86] We dip vegetables in salt water before the meal, hand out treats to the children during the meal, hide the *Afikoman* (see above), remove the Seder plate, and cover and uncover the *matzot* at various times. Certainly, enough is happening to inspire even tired children to wonder what is going on. Just in case nobody does ask, the Sages scripted certain questions into the Haggadah. Today, it is customary for children to sing or recite the famous "Four Questions" beginning with *Mah Nishtanah,* "Why is this night different from all other nights?"[87]

7. Symbols

The table is set with a Seder plate containing bitter herbs, a vegetable for dipping, a piece of broiled meat (symbolizing the paschal lamb), a broiled egg (symbolizing the festival offering in the Temple) and *charoset*, a finely ground mixture of apples, cinnamon, nuts, red wine, ginger and dates that resembles the mortar that the Jews were forced to use in Egypt (but tastes significantly better). Three *matzot* are placed in a special cover or under the Seder plate and are used to fulfill the commandment of eating *matzah*. The entire table is set beautifully, as if for a royal banquet.[88]

A Seder plate with all of the symbolic foods. Three hand-made matzot are beneath it.

The Order of the Seder

The Seder consists of fifteen segments. (For more detail on the Seder, see the following section of the Laws of Pesach.) The Hebrew names for the different parts of the Seder are written in rhyme at the beginning of all Haggadahs:

1. ***Kadesh*** — The person conducting the Seder takes a cup of wine and recites the *Kiddush*. Everyone then drinks the first cup of wine. (Children, of course, use grape juice.)

2. ***Urchatz*** — We wash our hands in preparation for *karpas*.

3. ***Karpas*** — We eat a vegetable dipped in salt water, to arouse the children's curiosity.

4. ***Yachatz*** — The *matzah* is broken into two pieces, just as a poor person would do when he does not know where his next meal will come from.

5. ***Maggid*** — The children ask the Four Questions, "*Mah Nishtanah*," and we respond with *Maggid*, telling the story. We then read, discuss and explain the story of the slavery and the Exodus from Egypt to all present. We conclude the story with the first part of *Hallel*, songs of praise to God, and drink the second cup of wine.

6. ***Rachtzah*** — We wash our hands in preparation for eating *matzah*.

7. **Motzi** — A blessing is made for eating bread (in this case *matzah*, but the blessing is the same).

8. **Matzah** — A blessing is made on fulfilling the commandment of eating *matzah* and the *matzah* is then eaten.

9. **Marror** — We eat *marror*, the bitter herbs, as a reminder of slavery.

10. **Korech** — We eat a sandwich of *matzah* and bitter herbs, as was done in ancient times when the lamb was eaten together with *matzah* and the bitter herbs.

11. **Shulchan Orech** — The festive meal begins, accompanied by further discussion about the Exodus, songs and traditional, delicious Passover foods.

12. **Tzafun** — The meal ends with the eating of the hidden piece of *matzah*, the *Afikoman,* symbolizing the paschal lamb that the Jews ate in Egypt.

13. **Barech** — Grace After Meals is recited while holding the third cup of wine, which we then drink.

14. **Hallel** — We complete the *Hallel*, end with a blessing and then drink the fourth cup of wine.

15. **Nirtzah** — We pray that God accepts our service and conclude the Seder with the declaration and prayer, "Next Year in Jerusalem!" We then sing traditional Pesach songs, and discuss the Haggadah until sleep overtakes us!

The Levy Family Unleavens

About two months before Pesach, the Levys begin to prepare the house for the upcoming festival. Gradually, everyone goes through his or her bedroom, inspecting toys, clothing, pocketbooks and jacket pockets, throwing away any chametz that may have been left there. Inevitably, a six-month-old peanut butter sandwich will be found in some dark corner of a child's knapsack, or a piece of a cracker that someone fed to the teddy bear will be found inside its overalls. As each area of the house becomes a chametz-free zone, Mrs. Levy crosses it off her "to do" list and Eli hangs a "NO CHAMETZ!" sign of his own design on the door. As Pesach approaches, the tempo of the cleaning picks up and the areas most often used for food preparation and consumption are given most attention.[89]

Mr. and Mrs. Levy start to think about whom they will invite to the Seder and other meals well before the holiday. The Levy grandparents will, of course, join them, but in addition, the Levys usually have people at the Seder who might otherwise have nowhere else to go. They often invite an elderly neighbor or students who are living away from home. Several times, they have hosted a family who had never before experienced a traditional Seder.

By the time Pesach is only a few days away, the entire home is sparkling and the children are getting used to eating in the garden or on the front porch. They are careful (most of the time) to shake off any crumbs before entering the house (or else!). The dining room table and sideboard have been covered with plastic and the last refuge of chametz, the kitchen, is ready for cleaning.

The Levys usually plan to have the kitchen kosher for Passover about two days before the festival begins, so they will have time to cook and prepare for Yom Tov. Most people organize their preparations in a similar way, so the local kosher pizza store does as much business in these few days as it usually would in an entire month.

A number of items containing chametz still remain in the house:[90] Two bottles of fine, single malt Scotch whiskey that Mr. Levy was given on Purim, several cosmetic items[91] and three bottles of vitamins[92] would all entail significant financial loss if they were thrown away. Mr. Levy therefore decides that these products must be sold to a non-Jew. He goes to his rabbi one evening during the week preceding Pesach and grants the rabbi power of attorney to sell his chametz. The rabbi will later sell the chametz of the entire community to a non-Jew for the duration of Passover. At the time of sale, Mr. Levy gives the rabbi a token sum of money.

Koshering the kitchen for Pesach is done largely by Mr. Levy and his son, Shlomo. They begin by thoroughly cleaning every surface, nook and cranny of the stove, refrigerator, counters, sinks and open shelves. They do not clean the cabinets containing all the chametz utensils, since the Levys include these in the sale of chametz and close them up for Pesach with a piece of masking tape that states "Chametz — SOLD."[93] They pour boiling water from the kettle on the entire surface of their marble countertops and over the entire surface of the sinks, self-clean the oven, and replace the stovetop grates with ones that they bought for Pesach. Finally, they cover the countertops with pieces of vinyl cut to the correct size and shape; the shelves of the fridge with plastic mats *(open weave to allow for air flow); and the stovetop and oven with heavy-duty aluminum foil.*

Once the kitchen looks like a Star Trek set, it is ready for Pesach. At this point (usually around 2 a.m.), Mr. Levy and Shlomo bring up all the boxes containing Pesach utensils from the basement. Later, Mrs. Levy and Tova will arrange them in the kitchen.

Besides all this physical labor, the Levy family has also been involved in intellectual preparation for Pesach. Each of the children studies the Haggadah in school for about a month before the holiday. The younger children create their own illustrated Haggadahs, and the older ones prepare notebooks filled with questions, comments and insights relating to the Haggadah. They plan to share these with everyone at the Seder. (It's going to be a long Seder.)

Once the house is thoroughly cleaned, the children take out the family's large collection of Haggadahs, dust them off and put them on a shelf in the dining room. Mr. Levy has a favorite Haggadah with commentaries in which he has written notes through the years. He likes to study a new commentary each year, however, in order to provide some fresh insights at the Seder. Shlomo has been studying the Talmudic tractate of Pesachim all year. He hopes to complete the tractate in time to make a siyum, a meal celebrating his achievement, on the day Passover begins.

On the night before the Seder, the Levy family does "bedikat chametz": They search in all places where chametz may have been found during the year.[94] (In the Levy household, thanks to 3-year-old Esther, this could be almost anywhere.) Even though the house has been cleaned and all chametz has been removed (except for breakfast), every household is obligated to actively search for chametz, annul it and to burn anything found. Following an ancient custom, the younger Levy children take 10 pieces of bread and hide them throughout the house to ensure that Mr. Levy will find at least some chametz in the pristine, sterile environment of their home.[95] (Mrs. Levy insists that the children record the location of each piece, just in case they are not all found.) Mr. Levy searches for the pieces of chametz with a candle. When he finds one, he brushes it into a wooden spoon using a feather, then transfers the pieces into a paper bag. Shlomo, Tova and Eli also participate in the search using flashlights, but aside from the 10 pieces, other chametz is rarely found at this stage.

Early the next morning, after finishing off a "chametzdik" breakfast, the Levys take all the leftover chametz to a local park where a community chametz-burning is organized under fire department supervision. The rest of the day is devoted to preparations for the Seder. Mrs. Levy and Tova are busy cooking; Shlomo takes care of cleaning and grating the marror, grilling the egg and the shank bone, ensuring a supply of unbroken matzot for the Seder table, opening wine bottles and getting the Seder plate and table ready. Mr. Levy always makes the charoset, which is so popular that he prepares enough to last for several festival meals in addition to the Seder. He also organizes "props" for the Seder to keep the younger children awake and involved. Bars of chocolate are standard (kosher for Passover and pareve,[96] of course), ready to be distributed to the children at intervals. This year, he has also found small plastic toys to represent each of the plagues.

Just before the festival, when all the children are in their Yom Tov clothing (and still clean!) and the Seder table is beautifully set, Mrs. Levy finds a moment to take a photo of the scene. Then she lights the Yom Tov candles and ushers in Pesach, as Mr. Levy goes with the older children to the evening services. The younger children had naps in the afternoon, so that they could stay up as late as possible. By the time Mr. Levy returns from the synagogue, everything is ready and the children are eager to start the Seder.

For the first night, the Levys have invited the Jacobovs, a family of four that recently immigrated to the United States from Russia and are celebrating their first traditional Seder. Mrs. Levy, who studied Russian language and literature in college (and even remembers some of it), will be able to help with some translation. Shlomo has also invited an Australian friend from his yeshivah who will be remaining in the United States for Pesach instead of going home.

Mr. Levy conducts the Seder smoothly, after years of experience. Much of the text of the Haggadah is sung by the family in both traditional and contemporary tunes. Every few minutes, one of the children or adults interjects a question that everyone does his or her best to answer. Best of all are the questions asked by the Jacobovs. Their perspective on the Exodus story is refreshing and they pinpoint many concepts the Levys had never had to explain before. Mr. Levy tries to answer the questions and offer explanations. He saves the more in-depth discussion and commentary for during the meal so that the little ones can stay awake to eat the matzah and marror.

The plastic plagues are a big hit! The children seem more awake than ever, even though the hour is late. They take turns singing and translating the Four Questions, starting with the youngest, and of course, they manage to steal the Afikoman and hide it. The Levys do not get to the meal until about 11 p.m. By then, the Russian family is a little puzzled (as they thought they had been invited for a meal), and everyone else is hungry too. But they are still in good spirits, helped along by two cups of wine consumed during the early part of the Seder. The meal is delicious but not elaborate, since everyone has already eaten considerable quantities of matzah, marror, and charoset. They are also aware that they must leave room for the Afikoman and two more cups of wine.

At the end of the meal, Mr. and Mrs. Levy "bargain" with the children for the return of the Afikoman. This year, each child is promised a book of his or her choice from the Jewish bookstore. After the meal, the Seder continues with more singing and discussion. By the time they reach the end, it is 1:30 a.m. Most of the children have been put to bed or have fallen asleep on couches in the living room, but everyone has had an inspiring and enjoyable experience that will stay with them forever. The Jacobovs leave amidst a flurry of tired, but warm farewells.

The next day is Yom Tov, and is spent much like a regular Shabbat (although everyone is still exhausted from the previous night!). The second Seder is similar to the first, but not an exact replica. Mr. Levy and the older children have held some comments and questions in reserve for the second night, and Shlomo and his friend teach everyone some new tunes. Mrs. Levy, who has had a chance to recuperate from the Pesach preparations, participates more tonight than at the first Seder, contributing her own questions and insights on the Haggadah.

After the first two days of Yom Tov are over, the Levy family looks forward to an enjoyable and relaxing Chol Hamoed. They plan to go on at least one hike in the country, taking along a large kosher-for-Passover picnic. They will visit some friends and relatives, go to a Jewish music concert and enjoy special meals and treats every day. Mr. Levy has arranged a time to study Torah with each child every morning. Afterward, they all enjoy special Pesach delicacies. Their favorite is matzah brie, a mixture of matzah and eggs which is fried, then drizzled with honey.[97]

The eight days of Passover go by very quickly. The last day of Yom Tov ends with a final meal of matzah in the late afternoon, followed by the evening service and Havdalah. (See chapter on Shabbat.) The Levys clean and pack away the special Passover dishes and utensils, the Haggadahs and all the Pesach paraphernalia. They will put it away until Passover next year, which they fervently hope they will celebrate in Jerusalem.

Selected Laws of Passover

Selected Laws of Yom Tov (Festivals)[98]

1. The purpose of the prohibition of work on the festival is to enable us to properly focus on the ideas of the festival. For this reason, the prohibition only applies to activities that transform and improve the material world. However, where enjoyment and fulfillment of the festival requires certain specific activities, they are permitted.[99]

2. Activities which directly produce things "that must be eaten (by a person)"[100] are permitted.[101] This Biblical verse refers almost exclusively to the preparation of food. No work is permitted simply to gratify by smell, sight or hearing,[102] or for commercial, industrial or other purposes.

3. Permission for food preparation is limited to:

    ▶ Preparation of food that could not be done on the previous day.[103]

    ▶ Food whose quality is improved by being prepared on the same day it is eaten.[104]

    ▶ All food preparation that results in the use of food for that day only.[105]

4. Specifically, one is permitted to bake, roast, cook, grind spices (that would otherwise lose flavor),[106] select (by hand),[107] carry,[108] increase a flame and decrease a flame (if indispensable to the food preparation).[109]

5. Rabbinic law prohibits lighting a new fire, so all cooking is done on a fire that was already in existence before the festival began. It is permitted to transfer a flame, so a candle can be left burning and used to light other fires.[110]

6. The rest of the 39 prohibited activities of Shabbat,[111] e.g., any agricultural work, fixing of utensils, sewing, writing, building, etc. are prohibited on festivals.[112]

7. Rabbinic prohibitions include the following categories:

    ▶ Activities similar to a *melachah* (activity forbidden on Shabbat) — e.g., sharpening knives, producing fire.[113]

    ▶ Things that might lead to *melachah* — e.g., moving objects that may not be used, such as pens, money, etc.[114]

8. All of these laws apply equally to the second day of a festival in the Diaspora.[115]

9. Special prayers are recited every day throughout Passover, including *Hallel* and *Mussaf* (the additional festival prayer); and "*Yaaleh veyavo*"[116] is included in the *Amidah*.[117]

10. The Torah is read in the synagogue every day of Passover.[118]

11. On Yom Tov, *Kiddush* is recited while holding a cup of wine at the beginning of the evening and morning meals, as on Shabbat.[119] A blessing is also made over two *matzot* (instead of challah) at these festival meals.

12. One should invite guests to join in the festival meals, as Maimonides writes: "When one eats and drinks on the festival, one is obligated to feed the stranger, the orphan and the widow together with others who are poor and unfortunate. However one who closes the doors of his courtyard and eats and drinks with his wife and children and does not give food and drink to the poor and the depressed — [he celebrates] not the happiness of a *mitzvah*, rather the happiness of his stomach. About these people the verse[120] states, "... all who partake will be defiled, for their bread is only for themselves."[121]

13. Before the holiday, every Jew in the community contributes to a special fund that helps needy people purchase items for the festival. The fund, called *Maot Chittim*, is necessary above and beyond the regular charitable funds, because Pesach is such a costly festival.[122]

14. Firstborn males should fast on the eve of Pesach,[123] to commemorate the miracle of the plague of the first-born Egyptians, and the saving of the Jewish firstborn.[124] It is a widespread custom for the firstborn to participate in a *siyum*, a meal celebrating the completion of a tractate,[125] in which case he does not have to fast.[126]

15. After Yom Tov, *Havdalah*[127] is said over a cup of wine, but the spices and candle normally blessed after Shabbat are not used.[128]

Chol Hamoed – Intermediate Days of Festival

1. All labor is forbidden on Chol Hamoed[129] except for:

   ▶ That which will cause loss if not done immediately.[130]

- ▸ Things that are necessary to obtain or prepare food for the festival, and could not have been done beforehand.[131]

- ▸ Unskilled labor which involves little effort, e.g., turning on a light, driving a car.

- ▸ Communal needs.[132]

- ▸ Any work, in the case of a person who will have nothing to eat for the festival if he does not work.[133]

2. The main purpose of Chol Hamoed is to absorb the lessons of the festival without being distracted by mundane affairs. Therefore, it is appropriate to use this time to study more Torah than usual.[134]

3. One should wear festive clothing, and enjoy festive meals (generally, these should include meat and wine) every day during Chol Hamoed.[135]

4. One should shave and take a haircut before the festival.[136] It is prohibited to shave or take a haircut during Chol Hamoed.[137]

5. It is prohibited to do laundry[138] or to repair clothing[139] on Chol Hamoed. The clothing of young children may be washed, if needed.[140]

6. One should not engage in business during Chol Hamoed (unless it is included in categories 1. a. — e.).[141]

7. The prayer service on Chol Hamoed contains elements of festival prayers and elements of weekday prayers.

Chametz and Cleaning for Passover[142]

1. All places or articles into which *chametz* (leavened grain products, e.g., bread, crackers, cake) is usually brought during the year must be cleansed and checked for *chametz* before the evening preceding the Seder.[143] The official search for *chametz* (details of the ritual can be found in most Haggadahs as well as *The Complete ArtScroll Siddur*)[144] is started at nightfall on the evening preceding the Seder.[145] Any *chametz* that is found on the search, and any leftover *chametz* from the next morning's breakfast, should be burnt that morning, before the time that it becomes prohibited to possess *chametz*.[146] When burning the *chametz*, local fire codes and all fire-safety precautions should be observed. Children should never be allowed near the fire without strict adult supervision.

2. The owner of the *chametz* declares that the *chametz* is worthless to him and renounce his ownership.[147] This declaration is made at night after the search, and in the morning while the *chametz* is being burnt. (For the precise wording of this declaration see *The Complete Artscroll Siddur, Ashkenaz*, pp. 654 — 655 or any Haggadah.)

3. Any article or place that is not used on Pesach, which is closed up and sold, does not have to be checked for *chametz*.[148]

4. *Chametz* that has been rendered inedible (even to an animal) by being soaked in a foul-tasting liquid such as bleach or ammonia is not considered *chametz*.[149]

5. There is no obligation to check and destroy *chametz* that is less than the size of an olive (approx. 1 oz.) *and* so dirty that a person would not eat it.[150]

6. Surfaces, closets and cracks where it is possible that *chametz* has fallen should be washed, ensuring that detergent enters all cracks and crevices.[151]

7. The kitchen must be thoroughly cleaned and *kashered* (made kosher) for Passover use. Anything that is to be koshered may not be used for 24 hours prior to the koshering process.[152] A rabbi should be consulted for detailed instructions regarding koshering. Ideally, one should have a complete set of eating and cooking utensils specifically for Passover use. If this is difficult, a rabbi should be consulted regarding *kashering* utensils used year-round for Pesach.

8. It is also customary to cover any surfaces that have been *kashered* and will be used for food or utensils on Pesach — e.g., tables, countertops, cabinets and stovetops.[153] Plastic, cardboard or aluminum foil are most commonly used to cover these surfaces.

9. Any *chametz* that will not be consumed or destroyed before Pesach must be sold to a non-Jew before the time that *chametz* becomes prohibited (the precise time is printed in Jewish calendars and newspapers). This transaction should performed by a rabbi, as the laws are complex and a contract is necessary. The sale is not a legal fiction, therefore the nature, amount and location of the *chametz* must be detailed in the contract. The contract also specifies that the place in which the *chametz* is stored will be rented to the buyer and that he will have access to the *chametz* should he so desire. It is rare for the buyer to come into one's

house and demand the goods, but if he does, Jewish law clearly says that he can take it. The *chametz* that has been sold must be put away and clearly marked, until after the holiday.[154]

10. The prohibition against eating *chametz* begins in the morning, before the first night of Pesach. All *chametz* should be removed from one's property (or sold) by that morning.[155]

11. All food, medicine, cosmetics or cleaning products should either have supervision to ensure that they contain no *chametz*, i.e., are certified "Kosher for Passover," or should be included in a Kashrus agency's list of products used year-round that are acceptable for Passover. These lists are published every year by the major agencies of kosher supervision.

Selected Laws of the Seder

1. The Seder table should be prepared before nightfall, complete with the Seder plate, *matzot*, cups, etc. The table should be set as beautifully as possible.[156]

2. The Seder plate should contain: an egg (*beitzah*) lightly broiled over a fire (hard-boil it first); a piece of meat (*zroa*) broiled over a fire (chicken is also fine); *charoset* (usually made of grated apple, ground walnuts, cinnamon, red wine, ginger and dates),[157] a vegetable (*chazeret*); a potato or parsley (*karpas*); and the bitter herb (*marror*), usually fresh horseradish or romaine lettuce. A bowl of salt water should be placed on the table, but is not placed on the plate.[158] There are different customs regarding the order in which the items are placed on the Seder plate. Several variations are usually depicted at the beginning of the Haggadah. The most common is illustrated below.

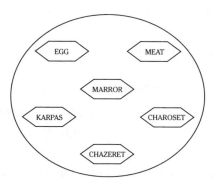

3. Three whole (not broken) *shmurah matzot* should be placed under or in front of the Seder plate. They should be covered and separated from each other by a napkin or cloth.[159] *Shmurah* means "guarded" — these are *matzot* that were made with the specific intention of using them for this *mitzvah*. They are made from wheat that was "guarded," carefully kept away from moisture, from the time of its harvest. *Shmurah matzah* should be used to fulfill the requirements of the Seder.[160]

4. Pillows should be placed on each seat so the participants can each lean on his left side, in the manner of royalty, while eating and reciting the Haggadah (but not while eating the *marror*).[161]

5. Everyone should have a cup that holds at least 3 fluid ounces. Red wine is preferable, but white wine may also be used. Children, pregnant women or people who cannot drink alcohol for health reasons may fulfill the obligation with grape juice (preferably, with a little wine mixed in). The cups should be filled to the brim for each of the four cups of wine.[162]

6. For detailed instructions on how to conduct the Seder, see *The Family Haggadah*, Mesorah Publications, NY, 1981. Literally hundreds of editions of the Haggadah exist, and illuminating commentaries explaining the concepts in the Haggadah have been written by great scholars throughout history. Translations of many editions, along with commentaries, laws and instructions are available. Although at first it may seem overwhelming, with the right text and a little preparation anyone can conduct a beautiful, inspiring Seder.

For Further Reading

▸ *In Every Generation* by Rabbi Moshe Grylak (ArtScroll/Mesorah, 2003)

▸ *From Bondage to Freedom* by Rabbi Abraham J. Twerski, M.D. (Shaar Press, 1995)

▸ *Passover Survival Kit* by Shimon Apisdorf (Leviathan Press, 1997)

▸ *The ArtScroll Family Haggadah* (ArtScroll/Mesorah, 1981)

▸ *The Haggadah with Answers* by Rabbi Yaakov Wehl (ArtScroll/Mesorah, 1997)

▸ *The Pesach Haggadah* by Rabbi Berel Wein (Shaar Press, 2004)

NOTES

References to books of the Talmud refer to the Babylonian Talmud unless otherwise noted.

1. For information on the historicity of the Egyptian exile and Exodus see Leah Bronner, *Biblical Personalities and Archaeology*, Keter Publishing, Jerusalem, 1974; James K. Hoffmeier, *Israel in Egypt*, Oxford University Press, NY, 1996; David Rohl, *A Test of Time*, Century Publishing, London, 1995.

2. Deuteronomy 4:34.

3. Rabbi Aaron of Barcelona, *Sefer Hachinuch,* Mitzvah 306.

4. *Nedarim* 32a; *Tanna Debei Eliyahu Rabba* 14:5, *Shabbat* 10b; Cf. Maharal, *Gevurot Hashem*, Chap. 9.

5. Exodus 22:20; 23:9; Leviticus 19:34; Deuteronomy 10:19.

6. Exodus 23:9.

7. I Kings 8:51.

8. Rabbi Isaac Luria, *Likutei Ha'AriZal*, beginning of Exodus.

9. Heard from Rabbi Moshe Shapiro, based on Rabbi Isaac Luria, the AriZal.

10. Rabbi Samson Raphael Hirsch, *Horeb*, pp. 84-85, para. 161-162.

11. Rabbi Aaron of Barcelona, *Sefer Hachinuch, Parshat Bo,* Mitzvah 20, Mossad Harav Kook, Jerusalem, 1984.

12. When it occurs in the Land of Israel.

13. Exodus 12:1-2.

14. Ibid. 23:15.

15. The Jewish Calendar.

16. Joshua 4:19.

17. Ezra 7:9; 8:31.

18. Rabbi Eliyahu Dessler, *Michtav M'Eliyahu*, vol. 1, p. 103; vol. 2, p. 21; Rabbi Shlomo Eliashiv, *Leshem Shvo Ve'achlamah*, Sefer Hadeah, 2, Drush 4, 24:8; Ibid. Drush Miut Hayare'ach, 6; Rabbi Yitzchak Ze'ev Soloveitchik, *Chidushei Hagriz al HaTorah*, No. 131.

19. *The Complete ArtScroll Siddur, Ashkenaz,* pp 228-229.

20. Song of Songs 2:10.

21. *Midrash Rabbah* ibid., ad loc.

22. Some translate this as "sacred convocation."

23. Exodus 12:16.

24. See chapter on Shabbat for a full explanation of *Kiddush.*

25. *Code of Jewish Law, Orach Chaim,* 530:2, *Mishnah Berurah* 2.

26. Ibid. *Mishnah Berurah* 1.

27. *Berachot* 9b; *The Complete ArtScroll Siddur, Ashkenaz,* pp. 262-263 — "eternal freedom."

28. Exodus 1:14.

29. Leviticus 25:39-43.

30. *matzah*, sing; *matzot* or *matzos*, pl.

31. Exodus 12:15-18.

32. Ibid. 12:39.

33. Maimonides, *Mishneh Torah*, Laws of Chametz and Matzah, 5:1.

34. These include several alpha-amylase isoenzymes, several beta-amylase isoenzymes, pullulanase, isoamylase, proteases, lipoxygenase, lipases, esterases and phosphatases.

35. CO_2

36. *Code of Jewish Law, Orach Chaim,* 459.

37. Rabbi Aharon Hacohen of Lunel, *Orchot Chaim on the Haggadah, Haggadat Torah Chaim,* Mossad Harav Kook, Jerusalem, 1998, pp. 15-16; Maharal, *Gevurot Hashem,* Chap. 50.

38. Deuteronomy 16:3.

39. Rabbi Samson Raphael Hirsch, *Horeb,* II Edoth, Chap. 26, para. 199.

40. *Mechilta* and Commentary of Rashi on Genesis 15:13.

41. Maimonides, *Mishneh Torah*, Laws of Idolatry, 1:3.

42. *Mechilta,* Introduction to *Parshat Shelach*; Commentary of Rashi on Exodus 13:18.

43. Heard from Rabbi Uziel Milevsky, of blessed memory.

44. Scholars of Jewish mysticism.

45. Rabbi Chaim ibn Attar, *Ohr Hachaim*, Exodus 3:7.

46. Exodus 12:11, Deuteronomy 16:3.

47. *Zohar*, Exodus, 40b.

48. Maharal of Prague, *Gevurot Hashem*, Chs. 50-51; Rabbi Yitzchak Hutner, *Pachad Yitzchak*, Pesach, Ma'amar 1, Gur Aryeh Institute, NY, 1984.

49. Deuteronomy 16:3.

50. Maharal, ibid., Chap. 35.

51. Rabbi Yeshayahu Horowitz, *Shnei Luchot Habrit, Derech Chaim Tochachat Mussar, Parshat Miketz*.

52. *Midrash Shmot Rabba*, 25:12.

53. Exodus 12:18-20.

54. Maimonides, *Mishneh Torah*, Laws of Chametz and Matzah 1:1-2, 2:1, 4:2.

55. Exodus 12:19-20.

56. *Code of Jewish Law*, 445; *Be'er Heitev, Shaarei Teshuvah* and *Mishnah Berurah* ad loc.

57. Ibid. *Orach Chaim*, 445:1-3.

58. Ibid. *Orach Chaim*, 447:1.

59. Maimonides, *Mishneh Torah*, Laws of Idolatry, Introduction to Chap. 1.

60. *Berachot* 17a, Rashi ad loc.

61. Rabbi Aharon of Barcelona, *Sefer Hachinuch*, Mitzvah 117.

62. Rabbi Yeshayahu Horowitz, *Shnei Luchot Habrit*, Masechet Pesachim, Perek Torah Ohr, 13.

63. *Sefer Hachinuch*, ibid.; Rabbi Moshe Chaim Luzzatto, *Path of the Just*, Chap. 6.

64. Jeremiah 2:27.

65. Isaiah 47:8.

66. Rabbi Samson Raphael Hirsch, *Horeb*, II Edoth, Chap. 26, para. 204.

67. Exodus 7:10: Chaps. 8-12; Chap. 14.

68. *Sotah* 2a, Rashi ad loc.; *Shabbat* 53b; *Avodah Zarah*, 54b, 55a; Maimonides, *Guide for the Perplexed*; Rabbi Chaim ibn Attar, *Ohr Hachaim*, Genesis 31:12; *Sefer Hachinuch*, Mitzvah 132.

69. Exodus 8:18, 9:29, 9:14 respectively.

70. Author's translation of Commentary of Nachmanides on Exodus 13:16;

71. Exodus 12:3-8.

72. Ibid. 8:22; *Targum Onkelos*, Genesis 43:32; Herodotus 2:41.

73. Ian Shaw, *The Oxford History of Ancient Egypt*, Oxford University Press, 2000, pp. 94, 99; David P. Silverman, *Ancient Egypt*, Oxford University Press, 1997, p. 19.

74. *Zohar, Parshat Bo*, Raayah Meheimnah, 2.

75. Commentary of Rashi, Exodus 12:6; *Midrash Rabbah*, Exodus, 16:2.

76. *Code of Jewish Law, Orach Chaim*, 473:4.

77. Mishnah and Talmud *Pesachim* 119b, Commentaries ad loc.

78. Number 9:11. In the absence of the Pesach offering, eating the bitter herbs today is a Rabbinic commandment — *Pesachim* 120a.

79. Exodus 13:8; 13:14; Deuteronomy 6:20.

80. Mishnah *Pesachim* 10:4.

81. Ibid. 10:5.

82. *Pesachim* 117a; *The Complete ArtScroll Siddur, Ashkenaz*, pp. 632-643.

83. *Berachot* 56a, Rashi "*hallelah mitzraah*."

84. Mishnah *Pesachim* 10:1.

85. *Pesachim* 109b.

86. Ibid. 109a, 115b.

87. Found in every Passover Haggadah.

88. *Code of Jewish Law, Orach Chaim*, 472:2, 473:4-5.

89. *Code of Jewish Law, Orach Chaim*, 433:11 Ramah.

90. Before every Passover, kosher supervision organizations and rabbis publish lists of acceptable and unacceptable Passover products. It is important to obtain a new list each year.

91. Perfumes and aftershave often contain grain alcohol, which is *chametz*.

92. Vitamins often contain grain products or derivatives as binders.

Mossad Harav Kook, Jerusalem, 1976.

93. *Code of Jewish Law, Orach Chaim,* 451:1.

94. Ibid. 431:1.

95. Ibid. *Orach Chaim,* 432:2 Ramah, *Mishnah Berurah* 13.

96. Neutral — containing no milk or meat products. See chapter on Kashrut.

97. Some people have a custom not to eat *matzah* that has been mixed together with any liquid. The resulting mixture is called *gebrochts.* There are differing traditions concerning its use on Passover.

98. Many thanks to Rabbi Moshe Newman and Ohr Somayach Institutions, Jerusalem, for permission to use material that we wrote for their website www.ohr.edu.

99. Rabbi Samson Raphael Hirsch, *Horeb,* II, Edoth, Chap. 23.

100. Exodus 12:16.

101. *Code of Jewish Law, Orach Chaim,* 495:1.

102. *Horeb,* ibid.

103. *Code of Jewish Law,* ibid.

104. Ibid. Ramah.

105. Ibid. 503:1.

106. Ibid. 504:1.

107. Ibid. 510:2.

108. Ibid. 518:1

109. Ibid. 495:1, 502:1, Rabbi Moshe Feinstein, *Igrot Moshe, Orach Chaim,* 1:128.

110. *Code of Jewish Law,* Ibid. 502:1.

111. See chapter on Shabbat.

112. *Code of Jewish Law, Orach Chaim,* 495:1, 2.

113. Ibid. 502:1.

114. Ibid. 495:4.

115. Ibid. 496:1.

116. *The Complete ArtScroll Siddur, Ashkenaz,* pp. 632-643, 674-692, 110-111 respectively.

117. *Code of Jewish Law,* ibid. 488:1.

118. Ibid. 488:3, 490:1.

119. *The Complete ArtScroll Siddur, Ashkenaz,* pp. 492-493, 656-659.

120. Hosea 9:4.

121. Maimonides, *Mishneh Torah,* Laws of Festivals, 6:18.

122. *Code of Jewish Law, Orach Chaim,* 429:1, Ramah.

123. *Code of Jewish Law, Orach Chaim,* 470:1.

124. Ibid. *Mishnah Berurah* 1.

125. See chapter on Torah Study.

126. Ibid. *Mishnah Berurah* 10.

127. See section on Shabbat.

128. *Code of Jewish Law, Orach Chaim,* 491:1.

129. Ibid. 530:1, *Mishnah Berurah* 1.

130. Ibid. 537, 538.

131. Ibid. 533:1.

132. Ibid. 544.

133. Ibid. 542:2.

134. Ibid. *Mishnah Berurah* 2.

135. Ibid. *Mishnah Berurah* 1.

136. Ibid. 531:1.

137. Ibid. 531:2.

138. Ibid. 534.

139. Ibid. 541:4.

140. Ibid. 534:1, Ramah.

141. Ibid. 539:1.

142. Based on classes by Rabbi Chaim Pinchas Scheinberg, Jerusalem.

143. Mishnah *Pesachim* 1:1.

144. *The Complete ArtScroll Siddur, Ashkenaz,* pp. 654-655.

145. Mishnah, ibid.

146. Local calendars should be consulted.

147. *Code of Jewish Law, Orach Chaim,* 434:2, 3.

148. Mishnah, ibid.

149. *Code of Jewish Law, Orach Chaim,* 442:9.

150. Ibid. 442, *Mishnah Berurah* 33.

151. *Code of Jewish Law, Orach Chaim,* 442:9.

152. Ibid. 452:2, Ramah.

153. *Code of Jewish Law, Orach Chaim,* 451:20, *Mishnah Berurah* 115.

154. Ibid. 448:3, *Mishnah Berurah* and *Shaarei Teshuvah* ad loc.

155. Ibid. 443:1.

156. *Code of Jewish Law, Orach Chaim,* 472:1.

157. Ibid. 473:5, Ramah.

158. Ibid. 473:4, Ramah, *Mishnah Berurah* ad loc.

159. Ibid.

160. Ibid. 482:1.

161. Ibid. 472:2-3.

162. Ibid. 472:8-11.

Back to Sinai: Shavuot

Revelation at Mt. Sinai and celebration of the Torah

Countdown to Sinai

*T*he Jewish people's journey toward nationhood began on Passover. The Exodus redeemed them from physical slavery and subjugation, but they still lacked a national identity and purpose. This was conferred upon them only later — when the Jewish people both heard and saw the words of God at Mt. Sinai.[1] In those moments, the newly formed nation obtained its spiritual identity and national calling through the Torah,[2] and the redemption was complete.[3] This world-altering event, the Revelation of the Torah to the Jews at Mt. Sinai, took place on the seventh day of the month of Sivan, in the year 2448 (1313 B.C.E.). Every year, the seventh of Sivan is celebrated as the festival called Shavuot.[4]

The Torah emphasizes the link between Passover and Shavuot, the very beginning of the redemption from Egypt and its culmination, through the commandment of *Sefirat Ha'omer*. We count the days and weeks from the second day of Passover until the festival of *Atzeret*, The Day of Assembly, as Shavuot is called in the Torah.[5] (We begin the counting only on the second night of Passover, not on the first, in order not to detract from the celebration and joy of the Exodus with a reminder that the redemption was not yet complete.[6])

The words *Sefirat Ha'omer* actually mean, "the counting of the *Omer*." The *Omer* was an offering of newly harvested barley that was brought to the Temple in Jerusalem on the 16th of Nissan, the second day of Passover.[7] In contrast to the Passover barley, the offering on Shavuot was bread made from wheat flour.[8] Barley is often used as animal fodder,[9] while wheat is predominantly for human consumption — and bread is an exclusively human food.[10] Thus, as we count from Passover to Shavuot, we also mark our progression from slavery to our material animal needs, to the increasingly human realm of free will, intellect and attachment to God.[11]

The Best of Times, The Worst of Times

For the Jewish people who came out of Egypt, the period between the Exodus and the Revelation at Mt. Sinai was one of continuous spiritual awakening. Their relationship with God grew stronger and closer. Miraculous events occurred daily. For the Jewish people in subsequent generations, this period continues to be one of the greatest times of the year, in which we prepare ourselves for a renewal of our commitment to the Torah on Shavuot.

Jewish mystical tradition teaches that there are 50 levels of sanctity and opposing them, 50 levels of impurity.[12] The Jewish people in Egypt (with some exceptions) had sunk to the 49th level of impurity. Most of them believed in Egyptian deities and superstitions and were almost completely devoid of faith in God.[13] It was only God's decision to save them from Egypt when He did, that prevented them from falling to the 50th and lowest level,[14] from which they would never have been able to rise. The 49-day period from the Exodus until Shavuot was (and still remains) a time when the Jewish people are able to ascend through the levels of sanctity and knowledge to reach the level of Revelation of the Torah on the 50th day at Mt. Sinai.[15] Accordingly, counting the *Omer* measures our readiness to accept the Torah.

In the first century of the Common Era, the Jewish people experienced a major tragedy during the period of counting the *Omer*. The greatest sage of the generation was Rabbi Akiva, who taught vast numbers of people. The Talmud relates that 24,000 (!) of Rabbi Akiva's students, who constituted the primary chain of Torah transmission, died as a result of an epidemic between Passover and Shavuot. It further states that the reason for this Divine punishment was that they did not treat one another with sufficient respect.[16]

One of the greatest Jewish philosophers and Kabbalists, the Maharal of Prague, explains the Talmud's statement in this way: Since the period from Passover to Shavuot is the time of preparation for receiving the Torah — and these students were the central transmitters of Torah — any flaw in the process of receiving and transmitting the Torah was judged by God with extreme gravity. The lack of proper respect for a colleague demonstrates deficient understanding of the intrinsic, infinite potential of the human soul. Had the students fully appreciated this hidden potential, had they looked at their colleagues beneath the surface, their respect for each other would have been tremendous.[17]

Respect for a colleague with whom one studies Torah is also a reflection of the respect one has for the Torah itself and for the vast treasure hidden beneath its surface. During the counting of the *Omer*, one of our primary tasks is to develop respect and honor for the Torah and for those who are devoted to it. The students of Rabbi Akiva failed in this task and therefore could not be the primary transmitters of the Torah. They had to be replaced. Rabbi Akiva however, did not give up hope. He continued to teach, and ordained other students who eventually became the major authorities of the Mishnah,[18] the central work of Jewish law.[19]

To commemorate this tragedy, many Jewish communities observe customs associated with mourning. During the period of *Sefirat Ha'omer* (known simply to many as the period of *Sefirah*) marriages are not performed, people forgo haircuts and men do not shave. Among the Jews of Europe (*Ashkenazim*), *Sefirah* was also a time of tremendous suffering during the Crusades, and therefore *Ashkenazim* are stricter about the mourning laws than the Jews of Spain, the Middle East and North Africa (*Sephardim*).[20]

Lag B'Omer – The 33rd Day of the Omer

The term *"Lag"* (pronounced "log") is the abbreviation of the Hebrew letters *lamed* (L) and *gimmel* (G) whose numerical equivalents are 30 and 3 respectively. *B'Omer* means "the [counting] of the Omer."

Two significant events occurred on this date, and though separated by many years, they both contribute to its special status. On the thirty-third day of the counting of the *Omer*, the epidemic rampant among Rabbi Akiva's students abruptly ceased. Because the epidemic lasted 33 days, the common custom is to observe 33 days of mourning during the *Omer* period, ending on Lag B'Omer. It is also customary to mark the day with festive practices.[21] The most colorful of these is a grand celebration on Mount Meron in Israel, at the grave of Rabbi Shimon *bar* (son of) Yochai.

The greatest scholar of the *Kabbalah* (Jewish mysticism) who ever lived, Rabbi Shimon died on Lag B'Omer, and on that day he revealed many of the deepest ideas of the *Kabbalah* to his students.[22] They recorded his teachings in a book known as the *Zohar*, the Light.[23] Ancient Jewish custom dictates that the anniversary of the death of a great scholar should be noted as a means of inspiring people with his lessons and teachings.[24]

For hundreds of years on Lag B'Omer, people have gone to the grave of Rabbi Shimon on Mount Meron in the Galilee region.[25] There they celebrate by lighting bonfires[26] to symbolize the light of Torah that Rabbi Shimon revealed, and by dancing, singing and studying Rabbi Shimon's teachings. Today it is common to see people all over Israel celebrating Lag B'Omer with bonfires and singing, while at Mt. Meron itself, hundreds of thousands participate in the festivities.

The Grand Finale

The *Omer* is counted for the final time on the 49th night. The following evening, the festival of Shavuot begins at sundown. Shavuot is the anniversary of the Revelation on Mount Sinai,[27] when God communicated the Torah to the entire Jewish people and in so doing, revealed to them their national mission and purpose. In our prayers, Shavuot is referred to as *Zman Matan Torateinu,* the Time of the Giving of Our Torah.

Unlike all the other holidays, no particular *mitzvah* is associated with Shavuot: On Passover, we eat *matzah,* on Sukkot we dwell in a *sukkah* and on Rosh Hashanah we blow the *shofar,* but no specific commandment is related to the giving of the Torah. Shavuot celebrates the totality of Torah. The Torah is all encompassing, it sanctifies and elevates every aspect of life; therefore it cannot be encapsulated in any single ritual, or any one experience.[28]

On all festivals, the spiritual light that originally encompassed the world on the first occasion of that festival (for instance, the very first Passover) flows again *every year* at that same time.[29] This increased spirituality is available to us if we are attuned to it.

On Shavuot, God spoke to the entire Jewish people and gave us the gift and the responsibility of studying and observing the Torah. The Jewish people responded with the famous words, "Everything that God has said, we will do and we will hear."[30]

With these words, our ancestors expressed the depth of their trust in God and their commitment to His words. Saying, "we will do" even before "we will hear," they accepted whatever obligations He might give them, sight unseen. On Shavuot, the light of that commitment still burns and can be re-experienced through the observance of this festival.

One of the customs of Shavuot that helps us capture this special light is all-night Torah study. After the evening service and a festive dinner, virtually the entire community returns to the synagogue to study and hear classes on Torah. Most will remain to learn the entire night.[31] At dawn, the festival morning service is recited and the congregation returns home to have breakfast (and usually to sleep until lunchtime). It is customary to study selections from every different part of the Torah,[32] to demonstrate our desire to know and fulfill the Torah in its entirety.

What Happened at Mount Sinai?

Receiving the Torah at Mt. Sinai was an overwhelming experience for the Jewish people. The Torah describes in great detail how every man, woman and child experienced the word of God with all of their senses.[33] The uniqueness of this account cannot be overemphasized. God did not whisper to a lone individual on a mountaintop, on a rooftop, on a secluded road or in a cave. We do not need to trust an individual's word that he or she had prophecy in order to accept the reality of this communication.

In this critical respect, the Revelation at Sinai stands in marked contrast to all other claims of prophetic revelation that we find in history. The standard revelation story goes something like this:

"Yesterday I was alone on a mountaintop in New Jersey, praying and meditating. God came to me in a vision and said, 'Becher, you are My prophet. Go out and command the people and establish for Me the United Church of Becherology.' I was terrified and yet filled with love, humbled and yet encouraged to fulfill my unique destiny, and so I come to you as your prophet and seer."

The claim that God spoke to an *individual* and that individual conveyed the message to others is common to every story of revelation (except the Torah account).[34] It is relatively easy to disseminate this type of story even if it is false. An eloquent and charismatic leader can convince people that God spoke to him, as indeed people have done throughout history. They are able to succeed because the revelation is described in such a way that even if it had actually occurred there would be no reason to expect any evidence to remain. The lack of tangible evidence does not, therefore, elicit any skepticism. Neither is there any possibility of an eyewitness other than the "prophet," so no one can dispute his claims.

At Mt. Sinai, *the entire Jewish nation experienced prophecy*; each and every one heard God say, "I am the Lord your God Who took you out of Egypt," the only God, the One Who designated Moses as His prophet. The Jews did not have to trust Moses and rely on his testimony: they themselves heard the voice of God.[35] Everyone also heard God speak with Moses and appoint him as God's prophet and leader of the Jewish people.[36]

If this event had not actually happened with thousands of eyewitnesses, as described in the Torah, it would be extremely difficult, if not impossible, to convince people that it had. Thousands of people would be able to attest to the absence of this experience and refute even an eloquent and charismatic leader.[37] This is one reason that the Torah's account continuously mentions the public nature of the Revelation and the fact that the Jewish people were witnesses to both the commands of God and His appointment of Moses as a prophet.

So what did they see? The account in Exodus records:

> God said to Moses, "Behold! I come to you in the thickness of the cloud, **so that the people will hear as I speak to you, and they will also believe in you forever.**" Moses related the words of the people to God.
>
> God said to Moses, "Go to the people and sanctify them today and tomorrow, and they shall wash their clothing. Let them be prepared for the third day, for on the third day **God shall descend in the sight of the entire people on Mount Sinai.**"
>
> ...On the third day when it was morning, there was thunder and lightning and a heavy cloud on the mountain, and the sound of the shofar was very powerful, and the entire people that were in the camp shuddered. Moses brought the people forth from the camp toward God, and they stood at the bottom of the mountain.
>
> All of Mount Sinai was smoking because God had descended upon it in fire; its smoke ascended like the smoke of the furnace, and the entire mountain shuddered exceedingly. The sound of the shofar grew continually much stronger; **Moses would speak and God would respond to him with a voice.** God descended upon Mount Sinai to the top of the mountain; **God summoned Moses to the top of the mountain, and Moses ascended.**[38]

The Torah emphasizes, as well, the uniqueness of the Jewish people's experience in having a national encounter with God:

> For inquire now regarding the early days that preceded you, from the day when God created man on the earth, and from one end of heaven to the other end of heaven — Has there ever been anything like this great thing or has anything like it been heard? **Has any nation ever heard the voice of God speaking from the midst of the fire as you have heard, and survived?** Or has any god ever miraculously come to take for himself a nation from amidst a nation, with challenges, with signs, and with wonders, and with war, and with a strong hand, and with an outstretched arm, and with greatly awesome

deeds, such as everything that God, your God, did for you in Egypt before your eyes?

You have been shown in order to know that God, He is the God! There is none beside Him. **From heaven He caused you to hear His voice in order to teach you, and on earth He showed you His great fire, and you heard His words from the midst of the fire.**[39]

The prophets refer to the Jewish people as the witnesses of God, "You are My witnesses, says God, and the servant that I have chosen."[40] We are identified this way because the entire nation witnessed God's revelation and continuously testify to that revelation by following the commandments of the Torah. There is, in fact, a specific *mitzvah*[41] to pass on the testimony and memory of the events of Mt. Sinai to our children, as the Torah states in the fourth chapter of Deuteronomy:

> *Only beware for yourself and greatly beware for your soul, lest you forget the things that your eyes have beheld and lest you remove them from your heart all the days of your life; make them known to your children and your children's children. The day that you stood before the Lord your God, at Horeb [another name for Mt. Sinai], when God said to me, "Gather the people to Me and I shall let them hear My words, so that they shall learn to fear Me all the days that they live on the earth, and they shall teach their children."*

The festival of Shavuot is a communal fulfillment of this obligation. It is a time when the Jewish people testify together that God spoke to them at Mount Sinai and that they will continue to transmit His message through all time.

Milk and Honey

It is customary to eat dairy foods on Shavuot, possibly as one component in re-enacting Sinai. Having just received the laws about kosher food, the Jewish people had no choice but to limit themselves to dairy or plant-based foods, instead of meat that would require kosher slaughter, salting and other preparations before it could be eaten.[42] Some observe the custom of eating milk and honey, because the Torah is compared to their sweetness and pleasure.[43] As it says in Song of Songs: "Honey drops from your lips, O bride, honey and milk are under your tongue."[44]

Milk and honey also symbolize the idea that the Torah teaches us how to live in harmony with the physical and spiritual worlds. "Its ways are ways of pleasantness and all its paths are peace."[45] Milk and honey are both foods that do not require the taking of life or even the interruption of growth to be obtained. They, like the Torah, are in harmony with nature.

The Scroll of Ruth

During the morning service on Shavuot we read the Book of Ruth, *Megillat* (Scroll of) *Rut* (pronounced "root").[46] It tells the story of Ruth, a Moabite woman who converted to Judaism and became the epitome of a righteous convert. Why was this reading chosen for the festival of receiving the Torah? Some explain that Ruth's tremendous self-sacrifice in abandoning her country, her wealth and her comfort in order to become part of the Jewish people is a lesson to us all about priorities in life. Ruth teaches us that the truth of Torah is worth any sacrifice. If necessary, we too must be ready to give up what we erroneously thought was valuable for that which is truly valuable, the Torah.[47]

Another possible reason for reading Ruth publicly is that on Shavuot we all look upon ourselves as converts to Judaism. When the Jewish people came to Mt. Sinai, they unconditionally accepted the entire Torah and God's sovereignty. They purified themselves, the men were circumcised and the entire people entered into a covenant with God. Each of these steps is repeated by every convert to Judaism, in order to recreate the experience of Mt. Sinai, which is necessary to become Jewish. All the laws governing conversion are actually derived from the "mass conversion" of the Hebrews who came out of Egypt and became the Jewish people.[48] It is appropriate, therefore to read the story of the prototype of the righteous convert, Ruth, to see the greatness that she achieved despite her pagan background. Another reason the Book of Ruth is recited is that Ruth's great-grandson was King David,[49] who was born on Shavuot (and 70 years later, died on Shavuot).[50] The Messiah will ultimately trace his lineage to King David.

The First Fruits – Chag Habikurim

Shavuot was also the time when the first fruits, *Bikurim*, were brought to the Temple in Jerusalem from all over Israel. The Torah commands us, "The choicest first fruit of your land you shall bring to the House of the Lord, your God..."[51] and in fact, Shavuot is identified in the Bible as the Festival of the Harvest.[52]

Offering the first fruits is perhaps one of the ultimate expressions of gratitude to God. A farmer works hard for months, even years, in order to produce a crop. His elation at seeing the first fruits of his labor is incomparable to other joys. But, instead of keeping those fruits and celebrating his own achievements, he brings them to Jerusalem and gives thanks to God for His benevolence. He recognizes that even with all his work, his success is totally dependent on God. The rain, the wind, the climate and the water are all beyond his control. Therefore, as he plants the seeds he must have faith,[53] and gratitude when he harvests the fruits.

This festival was a major event in ancient Israel, full of pageantry and beauty, as described in the following selections from the Mishnah:[54]

> *A man would go down to his field and see a fig growing, a bunch of grapes forming or a pomegranate that ripened; he would tie a string around the fruit and would say, "These are bikurim." People from small villages would gather together in a central location… and the appointed person would declare, "Let us get up and go to Zion, to the House of the Lord, our God."[55]… Those closest to Jerusalem would bring (fresh) figs and grapes; those from further away would bring dried figs and raisins.*
>
> *An ox with gold-covered horns would walk before them and it would be adorned with a wreath of olive branches on its head. Flutes would be played in front of the procession until they came close to Jerusalem. When they neared Jerusalem, they would send messengers to the city… the leaders and officers would come out to greet them… and all the workers and tradesmen of Jerusalem would stand and greet them, saying, "Our brothers from___ , you have come in peace."*
>
> *They would be accompanied by music until they came to the Temple Mount… then they would take their baskets on their shoulders and bring them into the courtyard of the Temple… The Levites would sing, "I will exalt You, God, for You have drawn me up and not let my foes rejoice over me…"[56] As each person would give his basket to the priests he would read the section of the Torah from [the passage that begins], "I declare today to the Lord, your God, that I have come to the Land that God swore to our forefathers to give us…" until the end of the section, "He brought us to this place, and He gave us this Land, a Land flowing with milk and honey. And now, behold! I have brought the first fruit of the ground that You have given me, O God!"[57]*

Due to the destruction of the Temple this *mitzvah* cannot be fulfilled today, and it has become a lesser-known component of Shavuot. It is still commemorated, however, in the Torah reading for Shavuot and in our festival prayers.

It is also customary to decorate synagogues and homes with flow-ers and branches on Shavuot, because that is the time that God judges the Jewish people regarding the success of their fruit trees.[58] In addi-tion, Rabbi Samson Raphael Hirsch points out that just as on Shavuot the first summer fruits ripen, so too, the Jewish people "ripen" as a nation. The seeds of our nationhood were planted at the Exodus, but we only truly ripened into a mature nation when we received the Torah on Shavuot.[59]

Insomnia at the Levy House

Shlomo Levy's Palm Pilot® beeps at 9 p.m. to remind him to count the Omer. Tonight is the last night of the Omer, so he recites the blessing and counts 49 days, 7 weeks. Tomorrow night, Shavuot will begin and Shlomo will be spending the holiday at his yeshivah in order to study with his chavruta (study partner) through Shavuot night.

The Levy house is already filled with the delicious smells of cooking for the festival. Like most families, the Levys have cheesecake, cheese blintzes and various other dairy treats on Shavuot. They usually eat a dairy meal on the first night so that during the all-night learning they can take breaks for infusions of coffee with milk, and cheesecake.

The following afternoon, Tova, Eli, Esther and several of their friends spend a few hours decorating the synagogue with greenery and flowers. They are eagerly awaiting the arrival of their grandparents who are coming to spend Shavuot with them.

On Shavuot evening the service starts late. It is almost 10 p.m. by the time the men arrive home for the festive Yom Tov meal. Mr. Levy says Kiddush[60] over wine and a blessing over two loaves of challah. The family then enjoys a sumptuous dairy meal (blintzes, cold fruit soup, grilled salmon, cheese soufflé, assorted salads and dessert of New York-style cheesecake, cherry cheesecake and/or ice-cream). The meal is accompanied by singing and discussion of Torah ideas related to the festival and to topics that the children are studying in school.

The older Levy children have made arrangements to study Torah with a partner throughout the night. The younger children take turns learning with Mr. Levy immediately after dinner. They delight in the fact that they are allowed to stay up as late as they like on Shavuot night (kept awake by cheesecake and chocolate), as long as they continue learning Torah. The children's teachers usually give out source books and study materials for Shavuot night.

A little after midnight, Mr. Levy goes to the synagogue to study with Ben, his regular chavruta. He and Ben meet every night after work to learn Talmud together, and over the years they've accomplished quite a lot. Tonight, they will review the sections of Talmud that they have been studying most recently. Once the younger children are finally settled down, Mrs. Levy arranges chairs and source materials in preparation for a class that she will teach about the Book of Ruth. Women begin to arrive at her home a short time later, anxious to hear her insights on this poignant story.

The morning service on the first day of Shavuot begins at the crack of dawn, after a complete night of learning. A later service is also held for those who slept. The prayers are enhanced by beautiful, traditional festival melodies and are followed by the Torah reading. On the first day, the reading is of the stirring account of God's giving of the Torah to the Jews at Mt. Sinai, and the Ten Commandments.[61] This reading is preceded by an 11th-century Aramaic poem that describes the awesome and infinite nature of the Torah, the holiness of God as the Ruler of the (spiritual) Heavens and (material) earth, and asks His permission to read His holy Torah:

> His is eternal strength that could not be described —
> Even if the heavens were parchment, and the forests quills,
> If all oceans were ink ...[and even]
> If the earth's inhabitants were scribes and recorders of words ...[62]

After services, the synagogue sponsors a light breakfast, where people can make Kiddush, eat a cheese Danish (or two) and then go home to sleep until it is time for a late lunch.

The rest of the festival is much more relaxed. The first day is usually spent recovering from being up all night studying. (It is not customary to stay up the second night). The second day's prayers are similar to the first, except for a different Torah reading, the Scroll of Ruth and the addition of the special memorial prayer for the departed, Yizkor.[63]

In the late afternoon of the second day, the rabbi gives a class for the community, followed by the afternoon service, a light snack and the evening service. The Levy family ends the festival with the Havdalah[64] prayer over a cup of wine, then joyfully wish each other shavua tov (Hebrew, "[Have a] good week.") or gutt voch (Yiddish).

Selected Laws and Customs
of Counting the Omer and of Shavuot

1. On the second night of Passover, we begin counting the *Omer*.[65]

2. The *Omer* is counted every night until the eve of Shavuot.

3. The *Omer* should be counted after nightfall and is customarily counted immediately following the Silent Prayer of the evening service. One may count the *Omer* anytime during the night.[66]

4. One should stand when counting the *Omer*.[67]

5. The *Omer* can be counted in any language one understands.[68] However, Hebrew may be used even if one does not understand Hebrew. (Translations are available!)

6. One should count both the days and the number of weeks (and days of the *Omer*).[69] For example: "Today is 9 days, which are 1 week and 2 days of the *Omer*."

7. A blessing is said before counting. Be aware of the number for that night before saying the blessing.[70] Some people also add prayers before and after the counting.[71] For the complete version of the counting, see *The Complete ArtScroll Siddur, Ashkenaz*, pp. 282 – 287.

8. If one forgot to count at night, one should count during the day without saying a blessing. One may then continue to count on subsequent nights with a blessing. If, however, one did not count at all, even during the day, then on subsequent nights one should count till the end of the *Omer* without saying a blessing.[72]

9. For 33 days of the *Omer* one should not take a haircut, shave or listen to music. Weddings are not held during this period.[73] There are some exceptions and leniencies regarding these laws; therefore one should consult a rabbi if there are extenuating circumstances.

10. There are various customs as to when the 33-day semimourning period could begin. Some people start from the beginning of the *Omer* and end at the 33rd day of the *Omer*. Others begin the first or second day of the Hebrew month of Iyar and continue until three days before Shavuot.[74]

11. Shavuot is celebrated on the 50th day after Passover,[75] the seventh of the Hebrew month of Sivan, from just before sundown until after nightfall. Outside of Israel, Shavuot is a two-day festival. In Israel it is celebrated for one day.

12. Candles are lit (usually by the lady of the house) just before Shavuot begins on the first night and after the onset of the second night. (On the second night one lights from a preexisting flame.) (Some people have the custom of lighting festival candles after nightfall from a pre-existing flame, unlike Shabbat when candles must be lit before sundown.) Two blessings are recited before lighting the candles: "Blessed are You, our God, King of the universe, Who has sanctified us with His commandments and commanded us to kindle the light of the festival;" and (Shehecheyanu) "Blessed are You, our God, King of the universe, Who has kept us alive, sustained us and brought us to this season."[76]

13. As on all other Yamim Tovim (Festive Days, pl.), it is prohibited to do any work on Shavuot, with the exception of activities directly related to the preparation of food that cannot be done in advance. (For example, one may place something on an existing fire to cook, but not light the fire.)[77]

14. One should honor and enjoy the festival. We honor the day by getting a haircut and/or shaving, bathing and putting on nice clothing in preparation for the festival. Ensuring that our home is clean and the table elegantly set is also part of the honor of the festival. It is also customary for men to immerse in a mikveh (ritual pool) on the eve of Shavuot. A husband should buy new clothing or jewelry for his wife (or encourage her to do so herself!). Parents give sweets and presents to their children.[78]

15. One should eat (at least) two festive meals on each day of Shavuot. One should make Kiddush before each meal, and say a blessing over two loaves of bread as on other festivals and Shabbat.[79]

16. It is customary to eat dairy foods on Shavuot. Due to the custom of eating meat on Shabbat and festivals, however, there is usually an attempt to include meat meals as well. Some people eat dairy hors d'oeuvres, then change the table settings and continue with a meat meal, eating something neutral (parve) in between. Others have one meal that is entirely dairy, and some

have a dairy snack for the *Kiddush* after morning service and then proceed to meat meals.[80]

17. Special festive prayers are recited on Shavuot, including *Hallel* (*The Complete ArtScroll Siddur Ashkenaz*, pp. 632-643), the festival silent prayer (ibid. 660-671) and the additional service for festivals (ibid. 674-691). There are specific Torah readings for Shavuot also (ibid. 966-970), as well as the reading of the Scroll of Ruth.

18. It is customary to stay up all night on the first night of Shavuot and study Torah until dawn.[81] Many people study selections from all the classic texts of the Torah, Prophets, Writings, Mishnah and Talmud. These selections are found in the *Tikkun Leil Shavuot*.

19. *Havdalah* (separation prayer) is recited over a cup of wine at the end of Shavuot.[82]

For Further Reading

▸ *Permission to Receive* by Rabbi Leib Keleman (Feldheim/Targum, 1996)

▸ *Shavuos: Its Observance, Laws, and Significance* (ArtScroll/Mesorah, 1995)

▸ *The Book of Ruth* (ArtScroll/Mesorah, 1976)

NOTES

References to books of the Talmud refer to the Babylonian Talmud unless otherwise noted.

1. Exodus Chaps. 19 and 20.
2. Rabbi Sa'adiah Gaon, *Haemunot Vehadeot*, 3:7.
3. Nachmanides, *Commentary on Exodus*, Introduction.
4. Exodus 19:1; Leviticus 23:15-22.
5. Leviticus ibid.
6. Rabbi Aaron Halevi, *Sefer Hachinuch*, Parshat Emor, Mitzvah 306.
7. Leviticus 23:10-14.
8. Ibid. 23:17.
9. *Sotah* 9a.
10. Genesis 3:19, Deuteronomy 8:3.
11. Maharal, *Tiferet Yisrael*, Chap. 25.
12. *Rosh Hashanah* 21b.
13. Maimonides, *Mishneh Torah*, Laws of Idolatry, 1:3; Nachmanides, *Commentary on the Torah*, Exodus 12:40.
14. *Likutei Torah*, Vayera; Rabbi Chaim ibn Attar, *Ohr Hachaim*, Exodus 3:7 and Deuteronomy 32:10.
15. *Zohar, Raya Mehemena*, Emor 97a; *The Complete ArtScroll Siddur*, Ashkenaz, pp. 284-285, last paragraph.
16. *Yevamot* 62b.
17. Maharal, *Chidushei Aggadot, Yevamot* 62b; *Netivot Olam*, Netiv Hatorah, Chap. 12.
18. Compiled and edited by Rabbi Judah the Prince circa 200 C.E. in Israel.
19. Ibid. *Yevamot*; Maimonides, *Commentary on the Mishnah*, Introduction.
20. *Code of Jewish Law, Orach Chaim* 493:1-4.
21. *Code of Jewish Law*, ibid.
22. *Zohar, Idra Zutta,* Introduction.
23. The central text of the *Kabbalah*, arranged as a commentary on the Five Books of Moses and other parts of the Bible, is attributed to the students of Rabbi Shimon bar Yochai, who wrote down his teachings and compiled them c. 200 C.E. It was first published in 1290 by Rabbi Moshe de Leon in Spain.
24. Rashi on *Yevamot* 122a, "*Tilta riglei.*"
25. *Code of Jewish Law, Orach Chaim* 531, *Shaarei Teshuvah* 2.
26. Rabbi Ovadiah of Bartenoro, Letter to his brother, 5249 (1489).
27. *Shabbat* 86b-87b.
28. Heard from Rabbi Moshe Shapiro.
29. See chapter on the Calendar.
30. Exodus 24:7.
31. *Zohar*, Leviticus 3:98a; *Code of Jewish Law, Orach Chaim* 494:1, *Mishnah Berurah* 1.
32. These selections are compiled in a book called *Tikkun Leil Shavuot.*
33. Exodus 20:15; *Midrash Rabbah*, Exodus ad loc. 5:16.
34. For instance, the story of Mohammed on the mountain (Islam), Joseph Smith in a cave (Church of the Latter Day Saints — Mormon), and the private "resurrection" of Jesus (Christianity).
35. Exodus 20:1-3.
36. Maimonides, *Mishneh Torah*, Laws of Foundations of the Torah, Chap. 8 and Letter to Yemen.
37. Rabbi Yehudah Halevy, *The Kuzari*, 1:87; Lawrence Kelemen, *Permission to Receive*, pp. 50-78. Targum Press, Jerusalem, 1996. Rabbi Dr. Dovid Gottlieb, *Living Up to the Truth*, www.dovidgottlieb.com or www.ohr.edu.
38. Exodus 19:9-11; 16-20.
39. Deuteronomy 4:32-36.
40. Isaiah 43:10.
41. According to Nachmanides, *Critique of Maimonides' Book of the Mitzvot,* Negative Mitzvot 2. Although Maimonides does not list this commandment, he certainly maintains that it is an obligation. He does not list it, either because he believes that it is part and parcel of the commandment to teach Torah (according to Rabbi Moshe Shapiro) or because it

is an all-encompassing general obligation rather than a specific *mitzvah* (*Megillat Esther* ad loc.).

42. *Code of Jewish Law, Orach Chaim*, 494:3, Ramah; *Mishnah Berurah* 12.

43. Ibid. *Mishnah Berurah* 13.

44. Song of Songs 4:11.

45. Proverbs 3:17.

46. Ibid. 490:9, Ramah.

47. Ibid. *Mishnah Berurah* 17.

48. Maimonides, *Mishneh Torah*, Laws of Forbidden Relationships, Chap. 13:1-5.

49. Scroll of Ruth, 4:18-22.

50. *Shaarei Teshuvah* 2 on *Code of Jewish Law* 494.

51. Exodus 23:19 and 34:26.

52. Ibid. 23:16.

53. *Shabbat* 31a, Tosafot ad loc. "*Emunat.*"

54. Mishnah *Bikurim*, Chap. 3, 1-9.

55. Based on Jeremiah 31:5.

56. Psalm 30:2.

57. Deuteronomy 26:3-10.

58. *Rosh Hashanah* 16a; *Code of Jewish Law, Orach Chaim*, 494:2 Ramah, Magen Avraham ad loc. *Mishnah Berurah* 9.

59. Rabbi Samson Raphael Hirsch, *Horeb,* II Edoth, Chap. 23, para. 166.

60. A blessing regarding the sanctity and significance of the festival. *The Complete ArtScroll Siddur, Ashkenaz,* pp. 657-659.

61. Exodus 19:1-20:23.

62. *The Complete ArtScroll Siddur, Ashkenaz*, pp. 714-719.

63. Ibid. pp. 810-815.

64. Ibid. pp. 618-621.

65. *Code of Jewish Law, Orach Chaim*, 489:1.

66. Ibid.

67. Ibid.

68. Ibid. *Mishnah Berurah* 5.

69. *Code of Jewish Law*, ibid.

70. Ibid. 489:6.

71. *Code of Jewish Law*, Ibid. *Be'er Heitev* 9; *Mishnah Berurah* 10.

72. *Code of Jewish Law,* ibid. 489:7.

73. Ibid. 493: 1-2.

74. Ibid. 493:2-3. *Mishnah Berurah* 14.

75. *Code of Jewish Law*, ibid. 494:1.

76. *The Complete ArtScroll Siddur, Ashkenaz*, pp. 296-297.

77. Leviticus 23:24-25; *Code of Jewish Law, Orach Chaim*, 495:1.

78. *Code of Jewish Law, Orach Chaim*, 529:1-2.

79. Ibid. 529:1.

80. Ibid. 494:3, Ramah. *Mishnah Berurah* ad loc.

81. Ibid. 494:1, *Mishnah Berurah* 1.

82. *The Complete ArtScroll Siddur, Ashkenaz*, pp. 618-619.

Slow Down, It's a Fast Day

The history and purpose of the Jewish fast days

he Jewish calendar includes six days of fasting. Four of these days are linked to the destruction of the First and Second Holy Temples in Jerusalem and the exile of the Jewish people from the Land of Israel.[1] These will be the focus of this chapter. The other two — Yom Kippur (sometimes known as the Day of Atonement) and Ta'anit Esther (the Fast of Esther) — are discussed in the chapters dealing with the holidays to which they are closely related: Yom Kippur and Purim.

Fasting – Means to an End

Eighty days of the year we are commanded to feast,[2] while we are forbidden to eat or drink for only six days of the year — a 13 to 1 ratio of feasting to fasting! Rather than being ascetic, Judaism clearly rejoices in life and seeks to elevate the material world through the commandments. We have even been described as "gastrocentric," since virtually all Jewish celebrations and festivals involve food.

The purpose of the fast days is to achieve a certain mood or state of mind, not self-torture. Maimonides states:

> The Torah commands us to cry out [to God]... when any tragedy strikes the community... This is part of the process of repentance — when a misfortune occurs and the community prays, cries out and assembles, they will realize that this has happened as a result of their sins... And the Sages further obligated the community to fast on the occasion of any tragedy...[3]

The prophets mention the obligation to mourn the exile through fasting,[4] but they stress that the fast is primarily a means to gather the entire community together for prayer:

> Blow the shofar in Zion; decree a fast; call an assembly; gather the people; summon the congregation; assemble the elders; gather the children... and let them say, "Have pity, God, upon Your people..."[5]

In the Book of Jonah, God calls upon Jonah to inform the citizens of the city of Nineveh that unless they change their ways, correct the injustices in their city and refrain from theft, God would destroy their city.[6] The people of Nineveh took the warning seriously: *The people of Nineveh believed in God, so they proclaimed a fast and donned sackcloth.*[7] Even the king proclaimed a public fast day, and concluded his command with the following words: *Every man shall turn back from his evil way, and from the robbery that is in his hands.*[8]

The Talmud points out that the fasting, sackcloth and mourning of the people of Nineveh were means to an end, vehicles to behavior modification.[9] God considered the end result in His favorable judgment of Nineveh: *And God saw their* actions, *that they turned away from their evil way ...*[10]

While the examples above are on a communal level, this principle applies to us as individuals as well. The end result of a day of fasting should be self-improvement and positive change, or at the very least, acknowledgment that there is a need for change. The external aspects of the fast days are important, but the internal aspects are even more critical. If a person observes the fast meticulously, does not let a drop of water pass his lips or a crumb of bread enter his mouth, but does not engage in reflection or introspection, he or she has missed the point.[11] The prophet Joel rebuked the Jewish people for precisely this fault when he said, "Tear your hearts, not your garments!"[12]

Fasting for an entire day is certainly not pleasant, but this unpleasantness helps us to identify with the suffering of our fellow Jews throughout the exile. Through this process we should be inspired to improve our lives and become better people.

What Happened, and When?

The fast of the Ninth of Av, in Hebrew Tishah B'Av, is the most famous and the most stringent of all the fasts relating to the destruction of the Holy Temple and the exile of the Jews from the Land of Israel. (The concept is so important that "the Exile" is often capitalized, for it describes a continual state of being more than just a political event.) Yet even before the first destruction and exile by the Babylonians in 421 B.C.E., the ninth day of the Hebrew month of Av was earmarked for tragedy.

The very first tragedy to occur on this day took place soon after the Exodus from Egypt.[13] Spies had been sent to the Land of Israel, in preparation for its conquest. When the spies returned with a discouraging report, the men lost hope (though not the women)[14] of ever reaching the Holy Land. That first Tishah B'Av night, they cried in despair, thereby establishing the character of that date for the rest of history. The Babylonians destroyed the First Temple on the Ninth of Av. On the same date in 70 C.E.[15] the Romans destroyed the Second Temple; brutally put down the Bar Kochba revolt; slaughtered the inhabitants of Betar;[16] and plowed over the site of the Temple.[17]

The destruction of Jerusalem and the exile of the Jewish people from their land were, without doubt, the greatest tragedies in Jewish history. Spiritually, they signified that the Jewish people had alienated themselves from God: This distance is acutely felt and powers our yearning to return to the devotion of former years. In physical terms, these two events were the ultimate cause of all the pogroms, Inquisitions, *jihads*, expulsions and suffering of our people for more than 2,000 years.

Throughout Jewish history, the Ninth of Av has recurred as a day of calamity. The Jews were expelled from England on Tishah B'Av, 1290, and the Spanish Inquisition culminated in the expulsion of the Jews from Spain on Tishah B'Av, 1492. Germany declared war on Russia on Tishah B'Av in 1914, precipitating the First World War, which had tragic repercussions on the Jews of Europe and also ultimately led to the Second World War and the Holocaust.

Great Jewish scholars and poets throughout the centuries composed *Kinot,* elegies that lament these and other tragedies. Recent scholars have written *Kinot* about the Holocaust, adding further to this large collection of poems and prayers.[18] Traditionally, we recite these *Kinot* on Tishah B'Av while sitting in an attitude of mourning, on low benches or the floor.

The Light in the Darkness

Despite the dreadful, heartbreaking nature of Tishah B'Av, an element of happiness is concealed within it. Tishah B'Av is called a *mo'ed*,[19] meaning festival, and certain prayers associated with sadness are, in fact, not said on this day.[20] What is the source of the joy that lightens our mourning on Tishah B'Av? Some commentaries explain that it springs from the knowledge that eventually, at the time of the Redemption, Tishah B'Av and the other fast days will become festivals and times of joy, as Zechariah prophesied:

> The fast of the fourth [i.e., in the fourth month, the Seventeenth of Tamuz], the fast of the fifth, [the Ninth of Av] the fast of the seventh [the Fast of Gedaliah] and the fast of the tenth [the Tenth of Tevet] will be to the House of Judah for joy and for gladness and as happy festivals.[21]

The Talmud relates the following incident that occurred approximately 50 years after the destruction of the Temple:

> [Rabbi Gamliel, Rabbi Elazar Ben Azariah, Rabbi Yehoshua and Rabbi Akiva] were walking to Jerusalem… At the Temple Mount they saw a fox leaving the ruins of the Holy of Holies, the innermost sanctuary of the Temple.[22] They [the first three] cried and Rabbi Akiva laughed. They asked, "Why are you laughing?"
> He asked them, "Why are you crying?"
> They answered, "The place about which it is written, 'any alien [non-Kohen] who approaches shall die,'[23] now has foxes walking in it! Shouldn't we cry?"
> He said to them, "That is why I am laughing… The prophecy [of the ultimate Redemption] of Zechariah is contingent upon the prophecy [of destruction] of the prophet Uriah. Regarding Uriah it is written, 'And, therefore, because of you, Zion shall be plowed like a field.'[24] In Zechariah it is written, 'The old men and women will return and sit in the streets of Jerusalem…'[25] Now that the prophecy of Uriah has been fulfilled, we know that the prophecy of Zechariah will also be realized…"
> They said to him, "Akiva, you have comforted us! Akiva, you have comforted us!"[26]

Rabbi Akiva saw that destruction was only a prelude to Redemption. Just as the plowing of a field prepares it for planting, so the plowing of Jerusalem was a preparation for planting the seeds of Redemption.

To better understand Rabbi Akiva's perspective, let us imagine the case of an alcoholic who continuously denies that he has a problem and blames every mishap and mistake on others. After months of warnings, he is dismissed from his job. He arrives home to find a note from his wife that she has left him and taken the children with her. The bank manager phones to inform him that they are foreclosing on his mortgage and are also repossessing his car. In a deep depression, he sits down to watch television and is interrupted by a knock on the door. The final blow has arrived — a technician has come to disconnect his cable. On one black day, he lost his family, his income, his house and his car. All these events occurring on the same day finally force him to recognize the connection between them and to acknowledge that his alcoholism was the cause of these tragedies.

As a result, he checks into a rehabilitation clinic, dries out, sobers up and comes out a new man. He gets his job back, makes his car and mortgage payments and shows his wife that he has really changed. She returns home with the children, the cable is reconnected and they live happily ever after.

Will this man look at the day he was fired as a day of misfortune or as the luckiest day of his life? If, because of that day, his life changed dramatically for the better and he found the happiness that had eluded him until then, he will celebrate that date every year as a festival. This may be a metaphorical meaning of the statement that "the Messiah was born on the day of the Temple's destruction"[27] — the seeds of the Redemption already existed at the time of destruction.

In the future, when the Jewish people achieve full spiritual rehabilitation, we will look back on Tishah B'Av with appreciation. We will understand that if not for the incredible Divine Providence manifested on that day throughout history, we might have shrugged off every misfortune as "bad luck." It is for this reason that Tishah B'Av is called a "festival." Only someone with the insight of Rabbi Akiva was able to perceive the light even in the midst of destruction; for most of us, this is possible only with hindsight.

Another explanation for Rabbi Akiva's laughter is suggested by Rabbi Sa'adiah Gaon, a tenth-century Jewish philosopher.[28] He explains that all laughter is caused by the soul gaining a correct perception of reality. Truth shows us the absurdity of our previous false perception and the soul reacts with joy, which is manifested in laughter. Rabbi Akiva[29] had a deeper perception of reality than others and therefore he was always in a state of happiness, and was able to laugh even when foxes ran in the Holy of Holies.[30] His acute perception of reality allowed him to immediately see the true message of hope in the very event that caused his colleagues to mourn.

The Siege of Jerusalem

The Babylonian Empire first laid siege to Jerusalem on the Tenth of Tevet, 423 B.C.E., cutting it off from the outside world.[31] This not only laid the groundwork for the destruction of the Holy Temple but also caused horrific suffering for the besieged population of Jerusalem, thousands of whom died from starvation and disease.[32]

Another tragedy lies within this day, however, that is less obvious. Jerusalem is meant to be the source of inspiration to the world and the place from which Torah and the word of God reach out to everyone.[33] A siege prevents supplies from entering a city, and it also prevents any communication from the city reaching the outside world. Ever since Nebuchadnezzar, king of Babylon, laid siege to Jerusalem, the voice of this holy city has been muted. It ceased to be the spiritual beacon for the world, it lost its role as the primary center of Torah study, and the "word of God" could no longer be heard coming forth from its gates.[34]

Other voices now issued from Jerusalem — the sounds of the Crusaders, the Moslems and all her other conquerors and their cultures drowned out the sounds of Judaism. Even though the physical siege ended with the destruction of the Temple, Jerusalem remains under a spiritual siege. We fast on the Tenth of Tevet because the glory of Jerusalem as the moral and spiritual center of the world has not been fully restored — it is as if the siege of the Babylonians still continues to this day.[35]

Broken Tablets and Burnt Scrolls

The Seventeenth of Tamuz, which occurs exactly three weeks before Tishah B'Av, is the next most significant fast day. The Mishnah states:

> Five things happened to our ancestors on the Seventeenth of Tamuz: The First Tablets were broken,[36] the daily offering ceased,[37] the walls of Jerusalem were breached,[38] the evil Apostomus burnt a Torah scroll and an idol was set up in the Sanctuary.[39]

Let's look at the significance of these events. The first calamity to occur on the Seventeenth of Tamuz was the sin of the Golden Calf. Only 40 days after hearing God speak on Mt. Sinai, the Jewish men (again, not the women)[40] created and worshipped an idol. When Moses came down from Mt. Sinai and saw what had happened, he broke the Tablets of the Law that God had given to him.[41] The Jews were forgiven for this sin on the Day of Atonement and received the second set of Tablets. Nevertheless, the perfect unity of the Jewish people with the Torah, which had been created at Mt. Sinai, was now damaged. With the sin of the Golden Calf they weakened their connection to the Revelation at Mt. Sinai and created the possibility that in the future, other Jews would also sever their connection to the teachings first begun at Mt. Sinai. Had they not sinned in this way, such a possibility would never have existed.

Similarly, when the Jews rejected the Land of Israel by despairing at the report of the spies on Tishah B'Av, they cut off their connection to the Land and thereby created the possibility of a Jewish people disconnected from the Land of Israel. In essence, all the tragedies of the Exile are products of our separation from Torah and from the holiness of the Land of Israel.[42] This idea is alluded to in Lamentations, which is read in the synagogue on Tishah B'Av: "All her pursuers overtook her, in dire straits."[43]

The words "in dire straits"[44] can also be translated as "between the calamities," a reference to the period between the Seventeenth of Tammuz and the Ninth of Av. The commentaries point out that every punishment visited upon the Jewish people carries within it a tiny measure of punishment of the sin of the Golden Calf and that of the spies that took place on those dates.[45]

The second tragedy mentioned by the Mishnah was the cessation of the daily offering. This was a communal offering which was brought in the Temple in Jerusalem every morning and every afternoon on behalf of the entire Jewish people.[46] It was a continual reminder to the Jewish people of their connection to God and their obligation to Him, as well as of their connection to one another as parts of a single body. It reminded them that the focus of their national life was in the spiritual realm, and that as individuals their connection with God could only be guaranteed by observance of the Torah and affiliation with the nation.[47] During the siege of Jerusalem, supplies ran out, and for the first time in over half a millennium, the daily offering ceased.

Both the Babylonians[48] and the Romans[49] laid siege to Jerusalem and caused the death of thousands by starvation, disease and violence. During both sieges, the walls of Jerusalem were breached on the Seventeenth of Tamuz,[50] beginning the bloody battles for possession of Jerusalem and the Temple Mount.

The next two catastrophes listed in the Mishnah do not seem as serious as the first three — the burning of a Torah scroll and the setting up of an idol seem to be minor events in comparison to the destruction of Jerusalem and its population. In order to understand the magnitude of these events, we must take a deeper look at the tragedy of exile.

Perhaps the most terrible aspect of exile and destruction is the illusion it creates that God is not present or is not concerned with our fate. The prophet Joel expressed this concern:

> Have pity, God, upon Your people — let not Your heritage be an object of scorn, for nations to dominate them. Why should they say among the peoples, "Where is their God?"[51]

To all appearances, the Divine Presence was absent when a pagan Roman general, Apostomus, was able to publicly burn a Torah scroll, and an idol was erected in the Temple itself. The Hebrew expression for this illusion is "chillul Hashem," usually translated as "desecration of God's Name." The literal translation, "absence of God's Name," reflects this idea, because any action of blatant rebellion against God that occurs without hindrance creates the impression that "God is not here." In reality, God is everywhere. Even at the moment that an evil person commits a sin, it is God Who sustains him and gives him life and the free will to act as he chooses.[52] When confronted with the falsehood of a *"chillul Hashem"* we surely have reason to mourn.[53] It is during these times of suffering that the whole world asks, "Where is your God?"

The Fast of Gedaliah

The Book of Jeremiah[54] relates the horrific downfall of the Jewish king Zedekiah[55] and the subsequent destruction of Jerusalem. The king's sons were slaughtered in front of him, after which he was blinded so that the last thing that he would ever see was the death of his children. Bound in chains, he was taken to Babylon as a prisoner. King Nebuchadnezzar of Babylon exiled the rest of the Jews from the Land of Israel but "appointed Gedaliah, son of Ahikam, over the land … and entrusted him with men, women and children and some of the poor people of the land who were not exiled to Babylon."[56] Eventually many Jews who had fled Israel heard that the king of Babylon had appointed a Jewish governor. They returned to Israel and the community grew and prospered. Baalis, king of Amon, was distressed by the success and growth of the community in Israel and he sent Yishmael, son of Nethaniah, to assassinate Gedaliah. Although Gedaliah was warned about the assassination attempt, he ignored the warning.[57] He was murdered along with many of his Jewish and Babylonian colleagues.

The assassination of Gedaliah put an end to the newly revived Jewish community in Israel. Thousand died in the violent upheavals following the assassination, and thousands more fled the Land of Israel in fear of Babylonian reprisals. This event extinguished the last spark of Jewish government in Israel[58] and was therefore established as a public fast day. The Fast of Gedaliah immediately follows the New Year, Rosh Hashanah, on the third of the Hebrew month of Tishrei, and is referred to in the prophets as the "fast of the seventh [month]."[59]

The Talmud notes an essential lesson of this fast day: *This teaches you that the death of a righteous person is equivalent to the burning of the Sanctuary of God.* [60]

What does this statement mean? The Kabbalists describe the Holy Temple as comprised of both spiritual and physical elements, just as a human being has a physical body housing his immortal, spiritual soul.[61] Therefore, when the spiritual Temple was undermined through the corrupt and hypocritical actions of the Jewish people, the physical Temple became vulnerable. It was only when the Jewish people had completely destroyed the inner spiritual Temple with their sins that the Babylonians and Romans were able to destroy the physical Temple.[62]

Now on to the next step: Just as the Divine Presence was manifested in the Temple in Jerusalem, so too the Divine Presence is manifested in a righteous person. Thus the death of a righteous person is equal to the destruction of the Temple. This insight is manifested in the observance of the Fast of Gedaliah.

Causes of the Destruction

Why did God allow these tragedies to befall the Jewish people? What terrible deeds led to the destruction of the Temple and the exile of the Jewish people? If we understand the fundamental flaws that precipitated these events, we can begin to take the first steps toward Redemption. The Talmud tells us: *Any generation in whose days the Temple was not rebuilt is considered as though the Temple was destroyed in its days.*[63]

The fact that we have not yet merited the Redemption means that at some level we are still guilty of the very sins that caused the Exile! The Talmud describes the transgressions that led to the destruction of the First and Second Temples:

The First Temple was destroyed because the Jewish people transgressed the three cardinal sins of idol worship, murder and sexual immorality. However, during the Second Temple period the Jews engaged in Torah study and fulfilled the commandments! For what sin was it destroyed? For the sin of groundless hatred, i.e., hatred that is not a response to another's evil actions.[64] This teaches us that the sin of hatred is equivalent to transgressions of idol worship, murder and sexual immorality.[65]

It would appear that the two Temples were destroyed for quite different, although equally serious, sins. A closer examination of these transgressions, however, reveals their common origin. Idol worship is the most extreme form of severing one's relationship with God. Murder reflects the complete breakdown of one's relationship to other human beings. Sexual immorality is a "victimless crime" but it undermines the individual's spiritual purity; *the victim is his own soul.*[66] The cause of the destruction of the Second Temple, "groundless hatred," springs from egocentric self-worship. "I hate others because something has offended *me*, someone has more than *me*, someone is happier than *me*, or someone is different from *me*." Placing oneself at the center of existence to the exclusion and negation of everyone else is the ultimate cause of all other sins — therefore the Talmud equates it with idol worship, murder and sexual immorality.[67] The totally self-centered person cannot have a relationship with God nor with other people, and even his relationship with his own soul is corrupted.

In order to correct this sin, we must develop the opposite characteristics of selflessness, generosity and "groundless love." Rabbi Abraham Isaac HaCohen Kook, the first Ashkenazic Chief Rabbi of Palestine (1921), is often quoted on this point: "If the Temple was destroyed because of unfounded, baseless hatred, then it can only be rebuilt by unfounded, baseless love."

Selected Laws of the Fast Days

1. With the exception of the Ninth of Av and the Day of Atonement, all fast days start at dawn and end at nightfall.[68]

2. One may not eat or drink on a fast day.[69]

3. If a person is sick, pregnant or nursing, he or she may not have to fast, depending on the situation.[70] A rabbi should be consulted.

4. If there is the slightest possibility that fasting will endanger a person, that person is exempt from fasting. (E.g., diabetics and/or people prone to dehydration should consult their physician and a rabbi for details.)[71]

5. Special prayers and Torah readings are recited on fast days.[72]

The Three Weeks

1. The Seventeenth of Tamuz marks the beginning of a three-week period of mourning (popularly known as "the Three Weeks") and culminates in the fast of the Ninth of Av.[73]

2. During The Three Weeks weddings are not held, no music is played and Ashkenazic Jews[74] do not shave or take haircuts. Sephardic Jews[75] observe these restrictions only during the week in which Tishah B'Av falls.[76]

The Nine Days

1. Mourning increases at the beginning of the month of Av and continues for nine days until the Ninth of Av.[77]

2. During the Nine Days, beginning with the eve of Rosh Chodesh Av and ending at noon on the Tenth of Av (unless the Tenth of Av falls out on a Sunday), the following rules apply:

▶ No meat (including poultry) or wine may be consumed, except on Shabbat.[78]

▶ Clothing should not be laundered or dry-cleaned, even for use after Tishah B'Av.[79]

▶ Clothing which was previously laundered or cleaned should not be worn for the first time during this period, except for Shabbat.[80]

▶ One should refrain from swimming or bathing for pleasure during this period. (Washing or showering in order to remove dirt or perspiration is permitted, as is washing or showering for Shabbat.)[81]

Laws of the Ninth of Av

1. Tishah B'Av is observed from the eve of the Ninth of Av (sunset of the eighth of Av) until the eve of the tenth of Av (when the first stars appear on the night following the Ninth of Av). If the Ninth falls on Shabbat, Tishah B'Av is observed from Saturday night until the first stars appear on Sunday evening. Eating is forbidden from sunset on Saturday.[82]

2. A special meal symbolizing mourning is eaten before Tishah B'Av. It consists of bread, and an egg dipped in ashes. The meal should not be eaten with a group of people.[83] Of course, one should eat well and drink plenty of water the day before Tishah B'Av. The special meal of mourning is generally eaten after a hearty meal.

3. The following activities are prohibited for the entire 24 hours of Tishah B'Av:[84]

▶ Eating or drinking (including rinsing the mouth)

▶ Washing (even with cold water). Morning ritual washing of hands or washing after using the bathroom is permitted.[85]

▶ Using lotions or body oils[86]

▶ Wearing leather shoes[87]

▶ Sexual intimacy[88]

▶ Study of Torah subjects not related to the day[89]

4. From the eve of the Ninth of Av until noon the next day, it is forbidden to sit on regular seats. It is customary to sit on low benches or cushions placed on the floor.[90]

5. One should not work or engage in business on Tishah B'Av.[91]

6. *Tefillin* are not worn at the morning service, nor is a blessing made on *tzitzit*. *Tefillin* are worn for the afternoon prayers, at which time the blessing on the *tallit gadol* is also said, as well as for the *tallit katan* (for one who does not wear a *tallit gadol*).[92]

7. At the afternoon service, the prayers *Nacheim*[93] and *Aneinu*[94] are added to the Silent Prayer in the blessing of *V'liYerushalayim* and *Shma Koleinu* respectively. We also say *Sim Shalom* in place of *Shalom Rav*. If one forgot these additions or changes and completed that blessing, one need not repeat the prayer.[95]

For Further Reading

▶ *A Time to Weep* by Rabbi Leibel Reznick (CIS Publishers, 1993)

▶ *Eichah/Lamentations* (ArtScroll/Mesorah, 1976)

▶ *Jerusalem, The Eye of the Universe* by Rabbi Aryeh Kaplan (also available with photos as *Jerusalem, the Eye of the Universe: A Pictorial Tour of the Holy City*) (OU/NCSY, 1997)

▶ *Kinnos/Tishah B'Av Service* (ArtScroll/Mesorah, 1991)

▶ *Tishah B'Av: Texts, Readings, and Insights* (ArtScroll/Mesorah, 1992)

NOTES

References to books of the Talmud refer to the Babylonian Talmud unless otherwise noted.

1. *Code of Jewish Law, Orach Chaim,* 503:1.

2. Most years, there are about 50 Sabbaths, 2 days of Rosh Hashanah, 8 days of Passover, 9 days of Sukkot, 2 days of Shavuot, 1 day of Purim, 8 days of Chanukah, and the day preceding Yom Kippur.

3. Maimonides, *Mishneh Torah,* Laws of Fast Days, 1:1-4.

4. Zechariah 8:1.

5. Joel 2:15-18.

6. Jonah 1:2, 3:2-4.

7. Ibid. 3:5.

8. Ibid. 3:6

9. *Ta'anit* 15a.

10. Jonah 3:10.

11. Isaiah 58:6; *Code of Jewish Law, Orach Chaim,* 579:1; *Mishnah Berurah,* 576:36.

12. Joel 2:13; see also *Ta'anit* ibid.

13. 1312 B.C.E.

14. Rashi, Numbers 26:64.

15. Mishnah *Ta'anit* 4:6.

16. 132 C.E.

17. 133 C.E.

18. See *Complete Tishah B'Av Service/ Kinnos,* ArtScroll/Mesorah Publications, NY, 1991.

19. Lamentations 1:15, 2:7.

20. *Tachanun — Code of Jewish Law, Orach Chaim,* 552:12.

21. Zechariah 8:1.

22. The innermost sanctuary of the Temple, where the Ark of the Covenant was kept. Only the High Priest entered there, and only on Yom Kippur.

23. Numbers 3:38.

24. Micah 3:12.

25. Zechariah 8:4.

26. *Makkot* 24a.

27. Midrash, *Eichah Rabbati,* 1:57. See also *Kitvei HaRamban, Vikuach-Milchamot Hashem,* Mossad Harav Kook, Jerusalem, 1986, vol.1, p. 306, para. 19-24.

28. Rabbi Sa'adiah Gaon, *Haemunot Vehadeot.*

29. The last letters of each word in the verse in Psalms 97:11, "Light is sown for the righteous and for the upright of heart, gladness," spell Rabbi Akivah — Rabbi Shlomo Luria, *Yam Shel Shlomo, Gittin* 4:31, "*Ayin.*"

30. See *Berachot* 61b; *Sanhedrin* 101a; Jerusalem Talmud, *Berachot* 9:5.

31. II Kings 25:1.

32. Nachmanides, Deuteronomy 28:42; Josephus Flavius, *The Jewish War,* Translated by G. A. Williamson, Penguin Classics, London, 1959, Chap. 17 "The Siege of Jerusalem."

33. Isaiah 2:3, Micah 4:2.

34. Ibid. Isaiah and Micah.

35. Heard from Rabbi Moshe Shapiro.

36. (In 1313 B.C.E.) See Exodus 32:19; *Ta'anit* 28b; Rashi, ibid. Exodus 32:1.

37. (In 423 B.C.E). *Ta'anit* ibid.

38. (In 423 B.C.E.) Jeremiah 39:2; ibid. 52:6; Chronicles I, 27:7.

39. (In 70 C.E.) Mishnah *Ta'anit* 4:6; Talmud *Ta'anit* ibid.

40. *Midrash Bamidbar Rabbah,* 21:10; *Midrash Tanchuma,* Pinchas 7.

41. Exodus, Chap. 32.

42. Heard from Rabbi Moshe Shapiro; see also Maharal, *Derech Hachaim,* Chap. 5, p. 228.

43. Lamentations 1:3. Written by the prophet Jeremiah, in mourning over the destruction of the First Temple.

44. In Hebrew, "*bein hametzarim.*"

45. Rashi, Numbers 14:33; See also *Sanhedrin* 102a.

46. Numbers 28:1-8.

47. Rabbi Samson Raphael Hirsch, Commentary on Numbers 28:2.

48. Under their king, Nebuchadnezzar.

49. Under Vespasian and Titus.

50. Jerusalem Talmud, *Ta'anit* 4:5; Babylonian Talmud, *Ta'anit* 28b, Maharsha ad loc.

51. Joel 2:17.

52. Rabbi Moshe Cordovero, *Tomer Devorah*, Chap. 1.

53. Rabbi Chaim of Volozhin, *Nefesh Hachaim*, 2:11.

54. Chaps. 39-41.

55. King of Judea at the time of the Babylonian invasion, a contemporary of Jeremiah.

56. Jeremiah 40:7.

57. *Niddah* 61a.

58. Maimonides, *Mishneh Torah*, Laws of Fasting, 5:2.

59. Zechariah 8:19.

60. *Rosh Hashanah* 18b.

61. *Nefesh Hachaim*, 1:4, Hagah "*lezot.*"

62. *Sanhedrin* 96b; *Nefesh Hachaim*, 1:4.

63. Jerusalem Talmud *Yoma* 1:1.

64. Rashi, Commentary on *Shabbat* 32b — *Sinat chinam*.

65. Ibid. *Yoma* 9b; Tractate *Kallah Rabati*, Chap. 8.

66. Maharal, *Derech Hachaim, Pirkei Avot* 1:2.

67. Rabbi Eliyahu Dessler, *Michtav M'Eliyahu*, vol. 2, p. 51.

68. *Code of Jewish Law, Orach Chaim*, 550:2.

69. Ibid. 550:1.

70. Ibid. 550:1, 554:5, *Mishnah Berurah* 9.

71. Ibid. 554:6, *Mishnah Berurah* 11 — Even if his life is not in danger.

72. *The Complete ArtScroll Siddur Ashkenaz*, NY, 1984, pp. 816-869 and pp. 952-954.

73. *Code of Jewish Law, Orach Chaim*, 551:9.

74. Jews of European origin.

75. Jews of Middle Eastern, African or Oriental origin.

76. Ibid. 551:2-3.

77. *Ta'anit* 26b; *Code of Jewish Law, Orach Chaim*, 551:1.

78. Ibid. 551:9.

79. Ibid. 551:3.

80. Ibid.

81. Ibid. 551:16; *Mishnah Berurah* 88; *Yoreh Deah* 381, *Pitchei Teshuvah* 2.

82. *Code of Jewish Law*, Ibid. 553:1.

83. Ibid. 553:1-2.

84. Ibid. 554:1.

85. Ibid. 554:7.

86. Ibid. 554:15.

87. Ibid. 554:16.

88. Ibid. 554:19.

89. Ibid. 554:1-3.

90. Ibid. 559:3.

91. Ibid. 554:22-24.

92. Ibid. 555:1.

93. Ibid. *The Complete ArtScroll Siddur, Ashkenaz*, pp. 240-241.

94. Ibid. pp. 242-243.

95. *Code of Jewish Law, Orach Chaim*, 557:1.

The Torah and Its Home

The Torah Scroll; history, purpose and appearance of the synagogue

The First Torah Scroll

orty years after the Exodus from Egypt, when the Jewish people were finally preparing to enter the Land of Israel, Moses wrote down everything that God had told him on Mt. Sinai and in the desert.[1] He wrote 13 scrolls on parchment, one for each of the 12 tribes of Israel, and one to place in the Tabernacle near (or inside) the Holy Ark.[2] All Torah scrolls throughout the generations are ultimately copies of these original scrolls, meticulously copied by a scribe (*sofer,* in Hebrew) from an existent scroll.[3]

The Torah is written on specially prepared parchment (*klaf*) made from a kosher animal. The scribe uses an ink that is formulated to last a long time and to retain its black color. The parchments are sewn together and wrapped around two wooden poles called *Atzei Chaim,* "Trees of Life." Silver ornaments are placed on the *Atzei Chaim,* and often a silver breastplate, held by a silver chain, adorns the front of the Torah. Ashkenazic[4] custom is to drape the Torah with a beautifully embroidered cloth cover. Sephardic Jews[5] encase the scroll in an ornately decorated wooden container, often overlaid with silver.

A Silent Witness

The last of the 613 commandments to appear in the Torah, is the *mitzvah* for every individual to write a Torah scroll:[6] "And now, write this song for yourselves, and teach it to the Children of Israel, place it in their mouths, in order that this song shall be a witness for Me among the Jewish people."[7]

What purpose does a Torah scroll serve? The presence of a Torah testifies that there was once a direct communication from the Creator to His creations, in which He informed humanity of His will. Since the Torah is the word of God, it must be preserved accurately and treated with respect. The care with which every Torah scroll is copied ensures that it will serve as a standard against which all printed and spoken excerpts can be compared. It is like a standard measure of length or weight against which all other measurements are evaluated.

The Torah is also the national treasure of the Jewish people, but unlike any other. The original Constitution of the United States is preserved under bulletproof glass and guarded by the Secret Service, but every Jewish community possesses a copy of the Torah.

The Torah scroll is revered as the repository of our nation's destiny, law and charter. In a way, it is also like a memento of our national encounter with God at the Revelation at Mt. Sinai — the event that created our national identity. The ninth-century Jewish philosopher, Sa'adiah Gaon, went to far as to say, "Our nation is a nation, only by virtue of its Torah."[8]

The Ultimate Reminder

According to Jewish law, a Jewish king is commanded to have two Torah scrolls: one to place in his treasury and one to carry with him always.[9] The scroll in his treasury indicated that the Torah is our greatest treasure, both for the truth it embodies, as well as a witness to our relationship with the Creator. The scroll kept with him reminded the king that even he is bound by its commandments. The Jewish leader is not followed by a soldier carrying nuclear weapons codes, but by a soldier in a *tallit,*[10] carrying a Torah scroll. The presence of the Torah scroll acts as a restraint on his behavior and helps the king to be a just and moral leader.

A student of mine once related an incident that vividly illustrates this idea. When he was about 17 years old, he was asked to transport a Torah scroll from Israel to America. In addition to his seat, a second seat next to him was reserved for the Torah. When the trip was over, he told me that traveling with the Torah was "worse than sitting next to a rabbi." He complained that he had to be extra careful about his movie selection, the books and magazines he read, how he spoke and with whom he struck up conversations, what he ate and how much he drank. In his words, "That scroll sitting next to me really cramped my style."

This is precisely what the Torah is meant to do for the king and indeed for every Jew — to make us aware of our responsibilities, to remind us of what we represent and to ensure that we act accordingly.

Copying the Torah scroll faithfully in every generation is a way of transmitting the *content* of the Revelation at Mt. Sinai throughout history. The reverence with which we treat the scroll is one of the ways we transmit the *experience* and *feeling* of that moment of revelation. I once attended Shabbat afternoon service in the Bayit Vegan neighborhood of Jerusalem. It was the Shabbat of a Bar Mitzvah, a very special one that I will never forget. The Bar Mitzvah boy was the tenth son of a retired teacher who had completed writing his own Torah scroll in time for the celebration. This man, praying together with a *minyan*[11] of his own children, whose son was reading the Torah portion from a scroll that his father had written, exemplified to me the ideal of the *mitzvah* of writing a scroll. He was handing down both the content and the feeling of the Revelation to the next generation, ensuring continuity of the encounter between God and the Jewish people begun at Sinai.

People of the Books

The commandment to write a Torah scroll includes the phrase, "… teach it to the Children of Israel, place it in their mouths…"[12] This passage tells us that the main purpose of the Torah scroll is instruction. Originally, the only text used to teach Jewish law, philosophy and ethics was the Torah scroll. All information not found in the verses was conveyed by oral tradition. Eventually this was written down in the form of the Mishnah,[13] Talmud[14] and commentaries, and the scroll was no longer the exclusive vehicle for studying and teaching. For hundreds of years, books have served as the principal source of Torah knowledge, while the scroll is used for the public reading of the Torah in the synagogue.[15]

Because the verse in Deuteronomy emphasizes the obligation to teach and study from the Torah that we write, most legal authorities maintain that the obligation to write a Torah scroll is now fulfilled through the writing and purchase of the books that we use to study the Torah.[16] (Yes, this *is* a plug.)

The books of Torah in a Jewish home take the place of the Torah scroll, but convey the same message. The six-foot diagonal, high-definition, digital, rear-projection television with surround sound should not be the centerpiece of a Jewish living room. Rather, the focus should be on our version of the Holy Ark — the bookshelves laden with Jewish books. Think of the message that children absorb from our reverence and enthusiasm for our books. Consider also the impact that the books have on the use of "spare time." Does our hand automatically reach for the remote, the joystick, the game-control pad, or do we reach for the well-worn volume of the Talmud, the book of ethics, or the new commentary on the Torah portion of the week?

Traditional Jewish homes usually have an extensive library of Jewish books. Just "the basics" of Torah, Prophets, Writings and commentaries, the Talmud and commentaries, the codes of law, works of ethics, philosophy and history amount to a few hundred books. A close friend of mine once served as the rabbi of a small community in Australia. His house was crammed with hundreds of Jewish books in Hebrew, Aramaic, Yiddish and English. Most members of the community were quite distant from Jewish tradition and were shocked and amazed by the vast numbers of books in his house. They had no idea that there was so much Jewish knowledge out there. The rabbi believes that many people were inspired to begin studying Judaism merely by seeing his library. Its presence posed a challenge to people's ignorance and stood as witness to the breadth, depth and grandeur of their Jewish heritage.

When I contemplate a large Jewish library I recall a pie chart that a science teacher once drew for me, and I am reminded anew of how much I have to learn.

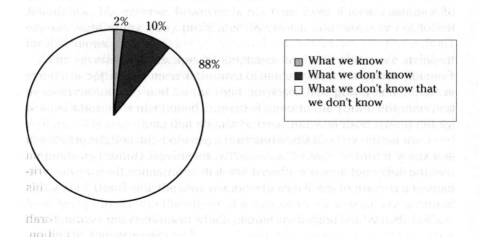

2%   10%

88%

☐ What we know
■ What we don't know
☐ What we don't know that
   we don't know

Beit Knesset —The Synagogue

Moving the Mountain

The Jewish people experienced a unique event at Mt. Sinai. God spoke to an entire people and elevated every member of the nation, at least momentarily, to the level of prophecy. How could the Jewish people preserve to the greatest possible degree that connection to God and the clear perception of His presence for all time? Our Sages answer that building the Tabernacle, the portable Temple, in the desert was really the construction of a portable Mt. Sinai. The Torah records that God commanded the Jewish people to build a sanctuary so that the Divine Presence would always be among them:

> And they shall make a sanctuary for Me and I will dwell in their midst.[17]

The sanctuary would facilitate the continuity of the Revelation and communication that took place at Mt. Sinai. Nachmanides explains:

> And in the Tabernacle the honor of God that rested on Mount Sinai would be continuously manifested to the Jewish people... And the word of God that came to Moses on Mount Sinai would continue to come to him from the Tabernacle...[18]

Eventually, the Jewish people established a Jewish state and homeland in the Land of Israel and built a permanent Temple in Jerusalem that continued to serve as the "interface" between the people and God. When the Jews went into exile, however, and the Temple in Jerusalem was destroyed, something else had to replace it for the scattered, far-flung nation. The prophet Ezekiel comforted the Jewish people by telling them that the synagogue would fill this need:

> Thus said the Lord God: Although I have removed them far away among the nations, and although I have scattered them among the lands, yet I have been for them a small sanctuary in the lands where they arrived.[19]

The Talmud explains that the expression "a small sanctuary" refers to the synagogues and houses of study in the Diaspora.[20]

Nachmanides adds that another purpose of the synagogue is to proclaim and publicize our relationship with the Creator:

> The purpose of raising our voices in prayer, the purpose of synagogues and the merit of communal prayer is in order to

*provide people with a place to gather and to acknowledge
that God is the Creator Who brought them into existence. And
they publicize this and declare before Him, "We are Your creations."*[21]

Synagogue Decor

Like the Temple, the synagogue has as its focal point, the Holy Ark, the
Aron Kodesh. The Ark is a cabinet covered with an embroidered curtain
called the *parochet.* It is built on the wall of the synagogue facing Israel
(in Israel, facing Jerusalem).[22] The original Holy Ark was a receptacle for
the Tablets of the Law that Moses brought down from Mt. Sinai. The synagogue Ark contains the closest thing to the Tablets that we have — the
Torah scrolls. Above the Ark hangs a lamp, known as the *Ner Tamid* (literally, the Eternal Candle, and often referred to as the Eternal Light), which
symbolizes the Menorah, the candelabrum that stood in the Temple. Just
as the middle candle of the Menorah always remained alight,[23] the *Ner
Tamid* in the synagogue is always lit. The design of the Ark is not specified: It may be a simple wooden box or an imposing marble structure, as
long as it reflects the sanctity of what it holds.

Ideally, the orientation of the synagogue should be towards the Land
of Israel, and it should have 12 windows facing in the direction of Israel, to
remind us of the Twelve Tribes of Israel and to help inspire us.[24] The synagogue should also be built so that it is at the highest point of the city.[25]
Where logistical considerations make it difficult to meet these criteria,
virtually any room can serve as a synagogue.

When the Jews received the Torah at Mt. Sinai, they camped around
the mountain. Similarly, the elevated platform and table where the Torah
is read publicly, the *bimah,* should be in the center of the synagogue, surrounded by the congregation.[26] The *bimah* becomes a miniature Mt. Sinai,
and also enables the entire congregation to hear the Torah reading clearly.[27] Placing the *bimah* in the center also recalls the placement of the altar
in the Temple, in the middle of the Temple's courtyard.[28] In many Jewish
communities, most commonly among *Sephardim,* the Torah is read from a
platform elevated much higher than the congregation, to give the allusion
that one is hearing the Torah coming from the top of Mt. Sinai.

A small lectern, the *amud,* is placed toward the front of the synagogue
for the person who leads the prayers. The *amud* usually has candles or
lights on it and is often decorated with inspirational designs and artwork.
In some synagogues, the *amud* is placed in an area that is lower than the
rest of the synagogue, to fulfill the words of Psalms, "From the depths
I called You, God."[29] The person who leads the prayers is known as the
shliach tzibur, "representative of the community." He sets the pace of the

prayers, coordinates the communal prayers and leads the recitations of the responsive sections. A leader who is proficient in the traditional melodies is known as the *chazzan* or cantor.

Since the times of the Temple in Jerusalem, there has always been a partition (*mechitzah*) between men and women during times of prayer and festivity.[30] In most European synagogues, the women's section, the *ezrat nashim*, was built as a balcony surrounding the inside of the synagogue on three sides (excluding the side on which the Ark was placed). Due to financial and structural constraints, however, many synagogues, particularly in the United States, the women's and men's sections are placed side by side or one in back of the other on the same level, using a partial wall or a curtain as a division.

The law requiring a *mechitzah* between men and women during prayer is of Biblical origin[31] and is discussed in the Babylonian Talmud.[32] By creating a division between men and women, the *mechitzah* facilitates an appropriate atmosphere during prayer,[33] which should be serious and focused.[34] Since the main purpose of the *mechitzah* is to prevent socializing, it should stand at least at shoulder height, about 5 feet tall.[35] The *mechitzah* also prevents distractions which can be caused by the presence of members of the opposite sex, to whom there is a natural and normal attraction.[36] With men and women sitting separately, everyone can better focus on talking to God.

An original insight into the effects of the *mechitzah* comes from an Australian professor of social work:

> *I have mixed feelings about the separation. While I know some people regard it as an affront to equal rights for women, I quite like the idea that my family status is anonymous. When we are not seated together, I am not automatically regarded as someone's wife and mother; rather I can have some time to myself.*[37]

Perhaps one important function of the *mechitzah* is to make it clear that no one is automatically defined as a wife, husband, father or mother, single or married, but rather as an individual seeking a relationship with God.

House of Prayer

The synagogue is meant to create a space conducive to prayer. The very fact that it is designated specifically for prayer helps one to focus merely by being there. Therefore, even when no *minyan* is present and no regular service is going on, it is preferable to pray in a synagogue.[38] It is a little like going to the health-club to work out. As soon as I walk into the weight room, my heart rate goes up, adrenalin shoots into my system and I become physically and psychologically prepared for exercise. Similarly, when we walk into the synagogue, we feel ourselves going into "prayer-mode"; we become psychologically and spiritually prepared for prayer. It is appropriate to have a specific place in the synagogue where one usually sits, both to help one's concentration and also to express the importance and gravity of prayer.[39]

For this reason it is customary for congregants to buy permanent seats in the synagogue. If one is new to a synagogue, it is proper etiquette to check that the seat is not someone's regular place, before sitting down to pray. (A reminder to the seat owner: It is also inappropriate to greet a guest in the synagogue with the phrase, "That's my seat, buddy!")

House of Study

The synagogue is called a *shul* in Yiddish, which actually means "school." In fact, a primary function of the synagogue is to be a place for Torah study, a *beit midrash*, or house of study. Today, as throughout history, classes on Torah (*shiurim*) are given in the synagogue. Before, after and in-between prayer services, it is the norm to have classes attended by congregants. Many synagogues organize educational programs, lectures and study groups that meet on a regular basis. Individuals frequently go to the synagogue to study Torah with their children or with a *chavruta*, a study partner.[40] Before the Second World War, synagogues in Europe were often used as schools for young children. Among Chassidim in Poland, most advanced Torah learning took place in small synagogues, known as *shtieblach*[41] rather than in yeshivot.[42]

House of Community

The synagogue also serves as a place for the community to gather. In times of danger or tragedy, Jews come to the synagogue to recite Psalms together, to pray and to attempt to address any spiritual and moral weaknesses of the community.[43] On happy occasions, people come to the synagogue to celebrate. Circumcisions are often performed in the synagogue, and Bar/Bat Mitzvahs, engagements and weddings frequently take place in an adjacent hall. Community meetings are held in the synagogue, and the local rabbinic court, the *beit din*, is often located there. The rabbi's office — an address for counseling, *halachic*[44] decisions, mediations and teaching — can usually be found there as well.

For centuries, the synagogue has been the focal point of Jewish communal life. Even poor *shtetlach*[45] in Europe often had beautifully painted and carved wooden *shuls* that were the pride and joy of the community. People living in poverty, nevertheless, contributed happily to the building and upkeep of the synagogue.[46] In some cities, every group of tradesmen maintained its own synagogue, where the members would be able to pray and study together with other people who had similar schedules. From Calcutta to Venice,[47] from Sao Paulo to Halifax, wherever there is a Jewish community, there are synagogues. The architecture varies widely, from the Moorish designs of Moroccan synagogues to the Victorian synagogues of London, but the heart and soul of the synagogue remain constant — the Torah that is studied there, the prayers that are recited and the communities that are created.

Selected Laws of the Torah Scroll

A scribe filling in the first letter of a Torah scroll

1. For a Torah scroll to be kosher (fit for use), it must be written by a God-fearing, expert scribe according to the prescribed laws and customs.[48]

2. The scribe must have the conscious intent to sanctify the scroll as a Torah.[49]

3. If even one letter is missing, illegible or written incorrectly, or if even one extra letter is added, the entire scroll is not *kosher* and may not be used for the public reading of the Torah.[50] (It can be repaired by a competent scribe, however, and used afterward.)

4. The Torah scroll must be treated with great respect. A special place should be designated for its storage.[51]

5. One who sees a Torah scroll being carried should stand up until it is placed in the Ark or on the *bimah*, or until it is out of sight.[52]

6. One may not sit on a surface upon which a Torah scroll is placed,[53] nor may one place anything on top of a Torah scroll.[54]

7. One should not directly touch the actual parchment of the Torah scroll with one's hand.[55] For this reason, when one is given an *aliyah* during the reading of the Torah, one customarily touches the *tzitzit* of one's *tallit* to the parchment, then kisses the *tzitzit*.

8. It is customary to kiss the cover of the Torah scroll as it is carried to and from the Ark.

9. A Torah scroll which is worn out and is no longer usable should not be discarded, but should be buried in a clay container in a Jewish cemetery.[56]

Selected Laws of the Synagogue

1. Everyone in the community contributes to the building and upkeep of the local synagogue.[57]

2. The synagogue should be treated with the utmost respect and one should behave in a dignified manner while inside.[58]

3. One should not go through the sanctuary as a shortcut, or use it as a shelter from the weather. One should not eat, drink or sleep in a synagogue or engage in idle conversation there.[59]

4. One may eat and drink in a synagogue that is also designated as a place of learning (a *beit midrash*).[60]

5. One should not enter a synagogue with a weapon, or without a head-covering.[61]

6. It is proper to enter a synagogue only when wearing clean clothing.[62]

7. Every time one enters a synagogue, even if not for the purpose of praying, one should either study a small portion of Torah, or at least recite a verse from Psalms, while seated.[63]

For Further Reading

▶ *The Gabbai's Handbook* (ArtScroll/Mesorah, 1984)

▶ *Tikkun — The Torah Reader's Compendium* (ArtScroll/Mesorah, 2002)

NOTES

References to books of the Talmud refer to the Babylonian Talmud unless otherwise noted.

1. Deuteronomy 31:24.
2. *Midrash Rabbah*, Deuteronomy 9:9.
3. Maimonides, *Mishneh Torah*, Laws of the Torah Scroll, Chaps. 7-10.
4. Jews of European origin.
5. Jews of African or Middle Eastern origin.
6. Maimonides, ibid. 7:1; *Code of Jewish Law, Yoreh Deah*, 270:1.
7. Deuteronomy 31:19.
8. Rabbi Sa'adiah Gaon, *HaEmunot VeHadeot*, 3:7.
9. Ibid. 7:2.
10. Fringed prayer shawl — see chapter on Material Witnesses.
11. Quorum for prayer of ten adult Jewish males — see chapter on Prayer.
12. Deuteronomy 31:19
13. By Rabbi Judah the Prince, in Israel in about 200 C.E.
14. Jerusalem Talmud, edited by Rav Munah and Rav Yonah in 350 C.E., Babylonian Talmud, edited by Ravina and Rav Ashi in 500 C.E.
15. See chapter on Prayer.
16. Rabbeinu Asher, Menachot, *Hilchot Sefer Torah*; Tur and *Code of Jewish Law, Yoreh Deah*, 270:2; Bach, Shach and Taz ad loc.
17. Exodus 25:8; Rabbi Chaim ibn Attar, *Ohr Hachaim*, Exodus ad loc.
18. Nachmanides, *Commentary on the Torah*, Exodus 25:1.
19. Ezekiel 11:16.
20. *Megillah* 29a.
21. Nachmanides, *Commentary on the Torah*, Exodus 13:16.
22. Maimonides, *Mishneh Torah*, Laws of Prayer 11:2-3; *Code of Jewish Law, Orach Chaim* 150:5.
23. *Shabbat* 22b.
24. *Code of Jewish Law, Orach Chaim*, 90:4
25. Ibid.
26. Ibid. 150:2.
27. Maimonides, ibid.; *Code of Jewish Law*, ibid.
28. Rabbi Moshe Sofer, *Responsa Chatam Sofer*, Orach Chaim 28.
29. Psalms 130:1; *Code of Jewish Law*, ibid. 90; *Magen Avraham, Be'er Heitev* 1; *Mishnah Berurah* 5.
30. *Sukkah* 51b.
31. Rabbi Moshe Feinstein, *Igrot Moshe, Orach Chaim* 1:39-42; Aaron Rakeffet-Rothkoff, *The Silver Era*, Appendix A — Court deposition of Rabbi Eliezer Silver.
32. Ibid. *Sukkah* 51b-52a.
33. Ibid. *Sukkah*.
34. *Berachot* 31a.
35. Rabbi Moshe Feinstein, ibid. 1:39 3 *amot* = 18 *tefachim* = 60 inches = 152.4 cm.
36. Ibid.
37. Sally Berkovic, *Under My Hat*, Joseph's Bookstore, London, 1997, p. 190.

38. *Code of Jewish Law*, 90:9.
39. *Berachot* 6b; *Code of Jewish Law*, ibid. 90:19.
40. See chapter on Torah Study.
41. Rabbi Berel Wein, *Faith & Fate: The Story of the Jewish People in the Twentieth Century*, Shaar Press, NY, 2001, p. 122.
42. See chapter on Torah Study.
43. See Chapter 13.
44. Jewish law.
45. Jewish villages in Eastern Europe.
46. Albert Barry, Dr. Henry Abramson, and Florida Atlantic University, *The Lost Wooden Synagogues of Eastern Europe*, 2000 — Video.
47. Synagogues from these cities have been relocated to the Israel Museum in Jerusalem.

48. *Code of Jewish Law, Yoreh Deah* 281:1-5.
49. Ibid. 274:1.
50. Ibid. 274:2-7.
51. Ibid. 282:1.
52. Ibid. 282:2.
53. Ibid. 282:7.
54. Ibid. 282:19.
55. Ibid. 282:4.
56. Ibid. 282:10
57. *Code of Jewish Law, Orach Chaim*, 150:1.
58. Ibid. 151:1.
59. Ibid. 151:1, 3, 5.
60. Ibid.
61. Ibid. 151:7.
62. Ibid. 151:8.
63. Ibid. 151:1.

The Land of Israel

The Jewish national homeland –
historical, spiritual and legal significance

Land of Our Fathers ... and Mothers and Grandparents, Uncles, Aunts and Cousins

*T*he first commandment God ever gave to the first Jew in history was to go to the Land of Israel. The Torah relates that God spoke to Abraham, and said:

> Go [for your benefit], from your land, from your relatives and from your father's house to the land that I will show you. And I will make of you a great nation; I will bless you, and make your name great, and you shall be a blessing.[1]

Abraham, his wife Sarah, their extended family and their retinue[2] all came to Israel, then known as Canaan. They traveled throughout the land, engaged in commerce and, of course, in spreading the idea of monotheism.[3] At various times, they lived in the mountains of Beit-El,[4] on the west bank of the Jordan; Beersheva[5] in the Negev Desert; and the city of Hebron.[6] God promised Abraham that although his descendants would go into exile and be enslaved, ultimately He would free them, bring them back to Israel and make Israel the eternal homeland of the Jewish people.[7]

One of the earliest recorded purchases of land was Abraham's purchase of the Machpelah cave and field in Hebron for the burial of his wife, Sarah. The Torah provides us with the details of his protracted negotiations with the Hittites, Abraham's insistence on paying "full price," and his concern that the elders of the Hittites should agree to and witness the purchase — for this purchase was the beginning of God's promise turning into reality.[8]

All the Patriarchs, Matriarchs and the Children of Jacob (the Twelve Tribes) lived in and were buried in Israel. Abraham and Sarah, Jacob and Rebecca, Isaac and Leah were all buried in Hebron, in the cave purchased by Abraham. Rachel was buried on the road to Bethlehem[9] and even Joseph (who died in Egypt) was buried in the city of Shechem (Nablus).[10] Joseph had specifically ordered that the Jews should take his remains with them at the time of the Exodus and bury him in Israel.[11]

Following Joshua's conquest of Israel, the Jews lived there as an independent commonwealth (and later under a monarchy) for 800 years. Judges ruled the people for almost 400 years until the coronation of the first king, Saul. Saul was succeeded by King David, who was followed by his son, Solomon. King Solomon built the First Holy Temple in Jerusalem, the capital of Israel.[12] This Temple stood for 410 years until it was destroyed by the Babylonians, who conquered Israel and exiled the Jews to Babylon (modern-day Iraq).

By the Rivers of Babylon ...

Although the Jewish people were in exile they did not forget the Land of Israel. Their emotions were prophetically described by King David in Psalm 137:[13]

> By the rivers of Babylon, there we sat and also wept when we remembered Zion. On the willows within it we hung our lyres. For there our captors requested the words of song from us, with our lyres [playing] joyous music. "Sing for us from Zion's song!" "How can we sing the song of God upon alien soil?" If I forget you, O Jerusalem, let my right hand forget its skill. Let my tongue adhere to my palate, if I fail to recall you, if I fail to elevate Jerusalem above my foremost joy...

After 70 years in Babylon, the prophets Ezra[14] and Nehemiah[15] led many of the exiles back to Israel where they built the Second Temple. The Jewish Commonwealth was renewed and the Temple services were once again performed in Jerusalem. The Jews lived in Israel from the time of their return until the Roman destruction of the Temple and subsequent exile in about 70 C.E.

The era of the Second Temple, which lasted approximately 420 years, was a time of great upheaval. The Jewish state experienced invasion by the Greek Seleucids, which led to the Maccabean revolt in 165 B.C.E. (the Chanukah story[16]). Later came the Roman occupation, the despotic rule of Herod and the Jewish revolts against Roman rule that ultimately ended in the disastrous events of 70 C.E.

We Shall Not Be Moved

Despite all the invasions, exiles and hardship, two Jewish states existed in Israel during this time, the first lasting for 840 years, the second for 420 years. Even during the long exile that followed the Roman destruction of the Temple, a continuous Jewish presence (albeit, sometimes quite small) was maintained in the Land of Israel. The land was invaded by Arabs, Crusaders, Saracens, Mongols, Mamluks, Ottoman Turks and the British Empire, but through it all Jews not only remained, but produced monumental works of learning and liturgy. Rabbi Judah the Prince, for example, wrote the Mishnah in the north of Israel in 200 C.E.; and the Jerusalem Talmud was edited there in 350 C.E. Throughout the centuries, Jews undertook the dangerous journey to Israel from other lands. The great scholar Nachmanides came from Spain and established a synagogue in Jerusalem in the 13th century. In the 16th century, Rabbi Yosef Karo wrote the *Code of Jewish Law* in the city of Safed[17]; and the song *Lechah Dodi*[18] was composed and first sung there by Rabbi Shlomoh Alkabetz, student of the great Kabbalist of Safed, Rabbi Yitzchak Luria (known by the acronym AriZal).

In the 19th century, during the Ottoman rule, groups of Chassidim[19] came to Israel on the instruction of their leaders in Europe. The famous Lithuanian rabbi known as the Gaon of Vilna[20] sent many students to settle in Israel. In the late 19th century, the Zionist movement brought thousands of people to Israel to establish agricultural settlements and industry there. The attachment of the Jews to their land throughout 1,900 years of exile culminated in the establishment of the modern State of Israel in 1948, now home to more than five million Jews from all over the world.

Jews of the 21st century take for granted the presence of Jewish communities in Israel. From a historical point of view, however, the return of a people to their Land after nineteen centuries of exile (in the case of some, 2,500 years of exile[21]) the establishment of an independent Jewish state and the ingathering of Jews from virtually every country in the world are miraculous and unprecedented events in world history.

The building in which I lived in Jerusalem[22] represents a microcosm of the "ingathering of the exiles" that has taken place. Although it contains only fifteen apartments, at one point, the countries of origin of the inhabitants of our building included Australia, Canada, France, Gibraltar, Greece, Morocco, South Africa, the United Kingdom, the USA and Israel!

Historian Paul Johnson says the following about the Jewish attachment to Israel:

> The Jews are the most tenacious people in history. Hebron is there to prove it ... There, in the cave of Machpelah, are the Tombs of the Patriarchs. Hebron reflects the long, tragic history of the Jews and their unrivaled capacity to survive their misfortunes. David was anointed king there ... When Jerusalem fell, the Jews were expelled and it was settled by Edom. It was conquered by Greece, then by Rome, converted, plundered by the Zealots, burned by the Romans, occupied in turn by Arabs, Franks and Mamluks. From 1266 the Jews were forbidden to enter the Cave to pray. They were permitted only to ascend seven steps by the side of the eastern wall ...
>
> In 1518 there was a fearful Ottoman massacre of the Hebron Jews. But a community of pious scholars was re-established. It maintained a tenuous existence ... The Jewish community, never very numerous, was ferociously attacked by the Arabs in 1929. They attacked it again in 1936 and virtually wiped it out. When Israeli soldiers entered Hebron during the Six Day War in 1967, for a generation not one Jew had lived there. But a modest settlement was re-established in 1970 ...
>
> Hebron is thus an example of Jewish obstinacy over 4,000 years ... No race has maintained over so long a period so emotional an attachment to a particular corner of the earth's surface.[23]

Land of the Spirit

It is not only the historical attachment of the people of Israel to the Land of Israel that makes it special, but its intrinsic, spiritual qualities as well. Most of the prophets either lived in Israel or prophesied about it.[24] In Jewish philosophy, prophecy is considered to be a "product" of the Land of Israel.[25] Based on the principle that the structure and nature of the physical world reflects the underlying spiritual nature of reality, Rabbi Yehudah Halevy explains that the spiritual capacity to produce prophecy is similar to the physical capacity to grow crops. Different regions have the capacity to grow certain crops better than other places — Idaho potatoes, French grapes and the rubber trees of India are some examples. So too, different areas have different spiritual influences and potentials. Israel has the capacity to cultivate prophecy, connection to God and intense spirituality more than any other place in the world.[26] It is not a coincidence that many religions feel a special connection to Israel,[27] that the bulk of the Bible was written in Israel and that the Psalms, which form the basis of prayer for literally hundreds of millions of people around the world, were written in Israel.

Of the 613 commandments of the Bible, 343 are directly dependent on the Land of Israel — that is, fully 56 percent of Jewish law is, in some way, contingent upon being in Israel.[28] Even those commandments that are not directly dependent upon the Land will have a different and deeper spiritual dimension when performed in Israel.[29] Maimonides maintains that if, in theory, a time ever came when no Jews at all lived in the Land of Israel, the entire Jewish calendar would lose its validity, and we would not be able to observe any of the festivals.[30]

It is still possible today to feel the intensity of spirituality in Israel. People of every race and nationality sense the Divine Presence in Jerusalem — especially at the Western Wall, the remnant of the Holy Temple. One can often see ostensibly secular Jews praying and crying at the Western Wall. It is not uncommon for people who have never read the Bible to be inspired to study it after seeing and experiencing the Land of Israel, because the Land is one in which the very air is permeated with the spiritual.

The Model State

The Land of Israel is also central to Judaism because it is the best vehicle for demonstrating Jewish values and ethics in practice. Israel is supposed to be the place to which the people of the world look for guidance in moral behavior.[31] The tremendous media scrutiny of Israel and the extraordinary amount of attention paid to this tiny country in the Middle East may well be due to the fact that, deep down, people expect something more of Israel and the Jews. There is a sense that the State of Israel should have higher standards than its neighbors and the rest of the world — and indeed it should. This idea is beautifully expressed in the following verses in the Book of Isaiah:

> And many nations will go and say, "Let us go and ascend to the mountain of God, to the Temple of the God of Jacob; and we will be instructed in His ways, and we will walk in His paths"; for from Zion shall come forth the Torah, and the word of God from Jerusalem.[32]

The Jewish ideal is not withdrawal from the physical world in an attempt to become an angel.[33] On the contrary, we want to be involved in many different facets of the world and apply the moral and spiritual guidance of the Torah to every aspect of life. This is one of the reasons that the Twelve Tribes of Israel were so diverse in their characters. They represented a microcosm of all humanity and demonstrated that it was possible for anyone to be a righteous person. Rabbi Samson Raphael Hirsch discusses the reason for this diversity within the Jewish people:

> *The Jewish nation is to represent agriculture as well as commerce, militarism as well as culture and learning. The Jewish people will be a nation of farmers, a nation of businessmen, a nation of soldiers and a nation of science. Thereby, as a model nation, to establish the truth that the one great personal and national task which God revealed in His Torah is not dependent on any particular kind of talent or character trait, but that the whole of humanity in all its shades of diversity can equally find its calling in one common spiritual and moral mission and outlook in life.*[34]

There is no better way to teach people how to live than by personal example.[35] If a person is successful in all spheres of life while remaining moral and good, others will be more inclined to imitate him than if he were a moral, noble pauper.[36] Although the modern State of Israel is far from perfect (as virtually every Israeli will be happy to tell you for hours on end), there are still ways in which it can teach the world Jewish ideals by example.

During one stint on reserve duty in the Israeli army, I noticed an amazing picture on the cover of an army magazine.[37] A senior member of the Argentinean military had come to visit Israel and was meeting with Ehud Barak, then Chief of Staff of the Israel Defense Forces. The Argentinean was covered with medals, braid, campaign ribbons and badges from head to foot — there was not an inch that did not brilliantly reflect the camera's flash. Barak, on the other hand, was wearing a simple khaki uniform with paratrooper wings and a few stars on his shoulder boards to indicate his rank.[38] Now, consider the fact that Barak was the most highly decorated soldier of a very successful army, while the Argentineans had recently lost the Falkland Islands! This photo was a demonstration of the Jewish abhorrence for war and violence that still prevails in Israel, even though we have fought and won so many wars. The glorification of military prowess that exists in some countries is thankfully absent in Israel. The contrast between Barak's modest attire and his counterpart's shining armor painted a striking picture of their opposing values.

Jewish values and priorities come to the fore even in the most mundane situations. Permit me a personal recollection of one of my favorites:

During my first week in Israel in 1978, I went to a bank in the Meah Shearim neighborhood of Jerusalem at about noon. The bank was scheduled to close at 12:30 p.m. and I expected to perform a minor transaction and leave. After waiting in line for about 20 minutes and listening to the teller argue with his wife on the phone for another eight minutes, I was finally able to complete my business. As I walked to the exit, the security guard rushed over and locked the door before I could get out. I asked him, very politely, to open the door, but he gestured for me to wait. I pointed out to him (a little less politely this time) that I had come in for a two-minute transaction that ended up taking half an hour! Now that I had finally finished, how dare he actually imprison me in the bank against my will? He yawned and again gestured for me to wait. Just then, one of the tellers stood up and announced, *"Minchah!"* (afternoon service). I did a quick count and realized that together with myself, the security guard and the tellers we had exactly the 10 men required for a *minyan* (quorum for prayer). I realized then that I was being "held hostage" for prayers! Only in Israel!

The Shechinah Is Here

The Hebrew word *Shechinah* means "Divine Presence." Although in reality, God permeates all of time and space equally,[39] we are not able to perceive His presence equally in all times and all places.[40] Venice Beach, California (as a purely random example) is a *place* where the Divine Presence is well concealed, and Super Bowl Sunday is a *time* when the Divine Presence is difficult to perceive.

There are moments when God allows us more of a glimpse of the Divine Presence — at sunset toward the end of Yom Kippur, for instance.[41] There are also places where God allows us a greater degree of perception, such as in the Land of Israel. The Torah calls Jerusalem the "Gates of Heaven"[42] and our Sages point out that even after the destruction of the Temple, the Divine Presence has never left the Western Wall.[43]

Tens of thousands of Jews from all over the world, representing every level of religiosity, ignorant and learned, Zionist and non-Zionist, visit the Western Wall every year. The Western Wall (*Hakotel Hama'aravi* or, simply, the *Kotel*) is the westernmost retaining wall of the Temple Mount, and dates from the Second Temple era. (In the late 19th and early 20th centuries the English began referring to the Western Wall as the Wailing Wall, based on the old Arabic name for it, *El Mabka*, the place of weeping. Jews, however, have always referred to the wall as the Western Wall, preferring to relate it to the Holy Temple.[44]) Many Jews who visit have no knowledge of the Temple at all; many know little or nothing about Judaism or Jewish history. And yet, the Western Wall draws them like a magnet and often elicits from them deep spiritual feelings. For many people, a single visit to the Western Wall has changed their lives by prompting them to investigate their Jewish roots. We believe that much of this remarkable energy is due to the fact that "the *Shechinah* never left the Western Wall."

Once on a trip outside of Israel with my two oldest sons, we had a long stopover in Athens. I decided to take the boys to see the Acropolis, one of the most famous and magnificent archaeological sites in the world. On top of the Acropolis, a hill overlooking Athens, stands the remains of the Parthenon — a massive pagan temple dedicated to the Greek goddess, Athena. I asked my children to compare the Parthenon with the Western Wall. They pointed out that the Parthenon is made of white marble, while the *Kotel* is made of limestone; the Parthenon is supported by scaffolding and the *Kotel* stands unassisted. The *Kotel* has hyssop growing out of it, while the Parthenon is quite bare of vegetation. The most astute observation made, however, was, "Hey! No one is *davening* (praying) at the Parthenon!" My children saw through the pomp and grandeur of the Parthenon. They saw that the Parthenon and what it represented is dead and long gone, while Judaism and the Divine Presence that can be felt at the *Kotel* are living entities. Many tourists visit the Parthenon, but very few, if any, find the same inspiration and feeling of connection that is regularly experienced at the Western Wall.

In 1967, toward the end of the Six Day War, when the *Kotel* returned to Jewish hands after 1,900 years, there was an unprecedented outpouring of emotion from all Israelis.[45] Although rarely articulated publicly, there is a widespread recognition that the *Kotel* is more than just a place — it is a portal to a spiritual dimension and an opportunity to connect with God.

Special Surveillance

The Torah describes Israel as, "A land that the Lord, your God, seeks out; the eyes of the Lord, your God, are always upon it, from the beginning of the year to year's end."[46] What does this expression mean? It teaches that the degree to which Divine Providence is manifest in Israel is much greater than anywhere else in the world.

A striking example of the special Divine Providence in Israel is described in the prophecies of Exile and Redemption. The Torah predicted that the Jews would eventually be exiled from the Land of Israel and that during that time the Land would be desolate: "I will make the land desolate; and your enemies who dwell upon it will be desolate. And you, I will scatter among the nations ..."[47]

Two of the great commentators, Rashi[48] and Nachmanides,[49] explain that this ominous prediction is actually a blessing as well. God guarantees to the Jewish people that while they are in exile the land will not accept other inhabitants and will remain barren and desolate until their return. In fact, during the period of the first two Jewish commonwealths, the Land of Israel was renowned for its produce, was heavily forested and supported a large population. It was accurately described by the Torah as "flowing with milk and honey,"[50] "a Land with streams of water, of springs and underground water coming forth in valley and mountain; a Land of wheat, barley, grapes, figs, and pomegranates; a Land of oil [-producing] olives and [date-] honey."[51] The Roman-Jewish historian, Josephus Flavius, describes the northern (Galilee) region of Israel when the Jews still inhabited it in his day:

> ... although small in size ... [the land] is fertile and has rich pastures ... the whole land is cultivated by its inhabitants without even the smallest area left barren, and the cities are populated and plentiful.[52]

The special connection between the Jewish people and the Land of Israel becomes apparent when we see how precisely the Biblical prophecy has been fulfilled. Contrast the account of Josephus with the eyewitnesses report by Nachmanides, who immigrated to Israel in the 13th century, during the exile. He wrote the following letter to his children:

> What shall I tell you about the Land? There are so many forsaken places, and the desolation is great. It comes down to this: The more sacred the place, the more it has suffered — Jerusalem is most desolate, Judea more so than the Galilee. Yet in all its desolation it is an exceedingly good Land.[53]

When Mark Twain visited Israel (then called Palestine) 600 years later, the landscape was just as bleak:

> ... [a] desolate country whose soil is rich enough, but is given over wholly to weeds — a silent mournful expanse .... A desolation is here that not even imagination can grace with the pomp of life and action .... We never saw a human being on the whole route .... There was hardly a tree or a shrub anywhere ... Even the olive and the cactus, those fast friends of the worthless soil, had almost deserted the country ... No landscape exists that is more tiresome to the eye than that which bounds the approaches to Jerusalem ... Jerusalem is mournful, dreary and lifeless. I would not desire to live here. It is a hopeless, dreary, heartbroken land ... Palestine sits in sackcloth and ashes.[54]

Today Israel has flowered once again (It exports tulips to Holland![55]), has a thriving, internationally acclaimed wine industry, and produces an incredible variety of fruits, from tropical pineapples, mangos and bananas to cold-climate fruits such as apples and pears. In the Jerusalem forest, a 10-minute walk from a number of modern neighborhoods, all the species that flourished in Biblical times grow wild. Israel's children have started to come home and the Land is proclaiming its welcome. As Ezekiel wrote some 2,500 years ago, "But you, O mountains of Israel, shall give forth your branch and bear your fruit for My people Israel, for they are soon to come."[56]

This Land Is Your Land, This Land Is My Land

The Bible is replete with promises that the Land of Israel will be given to the Jewish people. God completes His Covenant with Abraham with the words, "To your descendants I have given this Land ..."[57] He repeated the promise to Isaac,[58] to Jacob[59] and later to Moses.[60] Before the Exodus, God promises that, "I shall bring you to the Land about which I raised My hand [in an oath] to give to Abraham, Isaac and Jacob, and I shall give it to you as a heritage ..."[61]

Nevertheless, there have always been those for whom the Bible is insufficient evidence, and who have challenged our right to the Land of Israel.[62] Some arguments against our claim to Israel have been stunning in their audaciousness. The following quotation from the Palestine National Covenant, the founding charter of the Palestine Liberation Organization, for instance, attempts in one short paragraph to erase 3,500 years of history as well as a large part of Jewish law, philosophy and tradition. Article 20 of the covenant reads as follows:

> *Claims of historical or religious ties of Jews with Palestine are incompatible with the facts of history and the true conception of what constitutes statehood. Judaism, being a religion, is not an independent nationality. Nor do Jews constitute a single nation with an identity of its own; they are citizens of the state to which they belong.*

The first part of this chapter has shown that the "historical or religious ties of Jews with Palestine" are indisputably borne out by the facts of history. The existence of independent Jewish states and monarchies in Israel for over 1,000 years demonstrate that we are indeed "an independent nationality." Nevertheless, we will address the question of whether, after 2,000 years of exile from our Land, our claim is still valid. The following parable (with apologies to Mario Puzo) will illustrate our explanation.

The Godfather

Once upon a time a family lived happily in their ancestral home. They lived there for many generations until one dark and stormy night, when a gang decided to make them an offer they could not refuse. They were forced to leave their house — but they never gave up hope that someday they would return. The family innocently asked the police and the courts to intervene, but of course, these authorities had been corrupted by the gang and would not help the family. They approached the government, but were just shunted from one bureaucrat to the next. Still, they did not give up hope.

The generation that had been expelled from their home did not want their children to forget the family history, so they set up a legal fund for reclamation of the ancestral home to which all family members contributed. They arranged for everyone to see the house at least once in their lifetime, and they instituted a ritual pledge of allegiance to the home, which would be recited while facing toward it three times every day. On numerous occasions, some of the braver family members tried to take the house back by force; but they were easily repelled by gang's hit men. After a few generations, the descendants of the gang became respectable citizens and were blissfully unaware of the fact that they were living on stolen property. They became quite offended at the letters, protests and visits by descendants of the expelled family. They even sued for libel and slander, and thanks to their wealth, power and prestige easily won the court case and obtained a restraining order against the exiled family.

Squatters and Owners

In both Jewish and secular law there is a principle that living on land and using it for a certain period of time can be considered proof of ownership.[63] Proof can only be established, however, on condition that no protests have been made by the original owners of the land. The law assumes that no normal person would be silent when his land or house is being used by someone else. If he does remain silent, this constitutes *de facto* evidence that he has relinquished ownership or that it was never his to begin with. If, however, the squatter lived on the land for ten, twenty or even fifty years, and during that time the real owner made loud, frequent and passionate protests about the theft of his property, then no evidence of ownership is established for the squatter. In the case of the evicted family in our parable, most courts would award them their house because of their refusal to relinquish hope of return. The original gang leader would be a thief, and his descendants would be squatters — that is, a person who occupies real property without a claim of right or title.[64]

The Jewish nation was forcibly exiled from the Land of Israel by the Babylonians. Eventually, we returned and re-established a Jewish commonwealth, but were exiled again by the Romans. Like the family in our story, however, we never gave up hope that someday we would return. Wherever a Jew finds himself in the world, he or she always prays in the direction of the Land of Israel. For thousands of years, from Yemen to Krakow, Jews have prayed every day, three times a day, for the restoration of Jewish government in Israel, for the ingathering of all Jews to Israel and for the rebuilding of Jerusalem.

One way in which our bond with Israel, Jerusalem and the Temple expresses itself is in certain practices that commemorate the destruction of the Temple and the ensuing exile. The Sages decreed that at every celebration something must be done to remind us of the destruction of the Temple,[65] in order to fulfill the mandate of Psalm 137: "If I forget you, O Jerusalem, let my right hand forget its skill. Let my tongue adhere to my palate, if I fail to recall you, if I fail to elevate Jerusalem above my foremost joy ..." For this reason, a glass is broken at weddings, and we are required to leave a small section of the wall in a new house unfinished.[66]

Jews have visited Israel, immigrated to Israel and have arranged to be buried in Israel through the entire course of the exile. Jewish communities all over the world have sent money to help the inhabitants of Israel. There has always been a Jewish presence in the Land of Israel and our connection to the Land has been almost universally recognized throughout our history. We have never relinquished our title and we have never given up hope.

Holy to Three Faiths?

Although other religions also have connections to Israel, the relationship is not the same as that of Judaism. Moslems, even in Israel, always pray in the direction of Mecca in Saudi Arabia. The Land of Israel and Jerusalem are not mentioned in the Koran at all. No Pope has ever moved his throne to Israel, and Christians do not live with the hope of return to the land of their founder. No other nation or religion ever claimed Israel as its homeland until the 20th century.

The Torah, on the other hand, mentions Zion 161 times, and Jerusalem 664 times![67] The Christian historian, James Parkes, provides some insight into this contrast:

> For Moslems, the issue is not Palestine as a Holy Land, but Jerusalem as a Holy City. For, according to Muslim belief, the Temple of Solomon was miraculously built, and it was to and from Jerusalem that Mohammed was transported in order to

*make his ascent into heaven where his vocation was recog-
nized by his prophetic predecessors. Jerusalem is therefore the
third holiest shrine in Islam. For Jews the Land is a Holy Land
in the sense of being a Promised Land, and the word indicates
an intensity of relationship going beyond that of either of the
other two religions. The common phrase that Palestine is the
Holy Land of three faiths is not strictly accurate.*[68]

Jews all over the world, throughout the centuries, have held on to the belief that they would eventually return to Israel, just as God promised in the Torah:

*And the Lord your God shall return you from your captivity, and
have compassion upon you; and He shall return and gather
you from among all the nations to which the Lord your God has
scattered you ... And the Lord your God shall bring you into the
Land that your fathers inherited.*[69]

Jerusalem – Palace of the King

The Jewish people have a special relationship with the entire Land of Israel, but our bond specifically with the city of Jerusalem is as deep as the bond between mother and child. Jerusalem is first mentioned as the city of Malchizedek, the grandson of Shem, a monotheistic priest who greeted Abraham with bread and wine.[70] It was to the mountain at the center of the city, Mt. Moriah, that Abraham later came for the binding of Isaac.[71] The city was originally called *Shalem*, which means "whole" or "peaceful" but Abraham renamed it "*Yireh*," "God will see." God combined these two names and called the city "*Yerushalayim*," Jerusalem.[72]

The Bible relates that when Jacob fled Israel to escape his murderous brother Esau, he went to sleep on Mt. Moriah the night before leaving the Land. There he dreamed of a ladder that extended from the earth to the heavens.[73] The ladder symbolized the future role of Jerusalem as the site of the Holy Temple which joined together heaven and earth.

Jerusalem was the capital during both the First and Second Jewish Commonwealths. It was chosen to be the capital by King David with the assistance of Samuel the prophet,[74] and King Solomon built the Temple there.[75] The Sanhedrin, the supreme court of Israel, had its seat in Jerusalem,[76] and Jews from all over Israel and the Diaspora would come to them for guidance. Today, Jerusalem is the capital of the State of Israel.

It is fascinating to note how the geography of Jerusalem precisely reflects the role that the city is meant to play. Jerusalem is situated near the trade routes connecting Europe, Asia, Africa and the Middle East. It is in proximity to, but not part of, the great civilizations of Egypt, Babylon,

Greece, Phoenicia, Rome, Persia, Arabia and Assyria. Jerusalem is located on a mountain, because it is meant to be a beacon, but it is also surrounded by mountains,[77] as if to show that it must remain somewhat isolated[78] and insulated from foreign influences. Jerusalem is meant to be a place where people absorb spirituality, learn morality and find a connection to the Divine. Many empires have conquered Jerusalem, many pilgrims have passed through it and Jerusalem has left an imprint on them all.

Mitzvot of the City

Numerous commandments, laws and customs relate specifically to Jerusalem. In ancient times, Jews from all over Israel would gather to celebrate in Jerusalem on the pilgrimage festivals of Passover, Shavuot and Sukkot. Every seven years, the entire Jewish people would assemble in Jerusalem, and the king would read from the Torah in their presence. The new moon (the beginning of each Jewish month) was proclaimed by the Sanhedrin in Jerusalem, and even today our calendar is coordinated with the first appearance of the new moon over Jerusalem. The city was the focus of religious, national and legal events to such an extent that the Sages wrote, "Jerusalem is the city that joins together all the Jewish people."[79] Even today, when a Jew arrives in Jerusalem for the first time, there is a feeling of having come home to the most beautiful city in the world.

Some Laws of the Land

Living in Israel

Aliyah, going to live in the Holy Land, has been the cherished dream of Jews throughout the centuries. In fact the very word *aliyah* means to "go up" because the Jewish people have always regarded moving to Israel as an ascent, an act of spiritual elevation.[80] At times, this dream was realized, but more often, circumstances prevented it becoming anything more than a faint hope. Today, *aliyah* to Israel no longer involves sailing a pirate-infested Mediterranean, risking attacks by Crusaders or Saracens, or living in poverty. One can travel to Israel on a comfortable jet, live there in a modern house or apartment, own a car (or two), and enjoy a rich, religious life.

Beyond the emotional and philosophical significance of *aliyah*, what is the halachic (Jewish legal) perspective on living in Israel? In the Book of Numbers, God commands the Jewish people to "possess the Land and settle in it."[81] This commandment was fulfilled when the Jews entered Israel under Joshua's leadership, fought the Canaanites and settled the Land.

After centuries of oppression and exile does this *mitzvah* apply? Does this verse constitute an obligation on Jews today to live in the Land of Israel or did it refer only to a particular time in history? Nachmanides[82] maintains that the verse is timeless. Every Jew in every generation is obligated to live in the Land of Israel. He notes that the Mishnah considers it grounds for divorce if a spouse prevents his or her partner from going to Israel.[83] The Talmud even permits arranging for a non-Jew to write a purchase contract for Land in Israel on the Sabbath.[84] A later authority expressed this obligation in the following way:

> *Every Jew must make an unwavering, firm commitment in his heart to go up to live in the Land of Israel and he should aspire to merit to pray there before the palace of the King, which the Divine Presence has never left, even though it has been destroyed ...*[85]

Maimonides took a different view however. In his authoritative listing of the *mitzvot*, he does not mention the commandment to live in Israel. Some authorities maintain that Maimonides believed the *mitzvah* was only applicable during an era of Jewish monarchy, when the Temple in Jerusalem existed, and will only be obligatory once again in the Messianic Era.[86]

Some commentaries maintain that although the commandment may no longer apply to the Jewish nation as a whole, nevertheless, individuals still fulfill a *mitzvah* by living in Israel.[87] One of the most respected halachic authorities (*halachah* is Jewish law) of our times, Rabbi Moshe Feinstein,[88] wrote that he felt inadequate to resolve a controversy between two such great authorities as Maimonides and Nachmanides. He rules, however, that even though there may be no obligation today (according to Maimonides), it is nevertheless a praiseworthy act to live in Israel.[89] Ultimately, the choice of where to live affects virtually every aspect of a person's life — physically, spiritually and emotionally. The decision of whether or not to make *aliyah* must take into account all these factors, and should be made with rabbinic guidance.[90]

Agricultural Ethics

The Land of Israel and its agricultural products are considered holy, therefore there are special laws that apply to them. The most well known is the obligation in Biblical and Temple times is tithing — to separate a specific percentage of the crop and give it to the *Kohanim* (Priests of the Holy Temple), the Levites and the poor. Some of the produce would be separated from the crop and later brought to Jerusalem, where it would be eaten by the owners, and with whomever they wanted to share it. The distribution of the tithing worked according to a precise schedule that ran in seven-year cycles.[91]

The lesson of the tithes is that the world and everything in it belongs to God: By obligating the farmer to either give away part of the crop or eat it in a specific city, the idea that God — not the human — is the ultimate landowner was well learned. The other purpose of the tithes was to support those who did not have land of their own, and who worked for the communal good. The Levites and the *Kohanim* were dedicated to working in the Temple in Jerusalem and to teaching Torah, and therefore they did not inherit land like the rest of the nation. Because of this, the Torah granted them the income from these taxes as their means of livelihood.[92] Another purpose of these agricultural laws is to inculcate in the Jewish people the positive character traits of compassion, justice and humility.[93]

Today, since most Jews do not live in Israel and the *Kohanim* are not in a state of ritual purity (prerequisite to eating tithed food), tithes are not given, nor are they eaten in Jerusalem.[94] There is still an obligation, however, to separate the tithes from agricultural produce of the Land of Israel and dispose of them in a respectful fashion. The law requires that one separate a little more than 1 percent of any produce grown in Israel and recite a declaration before the fruit or vegetables may be eaten.

There is yet another symbolic remembrance of agricultural tithes observed today, both inside and outside the Land of Israel. When one makes dough for bread, a small amount is taken off and burnt. In Holy Temple times, when the *Kohanim* were in a state of ritual purity, this separated dough was given to them. The separated dough was called *challah*, from which our term for special Sabbath and festival bread is taken.[95]

The Biblical laws of tithes only apply to agricultural produce. Jewish practice has extended the idea,[96] however, to tithing one's income as well. It has become the universal custom, (according to some authorities, it's the law) that we give at least 10 percent of our income to charity. This practice is known as *ma'aser kesafim,* tithes of money.[97] In setting aside a part of our incomes for charity in this way, we are acknowledging that our money was not earned through our efforts alone, but is a gift from God. As He has chosen to reward us with financial gain, it is our duty to share it with others.

Sabbath of the Land

The seventh year of the agricultural cycle is known as *Shmittah*, the Sabbatical year.[98] In Israel, no new crops are planted and only maintenance work is done on crops and trees that already exist. Farmers may not sell their produce or prevent people (or animals) from entering their fields and consuming the crops.[99] Maimonides maintains that one of the effects of this law is to increase the productivity of the land, by having it lay fallow for a year.[100] He and most other commentaries agree, however, that the primary purpose of *Shmittah* is to allow everyone equal access to the land, and to have the landowners feel like tenants once in a while. This experience will help them understand that "the earth is the Lord's"[101] and that the main purpose of life is not the accumulation of possessions.[102] The Sabbatical year also provides an opportunity for hard-working farmers to devote more time to Torah study. The observance of *Shmittah* fell into disuse during the long Jewish exile from the Land. Today, however, with the return of Jews to their homeland and the increase in Jewish observance among Israeli farmers, there are farms and kibbutzim that strictly observe the *Shmittah* laws. These farmers spend much of their time during the *Shmittah* year revitalizing their connection to God by studying Torah.

A Noble Harvest

In earlier times, Jewish law governed the harvest of crops in Israel. These laws were designed to channel support to poor people, while at the same time allowing them to retain their dignity by having them work for what they received. When a farmer harvested his field he was obligated to leave one corner (*peah,* in Hebrew), unharvested, so that the poor could harvest it themselves and keep the produce.[103] When he gathered his sheaves together, any sheaves that he forgot (*shikchah*) had to be left for the poor to gather for themselves.[104] If he inadvertently dropped any stalks during the harvest (*leket*), he would leave them for the poor as well.[105]

These laws only apply when there are, in fact, poor people who go to the fields to collect or harvest the grains. Nowadays, however, poor people do not wait near farms for the harvest. Instead, they are generally supported by various charitable organizations, and therefore some of these laws are not applied in practice today.[106]

First Fruits, Mixed Fruits, Forbidden Fruits and New Fruits

In Temple times, laws (that were not related to supporting the needy) also regulated planting and harvesting. Some of these laws are still implemented today, while others cannot be. The first fruits to appear on a tree, for example, were taken to the Temple in Jerusalem as an offering.[107] This offering of the first fruits, *Bikurim,* was another way of expressing gratitude to God for His blessings. Since the destruction of the Temple, this *mitzvah* cannot be fulfilled until the Messianic Era, when the Third Temple will exist.

For the first three years after a tree is planted, the fruit is known as *orlah,* and we may not eat it. Rather, it is left for birds and animals to eat. The fruit of the fourth year is holy, and therefore we wait for the fifth year to eat of the fruit.[108] In Israel, any fruit that might possibly be *orlah* is prohibited. Outside of Israel, however, unless one knows that the fruit is definitely *orlah,* it may be eaten.[109]

Similarly, wheat, barley, rye, spelt and oat grains from a new harvest was, in Temple times, not to be eaten until the first sheaf is cut in a special manner and brought as an offering in the Temple on the second day of Passover.[110] Any grain that was sown after the bringing of this offering, known as the *Omer,* was not to be eaten until after the next year's offering. This prohibition is known as *chadash,* "new," referring to the new harvest. Since the destruction of the Temple, we can no longer bring the *Omer* offering. Nevertheless, grain from the new harvest is still forbidden until the day after the offering would have been brought. There is some controversy about whether this prohibition applies only in Israel or outside as well.[111] Today, though some follow the more stringent view, most Jews outside of Israel follow the lenient view that *chadash* does not apply in the Diaspora.[112]

The underlying message of both *orlah* and *chadash* is one of restraint and self-control, and the acknowledgement that, since everything ultimately belongs to God, it may only be used for purposes that are in keeping with God's plan for the world. We are only free to use the fruit or grain after bringing some to Jerusalem to eat or for use as an offering, acts which impress upon us that everything we have is a gift of God.[113]

The prohibition against mixing seeds and grafting different species together, know in Hebrew as *kilayim,* applies both in and outside Israel.[114] One of the ideas behind this prohibition is the principle that just as in nature there are laws that delineate species, so too there are moral laws that are part of the fabric of Creation. The same God Who commanded the plants and animals to appear "in their own species"[115] also has moral demands on the human being. Do not change the nature of Creation is the central idea of this command.[116]

Showing Appreciation

It is customary to say Psalm 126 before reciting the Grace After Meals:[117]

A Song of Ascents: When God will return the captivity of Zion, we will be like dreamers. Then our mouth will be filled with laughter and our tongue with glad song. Then they will declare among the nations, "God has done greatly with these." God has done greatly with us; we were gladdened. O God — return our [people in] captivity like springs in the desert. Those who tearfully sow will reap in glad song. He who bears the measure of seeds walks along weeping, but will return in exaltation, a bearer of his sheaves.

Today, when we eat fruit that has been grown in Israel and observe its agricultural laws, we engage in activities that were not possible for most Jews throughout history. The haunting, yet joyous words of the psalm describe our experience beautifully.

For Further Reading

▶ *Faith & Fate: The Story of the Jewish People in the Twentieth Century* by Rabbi Berel Wein (Shaar Press, 2001)

▶ *Jerusalem: Eye of the Universe* (also, in an edition with pictures with added subtitle *A Pictorial Tour of the Holy City*) by Rabbi Aryeh Kaplan (OU/NCSY, 1993)

▶ *The Land of Our Heritage* by David Rossoff (Feldheim, 1987)

NOTES

References to books of the Talmud refer to the Babylonian Talmud unless otherwise noted.

1. Genesis 12:1-2.
2. Ibid. 12:5, Rashi ad loc.
3. Ibid. 12:8, Nachmanides ad loc.; ibid., 21:33, Rashi, ad loc.
4. Ibid. 12:8.
5. Ibid. 22:19.
6. Ibid. 13:18.
7. Ibid. Chap. 15.
8. Ibid. Chap. 23. See also Leah Bronner, *Biblical Personalities and Archaeology*, Keter Publishing House, Jerusalem, 1974, p. 21.
9. Genesis 35:19.
10. Ibid. 23:19, 25:9, 35:19, 35:29, 50:13; Joshua 24:32.
11. Genesis 50:24-26.
12. I Kings 6:1. The Temple was completed by King Solomon 480 years after the Exodus.
13. *Gittin* 58a.
14. Ezra, Chap. 1.
15. Nehemiah, Chap. 2.
16. See chapter on Chanukah.
17. *Tzfat* in Hebrew — a city in the mountains of the Galil region, in the north of Israel.
18. Incorporated as part of the standard Friday night service. See *The Complete ArtScroll Siddur, Ashkenaz,* pp. 316-319.
19. The Chassidic movement was started circa 1700 by Rabbi Israel Baal Shem Tov. Most of its early adherents lived in Russia, Podolia, Poland and the Ukraine. The movement emphasized joy, spontaneity and sincerity in the service of God and encouraged people to attach themselves and emulate a pious rabbi, known as a *Rebbe*. They formed communities around their particular *Rebbes,* and wore specific clothing identifying them as members of a Chassidic group. Today Chassidism is prevalent worldwide.

20. Literally, the "Genius of Vilna," Rabbi Elijah Kramer, the foremost Torah scholar of the 18th century.
21. The Jewish community of Iraq, for example, has been in existence since the destruction of the First Temple by the Babylonians.
22. In the Har Nof neighborhood of Jerusalem.
23. Paul Johnson, *A History of the Jews,* Harper and Row Publishers, New York, 1987. Part One, Israelites.
24. Rabbi Yehudah Halevy, *Sefer Hakuzari,* (also known simply as *Kuzari*) Israel, 1979. 2:14, 4:3.
25. Nachmanides, Commentary on Deuteronomy 18:15.
26. *Sefer Hakuzari,* 2:8-14. See also Rabbi Eliyahu Dessler, *Michtav M'Eliyahu,* III, pp. 193-196.
27. Christianity, Islam, Bahai; *Kuzari,* 4:11.
28. Calculation of Rabbi Yishayahu Halevi Horowitz, *Shnei Luchot Habrit,* Heichal Hasefer, Bnei Brak. Notes to Introduction of Torah Shebichtav. In exile, we are obligated to 270 commandments, hinted at in Song of Songs 5:2, "I was asleep [but] my heart was awake." The numerical value of the Hebrew word for "awake" is 270. See also Rabbi Yitzchak Hutner, *Pachad Yitzchak,* Rosh Hashanah 4.
29. Nachmanides, Commentary on Leviticus 18:25; Deuteronomy 11:18.
30. Maimonides, *Book of the Commandments,* Positive Commandment 153.
31. *Kuzari,* 2:16.
32. Isaiah 2:3.
33. Rabbi Moshe Sofer, *Teshuvot Chatam Sofer,* Mekor Press, Jerusalem, 1970. Introduction to Responsa on *Yoreh Deah,* Pituchei Chotam.
34. Rabbi Samson Raphael Hirsch, Commentary on Genesis 48:3-4. See also Rabbi Yechiel Yaakov Weinberg,

Responsa Seridei Aish Vol. 4, p. 365; *Shem MiShmuel, Parshat Balak.*

35. *Otzar Midrashim*, Tzedakot 3 — *Gadol shimushah yoter milimudah.*

36. Nachmanides, Commentary on Genesis 25:34.

37. *Bamachaneh* (In the Camp).

38. In Israeli slang, a general's stars are called "falafels" and an officer's bars are called "coffins."

39. *Zohar, Raya Meheimnah* 3:225a; Rabbi Chaim Volozhin, *Nefesh Hachaim*, Sha'ar 3, Chap. 4.

40. Ibid. Sha'ar 3, Chaps. 5-6.

41. *Yoma* 87b.

42. Genesis 28:17. See also *Shnei Luchot Habrit*, Notes to Tractate *Tamid*, Ner Mitzvah 13, First Note; *Teshuvot Chatam Sofer*, Responsa *Yoreh Deah*, 233.

43. *Midrash Shmot Rabbah*, 2:2; *Midrash Tanchuma, Shmot* 10; *Midrash Tehillim* 11:3.

44. Hillel Halkin, "Philologos" column from *The Forward*, January 12, 2001.

45. Noted in a speech by Yitzchak Rabin at Hebrew University on receiving an honorary doctorate. See also *Follow Me*, a video of the Six Day War, filmed by Israeli combat photographers, produced by *The Jerusalem Post.*

46. Deuteronomy 11:12.

47. Leviticus 26:32-33.

48. Rashi, ad loc.

49. Nachmanides, Commentary on Leviticus 26:16.

50. Exodus 3:8, 13:5, 20:24.

51. Deuteronomy 8:7-8.

52. Josephus Flavius, *The Complete Works of Josephus Flavius, The Jewish Wars*, Bigelow, Brown and Co., N.Y. Book III, 3:2.

53. Nachmanides, *Collected Writings of Nachmanides*, Edited by Charles B. Chavel, Mossad Harav Kook, Jerusalem, 1978, p. 378.

54. Mark Twain, *Innocents Abroad or the New Pilgrims Progress: Being Some Account of the Steamship Quaker City's Pleasure Excursion to Europe and the Holy Land*, London: 1881 (New American Library, 1997).

55. In 1999, Israel shipped some 1.124 billion flowers to Dutch flower bourses, according to Israel's Production Marketing Board of Ornamental Plants (PMBOP).

56. Ezekiel 36:8. See also *Sanhedrin* 98a; Rashi ad loc.

57. Genesis 15:18; Rashi ad loc.

58. Ibid. 26:3-4.

59. Ibid. 28:13.

60. Numbers 33:50 — 34:1-29.

61. Exodus 6:8.

62. Rashi, Commentary on Genesis 1:1.

63. *Chazakah,* in Hebrew. See *Bava Batra,* Chapter 3.

64. *Merriam-Webster's Dictionary of Law*, Merriam-Webster Incorporated, 1996.

65. *Code of Jewish Law, Orach Chaim*, 560:1, *Mishnah Berurah* ad loc. 1

66. Ibid.

67. *Judaic Classics Library*, CD-Rom, Version IIc2, Institute for Computers in Jewish Life and Davka Corporation, 1991-1996.

68. James Parkes, *Whose Land?* Oxford University Press, London, 1949.

69. Deuteronomy 30:3-5.

70. Genesis 14:18.

71. Ibid., Chap. 22.

72. *Pesikta DeRav Kahana, Vayera* 22:14.

73. Genesis 28:11, Rashi ad loc.

74. *Zevachim* 54b.

75. I Kings, 6:14.

76. *Yoma* 19a.

77. Psalms 125:2.

78. Tosafot *Bava Kama* 82a *"ve'eina"*; Tosafot *Bava Batra* 23b *"beyoshevet."*

79. Jerusalem Talmud *Bava Kama* 7:7.

80. Mishnah *Ketuvot* 110b — *"hakol ma'alin."*

81. Numbers 33:53.

82. Nachmanides, Commentary on the Torah, ad loc.; Nachmanides, Critique

of Maimonides' *Sefer Hamitzvot, Mitzvot aseh shechachach otan harav,* 4.

83. *Ketuvot* 110b.

84. Ibid. *Gittin* 8b.

85. Rabbi Ya'akov Emden, *Siddur Beit Ya'akov,* Pe'er Hatorah, Jerusalem, 1973, *Sulam Beit-El,* 6.

86. Rabbi Yitzchak De Leon, *Megillat Esther, Mitzvot aseh shechachach otan harav,* 4; Rabbi Yoel Teitelbaum, *VaYoel Moshe,* p. 198.

87. Rabbi Israel of Shklov, *Pe'at Hashulchan,* Yad Binyamin Publishing, Jerusalem, 1968, Chap. 1, par. 3.

88. 1895 – 1985.

89. Rabbi Moshe Feinstein, *Igrot Moshe,* New York, 1957. *Yoreh Deah* 3:122, *Even Haezer* 1:102.

90. See *Pitchei Teshuvah* 6 on *Shulchan Aruch, Even HaEzer* 75; *Pe'at Hashulchan* 1:3; Rabbi Eliezer Yehudah Waldenberg, *Responsa Tzitz Eliezer* 14:72; Rabbi Isaiah Karelitz, *Igrot Chazon Ish* 1:177.

91. Leviticus 22:10; Numbers 18:21; Ibid., 18:26-29; Deuteronomy 14:22-27; Ibid., 14:28. The tithes took the form of taxes and followed a seven-year cycle. *T'rumah,* the tax for the *Kohanim,* and *Ma'aser Rishon* (First Tithe), which was given to the Levites, was taken every year except the seventh. The Levites, in turn, also gave a portion of the tithes they received to the *Kohanim* (*t'rumat ma'aser*). *Ma'aser Sheni* (Second Tithe) either was taken to Jerusalem and eaten there, or was exchanged for money to buy food in Jerusalem. The Second Tithe was only taken on the first, second, fourth and fifth years of the cycle. (Since this was not eaten exclusively by the owner, but usually shared with the people in Jerusalem, some suggest that this was compensation for the population of Jerusalem who hosted the entire Jewish people on the pilgrimage fes-

tivals, three times a year. The tithes of the third and sixth years (*Ma'aser Ani*) went to the poor. The seventh year was the Sabbatical year and no tithes were taken.

92. Deuteronomy 18:8-24.

93. Dayan Dr. I. Grunfeld, *The Jewish Dietary Laws,* The Soncino Press, London, 1972. Vol. II, Chap. 1.

94. Ibid. vol. II, Chap. 3.

95. For the declaration and procedure, see *The Complete ArtScroll Siddur, Ashkenaz,* pp. 226-227.

96. Tosafot *Taanit* 9a "*aser te'aser.*"

97. *Code of Jewish Law, Yoreh Deah,* 249:1, Ramah, Gaon of Vilna, ad loc.

98. Leviticus 25:6.

99. Ibid. 25:1-7; Exodus 34:21.

100. Maimonides, *Guide for the Perplexed,* Mossad Harav Kook, Jerusalem, 1977. Section 3, Chap. 39.

101. Psalms 24:1.

102. Grunfeld, ibid.

103. Leviticus 19:9; 23:22.

104. Deuteronomy 24:19.

105. Leviticus 19:10; 23:22; Deuteronomy 24:20-22.

106. *Code of Jewish Law, Yoreh Deah* 332:1, Rama ad loc.; Notes of the Gaon of Vilna, 1.

107. Exodus 23:19; 34:26.

108. Leviticus 19:23-24.

109. *Berachot* 36a; Maimonides, *Mishneh Torah,* Ma'achalot Asurot 10:11.

110. Leviticus 23:9-14.

111. *Kiddushin* 37a; *Menachot* 68b.

112. *Shulchan Aruch, Yoreh Deah,* 293, *Be'er Hagolah* ad loc.

113. Grunfeld, Vol. II, p. 43.

114. Leviticus 19:19; Deuteronomy 22:9.

115. Genesis 1:12.

116. Rabbi Samson Raphael Hirsch, *Horeb,* The Soncino Press, London, 1981, Chap. 57.

117. *Shulchan Aruch, Orach Chaim* 1; *Mishnah Berurah* 11.

Looking Jewish

Modest clothing, head coverings, beards, tatoos

Modesty, Shmodesty!
As Long As You Look Good!

> *What does God require of you but to do justice, to love kind-*
> *ness and to walk modestly with your God?*[1]

Modesty (*tzniut*) is an attitude to life that informs the way we speak, walk, think and dress. It dictates that we not put every quality on display; not flaunt our wealth, beauty or success; and recognize that the inner, spiritual world is more important than the external world. These ideas are most overtly expressed in the way we dress.

Clothing is worn by people all over the world; it distinguishes humans from animals. It testifies to the inner dignity and honor of the human being, who possesses a Divine soul. That is why one Talmudic Sage used to refer to his clothing as that which gives honor.[2]

Clothing and appearance play important roles in society. They are used to identify the wearer with a particular group or ideology; they may express one's status in society and they often serve to enhance the wearer's beauty. When choosing clothing, a person may decide to emphasize the physical self and conceal his or her spiritual essence or to reveal more of the spiritual self by de-emphasizing the physical. The way a person dresses can either send the message, "Look at my body, this is me!" or it can declare, "Listen to what I say, I have spiritual presence."

Our clothing affects not only the way others perceive us, but also the way we perceive ourselves. Do we identify primarily as a body (e.g. "The Material Girl" and Jesse "the Body" Ventura) or as a soul with intellect and emotions?

This is not to suggest that one should dress in an unattractive manner. On the contrary, the Torah instructs always to present a pleasant, neat and dignified appearance.[3] In our interactions with other people, our clothing should serve to focus attention on the face and the personality, not the body.

A person's face is the one part of the body that reveals his or her inner spiritual essence. The Hebrew word for face, *PaNiM,* has the same three-letter root as *PNiM,* meaning "inside" — because the face is a window into one's inner being.[4] For this reason, the Jewish tradition of modesty never required, or even encouraged, covering the face. The Jewish laws of modesty do, however, require that neither men nor women dress in a provocative or suggestive fashion, or in clothes designed to highlight the sexuality of the body.[5] Because of its inherent sexuality, one's torso should be covered; for the same reason, women are also required to cover thighs and upper arms.[6] Jewish law also obligates us to conform to local custom when it goes beyond these minimum objective requirements.[7] For example, in Victorian times, a woman who would wear her skirt above her ankle would be seen as brazen. Therefore a Jewish woman at that time was required to meet local standards of modesty that went beyond Jewish law. The reverse, however, is not true. Even if local custom is to expose parts of the body prohibited by Jewish law, one may not follow local fashions.

For several reasons, special emphasis is placed and more stringent standards apply to women in the area of modesty. Anything powerful must be used responsibly and for the right purposes. The power and impact of women's beauty is mentioned numerous times in the Torah, Prophets and Writings. It is something that should be treasured and used appropriately, in a loving relationship between a husband and wife. The root of the word for modesty *(tzniut)* also means to "hide" or "treasure";[8] by dressing modestly, a woman demonstrates that she treasures one of her great powers, her beauty. Observing the laws of modesty also helps to prevent a woman from being turned into the object of someone else's sensual gratification. It encourages interactions in which people are judged not by their bodies, but by their inner essence.[9]

We are not ashamed of our bodies, nor do we look at them as impure; on the contrary, we care for our bodies and value their beauty. We believe, however, that the appropriate time and place for using that beauty and sensuality is not in the public arena, but in the privacy of a holy and loving relationship between a man and woman, a relationship that is spiritual and emotional, as well as physical. As the Jewish commentator Nachmanides writes, "When husband and wife are intimate ... there is nothing so holy and pure ... God did not create anything that is ugly or shameful. If the reproductive organs are said to be shameful, how can it be said that the Creator fashioned something blemished?"[10]

Dressed to Kill

It is one of the great tragedies of our times that many women dress in ways that are calculated to please the casual male spectator. By dressing this way, they cultivate an image of themselves that is based entirely on their external appearances and their value as an object of pleasure to a man,[11] when in reality, the truest beauty of a woman is internal. A verse in Psalms informs us, "The entire glory of the daughter of the King is within ..."[12]

This is one reason that the Torah actually prohibits men to stare at women for their pleasure.[13] When a man disregards the fact that a woman is much more than a beautiful body or pretty face, and focuses on her for his own pleasure, he objectifies and degrades her.

Often, the way a person dresses indicates whether or not they treasure that internal, essential self. A Jewish woman dresses to look attractive, but she does not dress to attract; she may wear elegant and beautiful clothing, but the message of her clothing should be that there is more to her than meets the eye, that her beauty is not merely skin deep.[14]

Women's Hair Covering

A Biblical commandment obligates married women to cover their hair.[15] Although the Torah offers no explanation of this commandment, from the context it appears to be connected to a woman's relationship with her husband and her mastery of her sensuality.[16] As any shampoo commercial demonstrates, a woman's hair can greatly enhance her beauty; it can be incredibly seductive and exciting.

Covering her hair is an assertion of the woman's bond of intimacy with her husband; it is, in a sense, a "crown of modesty."[17] When a married woman covers her hair[18] it is an act of dedication to the ideals of modesty.

The Talmud relates this obligation to the general laws of modesty.[19] As mentioned earlier, the Hebrew term for modesty also means to treasure something. Perhaps the idea is that since the hair is an object of feminine beauty, by covering it when she gets married, the woman is treasuring her new and exclusive relationship with her husband. She demonstrates that there is only one person with whom she wants to share all of her beauty — only one person with whom she wants to share intimacy — her husband.

A woman may cover her hair with a hat, scarf (Yiddish, *tichel*), kerchief or wig (Yiddish, *sheitel*).[20] To a large extent, the particular way in which a woman covers her hair is a matter of personal preference, although customs do vary among different communities. In many Sephardic communities, wigs are considered unacceptable[21] and women only wear scarves or hats. In some Chassidic communities, a small hat or scarf is worn together with a wig, to make it obvious that the woman is wearing a head covering. Many women choose scarves or kerchiefs for casual wear and a hat or *sheitel* on more formal occasions.

Differences of opinion and custom also exist regarding how much hair to cover and how much may be left uncovered;[22] whether to cover hair in one's house[23] or only outside the house;[24] and at what point in the marriage ceremony to begin covering the hair. Generally, these issues are decided between a husband and wife, in consultation with their rabbi, taking local custom into account.

Men's Head Covering – Yarmulka

The head covering worn by Jewish men is known as a *kippah* (literally, dome) or *yarmulka*. The word *yarmulka* is made up of two Aramaic words, *"yarei"* and *"malka,"* which mean "fear of the King."[25] This name expresses one purpose of the head covering, which is to remind us that we are always in God's presence. It is worn constantly to encourage a feeling of awe that this awareness should bring. As early as Talmudic times, the Sages advised a mother to cover her son's head so that he would know that the power of God is above him at all times.[26] Today, it is customary to educate boys to wear *yarmulkas* even when they are very young,[27] most commonly from age three.

The Sages also associated covering the head with the characteristic of humility,[28] related perhaps to the fact that in ancient times, slaves would wear a head covering.[29] The practice of men covering their heads became so widespread that by the 17th century it was recorded in the *Code of Jewish Law*.[30] Later in history, it became customary for Gentiles to uncover their heads when praying or entering a church. Since the Torah prohibits imitating the customs of other religions,[31] Jews are obligated specifically to cover their heads during prayer.[32]

No particular requirements regulate the color, material[33] or size[34] of the headcovering. Multicolored crocheted *kippot*, black felt *yarmulkas*, baseball caps and black fedoras are all acceptable. It is interesting to note, however, that today the different types of headcoverings usually identify a wearer's affiliation within Judaism. Some people always wear a hat anytime they go outside, as well as for prayer. Others have specific headcoverings that are used for special occasions. Members of many Chassidic groups, for example, wear *shtreimlach* or *spodeks*,[35] fur hats similar to those that were once worn by the nobility in Eastern Europe. They wear these on Shabbat and festivals, to show that at these times, every Jew becomes like royalty.

The standard *kippah* of religious Zionists is white or colored and intricately crocheted, while a typical American *yeshivah*[36] student might wear a black velvet or leather *yarmulka*. Certainly, the style of *yarmulka* that someone wears should never determine how we evaluate that person; it is merely one way in which individuals identify themselves with a particular group or ideology to which they feel an affinity.

Since wearing of a head covering at all times is a custom (albeit very widespread) and not a legal requirement,[37] Jewish law allows one to remove the head covering in situations where wearing it would jeopardize one's livelihood.[38] The exception may be made, for example, for lawyers appearing in court, or people doing business in a place where observant Jews are a rarity. (A halachic authority should be consulted in specific cases.) Most men, however, will wear a head covering at all times (except, of course, when bathing, swimming and sleeping[39]). When studying Torah, praying or saying a blessing, wearing a head covering is obligatory.[40]

It's Not Greek to Us!

A further insight into the significance of covering one's head or hair emerges when one examines the contrast between statues of the Greek philosophers who were almost always portrayed bareheaded,[41] and the attitude of the Talmudic Sages, who were "repelled by an uncovered head."[42] This distinction reflects two profoundly divergent philosophies. The Greeks believed that their minds were the ultimate judges of reality and morality, that there is no cap or limitation on the human brain.[43] The Jewish view accepts that our perception is limited, that human beings are not the ultimate arbiters of moral standards — that these must come from an absolute source — God. We cover our heads to demonstrate our understanding that the human mind is limited, that an Authority exists above and beyond us.[44]

Vive La Difference!

> *Male garb shall not be on a woman, and a man shall not wear a feminine garment, for anyone who does so is an abomination of God.*[45]

The Torah celebrates the individuality of the sexes and does not want us to blur the distinction between men and women.[46] Just as men and women are physically distinct, they are spiritually unique as well.[47] Each has his or her own vital role in the world, each has a path to God and an individual perspective on life. In part to preserve these differences, the Torah prohibits men to dye their hair, wear women's clothing, shave their body hair, or engage in other specifically feminine practices.[48] Women are likewise prohibited to wear men's clothing or uniquely masculine ornaments.[49]

The way a person acts, and even the clothing one wears, has a tremendous impact on one's personality.[50] The Kabbalists explain that the clothing we wear affects our thoughts and souls, and can even distort the spiritual integrity of the wearer.[51] The prohibition against wearing clothing of the opposite sex is therefore a critical element in maintaining the uniqueness of masculine and feminine roles in life. These restrictions are also designed to curtail homosexuality and other immoral practices that are encouraged by cross-dressing.[52]

Keep Your Whiskers!

> *You shall not round off the edge of your scalp and you shall not destroy the edges of your beard.*[53]

Some commentaries explain that the prohibition against a man eradicating his beard and sideburns (*payot* or *payos*) is related to the idea of maintaining and emphasizing the distinction between men and women.[54] Other authorities suggest that it is intended to avoid any similarity to pagan practice. Since the pagans would shave their heads completely, or shave around their heads and remove the sideburns,[55] Jews specifically allow hair to grow in these areas.

Jewish law only prohibits shaving the beard and sideburns with a razor blade. Using scissors or a scissorslike device[56] (e.g., certain electric shavers[57]), is permitted. It is not unusual, therefore, to see observant Jewish men who are cleanshaven or have a trimmed beard. Even with scissors, the sideburns should not be trimmed above the point where the skull joins the jawbone.[58] Some groups, such as Chassidim, do not trim their beards, sideburns or sidelocks at all.[59] Many Chassidim grow their *payos* exceptionally long, and curl them, in order to enhance and beautify this Biblical commandment.[60]

Tattoo Taboo

... You shall not place a tattoo upon yourselves — I am God.[61]

The Torah prohibits us from placing any permanent tattoo on our bodies, whether it consists of words or pictures, regardless of what message is written or conveyed.[62] A tattoo is defined in Jewish law as any word, letter or picture that is marked on the skin by means of dye or ink, which is introduced under the surface of the skin, either through piercing with a needle, scratching or cutting.[63]

The human body is holy and is perfectly designed by the Creator to fulfil its task in this world. The only permanent sign that may be made on a Jewish person is the sign of circumcision, the Covenant between God and Abraham and his descendants.[64] Any other permanent mark or mutilation is a desecration of the human body. Some commentaries suggest that the prohibition against tattoos is also intended to prevent us from imitating idolaters and their practices.[65]

It is important at this point to dispel a widespread misconception. If, for whatever reason, a Jewish person does have a tattoo, nevertheless, he or she unequivocally can and must be buried in a Jewish cemetery.[66]

Kosher Clothing

You shall observe My decrees — you shall not mate your animal with another species, you shall not plant your field with mixed seed; and a garment that is a mixture of combined fibers shall not come upon you.[67] *...You shall not wear combined fibers, wool and linen together.*[68]

This law, which prohibits wearing a garment made of wool and linen,[69] is described in the Torah as a *chok* (plural, *chukim*), a decree or statute. This is the same word that is used to refer to a "law of nature." Just as there are physical realities in the world which operate whether or not we can understand or even observe them, so too, there are spiritual laws of the universe which do not depend on human understanding for their validity.[70]

The prohibition of wearing a garment made of wool and linen, *shaatnez,* is one such law. The effects are not discernable and the rationale is not apparent; it is a *chok*. The laws of *shaatnez,* like all *chukim,* teach us humility and obedience to the Torah. We accept them, even when our intellect does not understand their purpose.

Even though the laws of not mixing species are statutes, commentators have offered several possible rationales.[71] Some explain that God created an orderly systematic world which is nevertheless filled with infinite variety. In order to maintain both the harmony and the unique character of all parts of creation, we are forbidden to combine species that do not naturally mix.[72]

Others suggest that this prohibition is also intended to prevent us from imitating pagans, whose priests used to wear garments made of wool and linen.[73] Some understand it as an allusion to the tragedy of the first murder, when Cain (the farmer) killed his brother Abel (the shepherd).[74] Kabbalistic sources indicate that Cain brought flax as an offering to God, while Abel brought wool. The Torah does not want us to wear a reminder of that sin by mixing the two offerings, wool and linen.[75] Others explain that linen is a symbol of those functions that we have in common with all plant life, sustenance and reproduction, while wool symbolizes those functions that we have in common with the animal world, will and intellect. The prohibition of *shaatnez* is a way of stating that one should not degrade his will and intellect (wool) by allowing them to become completely intertwined with merely fulfilling the needs of sustenance and reproduction (linen).[76]

Check It Out

When one buys a garment made of wool or linen it must be checked for the presence of the other fiber.[77] It is impossible for a layperson to determine whether or not *shaatnez* is present; therefore, one should take the garment to someone who is trained in this area.[78] Linen is often found in linings, shoulder pads and the collars of wool suits, but is usually not listed in the fiber content. Checking a garment for *shaatnez* usually takes less than half an hour, and often, even if linen is found, it can be removed. In areas with a large concentration of observant Jews, many clothing stores will send garments to a *shaatnez* lab as a service to their customers.

Torah, Science and Shaatnez

When Rabbi Levi Yitzchak Horowitz, the "Bostoner Rebbe,"[79] first moved to Boston he wanted to set up a *shaatnez*-testing facility there. He heard that a professor at M.I.T. was an expert in textiles and fabrics and set up an appointment with him. After determining the best way of checking whether a material contains linen, wool or other fibers, the Rebbe said, "Professor, as you know our Torah prohibits us from wearing any garment made of a combination of wool and linen. From your experience, can you determine any negative effect of mixing these fibers?"

The professor replied, "I don't know of any detrimental effect whatsoever caused by a mixture of wool and linen. But Rabbi, my field of science has only been around for about 200 years, and your Torah has existed for over 3,000 years. My tests and studies are limited to the physical, but your Torah looks into the spiritual dimension. I am sure that God knew what He was doing when He prohibited *shaatnez,* even though I can't offer any scientific explanation."[80]

Funny, You Do Look Jewish!

What does a Jew look like? There are black Ethiopian Jews, Caucasian European Jews, Moroccan, Yemenite, Argentinean and Indian Jews. Ethnic groups within Judaism eat differently, speak differently and look different from one another, yet they are one people by virtue of their Judaism.[81]

How Jews look (or should look) is a function of their Judaism as well. Modest dress, head coverings and distinctly male and female styles of dress are some of the distinguishing features of the Jewish look, no matter what culture surrounds us. In many Jewish communities it is customary to dress in a way that is consciously different from the surrounding non-Jews. Through our behavior, appearance and demeanor we identify as Jews and proclaim our pride in being Jewish.

When the prophet Jonah was asked about his occupation, where he came from and to which nation he belonged, he offered a single response, "I am a Hebrew and I fear God!"[82]

Our ancestor Abraham was the world's first revolutionary: He questioned, debated and challenged idolatrous beliefs and stood alone against the whole world.[83] This is one reason that he was called "*Avraham HaIvri,*" Abraham the Hebrew. The word "*Ivri*" (Hebrew) is related to the word "*ever,*" meaning "the other side," because the whole word stood on "one side" and Abraham stood on the "other side."[84] This fact has been true of his descendants for much of history as well. Our independence is reflected in our appearance: The dictates of fashion and current trends do not govern our behavior — we remain securely on the other side, proud of our distinct origins and traditions.

For Further Reading

▸ *Outside/Inside: A Fresh Look at Tzniut* by Gila Manolson (Targum, 1997)

▸ *Living Jewish: Values, Practices and Traditions* by Rabbi Berel Wein (Shaar Press, 2002)

NOTES

References to books of the Talmud refer to the Babylonian Talmud unless otherwise noted.

1. Micah 6:8.
2. *Shabbat* 113a.
3. Maimonides, *Mishneh Torah*, Laws of Character, 5:1, 5:9; Rabbi Isaiah Horowitz, *Shnei Luchot Habrit*, Shaar Haotiyot, 4, Derech Eretz 9.
4. Rabbi Yitzchak Hutner, *Pachad Yitzchak*, Shabbat, Maamar 1, 2:8.
5. Maimonides, *Mishneh Torah*, Laws of Marital Relations, 24:12.
6. Ibid.
7. *Code of Jewish Law, Orach Chaim*, 75:2, Biur Halachah "*michutz.*"
8. Mishnah *Shabbat* 7:4.
9. Tziporah Heller, *Our Bodies Our Souls*, Targum/Feldheim, NY, 2003, pp. 50-55.
10. Nachmanides, *Iggeret Hakodesh*, NY, Ktav, 1976.
11. Wendy Shalit, *A Return to Modesty*, Free Press, NY, 2000, Chaps. 1-3.
12. Psalm 45:14.
13. *Berachot* 61a; *Avodah Zarah* 20a; *Code of Jewish Law, Even Haezer* 21:1.
14. Gila Manolson, *Outside Inside*, Targum/Feldheim, Jerusalem, 1997, pp. 24-28.
15. Numbers 5:18; *Ketuvot* 72a-b.
16. Numbers ibid.
17. Rabbi Samson Raphael Hirsch, *Commentary on the Pentateuch*, Numbers ad loc.
18. Ibid. *Ketuvot*; Sifri, Numbers 5:56; *Midrash Rabbah*, Numbers, 9:16.
19. *Berachot* 24a.
20. *Code of Jewish Law, Orach Chaim* 75:2, Ramah; Beer Heitev 8 ad loc.
21. Rabbi Ovadiah Yosef, *Responsa Yabia Omer*, 5, Even Haezer 5.
22. Rabbi Moshe Feinstein, *Igrot Moshe, Orach Chaim* 4:112-4; *Mishnah Berurah* 75:14 and *Biur Halachah* 75:2.
23. Rabbi Moshe Sofer, *Responsa Chatam Sofer, Even Haezer* 36.
24. *Igrot Moshe, Even Haezer* 1:58; *Mishnah Berurah* ibid.
25. Rabbi Yehoshua of Belz, *Ohel Yehoshua*, quoted in *Minhagei Yisrael, Orach Chaim*, 1.
26. *Shabbat* 156b.
27. *Mishnah Berurah*, 2:11.
28. *Kiddushin* 31a.
29. Commentary of Rav Menachem Hameiri on Talmud, *Rosh Hashanah* 8b.
30. *Code of Jewish Law, Orach Chaim*, 2:6.
31. Leviticus 18:3.
32. *Code of Jewish Law, Orach Chaim*, 2:8, *Turei Zahav* 3.
33. Rabbi Moshe Sofer, *Responsa Chatam Sofer*, Likutei Teshuvot, 2.
34. Rabbi Moshe Feinstein, *Igrot Moshe, Orach Chaim*, 1:1.
35. A *shtreimel* is a flat round fur hat with a velvet skullcap in the middle. A *spodek* is a taller, cylindrical fur hat.
36. See chapter on Torah Study.
37. *Mishnah Berurah*, 2:11.
38. Rabbi Moshe Feinstein, *Igrot Moshe, Orach Chaim* 4:2.
39. *Mishnah Berurah*, ibid.
40. Mishnah Sofrim, 14:15; *Mishnah Berurah*, 2:12.
41. Statues of Plato, Socrates, Aristotle and Pythagoras are all bareheaded.
42. Maimonides, *Guide for the Perplexed*, 3:52.
43. Nachmanides, Commentary on the Torah, Leviticus 15:8.
44. See chapter on Chanukah.
45. Deuteronomy 22:5.
46. Rabbi Samson Raphael Hirsch, *Horeb*, IV Chukim, Chap. 64, para. 433.

47. Rabbi Isaiah Horowitz, *Shnei Luchot Habrit*, Parshat Ki Teitzei, Torah Ohr 3.

48. Deuteronomy 22:5, Targum Onkelos ad loc.; *Nazir* 59a; *Code of Jewish Law, Yoreh Deah*, 182.

49. *Code of Jewish Law*, ibid.

50. Rabbi Aaron of Barcelona, *Sefer Hachinuch* Mitzvah 16.

51. *Shnei Luchot Habrit,* ibid.

52. *Nazir* ibid.; Commentary of Rashi, Deuteronomy ibid.; *Sefer Hachinuch,* Mitzvah 542.

53. Leviticus 19:27.

54. *Horeb* ibid.

55. *Sefer Hachinuch,* Mitzvah 251 and 252; Maimonides, *Mishneh Torah,* Laws of Idolatry, 12:7, *Guide for the Perplexed* 3:37.

56. Commentary of Rashi, Leviticus 19:27; *Sifrah*, Kedoshim 6:4; *Makot* 21a; *Code of Jewish Law, Yoreh Deah* 181.

57. Institute for Technology and Halachah, *Electricity in Halachah,* Vol.1, Jerusalem, 1978, pp. 136-143.

58. *Code of Jewish Law, Yoreh Deah,* 181:1; *Biur Halachah*, 251, "*afilu.*"

59. Rabbi Zvi Hirsch Shapira, *Darchei Teshuvah, Yoreh Deah* 181:9 para. 16, 181:10 para.16-19.

60. *Shabbat* 133b.

61. Leviticus 19:28.

62. *Code of Jewish Law, Yoreh Deah,* 180:1, *Siftei Cohen* 2.

63. *Makot* 21a; *Code of Jewish Law*, ibid.

64. Rabbi Ovadiah Sforno, *Commentary on Leviticus* 19:27; Rabbi Samson Raphael Hirsch, *Horeb*, IV Chukim, Chap. 63.

65. Maimonides, *Mishneh Torah,* Laws of Idolatry, 12:11.

66. Rabbi David Zvi Hoffman, *Responsa Melamed Lehoil,* 2:114; Rabbi Yekutiel Yehudah Greenwald, *Kol Bo Al Aveilut*, pp. 191-196.

67. Leviticus 19:19.

68. Deuteronomy 22:11.

69. *Code of Jewish Law, Yoreh Deah* 298.

70. Rabbi Samson Raphael Hirsch, *Nineteen Letters*, Letter 18, Feldheim Publishing, Jerusalem/NY, 1994.

71. Maimonides, *Mishneh Torah*, Laws of Exchanged Offerings, 4:13.

72. Rabbi Samson Raphael Hirsch, *Horeb,* IV Chukim, Chap. 57, para. 402, 408-410.

73. Maimonides, *Guide for the Perplexed*, 3:37.

74. Genesis, Chap. 4; *Tikunei Zohar* 69, p. 112a; Rabbi Isaiah Horowitz, *Shnei Luchot Habrit,* Leviticus, Torah Ohr, 19.

75. Rabbi Menachem Recanati, *Sefer Taamei Hamitzvot*, Negative Mitzvah 320.

76. *Horeb*, ibid. para. 409.

77. *Code of Jewish Law, Yoreh Deah*, 302:2.

78. For US and worldwide listing see http://home.comcast.net/~shatnez/testing_labs.html

79. Spiritual leader of the Bostoner Chassidim, Boston and Jerusalem.

80. Author's paraphrasing of story as heard from the Rebbe, Rabbi Levi Yitzchak Horowitz.

81. Rabbi Sa'adiah Gaon, *Haemunot Vehadeot*, 3:7.

82. Jonah 1:8-9.

83. Maimonides, *Mishneh Torah*, Laws of Idolatry, 1:3.

84. *Midrash Rabbah* Genesis 42:8, "Rabbi Yehudah."

Soul Food:
The Kosher Dietary Laws

The practice and purpose of keeping kosher

ew activities are as instinctive as eating, and few activities have such a profound impact on us physiologically, psychologically and spiritually. Many people do not give much thought to when, what and how they eat until their cardiologist tells them to lower their cholesterol level. Jews who observe the dietary laws *(Kashrut),* however, make regular decisions about what they eat, when they eat and how they prepare their food: for the observant Jew, eating ceases to be a totally instinctive activity. The dietary laws force us to stop and think about daily activities and deter us from going through life on autopilot.

Misconceptions abound about *Kashrut,* among both Jews and Gentiles. A friend of mine ordered kosher meals for his flight but the airline forgot to load the meals. A flight attendant approached apologetically with a nonkosher meal and suggested, "Sir, we did not receive your kosher meal, but maybe you can bless this meal before we heat it up, and have it instead." *Kashrut* does not mean that a rabbi blessed the food, nor does it mean that the food is from Israel (in fact, not all food from Israel is kosher).

Some people think *Kashrut* is an antiquated custom observed by a handful of Orthodox Jews. In reality, in 1988 the worldwide kosher market was estimated to be 8.5 million kosher consumers who spent $3.5 billion annually on kosher food. Overall, the general public spent $45 billion on kosher products in the year of 1998. Since 1992, sales of kosher food have been increasing at a yearly rate of 13-15 percent.[1]

The following discussion of the dietary laws, their philosophy and rational, will help clarify what *Kashrut* is really about. Once we understand the meaning of these laws, we can begin to appreciate the moral lessons that they teach.

Is It Kosher?

The Hebrew word *kosher* means proper, or acceptable.[2] The word is used in many contexts other than the dietary laws. A kosher Torah scroll, for example, is one that is free of mistakes and may be used for reading the Torah in the synagogue. This meaning of the word has also entered the English language as a slang term for something that is legitimate or permissible.[3] The most common use of the word, however, is to describe food that fulfills the requirements of the Jewish dietary laws. We will use the term *Kashrut* to refer to the dietary laws in their entirety. The Hebrew word *treifah* is colloquially used to mean "not kosher." Technically, it refers to an animal that has been slaughtered correctly but is not kosher due to injuries or disease.

Meaning of the Laws

What They Are Not

Anthropologists have viewed the laws of *Kashrut* as superstitious taboos,[4] or as a reflection of the eating habits and norms of the ancient Near East. One author explained the prohibitions of *Kashrut* as purely a matter of economic necessity.[5] A number of scholars explain the laws as being an ancient attempt at a health-food diet.[6] The law against consumption of pork, for example, is explained as an attempt to avoid contracting trichinosis.[7] The existence of about one billion Chinese people, who eat pork as a staple of their diet, would seem to indicate that pork eaters are not in any imminent danger of extinction. As one of our greatest Biblical scholars once wrote:

Is our Torah merely a concise medical guide ...? We see that those who eat the pig, and all forbidden animals and birds are healthy, great in number and without weakness or disease ... And if these laws are only for the purpose of health, what of all the poisonous herbs and plants that cause serious injury and even death, which are not prohibited by the laws of Kashrut?[8]

It is true, as some of Judaism's greatest philosophers and sages have pointed out, that the laws of *Kashrut* do confer certain health benefits.[9] None, however, suggest that this is the motivation behind the laws.[10]

What They Are

Textual evidence indicates as well that *Kashrut* is not concerned with health, economics or with superstition. When the Torah speaks about these laws it always refers to nonkosher animals as *tamei,* or spiritually impure.[11] Kosher animals are described as *tahor,* pure,[12] and the diet is associated with *kedushah,* holiness.[13] The Torah uses the same concepts of purity, impurity and holiness when discussing sexual ethics[14] and idolatry.[15] The use of these terms with regard to *Kashrut* clearly indicates that the ideas behind the dietary laws are spiritually and morally based.[16] Nowhere does the Torah refer to nonkosher food as dirty or unhealthy, and nowhere does the Torah give explicit reasons for these laws.

Jewish scholars have always understood these laws as being in the category known as *chukim,* Divine statutes that the human mind cannot completely comprehend.[17] The purpose of the *chukim* is to teach us that human understanding is not a prerequisite for doing that which is right, and the criteria for determining good and evil are not within the province of the human being. In Judaism, absolute good and absolute evil do exist and the concepts are neither relative nor subjective, but they must be defined by Divine law.[18] Morality based solely upon human reason or conviction is inadequate;[19] sincerity and belief do not ensure moral behavior. A sincere, believing Nazi is still doing that which is evil, and an insincere philanthropist is doing that which is morally correct. Our lack of understanding of the laws of *Kashrut* also teaches us humility. True morality requires humility in our relationship with God, Who is the ultimate source of moral authority.

The Hebrew word for statutes, *chukim,* is the same as the word used to refer to the laws of nature.[20] The parallel usage of *chukim* for Torah commandments and natural law teaches us an important lesson in our attitude toward fulfilling the commandments. The laws of nature are completely unaffected by human understanding or lack of understanding. Gravity will cause someone to fall even if he does not understand how it works, and fire will burn even if we do not know the chemistry of combustion. Rabbi Samson Raphael Hirsch points out that in precisely the same way "the components of the Torah remain the law even if we have not discovered the cause and connection of a single one."[21]

Although we may never fully understand the rationale behind the *chukim,* scholars throughout the centuries have described their effect and impact on the Jewish people and have enhanced our fulfillment of these laws by showing some of the deep ideas behind them.[22] Some of these explanations will be discussed below, but first we must familiarize ourselves with the basic dietary laws.

Basic Rules of Kashrut

Animal Kingdom

An animal is kosher if it has the "signs of *Kashrut,*" i.e., it chews its cud[23] and has split hooves; therefore cows, sheep, goats, deer, oxen and buffalo are all kosher. Pigs, which have cloven hooves, but do not chew their cud, are not kosher. Conversely, camels, llamas, vicunas, alpacas and guanacos that chew their cud, but do not have cloven hooves, are also not kosher. Lions, and tigers and bears, horses and elephants have no signs of *Kashrut* at all and are not kosher.[24]

Most common fowl, such as chickens, ducks, geese and turkeys, are kosher, but birds of prey like hawks, eagles and falcons are not kosher. Ostriches, emus, penguins, parrots and vultures are examples of other nonkosher birds.[25] I was once asked by an Australian emu farmer what he needed to do in order to make his emus kosher for export to Israel. I replied that, short of rewriting the Bible, there was nothing he could do — a nonkosher species of animal can never become kosher.

A sea creature is kosher if it has fins and scales. This classification includes most species of fish such as tuna, salmon, flounder, herring, perch and sole. All shellfish are not kosher; however, neither are catfish, dolphins, whales, squid, eels or giant Chinese sea slugs.[26]

Any food product of a nonkosher animal is also nonkosher.[27] Horse milk, for example, would not be kosher and rennet from a non-kosher animal is also prohibited. The exception to this rule is bee's honey. In this case, the food product, honey, comes from the nectar of the flower and is not actually part of the animal. The bee merely stores it and injects it with enzymes.[28]

Kosher Slaughter and Preparation

An animal or bird[29] must be slaughtered according to Jewish law.[30] In Hebrew, slaughtering is *shechitah*. It may not be eaten if it died in any other way.[31] The laws of *shechitah* require cutting the animal's trachea and esophagus with an extremely sharp knife. The knife must be carefully checked for nicks on the sides and edge of the blade to ensure that it will not tear the animal's flesh. The *shechitah* must be performed by an expert, competent *shochet* (ritual slaughterer), as there are many complex laws pertaining to *shechitah*.[32] He (or she) must accomplish the slaughter swiftly, and without pausing or chopping.[33] This method of slaughter also cuts the carotid artery, jugular vein and many of the major blood vessels supplying blood to the brain. This procedure almost instantaneously reduces the blood pressure in the brain to zero, so the animal loses consciousness in a few seconds and dies in minutes.[34]

The animal must be free of *treifot*, which are 70 different categories of injuries, diseases or physical abnormalities that render the animal non-kosher.[35] A kosher animal slaughtered correctly may still not be eaten if defects such as spinal injuries, holes in the lung or a severed limb are found subsequent to *shechitah*. If the animal's lungs are smooth (*chalak* in Hebrew, *glatt* in Yiddish) then the animal is considered "*glatt* kosher." All Sephardim and many Ashkenazim eat only meat that is *chalak* or *glatt*. If the lungs have adhesions on them, they must be checked for holes; but even if found to be without holes they are kosher, but not *glatt*.[36] Since most animals are naturally healthy, the animal is only checked for some of the most common *treifot* (usually damage to the lungs or the esophagus).[37]

Once the animal is declared kosher, certain parts are still prohibited and must be removed. Fat in specific areas, such as the animal's kidneys, known as *chelev,* may not be eaten.[38] The sciatic nerve in the hind legs and the surrounding fat must also be removed.[39]

Blood must be removed from the meat by soaking, salting and rinsing, or by broiling over fire. (Even an egg with a spot of blood in it may not be eaten.)[40]

Meat and Milk Don't Mix!

It is forbidden to cook or eat mixtures of milk and meat. We are also not allowed to use this mixture for our benefit, such as using a skin cream made of meat and milk, or feeding a pet with such a mixture. Dairy products also cannot be cooked or eaten together with poultry.[41]

Meat and dairy products may not be eaten at the same meal even if they are not mixed together. In fact, one must wait after eating meat before eating dairy foods. Times of waiting vary based on custom, from one hour to three or six hours.[42] After eating dairy products, such as milk, cream cheese, cottage cheese, yogurt, ice cream and butter, it is not necessary to wait before eating meat; however, one should rinse one's mouth or have something neutral (*pareve*, see below) to eat or drink in between.[43] (However, some people have the custom of waiting a half-hour before eating the meat.) After eating cheddar, Dutch or any strong-tasting cheese it is also obligatory to wait about six hours before eating meat.[44]

The category of foods designated as *pareve* are those that contain no specific meat or milk products. This includes foods such as eggs, bread, juices and water, though there are many more. These foods may be eaten with either meat or dairy meals.

We keep the dishes, cutlery and cooking utensils used for milk and meat separate from each other. A kosher kitchen will therefore contain at least two sets of all cooking, serving and eating utensils — one for meat and one for milk.[45] Milk and meat meals are served on different tablecloths.[46] Separate dishwashers are used.[47] Meat and milk dishes may be washed in the same sink at different times,[48] although many kosher kitchens have separate sinks. It is common to have a set of cooking and serving utensils that are *pareve* as well.

Processed foods require rabbinic supervision to ensure that all ingredients are kosher and that no milk and meat derivatives are mixed together in the product. Casein, for instance, is a milk derivative that is added to many processed foods, sometimes when least expected. One summer, while engaged in a favorite Australian pastime, the barbecue, I was about to drink some New Zealand beer. A friend happened to look at the label and pointed out that it contained casein.[49] Naturally, I was disappointed that I couldn't drink it during the meal, but I did feel that I had learned a lesson in *Kashrut* (as well as a lesson in loyalty to Australian beer, which is not dairy!)

Milk, Vegetables and Processed Foods

All fruits and vegetables are kosher (and *pareve*). Jewish law, however, prohibits eating insects or worms, so all produce that has a high probability of infestation has to be cleaned and checked.[50] Wheat, barley, fruit or vegetables grown in Israel are actually not "kosher"[51] until the commandments of tithing have been fulfilled. (See the chapter about the Land of Israel for a full explanation of these laws.)

Kosher milk products must come from kosher animals. Milk must be produced under supervision to ensure that no milk from nonkosher animals is mixed in. Many halachic authorities require supervision by a Jew who observes the laws of *Kashrut*. Dairy products using this milk are known as *cholov Yisrael*, "Jewish milk." Other authorities maintain that government supervision is sufficient, and as long as the product has a *Kashrut* certification it is acceptable. [52] (Milk may be certified kosher, but not necessarily be *cholov Yisrael*. These terms are printed on the label.) All cheese, even if made from kosher milk, requires *Kashrut* certification because of the likelihood that the rennet used was from nonkosher animals.[53]

Processed foods require certification by a rabbinic authority to ensure that they contain only kosher ingredients, and are not produced on machinery used for nonkosher foods.[54] The list of ingredients on the package does not provide definitive information, because small amounts of nonkosher ingredients are significant in Jewish law, but need not be listed according to government regulations. In addition, the same ingredient may sometimes be kosher and at other times nonkosher, depending on how it was produced. Glycerin, for example, can be of animal or vegetable origin, and flavors are composed of scores of ingredients, even though only the word "flavor" need appear on the label. Certain commonly used flavors may contain castorium, a beaver extract, or civet, a cat extract![55]

In most countries with significant Jewish populations, symbols indicating rabbinic supervision are usually printed on the label, making it easy to identify kosher foods.[56] The symbol usually includes information about whether the product is meat, dairy or neutral. In Hebrew, this certification is called a *hechsher*. When kosher consumers go shopping, they look at the *hechsher* first, and the price tag second. In the United States, four of the larger, well-known certifications are the OU, Chof K, OK and Star K. Products bearing these symbols may be found worldwide. There are many other reliable rabbinic supervising agencies as well. An "R" on the label is not a kosher certification; it simply means the product has a registered trademark! The letter K is not a copyrighted *Kashrut* symbol. It stands for no specific certification and does not guarantee that the product is actually kosher.

I was once in the Honolulu airport, browsing through the duty-free store, when one of the salespeople approached me with a box in his hand. "These are extremely good for *you,* sir," he said with great enthusiasm, "just what *you* need." I asked him why he thought that the chocolate-covered macadamia nuts were good for me — perhaps, I thought, he mysteriously knew about my passion for chocolate, or maybe I just looked hungry. He smiled broadly, turned over the box and proudly showed me a familiar *Kashrut* symbol. Naturally I bought them, even though the price was as high as the calorie content.

The Food Barrier

Wine and grape juice products that are not produced by Jews are prohibited.[57] There are two major reasons for this prohibition. The first is based on the Biblical prohibition against using anything that was dedicated to idolatry. Since many pagans used wine in their religious ceremonies, a blanket prohibition was instituted against using any wine of any Gentile. The main reason for the prohibition today, however, is to discourage socializing between Jews and non-Jews. What's a party without a good wine? Not drinking together acts as a barrier to sharing and intimacy, the first steps toward intermarriage. Because intermarriage is something to be avoided in every way possible, this rule is employed as an effective deterrent.[58]

Effects of the Laws

Chosen People – Chosen Food

Kashrut has contributed very significantly to our survival as a distinct nation. Jews all over the world have common dietary patterns. I can be confident that the curried *hamin* of the Calcutta Jews has no milk and meat mixed together in its ingredients. When I eat kosher French cuisine I know that the meat is not pork and that the animals have been slaughtered according to Jewish law. Jews meet each other at the local kosher bakery; they shop at the same grocery and patronize kosher butchers and restaurants. These laws are a major force in maintaining Jewish unity, and act as a social barrier against assimilation by creating a feeling of community among the Jewish people. This effect of the dietary laws is, in fact, alluded to in the Torah itself:

> *You shall distinguish between the clean animal and the unclean and between the clean bird and the unclean ... You shall be holy for Me, for I, God, am Holy; and I have separated you from the peoples to be Mine.*[59]

These verses suggest that there is a link between observing the laws of *Kashrut* and maintaining our identity as a distinct and unique people among the nations of the world.[60]

When my sister and I were teenagers, we once traveled by bus from Miami to Disneyworld in Orlando. It was a long trip and the bus stopped at a restaurant for supper. We could not eat there since the food was not kosher, so we went into the game room to play pinball instead. The manager came over to us from behind his desk and whispered, "I can see that you're not eating because our food isn't kosher. Listen, I'm also Jewish —

here, play as many games as you want for free." He then took out a key and set the machine for free play. Our observance of *Kashrut* and his respect for *Kashrut* had created this feeling of kinship.

The outside world has often identified Jews by their diet. The Cherokee Indians, for example, called Jewish peddlers "egg eaters" because they did not eat the food offered to them. (It had obviously not been prepared according to Jewish dietary laws.) Instead, the peddlers asked for (chicken) eggs, and subsisted on a diet of eggs and vegetables until they returned to their kosher homes.[61]

The laws of *Kashrut* also serve to remind the Jewish people themselves that they are different and distinct. Every time we eat, every time we go grocery shopping, or to a restaurant, these laws remind us that we have special obligations, a unique identity and a national mission.[62]

Discipline and Self-Control

One of the most obvious effects of the laws of *Kashrut* is self-control and discipline.[63] Let me illustrate this with a real-life example. Most parents are familiar with the horrors of going to the supermarket with young children. The worst part of this ordeal is waiting in line at the checkout counter. You have only five items, so you wait in the "Eight Items or Less" express line. The lady in front of you has 25 items at least; she is trying to pay with a third-party check from Paraguay, and she's negotiating with the clerk over her expired coupons (and her mortgage). You are waiting with two children under the age of six, surrounded on both sides by four-foot-high walls of sugar-based products. The children become increasingly impatient and beg for candy. Most kids will manage to scream, beg or embarrass their parents into buying the candy.

Now for my story: I moved with my family from Israel to Toronto for a four-year stay, and in the first week after our arrival, was waiting in line at the supermarket with one of my children. He asked me for the chocolate bar on display at his fingertips. I looked at the bar, did not find a *Kashrut* symbol and told him that it was not kosher. His response was silence, accepting the decision without tantrums, threats, tears or hysteria. It struck me then, that my 5-year-old son, who had been brought up with the laws of *Kashrut,* had more self-control than millions of adults. How many people accept "no" as an answer when denied a pleasure that they want *now*? If they are told something is dangerous, they answer, "I'll take precautions." Unhealthy? "I'll stop after a few." Addictive? "Not to me." Illegal? "I won't get caught." For them, not to indulge is simply not an option. But for those habituated to the self-discipline of *Kashrut*, restraint is second nature.

Of course, keeping kosher doesn't mean that everyone is a tower of strength in all situations, but there is surely a carry-over to other forms of temptation. I was told by a mother of a highly allergic child that "You can't eat this; it's bad for you," is perfectly acceptable to her *kashrut*-trained daughter. Moreover, as the child grew older, the habit of checking product labels for the kosher certification trained her to automatically peruse labels for ingredients to which she is allergic as well. Her friends from non-kosher homes threw tantrums when they were denied tempting foods and looked for ways to sneak a bite when their parents weren't looking. As she matured, the girl realized that just as allergens in her food could trigger a dangerous allergic reaction, non-kosher food triggers a negative spiritual reaction. She has no problem staying away from either.

Character Improvement

I once read an interview with a presidential candidate whose election promise was to create "a kinder, gentler America." The interview was conducted while he was engaged in hunting grouse on his estate. To an observant Jew, the contradiction between his recreational activity and his slogan is jarring. How can a person entertain himself by pursuing and killing a helpless animal and at the same time espouse a "kinder, gentler America"? A rabbi, who was asked for his opinion on hunting for sport, responded:

> *I am shocked by this activity of hunting for sport; the only hunters that are found in the Torah are the wicked Nimrod and Esau. This is certainly not appropriate for the children of Abraham, Isaac and Jacob... as it is written, "His mercy is upon all his creatures." How can a Jew kill living beings, without any other need than to pass his time?!... This activity causes cruelty and is forbidden...*[64]

In Jewish tradition we are permitted to use animals for food, however, we are not supposed to rejoice in this, and we are certainly not supposed to make a sport of it. Obtaining leather shoes or clothes also involves the death of an animal. Even though we are permitted to wear leather clothing, the common custom is to be sensitive to the suffering of the animal that had to die in order to produce the garment.[65]

Some of the laws of *Kashrut* are designed precisely to prevent us from becoming callous and cruel; they discourage, if not forbid, hunting as a form of recreation. The laws of *shechitah*, for example, ensure that the animal is killed in the quickest and least painful way possible.[66] The legal requirement of *shechitah* and *treifot* make it virtually impossible to eat meat from an animal that was killed by hunting, and ensure that the killing of the animal will only be performed by an expert.[67] By keeping these laws, we recognize that animals are not objects, but rather living beings that feel both physical and emotional pain. One of the messages of the laws of *Kashrut,* therefore, is that we may use animals for legitimate purposes, but not abuse them.[68]

Reminders

The prohibition against mixing meat and milk also serves to increase our sensitivity and awareness by reminding us of where our food comes from. Both milk and meat have their origin in living creatures, but obtaining meat necessitates the animal's death, while milk is that which nourishes life and which can only be obtained from a living animal. By commanding us to keep these elements separate, the Torah is telling us "do not be callous."[69]

Some commentaries compare the prohibition of milk and meat mixtures to the prohibition against simultaneously taking both the mother bird and her egg from a nest, or the prohibition against slaughtering a cow and her calf on the same day.[70] These acts are a symbolic annihilation of a species — by taking the parent and offspring, the "tree and the fruit" at the same time, we are overstepping our right to use nature.

Pursue Justice and Kindness

The Hebrew word for charity, *tzedakah,* has the same root as the word *tzedek,* which means justice. In Jewish law, giving to the poor is not something beyond the call of duty, it is a moral and legal obligation.[71] The Jewish farmer who worked hard in his field all year is forbidden to eat from his own crop until he has given tithes to those without land of their own. He is not being extra nice in giving away a certain percentage of his income to those less fortunate; he is simply doing what ought to be done according to the principles of justice. The Torah emphasizes this idea by declaring the food not "kosher" until tithes have been given.

One of the nonkosher birds, the white stork, is known in Hebrew as the *chassidah,* which means "the pious one." The bird is named "the pious" because it treats its fellow birds with affection.[72] My father taught me this section of the Torah when I was a child.[73] He asked, "Why is a bird with such a beautiful name and such 'piety' not kosher?" He then explained that its generosity and kindness is extended *only* to its immediate family. That type of piety is not kosher. Certainly there are priorities in giving charity and doing kindness, but it is wrong to limit our concern only to those who are exactly like us.

Symbolism

The types of animals we eat are significant also for their symbolism. The ruminants that have split hooves tend to be tranquil, herbivorous animals that rarely, if ever, attack other animals. They demonstrate characteristics that we should try to emulate — tranquility and nonviolence. Most kosher animals are also easily domesticated and trained. This idea teaches us that the animal forces within the human being should be harnessed for positive purposes and trained to be willing servants of our spiritual side.[74] We may not eat scavengers, carnivores or birds of prey — their characteristics are not those that the Torah wants us to emulate.

The Body-Soul Connection

Our concern with the characteristics of the animals that are part of our diet also goes a step beyond symbolism. Consider the common expression "You are what you eat," generally understood in the physical sense. The *Kashrut* laws take into account the fact that our nutrition also affects our spirituality in ways too subtle to discover through observation of physical phenomena. We believe that when we eat something, we actually absorb certain characteristics of the food source. The Torah selects animals that are passive, because its goal is to create a body that is a willing servant of the spirit and the intellect. We refrain from eating animals that are too active, like the carnivores and nonruminants, because their excessive physical activity reinforces the independence of the body from the soul. For similar reasons, we do not eat the most continuously active part of the kosher animal, its blood.

At the other extreme, some foods are forbidden because of their excessively dulling and slothful nature. The fat of cattle (known as *chelev)* that grows as a result of inactivity, as well as mollusks and carcasses all represent the excessive passivity that we do not want to absorb.[75]

Dignity

Another aspect of *Kashrut* is the encouragement of aesthetic sensibility. Judaism prohibits the consumption of animals that have died of natural causes or those that are injured or diseased. It also prohibits the consumption of insects and loathsome foods.[76]

It is possible that one idea behind these prohibitions is to encourage us to recognize that a human being should always behave with dignity. One of the best defenses against immorality is a strong sense of self-esteem and honor.[77] Evil should be regarded as beneath our dignity, stealing as stooping too low, gossip as petty and small minded. To help us achieve and maintain this level of self-respect, the Torah prohibits foods such as meat from carcasses, diseased animals and worms.[78]

Health and Hygiene

Although, as discussed earlier, issues regarding health are not the motivating force behind the *Kashrut* laws, they do confer certain health benefits. The prohibitions against consumption of carcasses and diseased animals, for example, have helped the Jewish community avoid common diseases and infections, even in times when little was known about hygiene and health. Avoiding pork, the principal carrier of trichinosis, meant that Jews who observed the dietary laws were free of that disease. In addition, the obligation to soak, salt and rinse meat before cooking results in a cleansing and sterilizing process.[79]

The Middle Path

Some religions seek spirituality through withdrawal from the physical world. A monastic life is glorified, celibacy and asceticism are seen as ideals.[80] At the other extreme, many pagan religions view the human as essentially an animal, incapable of elevating itself beyond the struggle for survival, so they encourage a life of hedonism and materialism.

In contrast to these approaches, Judaism chooses a middle path.[81] The Torah teaches us to elevate the physical world, neither to deny nor to idolize it. Judaism sees the physical world as essentially pure, as something that can be used correctly or misused. The human is an essentially spiritual being, clothed in a physical body.

In Judaism, the physical is not evil and is not an illusion. It is real, but it is not all of our reality. The body created by God is morally neutral, meant to be used as a vehicle for spiritual and moral accomplishments. Far from ignoring the physical, we are commanded to nourish and care for our physical bodies in every way. Even nonessential needs are to be gratified as long as this is done appropriately. In order to live a healthy life, human beings must experience pleasure in addition to having their basic needs satisfied. This is one reason that Jewish law considers it a sin to deny oneself permissible physical pleasures.[82]

A great Jewish philosopher and poet wrote the following description of the ideal righteous person:

The way of the Jewish servant of God is as follows: He does not withdraw from life so that he becomes a burden to the world, and the world a burden to him. He does not reject life, since it is a good gift that God has given him. On the contrary, he loves the world and long life, for it gives him opportunities to earn the World to Come.[83]

The laws of *Kashrut* allow us to enjoy the pleasures of the physical world, but in such a way that we sanctify and elevate our pleasure through consciousness and sensitivity. *Kashrut* recognizes that the most essential human need is not for food, drink or comfort, but for meaning.

Through the dietary laws, Judaism injects meaning even into something as commonplace and instinctive as eating.

A Jewish Army Story

Israeli law mandates that all food served to the Israel Defense Forces must be kosher. As a reserve chaplain in the Israeli army, ensuring *Kashrut* was one of my duties.[84] One afternoon, after a combat exercise in the Golan Heights, we were resting in our tent, and, as is common in Israel, the conversation turned to religion and politics. One soldier commented that if Israel's security relied on our unit we really have reason to worry — everyone agreed wholeheartedly. Another soldier, a member of a secular kibbutz, replied that the only thing Israel's security relied on absolutely was miracles. He quoted David Ben-Gurion,[85] first prime minister of the State of Israel, who said, "If you live in Israel and do not believe in miracles, you are not a realist."

The soldier concluded that the fact that the army keeps kosher probably has more to do with its success than training exercises or anything else. I was pleasantly surprised to hear him voice this opinion and shocked to see nods of agreement from the others with equally secular background. One soldier put it this way, "Keeping kosher means that we are a Jewish army, like Joshua's army, the Maccabees and Bar Kochba's rebels.[86] As long as we follow the same traditions, God will help us just as He helped them."

As these soldiers aptly demonstrated, eating kosher creates a link to Jewish tradition that goes beyond ethnic food. It is a way of life and a way of thinking that connects us to Jewish philosophy, Jewish history and the Jewish people.

Something's Cooking at the Levys

When the Levys built their house, they designed the kitchen to make keeping kosher as convenient as possible. There are two kitchen counters, divided by the stove.[87] One side is the dairy side. (The Levys use the Yiddish word for dairy, milchig.) The dairy side has a sink, as well as drawers and cupboards for a complete set of dairy cooking, serving and eating utensils.[88] On the meat (fleishig) side there is another sink and a duplicate set of drawers and cupboards for all the meat dishes and utensils. They chose distinctive patterns for the different sets of dishes and cutlery to avoid confusion.[89] Some families have two dishwashers,[90] one for meat and one for dairy. The Levys have an electric dishwasher for meat, and Shlomo, their oldest son, for washing the dairy dishes.

They use separate dishtowels for meat, dairy and neutral (pareve) — red ones for meat, blue for milk and yellow for pareve. There is no law about which color to use, but red and blue are the most common color codes for meat and milk, respectively. An additional set of cupboards is reserved for the pareve cooking utensils.

The kitchen contains a large double oven. One oven is used only for meat and pareve, and the other for dairy.[91] Although it is possible to use one oven for both, that would require heating the oven in between uses of meat and milk. The Levys prefer separate ovens to avoid the hassle of "changing over" the oven regularly. The Levys, however, do use one microwave for both dairy and meat, but they always cover anything that they heat in the microwave and ensure that they cover the turntable with a different cover for meat and dairy.[92] Some families prefer to have two microwaves.

Separate areas are not required for storing cold foods, so the refrigerator is a standard model. The family recently purchased a large freezer to better accommodate the large meals that they prepare for Shabbat and festivals, when numerous guests join them.

Mrs. Levy keeps her favorite cookbooks on a handy shelf, along with a Kashrut newsletter that keeps her informed of products incorrectly labeled as kosher, new kosher products on the market, or products that have had supervision removed. She also has a guide to the checking and cleaning of worms and insects from produce.

On the wall near the table is a colorful, laminated chart of blessings on various foods for the benefit of the younger children who do not yet know them by heart. Next to this is a holder for birchonim (bentchers), small pamphlets containing Grace After Meals.

Tonight is Shlomo's birthday, and the Levys are planning to take the children out for ice cream after supper, so Mrs. Levy is cooking a dairy meal. They usually have dairy for breakfast and lunch, and meat meals most nights. Occasionally, on Thursday nights, when Mrs. Levy is busy preparing for Shabbat, they will pick up a pizza pie at the local kosher pizza shop.

Keeping kosher at home is second nature to the Levy family and does not require any special effort. When traveling on vacation, however, or to visit relatives, observing the dietary laws requires more conscious attention. They ask their travel agent to order kosher meals on all flights[93] — with the exception of Iraq Air, this is usually not a problem — but they always take along extra food for snacks and in case of emergencies.

Occasionally, however, they find themselves in challenging situations. Once, to the children's delight, they were delayed in an airport for eight hours and forced to have a supper of soda, potato chips and cookies, the only items they could find with kosher certification. As gastric adventure is not Mrs. Levy's idea of fun, she now insists that they take along sandwiches on all their trips!

For Further Reading

▸ *Kashruth* by Rabbi Yacov Lipschutz (ArtScroll/Mesorah, 1988)

▸ *Kosher By Design* by Susie Fishbein [cookbook with information on *Kashrut*] (Shaar Press, 2003)

▸ *The Jewish Dietary Laws* by Rabbi Isidore Grunfield (Soncino Press, 1975)

NOTES

References to books of the Talmud refer to the Babylonian Talmud unless otherwise noted.

1. Information was obtained from the Union of Orthodox Jewish Congregations of America website at http://www.ou.org.

2. See Esther 8:5; Targum Onkelos ad loc. "*vetakin*"; Commentary of Rabbi Avraham ibn Ezra, ad loc.

3. *The American Heritage Dictionary of the English Language*, Third Edition, Houghton Mifflin Company, 1992.

4. W.R. Smith, *Lectures on the Religion of the Semites*, Ktav, NY, 1969, p. 357.

5. Marvin Harris, *The Sacred Cow and the Abominable Pig: Riddles of Food and Culture*, Simon and Schuster, NY, 1985.

6. See article by H. Rabinowicz on Dietary Laws in the *Encyclopedia Judaica*.

7. Trichinosis is the common name applied to a disease of rats, swine, bears, cats, dogs and humans, caused by infection with the larvae of a parasitic nematode worm, the trichina worm, *Trichinella spiralis*. Trichinosis is most often contracted in humans by eating infected pork. Information obtained from Microsoft® Encarta® '98 Encyclopedia. In fact, Jews have avoided trichinosis by not eating pork, but this is certainly not the purpose of the prohibition.

8. Don Isaac Abarbanel, Commentary on Leviticus 11:13, "*issur hama'achalim.*"

   In fact, beef can be a source of tapeworms. Anthrax, which can be a fatal disease, is transmitted by cattle, sheep and goats — all kosher animals.

9. Maimonides, *Guide for the Perplexed*, 3:48; Nachmanides, Commentary on Leviticus 11:13.

10. Even though Maimonides believed that there were health benefits to the laws, he nevertheless maintains that they are statutes that are ultimately beyond our understanding.

11. For example, Leviticus 11:4-8.

12. Ibid. 11:47; Deuteronomy 14:11, 20.

13. Leviticus 20:26; Deuteronomy 14:21.

14. Leviticus 18:19-30.

15. Ibid. 19:31; 20:7. Douglas, *Purity and Danger*, Routledge & Kegan Paul, London, 1966.

16. Some anthropologists have recognized that there are moral lessons in the laws.

17. *Yoma* 67b; Maimonides, *Mishneh Torah*, Laws of Misuse of Sacred Objects 8:8; *Shemonah Perakim*, Chap. 6.

18. Ibid. 67b; Maimonides, *Shemonah Perakim,* Chap. 6.

19. Maimonides, *Mishneh Torah*, Laws of Kings 8:11.

20. Jeremiah 33:25.

21. Rabbi Samson Raphael Hirsch, *Horeb*, Foreword; ibid., paragraph 454; *The Nineteen Letters*, footnote to Letter 18.

22. Ibid. *Pesachim* 119a, Maharsha ad loc.; Maimonides, *Mishneh Torah*, Laws of Exchanges 4:13; Laws of Mikvah 11:12; Dayan I. Grunfeld, *Introduction to Horeb*, xcviii-cv.

23. Animals that chew their cud are known as ruminants. They have several chambers in their stomachs requiring that their food be chewed more than once.

24. Leviticus 11:1-8; Deuteronomy 14:4-8.

25. Leviticus 11:13-19; Deuteronomy 14:11-20.

26. Leviticus 11:9-12; Deuteronomy 14:9-12.

27. Mishnah, *Bechorot* 5b; *Code of Jewish Law*, Yoreh Deah 81:1.

28. *Bechorot* 6b, ibid. 81:8. The nectar of flowers is ingested by worker bees and converted to honey in special sacs in their esophagi. Bee honey is composed of fructose, glucose and water, in varying pro-

portions and also contains several enzymes and oils.

29. But not fish — Numbers 11:22; *Chullin* 27b.

30. Deuteronomy 12:21.

31. Ibid. 14:21.

32. *Code of Jewish Law, Yoreh Deah*, 1:1.

33. *Chullin* Chaps.1 and 2; *Code of Jewish Law, Yoreh Deah*, Chaps. 1-26.

34. M. and E. Munk and I. M. Levinger, *Shechita: Religious, Historical and Scientific Perspectives*, Feldheim Publishers, NY, 1976, Chaps. 4-12; *An Electroencephalographic Study of the effect of Schechita Slaughter on Cortical Function in Ruminants*, Physiology Department, New York State Veterinary College, Cornell University, Ithaca, NY, 1963.

35. Maimonides, *Mishneh Torah*, Laws of Slaughter 10:10.

36. *Code of Jewish Law, Yoreh Deah*, Chaps. 29-60.

37. *Chullin* 11a, 12a; Rashi ad loc.; *Code of Jewish Law*, ibid., 39:1.

38. Leviticus 3:17; 7:23; ibid. *Yoreh Deah* 64.

39. Genesis 32: 33; ibid. *Yoreh Deah* 65: 5-14.

40. *Yoreh Deah*, ibid.; *Code of Jewish Law, Yoreh Deah*, 65-78.

41. Exodus 23:19, 34:26; Deuteronomy 14:21; *Chullin* 113a-116b; *Code of Jewish Law, Yoreh Deah* 87.

42. Ibid. 89:1. Some communities wait one hour, many wait three hours, but the most common custom is six hours. See Ramah, *Aruch Hashulchan* and *Darchei Teshuvah* ad loc.

43. Ibid. 89:2.

44. Ibid. Ramah 89:2; *Aruch Hashulchan, Yoreh Deah* 89; Sephardim do not wait after cheese.

45. Ibid. 89:4.

46. Ibid. 88:1-2.

47. Ibid. 95:3.

48. Rabbi Moshe Feinstein, *Igrot Moshe, Yoreh Deah* 1:42. If only one sink is available, it is permissible to wash dairy and meat utensils in the same sink at different times, providing that separate racks for dairy and meat are placed in the sink and that the sink is cleaned in between uses.

49. Many beers from New Zealand are considered dairy — *Kashrut Guide*, Mizrachi Kashrut Commission, Melbourne, 2002.

50. *Yoreh Deah* 84:8.

51. *Tevel* is the Hebrew term that describes the produce before tithes were taken.

52. Mishnah, *Avodah Zarah* 35b and 39b; *Code of Jewish Law, Yoreh Deah* 115:1. See Rabbi Moshe Feinstein, *Igrot Moshe, Yoreh Deah* 1:47-49; Rabbi Isaiah Karelitz, *Chazon Ish, Yoreh Deah* 41:4.

53. *Avodah Zarah* 35a; *Code of Jewish Law, Yoreh Deah* 87:11.

54. If the machinery is *koshered* — undergoes a special cleansing process under rabbinic supervision — it may be used for production of kosher food. Also, foods must be cooked or prepared with the participation of a Jew in the process.

Mishnah, *Avodah Zarah* 35a; *Code of Jewish Law, Yoreh Deah* 113.

55. A product labeled as "pure vegetable oil" may legally contain up to 2 percent animal fats. Products may have been produced on nonkosher equipment. Cookies may contain a nonkosher emulsifier, derived from animal fat. Potato chips may be fried in animal oil. Information was obtained from the Union of Orthodox Jewish Congregations of America http://www.ou.org.

56. In the USA, the most common symbols are a 'U' inside an 'O', a 'K' inside an 'O', a 'K' inside a star and the Hebrew letter *chaf* surrounding a 'K'; in Canada, 'COR' inside an oval, or 'MK' in a circle. The letter 'K' alone without any accompanying symbol is not a *Kashrut* certification. Since it is not a registered trademark, companies can, and do, print

it on the label even if the product is not kosher.

57. In fact, even wine produced by Jews is prohibited if poured by a Gentile, unless it has the designation "*Mevushal.*" Most kosher caterers use *mevushal* wines to avoid halachic problems of non-Jewish waiters serving their wine.

58. Mishnah, ibid. 29b, Gemara, Tosafot and Tiferet Yisrael ad loc.; *Avodah Zarah* Chap. 4; Tosafot, *Shabbos* 17b; *Tur, Yoreh Deah* 123.

59. Leviticus 20:25-26; see also Deuteronomy 14:2-4.

60. Rabbi Chaim ibn Attar, *Ohr Hachaim,* ibid. ad loc., *"ki kadosh."*

61. Elizabeth Van Steenwyk, *Levi Strauss — The Blue Jeans Man*, Walker and Co., NY, 1988.

62. Jacob Cohn, *The Royal Table*, Feldheim Publishers, NY, 1973, p. 30.

63. Rabbeinu Bachya, Commentary on Leviticus 11:43; Dayan Dr. I. Grunfeld, *The Jewish Dietary Laws*, Soncino Press, London, 1972, vol. 1, pp. 11-12.

64. Rabbi Yechezkel Landau, *Responsa Noda BiYehudah, Yoreh Deah* 1:10.

65. *Code of Jewish Law, Orach Chaim* 223:6 Ramah.

66. M. and E. Munk and I. M. Levinger, *Shechita: Religious, Historical and Scientific Perspectives*, Feldheim Publishers, NY, 1976, Chaps. 4-12.

67. *Code of Jewish Law, Yoreh Deah* 1, Ramah.

68. Nachmanides, *Commentary on the Torah,* Deuteronomy 22:6; Maimonides, *Guide for the Perplexed* 3:48.

69. Nachmanides, *Commentary on the Torah*, Deuteronomy 14:21; Avraham ibn Ezra, *Commentary on the Torah*, Exodus 23:19.

70. Avraham ibn Ezra, ibid.; Abarbanel, ibid.

71. Maimonides, *Mishneh Torah*, Laws of Gifts to the Poor, 7:1-2; 10:1-3; *Code of Jewish Law, Yoreh Deah*, 247:1.

72. *Chullin* 63a; Rashi, Leviticus 11:19; As to the identity of the *chassidah,* see I. M. Levinger, *Mazon Kasher Min Hachai*, Institute for Agricultural Research According to the Torah, Jerusalem, 1980, p. 76.

73. Mr. Solomon Becher of Melbourne, Australia; see *Chidushei HaRim, Pardes Yosef*, Leviticus ad loc.

74. Rabbi Samson Raphael Hirsch, *Horeb*, Soncino Press, London, 1962, Chap. 68.

75. Ibid.; Rabbi Menachem Recanati, *Taamei Hamitzvot*, Positive Commandment 70; *Sefer Hachinuch*, Parshat Mishpatim, Mitzvah 79.

76. *Code of Jewish Law, Yoreh Deah* 116:6. For example, live fish or rotting food.

77. Rabbi Zerachiah Halevy, *Baal HaMaor*, Introduction to Commentary on the Talmud. "The soul is called *kavod,* honor." My revered teacher, Rabbi Moshe Shapiro, explained that the primary feelings of obligation and morality that a person has stem from honor.

78. For a similar idea, see Abraham J. Twerski, *Generation to Generation,* Traditional Press Inc., NY, 1986, pp. 15-16.

79. Dr. Elizabeth Kauffman, Veterinary Surgeon, Biblical Zoo, Jerusalem.

80. Trude Weiss-Rosmarin, *Judaism and Christianity: The Differences,* The Jewish Book Club, NY, 1963, Chap. 5.

81. Gabriel Sivan, *The Bible and Civilization*, Keter Publishing House, Jerusalem, 1973, pp. 8-9.

82. *Nedarim* 10a; *Bava Kamma* 91b.

83. Rabbi Yehudah Halevy, *The Kuzari,* 3:1.

84. The Rabbinate of the Israeli army has three main tasks: 1) education and counseling; 2) religious needs of soldiers, such as Sabbath, festivals, prayer and *Kashrut*; 3) corpse identification, preparation and burial.

85. Born 1886, died 1973 — Israeli statesman and prime minister of

Israel from 1948 to 1953 and from 1955 to 1963.

86. Joshua succeeded Moses as leader of the Jewish people and conquered Israel from the Canaanites c.1270 B.C.E. The Maccabees led a successful revolt against Syrian-Greek rule of Israel c.140 B.C.E. Shimon Bar Kochba led a rebellion against Roman rule of Israel c.120 C.E.

87. *Code of Jewish Law*, *Yoreh Deah* 88, Yad Avraham ad loc.

88. Ibid. 93:1; 89:4.

89. If the sets are similar, it is customary to mark the dairy set of utensils — ibid. Ramah, 89:4.

90. Rabbi Moshe Feinstein, *Responsa Igrot Moshe*, *Yoreh Deah* 2:28, 29.

91. *Code of Jewish Law*, ibid., 108:1.

92. Ibid. 108:2. Some are stringent regarding use of the microwave and require either double wrapping or cleaning between meat and dairy uses. The cleaning is performed by wiping out the inside and then boiling a cup of water in the microwave until it fills with steam.

93. Kosher meals can be ordered on almost every airline for no extra charge. Standard vegetarian meals are not kosher.

Material Witnesses

Physical symbols of Jewish life: mezuzah, tefillin, tzitzit, tallit

Symbols

All human communication utilizes symbols. Spoken and written words are symbols for thoughts and feelings. Gestures, nuances of tone and facial expression convey meaning without words: A handshake may symbolize friendship; a smile, happiness. We cannot communicate directly by thought (Vulcan mind-melds notwithstanding), because we are creatures that exist in a physical medium.

Thought, which originates in the spiritual realm, must be translated into a form that can be understood in the physical world. The Torah accomplishes this type of translation by using physical objects to teach a spiritual message that would otherwise be inaccessible to human beings. Many commandments concern the use of physical objects that stand as "material witnesses"[1] for spiritual ideas. Rabbi Samson Raphael Hirsch discusses two primary advantages that concrete symbols have over the spoken word:

a) Symbols employed, or symbolic acts performed by hundreds of thousands of individuals at the same time, underscore their sense of unity, uniformity and recognition of the teachings and principles that hold them together.

b) By accompanying us throughout our lives, regardless of our momentary concerns, symbols serve us as constant reminders of the ideas they represent — an advantage that can never be attained by the spoken word or even by the written word.[2]

In this chapter we will focus on some of the more ubiquitous symbols of Jewish life: private, communal and national.

Mezuzah = Jews Live Here!

The word *mezuzah* literally means doorpost. Common usage of the term, however, refers to parchments (usually encased in a strong material) that are attached to the doorpost. The two paragraphs of *Shema*[3] — a Biblical quotation affirming the Oneness of God — are written on a parchment, placed in a container and affixed to the right doorpost of every door in the house.[4] Throughout the world and throughout history, *mezuzot* (pl.) have adorned and identified Jewish homes. *Mezuzot* have been found in Qumran, Israel dating back about 2,000 years.[5] In the Old City of Jerusalem, rather than attaching the *mezuzah* onto the doorpost, a niche was typically carved into the Jerusalem stone of the house doorpost and the parchment placed directly inside. In the "Moslem Quarter" of the Old City, one can still identify former Jewish homes by the presence of a stone with a carved-out niche in the doorframe.

Volumes could be written on the rich history of the *mezuzah*, from an artistic, historical and sociological perspective. Artists have designed beautiful *mezuzah* cases of sterling silver, marble, glass, wood and leather. In a kibbutz[6] in the north of Israel, a farmer who works in the olive groves carves cases out of the olivewood that he cultivates. *Mezuzot* abound with the designs of renowned artists such as Marc Chagall and Ron Agam. From Singapore to San Francisco, Jewish homes are identified by the *mezuzah* on the door. The outer case is only a container, however. The true essence of the *mezuzah* lies within, contained in the words of *Shema,* so carefully written on the parchment.

An acquaintance of mine, the principal of a Jewish high school in California, once noticed a captain in the United States Navy saying *Kaddish*[7] at a local synagogue. He greeted the officer, introduced himself and, in due course, learned that the captain was the commander of a nuclear aircraft carrier that had just come into port. Naturally, he asked if he could bring his students to tour the aircraft carrier and after some (ok, a lot of) nagging, the captain agreed. As a gesture of appreciation, the principal decided to bring a *mezuzah* in a beautiful sterling silver case for the officer's personal cabin. After the tour, the students presented the *mezuzah* to the captain. But they were keenly disappointed to hear that it was against Navy regulations to attach anything unofficial to the vessel. When the captain saw how upset the students were, he phoned the admiral of the fleet to request permission to put up the *mezuzah*. The admiral agreed, on condition that they paint it battleship gray. The *mezuzah* was set in place to everyone's satisfaction. Even when it is no longer an *object d'art,* the *mezuzah's* spiritual beauty and effect remain untouched.

Inside the Mezuzah

> **"...Write them [these words] on the doorposts (*mezuzot*) of** your house and upon your gates."[8]

As noted above, the phrasing of the Torah commandment suggests that the words of *Shema* be inscribed on the house itself, carved into its stones and bricks. Since the Torah also specifies that the writing must be clear and precise, however, the Oral Tradition tells us that we are to write the paragraphs on parchments, which are then affixed to the doorpost.[9] The Torah presents the commandment in this way to teach us that the effect of attaching a *mezuzah* to a doorpost is to transform the entire house into an object of holiness.[10]

The parchments are written by a scribe, with special ink,[11] in *Ktav Ashurit,* a specific Hebrew lettering style used exclusively for the Torah, *tefillin* and *mezuzah.* Even a slight flaw in the writing will render the *mezuzah* unfit for use.[12] We can appreciate this need for precision by considering the production of computer chips, where even the slightest error can make them useless. The verses must be transcribed *exactly* as they appear in the Torah. Because the Torah is the word of God — whose perfection means that He is also completely perfect — every word, every letter and even the very shapes of the letters convey meaning and have significance.

A mezuzah case and the parchment scroll that is placed inside

Home Security System

Jewish tradition teaches that in the merit of the *mezuzah* God protects our houses.[13] How does this happen? There is no magic involved, and the explanation is relatively simple. Because the degree of God's involvement in our lives is directly proportional to the degree that we are conscious and aware of Him,[14] the more that we are reminded of God's presence, the more of His presence we will experience. The *mezuzah* is a vital element in creating and maintaining that awareness — and Divine protection is the result.

The Talmud[15] states that the *mezuzah* also protects individuals from committing sin. Maimonides explains this idea:[16]

> ... *Every time a person enters or leaves his house [and notes the mezuzah on the doorpost], he will encounter the unity of the Name of the Holy One, Blessed be He, and he will remember His love, and will wake up from his slumber and his obsession with the frivolities of the moment. He will realize that there is nothing that exists eternally except for the knowledge of the Rock of Ages.[17] Immediately he will turn to contemplation [of the truth] and will walk in the path of the just. Our ancient Sages said, "Anyone who has tefillin on his head and arm, tzitzit on his clothing, and a mezuzah on his door, is assured that he will not sin"[18] — for he has many reminders, and they [tefillin, tzitzit and mezuzah] are the very angels that save him from sinning — as it says, "The angel of God camps around the reverent ones and saves them."[19]*

Home Hardware for the Heart

One obvious lesson that the *mezuzah* teaches is that we should build homes on which the words of the Torah are indeed inscribed. Through our activities, speech, hospitality and family life we can transform the house itself into a holy object. This may explain the Talmudic law which prohibits taking the *mezuzah* off of a house when leaving it.[20] To do so would be tantamount to destroying a holy object.[21]

The *mezuzah* serves as a constant reminder of key Jewish values. The two paragraphs inscribed on the parchment contain almost all of the most basic principles of Jewish belief. The first verse begins with the famous proclamation of God's unity, *Shema Yisrael,* and continues with the ideas of love of God, the study of Torah, the fulfillment of the commandments, Divine providence and the concept of reward and punishment. The *mezuzah* reminds us of these ideas and increases our awareness of God's presence in our lives. In order to remember the presence and significance of the *mezuzah*, it is customary to touch the *mezuzah* (some also kiss the fingers with which they touch the *mezuzah*) as one passes through a doorway.[22]

Nachmanides points out that the text of the verses, the parchment, and the *mezuzah's* position on the doorpost together encapsulates virtually all the major principles of the Torah. The parchment contains the words of *Shema,* the most fundamental statement of our faith in God. The *mezuzah* is placed on the doorpost, just as the Jewish people in Egypt placed the blood of the Passover lamb on their doorposts,[23] to show their allegiance to God and their devotion to His commandments. Nachmanides explains this idea beautifully in his commentary on the Torah:

> ... One who buys a mezuzah for one zuz, [Talmudic currency] ,sets it in his doorway and thinks about its purpose has already acknowledged creation, God's knowledge and involvement in the world, and also prophecy, and has declared belief in all the foundations of the Torah. In addition, he has acknowledged the great kindness of the Creator upon those who fulfill His will, whom He took from slavery to freedom ...[24]

Tzitzit and Tallit

Fringe Observance

The Torah commands us to tie fringes, called *tzitzit*, to the corners of every four-cornered garment:

> God said to Moses, saying, "Speak to the Children of Israel and say to them that they shall make themselves fringes [tzitzit, in Hebrew] on the corners of their garments, throughout their generations. And they shall place upon the fringes of each corner a thread of turquoise wool[25] ... that you may see it, and remember all the commandments of God and perform them; and do not follow your heart and your eyes after which you stray. So that you may remember and perform all My commandments and be holy to your God. I am the Lord your God, Who has removed you from the land of Egypt to be a God unto you; I am the Lord your God.[26]

The specially tied tzitzit fringes. The knots (left side of picture) and strings express Kabbalistic concepts.

The *tzitzit* consist of white[27] woolen strings tied in a very specific way to each of the four corners. A *tallit* is a large square woolen shawl that has *tzitzit* attached, which is worn specifically for prayers. Because most modern clothing does not have four corners, it is customary for men to also wear a square garment called a *tallit katan,* a small *tallit,* under their clothes, in order to fulfill the Biblical commandment of wearing fringes.[28] It is interesting to note that women are not obligated to wear *tzitzit* or a *tallit* for prayer. A woman who dresses in accordance with Jewish standards of modesty expresses the fact that she is fully aware of God's commandments without the use of other reminders. See more about this in the section below titled "For Men Only?"

Strings Attached

Virtually all societies mandate some type of clothing, no matter how minimal or crude. Often, the purpose is obviously not utilitarian, and sometimes it is completely impractical, like a man's tie. What then is the explanation for this universal human practice? The key can be found in a statement of the Talmud, in which the sage, Rav Yochanan, referred to his clothing as "that which gives me honor."[29]

Clothing expresses the human desire to be distinguished from the animals. A human being's innate feeling of dignity is an expression of the soul, the image of God within the person, which says, "I am more than an animal!" Dignity and self-respect taken to negative extremes can become selfishness and egocentricity. Used in a positive way, however, they act as barriers against immorality. Sin and immorality are seen as "beneath" us, as simply inappropriate for a being with a soul, created in "the image of God."[30]

Tying *tzitzit* onto our clothing emphasizes and reminds us that our dignity has strings attached. *"Noblesse oblige"* — nobility obligates, and indeed our nobility as humans obligates us to act morally. The fringes attached to our clothing, the symbol of our nobility and honor, are there, "So that you may remember and perform all My commandments and be holy to your God."[31]

The Kabbalists[32] suggest another meaning behind the *mitzvah* of *tzitzit*. They explain that clothes symbolize the body. Just as clothing surrounds, protects and helps the body to survive, so the body surrounds, protects and helps the spiritual soul to operate in the physical world. Thus, the clothing to which the fringes are attached symbolizes the physical body, and the fringes themselves represent the *mitzvot*, the fine threads that bind us to a spiritual reality.

Blue and White Are My Colors

Ideally, as the verse in Numbers states, the fringes should consist of white threads tied together with one blue thread, the *tcheilet*. The purpose of the blue thread, like all the threads in fact, is to remind us of higher spiritual goals and realities. The Talmud asks:

> *Why is tcheilet the color chosen for the thread? Because tcheilet is similar to the color of the sea, the sea is similar to the color of the sky, and the sky is similar to the color of the Throne of Glory.*[33]

Apparently, it was obvious to the Sages that there must be a colored thread in the *tzitzit*; their only question was why specifically *this* color. One of the commentaries[34] explains that the white of *tzitzit* symbolizes purity of action, activity free of any wrongdoing. The Sages understood, however, that simply refraining from doing evil is insufficient if one wants to attain spiritual and moral perfection. One must also actively engage in performing good deeds. These positive actions are symbolized by color, which improves a garment and elevates its status, just as the positive commandments elevate and improve human character.

The question the Talmud asks, then, is "Why *tcheilet*?" As quoted above, the Talmud answers that, "*tcheilet* is similar to the sea." In another section of the Talmud,[35] the Sages explain that the sea is a metaphor for total immersion in the Torah. The blue-sea color of the *tcheilet* string in the *tzitzit* teaches that the first step toward actualizing the Torah's teachings in one's life is commitment. Even if one's intentions are less than pure, "from impure intentions will eventually come fulfillment of the Torah and *mitzvot* for altruistic reasons."[36] This will only come about, however, if the starting point is commitment, swimming like a fish in the sea of Torah. The Talmud continues, "the sea is similar to the sky" — the heavens symbolize the performance of *mitzvot* for the sake of Heaven, i.e., altruistically. From this ideal level of *mitzvah* fulfillment a person can eventually reach the highest possible level of connection to God, symbolized metaphorically by His Throne of Glory.

Tying the Knot

The Torah states explicitly that when we see the *tzitzit* we will "remember all the commandments of God and perform them."[37] We have explained how the very presence of fringes on our clothing and the color of the fringes remind us of the commandments.

A number of deep Kabbalistic concepts are expressed in the manner in which the *tzitzit* are constructed and tied. For example, the *tzitzit* consist of eight threads tied in five knots,[38] adding up to 13, which calls to mind the Thirteen Attributes of Divine Mercy.[39]

There are no numerals in Hebrew; instead, each letter has a numerical value. The numerical value of the word *tzitzit* is 600. When this number is added to the 13 of the fringes, the total is 613, the number of commandments in the Torah (thereby reminding us to keep all of the commandments).[40] The five knots on each fringe remind us of The Five Books of Moses. When we look at the two sets of fringes on the front of the *tallit katan*, the 10 knots (five on each fringe) should remind us of the Ten *Sefirot*, or Emanations of God's Will.[41] One thread is intentionally made longer, and this longer thread is wound around the others a number of times. The number of times it is wound around the others[42] alludes to the letters in the Names of God.[43]

The knots themselves teach us that we should always be bound to God and to His Torah with a permanent knot, just as the *tzitzit* are tied to our garments. The four fringes, one on each corner of the *tallit katan*, remind us that no matter in which direction we go, or where we turn, we are always in God's presence.[44]

Tefillin

Bound Together

In the Book of Deuteronomy, God gives a commandment to the Jewish people that seems enigmatic:

> *And these words, that I command you today, shall be upon your heart. You shall teach them thoroughly to your children, and shall speak of them while you sit in your home, while you walk on the way, when you retire and when you arise.* **Bind them as a sign upon your arm and let them be ornaments**

A pair of tefillin.
The one on the left is placed on the head; the one on the right is bound to the arm.

between your eyes.[45] *You shall place these words of Mine upon your heart and upon your soul;* **you shall bind them for a sign upon your arm, and let them be an ornament between your eyes.**[46]

There is no further explanation in the Written Torah, but the Oral Tradition received by Moses at Mount Sinai clarifies the commandment to "bind the words of Torah on our arms and put them on our eyes": It is the *mitzvah* of wearing *tefillin*. Known in English as phylacteries,[47] *tefillin* are black, square, leather boxes that contain four parchments. Written on these parchments are the four sections of the Torah where the commandment regarding *tefillin* appear.[48] One box is bound to the left arm[49] with leather straps and the other box is placed on the forehead (held by a leather loop), aligned with the midpoint between the eyes. *Tefillin* are put on every day and worn during prayer, with the exception of Sabbath and festivals.

The placement of the *tefillin* conveys the idea that our actions, symbolized by the arm and hand; our emotions, symbolized by the heart (which is slightly to the left of the body's center); our intellect, symbolized by the head; and our senses, symbolized by the eyes, should all be directed toward a meaningful existence, bound by the commandments of the Torah and the love of God.[50] It is customary to recite a prayer before putting on the *tefillin,* to help one focus on the significance and effect of the commandment. This prayer expresses many of the ideas behind *tefillin* in a beautiful way:

... By putting on tefillin I intend to fulfill the commandment of my Creator ... so that we will recall the miracles and wonders that He did for us when He took us out of Egypt; and that He has the strength and dominion over all of creation to do with them as He wishes. He has commanded us to put tefillin upon the arm to recall the "outstretched arm" [of the Exodus] and that it be opposite the heart to thereby subjugate the desires and thoughts of our heart to His service ... and upon the head near the brain, so that my soul ... together with my other senses and abilities may all be subject to His service ...[51]

Although the text of the Torah commandment does not tell us anything about the appearance of *tefillin,* the Oral Tradition specifies the details.[52] Around the world, in all Jewish communities, *tefillin* are black, square, leather boxes containing specific parchments. Archaeologists in Israel have uncovered *tefillin* dating back 1,800 years,[53] and they too are black (although somewhat faded), square, leather boxes containing the same parchments. Our ancestors living in Israel just after the Roman destruction of the Second Temple[54] wore the same *tefillin* that we wear today, as taught by the same Oral Tradition. What messages and symbols lie in these detailed laws that we have so carefully preserved?

Shape

The Talmud specifically invalidates round or rounded *tefillin,*[55] they must be square. Rabbi Samson Raphael Hirsch interpreted the square shape of *tefillin* as being reminiscent of a home. We are obligated to make the entire world, starting with ourselves, into a "home" for the presence of God. He goes on to explain that the square shape has a deeper significance as well:

We note that the square was the predominant shape in the construction of the Temple and its accessories. If we consider the shapes created by the vital forces of nature, i.e., all the physical forms produced by organic energies operating without a free will of their own, we will note that most of these formations have a rounded shape ... Of all the creative organic forces it is only the energy of man, who thinks and acts freely, that constructs linear or angular forms. We therefore maintain that the circle characterizes the structures produced by organic forces not endowed with free will, while angles and squares are hallmarks of man, who can use his intelligence and free will in building his creations and structures. We may thus understand why the circular form was not used in the makeup of any sacred structure or object in Judaism. We will then understand, too, why the same rule was applied to the shape of tefillin: The tefillin represent, in miniature, the abode we must prepare on earth for the Law of God. This type of construction is expected from man because he is a human being endowed with the Divine freedom, not a creature restricted in its development by the forces of nature. The circle is associated with constraint and lack of freedom; the square is the mark of human freedom which masters the material world.[56]

Material

If we understand the *tefillin* as representing homes for Godliness, then perhaps we can understand why they are made of leather.[57] The true abode of Godliness in this world is only found in human beings, not in structures or objects. Making the *tefillin* out of any materials normally used for the construction of permanent dwellings, such as wood, stone or clay, would give the impression that the Divine Presence automatically rests within an object or structure as long as it is built correctly. *Tefillin* teach us that the presence of God will be manifest only through the involvement of a human being with free will. The materials of the *tefillin*, leather and parchment, come specifically from living beings, thus symbolizing the involvement of the living human being in the creation of holiness.[58]

Jewish law specifies that the leather from which the *tefillin* are made must come from a kosher animal, that is, specifically from an animal that we may consume.[59] This too is significant, as it teaches us that if we want to become better people (and ultimately homes for God's Presence), proximity to the ideals and laws of the Torah is not enough: We must incorporate them within ourselves. Therefore the *tefillin* are made from materials that we could, theoretically, eat (although, obviously we do not eat our *tefillin*), symbolizing complete absorption of the message of *tefillin* within ourselves.[60] In the words of a contemporary rabbi, "If you wear *tefillin* and don't think about what's in them, you may as well be wearing potatoes on your head!"

Black Is Beautiful

Both the boxes and the straps of the *tefillin* must be uniformly black.[61] Maimonides explains that this enhances the beauty of the *tefillin*,[62] and there is no question that *tefillin* with a deep, even black color have an elegant and dignified look. In addition to the aesthetic value, however, the Torah's choice of this color has a deeper meaning as well.

The sensation of blackness is due to a lack of stimulation of the retina. This occurs because little or no light is reflected from a black surface. The smooth, featureless black surface of the *tefillin* thus suggests the unique and indivisible Oneness of God, which is not reflected in anything else and to which nothing else can be compared.[63]

Black also indicates lack of illumination, as if the *tefillin* are saying to us that, although we must strive for closeness to God and we can achieve closeness, we must nevertheless not be under the illusion that we will ever be able to fully comprehend God and His infinite reality.[64]

Knots, Straps and Letters

The *tefillin* are bound to the arm and held to the head by black, leather straps. The knots of the straps and the way in which they are wrapped on the hand and fingers spell out the three-letter name of God, *Shin, Dalet, Yud – Sha-dai.*[65] The letter *shin* is also on the *tefillin* of the head. According to Rabbi Samson Raphael Hirsch, ... *the name [Sha-dai — which means "that is sufficient"] characterizes God as the One Who is sufficient for all things and in all things, but for Whom no description is exhaustive. Not even the whole universe is sufficient to encompass the infinite abundance of His being and His might...* [As the Talmud comments] "The world is not sufficient for His Godliness."[66]

A man praying while wearing a tallit and tefillin. The silver squares on the tallit are decorative additions which beautify the mitzvah.

The way the straps are wrapped around the fingers also creates a symbolic wedding ring made of the *tefillin,* through which we declare that we, the Jewish people, are betrothed to God. We recite the following verses from the prophet Hosea as we are tying the straps: *I will betroth you to Me forever, and I will betroth you to Me with righteousness, justice, kindness and mercy. I will betroth you to Me with fidelity, and you shall know God.*[67]

For Men Only?

The Oral Tradition rules that women are exempt from obligations that are "time bound,"[68] i.e., those commandments that must be performed at specific times. Some exceptions apply, such as Shabbat and festivals, which women are obligated to observe.[69] One of the more obvious consequences of this rule is that women do not wear *tefillin*[70] or *tallit*.[71] Since both are obligatory only during daylight hours (and are customarily worn only during prayer times), they are considered "time bound."[72] In all other areas, such as the *mitzvot* related to morality, all prohibitions and the overwhelming majority of *mitzvah* obligations, women and men are equally obligated.

What is the logic behind this exemption? Some commentaries[73] maintain that the Torah exempted women from the time-bound commandments because most women will be involved in educating and caring for children, a job that has no fixed hours, and few, if any, breaks. Infants do not care if it is time for the morning service, and toddlers want and need attention (now!) at any time. Something as essential as the creation of the Jewish people and the education of Jewish children may not be abandoned even temporarily for these other *mitzvot*. Just as we would not interrupt surgery to call the physician for jury duty, Jewish law does not interrupt the *mitzvah* of educating and parenting for other commandments, because it views these as having greater spiritual value than many other commandments.[74]

All *mitzvot* are finely tuned techniques to help us fulfill our greatest spiritual potential. Beyond any practical considerations, the fact that women are exempt from time-bound commandments must reflect particular spiritual qualities that differ from men. This also explains why the exemption also applies to women who are not involved in parenting.

Some commentaries see this exemption as an indication of women's spiritual advantage. Since men are generally regarded by Judaism as more aggressive and less likely to find calm moments of contemplation in which to connect to God, the Torah provides them with commandments that have specific time limitations which force men to calm down, slow down and meditate. Women are seen as naturally more calm, serene and contemplative and therefore require fewer physical reminders (such as *tzitzit*) and "timeouts" (such as specific times for prayer) than men.[75]

In a similar vein, Rabbi Samson Raphael Hirsch explains:

> *The Torah did not impose those mitzvot on women because it did not consider them necessary to be demanded from women. All time-bound positive commandments are meant ... to bring certain facts, principles, ideas and resolutions afresh to our minds from time to time — to spur us on afresh and to fortify*

us to realize them ... God's Torah takes it for granted that women have greater fervor and more faithful enthusiasm for their God-serving calling and that their calling runs less danger in their case than in that of men ... Accordingly, it does not find it necessary to give women those repeated spurring reminders to remain true to their calling ...[76]

Ultimately, the law that exempts women from these commandments remains a law not because of the explanations that are advanced for it, but because of its origin in the Torah. The explanations are *ex post facto* rationale for existent fact, not the cause of that fact.[77] They are useful to the extent that they help our understanding and increase our motivation. If the explanations prove unsatisfactory, however, the law remains unchanged. In the words of Rabbi Hirsch:

As in Nature, the phenomenon remains a fact although we have not yet comprehended ... its causes and connections, and its existence is not dependent on our investigation, but vice versa, thus also the components of the Torah remain the law even if we have not discovered the cause and connection of a single one.[78]

Selected Laws of Mezuzah

1. A *mezuzah* must be affixed to the doorposts of a home in which Jews live.[79]

2. The *mezuzah* must be written on parchment by a qualified scribe, in accordance with Jewish law.[80]

3. The *mezuzah* should be placed on the doorpost which is on the right-hand side as one enters the room.[81] Where possible, it should be placed on the outer part of the doorpost.[82] The *mezuzah* should be placed a little over two-thirds of the way up the doorframe,[83] and should be firmly affixed to the doorpost (e.g., nailed, screwed or glued in place).[84]

4. Sephardic Jews affix the *mezuzah* in a vertical position, while Ashkenazic Jews slant the *mezuzah,* with the top facing into the room.[85]

5. The *mezuzah* should be covered to protect it from the elements.[86]

6. One should not affix a *mezuzah* to the door of a bathroom, [87] nor does one affix a *mezuzah* to the door of any room that is less

---

than 7 x 7 feet.[88] Only doors or gates that have two doorposts and an architrave require a *mezuzah*.[89] A rabbi should be consulted regarding affixing a *mezuzah* to entrances and doorways that are not of the classic configuration.

7. If one rents a house for longer than a 30-day period, *mezuzot* must be put up. In Israel, one puts up a *mezuzah* even if the house is rented for less than thirty days.[90]

8. Before putting up a *mezuzah* one recites this blessing: "Blessed are You, our God, King of the universe, Who has sanctified us in His commandments and commanded us to affix a *mezuzah*."[91]

9. It is customary to touch the *mezuzah* upon entering or leaving a room; some have the custom to kiss the fingers that touched the *mezuzah*.[92]

10. All *mezuzahs* should be checked by a scribe for damage or deterioration twice in seven years.[93]

Selected Laws of Tzitzit and Tallit

1. Every Jewish male must have *tzitzit* tied on any four-cornered garment that he wears.[94]

2. Since it is unusual to wear a four-cornered garment nowadays, it is proper to wear a small four-cornered garment under one's clothing with *tzitzit* attached, in order to fulfill this commandment.[95] This garment is known as a *tallit katan,* small *tallit.* It can be purchased in stores specializing in Jewish books and religious articles. Some wear the *tzitzit* so that the fringes are visible outside their clothing, although this is not obligatory, especially for those who work and travel among Gentiles.[96]

3. The fringes should be made of white wool that was spun with the intent that the threads be made into *tzitzit*.[97]

4. A hole is made at each of the four corners of the garment and the *tzitzit* are threaded through the hole and tied with a double knot.[98]

5. The *tzitzit* should consist of four strings of woolen thread, each one spun from four strands, with one string longer than the others. When threaded through the hole, there will then be a total of eight strings.[99]

6. The longer string is wrapped around the others seven times, after which a knot is tied; it is then wrapped eight times and another knot is tied; then eleven times, followed by a knot; and finally, thirteen times and a knot, to form a total of five knots.[100] Some groups have different customs regarding the number of times the longer string is wrapped around the others. All the customs are valid, as long as there are five knots, with some wraps between.[101]

7. The *tallit* and the garment to which the *tzitzit* are attached should be white, so that they are the same color as the fringes.[102] It is customary to have black or dark blue stripes on the garment as a reminder of the color blue that was once used in the fringes.[103]

8. One is only obligated to put *tzitzit* on a garment large enough to cover the head and the majority of the torso of a 9-year-old boy. Ideally, however, the *tallit* or *tzitzit* should be at least about one and a half to two feet long from the shoulder to the bottom edge and about one and a half to two feet in width.[104]

9. Boys usually begin wearing *tzitzit* when they are about 3 years old.[105] One should wear a large *tallit*, known as a *tallit gadol*, for the morning prayers, especially for the recitation of the *Shema*.[106] In Sephardic and German communities, boys wear a large *tallit* when they become *bar mitzvah*, while in most Ashkenazic communities a large *tallit* is worn only by married men.[107]

10. One should say this blessing when putting on the *tallit gadol*: "Blessed are You, Hashem, our God, King of the universe, Who has sanctified us in His commandments, and commanded us to wrap ourselves in *tzitzit*."[108] The blessing is recited while standing and holding the *tallit* ready to put on, but before actually wrapping oneself in it. One should stand with one's head wrapped in the *tallit* for a few seconds after reciting the blessing.[109]

11. When putting on the *tallit katan* we say: "Blessed are You, Hashem our God, King of the universe, Who has sanctified us in His commandments, regarding the commandment of *tzitzit*."[110] If one will be using a *tallit gadol* for prayer later that morning, the blessing for the *tallit gadol* suffices for both.

12. This blessing is said only during the daylight hours.[111] The earliest time to recite this blessing is when it is light enough to distinguish between the blue and white threads in *tzitzit*,[112] usually about 54 minutes before sunrise.[113]

Selected Laws of Tefillin

Please note that the instructions regarding putting on tefillin listed below (#s 7-13) are halachic guidelines. To learn how to put on tefillin, one should ask a knowledgeable person to demonstrate the correct procedure.

1. Every adult Jewish male is commanded by the Torah to wear *tefillin* on his arm and head every day,[114] except on Sabbaths and festivals.[115] Custom vary regarding the wearing of *tefillin* on *Chol Hamoed,* the intermediate days of Passover and Sukkot.[116] Generally, one should follow the custom of the synagogue in which one prays.[117]

2. There are different customs as to when a boy starts putting on *tefillin.* Some start one month before turning 13, others start two or three months before, and some only begin when they actually turn 13.[118]

3. The *tefillin* are purchased from an expert, God-fearing scribe to ensure that they were produced for the sake of the *mitzvah,* made with appropriate materials and that the parchments were written according to Jewish law without mistakes.[119]

4. Although the *mitzvah* of *tefillin* ideally applies all day, it is customary to wear them only for morning prayers.[120] If one did not put *tefillin* on for the morning service, they may be worn any time during the day, but not after nightfall.[121] It is prohibited to sleep while wearing *tefillin* at any time, even for a short nap.[122]

5. The earliest time that one may put on *tefillin* in the morning is defined as the time one can first recognize an acquaintance at a distance of about 8 feet in natural light.[123] This is usually about 54 minutes before dawn.

6. The *tefillin* should be put on after the *tallit,* since the commandment of *tzitzit* is fulfilled more frequently.[124] (The Talmud generally rules that we fulfill a more frequently occurring *mitzvah* before a less frequent one.[125])

7. Many people recite an introductory prayer before putting on the *tefillin.*[126]

8. *Tefillin* should be put on while standing up.[127] (*Sephardim* put *tefillin* on the arm while sitting.[128]) The *tefillin* are tied on the left arm (or on the right, for a left-handed individual[129]) and the follow-

ing blessing is made while holding the strap, before tightening the knot:[130] "Blessed are You, Hashem, our God, King of the universe, Who has sanctified us in His commandments, and commanded us to put on *tefillin*."[131] The *tefillin* should be placed on the lower half of the bicep, facing inward toward the heart.[132] After saying the blessing and tightening the knot around the arm, the strap is wound seven times[133] around the forearm[134] and then loosely wrapped around the hand.

9. Nothing should intervene between the *tefillin* and the body.[135] One must therefore ensure that clothing or a band-aid does not intrude between the *tefillin* and the arm or, for example, that one's *yarmulka* does not come between the *tefillin* (or their straps) and one's head. When bandages or a cast cannot be removed, one should consult a rabbi.

10. No interruption at all is allowed between putting on the *tefillin* of the hand and those of the head. One should not talk, gesture, or even answer "*amen*" to a blessing during this time.[136]

11. *Tefillin* are placed on the head, with the box just above the hair-line (or where the hairline used to be!), aligned with the midpoint between the eyes. The knot at the back should be positioned just under the end of the skull, exactly in the middle.[137] A second blessing is recited immediately before positioning and tightening the *tefillin* on the head:[138] "Blessed are You, Hashem, our God, King of the universe, Who has sanctified us in His commandments, and commanded us regarding the commandment of *tefillin*." After the *tefillin* are in the correct position, a further blessing is recited: "Blessed is the Name of His glorious kingdom for all eternity."[139] (Most Sephardic Jews do not have the custom of reciting the bless-ings for the *tefillin* of the head.[140])

12. After completing the placement of the *tefillin* on the head, the straps that were lightly wrapped around the hand are wound around the middle finger and the hand. There are a number of different customs regarding how to wrap the straps.[141] Some wind the strap in a configuration that looks like the letters *shin*, *dalet* and *yud*, the letters of one of the names of God. While wrapping the strap around the fingers, we recite two verses from the prophet Hosea:[142] "I will betroth you to Me forever, and I will betroth you to Me with righteousness, justice, kindness and mercy. I will betroth you to Me with fidelity, and you shall know God."[143]

13. The remaining length of strap is then wrapped around the hand. One should ensure that all the straps have only the black side showing.[144]

14. While wearing *tefillin*, one should be aware of them and touch them occasionally to remind himself that he is wearing them and to ensure that they are placed correctly.[145]

15. It is obligatory to have a clean body[146] and pure thoughts[147] while wearing *tefillin*. One should not enter a bathroom while wearing them,[148] and one who needs to relieve himself should remove his *tefillin* immediately.

16. The *tefillin* should not be removed until the end of the morning service.[149] They should be removed while standing, reversing the order in which they were put on. One first unwinds the strap from the fingers, then removes the *tefillin* of the head and puts them away. The *tefillin* of the arm are then unwound and put away.[150]

17. *Tefillin* are objects of sanctity and are stored in special containers to protect them. They are kept in a bag specially made for the *tefillin*, usually decorated or embroidered. They should not be placed anywhere that is disrespectful or dirty.[151]

18. The *tefillin* must be completely black (including the straps on one side) and precisely square.[152] If one notices any cracks, loss of color or rounding of the corners, one should consult a rabbi or scribe before using the *tefillin* again. It is best to consult one immediately in order to have proper *tefillin* for the next day.[153]

19. *Tefillin* that are worn out should not be thrown away, since they are objects of *kedushah*, sanctity. A rabbi should be consulted as to how to dispose of them correctly.

For Further Reading

▶ *Living Jewish: Values, Practices and Traditions* by Rabbi Berel Wein (Shaar Press, 2002)

▶ *Tefillin* by Rabbi Aryeh Kaplan (OU/NCSY, 1973)

▶ *Tzitzith: A Thread of Light* by Rabbi Aryeh Kaplan (OU/NCSY, 1984)

NOTES

References to books of the Talmud refer to the Babylonian Talmud unless otherwise noted.

1. Thanks to Betzalel Karan for this phrase.
2. Rabbi Samson Raphael Hirsch, *Collected Writings,* Vol. III, pp. 7, 8. Feldheim Publishers, NY. Jerusalem, 1984.
3. Ibid. 6:4-9, 11:13-21. See chapter on Prayer.
4. See below regarding the details of placement.
5. Israel Antiquities Authority, Qumran Collection, Israel Museum, Jerusalem.
6. Kibbutz Tirat Zvi, in the Beit Shean valley.
7. Prayer recited after the passing of a close relative, and on the anniversary of their passing.
8. Deuteronomy 6:9.
9. *Menachot* 34a.
10. Heard from Rabbi Shlomoh Fischer — In Hebrew, "*cheftzah shel mitzvah.*"
11. The parchment, ink and lettering are discussed in the section about the Torah Scroll.
12. *Code of Jewish Law, Yoreh Deah,* 288:1-15.
13. *Avodah Zarah* 11a.
14. Maimonides, *Guide for the Perplexed,* Section 3:51 *He'ara*; Nachmanides, *Commentary on Job,* 36:7.
15. *Menachot* 43b.
16. *Mishneh Torah,* Laws of Mezuzah 6:13.
17. A term for God.
18. Ibid. *Menachot.*
19. Psalms 34:8.
20. Babylonian Talmud, *Bava Metzia* 102a; Jerusalem Talmud, *Megillah* 4:12.
21. Heard from Rabbi Shlomoh Fischer, Jerusalem.
22. *Code of Jewish Law, Yoreh Deah,* 285:2 Ramah.
23. Exodus 12:7.
24. Nachmanides, *Commentary on the Torah,* Exodus 13:16.
25. *Tcheilet* — may also be translated as sky-blue.
26. Numbers 15:37-41.
27. In ancient times, one thread was dyed a color called *tcheilet,* turquoise or sky-blue. Later the secret of producing this dye was lost due to persecution, exile and economic factors, and only white threads have been used since then. Recent evidence suggests that the dye was produced from a substance in the *murex trunculus,* a Mediterranean sea snail.
28. Tosafot on *Shabbat* 32b, "*be'avon tzitzit*"; Maimonides, *Mishneh Torah,* Laws of Tzitzit, 3:11.
29. *Shabbat* 113a.
30. Genesis 1:27.
31. Numbers 15:39.
32. Maharal of Prague, *Chidushei Aggadot, Sotah* 13a.
33. *Menachot* 43b.
34. Rabbi Chaim of Volozhin, *Ruach HaChaim on Pirkei Avot,* 3:1.
35. *Avodah Zarah* 13a.
36. *Pesachim* 50b.
37. Numbers 15:39.
38. See laws at end of chapter.
39. Exodus 34:6-7. See chapter on Yom Kippur for an explanation of these concepts.
40. *Code of Jewish Law, Orach Chaim,* 11:14, Commentaries ad loc.
41. Ibid. 24:5. A Kabbalistic concept, in which God's Infinite Will is manifested in our finite world in ten ways, each called a *Sefirah.* These parallel the ten statements of creation in Genesis.
42. See laws at end of chapter.
43. *Code of Jewish Law, Orach Chaim,* 11:14, Commentaries ad loc.
44. Ibid. 24:1.

45. Deuteronomy 6:6-8.

46. Ibid. 11:18.

47. Middle English *filaterie, philacterie,* from Old French *filatiere,* from Late Latin *phylactērium,* from Greek *phulaktērion,* guard's post, safeguard, phylactery, from *phulaktēr,* guard, from *phulax, phulak* — *The American Heritage® Dictionary of the English Language, Third Edition©* 1996, Houghton Mifflin Company.

48. The sections are: Exodus 13:1-10; Exodus 13:11-16; Deuteronomy 6:4-9; and Deuteronomy 11:13-21.

49. The left arm is defined in Jewish tradition as the weaker, less skilled arm. For the left-handed individual, the right arm is weaker, so he puts the *tefillin* on his right arm.

50. Based on the prayer recited before wearing *tefillin. The Complete ArtScroll Siddur,* pp. 6-7.

51. Ibid.

52. *Shabbat* 28b; *Menachot* 35a.

53. Yigal Yadin in Qumran. The *tefillin* are exhibited in the Shrine of the Book, in the Israel Museum, Jerusalem.

54. 70 C.E.

55. Ibid. *Menachot* 35a.

56. Rabbi Samson Raphael Hirsch, *Collected Writings Vol. III,* Feldheim Publishers, NY, 1988, p. 152.

57. *Shabbat* 28b.

58. Based on Rabbi Hirsch, ibid.

59. *Shabbat* 28b.

60. Based on Rabbi Hirsch, ibid.

61. Ibid. *Menachot.*

62. Maimonides, *Mishneh Torah,* Laws of Tefillin, 3:14.

63. *Yafeh Lelev,* 25:33.

64. Rabbi Menachem ben Meir Tzioni, *Tzioni, Parshat Bo.*

65. Rashi, *Menachot* 35a *"shin"*; Rabbeinu Bachya, *Kad Hakemach, Tefillin.*

66. Rabbi Samson Raphael Hirsch, ibid. pp. 156-157.

67. Hosea 2:21-22.

68. *Mishnah Kiddushin,* Chap. 1, Mishnah 7.

69. *Shevuot* 20b.

70. *Code of Jewish Law, Orach Chaim,* 38:3.

71. Ibid. 17:2.

72. Others are recitation of the *Shma,* dwelling in the *sukkah,* taking the *lulav,* hearing the *shofar* and the counting of the *Omer. Kiddushin* 32b.

73. Rabbi David Abudraham, 14th-century guide and commentary on prayers, section on weekday prayers.

74. Moshe Meiselman, *Jewish Woman in Jewish Law,* Ktav Publishing House, NY, 1978, Chap. 8.

75. Maharal, *Drush Al HaTorah,* pp. 27-28.

76. Rabbi Samson Raphael Hirsch, Commentary to Leviticus, 23:43.

77. Ibid. Meiselman, Chap. 1.

78. Rabbi Samson Raphael Hirsch, *The Nineteen Letters,* Letter 18, footnote.

79. *Code of Jewish Law, Yoreh Deah,* 285:1; 286:1.

80. Ibid. 288.

81. Ibid. 289:2.

82. Ibid. 285:2.

83. Ibid.

84. Ibid. 289:4.

85. Ibid. 289:6, Ramah ad loc.

86. Ibid. 289:1.

87. Ibid. 286:4.

88. Ibid. 286:13.

89. Ibid. 287:1.

90. Ibid. 286:22.

91. Ibid. 289:1.

92. Ibid. 285:2, Ramah and *Birkei Yosef,* ad loc.

93. Ibid. 291:1.

94. *Code of Jewish Law, Orach Chaim,* 9:1, 10:1.

95. Commentary of *Tosafot, Shabbat* 32b *"be'avon tzitzit." Code of Jewish Law, Orach Chaim,* 24:1.

96. *Code of Jewish Law, Orach Chaim* 8, *Mishnah Berurah,* 25.

97. Ibid. *Code of Jewish Law,* 11:1, 2.

98. Ibid. 11:9.

99. Ibid. 11:4,12.

100. Ibid. 11:14. *Mishnah Berurah* ad loc. 70.

101. Ibid. *Mishnah Berurah,* 65-70.

102. Ibid. 9:5.

103. Ibid. *Mishnah Berurah* ad loc. 16.

104. Ibid. 16:1, *Mishnah Berurah,* 2.

105. Ibid. 17:3, *Shaarei Teshuvah,* 2.

106. Ibid. 24:1.

107. Ibid. *Mishnah Berurah,* 10.

108. *The Complete ArtScroll Siddur*, pp. 2-3.

109. Ibid. *Code of Jewish Law*, 8:1-5.

110. Ibid. *The Complete ArtScroll Siddur.*

111. Ibid. *Code of Jewish Law,* 18:1.

112. Ibid. 18:3.

113. Ibid. 58:1, *Biur Halachah* ad loc.

114. Ibid. 38:3.

115. Ibid. 31:1.

116. Ibid. 31:2.

117. Ibid.; *Mishnah Berurah,* 8.

118. Ibid. 37:3; *Mishnah Berurah* 12, *Biur Halachah* ad loc.

119. Ibid. 39:8.

120. Ibid. 37:2.

121. Ibid. 30:2.

122. Ibid. 44:1.

123. Ibid. 30:1.

124. Ibid. 25:1.

125. *Berachot* 51b.

126. See above. *The Complete ArtScroll Siddur*, pp. 6-7.

127. Ibid. *Code of Jewish Law*, 25:11, Ramah.

128. Ibid.

129. Ibid. 27:6.

130. Ibid. 25:8.

131. Ibid. *The Complete ArtScroll Siddur.*

132. Ibid. *Code of Jewish Law*, 27:1.

133. Ibid. 27:8; *Mishnah Berurah* 31.

134. Ibid. 25:11; *Mishnah Berurah* 38.

135. Ibid. *Code of Jewish Law*, 27:4.

136. Ibid. 25:9-10.

137. Ibid. 27:9-10.

138. Ibid. 25:8, Ramah.

139. Ibid. 25:5, Ramah.

140. Ibid. 25:6.

141. Ibid. 27:8.

142. Hosea 2:21-22.

143. *The Complete ArtScroll Siddur*, pp. 8-9.

144. Ibid. *Code of Jewish Law*, 27:11.

145. Ibid. 27:1.

146. Ibid. 38:2.

147. Ibid. 38:4.

148. Ibid. 43:1-2.

149. Ibid. 25:13. At least they should be worn until the end of *"Uva letzion,"* *The Complete ArtScroll Siddur*, pp. 156-157.

150. Ibid. *Code of Jewish Law*, 28:2.

151. Ibid. 40.

152. Ibid. 32:39-40.

153. Ibid. 32:32.

19

Person to Person

Behavior toward other people: love, money, honesty and ethics

It's About People Too!

he Ten Commandments were inscribed on two tablets.[1] On the first tablet were five statements about the relationship between a person and his or her Creator (God and parents). The second five focus on the relationship between a person and his or her peers.[2] The design of the tablets teaches us that in order to be complete, people must cultivate proper relationships with their peers just as much as they form a connection with God.[3] A person who is devout and sensitive in matters relating to God, but is remiss in his treatment of other people, is neglecting half of the human purpose in the world. A famous story in the Talmud illustrates this idea:

> *A Gentile came to ... Hillel[4] and said, "Convert me, on condition that you teach me the whole Torah while standing on one foot." Hillel said, "That which is hateful unto you, do not do unto your friend — that is the whole Torah. The rest is commentary, go and learn."[5]*

Rashi[6] explains that Hillel is referring to two "friends": The Creator, Who is called "your Friend and the Friend of your father,"[7] and is referred to in our liturgy as "Beloved of the soul";[8] and to our literal "friends," our fellow human beings.[9] Acting with an awareness of and sensitivity toward the desires of both of these "friends" is the essence of Judaism. All of the laws and commandments are "commentaries" on exactly how to avoid doing that which "is hateful unto" your friend. In this chapter, we will summarize some of the primary obligations of the Torah that govern our relationships with people. The basis for most of these obligations can be found in the following verses in Leviticus:[10]

> *You shall not steal, you shall not deny falsely, and you shall not lie to one another. You shall not swear falsely by My Name, thereby desecrating the Name of your God — I am God. You shall not cheat your fellow and you shall not rob; you shall not withhold a worker's wage with you until morning. You shall not curse the deaf, and you shall not place a stumbling block before the blind; you shall fear your God — I am God. You shall not commit a perversion of justice; you shall not favor the poor and you shall not honor the great; with righteousness shall you judge your fellow. You shall not be a gossipmonger among your people, you shall not stand aside while your fellow's blood is shed — I am God. You shall not hate your brother in your heart; you shall reprove your fellow and do not bear a sin because of him. You shall not take revenge and you shall not bear a grudge against the members of your people; you shall love your fellow as yourself — I am God.*

More Than Political Science

In the ancient world, many codes of law preceded or existed concurrently with the Torah's code.[11] These systems provided societies with the legal framework necessary to prevent anarchy and to ensure that the life of man not be "solitary, poor, nasty, brutish, and short."[12] In contrast to the Torah, however, none speak in terms of love for others, absolute morality or moral demands emanating from God. They specify the consequences of certain actions, describe payments and judgments, but never enter the sphere of morality. Their main concern is pragmatism and economic security, while the Torah's primary concern is goodness, righteousness and the service of God.[13] Other codes deal only with legal matters; the Torah combines "legal, moral, and religious prescriptions" into a single entity.[14] In other codes, those given the most protection under the law are the nobility, the landowners and the priests; in the Torah, most protection is provided for the stranger, the widow, the orphan and the poor.[15]

These laws of the Torah are, therefore, not merely a social contract or bill of rights; they are Divine commandments designed to elevate the individual and society, and inculcate us with the qualities of God's justice and compassion. It is not only enlightened self-interest that should motivate us in our dealing with other people, but also a recognition that God, the Creator, demands that we treat His children with justice, compassion and love. The Torah is teaching us that these commandments come with the authority of God behind them. They were not formulated merely by human choice or communal will; that is why so many of these laws end with the phrase "I am God."

Love, Don't Hate

The commandment to love others means that we should really want all the happiness, success, health and honor that we enjoy to be enjoyed by everyone else as well.[16] This obligation is the inverse of the prohibition, "Do not covet."[17] A jealous person's primary concern is that another person not have more than or even as much as he has.[18] To love means to be concerned with another human being's physical and spiritual well-being; to feel his pain and rejoice in his happiness. It means not looking at others as competitors for resources, affection and honor, but as essential partners in life.[19] The verse, "Love your neighbor,"[20] ends with the words, "I am God," to explain why we should strive to achieve such love. We are all indeed children of God, and He loves all of us. If we love God, we express that connection by loving His children. If our love of God is sincere, we want to imitate Him, which we can best do by loving and giving.[21]

This *mitzvah*, beautiful as it is, poses a difficulty. How can the Torah command us to have a specific emotion? Either one feels love toward another person, or one does not. It does not seem realistic to expect a person to feel love on demand.

One way of understanding this dilemma is that the *mitzvah* of loving one's friend is multilayered. Ideally, we should feel love towards all of humanity. The Torah does not, however, expect this ideal, nor is it attainable for most people. We are, of course, prohibited to steal from,[22] murder,[23] or cheat[24] any human being. We are also commanded not to hate anyone, even one's enemy, as the Torah teaches us, "At the fall of your enemy, do not rejoice."[25] The exception is an evil person whom we are obligated to hate.[26] Even in that case, however, we should hate the evil that he does, but still retain a love for the essence of Godliness within him, his soul.[27]

When it comes to the positive commandment to love, however, the minimal requirement is more limited. According to Nachmanides, we are obligated to *act* with love toward one another, even when the corresponding emotion is absent.[28] We must not do anything to another person we would not like to be done to us.[29] Others disagree with this interpretation, and maintain that we are obligated to develop a feeling of love toward other Jews. How can we be asked to do this? Because a person's inner being is affected by his external reality.[30] To the extent that we consistently behave with sensitivity and perform acts of kindness toward others, a *feeling* of love will inevitably begin to grow.

Although there is a divergence of opinions regarding the legal implications of the *mitzvah*, the practical directive is the same: Act kindly and with respect toward others at all times. The Sages reinforced this idea over and over again in the Mishnah and Talmud:

> Receive every person with a cheerful face.[31]

> Who is honored? He who honors others.[32]

> One's dealings with people should always be in a pleasant manner.[33]

> Be among the disciples of Aaron, loving peace and pursuing peace, loving people and bringing them closer to the Torah.[34]

We must try to get closer and closer to the state where we wish for every Jew the same level of happiness and satisfaction that we wish for ourselves; where we love each one for who they are and realize that we are all part of a greater whole.[35] Ideally, we would wish to achieve this degree of love for every human being. The Torah is aware, however, that this is beyond the capacity of most people; therefore, the legal obligation only extends as far as members of the Jewish people.[36] Even this is a goal that most of us work all our lives to achieve.

More Equal Than Others

The Torah requires us to treat certain people with even greater sensitivity and kindness than would normally be expected. These are the convert, the widow, the orphan and the poor;[37] people who are disadvantaged or alone. As Maimonides writes: *A person must be careful with widows and orphans because their spirits are very low ... even if they are wealthy ... One should only speak with them gently, and treat them with honor. One should not oppress them physically with labor or with harsh words ... One should protect and care for their property as one protects and cares for his own property ...*[38]

Don't Get Even

"Do not take revenge nor bear a grudge"[39] is a commandment related to the *mitzvah* of love. If one is able to realize that he and the person who offended him are both part of a greater whole, taking revenge becomes absurd. It would be like punishing your right hand when it hits your left thumb with a hammer.[40] Maimonides considers the desire for revenge one of the most negative of character traits, the result of attributing too much importance to matters which, in reality, are trivial: *One who takes revenge on his friend has transgressed a Biblical prohibition... And even though he does not receive a punishment from the courts it is an exceedingly evil character trait. Rather, it is appropriate for a person to forgo his honor in all matters of this world, because they are all, in the eyes of the wise, trivial and inconsequential and are not worthwhile to take revenge for them ...*

> *And similarly, one who bears a grudge has transgressed a Biblical prohibition ... rather he should erase the matter from his heart and not keep it. Because as long as he remembers the matter in his heart, he may come to take revenge ... [Not bearing a grudge] is the correct attitude that will enable the survival of society and human interaction.*[41]

Another understanding of the prohibition against revenge is that when something happens to cause us distress, we are obligated to look inward at our own faults to discover the cause, rather than looking at others and blaming their faults: *The root of this commandment is that a person should be aware that everything that happens to him, whether it is good or bad, has been caused by God, may He be blessed, and nothing will be done by a man to his brother unless it is the will of God. Therefore when someone hurts him or insults him, he should realize that it is God's decree to punish us for our transgressions. And he shall not plan to wreak vengeance against his brother, because he is not the cause of the evil, rather it is his own sin which is the cause of the evil.*[42]

The intent of this approach is not to excuse the perpetrator of an evil act, but to have the victim focus on productive reflection rather than destructive thoughts of vengeance.

There is some disagreement as to whether this prohibition, in the strictest legal sense, applies only to financial matters, or whether it includes matters of personal injury and insult as well.[43] Since one may be transgressing a Biblical prohibition, it is appropriate to be very careful not to take revenge in these areas either.[44] The Talmud notes that it is also an act of piety to be forgiving in matters of personal offense, not to seek revenge or bear a grudge.[45]

These prohibitions in no way curtail a person's right to self-defense. If one is physically attacked, the Torah not only allows, but in fact, obligates him to defend himself.[46] If the attack is not violent or life threatening, a verbal attack, for example, one is still permitted to respond at the time of the incident, since in the words of one of our greatest 20th-century sages, the Chafetz Chaim, "A person cannot be a stone ..."[47] It is, nevertheless, considered an act of great piety and humility if one is able to remain silent.[48]

But Names Will Never Hurt Me ...

In Jewish tradition, an entire set of laws governs how we speak about, and to, other people. These are known as the laws of *Lashon Hara,* the "Evil Tongue." They include prohibitions against any speech that may damage another person or cause emotional distress. Insults, lies and breaches of confidence are all forbidden. When discussing the existence of these laws, a student of mine once reacted with shock and derision. "That's ridiculous!" he said, "How can you control human nature? Speaking about other people is as natural as breathing!"

Judaism maintains that, on the contrary, speech is very much under our control, that we can determine what we say and how we say it. The laws of *Lashon Hara* help us appreciate the incredible power of speech that has inspired people and saved lives, but has also caused death and destruction. As the verse in Proverbs states, "Death and life are in the power of the tongue."[49]

We bear tremendous responsibility for what we say, even beyond any tangible impact on the subject,[50] because when we speak about someone in a derogatory fashion we corrupt both ourselves and our listeners.[51] Even if what is said is true,[52] and even if it will not cause any measurable damage,[53] it is still forbidden to speak negatively about another person, because this is a misuse of the power of speech. Our tradition defines the human being as a "speaker."[54] *Lashon Hara* is a sin that corrupts and perverts the very essence of the human being, speech.[55]

It is significant that the verse most often repeated in the Torah teaches us a law about the ethics of speech. Virtually every time God speaks to Moses, the Torah writes, "God spoke to Moses, to say ..."[56] The Talmud notes that the Hebrew word for "to say" (*le'emor*) seems to be unnecessary. The redundancy teaches us that unless one is told "to say," anything a person hears should be kept in confidence:

> *"God called to Moses and spoke to him from the tent of meeting **to say...**" From here we see that one whose friend has told*

him something is prohibited from speaking of it to others until given permission to do so.[57]

It is commonly assumed that nothing is confidential unless we are told otherwise, but Jewish law teaches us precisely the opposite; we should treat everything we hear as confidential unless told otherwise.

Even worse than revealing secrets and breaking confidence is spreading dissent or hatred by being a "gossipmonger"[58] — one who tells others about negative things that someone has done to them or said about them. (In Hebrew, the term for this is *rechilut*.) Even if what he relates is true, the narration creates acrimony.[59] Such a person thrives on the ill feeling and damage that he causes with his tale-bearing. In the words of Maimonides, he "destroys the world"[60] through his speech.

The laws of *Lashon Hara* teach us to speak with great care and kindness and to avoid making negative statements about others. They direct us to be truthful, seek peace and value silence. As Mark Twain once said, "You always regret what you say much more than what you don't say."

Stumbling Blocks and Rebuke

You shall not place a stumbling block before the blind; you shall fear your God — I am God.[61]

This verse refers to someone who is blinded by ignorance or passion and cannot "see" what is the correct thing to do.[62] The Torah prohibits giving advice that is not in the best interests of the person, thereby "misleading the blind."[63] It also forbids us to cause anyone else, Jew or non-Jew, to do a sin.[64] Being the causative agent is a Biblical prohibition; even aiding and abetting the performance of a wrong deed is forbidden by Rabbinic law.[65]

Not only may we not participate in someone else's incorrect actions, the Torah expects us to actively discourage others from doing the wrong thing and encourage them to do what is right.

You shall not hate your brother in your heart; you shall reprove your fellow and do not bear a sin because of him.[66]

Maimonides states this obligation the following way: *One who sees that his friend has sinned or is going in a path that is not good, it is an obligation to turn him toward good and to inform him that he is hurting himself with his evil actions ...*[67]

In order for the rebuke to be effective, it must be delivered gently, with respect and love.[68] Words of rebuke spoken in anger are counterproductive; they will not be accepted,[69] and may even provoke the person to do something worse. In fact, according to Jewish law, if a person feels that he cannot control his anger, he is exempt from the obligation of rebuke.[70] The Talmud states that rebuke should generally take place in private — and even in private[71] it is prohibited to embarrass someone.[72] Publicly embarrassing someone must be avoided at all costs; it is considered the equivalent of murder.[73] The Talmud goes so far as to state: "It is better to throw oneself into a burning furnace than to embarrass someone in public."[74]

The commandment to reprove applies to cases of personal conflict as well. The verse quoted above teaches us that if someone is offended or hurt by another person, he should not hide his negative feelings, ("You shall not hate your brother in your heart") but should communicate his hurt to the other person ("You shall reprove your fellow"). In this way, the other person has an opportunity to apologize, explain or deny the wrongdoing. If the animosity is kept hidden, it will often grow and fester and may one day break out in negative, damaging action ("Do not bear a sin because of him").[75]

Honor of Parents

The obligation to love and respect others is even greater with regard to our parents. The Torah commands us:

> Honor your father and your mother, so that your days may be long on the land which the Lord your God gave you."[76]
>
> Every person shall fear his mother and his father...[77]
>
> Cursed is he who dishonors his father or his mother.[78]

The Talmud explains that we are obligated both to respect our parents (yirah) and to honor them (kavod). Respect generally refers to refraining from contradicting or arguing with one's parents, not disgracing them or treating them as equals. Honor usually refers to caring for, sustaining and generally making one's parents happy and comfortable.[79]

Just as we must be grateful to God for giving us life and maintaining our existence, so too we are obligated to be grateful to our parents, without whom we would not be alive.[80] Our parents can never be considered just like any other human beings; they were partners in our creation. There are three partners in every person: the father, the mother and God.[81]

Our parents also constitute our most immediate link in the chain of our heritage back to Mount Sinai. They are the ones who teach us Torah, instill us with faith and teach us how to be good people.[82] Even if the parents did not teach or care for their child, the Biblical commandment to honor them still applies.

The Sages compared honoring parents to honoring our ultimate Parent, God;[83] therefore, the honor due to a parent is so great that to properly fulfill this commandment is extremely difficult.[84] Under no circumstances may one insult or reproach his or her parents. Children must support their parents to the limit of their capability and treat them with the utmost respect, not even sitting in the place where the parent would normally sit.[85] The obligation to honor parents continues even after the parent dies.[86] A child must mourn for his parents and say *Kaddish* for a year, and must always refer to his parents with respect.[87]

Because of the seriousness of these obligations and the difficulty of fulfilling them perfectly, the Sages also warned parents not to be excessive in their demands for respect and not to "place their yoke too heavily on their children ... but to be forgiving."[88]

One must also honor one's step-parents,[89] his oldest brother, older siblings,[90] grandparents[91] and in-laws,[92] although the degree of obligation varies in each case.[93]

An Exception to the Rule

The Torah juxtaposes the obligation to respect parents to the obligation of keeping Shabbat: *A person shall fear his mother and father and keep My Shabbat.*[94]

The Talmud understands this to mean that although a person must "fear his mother and father" he should nevertheless "keep My Shabbat." In other words, since one's parents are equally obligated to obey God's will, their honor does not take precedence over the honor of God. If a parent were to tell his child to do something that is forbidden by the Torah, the child should not listen to him.[95] In addition, although a parent's advice must be heard respectfully, when it comes to choosing a spouse, a place to live, or a school for Torah study, the adult child should make the final decision.[96] In any decisions affecting a person's relationship with God and his own spirituality, one must ultimately act as his conscience dictates, even if parents disagree.[97]

Respecting Elders

> In the presence of an old person you shall rise and you shall honor the presence of a sage and you shall revere your God — I am God.[98]

The Torah obligates us also to respect an elderly person even if he or she is not a scholar (as long as one is not wicked) and to respect a Torah scholar, even if he is not old.[99] An elderly person who has learned much from life experience and a scholar who has gained understanding from learning God's Torah are both worthy of our respect. Each is a repository of wisdom and a source of guidance and advice.[100] Based on these verses, Jewish law requires one to literally stand up as a sign of respect when an elderly person[101] or a great Torah scholar approaches.[102]

The Prophets on Profits

From the Bible, through the writings of the Prophets and down to the Sages, Judaism has always placed tremendous emphasis on justice, honesty and righteousness. The eighth of the Ten Commandments, "Do not steal," encompasses all financial crimes, damages and issues of business ethics,[103] everything from the ultimate theft — kidnapping[104]— down to overcharging a customer. Elsewhere, the Torah also enumerates many specific financial crimes, such as:

> You shall not cheat one another ...[105]

> You shall not oppress your friend, nor rob him ...[106]

> You shall not move a boundary ...[107]

> You shall not commit a perversion in justice, in measures of length, weight, or volume. You shall have correct scales, correct weights, correct dry measures and correct liquid measures ...[108]

The prophets frequently chastised the Jewish people for not being honest, and reminded them that justice is what God most desires from us.

> It has been told to you, mankind, what is good and what God requires of you; only to do justice, love kindness and to walk humbly with your God.[109]
> ... [He who] does not oppress any man; does not keep collateral; does not rob any loot; gives his bread to the hungry and covers the naked with clothing; withholds his hand from harming the poor; does not take usury or interest; obeys my ordinances ... he shall surely live![110]
> Every man shall turn back from the robbery that is in his hands. He who knows shall repent, and God will relent...[111]

The Sages also stressed the critical importance of honesty in business and financial matters:

> When a person is brought to his final judgment [in the World to Come] he is asked the following question: "Did you deal with people in good faith? ..."[112]
>
> Come and see how great is the impact of theft! The generation of the flood committed all types of sins, but their final decree [of destruction] was signed because of stealing ...[113]

One reason for this emphasis on ethical conduct is that people judge the effectiveness and validity of Judaism by the behavior of its followers. Therefore, every Jew is — like it or not — a representative of Judaism:

> One who studies Torah ... but is not honest in his dealings with people, and does not speak pleasantly to others, what do people say about him? Woe to so-and-so who has learned Torah, woe to his father who taught him Torah, woe to his teachers who taught him Torah ...[114]

Even Yom Kippur, the Day of Atonement, can only atone for sins between a person and God. For offenses against other people, Yom Kippur is completely ineffective until the victim has been compensated, and has forgiven the one who injured him.[115]

An Honest Day's Work

Judaism places great emphasis on working and earning a living.[116] The Mishnah obligates every father to teach his son a trade[117] and requires every person to ensure for himself an honest means of obtaining a livelihood.[118] Labor is also valued because one who is engaged in productive activity is less likely to be drawn into inappropriate diversions.[119] Poverty is certainly not considered a positive state,[120] and is likely to lead a person to wrongdoing.[121] Working to earn an income also teaches a basic principal of life: that good only comes through effort.[122] Some of the greatest Sages, who were vital links in the chain of Torah transmission, also worked for their livelihood.[123] Rabbi Judah the Prince,[124] author of the Mishnah, was a wealthy businessman;[125] Maimonides[126] was a physician; Don Isaac Abarbanel[127] was an adviser to the government; Rashi[128] owned a vineyard and produced wine; and Rabbi Israel Meir Kagan (the Chafetz Chaim)[129] owned a grocery store.

The Talmud also requires that a person choose a profession that does not involve any wrongdoing, that is dignified[130] and that contributes positively to the "settlement of the world."[131] Based on this idea, a Jew would be forbidden to make a living from something like gambling,[132] since it does not contribute to the improvement of the world. Professional gamblers are actually disqualified as witnesses in a Jewish court.[133] Rashi offers a fascinating insight into why this is so: "Since they are not acquainted or familiar with people's efforts and pain [in the struggle for a livelihood], they do not care about causing others loss of money."[134] A person who understands what it means to struggle for a livelihood can sympathize with others who also value their hard-earned money. A righteous person does not acquire anything illicitly or without effort.[135] He values his possessions both because he has invested himself in obtaining them, and because he understands the tremendous potential for good inherent in his material wealth.

The Few and the Many

Concurrent with the Torah's positive view on working for a livelihood, there exists a tradition that some people should always be involved in full-time Torah study. Clearly, this is not an option for the vast majority of people, but if someone has a burning desire to study Torah and is capable of studying with diligence and understanding, that individual should dedicate himself entirely to Torah study.[136] The importance of this commitment overrides the obligation to earn a livelihood.[137] Jewish communities around the world recognize this need for continuous Torah study and have established institutions, *Kollels*, in which scholars study and receive a stipend from communal funds.[138]

An ancient tradition also allows for an arrangement in which one person contractually obligates himself to support a Torah scholar; in return, he shares equally the reward for that Torah study in the World to Come. Such an agreement is known as a Yissachar – Zevulun relationship, named after two of the Jewish tribes. The people of Zevulun were skilled traders, while the tribe of Yissachar produced a high percentage of brilliant Torah scholars. Zevulun invested its own money and natural resources in business endeavors along with that of the tribe of Yissachar. They gave half of the profits to the scholars of Yissachar, whose spiritual reward was, in turn, shared with Zevulun.[139]

Theft, Lies and Being a Fake

To most people, theft is a fairly obvious crime: taking something that belongs to another. In its broadest definition, however, it encompasses any situation in which one is in possession of something that should rightfully be in someone else's ownership.[140] This includes not only the glaring case of a mugging or robbery, but also not paying a worker, reneging on a contract or obligation, overcharging or underpaying, misrepresenting the value of an object and false advertising.[141]

Any form of theft is prohibited, even if it is done in jest or with the intention of later returning what was taken. Stealing, cheating, lying, withholding debts and evading obligations are all prohibited.[142] One is also prohibited to aid and abet theft by buying from a thief or smuggler,[143] whether the other person is a Jew or Gentile, adult or child, man or woman.[144]

The Talmud states that one could even be committing theft by giving someone a present.[145] If one were to buy a cheap cut-glass vase at a discount-closeout store, wrap it in tissue paper *and the distinctive bag of an exclusive boutique store* and then give the vase as a gift, one would, according to the Talmud, be a thief. What has been stolen in this case? The commentaries explain that one has stolen the undeserved gratitude for a $150 gift, after giving a gift worth $4.99 plus tax.[146]

In business, misrepresenting the qualities of an object, price gouging[147] and using inaccurate measuring devices[148] are all prohibited. One must always be true to one's word. A contract is considered a promise, even if it is only verbal, and one may not renege on any contract.[149] Workers must be paid on time by the employer,[150] and employees must work honestly and be careful not to waste the time for which they are paid. Chatting on the phone or Internet when one is paid by the hour is certainly a form of theft.[151]

Even beyond the vigilance necessary to avoid theft, the Torah requires us to be extraordinarily careful of other people's property. We are obligated to return lost objects to their owners,[152] to care for the lost property until it is retrieved[153] and to try to prevent damage to others' property whenever possible.[154] Jewish law requires us also to obey and respect the law of the country in which we live; to pay taxes honestly and to be loyal to the government.[155]

The Letter of the Law

In any matter of finance or business ethics, Jewish tradition encourages us to go beyond the letter of the law.[156] People should make decisions based not only on what is legal but what is "good and right in the eyes of God."[157] *Halachah* (Jewish law) does, however, distinguish between the average person and an "important person," someone whom the community is likely to observe and imitate, such as a scholar or teacher.[158] Such a person is required to go beyond the letter of the law, so that others will learn from his example.[159] The Talmud relates the following story, to illustrate this point:

> *Movers broke a barrel of wine belonging to Rabah, grandson of Chanan.[160] In order to guarantee their payment for the damage, Rabah took their coats as security. They came to Rav[161] [to*

complain] and Rav told Rabah to return their garments. Rabah asked Rav, "Is this the law?" He answered, "Yes, because it says in Proverbs[162] 'that you may walk in the paths of the good.'" He gave back their coats. The movers said to him, "We are poor and we worked a whole day, should we starve?" Rav said to Rabah, "Pay them for their work." Rabah asked, "Is this the law?" "Yes," he answered, "because the verse in Proverbs continues, 'and keep the paths of the righteous.'"[163]

Even though taking the garments as security and withholding the wages were legally acceptable under the circumstances, since Rabah was an "important person" he was required to go beyond the letter of the law so that others would see that the ways of the Torah are good and righteous.

Lending Money

It is a Biblical commandment to lend money to a fellow Jew,[164] and to do so without charging interest.[165] The Torah states the prohibition against charging interest immediately after the obligation to help support a fellow Jew. This juxtaposition teaches us that the reason we do not charge interest is not that it is somehow immoral. Rather, since we are *required* to help support other Jews, and the highest level of charity is giving someone the ability to support himself,[166] we may not charge a fee for doing what is simply our duty. The lender and his money are part of the organic unity of the Jewish people, therefore, as Rabbi Hirsch states, "It is neither entirely his own money that he is lending, nor is the decision to lend entirely his own good will."[167]

Lending money without interest also creates an entirely different relationship between the two parties, in which the lender now cares about the success of the borrower. Rabbi Hirsch continues:

*"If the prohibition [of lending money with interest] is strictly kept, all capital is in itself dead and unproductive, and can only be of use by wedding it to labour ... the rich man must either bring his otherwise dead capital to production by his own powers of work, or he must associate himself with the power of labour of the poor man, **share profit and loss with him**, and in his own interests further the interests of labour."[168]*

As Rabbi Hirsch mentions, lending money as a *partner* is acceptable, lending money as a *creditor* is not. According to Jewish law, if a contract is made in which the creditor shares in the profit from the debtor's venture,[169] he may be repaid the principle along with a percentage of the profit. The reason that this is not considered charging interest is that the debtor and the creditor become linked in both success and failure.[170] If the business goes well, the partners share the profit; if not, they will share the loss. This is as it should be for two members of a unified family, the Jewish people.

Damage, Torts and Liability

Jewish law holds us responsible for damage caused by our property or person, and for any damage that we enabled.[171] In fact, the Torah obligates us to be more careful not to cause damage to or hurt others than we would to avoid injury to ourselves.[172] A classic example of this obligation is the *mitzvah* to build a fence around any roof that is accessible:

> If you build a new house, you shall make a fence for your roof, so that you will not place blood in your house if a fallen one falls from it.[173]

Halachah understands this verse as a general requirement to ensure that our houses and properties are safe and will not, under normal circumstances, cause anyone harm. We would, therefore, also be obligated to put up a fence around a swimming pool, repair broken stairs or remove broken glass from our front yard.[174]

Our responsibility extends also to damage caused by our possessions or animals[175] within the limits of normal expectation.[176] A person is not held responsible however for situations beyond his control.[177] With regard to injury caused by one's own person, Jewish law considers one liable for all actions, whether intentional or not.[178]

"Justice, Justice You Shall Pursue"[179]

The Torah's message could not be clearer: Our first concern must be increasing harmony and justice within humanity. The Sages tell us, "The world stands on three things: Justice, truth and peace."[180] When we observe the laws that govern interpersonal relationships, when we act justly, speak words of truth and pursue peace, we do not just make the world a better place, we actually sustain its existence. This message is stressed repeatedly by nearly all the ancient prophets. For example:

> "What are your multiple sacrifices to Me?" says the Lord. "I have had enough of burnt offerings of rams, and the fat of fed cattle ... Wash yourselves, make yourselves clean; remove the evil of your deeds from My sight. Cease to do evil, learn to do

*good; **seek justice, reprove the ruthless, defend the orphan, plead for the widow.**"*[181]

When God praises Abraham, He offers the following reason for His closeness to our ancestor: "For I have loved him, because he commands his children and his household after him that they keep the way of God, doing charity and justice ..."[182] It is by acting with charity and justice that we most truly continue the tradition of Abraham and progress ever closer to the world's ideal state.

For Further Reading

▶ *Chofetz Chaim: A Lesson a Day* (concepts and laws of proper speech) by Rabbis Shimon Finkelman and Yitzchak Berkowitz (ArtScroll/Mesorah, 1995)

▶ *Chofetz Chaim: Lesson in Truth* (daily studies in honesty and fundamentals of Jewish faith) by Rabbi Shimon Finkelman (ArtScroll/Mesorah, 2001)

▶ *Chofetz Chaim: Loving Kindness — Daily lessons in the power of giving* by Rabbi Fischel Schachter/Chana Nestlebaum (ArtScroll/Mesorah, 2003)

▶ *Guard Your Tongue* by Rabbi Zelig Pliskin (Pliskin, 1975)

▶ *Journey to Virtue: The laws of interpersonal relationships in business, home and society* by Rabbi Avrohom Ehrman (ArtScroll/Mesorah, 2002)

▶ *Love Your Neighbor* by Zelig Pliskin (Aish HaTorah Publications, 1977)

▶ *Successful Relationships at Home, at Work and with Friends* by Rabbi Abraham J. Twerski (ArtScroll/Mesorah, 2003)

▶ *The Challenge of Wealth* by Meir Tamari (Jason Aaronson, 1995)

▶ *The Fifth Commandment: Honoring Parents* (ArtScroll/Mesorah, 1998)

NOTES

References to books of the Talmud refer to the Babylonian Talmud unless otherwise noted.

1. Exodus 20:2-24, Deuteronomy 5:6-18; Maharal, *Tiferet Yisrael* Chap. 35.
2. Jerusalem Talmud *Shekalim* 6:1.
3. Maharal, *Drush Al HaTorah,* p. 14b.
4. Mishnaic Sage, Israel, circa. 40 B.C.E.
5. *Shabbat* 31a.
6. France, 1040-1105 C.E.
7. Proverbs 27:10.
8. *"Yedid Nefesh"* — The Complete *ArtScroll Siddur* (Ashkenaz), pp. 590-591.
9. Rashi, Shabbat 31a, ad loc.
10. Leviticus 19:11-18.
11. Laws of Eshnunna, circa 1800 B.C.E.; Code of Hammurabi, 1750 B.C.E; Laws of Nuzi, 1500 B.C.E. – James B. Pritchard, *The Ancient Near East*, Princeton University Press, Princeton, NJ, 1958, pp. 133-172.
12. Thomas Hobbes, *Leviathan,* Collier Macmillan Publishers, London, 1962. Chap. 13, p. 100.
13. Barry L. Eichler, *Study of Bible in Light of Our Knowledge of the Ancient Near East,* in *Modern Scholarship in the Study of Torah*, Edited by Shalom Carmy, Jason Aronson, NJ, 1996, pp. 91- 93.
14. Leah Bronner, *Biblical Personalities and Archaeology*, Keter Publishing House, Jerusalem, 1974, p. 67.
15. Ibid. pp. 67-68.
16. Nachmanides, *Commentary on the Torah,* Leviticus 19:18; Rabbi Ovadiah Sforno, *Commentary on the Torah*, Leviticus ibid.
17. Exodus 20:14.
18. Nachmanides, ibid.; Rabbi Samson Raphael Hirsch, *Horeb,* I Toroth, Chap. 15, para. 120.
19. Ibid.
20. Leviticus 19:18.
21. *Horeb*, ibid.
22. Maimonides, *Mishneh Torah*, Laws of Theft 1:1.
23. Ibid. Laws of Homicide 1:1.
24. *Chullin* 94a.
25. Proverbs 24:17.
26. *Pesachim* 113b.
27. Rabbi Shneur Zalman of Liadi, *Tanya,* 1:32.
28. *Pesachim* 75a; Nachmanides, *Commentary on the Torah, Leviticus,* 19:18; *Sefer Hachinuch,* Mitzvah 243.
29. *Shabbat* 31a.
30. Rabbi Aharon of Barcelona, *Sefer Hachinuch, Parshat Bo*, Mitzvah 20, Mossad Harav Kook, Jerusalem, 1984.
31. Mishnah, Ethics of the Fathers 1:16.
32. Ibid. 4:1.
33. *Yoma* 86a.
34. Mishnah, Ethics of the Fathers 1:12.
35. Rabbi Shimon Shkop, *Shaarei Yosher*, Introduction.
36. Maimonides, *Mishneh Torah*, Laws of the Intellect 6:3.
37. Deuteronomy 10:18-19.
38. Maimonides, *Mishneh Torah,* Laws of Intellect 6:9.
39. Leviticus 19:17.
40. *Horeb*, Chap. 89, para. 581.
41. Maimonides, *Mishneh Torah*, Laws of the Intellect 7:7-8.
42. Rabbi Aharon of Barcelona, *Sefer HaChinuch*, Mitzvah 241.
43. *Yoma* 22b-23a; Commentaries ad loc.
44. Rabbi Israel Meir Kagan, *Sefer Chafetz Chaim*, Be'er Mayim Chaim, Prohibitions 8, 9.
45. *Yoma*, ibid.
46. *Sanhedrin* 72a.
47. *Sefer Chafetz Chaim*, ibid.
48. Ibid.
49. Proverbs 18:21.
50. Rabbi Israel Meir Kagan, *Chafetz Chaim*, Laws of Lashon Hara, 3:6.
51. *Pesachim* 118a.

52. *Chafetz Chaim,* Laws of Lashon Hara, 1:1.
53. Ibid. 3:6.
54. Genesis 2:7, *Translation of Onkelos,* ad loc.
55. Maharal, *Netivot Olam*, Netiv Halashon, Chaps.1,10.
56. See Exodus 6:10, 6:29, Leviticus 6:2, 6:13, Numbers 1:48, 3:5; Total occurrences – 78.
57. *Yoma* 4b.
58. Leviticus 19:16.
59. Maimonides, *Mishneh Torah,* Laws of the Intellect, 7:1-2.
60. Ibid.
61. Leviticus 19:14.
62. Maimonides, *Mishneh Torah*, Laws of Homicide 12:14.
63. Ibid.
64. *Avodah Zarah* 6b.
65. Ibid.
66. Leviticus 19:17.
67. Maimonides, *Mishneh Torah,* Laws of Intellect, 6:7.
68. Maimonides, ibid.; *Sefer Yereim,* 223 (37); Rashi on Talmud *Erchin* 16b.
69. *Shabbat* 34b.
70. Rabbi Chaim of Volozhin, *Keter Rosh (Siddur Hagra),* 143.
71. Maimonides, *Mishneh Torah*, Laws of the Intellect 6:8; *Chafetz Chaim*, Introduction, Be'er Mayim Chaim, 14.
72. *Erchin* 16b.
73. *Bava Metzia* 58b.
74. *Sotah* 10b; Tosafot ad loc. *"Noach."*
75. Ibid. 6:6.
76. Exodus 20:12; Deuteronomy 5:16.
77. Leviticus 19:3.
78. Deuteronomy 27:16.
79. *Kiddushin* 31b.
80. Rabbi Aharon of Barcelona, *Sefer Hachinuch,* Mitzvah 27.
81. *Kiddushin* 31b.
82. Proverbs 1:8.
83. *Kiddushin* 31a.
84. *Chullin* 145a.
85. *Kiddushin* 31a-32a.
86. Ibid. 31b.
87. See chapter on mourning and bereavement, "A Time to Cry...".
88. *Code of Jewish Law, Yoreh Deah* 240:19.
89. Ibid. 240:21.
90. Ibid. 240:22, Pitchei Teshuvah ad. loc. 19.
91. Ibid. 240:24, Ramah.
92. *Code of Jewish Law, Yoreh Deah* 240:24.
93. Ibid. 240, Commentaries ad loc.
94. Leviticus 19:3.
95. *Yevamot* 6a; *Bava Metzia* 32a.
96. *Code of Jewish Law, Yoreh Deah,* 240:25, Ramah.
97. *Aruch Hashulchan, Yoreh Deah.* 240:45; *Pitchei Teshuvah, Code of Jewish Law*, ibid. 22.
98. Leviticus 19:32.
99. *Code of Jewish Law, Yoreh Deah*, 244:1, Ramah.
100. Rabbi Samson Raphael Hirsch, *Horeb,* Mitzvoth V, Chap. 74.
101. 70 years of age and older — *Code of Jewish Law*, ibid.
102. *Code of Jewish Law,* ibid.
103. *Zohar*, Exodus 20:13.
104. *Sanhedrin* 86a.
105. Leviticus 25:17.
106. Ibid. 29:13.
107. Deuteronomy 19:14.
108. Leviticus 19:35-36.
109. Micah 6:8.
110. Ezekiel 18:16-17.
111. Jonah 3:8-9.
112. *Shabbat* 31a.
113. *Sanhedrin* 108a.
114. *Yoma* 86a.
115. Ibid. 85b.
116. Mishnah, *Ethics of the Fathers* 1:10.
117. Mishnah *Kiddushin* 4:14.
118. Maimonides, *Mishneh Torah*, Laws of Intellect, 5:11-13; *Code of Jewish Law, Orach Chaim*, 156:1.

119. Mishnah, Ethics of the Fathers 2:2; Commentary of Rashi and Rabeinu Yonah ad loc.

120. Contrast with the Christian concept.

121. *Code of Jewish Law*, ibid.

122. Heard from Rabbi Moshe Shapiro.

123. Maimonides, *Mishneh Torah*, Laws of Torah Study, 1:9.

124. Israel, circa 200 C.E.

125. *Berachot* 57b.

126. Author of numerous works of law, philosophy and commentary. Lived in Spain and Egypt, 1135-1204.

127. Author of commentary on the Bible and works of philosophy. Lived in Spain and Portugal, 1437-1508.

128. Author of commentary on Bible and Talmud. Lived in France, 1040-1105.

129. Author of books of law and ethics. Lived in Poland, 1838-1933.

130. Mishnah *Kiddushin* ibid.

131. *Sanhedrin* 24b.

132. Ibid.

133. Ibid.

134. Rashi, *Eruvin* 82a *"Bizman she'ein."*

135. *Chullin* 91a; Explanation of Rav Moshe Shapiro.

136. Maimonides, *Mishneh Torah*, Laws of Sabbatical and Jubilee Years, 13:12-13; Rabbi Moshe Feinstein, *Igrot Moshe, Yoreh Deah* 2:116.

137. *Berachot* 35b; *Biur Halachah*, on *Code of Jewish Law, Orach Chaim* 156:1.

138. *Code of Jewish Law, Yoreh Deah*, 246:21 Ramah and *Siftei Cohen*, ad loc.

139. *Midrash Rabbah*, Genesis 72:9; Commentary of Rashi on Genesis 49:13.

140. *Code of Jewish Law, Choshen Mishpat* 359.

141. Ibid.; *Zohar*, Exodus 20:13.

142. *Code of Jewish Law*, ibid. 348, 349; *Horeb*, Mishpatim III, Chap. 46, para. 337.

143. *Code of Jewish Law*, ibid. 369:1-4.

144. Ibid. 348, 349; *Horeb*, Mishpatim III, Chap. 46, para. 337.

145. Mishnah and Talmud *Chullin* 93b-94a.

146. Rashi, ad loc.

147. *Code of Jewish Law, Choshen Mishpat* 226.

148. Leviticus 19:35-36.

149. *Bava Metzia* 49a.

150. Deuteronomy 24:15.

151. *Code of Jewish Law, Choshen Mishpat*, 337:20.

152. Exodus 23:4.

153. Deuteronomy 22:1-2.

154. Exodus 23:5.

155. *Bava Kamma* 113a; *Code of Jewish Law, Choshen Mishpat* 369.

156. *Code of Jewish Law, Choshen Mishpat*, 259:5, 263:3, 264:1 Ramah.

157. Deuteronomy 12:28.

158. *Shabbat* 51a; *Moed Katan* 11b, 12a-b; *Ketuvot* 52b.

159. Rabbi Isaiah Horowitz, *Shnei Luchot Habrit*, Shaar Hamidot, Beasarah Ma-amarot, Maamar 7, 7-15.

160. Talmudic Sage, Babylon, circa 300 C.E.

161. Senior Talmudic Sage, Babylon and Israel, circa 270 C.E.

162. Proverbs 2:20.

163. *Bava Metzia* 83a.

164. Deuteronomy 15:8; ibid. Laws of Creditors and Debtors, 1:1.

165. Exodus 22:24; Leviticus 25:36-37.

166. Maimonides, *Mishneh Torah*, Laws of Gifts to the Poor, 10:7.

167. Rabbi Samson Raphael Hirsch, *Commentary on the Torah*, Exodus 22:24.

168. Ibid.

169. Known as a *heter iska*, "permission to do business."

170. Rabbi Shlomo Ganzfried, *Concise Code of Jewish Law*, 66:6-10.

171. Exodus 21:33; *Bava Kamma* 29b.

172. Tosafot, *Bava Kamma* 27b *"Amai patur."*

173. Deuteronomy 22:8.

174. Maimonides, *Mishneh Torah*, Laws of Homicide, 11:4.

175. Exodus 21:28-36.

176. Talmud, ibid.

177. Talmud, ibid. 19b.
178. *Bava Kamma* 26a.
179. Deuteronomy 16:20.

180. Mishnah, *Ethics of the Fathers* 1:18.
181. Isaiah 1:11-17.
182. Genesis 18:19.

Justice, Charity and Tzedakah

Jewish ideals and practice of philanthropy and kindness

A Giving Nation

For thousands of years the Jewish people have been noted for their philanthropy. Every Jewish community in the world, no matter how small or poor, has always had charitable societies and funds. A typical example was the Jewish community of Rome in the 17th century. Although numbering only a few thousand, they had 23 charitable organizations, including funds for the sick, for needy brides, schooling for the poor, a free burial society and a fund for the Jews in Israel.[1] Orthodox communities today have *Gemilut Chassadim*[2] funds that lend money free of interest. Goods and services are also available for loan: In some communities one can find just about any item from cribs to power tools. The local *Gemachs* (commonly used acronym for *Gemilut Chassadim*) are often established and run by one or two people. Others are larger organizations involving many volunteers, some of which service many communities and are supported by charitable contributions. Yad Sarah, an organization in Israel, for example, lends medical equipment free of charge to anyone who requests the service. It has branches at most hospitals in Israel and in many neighborhoods throughout the country, and helps thousands of people every year.

In addition to volunteering time and energy, it is customary for observant Jews to donate 10 percent of their income to charity. Giving charity and working for social justice have been hallmarks of the Jewish people from the very beginning. Our forefather, Abraham, epitomized these qualities. Referring to Abraham, God says in Genesis: "I have given him special attention, so that he will command his children and his household after him, and they will keep God's way, doing charity and justice."[3]

True to Abraham's teachings, righteousness and justice have been the recurrent themes of Jewish life throughout the ages. The prophets repeatedly exhorted the Jewish people to care for the widow, the orphan and the poor and to pursue charity as a priority in life.[4]

The Sages continued this tradition, teaching that: "The world stands on three things: The study of Torah, the worship of God and bestowing kindness.[5]

Maimonides writes in the *Mishneh Torah*, on Laws of the Festivals:[6]

> *And when he eats and drinks, he is obligated to feed the stranger, the orphan and the widow, together with all the other unfortunate poor. However, one who closes the doors of his courtyard and eats and drinks himself, with his children and his wife, and does not feed the poor and the miserable — this is not the celebration of a mitzvah, rather the celebration of the stomach. And regarding such people the verse states, "Their sacrifices will be unto them like the bread of mourners, of which all who partake are defiled, because their bread was only for themselves."[7]*

Strong words, indeed, but they are not mere sermonic hyperbole. This attitude of responsibility toward others is reflected in the codes of Jewish law and enshrined in the practices of the Jewish world. One month before Passover, for example, every Jewish community is obligated to collect money and food to distribute to the poor of that city for their holiday needs.[8]

Celebrating the festivals today, Jewish families fulfill Maimonides' mandate by inviting guests, especially those who are needy, to their homes. A travel guide[9] has even been published for Jewish students, listing the phone numbers and addresses of families around the world who are willing to have them as their guests. The fact that they are total strangers is irrelevant: They are fellow Jews. In addition, hospitality committees in many synagogues arrange accommodations and meals for visitors to the community. For children growing up in traditional homes, having new faces at the dining room table on Sabbaths and holidays is the rule, rather than the exception.

Are Tzedakah and Charity the Same?

The Hebrew word *tzedakah is* usually translated as charity, but there is a crucial difference between the two concepts. When we understand the word *tzedakah*, we learn a profound lesson about the Jewish attitude to giving. The root of the word *tzedakah* is *tzedek*, which means justice or righteousness. The word charity, however, carries intimations of benevolence. When we give *tzedakah*, we do not believe that we have gone above and beyond the call of duty; rather, we have simply fulfilled the demands of justice; we've done the right thing. This belief is based on the concept that everything that we possess is a gift from God, and He has specified that we should share that gift with others. Surely, if we share this gift, we cannot claim to be doing anything extraordinary, merely that which is morally correct. In fact, Jewish law mandates that the court estimate how much each individual is capable of donating to charity, and if he does not voluntarily give this amount, the court may force him to do so![10] This practice — which treats *tzedakah* as a fulfillment of justice rather than voluntary benevolence — was followed by Jewish communities for thousands of years.

Rabbi Samson Raphael Hirsch expressed the logic of giving in Jewish thought:[11]

> *Why should God give you more than you need unless He intended to make you the administrator of the blessing for the benefit of others, the treasurer of His treasures? Every penny you can spare is not yours, but should become a tool for bringing blessing to others — and would you close your hand on something that is not yours?[12]*

Biblical Sources

The Biblical source for the commandment of *tzedakah* is found in the section that discusses the laws of the Sabbatical Year.[13] The Torah states that any personal loans still outstanding at the end of this year are automatically cancelled. Nevertheless, God orders the people not to withhold loans close to the Sabbatical Year, but to lend the poor what they need. The fundamental principles and detailed laws of *tzedakah* are found in these few verses:

> *If there shall be a destitute person among you, any of your brethren, in any of your cities, in your land that the Lord, your God, gives you, you shall not harden your heart, nor close your hand against your destitute brother. Rather, you shall open*

your hand to him; you shall lend him his requirement, what-
ever is lacking to him … You shall surely give him, and do not
let your heart feel bad when you give to him, for as reward for
this matter, the Lord, your God, will bless you in all your deeds
and in your every undertaking. For the poor will not cease to
exist within the Land; therefore I command you, saying, "You
shall surely open your hand to your brother, to your poor and
to your destitute in your Land."[14]

As always, careful consideration of the details of the laws reveals their underlying philosophical outlook. In order to gain a clearer understanding of the Torah's perspective on *tzedakah,* we will present the verses and the laws derived from them along with the philosophical insights of the great Biblical commentators.[15] (As you read, note how sensitive the law is to human feelings!)

▶ *If there shall be a destitute person among you, any of your brethren* — Your family comes before anyone else. A person's first priority in charity must be his or her own family. If a parent is out working on a committee for abandoned children while his own child is suffering or neglected, this verse directs him to re-examine his priorities.

▶ *in any of your cities* — The poor of your own city come before the poor in other cities. Holding a benefit concert for the poor in a distant continent, when the slums and poverty of your own city stand in sight of the concert hall, is immoral.

▶ *in your land that the Lord, your God, gives you* — The poor of the Land of Israel take precedence over those outside of Israel. The Jewish people's national destiny is in the Land of Israel, therefore the Jews in Israel, who are working, defending and preserving our national heritage, deserve our support before any other community.

▶ *you shall not harden your heart* — Sometimes a person may give, but does so begrudgingly, with a heavy, hard heart. When we give, it must be with a joyful, generous feeling as well. It is difficult enough for someone to have to take charity: to increase the pain and humiliation of the recipient by giving in a bad-tempered, brusque manner adds insult to injury.

▶ *nor close your hand against your destitute brother.* — Do not decide to give and then close your hand. Follow through with your commitment to *tzedakah*. Do not treat your obligations to charity any less seriously than your obligation to the phone company, the government or a business associate. Your word, your pledge and your commitment should be firm and reliable.

- *Rather, you shall open your hand to him* — Translated literally, the verse reads, *you shall open, open your hand* — The repetition of the verb, "open" denotes repetition of the action which teaches us that the obligation to give is not a one time requirement but is an ongoing obligation. Therefore a person should not say, "I have already given once, I have performed the *mitzvah*," rather, he should be prepared to give again and again.

- *you shall lend him his requirement* — You are not obligated to make another person rich, but you must give him what he requires.

- *whatever is lacking to him.* — We must be aware that what is lacking is a subjective judgment. What is luxury for one person may well be a necessity that is lacking for another. Is an air-conditioner a luxury? If a family lives in a hot, humid climate and before they hit hard times, they owned an air-conditioner, the verse "whatever is lacking *to him,*" teaches us that it is legitimate *tzedakah* to purchase an air-conditioner for this family.

- *You shall surely give* — The word "give" is repeated, teaching us that we must give even a hundred times.

- *him* — Let it be between you and him. Do not publicize the charity and cause him embarrassment. *Tzedakah* should ideally be given as anonymously as possible.

- *and do not let your heart feel bad when you give to him, for as reward for this word* (Hebrew: *davar*, also translated as "matter") *the Lord, your God, will bless you in all your deeds and in your every undertaking.* — You will even be rewarded for your *word* to give if, through circumstances beyond your control, you were not able to follow through. You will also be rewarded if your *word* makes others give, as it is a great *mitzvah* to encourage others to give *tzedakah*.[16] (It is for this reason that publicizing donations is permitted. When people see an influential person, or many people of their financial status, giving to a charitable institution, they are more likely to follow suit and support it also.) In addition, if you cannot *afford to* give money, you will even be rewarded if you offer the poor at least *words* of encouragement and hope.

- *You shall surely open your hand to your brother, to your poor and to your destitute.* — You shall give to each of the poor according to his needs and dignity. To one you may have to give only money, for another, you may also have to help him purchase what he needs or prepare his food; some you may have to actually feed with your own hands.

To people whose experience of giving has been solely through donations to large organizations, the notion of personally giving money to a beggar may sound foreign, even disturbing. (Imagine, you actually must see the face of the recipient!) Yet, in Orthodox communities it is quite common for the Jewish poor to go from door to door asking for aid. In many cases, the person's financial needs have already been investigated by the local rabbi and the beggar will carry a discreet letter from him certifying that he or she is truly needy. With or without such credentials, however, the poor can usually rely on their fellow Jews to help them, even with a small amount. The fact that this practice is still alive and well is testimony to the inbred mechanism of *tzedakah* in these communities. The laws regarding one's demeanor when giving are therefore as relevant today as in the past.

Maimonides on Tzedakah

One of the most beautiful and authoritative explications of the laws of *tzedakah* is presented in the *Mishneh Torah,* Maimonides' legal work. Departing from his customary style, Maimonides does not restrict himself to listing the pertinent laws, but also discusses the merit and philosophy of the *mitzvah*, and the appropriate mind-set when giving *tzedakah*. The following selection provides a sense of the significance that Maimonides ascribes to this *mitzvah*.

> *We are obligated to be careful in tzedakah more than in all positive commandments. For tzedakah is a sign of the righteous descendants of Abraham, our Patriarch … And Israel will only be redeemed through tzedakah, as it states (Isaiah 1:27), "Zion shall be redeemed through justice, and those who return to her through tzedakah."*[17]
>
> *A person will never become poor from giving tzedakah and no damage or anything negative will come of giving tzedakah. And one who is merciful toward others, Heaven will be merciful toward him …*[18]

Divine rewards and punishments are always "measure for measure."[19] The reward for a *mitzvah* is an inevitable effect of its performance, much like the benefit that results from taking medicine or eating healthy food. By showing our loyalty to the principles of Abraham, we merit the fulfillment of God's promises to Abraham. By redeeming others from the chains of poverty, we merit redemption from the chains of exile. If we are merciful toward others, God will show mercy to us. Maimonides affirms that all of this will hold true when we give *tzedakah* in the appropriate way. But —

> One who gives tzedakah to the poor with an unpleasant demeanor and a sour face, even if he gave him a thousand gold coins, has destroyed and lost his merit. Rather, he should give it with a pleasant expression and with joy, and he should sympathize with the recipient over his plight ... and speak words of sympathy and comfort ...[20]

Often, words of encouragement, sympathy and hope do more for a poor person than money. Words alone can help someone regain their self-confidence, lift them out of depression and fill them with new hope. Sometimes, this kind of emotional boost may give a person the courage to begin an initiative that ultimately leads him out of dependency. In contrast, one who gives money to the poor, but in a way that depresses and humiliates the recipient, shows that he does not care for this person as a human being. In addition, by so blatantly demonstrating the "inferior" status of the recipient he strips him of hope and confidence, and actually contributes to the perpetuation of his poverty.

Employment – The Ultimate Tzedakah

Even when *tzedakah* is given anonymously, and in a pleasant, sensitive manner, the recipient still feels some degree of humiliation and degradation. The source of this feeling goes back to the creation of the first humans. Adam and Eve were created "in the image of God,"[21] which means that in the human soul there are similarities to God.[22] Just as God is totally self-contained, needs nothing and is the ultimate Giver, so too, human beings desire to be independent and to be givers, not takers.[23] This is why it is easier, emotionally, to give a loan than to ask for one. It also explains why my 16-month-old son insists on feeding himself with a spoon, even though more food ends up in his hair, nose and ears than in his mouth.

Let's look at this concept in the context of the Jewish understanding of why the world exists.[24] God wants to give His creations the ultimate good, which is closeness to God. However, in order to achieve this closeness and to establish a relationship with God, it is necessary that the creature be similar to and compatible with the Creator. (You can't have a relationship with someone or something that is entirely out of your experience.) This similarity is only real if the creature freely chooses to emulate God: Just as God's goodness is self-contained and not a result of anything external, so too, the creature's goodness must be from *within* and not the result of anything external. This requires an environment in which there is the possibility of making right and wrong choices — namely, the world of free will in which we live. In this world, when we choose to do what is right and good, in the face of all the various challenges and desires of the world, that good comes from within us and is really ours. Without our own free-will choice and efforts, any benefit that we receive would be what Kabbalists refer to as "bread of shame."[25]

"Bread of shame" is what a poor person eats when he receives *tzedakah;* therefore Jewish tradition tells us that the highest level of *tzedakah* is doing something to enable a poor person to become financially independent. Maimonides writes:

> *The highest level of tzedakah, above which there is no other, is to strengthen the hand of a Jew who has come upon hard times, to give him a present or a loan, or to make a partnership with him, or to provide him with work in order to strengthen his hand so that he will not have to become dependent upon others and have to beg money from them. And regarding this it is said, "If your brother becomes impoverished ... you shall strengthen him ..."[26] — that is, you should "strengthen him" before he falls and needs charity.[27]*

The next best level of *tzedakah* is a situation in which the donor does not know who the recipient of his *tzedakah* is, and the recipient does not know who the donor is. In this way the dignity of the recipient is preserved and the altruism of the donor remains untainted. Giving money to a trustworthy organization or individual who will distribute it to the needy is usually the most practical way to fulfill this level of *tzedakah*. Maimonides lists eight different levels of *tzedakah*.[28] From highest to lowest they are:

1. Giving someone a loan, job or partnership so that he can support himself.
2. Giving anonymously, the donor not knowing the recipient, and the recipient not knowing the donor.
3. The donor knows who the recipient is, but the recipient does not know the donor. Although the donor may have the satisfaction of knowing to whom he gave, at least the recipient does not feel embarrassed in his presence.
4. The recipient knows the donor, but the donor does not know the recipient.
5. Giving directly to the poor, but doing so even before being asked, thus saving the poor from the added humiliation of asking.
6. Giving only after being asked, but giving the appropriate amount.
7. Giving directly to the poor, only after being asked, a sum that is less than appropriate, but doing so cheerfully, with a pleasant demeanor.

8. Giving less than an appropriate amount, and doing so in an unpleasant manner.

How Much?

Jewish law specifies an absolute minimum amount which one must give per year in order to fulfill the obligation of *tzedakah*.[29] The most ancient and most prevalent custom, however (according to some, a Biblical obligation), has been to give a tenth of one's income to charity.[30] This is known as *ma'aser kesafim*, the tithing of money, and actually dates back to the Patriarch Jacob, who promised that he would give "to God" a tenth of everything that God would give to him.[31]

Some authorities see the Biblical obligations to tithe agricultural produce of the Land of Israel[32] as a source, or at least as a model, for the tithing of all forms of income.[33] This custom is widely practiced across the economic spectrum. Regardless of their own standard of living, people keep careful accounts of how much they have given and still have to give in order to fulfill the obligation of *ma'aser kesafim*.

The details of this law can be quite complex and it is appropriate to consult a rabbi to determine what income is included or excluded from the calculation, as well as the purposes for which the tithe may be used.

Ideally, the tithed funds should go to the poor, or to the needs of the community, such as for the building of a synagogue or *mikveh*.[34] It should not be used to pay for the fulfillment of personal obligations, such as the purchase of *tefillin*[35] or to buy Shabbat necessities,[36] even though both are *mitzvot*.[37]

Can You Give Too Much?

Generally speaking, the average person should give one-tenth of his income to *tzedakah*. One who is blessed with more wealth, however, should, if he is able, give one-fifth of his income.[38]

It is interesting that the Sages imposed a limit on the amount one should give to *tzedakah*, and actually forbade a person from giving more than a fifth.[39] (There are some exceptions to this rule, such as a very wealthy person, or one who is giving a donation to *tzedakah* on his deathbed.[40])

The logic of this limitation is clear: The Torah does not want one person to become destitute so that another could become rich. Neither does the Torah want a person of lesser means to give so much that he would end up needing charity himself. Since it is impossible to foresee all eventualities, we are expected to take reasonable precautions with our finances.[41]

Kindness and Chessed

The *mitzvah* of giving encompasses much more than monetary gifts. One may help a person in need in dozens of different ways that do not involve any transfer of funds. This type of giving is defined as *chessed,* kindness. It is interesting that the Torah obligates us to practice *chessed* whenever possible. One prototypical case of *chessed* is discussed in the Book of Exodus: "If you see the donkey of someone you hate crushed under its burden, would you refrain from helping him? — You shall help repeatedly with him."[42]

In other words, the Torah obligates us to help even a person we dislike, by unloading his donkey — or in modern terms, changing a tire or loading a roof rack. In fact, the Talmud states that if it is a choice between helping a friend or helping an enemy, one should help the enemy first.[43]

The Talmud rules that we should help an enemy because doing so subdues the inclination toward hatred. How does this work? Rabbi Eliyahu Dessler[44] explains that when one person gives to another, he is investing himself in the other person. This means that he will begin to see more of himself in the other person and will feel he has more in common with him. Eventually, he will grow to love the other person. A mother gives so much to her child in its infancy and receives little in return, yet her love grows the more she gives and nurtures the child. According to Rabbi Dessler, one could say, "It is true that one gives to the ones he loves, but it is also true that one loves those to whom he gives."

Chessed – Practical Applications

With a little thought, we can find countless opportunities to do acts of kindness every day, from smiling at a co-worker, taking time to give a stranger directions or letting someone merge into traffic. The following are a few of the classic examples of *chessed* discussed in Jewish sources:

Lending — Giving interest-free loans, lending tools, or finding someone a job. These can also constitute the highest level of *tzedakah*, when they enable the recipient to become independent.

Visiting the Sick — The Hebrew term for this kindness is *bikur cholim,* which more correctly translates as "scrutiny of the sick." When we visit the sick it is our obligation to scrutinize their needs and see what we can do for them. Does the family need a respite from being in the hospital? Do the children need to be car-pooled when a parent is sick? Does the patient need food, snacks, books or a telephone? We have not fulfilled our obligation of visiting unless we also pray for the patient, inquire about his needs and help improve his frame of mind.

The Talmud relates that a student of Rabbi Akiva was once very ill, and Rabbi Akiva came to visit him — and cleaned the house while he was there. The student recovered from his illness and proclaimed "Rabbi! You have given me life!"[45] We know that one's attitude, frame of mind and degree of hope have an enormous impact on recovery and well-being. Something as seemingly insignificant as cleaning a house may make such a difference to the patient that it can raise his spirits and maybe even save his life.

Helping a Bride to Marry — The Sages point out that the Torah begins with God Himself being involved in marrying Eve to Adam, thereby teaching us that kindness is a central theme of the Torah.[46] A bride and groom are often nervous about the wedding, and concerned about the many arrangements and expenses. The whole event can be stressful, as well as an enormous financial burden. As the marriage of a Jewish couple enables the very continuity of the Jewish people, we should contribute to it in any way that may be necessary. This can take the form of making some of the arrangements, giving (useful) gifts to the couple, attending the wedding and helping to make it a joyous occasion.

According to the *Code of Jewish Law*, a first priority for any *tzedakah* fund, and one of the greatest merits that an individual can have, is giving money or services which enable a wedding to take place.[47]

Burial of the Dead and Comforting the Mourners — Kindness performed for the deceased is described in Jewish tradition as *chessed shel emet*, a true kindness because it is almost always done for altruistic reasons.[48] Burial societies in most traditional Jewish communities are comprised of volunteers who care for the body of the deceased, prepare it for burial and arrange and perform the funeral. The society is known as the *Chevra Kadisha*, Aramaic for Holy Society. Comforting of mourners and taking care of the needs of the bereaved are also classic acts of great *chessed*. Attending a funeral, visiting the mourners, talking with them, supplying them with meals and helping them with their family's needs are all part of the *mitzvah* of *chessed*. (See the section on Death and Mourning for more detail.)

The Jewish chairman of a major United States corporation once visited Israel and received a lesson from one of the great scholars of Jerusalem regarding the idea of *chessed*. He describes the experience in the following excerpt from his acceptance speech after winning a community service award:

"When I was in Israel, I went to Meah Shearim, the ultra-Orthodox area within Jerusalem. Along with a group of businessmen I was with, I had the opportunity to have an audience with Rabbi Finkel, the head of a yeshivah there. I had never heard of him and didn't know anything about him. We went into his study and waited 10 to 15 minutes for him. Finally, the doors opened. What we did not know was that Rabbi Finkel was severely afflicted with Parkinson's disease. He sat down at the head of the table, and, naturally, our inclination was to look away. We didn't want to embarrass him. We were all looking away, and we heard this big bang on the table: 'Gentlemen, look at me, and look at me right now.'

"His speech affliction was worse than his physical shaking. It was really hard to listen to him and watch him. He said, 'I have only a few minutes for you because I know you're all busy American businessmen.' You know, just a little dig there.

"Then he asked, 'Who can tell me what the lesson of the Holocaust is?' He called on one guy, who didn't know what to do — it was like being called on in the fifth grade without the answer. And the guy says something benign like, 'We will never, ever forget …' And the rabbi completely dismisses him. I felt terrible for the guy until I realized the rabbi was getting ready to call on someone else. All of us were sort of under the table, looking away — you know, please, not me. He did not call me. I was sweating.

"He called on another guy, who had such a fantastic answer: 'We will never, ever again be a victim or a bystander.'

"The rabbi said, "You guys just don't get it. Okay, gentlemen, let me tell you the essence of the human spirit. As you know, during the Holocaust, the people were transported in the worst possible, inhumane way by railcar. They thought they were going to a work camp. We all know they were going to a death camp. After hours and hours in this cold, inhumane corral with no light, no bathroom, they arrived at the camps. The doors were swung wide open, and they were blinded by the light. Men were separated from women, mothers from daughters, fathers from sons. They went off to the bunkers to sleep.

"As they went into the area to sleep, only one person was given a blanket for every six. The person who received the blanket, when he went to bed, had to decide, 'Am I going to push the blanket to the five other people who did not get one, or am I going to pull it toward myself to stay warm?'

"And then Rabbi Finkel says, 'It was during this defining moment that we learned the power of the human spirit, because we pushed the blanket to five others.'

"And with that, he stood up and said, 'Take your blanket. Take it back to America and push it to five other people.' "[49]

Kindness and Charity, Levy Family Style

Every month, immediately after receiving his paycheck, Mr. Levy and his wife sit down together to pay the bills. In addition to the gas, electric and phone companies, one check is always written out to a fund administered by the rabbi of their synagogue which distributes food to needy families in the city. This first donation constitutes about half of the Levys' designated tzedakah money. Most of the rest is sent to various charitable organizations in Israel, while some is left in cash to put into charity boxes in the synagogue and to people who come to their door requesting donations. In traditional Jewish communities, it is very common for people to collect from door to door for charitable institutions, or for themselves, if they are in need. Mrs. Levy always offers them a cold drink, which they usually accept. A letter from a rabbi or rabbinic court is usually shown to confirm that they are collecting for an authentic charity. The Levys give a predetermined minimum amount, unless they feel that the need is particularly urgent.

Both Mr. and Mrs. Levy are volunteers in communal organizations. Mr. Levy runs a "tool Gemach." He maintains a large collection of home repair and gardening tools which he lends free of charge to anyone who needs them. Mrs. Levy is active in the community Hachnassat Kallah[50] organization, which helps couples who are about to get married. The organization makes available dresses for loan to brides, centerpieces for the tables, as well as discount vouchers for bands, caterers and local stores.

Their son, Shlomo, is an Emergency Medical Technician, who volunteers time for Hatzoloh, an organization with branches in major cities throughout the world. Hatzoloh sends ambulances and E.M.T.s as first responders for medical emergencies. Shlomo recently led a campaign to provide complete first-aid kits for all the synagogues and schools in the community.

Every Sunday morning, Tova Levy joins a group of friends who go to visit a local senior citizen residence. They spend time talking to the seniors and singing some familiar Jewish and Yiddish songs. These hours are the highlight of the week for many of the elderly residents, especially for those who rarely have young people coming to visit them.

Eli and Esther love taking a few coins to school and dropping them in the tzedakah pushke[51] in their classroom. When the box is full, their teachers tell the class about the charity to which the money will be sent.

An equally important chessed, their parents have taught them, is one they do almost every morning. As the Levy children leave for school, they usually see their elderly neighbor out walking his dog. Even though everyone is in a hurry, they always take a minute to smile and say hello. This is training that will last them throughout their lives.

For Further Reading

▸ *The Laws of Tzedakah and Maaser* by Rabbi Shimon Taub (ArtScroll/Mesorah, 2001)

▸ *The Tzedakah Treasury* by Rabbi Avraham Chaim Feuer (ArtScroll/Mesorah, 2000)

NOTES

References to books of the Talmud refer to the Babylonian Talmud unless otherwise noted.

1. Joseph Telushkin and Dennis Prager, *Why the Jews? The Reason for Antisemitism,* Simon and Schuster, NY, 1983, pp. 52-54.
2. A Hebrew term meaning, "giving kindness."
3. Genesis 18:19 (Translation of Rabbi Aryeh Kaplan, *The Living Torah*).
4. See, for example, Isaiah 1:17 and Micah 6:8.
5. Mishnah, *Ethics of the Fathers* 1:2.
6. Maimonides, *Mishneh Torah,* Laws of the Festivals, 6:18. See also *Zohar, Parshat Yitro* (In *Sephard* prayer books, *Tikunei Shabbat, Seudat Hayom*).
7. Maimonides is quoting Hosea 9:4.
8. *Code of Jewish Law, Orach Chaim,* 429:1, Ramah. Known as *Kimcha dePischah,* Passover flour.
9. Jeff Seidel, *Jewish Student Information Center Travel Guide*, Targum Press, Jerusalem, 2002.
10. *Bava Batra* 8a-b; Maimonides, *Mishneh Torah*, Laws of Gifts to the Poor 7:10: *Code of Jewish Law, Yoreh Deah* 256:5.
11. Rabbi Samson Raphael Hirsch, *Horeb,* The Soncino Press. V, Mitzvoth, Chap. 88, para. 570.
12. See Rabbi Chaim ibn Attar, *Ohr Hachaim,* Commentary on Exodus, 22:24 for discussion of this idea.
13. See chapter on the Land of Israel.
14. Deuteronomy 15:7-11.
15. The following commentaries are based on the *Sifri, Rashi* and *Malbim,* Deuteronomy ibid., ad loc., and on Talmud *Ketuvot* 67b.
16. *Bava Batra* 9a.
17. Maimonides, *Mishneh Torah,* Laws of Gifts to the Poor, 10:1.
18. Ibid. 10:2.
19. *Sanhedrin* 90a.
20. Maimonides, ibid. 10:4.
21. Genesis 1:27.
22. Rabbi Chaim of Volozhin, *Nefesh Hachaim,* 1:1.
23. Rabbi Eliyahu Dessler, *Michtav Me'Eliyahu,* Volume 1, *Kuntres Hachesed* 1.
24. Rabbi Moshe Chaim Luzzatto, *Derech Hashem,* Chaps. 1-5.
25. Kabbalists are scholars of Jewish mysticism. Rabbi Yosef Caro, *Magid Meisharim, Parshat Noach.*
26. Leviticus 25:35.
27. Maimonides, *Mishneh Torah*, Laws of Gifts to the Poor, 10:7.
28. Maimonides, ibid. 10:7-14.
29. One-third of a *shekel,* or about 17 grams of silver — *Code of Jewish Law, Yoreh Deah,* 249:2. In 2003, silver averaged about $5 per oz., so the currency equivalent is about $3.
30. *Bayit Chadash (Bach),* Commentary on Tur *Yoreh Deah,* 331; Rabbi Moshe Feinstein, *Igrot Moshe, Even Haezer,* 3:43. For further sources regard-

ing the nature of the obligation see Rabbi Avraham Chaim Feuer, *The Tzedakah Treasury*, p.126, ArtScroll/Mesorah Publications, NY, 2000.

31. Genesis 28:22.

32. See chapter on the Land of Israel.

33. A. C. Feuer, ibid.

34. Ritual pool. See chapter on marriage, "Two Become One."

35. Phylacteries. See chapter on Material Witnesses, physical symbols of Jewish life.

36. See chapter on Sabbath, "Who Invented the Weekend Anyway?"

37. *Code of Jewish Law, Yoreh Deah*, 249:1; Ramah and commentaries ad loc.

38. Ibid.

39. *Ketuvot* 50a, Ramah.

40. *Code of Jewish Law*, ibid. Ramah.

41. *Code of Jewish Law, Orach Chaim*, 529:1, *Biur Halachah* ad loc. "*ve'al yetzamtzem.*"

42. Exodus 23:5.

43. *Bava Metzia* 32b.

44. Rabbi Eliyahu Dessler, *Michtav Me'Eliyahu*, Volume 1, *Kuntres Hachessed 1.*

45. *Nedarim* 40a.

46. *Midrash Tanchuma, Parshat Vayera* 1.

47. *Code of Jewish Law, Yoreh Deah*, 249:15.

48. *Midrash Rabbah*, Genesis 96:5; *Midrash Tanchuma, Vayechi* 3.

49. From acceptance speech of Howard Schultz on winning the Columbia Business School's Botwinick Prize in Business Ethics, printed in *Hermes Magazine*, Columbia Business School, Spring 2001. Howard Schultz is chairman and chief global strategist of Starbucks. Through CARE and the Starbucks Foundation, the company works to give back to the communities in which it does business.

50. Literally, "bringing in the bride."

51. Yiddish for charity box.

Belief, Knowledge and Faith

The Thirteen Principles of Faith

The Need to Know

There is a popular misconception that "Judaism is not a religion of dogma"[1] and that it makes no demands on belief. However, it is clear from the Torah itself that there are obligations of the intellect as well as obligations of action.[2]

> *I am the Lord, your God, Who has taken you out of the land of Egypt, from the house of slavery. You shall not recognize the gods of others in My presence.*[3]

The first two of the Ten Commandments obligate us to acknowledge God's existence and His involvement in the world, and to deny the existence of any other power. Every Jew is required to affirm certain truths and to reject falsehood: truth, belief and knowledge are constant themes throughout the Torah.

In the account of the plagues in Egypt, for example, God repeatedly states that the purpose of the miracles is to demonstrate certain basic truths about His existence. God brings the first two plagues, "so that you will know that there is none like God, our God." After the fourth plague,

He says, "so that you will know that I am God in the midst of the land."[4] The fifth plague is followed by the statement, "so that you shall know that there is none like Me in all the world."[5] The Torah makes it very clear that God's purpose in performing the many miracles surrounding the Exodus was not simply to free the Jews and punish the Egyptians. The supernatural events that occurred during the Exodus were designed to be an educational experience (albeit, high impact) for the Egyptians and for the Jews. They were a graphic demonstration of the true nature of God.[6] It is only because God wanted to inform the entire world of certain eternal truths that the Exodus took place in such a dramatic and awe-inspiring way. God could have accomplished the same results much more easily and efficiently by simply removing the Jews from Egypt and placing them in the Promised Land.

Nachmanides, the 13th century Jewish philosopher from Spain, elaborates on this point:

> The intent of all the commandments is that we should believe in God and admit that He created us; and that is the purpose of the whole of creation ... And God's ... only desire in this lower world is that humans should know and acknowledge to God that He created us.[7]

Absolute Truth

Judaism is predicated upon the belief that there are absolute truths that are accessible to human beings.

> For this commandment that I command you today — it is not hidden from you and it is not distant. It is not in heaven, [for you] to say, "Who can ascend to the heaven for us and take it for us, so that we can obey it and fulfill it?" Nor is it across the sea, to say, "Who can cross to the other side of the sea for us and take it for us, so that we can obey it and fulfill it?" Rather, the matter is very near to you — in your mouth and in your heart — to fulfill it.[8]

A philosophy of pluralism or moral relativism, which denies the existence of absolute truths, is unacceptable to Jewish thought: The Torah has very definite moral pronouncements, imperatives and laws. The belief that all truth is relative, however, pervades modern society. As noted scholar and social commentator, Allan Bloom, writes:

> There is one thing a professor can be absolutely certain of: Almost every student entering the university believes, or says he believes, that truth is relative. If this belief is put to the

test, one can count on the students' reaction: They will be uncomprehending. That anyone should regard the proposition as not self-evident astonishes them, as though one were calling into question 2 + 2 = 4. These are things you don't think about.[9]

Although many people profess to believe that there are no absolutes, when challenged, it is clear that deep down they do accept certain absolutes. I was once traveling from London to Australia, and at about 3 a.m., somewhere over Bandar-Seri Begawan, we were served breakfast. As usual, I was served my kosher meal before anyone else received the regular meal. My neighbor looked at my elaborately wrapped tray and said, "Kosher food, huh? Well, I don't believe in absolute truth!" I replied, "Are you absolutely sure of that?" — a retort that usually makes the other party stop and think for a moment. This time, however, my fellow traveler immediately responded, "Ah, but you are using logic."

"If I understand you correctly," I answered, "you are saying that since you do not accept anything as absolutely true, logic is also in doubt. Therefore, I cannot use logic to refute you. Is that your claim?" He confirmed that I was correct in my understanding of his argument. "Well," I said, "That is quite logical." At that point he realized that even he does accept certain truths as absolute (such as the validity of certain logical rules) and he quickly ended the conversation.

Not only is a relativist often self-deluding, he is often intolerant of those who do believe in absolutes. The Chief Rabbi of the United Kingdom, Rabbi Jonathan Sacks, points out that to the same degree that Judaism rejects pluralism, pluralism rejects Judaism:

Theological, as opposed to political, pluralism presupposes the absence of absolute or normative truth and hence the falsehood of Orthodoxy. Orthodoxy stakes its being on the existence of some truth that transcends the relativities of man. This is the rock on which pluralism founders. Either the Torah is the unmediated word of God or it is not. Either Halachah [Jewish law] commands every Jew or it does not. Either God speaks to us through history or He does not. Where truth and falsity are at stake, the idea that both sides of a contradiction are true is itself a contradiction ... the [literature] on pluralism proceeds on the explicit or hidden premise that Orthodoxy is false. It could not be otherwise, for if Orthodoxy is true, pluralism would be false. But if so, pluralism is no more tolerant than Orthodoxy. Each represents a way of viewing the relationship between belief and truth, and each excludes the other.[10]

Knowledge

Many Jewish philosophers maintain that belief in God is not a commandment, but a prerequisite to the commandments. Such a commandment, they explain, would be irrelevant. For the believer it is unnecessary and for the atheist it is not compelling, since without a commander there can be no commandments![11]

Maimonides maintains, however, that the obligation to believe in God is indeed a commandment.[12] The key to understanding Maimonides' point of view can be found in the Hebrew word he uses to describe the nature of this belief. We must, he says, develop *da'at*. *Da'at* is usually translated as knowledge, but more accurately means the uniting of two entities as one. The Torah, in fact, uses this word to describe the sexual union of Adam and Eve.[13] In the context of belief in the principles of faith, the idea of *da'at* is to completely integrate these concepts into the way we think and see the world, so that the concepts become one with ourselves. Our knowledge of God's existence should be as clear as the knowledge of our own existence, and as certain as the existence of every physical object in the room. The quality of knowledge that constitutes *da'at* is defined by Maimonides in his *Guide for the Perplexed:*

> *Knowledge (da'at) … is the conviction that what we know exists outside our minds exactly as it is perceived in our minds. If we are also convinced that the matter cannot be different at all from what we believe it to be, and that no reasonable argument can be found for the rejection of the belief … then that knowledge is true knowledge.*[14]

It appears then, that even according to Maimonides, belief alone is not what is required by the commandment, "I am the Lord, your God." Rather, it is *knowledge* of God that we are commanded to pursue and achieve.

Belief and Faith

The Hebrew word for belief, *emunah,* is closely related to the word for reliability and faithfulness: *ne'eman*. Moses is described as, "*ne'eman*," trustworthy and faithful to God.[15] The simplest explanation of *emunah*, belief, is that one acts and lives in accordance with the principles of his belief, is faithful to them and can be trusted. Very few people go through their entire lives without experiencing times of uncertainty; nor does God expect such perfection. What the Torah does demand is that no matter what the challenges, we continue to act in a way that is consistent with belief in God. At the same time, we constantly strive to reach greater heights of *da'at* and belief in three primary ways:

- ▶ Fulfillment of the commandments helps us to absorb truths about the world by performing actions that symbolize and demonstrate these truths.[16] For example, observing the Sabbath demonstrates our belief that the world has a Creator.

- ▶ The study of Torah informs us of the principles of belief, reinforces them and brings the individual to a better understanding of these principles.[17]

- ▶ The study of nature and history shows us Divine wisdom and providence as manifested in the world.[18]

Clearly, none of these methods will automatically bestow upon a person *da'at* or belief. It is our task to struggle with, pursue and integrate the ideals of the Torah into our lives. The only limit to our knowledge of God is that we are creations, not the Creator. In the words of the Sages,[19] "If I would know Him, I would be Him." Just as an asymptote approaches the Y-axis but never touches it,[20] so we can continuously become closer and closer to God even though we will never "touch" Him.

Roots

Our belief in God and understanding of His relationship with the world is grounded in certain fundamental ideas. The Mishnah and Talmud refer to these core beliefs[21] as *ikarim*,[22] literally "roots," because they are indeed the roots of our actions, our attitudes and our lives; and they are the roots from which all the commandments grow.

On a deeper level, as we have mentioned earlier, the purpose of life is to have a relationship with God. For any relationship to be successful, the parties must be basically similar in their outlook on life and in the intellectual framework within which they function. The principles of belief are the roots of our relationship with God in that they constitute the necessary minimum conditions for that relationship to exist.[23]

Belief and Morality

The principles of belief are not mere philosophical ideas; they also have ethical ramifications. A 15th-century Jewish philosopher, Rabbi Yosef Albo, classified all of the roots under three major principles — belief in God, revelation of His will, and reward and punishment. He explained the ethical ramifications of each principle.[24]

Belief in God involves the belief that the world has an objectively true purpose, that life is meaningful and that everything that exists has a part to play in the Divine plan. The belief that He communicated His will to people teaches us that the concepts of good and evil are not dependent on consensus or belief and are not something that humans invented. Rather, there is a Source beyond the human mind from which morality is derived. The belief in a system of reward and punishment tells us that God did not create the world and then abandon it — He knows, cares and takes an active role in what goes on here. In addition, this principle tells us that there is justice and that our actions have consequences.

The Thirteen Principles

Writing in the 12th century, Maimonides[25] was the first Jewish scholar to systematically list and explain the principles of Jewish belief. His "Thirteen *Ikarim,* Principles of Faith," became the most authoritative formulation. They have been studied ever since in Jewish communities around the world.[26] The first five principles concern the existence of God and beliefs about His nature. The next four are beliefs about God's relationship and communication with the world and the Revelation of Torah, and the last four speak of reward, punishment and humanity's destiny.

A condensed version of the Thirteen Principles, known as *"Ani Maamin* [I Believe]," is printed in all standard prayer books just after the morning prayers.[27] The 12th principle, "I believe with perfect faith in the coming of the Messiah ..." has been the last words that Jews have sung and recited before going to their deaths at times of persecution. The beautiful poem, *"Yigdal Elokim Chai,"* said at the beginning of the morning prayers is also based on these 13 principles.[28]

The following is my translation[29] of Maimonides' Thirteen Principles as they appear in his commentary on the Mishnah.[30] It is not possible to delve into each of these ideas in great depth without devoting an entire book to them.[31] After each quotation of Maimonides' principle, however, I have included a short synopsis of the major themes of that principle.

1. The Existence of God

There is a completely perfect Being Who is the cause of everything else. He created everything, everything exists within Him and all continued existence depends upon Him.[32] If He did not exist, nothing else could exist. However, if nothing aside from Him existed, He would continue to exist as before, without any deficiency, because He does not need anything outside of Himself. Everything else, whether spiritual or physical, is dependent on Him.[33] This principle is stated in the verse, "I am the Lord, your God, Who took you out of the land of Egypt."[34]

Theme: We believe that God exists and that He is absolutely self-sufficient, not dependent in any way on human desire, belief or consensus. This belief is the basis for our dedication to a system of absolute morality and absolute values. If God is the source of our values, they are not subject to change and cannot be relative. If morality is a human invention, then it is nothing more than a matter of preference and taste. As Dostoyevsky's Ivan says, in *The Brothers Karamazov*, "If God does not exist, all is permitted."[35] Throughout history, moral systems created by human beings have been bent and molded to fit convenience and desire. It is significant that three of the most ruthless murderers in history, Hitler, Stalin and Pol Pot (who led the Khmer Rouge in a slaughter of millions of Cambodians), were all violently opposed to God and religion. Judaism maintains that in order to build a consistently moral society our worldview must have God at its center.[36]

2. **The Unity of God**

The Creator is One and is unique. His unity is not the same as the unity of a category (e.g., one species, which contains many individual animals) and is not similar to one object or body, which can be subdivided into many parts (e.g., skeleton, organs, limbs, soul, intellect). His unity is not even the same as the number one, because it too can be divided into smaller and smaller fractions. Rather, He is a totally unique Oneness, which cannot be compared to anything else at all.[37] This principle is based on the verse, "Hear O Israel: The Lord is our God, the Lord is One."[38]

Theme: We are monotheist — there is only one God and everything in the world is under His control. Pagans believed in gods of good and gods of evil. As a result, they did not expect the world to be harmonious or even comprehensible, since every natural power represented a different god and all were competing with one another. Monotheism, in contrast, sees all of existence as coming ultimately from one source, as expressed in Isaiah, "[I am the One] Who forms light and creates darkness; Who makes peace and creates evil; I am God, Maker of all these."[39] Monotheism taught people to look for uniformity and harmony in the universe. Albert Einstein pointed out that monotheism, in fact, laid the foundation for all scientific enquiry:

> *Science can only be created by those who are thoroughly imbued with the aspiration toward truth and understanding. This source of feeling, however, springs from the sphere of religion. To this there also belongs faith in the possibility that the regulations valid for the world of existence are rational, that is, comprehensible to reason. Without the belief in the uniformity of nature, no theoretical formula of universal character could be established.*[40]

Maimonides alludes to a similar idea at the beginning of the *Mishneh Torah*, "The foundation of foundations and the pillar of wisdoms is to know that there is a Prime Cause Who brought everything into existence."[41]

3. God Is Not Corporeal

The Creator is not a material being or a physical force. None of the phenomena of the physical world affect Him, and the conditions of the physical world cannot be applied to Him (e.g., movement and rest).[42] As the prophet Isaiah said, "To whom can you liken God, and what likeness can you attribute to Him?"[43] — i.e., since He is not physical in any way, there is nothing to which He can be compared. All the statements in the Torah that contain physical descriptions of God, depicting Him as walking, standing, sitting and speaking, are borrowed terms from the physical world, so that people can relate to the text.[44] As the Sages said, "The Torah speaks in the language of man."[45] The verse, "For you have not seen any image,"[46] teaches us this principle, that is, you did not perceive God in any physical form, because He is neither a material being nor a force of nature.

Theme: The French author Baron de Montisquieu once said, "If triangles made a god they would give him three sides."[47] All idol worship involves projecting human characteristics on one's god. It is the worship of gods made by man, in the image of man. In a sense, believing that God has physical characteristics is an act of ego worship; it suggests that one can only worship a god that can be "put into his pocket."[48] He can only relate to a god that is reduced to his own limited perspective.

Attributing physical characteristics to God also means ascribing to Him the limitations of the physical world. Since a physical god has weaknesses and needs,[49] the relationship between a pagan and his god is one of mutual benefit and mutual need. Judaism informs us that God is not physical, and therefore, He has no limitations, weaknesses or needs. We are the sole beneficiaries of our own good actions, and we alone suffer from our own evil — not God.[50]

4. The Eternity of God

God is eternal and infinite, and everything else is temporary and finite in comparison to Him. A Biblical verse describes Him as, "God, Who preceded all existence ..."[51] Another basic concept, which is a consequence of this belief, is that the world was created *ex nihilo*, from absolute nothingness. This means that space, time and matter did not always exist, but that they had a beginning. The only reality that always existed and always will exist is God Himself.[52]

Theme: Aristotle and other Greek philosophers believed that matter was eternal, and that God and matter had co-existed for all eternity.[53] Until the middle of the 20th century, most scientists also believed that the universe was infinitely old and that matter was eternal. In 1925, Edwin Hubble, an American astronomer, demonstrated that every galaxy was receding from the earth. This indicated that the universe was not static, but expanding, suggesting a beginning. In 1965, Arno Penzias and Robert

Wilson, discovered background radiation that constituted evidence of the "Big Bang." As a student of Einstein predicted, if an initial explosion created the universe, remnants of the released energy should still exist in the form of background radiation. They received a Nobel Prize for their discovery, and the paradigm of an infinitely old universe that had dominated the world since the time of Aristotle was dealt a deathblow. The view that the universe was not "always here," but rather, had a definite beginning is now accepted by most of the scientific world.[54] When it was first proposed, however, this view generated much opposition and argument,[55] perhaps because, as the famous physicist, Stephen Hawking, writes, "Many people do not like the idea that time had a beginning, because it smacks of *Divine intervention.*"[56]

The principle of creation and of God's eternity informs us of the possibility of miracles. Matter and nature are not eternal; they were created by God and are subject to His will. In contrast, the Aristotelian concept is of a god that is equal to and part of the world — and therefore bound by nature. In Aristotle's view, a god exists but cannot act upon the world.[57]

Perhaps the most important ramification of our belief that the world was created by an intelligent Creator is the logical extension that the world and all of existence have a purpose. If the world is merely a result of a chain of accidents, luck and random chance, existence has no intrinsic purpose or meaning.

Natural selection, the blind, unconscious, automatic process which Darwin discovered ... has no purpose in mind. It has no mind and no mind's eye. It does not plan for the future. It has no vision, no foresight, no sight at all.[58]

People can and do attempt to imbue existence with purpose that they subjectively create. Judaism, however, believes that God designed, created and sustains the world and He imbues it with a universal, objective purpose. He created (and continues to create) the world with a purpose and a plan, and our involvement in achieving that purpose is what invests life with true meaning.

5. Devotion to God

Only God may be worshipped ... and only He commands absolute obedience. We do not grant these privileges to anything or anyone at all aside from God, whether it is a spiritual entity, such as an angel, or a physical entity ... All things other than God are bound by the laws of nature that God created, and have no independent existence or power. Their existence and power are derived completely from God. Nor may we make these powers, or anything else, an intermediary between God and the human being. Rather, our thoughts, prayers and intentions should be focused and directed only toward God Himself.[59] This is the central idea behind the prohibition against idolatry, which is the theme of most of the Torah.[60]

Theme: Human beings have a direct, personal relationship with God, and therefore their prayers should be directed to Him alone. Nothing has the power to grant or deny our requests aside from God Himself. Ancient pagans often attempted to "appease" the various forces of nature. They would throw an innocent girl into a volcano to appease its god, or sacrifice a child to the sea gods to insure a good harvest of fish. Many superstitions that people still retain have their origins in this attempt to bribe the gods and influence the forces of nature in favor of human beings.[61] People make decisions based on horoscopes and omens, and request favors from angels, saints and "Lady Luck." Judaism rejects all of these activities as perverse and futile. It teaches us that our trust should be placed only in God and that we should pray to Him alone.

6. The Existence of Prophecy

There existed righteous people with exceptional abilities, whose intellects were highly developed and who were spiritually sensitive, upon whom God bestowed perception and Divine emanation. These individuals were the prophets[62] (mentioned throughout the books of the Torah). Many verses of the Torah testify to the concept of prophecy, and to the existence of prophets in the world.

Theme: We have already stated that we believe an intelligent Being created the world with purpose and continues to sustain it for that purpose. It is logical to assume that He would communicate instructions to His creations regarding the fulfillment of that purpose. Since human beings are the only creatures on earth capable of thinking about purpose, morality and spirituality, it follows that God would communicate with human beings. This is the essence of prophecy.

Maimonides explains that God communicated His will directly to human beings; He did not merely inspire thoughts that arise within them. Inspiration originates in the human mind and human desires, and therefore cannot "command the respect and authority necessary to bind man; rather it will become malleable in his hands."[63] Prophecy is a clear communication of the will of God that has its source *outside* the human mind and therefore carries Divine authority. Belief in God is easy enough if He does not tell us what He wants from us. It does not obligate or direct us and does not disturb our complacency. Maimonides explains, however, that belief in God actually obligates us to obey Him and listen to His instructions as conveyed through the prophets of the Torah. Monotheism, by itself, is insufficient for morality. Belief in prophecy enables us to embrace *ethical* monotheism — the belief in God Who communicated His moral imperatives to humanity.

7. The Prophecy of Moses

Moses is the "father" of all prophets, both of those who preceded him and those who succeeded him. All other prophets are inferior to Moses, as their communication from God was less direct. He was chosen by God from all people to know more of Him than any other human in the past or future. He achieved the highest possible level that a human can reach. No barriers stood between him and God, nothing clouded his vision and no physical, emotional or intellectual obstructions restrained him. His imagination, senses and emotions ceased to interpose, until he became a pure intellect who communicated with God without any intermediaries. There are four principal differences between the prophecy of Moses and that of other prophets:[64]

> ▶ God communicated with all other prophets through an intermediary (e.g. an angel), but He communicated with Moses directly, as the verse states, "Mouth to mouth I speak to him ..."[65]

> ▶ Other prophets received their prophecy when they were asleep at night, or in a dream-state or trance during the day, when their physical senses were inactive. Moses received his prophecy standing in the Tabernacle during the daytime, fully conscious and aware. As the verses states, "If there are prophets among you, I, God, will make Myself known to him in a vision; in a dream I shall speak with him. Not so is my servant Moses ..."[66]

> ▶ When other prophets received prophecy their strength failed, they trembled, and they experienced an overwhelming feeling of dread as though they were about to die. Moses did not experience any fear or trauma at all, as the verse states, "God would speak to Moses face to face, as a man would speak with his friend ..."[67] Just as one person speaks with another without fear or trauma, so Moses was able to speak with God.

> ▶ All other prophets were not able to receive prophecy at will, only when God granted them the prophecy. There were prophets who went for years without any prophecy; and there were some who waited for days, and even months, for a prophetic answer to a question. Sometimes there would be no answer at all. Some prophets prepared themselves for prophecy through joy and meditation, as Elisha did when he said, "Now call a musician for me ..."[68] When the musician played, the prophecy came to him. But there was no guarantee that any of the prophets would have prophecy, even with all their preparation. However, Moses, our teacher, was able to say at any time, "Stand and I will hear what God will command you."[69]

Theme: Verification of prophecy is not a simple matter. Miracles do not reliably prove that prophecy is authentic, since what appears to be miraculous to a headhunter from Malaysia may be run-of-the-mill technology to an Australian prospector with an SUV and satellite phone. The

Jewish people had doubts about Moses even after witnessing the Ten Plagues and the crossing of the Red Sea because they only had miracles to rely upon for verification.[70] Not until they arrived at Mt. Sinai, and all of them heard God speaking to Moses and declaring, "the people shall hear Me speak with you and they shall believe in you forever," did they whole-heartedly accept that Moses was a prophet.[71] Our belief in the prophecy of Moses is not based on miracles, predictions, faith or charisma, but rather on the personal experience and eyewitness testimony of the three million[72] Jews who stood at Mt. Sinai.[73]

All accounts of Divine revelation in the history of religion rely on claims that God communicated with an individual or a small, select group.[74] Faith in the testimony of those individuals was the only basis for believing that God had spoken to them. Judaism is the only religion claiming revelation occurred in front of an *entire* people who personally witnessed God communicating with Moses.[75] As no other prophet or claimant to revelation has or will ever duplicate this degree of revelation, verification and authority, no prophet who contradicts the Torah transmitted via Moses can be accepted by the Jewish people.[76]

Subsequent to the Revelation at Sinai, the Torah's criteria for verification of a prophet do include repeated predictions of future events or the performance of miracles.[77] Although, as we discussed, miracles do not provide absolute proof of prophecy, Jewish law mandates their use, just as we accept the evidence of witnesses in court, even though we can never be absolutely certain that they are telling the truth.[78] Nevertheless, a prophet accepted on the basis of these criteria cannot achieve the same degree of authority as Moses, whom God Himself identified as a prophet.[79]

8. Torah from Heaven

The entire Torah was given by God to Moses, and the Torah that is in our hands today is the same Torah as the original.[80] That is, the entire Torah was transmitted by God to Moses in a form that we call "speech" for want of a better term. And even though we do not fully understand the method of transmission, we know that Moses was like a scribe who faithfully recorded exactly what was dictated to him. There is, therefore, no difference between the verse, "The sons of Ham were Cush, Mizraim, Put and Canaan,"[81] and the verse, "Hear, O Israel: The Lord is our God, the Lord is One."[82] They are both of Divine origin, and both are part of the complete, sacred Torah of truth. This is what the Sages meant when they said that one who says "Torah is not from heaven"[83] has denied a basic principle of the Torah. This even includes one who will accept that the entire Torah is from God, but rejects even one verse, claiming that God did not dictate it, but that Moses wrote it independently.

Rather, every letter in the Torah bears within it wisdom and insights that are apparent to the perceptive and knowledgeable individual.

Similarly, the explanations of the Torah that were received by tradition [the Oral Law] are also from God.[84] This idea was expressed by Moses to the Jewish people in the verse, "Through this you shall know that God sent me to perform all these acts, that it was not from my heart."[85]

Theme: The entire Torah came directly from God. Not one phrase, word or letter of the Torah was invented by Moses himself. Moses acted solely as the conduit through which the Torah was transmitted to the Jewish people. He reached such great spiritual heights that he was able to convey God's words without the slightest change or nuance of interpretation.[86] An important ramification of this principle is that we cannot pick and choose which parts of the Torah to accept or which commandments to fulfill. People make distinctions betweens parts of the Torah that involve "rituals" and "ethics," "law" and "religion," and between commandments that govern our relationship with God and those that govern our relationships with other people. The Torah itself makes no such distinctions:[87] All the commandments are equally Divine, and we are obligated to fulfill them all to the best of our ability. To observe those parts of the Torah that we like and reject those that we do not like turns the Divine Torah into a matter of personal taste.

The Oral Law, which explains and clarifies the Written Torah, was also given by God to Moses. The Five Books of Moses are incomprehensible without additional explanation. Even a commandment as apparently simple as "You shall not murder"[88] requires clarification: What is the definition of death? When does life begin? Is self-defense a justification for killing someone? Is it right to defend your property with deadly force?

Some commandments are simply impossible to fulfill without additional information beyond what is found in the text. The Torah tells us, for example, to "Bind them (*tefillin*) as a sign upon your arm and let them be ornaments between your eyes."[89] What are we expected to do? Tattoo the Torah on our biceps? What is an "ornament"?[90]

It is a fundamental principle of our belief that God did not leave us in the dark about how to fulfill the Torah. Rather, He gave us all the information that we need, and will ever need, to observe His commandments. He also gave us the necessary rules and methodology to apply the Torah to changing times, places and circumstances.[91] All of this information is known as the Oral Torah, because it was transmitted verbally from God to Moses and by millions of fathers to their sons, mothers to their daughters and teachers to their students, until most of it was committed to writing in about 189 C.E., when Judah the Prince[92] compiled the Mishnah.[93]

9. The Eternity of Torah

The Torah of Moses will never be annulled, and no other Torah will ever come from God aside from it. God will never add to or subtract from it, neither in written form or orally.[94] As the verse states, "The entire word that I command you, that you shall observe to do, you shall not add to it and you shall not subtract from it."[95]

Theme: We must not be influenced by every charismatic, inspiring person who claims Divine revelation. God informed us of His will on Mount Sinai once in history. Prophets were sent afterward to reinforce our commitment to that Revelation but never to change or replace it.[96] One of the last prophets, Malachi, states the purpose of prophecy at the very end of his book, "Remember the Torah of Moses, My servant, that I commanded on Horeb[97] to the Jewish people, its laws and statutes."[98] All the prophets are doing are "reminding" us of what we already have received from Moses. Any prophet who claims to be bringing a message from God that the Torah has been changed is contradicting the Revelation at Mt. Sinai. There are those who claim that God "changed His mind," and gave the world a new Torah; there are those who say He added to or took away parts of the Torah. We believe, however, that God, Who is perfect, need not change or modify His word. Just as God does not change, so His morality and truth do not change with time and place. They are eternal and absolute.

10. God's Omniscience

God is aware of all the deeds of people and has not abandoned them.[99] Not [as heretics are quoted as saying that], "God has abandoned the world";[100] rather, as it states, "Great in counsel and mighty in deed, Your eyes are aware of all the ways of people, to give to each according to his ways and the consequences of his deeds."[101] And as it further states, "God saw that the wickedness of man was great upon the earth ..."[102] These verses clearly demonstrate this idea.

Theme: God is aware of everything that goes on in the world. As the saying goes, "You can run, but you can't hide." There are no places, there is no time and there are no circumstances in which we can avoid God.[103] Being a good person is a 24-hour-a-day, 7-day-a-week job. It encompasses our actions, speech and thoughts. *The Code of Jewish Law*, which guides a Jew throughout every moment of life, begins with this thought:

> *"I have set God before me always"*[104] — *This is a major rule of the Torah and of the ways of the righteous, who walk before God. For the way a person sits and behaves when he is alone in his house and his behavior in the presence of a great king are very different. He does not feel the same freedom of expression when he speaks in the presence of a great king as when he talks with his relatives and friends. How much more so, when a person realizes that God, the King of kings, Whose honor fills the whole world, is always present and knows his deeds.*[105]

Judaism, morality and spirituality are not restricted to Saturday mornings in the synagogue, to a Bar Mitzvah celebration, or to Hebrew school. The Torah gives us moral guidance in business, medicine, politics, sexuality, relationships and even in warfare. Just as God knows all things, at all times and in all places, we too are obligated to act as moral beings at all times and in all places. As a great scholar of the last century wrote:

"It is impossible for Judaism to be confined within the religious rituals of the synagogue; it strives to encompass all areas of life and to rule over them absolutely. Agriculture, society, art, science and politics — are all stamped with the seal of Judaism."[106]

11. Reward and Punishment

God rewards those who fulfill His commandments and punishes those who transgress them. The ultimate reward is the World to Come, and the ultimate punishment is excision of the soul [the soul is cut off from any connection to the spiritual existence of the World to Come].[107] As the verse states, "Moses returned to God and said to Him: 'The people have committed a grievous sin by making themselves a god of gold. And now if You would, please forgive their sin! — but if not, erase me now from Your book that You have written.' God replied to Moses: 'Whoever has sinned against Me, I shall erase him from My book.'"[108] God's reply to Moses shows that God is aware of who is faithful to Him, and who has sinned against Him; and that He will reward one and punish the other.

Theme: Fundamental to our understanding of the relationship between God and the world is the belief that all actions have consequences, whether good or bad. Any good that an individual does is ultimately rewarded and any evil is ultimately punished. In the physical world, every action creates certain inevitable effects. The first law of thermodynamics, for example, the law of conservation of energy, states that energy cannot be created or destroyed. Similarly, in the spiritual world there is a law of conservation of spiritual energy, which we call *kedushah* (holiness).[109] The spiritual energy of our actions is never destroyed; its impact is eternal and affects the state of the soul even after the death of the body.[110]

A central aspect of this principle is our conviction that God is just, as the Torah states, "The deeds of the Mighty One are perfect, for all His ways are just. He is a faithful God, never unfair; righteous and moral ...."[111] Even if we do not witness the reward of the righteous and punishment of the wicked in our lifetimes, we know that ultimately justice will be done.[112] The slightest act of goodness is noted and rewarded,[113] as are good intentions, even if they do not come to fruition. If someone tried to do the right thing but was unable to succeed due to circumstances beyond his control, that intention too will be rewarded.[114] At times, God may allow an evil person to be successful, but his deeds are not ignored; God "waits and eventually collects what is due to Him."[115] We realize that this world represents only a small part of reality, that our lifespan of 70 or 80 years is only a fraction of our complete existence. This understanding is central to the Jewish approach to life. We do not focus on other worlds (and life after death) to the exclusion of this world, but neither do we view this physical world as the totality of existence.[116]

12. The Days of the Messiah

We believe that the Messiah will come, and will not be delayed beyond the time that God has set for his arrival.[117] We wait for and expect his coming,[118] but we do not attempt to calculate the time of his arrival, nor do we attempt to derive from the Torah when he is supposed to come.[119] We believe in his prominence and his nobility and should love him and pray for his coming, in accordance with all the prophets from Moses to Malachi.[120]

Another element of this principle is that the only one fitting to be a king of Israel is a descendant of King David, through his son, King Solomon. As the prophet Nathan said to King David, "Your dynasty and your kingdom will remain steadfast before you for all time; your throne will remain firm forever."[121]

Theme: The Jewish people have been in exile for so long that the world has come to regard this as our natural state. Clearly, the opposite is true: To be scattered around the world — subject to the rule of other nations and under threat of annihilation — is completely unnatural.[122] The Land of Israel was designated as the homeland of the Jewish people from the beginning of time.[123] To exist independently — free of threats to our existence and secure in our land — should be the natural condition of the Jewish people.[124] An author visiting Israel once commented, "The Jews, because they are Jews, have never been able to take the right to live as a natural right."[125]

An unnatural state of existence cannot remain as it is forever. Everything in the universe returns to its natural *status quo* just as surely as water seeks its lowest level.[126] Therefore we believe that the inevitable conclusion to our long exile is the Messianic Age in which all Jews will return to Israel and live in peace in a sovereign Jewish commonwealth.

We also believe that the concept of being a Chosen People[127] is that we have a special destiny; namely, to bring the message of ethical monotheism to the world.[128] We can only be successful in achieving this goal when the full infrastructure of Judaism is in place in the Land of Israel.[129] This too is one of the functions of the Messiah, to provide us with an environment in which we can fulfill our purpose as a people.[130]

A third element of Messianic times is the revelation of the true purpose of the world and the truth of Torah in such a way that it will be obvious to all people. As the prophet Isaiah said, "For the earth will be as filled with the knowledge of God as water covers the seabed."[131] All the questions that have accumulated over the long and bitter years of our exile will be answered.[132] Why is there is so much anti-Semitism? Why did the Holocaust happen? How could false doctrines dominate the world for so long? In the time of the Messiah, we will look back on all of history and understand with absolute clarity the answers to all the "whys." This is the meaning of the beautiful psalm that describes the Messianic era:

> ... *When God returns the exiles to Zion, we will have been like dreamers. Then our mouth will be filled with laughter and our tongue with glad song ... Those who plant in tears will harvest in joy.*[133]

Finally, we wait in anticipation for the greatest of Messianic blessings, the blessing of peace, as expressed in the famous prophecy of Isaiah,

> ... *and they shall beat their swords into plowshares, and their spears into pruning-hooks; nation shall not lift up sword against nation, neither shall they learn war any more.*[134]

Jews have lived for centuries, through good times and bad, with the hope of the Messiah's coming. Our belief in the Messiah is an essential aspect of our recognition that the Jewish people have a national destiny. God has made a Covenant with us to fulfill that destiny: We observe the commandments, have faith and pray. God will then carry out His side of the "contract" by bringing the Messiah, returning all Jews to Israel and bringing peace to the world.[135]

13. Resurrection

The resurrection of the dead is a fundamental principle of the Torah of Moses.[136] One who denies this concept has no connection to the Jewish religion or to the Jewish people ... As Daniel himself was told, "As for you, go to [your] end; you will rest — then arise for your portion at the End of Days."[137]

Theme: Human beings are a combination of body and soul, the physical and the spiritual. Ultimate reward must therefore be conferred upon body and soul together.[138] The body alone is merely a physical animal without free will, unable to accomplish anything morally or spiritually significant. The soul by itself is a spiritual being but also lacks free will and can make no moral choices. Only when the body and soul are joined together does free will exist. Only then can meaningful accomplishments[139] be attained. And only when the body and soul are together can the consequences of these accomplishments be fully enjoyed.

The detailed laws regarding burial and respectful treatment of a dead body[140] originate in our appreciation of the human body as that which enables the soul to act with free will. It has served a holy purpose, just like a worn-out Torah scroll or *mezuzah,* and like them, deserves respect.[141]

This state of union between body and soul will be realized once again in the time of the resurrection of the dead. No matter what has happened to the original physical body, God will ultimately re-create the appropriate receptacle for every individual soul.

For God to resurrect the dead — and give the soul of the righteous a new body — is neither more wondrous nor more miraculous than initially placing a soul within every human body. We consider a type of resurrection that occurs regularly as quite natural: It is called birth.[142] Yet the type of resurrection that will occur at some point in the future is regarded as miraculous.

These descriptions are only valid, however, from the human point of view. From God's perspective, there is no difference between the two. A miracle requires no effort on His part, just as the ongoing functioning of nature requires no effort on His part. Every moment of life must be understood as a new act of creation; God continuously creates our existence from nothing and gives life to what is essentially a dead, material world.[143] If we look at life this way, the idea that God will one day resurrect the dead seems no more miraculous than waking up in the morning.[144] In other words, if we perceive our daily existence as supernatural, we will view resurrection as natural![145]

For Further Reading

▶ *Fundamentals and Faith: Insights into the Rambam's 13 Principles* by Rabbi Yaakov Weinberg (Feldheim, 1991)

▶ *Letters to a Buddhist Jew* by Rabbi Akiva Tatz and David Gottlieb (Targum Press, 2005)

▶ *Maimonides' Principles* by Rabbi Aryeh Kaplan (OU/NCSY, 1984)

▶ *Permission to Believe* by Rabbi Lawrence Keleman (Feldheim, 1990)

▶ *The Informed Soul* by Rabbi Dovid Gottlieb (ArtScroll/Mesorah, 1990)

NOTES

References to books of the Talmud refer to the Babylonian Talmud unless otherwise noted.

1. See for instance, Moses Mendelssohn, *Betrachtungen uber Bonnets Palingenesie, Gesammelte Schriften 111,* Berlin, 1843 Pp. 159-166, who appears to be a primary source of the misconception.

2. Rabbi Bachya ibn Pakuda's magnum opus, *Duties of the Heart,* was composed to address the fact that the duties of the intellect were ignored and the duties of the body were fulfilled. See Pakuda's Introduction to *Duties of the Heart.*

3. Exodus 20:2-3; Deuteronomy 5:6-7.

4. Exodus 8:18.

5. Ibid. 9:14.

6. Nachmanides, *Commentary on the Torah,* Exodus, 13:16.

7. Nachmanides, ibid.

8. Deuteronomy 30:11-14.

9. Allan Bloom, *The Closing of the American Mind,* Penguin Books, Great Britain, 1987, Introduction, p. 25.

10. Rabbi Jonathan Sacks, *Le'Ela: A Journal of Judaism Today,* Published by the Chief Rabbi's Office and Jew's College, London, Passover, 1990.

11. *Ba'al Halachot Gedolot,* cited by Nachmanides in his *Critique on Maimonides' Book of the Commandments,* Mitzvah 1; see also Rabbi Chananiah Kazis, *Kinat Soferim,* ad loc.

12. Maimonides, *Book of the Commandments,* Mitzvah 1; *Mishneh Torah,* Laws of Foundations of the Torah, 1:1-6.

13. Genesis 4:1, "And Adam knew (*vayeda*) Eve, his wife."

14. Maimonides, *Guide for the Perplexed,* 1:50; The Arabic word that Maimonides uses in the Book of the Commandments is *a'ataqad.* In the Guide he explains that the correct translation of *a'ataqad* is the Hebrew word *da'at.* See comments of Rabbi Yosef Kafach on *Guide for the*

Perplexed, Petichah, Note 7; 1:50, Note 1; Mossad Harav Kook, Jerusalem, 1977.

15. Numbers 12:7.

16. *Sfat Emet,* Commentary on *B'ha'alotcha,* 5431.

17. *Kinat Soferim,* ibid.; *Midrash Rabbah,* Eichah, Petichtah 2.

18. *Kinat Soferim,* ibid.; Maimonides, *Mishneh Torah,* Laws of Foundations of the Torah 2:2; Rabbi Bachya ibn Pakuda, *Chovot Halevavot,* Sha'ar Habechinah; Chazon Ish, *Emunah Ubitachon,* Chap. 1.

19. Quoted in Maharal, *Derech Hachaim, Pirkei Avot,* 5:6. See also Solomon ibn Gevirol, *Keter Malchut.*

20. A line that approaches but never meets the vertical Y – axis is an asymptote, as in the following diagram:

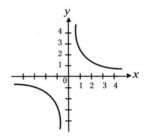

21. The concept that there are core principles of belief is the underlying rationale of the Mishnah in *Sanhedrin* 10:1 where it is stated that one who denies the concept of resurrection or is an *apikoros,* a heretic, loses his portion in the World to Come. Maimonides formulates his 13 principles of belief in his commentary on this Mishnah.

22. *Sanhedrin* 38b, 45b; *Bava Batra* 16b: See Rav Yosef Albo, *Sefer Haikarim,* Introduction: The word *ikar* refers to those principles without which the whole system of Divine religion would collapse.

23. Maimonides, *Commentary on the Mishnah, Sanhedrin* 10:1.

24. Rabbi Yosef Albo, *Sefer Haikarim.*

25. Born 1135, died 1204.

26. See also Rabbi Yosef Albo, ibid., and Rabbi Don Isaac Abarbanel in *Rosh Amanah*. There is some dispute as to the number and precise formulation of the principles, but none of the critics disputed that the principles were true. Maimonides' principles were the ones accepted by the vast majority of Jewish scholars and by the Jewish people as well.

27. *The Complete ArtScroll Siddur, Ashkenaz*, pp. 178-181.

28. Ibid. pp. 12-15.

29. Author's note: The translation is not literal, and there are words and phrases that have been omitted in order to make the text more readable.

30. From Maimonides, *Commentary on the Mishnah, Sanhedrin* 10:1 This translation is based on Rabbi Yosef Kafach's Hebrew translation of the original Arabic, Mossad Harav Kook, Jerusalem, 1965. See also *Mishneh Torah,* Laws of Repentance 3:6-8.

31. See Appendix for sources for further study.

32. *Mishneh Torah*, Laws of Foundations of the Torah, 1:1.

33. Ibid. 1:2-3, 1:4.

34. Exodus 20:2; Deuteronomy 5:6.

35. Fyodor Dostoyevsky, *The Brothers Karamazov*, Reissue Edition, Bantam Classics, 1995 (First published 1879-1880).

36. Rabbi Yaakov Weinberg, *Fundamentals and Faith*, edited by Rabbi Mordechai Blumenfeld, Targum/Feldheim, Jerusalem/NY, 1991.

37. *Mishneh Torah,* ibid., 1:7.

38. Deuteronomy 6:4.

39. Isaiah 45:7.

40. Albert Einstein, *Out of My Later Years*, Science and Religion, Secaucus, The Citadel Press, 1956, p. 26.

41. *Mishneh Torah*, ibid., 1:1.

42. Ibid. 1:7.

43. Isaiah 40:18.

44. *Mishneh Torah*, ibid., 1:9-12.

45. *Berachot* 31b.

46. Deuteronomy 4:15.

47. Baron Charles de Montisquieu, *The Persian Letters*, Translator C.J. Betts, Penguin USA, 1977.

48. Rabbi Moshe Shapiro.

49. *Mishneh Torah*, ibid., 1:7.

50. Job 35:6-7.

51. Deuteronomy 33:27 — Translation of Rabbi Yaakov Weinberg, ibid.

52. *Mishneh Torah*, ibid., 1:11.

53. Maimonides, *Guide for the Perplexed*, 2:25.

54. Brian Greene, *The Elegant Universe*, Vintage Books, NY, 2000, Chap. 14. Lawrence Keleman, *Permission to Believe*, Targum/Feldheim, Jerusalem, 1990, Chap. 3.

55. Kitty Ferguson, *The Fire in the Equations*, Bantam Books, UK, 1994, pp. 90-101.

56. Stephen W. Hawking, *A Brief History of Time*, Bantam Books, NY, 1988, p. 46.

57. *Guide for the Perplexed*, ibid.

58. Richard Dawkins, *The Blind Watchmaker*, W. and W. Norton & Company, Inc., NY, 1987, p. 5.

59. Maimonides, ibid. Laws of Idolatry, 2:1.

60. Maimonides, 2:4; *Guide for the Perplexed*, 3:37.

61. See James George Frazer, *The Golden Bough*, (a new abridgement), Oxford University Press, London, 1994, Books III and IV.

62. *Mishneh Torah*, Laws of Foundations of the Torah, 7:1.

63. Rabbi Yaacov Weinberg, *Fundamentals and Faith*, p. 70.

64. Maimonides, ibid. 7:6.

65. Numbers 12:8.

66. Ibid. 12:6.

67. Exodus 33:11.

68. II Kings, 3:15.

69. Numbers 9:8.

70. *Mishneh Torah*, Laws of Foundations of the Torah, 8:1.

71. Ibid.

72. *Mechilta* and *Targum Yonatan* on Exodus 12:37.

73. Ibid. 8:2.

74. For example, Christianity relies on the 12 apostles and the authors of the Gospels; Islam on Mohammed; and Mormonism on Joseph Smith and two others.

75. Rabbi Yehudah Halevy, *Kuzari*, 1:87; Maimonides, *Collected Letters and Responsa*, Letter to Yemen. For further elaboration on this idea see, Rabbi Dovid Gottlieb, *Living Up to the Truth*, Third Revised Edition, January 1997, available for free download, at http://www.ohr.edu/web/books; Lawrence Keleman, *Permission to Receive*, Targum/Feldheim, NY/Jerusalem, 1996, pp. 50-78.

76. Maimonides, *Mishneh Torah*, ibid., 8:3.

77. *Mishneh Torah*, Laws of Foundations of the Torah, 7:7; Maimonides, *Introduction to Commentary on the Mishneh*.

78. Ibid. 8:2.

79. Ibid. 8:3.

80. See Rabbi Yaakov Weinberg, ibid., p. 91: "The real emphasis of this Principle is that this Torah, which includes both the Written and Oral Law, is word for word, letter for letter from the Almighty, and absolutely none of it was edited by Moshe [Moses] in any way whatsoever."

81. Genesis 10:6.

82. Deuteronomy 6:4.

83. Mishnah, *Sanhedrin* 10:1.

84. Maimonides, ibid., Laws of Repentance, 3:8.

85. Numbers 16:28.

86. Rabbi Chaim of Volozhin, *Ruach Chaim* on *Ethics of the Fathers*, 1:1; Rabbi Meir Simchah Hacohen of Dvinsk, *Meshech Chochmah*,

Introduction to the Book of Exodus, Librairie Colbo, Paris, 1972.

87. Dayan Dr. I Grunfeld, Introduction to *Horeb*, The Soncino Press, London, 1962. Pp. cxxx-cxxxix.

88. Exodus 20:13; Deuteronomy 5:17.

89. Ibid. 6:8, Relating to the commandment to wear *tefillin.*.

90. Rabbi Yehudah Halevy, *Kuzari*, 3:35; Rabbi Avraham ibn Ezra, *Commentary on the Torah*, Introduction; Rabbi David Nieto, *Sefer Kuzari Sheni*, Jerusalem, 1986.

91. See for example, *The Complete ArtScroll Siddur, Ashkenaz*, pp. 48-53.

92. Roman Era sage, who was president of the Sanhedrin (descended from King David), who edited and redacted the Mishnah in the north of Israel.

93. Rashi, *Shabbat* 13b "Megillat"; *Iggeret of Rav Sherira Gaon*; Rabbi Zvi Hirsch Chajes, *Introduction to the Talmud*, 33; Maimonides, *Introduction to the Mishneh Torah*.

94. *Mishneh Torah*, ibid.; Laws of Foundations of the Torah, 8:3, 9:1.

95. Deuteronomy 13:1.

96. *Megillah* 2b. A prophet may not invent anything new.

97. Another name for Mt. Sinai, *Shabbat* 89b; Exodus 17:6, 33:6; Deuteronomy 1:2, 1:19, 4:10, 4:15, 9:8.

98. Malachi 3:22.

99. *Mishneh Torah*, Laws of Repentance, 5:5.

100. Ezekiel 8:12.

101. Jeremiah 32:19.

102. Genesis 6:5.

103. Jonah, Chapters 1 and 2; Psalms, Chap. 139.

104. Psalms 16:8

105. *Code of Jewish Law, Orach Chaim*, 1:1, Ramah; quoted from Maimonides, *Guide for the Perplexed*, 3:52.

106. Rabbi Yechiel Yaakov Weinberg, *Responsa Seridei Aish*, Mossad Harav Kook, Jerusalem, 1977. Vol. 4, p. 365. See also Rabbi Samson

Raphael Hirsch, Commentary on Genesis 48:3-4.

107. *Mishneh Torah*, Laws of Repentance, 3:5, 8:1, 8:5.

108. Exodus 32:31-33.

109. Rabbi Dr. Chaim Zimmerman, *Torah and Reason*, Tvuno Inc., U.S.A., 1979, pp. 78-79.

110. Rabbi Chaim of Volozhin, *Nefesh Hachaim*, Jerusalem, 1973, Sha'ar Alef, Chap. 12; *Ruach Chaim*, Introduction to *Pirkei Avot*, "Kol Yisrael."

111. Deuteronomy 32:4 — Translation from Rabbi Aryeh Kaplan, *The Living Torah*, Moznaim Publishing Corporation, Jerusalem/NY, 1981.

112. *Shabbat* 55b, Commentary of Rabbi Menachem HaMeiri, ad loc.; *Chullin* 7b; Maimonides, *Guide for the Perplexed*, 3:17.

113. *Pesachim* 118a; *Bava Kamma* 38b.

114. *Kiddushin* 40a.

115. *Midrash Bereshit Rabbah*, 67:2-4; *Pesikta DeRav Kahana* 24:14; Talmud Yeushalmi, *Shekalim* 21b.

116. Maimonides, *Commentary on the Mishnah*, ibid.; Deuteronomy 7:10, Commentaries of Rashi and Nachmanides, ad loc.

117. *Mishneh Torah*, ibid., Chapter 9; Laws of Kings, 11:1.

118. Habakkuk 2:3; Talmud, *Shabbat* 31a, "Did you wait for the Redemption?"

119. *Sanhedrin* 97b, "Let the spirits of the calculators of times explode."

120. Ibid. 11:1-2. Malachi was one of the last of the prophets, circa 350 B.C.E.

121. II Samuel, 7:16.

122. Maharal of Prague, *Netzach Yisrael*, Yahadut, Bnei Brak, 1980, Chap. 1.

123. Rashi, Commentary on Genesis 1:1.

124. Maharal, ibid.

125. Saul Bellow, *To Jerusalem and Back*, The Viking Press, 1976, p. 26.

126. Maharal, ibid.

127, Exodus 19:3, 6; Deuteronomy 4:20, 26:17-19; Isaiah 61:6.

128. Isaiah 2:1-3.

129. Rabbi Yehudah Halevy, *Kuzari,* 2:16.

130. Maimonides, *Mishneh Torah*, Laws of Repentance, 9:2; Commentary of Rabbi Samson Raphael Hirsch, Genesis 48:3-4.

131. Isaiah 11:9.

132. Rabbi Yaakov Weinberg, ibid., p. 119.

133. Psalm 126.

134. Isaiah 2:4; Micah 4:3.

135. Rabbi Yaakov Weinberg, ibid., p. 122.

136. Maimonides, *Commentary on the Mishnah*, *Sanhedrin* 10:1, Introduction to the 13 Principles; *Mishneh Torah*, Laws of Repentance, 3:6; Maimonides, *Collected Letters and Responsa*, Letter on the Resurrection.

137. Daniel 12:13.

138. Rabbi Moshe ben Yosef Matrani (Mabit), *Beit Elokim*, Sha'ar HaYesodot, Chap. 53.

139. *Sanhedrin* 91b; Rabbi Yaakov Weinberg, ibid., pp. 126-127.

140. Deuteronomy 21:23; *Mishneh Torah*, Laws of Sanhedrin, 15:8.

141. *Shabbat* 105b.

142. See *Shabbat* 129a; *Bechorot* 22a; *Niddah* 22b. In Mishnaic Hebrew, the word for womb is *kever,* which also means grave; in a sense, every grave is also a womb that will "give birth." — Rabbi Moshe Shapiro.

143. Rabbi Chaim of Volozhin, *Nefesh Hachaim*, Sha'ar Alef, Chap. 2.

144. *The Complete ArtScroll Siddur, Askenaz*, pp. 2-3, first prayer and pp. 18-19, first paragraph.

145. Rabbi Moshe Shapiro, in explanation of the statement in *Sanhedrin* 91a: "That which never existed — now lives. That which once existed — how much more so will it live again!"

Why Are There Commandments?

What are mitzvot and why do we do them?

The Problem

*O*ne of the most commonly voiced criticisms of Judaism is that it pays too much attention to details; that it is obsessed with hairsplitting and legalities. An initial look at Jewish law appears to justify this claim. The Torah comprises 613 commandments, divided into 365 prohibitions and 248 obligations,[1] with hundreds of rabbinical decrees and customs that govern every aspect of life. There are volumes upon volumes of detailed guidelines specifying how one should dress, eat, work and even talk. Of course, no individual Jew is obligated to fulfill all the commandments — unless that Jews is both male and female; single, married and divorced; *Kohen, Levi* and *Israelite*, all simultaneously.

This intricate structure can definitely give one the impression that the Torah is overly legalistic and that it places excessive demands on human beings without leaving them enough freedom to relax and enjoy life. Judaism's seeming obsession with laws and technicalities also makes one wonder about the point of it all. How does not eating lobster make one a better person? Why would lighting Shabbat candles bring one closer to God?

In order to comprehend why Jews have tenaciously adhered to this way of life for close to 3,500 years, we must gain a better understanding of the purpose of the commandments, called in Hebrew *mitzvot* (singular, *mitzvah*).

Being Like God

We believe that our primary obligation as beings created "in the image of God"[2] is to imitate God and to "walk in His ways."[3] What does this mean? The Sages defined the goal this way:

> *Just as He is merciful and kind, so you should be merciful and kind.*[4] *Just as He clothed the naked, so should you; as He visited the sick, so should you; as He comforted the mourners, so should you; as He buried the dead, so should you.*[5]

Each of the above statements refers to an instance in the Bible in which God demonstrated these qualities. The Sages are indicating that just as a parent teaches a child by doing rather than by preaching, God intentionally incorporated these instances into the Bible to teach us the behavior He expects of us.

Although Maimonides lists the obligation of "walking in God's ways" as just one of the 613 commandments,[6] it is also understood in the general sense as an underlying rationale for every one of the commandments.[7] In order to have a complete relationship with God it is necessary that we be as "Godlike" as possible. We must develop a similar intellectual framework, inculcating in ourselves the attributes of God, and act as He acts.[8]

Imitating the Creator is not an easy task and it is not always obvious what "being good" really entails in a given situation.[9] You may want to extend help to a needy person, but what is the best form for this kindness to take? Should you give him money, a loan or a job? Should you give a large sum to one person or small sums to many? How much of your own income is it appropriate to give? To address these complexities, God provided us with the ultimate guide to becoming like Him — the 613 commandments with all their attendant details.[10]

Refinement

Judaism accepts as axiomatic that neither the human being nor the world in which he lives is perfect. Rather, just as this world is incomplete and designed to be perfected, the human being is also designed to strive for perfection.[11] The Midrash[12] recounts a discussion concerning this idea between Rabbi Akiva[13] and the Roman official Turnus Rufus:

Turnus Rufus asked Rabbi Akiva, "What is better, the deeds of God or the deeds of man? If you say the deeds of man are better, then you are a heretic! If you say the deeds of God are better, then why do you circumcise your children? If God wanted them circumcised, why are they not born without a foreskin?"

Instead of answering directly, Rabbi Akiva showed Turnus Rufus a stalk of wheat and a piece of cake and asked him, "Which do you think is better? The deeds of God (the inedible, raw stalk of wheat) or the deeds of man (the delicious cake)?" The Roman was forced to admit that the deeds of man were better.

Rabbi Akiva demonstrated to Turnus Rufus that just as the wheat is inedible until it goes through many steps of refinement and is turned into bread or cake, the human being also needs refinement and perfection physically, morally and spiritually. The purpose of the commandments is to refine the human being and bring him closer and closer to perfection.[14]

Several ideas related to this process are expressed in a seemingly simple verse in Proverbs (30:5): "All the commandments of God are *tzerufah* (refined)."

The Midrash explains that the purpose of the commandments is the process called *tziruf*.[15] The Hebrew word *tzerufah* (from which *tziruf* derives grammatically) bears two opposing explanations. Depending on the context, the word can mean smelted, as in the method employed to separate the ore from metal through the application of heat. Alternatively, it can mean joining, as in soldering, where heat is used to join metals. In the present verse, these two explanations are to be taken metaphorically: i.e., God's commandments represent the source of heat, and the person represents the metal. Just as heat burns away waste matter, God gave us 365 prohibitions ("thou shalt not"s) to help eliminate the negative character traits contained within a person. And just as heat has the power to merge metals together, God gave us 248 obligations ("thou shalt"s) to consolidate positive traits and to connect human beings to a higher level of consciousness.

That humans need refinement is not a novel concept. Look at any infant: Is he or she a finished product? In our society, children receive 13 years of schooling before they are expected to contend with the challenges of life. Judaism believes that learning how to perfect oneself (and how to perfect the world) takes even longer — an entire lifetime of training.

All of us know adults who have yet to make the transition from infancy to adulthood. Their actions are governed by the instincts of a newborn baby. If they think that an object or a position or a title belongs to them, then by definition it must be theirs, and they will stop at nothing to obtain it. This adult code of behavior, "The Infant Rules of Ownership," is employed liberally at every level of our society.

When a small child wakes up in the early hours of the morning feeling thirsty, he cannot see beyond his basic human instincts, which tell him, "Thirsty — water — drink!" He does not think of his exhausted parents dragging themselves out of a deep sleep in order to bring him a cup of water (without which he could survive for a few hours). Compassion and consideration for others is not a built-in human instinct — it has to be learned and internalized. And like any other complex skill, the only way to master it is through intense training and self-conditioning. But where can a person take a course on compassion?

This is where the *mitzvot* of the Torah come in — they are God-given tools for refinement. Prohibitions enable people to identify their negative instincts and distance themselves from them, while obligations help channel their positive instincts toward becoming better people.

Consciousness Vs. Instinct

Another purpose of the *mitzvot* is to educate people to act consciously, rather than going through their lives on automatic pilot. God wants thinking beings to serve Him, not mindless robots. This is one explanation of what appears to be a strange statement by Rabbi Shimon ben Gamliel:

> A person should not say, "I do not like meat and milk mixtures ..."[16] Rather, he should say, "I would like them, but what can I do? My Father in Heaven has decreed upon me not to partake of them."[17]

The Talmud explains that Jews refrain from eating pork or meat and milk mixtures, not because they find such dishes offensive or unpalatable, but rather because God forbade them to partake of such foods. The Talmud suggests that a Jew should think, "Pork probably tastes excellent; however God has forbidden me to partake of it."[18]

The first time I read the Dr. Seuss book *Green Eggs and Ham*[19] to one of my children, he or she always asks, "Abba,[20] what is ham?" (For some reason, the child's mind is not bothered by green eggs; the school cafeteria probably plays a role in this.) I answer that ham is the meat of a pig. Their response is usually, "Uggh, yuck!" At this point I tell them that ham probably tastes very good and that billions of people eat it all the time. I try to emphasize that the reason we do not eat it is not due to its "bad" taste, but because God forbade us to.

I believe that Rabbi Shimon ben Gamliel would approve of my response. We could condition our children to be repelled by ham (yuck, gross!) but then we would merely have kosher robots, or *mitzvah* machines. This is far from the Torah ideal, which is for thinkers who make decisions about what to do or not to do based on moral commitments, not gut feelings. The commandments are designed to develop people's ability to serve God consciously, encouraging us not to rely on instinct, but to exercise our power of free will.

Revelation

I once met a student in California whose major in college was "Revelation." The goal of such a degree was a mystery to me, as was the curriculum. After speaking with the student about the course, it still remained a mystery. I mentally filed it with a long list of useless college courses, like "Empowering Women With Eating Disorders Through Fairy Tales and Native American Dance Movement Therapy."[21] The founder of the Chassidic movement, the Baal Shem Tov,[22] used to say that one has an obligation to learn from everything and everyone, so I tried to learn something from this encounter. After some consideration, it occurred to me that in reality, every Jew is majoring in revelation — our goal is to reveal the presence of God in this world of concealment.

The process of revelation is indeed a primary aim of the commandments.[23] On a mystical level, when we fulfill these commandments we reveal the attributes and presence of God in every aspect of space and time. For example, by doing an altruistic deed, we introduce into the world an aspect of God's image that was previously concealed: I.e., when a person gives selflessly to another, he is demonstrating that he has a soul (that imitates its Creator), and he is not merely a physical being concerned with his own survival. Upon encountering a truly righteous individual, one recognizes that this person is not merely a "naked ape,"[24] but a being created "in the image of God."

Similarly, when we use a physical object to perform a *mitzvah*, we reveal the concealed spark of Godliness that is contained in that object. When a tree is used to produce paper for a book that inspires someone to reach for higher spiritual and moral levels, the ultimate purpose of that tree — its "spark of Godliness" — becomes obvious to us. When a dining-room table is used as a place for hospitality, kindness and words of Torah, the "spark of Godliness" in that table has become more obvious. It is no longer merely a utensil for eating — a type of trough — rather it is a vehicle for holiness. Sometimes, by showing that everything in creation has a common goal and purpose in its existence we can reveal the idea that this unified, harmonious whole was created by a unified Being. Thus, every *mitzvah* that a person performs reveals another facet of God's existence and introduces it into the human plane of consciousness.

Conversely, if a person acts in a selfish, hedonistic manner, blindly following his baser instincts, his behavior conceals the image of God and emphasizes the animal component of the human. One contemporary American politician is known by the nickname "The Body." This person, to my surprise, was actually elected governor of a state, despite the fact that the qualities of a leader would probably be better found in someone whose nickname were "The Brain," "The Soul," or "The Heart" rather than "The Body." Our obligation in life is to act in such a way that we deserve to be nicknamed "The Soul," not merely "The Body."

The principal way in which we emphasize the spiritual component of humanity, time and space[25] is by fulfilling the commandments. Through the *mitzvot* we engage in the process of revelation, of uncovering elements of Godliness in the world[26] and the image of God within ourselves.

The Final Score

In summary, then, the purposes of the commandments/*mitzvot* are to:

▶ Become Godlike: to establish and deepen our relationship with God through imitation of Him.

▶ Refine humanity by helping people to eliminate their negative traits, strengthen their positive traits and connect them to a higher level of consciousness.

▶ Train people to act consciously as opposed to instinctively. This conditions us to make conscious decisions and not to go through life on autopilot.

▶ Reveal the unity, presence and the name of God in every aspect of the physical world — thought, speech, place, time and action.

Commitment + Action = A Tall Order

Let's say a person decides to become a better human being and lead a moral life. The first thing he would do is to make a firm commitment to this effect. Then he must attempt to consistently mold his behavior in accord with this commitment, exercising objective, non-arbitrary decision-making virtually every minute of the day. He must continually ask himself, "Is this act in tune with my original commitment, or not?"

Many people have tried this, and most fulfill only one half of the formula; some make a firm commitment to lead moral lives, others attempt to behave morally. But few people do both. We are all familiar with the type of scenario this can create:

Dad is berating little Johnny for telling lies. Just when his righteous indignation really begins hitting its stride, the phone rings. Mom picks up the receiver, listens and covers the mouthpiece. "It's George," she mouths silently to her husband. Dad thinks for a moment, and then wags his head firmly from side to side. "I'm sorry," says Mom into the phone, as little Johnny looks on in confusion, "my husband is not home right now. I'll tell him to call you just as soon as he comes back. No, his cell phone is not working at the moment either." Then Dad focuses his attention back on little Johnny and continues his lecture about honesty.

Johnny's parents are classic examples of people who have made a commitment to follow a code of morality, but do not follow up this commitment with consistent actions. Many people are like that. They are committed to honesty *as long as* it is not too inconvenient. Unfortunately this system doesn't work. Commitment to honesty is wonderful, but a person has to behave in a way that is consistent with this commitment if he really wants to lead an honest life. Our actions must reflect our commitment; otherwise, the commitment is a farce.

Children are particularly sensitive to such hypocritical behavior. If a child asks his parent for a cookie, the parent has two ways of saying no: "Sorry, there are no more cookies. We'll buy more tomorrow," or "No, you may not have a cookie. You've had too much sugar today." Obviously the second option is the more difficult of the two. Yet by following this approach, the parent would not only protect the child's teeth, but also educate the child through personal example, that he must always be honest, even if it is more difficult.

It is also possible to fulfill the other half of the formula, to behave well without a firm commitment. Consider the extreme example of people who live in a police state. They are very well behaved and hardly ever break the law. Yet remove the surveillance cameras for even a single day, and there would be complete mayhem in the streets.

In Singapore, for instance, all commercial vehicles are outfitted with special lights that flash on and alert police when drivers break the speed limit. While there is no denying that drivers in Singapore drive safely, they are not necessarily committed to safe driving. It all comes down to pragmatism: As a result of the country's laws, drivers find it more beneficial to obey traffic regulations than to defy them.

So we see that in order to truly become a good person, it is necessary to satisfy both parts of the formula: to make a firm commitment to moral values, and to do one's best to behave in accordance with these morals in all situations.

Thou Shalt Be Consistent

Consistency is much more difficult to achieve than one might expect. Imagine someone waking up one morning and making a firm decision to become a vegetarian. "From now on," he declares, "I will not benefit from the suffering of animals. I do not believe animals should have to suffer for human beings. It's wrong." Let's see what happens when he tries to act consistently with his commitment.

Okay, time to get dressed. He is about to reach for his clothes when he sees his leather shoes and leather belt. "Oh, no!" he groans. It's decision time. Well, would it be wrong to wear these things? The animal is already dead, so it wouldn't cause direct harm to any living being. But by supporting this industry, the person thinks to himself, I am essentially encouraging people to make animals suffer for the sake of human beings. Would wearing such articles of clothing be consistent with my commitment? After some more deliberation, he decides to keep wearing the articles he already owns, but never again to purchase leather goods. He feels satisfied that this is consistent with his philosophy.

Now it's time for breakfast. He walks to the nearest restaurant, asks the waiter what he recommends, and is startled by the response: "Steak and eggs."

"I can't have that," he snaps at the waiter. The waiter looks at him quizzically.

"Why not, sir?"

"Because," our vegetarian answers, "I believe animals shouldn't have to suffer for the sake of human beings." At this, the waiter's anxious look melts into a smile.

"Don't worry about that, sir. You see, these steaks are from the Happy Valley Ranch, where the steers are permitted to roam free on the range and never hear a discouraging word. There are no fences, they may eat all manner of herbs and grasses, drink only beer, and they receive a Shiatsu massage every day. Eventually, a steer dies, and then we make steaks out of it. So you see, sir — the steak that you would be eating is from a contented, happy animal and therefore this steak is kosher for vegetarians."

This sounds convincing, so our vegetarian orders a double helping and buys a few extra pounds to take home. That Sunday, he invites his friends for a barbecue. Just as he is putting the steaks on the grill, however, a disturbing thought occurs to him. "Wait a minute; is this consistent with my philosophy? I mean, *I* know these steaks are from the Happy Valley Ranch, but what about my friends and neighbors? They will think that I'm a big hypocrite. And what about the other people in my neighborhood? They'll smell the steaks and think, 'Hmm, I'm in the mood for a steak,' and they'll go the supermarket and buy a regular steak, and then more animals will have to be butchered! But then again, how far do I have to go with this commitment? Do I have to take such things into account?" Upon further consideration our vegetarian decides to dispose of the steaks. His friends are served salad and French fries.

The next day, at the supermarket, he heads directly to the dairy section, where he begins stacking his cart with food. "You must love cheese," a fellow shopper comments to him. "Not really," answers our vegetarian. "It's just that I've made a decision to stop eating meat. I'm against animals suffering for the sake of humans. I have nothing else to eat, so I have to get used to this stuff." The fellow shopper has a good laugh.

"Tell me," he says to the vegetarian, "do you think cows naturally produce milk all of their lives?"

"I don't know; to tell you the truth, I never thought about it before."

"Well, I have news for you — they don't. You know why? Because they start lactating when their calves are born, and they stop lactating when their calves grow older and stop suckling."

"Okay," says the vegetarian, "so far that makes sense."

"Well, the reason cows on dairy farms continue lactating for so long is that their calves end up in the veal section of the freezer over there, while they are injected with hormones and the electric pumps keep milking and milking them, for years afterward. Pretty cruel, huh?"

Our vegetarian is astounded by this revelation. In stunned silence, he empties his cart and heads over to the natural food section, where he picks up a high-energy power-bar. Now what possibly could be wrong with a power bar? He reads the label, but he can't decipher any of the ingredients, so he takes out his handy food-technology manual and decodes it. "Who would think this innocent-looking bar is full of products made from animal fat?" he gasps. "It's even got red food coloring, which is made from the cochineal beetle — I can't have this!"

By this time he is positively starving, so he goes to his grandmother's house. She serves him a steak. Now he has a value conflict. He has decided not to cause animals to suffer, but if he refuses to eat the food his sweet, little Jewish grandmother has served him, *she* will suffer!

"Is this consistent with my principles?" our vegetarian asks himself yet again. "Whose suffering is more important? My grandmother's or the cow's?"

We will leave our friend now as he agonizes, for the point is clear. We tracked a single person who made a commitment to uphold one ostensibly simple and straightforward moral directive, and in no time at all he was confronted by dozens of perplexing situations demanding complex and difficult decisions. Imagine what would happen if such a commitment would be made not by a single person, but by an entire nation that would live for several thousand years in every conceivable geopolitical and socio-economic circumstance. Would it be easy for them to behave consistently with this principle? What would they have to do in order to increase their chances of success?

They would have to write a Talmud, containing thousands of laws governing every aspect of life, investigating how to behave in all possible scenarios, establishing principles that could deal with any question that could arise. It all has one purpose — the pursuit of consistency.

The Torah is the ultimate guidebook that shows Jews how to behave consistently with the principles they received at Mount Sinai. The 613 commandments are really the details and explanations of the Ten Commandments[27] which enable us to properly observe these principles in all times and places.[28] When the goal of an entire nation is to live consistently according to certain ethical imperatives, things must be spelled out very clearly. And that means many laws and regulations.

Behavior-Modification Techniques

A great rabbi[29] once said that it is easier to memorize the entire 21 volumes of the Babylonian Talmud than to change one character trait. Self-improvement is one of the greatest and most difficult challenges that a person faces. How does one go about overcoming a negative trait?

The answer was supplied by my karate teacher (in a slightly different context). He said, "Always attack where the opponent is weakest." The same logic motivated Winston Churchill to attack Italy, "the soft underbelly of the Axis." Of all the manifestations of a particular character trait, the easiest to change is action; it is our weakest opponent. Speech, thought and emotion are extremely difficult to control, but most people are able to control their actions with relative ease. According to our martial arts principle, this should be the focus of our efforts toward self-improvement. It is in the field of action that we will find the least resistance and therefore have the most chance of success.

In addition to tactical considerations, the focus on action is based on a psychological principle formulated hundreds of years ago by a Jewish philosopher.[30] He was asked why there are so many commandments commemorating the Exodus from Egypt: We eat *matzah* and bitter herbs, drink wine, relate the story of the Exodus, clean the house to remove all leavened products, recite blessings and prayers, etc. Would it not have been sufficient for God to simply command us to remember the Exodus?

His reply is fundamental to understanding Judaism's emphasis on actions and concrete *mitzvot*.

> *Know that a person is affected by his actions, and his feelings and thoughts always follow the actions in which he is engaged, whether good or bad. Imagine a person who is completely evil*

in his heart and who only contemplates evil all day. If such a person is inspired to change and engages diligently in fulfilling the commandments of the Torah, even if not for the sake of Heaven, he will immediately incline toward good. And with the power of his actions he will slay the evil inclination — for the heart follows the actions. Imagine a righteous person, with pious and upright feelings, who engages in actions of folly and evil continuously ... If he is engaged in actions of evil continuously, eventually they will influence his thoughts and feelings and he will become an evil, corrupt person — for, as we know, the person is affected by his actions.[31]

The commandments of the Torah train us to become better people by focusing on our actions more than our thoughts and feelings. The act of giving charity, for example, makes the person into more of a giver every time it is done. Thinking and meditating about giving will not necessarily make a person more generous, but the act of giving will inevitably create this effect. Saying blessings to express appreciation to God for everything that we receive instills in us the attribute of gratitude.

Even *mitzvot* that appear to focus on our relationship with God can also have an impact on our ethical behavior in the world. Stopping work to observe the Sabbath, no matter how important or profitable that work may be, teaches a crucial lesson. Financial success is not the ultimate value in life, we will not do "whatever it takes" to get ahead. Each week we train ourselves to exercise self-control and to consider the moral impact of our actions.

The Mitzvah Candle

One of Auguste Rodin's[32] most famous sculptures, "The Thinker," is a physical object that immediately conveys to the viewer a full expression of an abstract idea: thought. The commandments too use mundane physical actions and objects to embody and convey eternal truths and make them readily accessible to every person. Placing a *mezuzah*[33] on the doorposts of our houses, for example, vividly communicates the reality that God's Presence is everywhere and that He is constantly watching over us.[34]

There is great depth in a commonly known verse in Proverbs (6:23): "For the *mitzvah* is a candle and the *Torah* is light." This verse compares the truth of Torah to light and the *mitzvah,* the commandment, to the candle that produces and sustains the light. Think about it. To produce a military jet that can fly at twice or three times the speed of sound, 760 mph, requires great resources, design, technology and investment. Yet to produce light, which travels at about 186,550 miles per second, only requires paraffin wax and a wick! The beauty of the *mitzvot* is that with simple, physical actions and material objects we are able to produce and maintain infinite, spiritual light.[35]

Obligations or Rights?

One of the primary effects of the abundance of *mitzvot* is a psychological shift in a person's focus in life. A person educated with the commandments sees him or herself as obligated. In Hebrew, the terms *bar mitzvah* and *bat mitzvah* mean "one who is obligated in the commandments," literally a "son/daughter of commandments."

The basis of morality is the feeling that one "ought to do the right thing," yet the origin of the sensation of "ought" is not clear. Immanuel Kant said, "Two things fill the mind with ever new and increasing admiration and awe, the oftener and more steadily they are reflected on: the starry heavens above me and the moral law within me."[36] Although we have an intuition about good and evil, it must be tutored and nurtured, if the feeling of "ought" is to be powerful enough to affect our actions, to enable us do good and avoid evil.

Many systems of law are based on individual rights and are primarily mechanisms for preventing one person's rights from impinging on another's. As the famous statement goes, "The right to swing my fist ends where the other man's nose begins."[37] In fact, the sole purpose of most legal systems and forms of government is to maintain an orderly society by defining and protecting individual rights. Judaism, on the other hand, seeks to elevate, perfect and improve society, not just preserve it, and the emphasis therefore, is on developing the feeling of "I ought." This is accomplished through *mitzvot* that affect every area of personal behavior and human interaction. One contemporary legal scholar wrote:

> *Jewish law, unlike rights jurisprudence, has a "systemic telos."*
> *All the laws of the Torah — civil, penal, and ritual — have a*
> *single purpose, the divine goal of aiding humanity in its striving*
> *for perfection. ... Jewish jurisprudence of duty has evolved for*
> *nearly two millennia, independent of an autonomous state or*
> *other hierarchical authority. In the absence of external institu-*
> *tions compelling obedience to the law, the internal structure of*
> *the law itself must promote adherence. The "common, mutual,*
> *reciprocal obligation" at the centre of the law makes possible*
> *continued adherence to the law without resort to violence. The*
> *notion of "obligation" in the Jewish legal system is not a mere*
> *linguistic reversal of the term "right"; rather, the Jewish legal*
> *system consists of commandments that specify precisely who*

is obligated to do what and for whom. Obedience to the law should not follow simply from threats of human punishment. Obedience should flow principally from love of God and secondarily from fear of God and divine punishment.[38]

Alexander The (Not So) Great

The Midrash relates the following story about Alexander the Great, which illustrates one of the basic differences between systems based on rights and one based on obligations:

> *Alexander of Macedon once visited Africa. While meeting with a king there, a case came before the royal court. One man had sold a field to another and while plowing the field, the buyer found a cachet of gold and precious stones. The buyer said, "I bought a field, not gold, the treasure is yours!" The seller claimed, "I sold you a field and everything in it. The treasure is yours!" The king asked them if they had children. One answered that he had a daughter; the other had a son. The king decreed that the children should marry each other and use the treasure for setting up their household. Alexander expressed his amazement at this decision. The king asked Alexander, "Do you disagree? What would you have done in your country?"*
>
> *Alexander replied, "I could not imagine such a case occurring in our country, but if it would come about, I would kill them both and take the treasure for myself."*
>
> *The king asked Alexander, "Does the sun rise and set every day in your country?" Alexander replied, "Of course!"*
>
> *"Are there animals in your country?" Alexander replied that there were.*
>
> *The king thought for a while and said, "If so, the sun must rise and set in your country in the merit of the animals — the humans certainly do not deserve it!"*[39]

In Greece, people focused on their rights. If someone found a treasure in his field, his impulse would be to keep it — "I found it in my field; it is my right to keep it." The other would say, "I left something in what used to be my field; it is my right to get it back." Alexander would say, "I am the king of my country; it is my right to have absolutely anything I want!" The Midrash uses the metaphor of the African country for the Jewish system of law, in which the dispute would be quite different:

"I found something in my field; it is my obligation to return it to its rightful owner."

"I signed a contract and sold the field and its contents to this person; it is my obligation to fulfill the details of this contract."

"I am the king; it is my obligation to ensure that my subjects are happy and live in harmony with one another."

In a society that is founded on the *mitzvot*, the underlying current is obligation; people consistently look at what they can do, what they can give and how they can contribute. In a society based on rights, people tend to focus more on what they can get, what they deserve and how much is owed to them. John F. Kennedy once said, "My fellow Americans, ask not what your country can do for you — ask what you can do for your country."[40] Through the *mitzvot* Judaism is saying, "Ask not what others can do for you — ask what you can do for others."

For Further Reading

▶ *Horeb* by Rabbi Samson Raphael Hirsch (Soncino Press, 1968)

▶ *Living Jewish* by Rabbi Berel Wein (Shaar Press, 2002)

▶ *Sefer Hachinuch: The Book of Mitzvah Education* (Feldheim, 1989)

▶ *The Mitzvot* by Rabbi Abraham Chill (Urim Publications, 2000)

▶ *Understanding Judaism: A Basic Guide to Jewish faith, history and practice* by Rabbi Mordechai Katz (ArtScroll/Mesorah, 2001)

NOTES

References to books of the Talmud refer to the Babylonian Talmud unless otherwise noted.

1. *Makkot* 23b.
2. Genesis 1:27.
3. Deuteronomy 28:9; see also Deuteronomy 13:5.
4. Jerusalem Talmud, *Peah* 3:1; *Mechilta, Parshat Shirah, Parshah* 3.
5. *Sotah* 14a.
6. *Sefer Hamitzvot*, Mitzvah 8; *Mishneh Torah, Hilchot Deot* 1:5-6.
7. *Mishneh Torah, Hilchot Tumot Ochlin* 16:11; *Hilchot Avadim* 9:8; *Orchot Tzaddikim*, Chap. 28 (toward end).
8. Rabbi Moshe Cordovero, *Tomer Devorah*, Introduction.
9. Maharal, Introduction to *Derech Hachaim* on *Pirkei Avot*; Rabbi Yehudah Halevy, *Sefer Hakuzari,* 1:79; Rabbi Sa'adiah Gaon, *Ha'Emunot VeHadeot*, 3:3.
10. Rabbi Moshe Chaim Luzzatto, *Derech Hashem*, Chap. 2.
11. Maharal, *Tiferet Yisrael,* Chap. 2.
12. *Midrash Tanchuma*, Leviticus, *Parshat Tazria* 5.
13. One of the greatest of the Sages of the Mishnaic period, circa 100 C.E.
14. Maharal, *Netivot Olam*, Netiv Hashalom, Chap. 1.
15. *Midrash Rabbah*, Genesis 44:1.
16. Which are prohibited by Torah law. See chapter on "Soul Food: The Kosher Dietary Laws."
17. As quoted by Maimonides, *Shmonah Perakim*, Chap. 6. See *Sifra*, end of *Parshat Kedoshim* with some differences.
18. See also *Chullin* 109b.
19. Theodore Seuss Geisel (Dr. Seuss) *Green Eggs and Ham*, Random House, NY, 1960.
20. Hebrew for "Daddy."
21. Charles J. Sykes, *A Nation of Victims*, St. Martins Press, NY, 1992, p. 5.
22. Rabbi Yisrael ben Eliezer, 1698-1760, Ukraine.
23. Nachmanides, *Commentary on the Torah*, Exodus 13:16.
24. British anthropologist Desmond Morris's book, *The Naked Ape* (1967) discusses the development of human culture and society.
25. *Olam*= space, *shanah* = time, *nefesh*= humanity.
26. *Tikkunei Zohar*, Tikkuna 29 (page 73a).
27. The Hebrew actually means "Ten Statements," not "commandments," because these statements contain within them more than 10 commandments.
28. See commentary of Nachmanides, *Commentary on the Torah*, Exodus 21:1-2; *Complete Writings of Nachmanides*, "The 613 Commandments As Derived from the Ten Statements," Mossad Harav Kook, Jerusalem, 1986.
29. Rabbi Israel Salanter, late 19th-century Lithuanian scholar and ethicist.
30. Author of the *Sefer Hachinuch*, published anonymously, but believed to be Rabbi Aaron Halevi of Barcelona, 1233-1300.
31. *Sefer Hachinuch, Parshat Bo*, Mitzvah 20, Mossad Harav Kook, Jerusalem, 1984.
32. François Auguste René Rodin, French artist, 1840-1917.
33. See chapter on Material Witnesses for a complete explanation of the *mitzvah* of *mezuzah*.
34. Nachmanides, *Commentary on the Torah*, Exodus 13:16.
35. Based on *Sfat Emet,* beginning of *Parshat B'Ha'alotcha*, from Year 5631.
36. Immanuel Kant, *The Critique of Practical Reason*, London, Macmillan Press, 1982.

37. This adage has been attributed to Abraham Lincoln, Benjamin Franklin, John Stuart Mill and Oliver Wendell Holmes.

38. Suzanne Last-Stone, "Harvard Law Review," Vol. 106, No. 4, February 1993, "In Pursuit of the Counter-Text: The Turn to the Jewish Legal Model in Contemporary American Legal Theory" (Excerpts).

39. *Midrash Rabbah, Parshat Noach*, Genesis 33:1.

40. Inaugural Address, Washington, D.C., January 20, 1961.

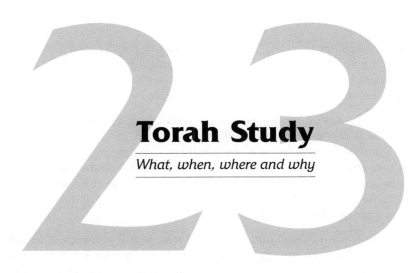

Torah Study

What, when, where and why

The People of the Book

*O*ne of the hallmarks of Jewish life throughout the ages has been a passion for study. This characteristic is so marked that for centuries we have been identified as the "People of the Book."[1] Unlike other religions and cultures, Judaism has never restricted academic learning to a particular caste, tribe or family. Torah study was and is the preoccupation not only of teachers and clergy, but of the entire nation. The renowned Jewish scholar of the 12th century, Maimonides, writes:

> *Among the great Sages of Israel were woodchoppers and water-bearers, and some who were blind. Nevertheless, they engaged in the study of Torah day and night, and they were part of the chain of transmission of the Torah, person to person, back to Moses our teacher.*[2]

Throughout history, Jews with widely varied backgrounds have been outstanding Torah scholars. Two of the greatest Talmudic Sages, Shmayah and Avtalyon,[3] were descended from Sennacherib, the Assyrian ruler who invaded Israel and exiled 10 of the 12 tribes. Onkelos,[4] whose Aramaic translation of the Torah is printed in almost every Hebrew Bible, was a convert and nephew of the Roman emperor, Titus. Judah the Prince,[5] editor of the Mishnah,[6] was a fabulously wealthy businessman;[7] Hillel,[8] a revered leader and president of the Sanhedrin,[9] was a pauper.

Among the great medieval commentators, Rashi[10] was a vintner, Rabbi Yehudah Halevy[11] was a professional poet; Maimonides[12] and Nachmanides[13] were both physicians. In short, the Torah is the universal inheritance of the entire Jewish people, regardless of their origin or social standing.[14]

The obligation to study and teach Torah is emphasized repeatedly in the Bible and in the works of the Sages, and the reward for this *mitzvah* is considered equal to that of all the others together.[15] Jewish law is unequivocal in exhorting people to study Torah:

> *Every Jewish man is obligated in the study of Torah, whether he is rich or poor, whether in good health or suffering, young and old, even if he is of an advanced age and very weak. And even if he was so poor that he was living on charity, and begging at doorways, and even one who must support a wife and children, is obligated to set aside time, every day and every night, for the study of Torah.*[16]

Although the Biblical obligation of Torah study is directed toward Jewish men,[17] women are not exempt from the commandment to study. The *Code of Jewish Law* rules: *Every Jewish woman is obligated to study all the laws of the Torah that are applicable to her.*[18]

Commenting on the obligation of women in Torah study, the Chafetz Chaim, one of the most influential of scholars of the last century, stated:

> *In the days that everyone lived in the place of their forefathers, and the chain of tradition was strong, it was possible to exempt women from study, since they could rely on what they had learnt and received from their parents. However, nowadays, when people do not live where their parents live, and the transmission of the Torah has been weakened, and especially since women study the languages and cultures of other nations, it is beyond any doubt, a great obligation to teach our daughters the Torah, the books of the Prophets and the Writings, and the ethical teachings of our Sages, such as the Ethics of the Fathers ... and other such works ...*[19]

Non-Jewish observers have often noted with wonder the degree to which the Jewish people have taken the obligation of universal education to heart, and have made Torah study a central part of Jewish life. A Christian scholar visiting Warsaw in the early 20th century recounted the following incident:

"Once I noticed a great many coaches in a parking place, but with no drivers in sight. In my own country, I would have known where to look for them. A young Jewish boy showed me the way; in a courtyard on the second floor was the *shtieble* [combination synagogue and study hall] of the Jewish drivers. It consisted of two rooms — one filled with Talmud volumes, the other a room for prayer. All the drivers were engaged in fervent study and religious discussions ... It was then that I found out... that all professions — the bakers, the butchers, the shoemakers etc. have their own *shtieble* in the Jewish district; and every free moment which can be taken off from work is given to the study of Torah."[20]

In my neighborhood in Jerusalem, literally thousands of people spend much of their spare time studying. Classes are offered in Hebrew, English, Yiddish, Spanish, French and Russian. There are Talmud classes that meet before sunrise, women's Bible study groups that meet every Shabbat afternoon and on weekday mornings, special programs in which parents and children study together at a synagogue, and public lectures attended by hundreds every Saturday night. Doctors, lawyers, accountants, refrigerator repairmen, storekeepers, university professors and police officers gather every evening to study Torah together. This scene is common in Jewish communities around the world, and was a widespread phenomenon in the lives of our ancestors, regardless of what was going on in the outside world. A 12th century monk observed:

"... the Jews, out of zeal for God and love of the law, put as many sons as they have to letters, that each may understand God's law ... A Jew, however poor, if he had ten sons, would put them all to letters, not for gain, as the Christians do, but for the understanding of God's law, and not only his sons, but his daughters."[21]

From This You Can Make a Living?

The pursuit of knowledge in modern society usually has a clear, utilitarian purpose — to make a living, to further a career, or to become famous. In contrast, Torah study for the layman does not advance his career, or increase his income. Even rabbis and accomplished scholars continue to study for their entire lives. Why isn't it sufficient to "qualify" and then stop learning? Why does the Torah place so much emphasis on the commandment to study continuously?[22]

The simplest and most obvious explanation is the practical aspect of studying Torah in order to properly observe Torah law. The Mishnah states, "An ignoramus cannot be fearful of sin; an unlearned person cannot be pious."[23] This vital function of Torah study is considered by some authorities to be the primary reason for the commandment.[24]

It is clear, however, that the obligation goes far beyond knowing the practical application of Jewish law. We study laws that are relevant, as well as those that have no direct application today, such as the laws of the Temple; we study the derivation and sources of the laws; we even study opinions that are not accepted as the final word in law; we study philosophy, mysticism and the text of the Torah. We must look further for an explanation of this obligation that goes beyond simple pragmatism.

According to Jewish belief, the purpose of existence is for human beings to create a relationship with God.[25] In order for a relationship to be meaningful and intimate the two parties must be compatible. We develop this compatibility with God by imitating His actions and traits. Through the performance of the commandments of the Torah we learn to act as God does; by improving our character traits we become similar to God in the realm of character, "just as He is merciful, you should be merciful; just as He is gracious, you should be gracious."[26] Full compatibility can only be achieved, however, when the intellect is also developed appropriately, when we learn to *think like God.*

A wonderful analogy for the idea of Torah study once occurred to me as I read a mystery novel called *Poodle Springs*.[27] Raymond Chandler had begun writing that book, but died after finishing only the first four chapters. Robert B. Parker decided to complete the book and managed to do an excellent job of imitating the style of the original author, even though his own works are written in a very different style. I began to consider the daunting task that faced Parker in continuing someone else's novel; he had to think and write just as Chandler would have thought and written. Clearly, Robert Parker would have to do more than just read the first four chapters of the book. He would have to read Chandler's notes, first drafts and corrections. He would probably have to read everything that Chandler ever wrote, including his books, diary, essays, memos and correspondence. It would help to go to the places that Chandler frequented, to speak to his family and friends, and perhaps to even sit in his office for a while.

I do not know whether or not Robert Parker did all of these things, but I believe we are asked to take on a similar task: to complete and perfect the unfinished novel of human life and history. A person who engages in this effort is called a "partner with God in the deeds of creation."[28] The Creator is Eternal and Omnipotent, but He deliberately left His "novel" unfinished so that we could participate in completing it. In this way, through our own efforts, we come closer to achieving perfection by understanding God's plan and purpose in creation. The study of Torah is one of the primary means available to humanity to approach the "Mind" of the Creator and His vision. This is why we study the Torah that God wrote, the books of the prophets with whom He communicated, works written by those inspired by His words and the books of those who probed and scrutinized every letter and nuance of these texts. We delve into the sources, the reasoning, the methodology and the theory in the hope that we can begin to think like the Torah, and to fathom God's "thoughts."[29]

The Ideal and Reality

The gym where I exercise prominently displays posters that portray the ideal to which we, the victims of the gym's physical trainer, are supposed to aspire. The posters inevitably depict an individual with perfect muscle tone and definition, a perfect tan and perfectly white teeth — he is the ideal. Reality is brutally exposed by the mirrors strategically placed in front of the exercise machines. Perhaps the gym's owners are inspired by Heinrich Heine's principle that "without tension there is no creativity." They hope that by sensing the tension between the real and the ideal, we will strive toward the ideal, although often the result is despair, not ambition.

The study of Torah is also an exposure to the ideal world, to what the world should look like and how people should behave — not in the realm of physical perfection like the health club, but in the realm of moral and spiritual perfection. The study of Torah teaches us how to apply the ideals of the Torah to the real world and how to elevate the real world to the Torah ideal. A contemporary Jewish philosopher, Rabbi Joseph B. Soloveitchik, expressed this concept succinctly:

> When Halachic man [one who adheres to Jewish law] approaches reality, he comes with his Torah, given to him from Sinai, in hand ... His approach begins with an ideal creation and concludes with a real one ... The essence of the Halachah, which was received from G-d, consists of creating an ideal world and cognizing the relationship between that ideal world and our concrete environment in all its visible manifestations and underlying structures. There is no phenomenon, entity, or object in this concrete world which the [pre-existing] Halachah does not approach with its ideal standard.[30]

Torah: The Toolbox for Life

Few things are as important in life as being aware of what is real and what is not, what is true and what is false. Unfortunately, in most educational systems, students are not given the necessary tools with which to discern and investigate truth. Instead, they are trained to absorb whatever the teacher says and faithfully duplicate the teacher's words on the final exam. Schools often train students to be like the famous horse, Clever

Hans. In the beginning of the 20th century, Hans was well known for his ability to do arithmetic, supplying answers to math problems by stamping his foot an appropriate number of times. Scientific investigation eventually found that Clever Hans was able to sense subtle cues that his trainer and the spectators unintentionally gave him, such as becoming tense or nodding slightly when Hans got to the right answer.[31] All too often, students in schools supply the answers that they think the teachers want to hear, rather than applying their own faculty of critical reasoning to the problem at hand.[32] The study of Torah, especially the in-depth analysis and discussion of the Talmud[33] and commentaries, teaches reasoning, critical thinking and logical analysis. A Jewish scholar of the early 18th century described Talmud study as the process of clarifying truth:

> *Analytical give and take involves the study and investigation of statements ... in order to determine if they are true or false. This ... is accomplished by setting forward claims that justify and support the truth of the statement ... and claims that refute or contradict the truth of the statement ... In this way the ... proofs and refutations may be compared and subjected to the evaluation of the intellect. This is the essence of Talmudic discussion ... the clarification of the truth by the presentation of conflicting arguments.[34]*

Although this methodology is the ideal of many educational systems, and is used in classes at law schools and by lecturers in philosophy, it is extremely rare to find it stressed throughout a student's educational career. The study of Talmud and its training in critical thinking starts for Jewish children in elementary school! It is not uncommon to hear boys of 11 or 12 years of age involved in a debate about a fine point of logic in the Talmud.

The Engine of Creation

"If not for My Covenant, day and night, I would not have set the statutes of heaven and earth."[35] The Sages understood that this verse in Jeremiah is stating a fundamental law of the universe. If not for the continuous study of Torah — "My Covenant, day and night" — then the laws of nature — "the statutes of heaven and earth" — would cease to function.[36] While this may seem like a farfetched notion, the concept that Torah study sustains existence is a logical extension of the idea that the human race was created "in the image of God."[37] The term means that we were created with a similarity to God, particularly in the area of creative capacity: just as God is a Creator Whose will is not bound by anything outside of Him, so also the human being is a creator, with free will. Just as the world's existence depends on

God willing it to exist, so also God granted human beings the power[38] to sustain the world or destroy it.[39] Since the whole purpose of creation is to provide an environment for humans to develop a relationship with God, humans sustain the existence of nature as long as they are fulfilling their purpose.[40] Should there be one moment in which not even one person is engaged in pursuit of a relationship with God, there would be no reason for the world to exist.[41] The study of Torah is the activity that, more than anything else, exemplifies the spiritual quest for closeness to God, and therefore, Torah is the engine on which the world runs.[42] When a person studies Torah, he should do so with the "consciousness that the non-existence of this world is just as possible as its existence"[43] and he should realize that his studies are contributing to the sustenance of all of creation.

While sustenance of the entire world may sound like a grandiose mission — perhaps even a *bit* overwhelming to the individual — the fact that Judaism invests every person's study of Torah with this responsibility infuses meaning and purpose to life. Understanding this deep concept also shifts our sense of reality from the mundane details we see before us to the hidden spiritual realms that actually govern the world.

It's a Mitzvah!

The study of Torah is a Biblical commandment, and as with every *mitzvah* a blessing is said before it is fulfilled.[44] As the law assumes that everyone will study some Torah every single day, the blessings are recited at the beginning of each day, and are incorporated into the daily liturgy.[45] Reciting the blessings before Torah study reminds us of its deeper dimensions that go far beyond any detached, intellectual exercise. Rather, our study should be full of passion and joy[46] and we should intend to fulfill everything that we learn about.[47]

At Mt. Sinai, when the Jewish people accepted the Torah from God, they said, "We will do and we will listen."[48] They recognized the binding power of the Torah and accepted all the obligations that it would confer, even before they had studied it or heard it. We emulate our ancestors by recognizing Torah study as both obligatory and as obligating even before we begin to study it. In his commentary on these blessings, Rabbi Samson Raphael Hirsch elaborates on this idea:

> As surely as the study of the Torah ... may well be the most important prerequisite for its fulfillment, so too, the spirit in which we study it, the attitude we have toward its value and purpose, and the aim we have in mind can certainly not be a matter of indifference. Only if we take the Torah to heart and study it as God's Torah ... are we able to acquire the proper

understanding ... to lead a good life before God. If it is not this proper attitude that motivates us to study the Torah ... then Torah study may fail to achieve its true purpose, which is the sanctification of life on the basis of the Torah.[49]

Where Do Jews Learn Torah?

In the Home

The Jewish home is the first and most essential source of Torah learning. Parents begin introducing Torah to their children well before any formal education starts,[50] and they continue throughout their lives. The pictures and decorations in the children's rooms will often have a Jewish theme, and the songs that are sung to them are drawn from prayers and other traditional sources. Snatches of simple prayers and blessings over food are often the children's first words. Selected portions of the Torah itself are told to the children in a simple manner in addition to stories from the ever-increasing body of Jewish children's literature. Because children learn best through observation and imitation, parents who live a traditional Jewish life will be continually teaching their child Torah through their words and actions. Many Jewish scholars maintain that acting as a role model is in fact the primary way in which parents fulfill their obligation to educate their children.[51]

A prominent feature in the traditional Jewish home is its library of Torah literature. Even a basic collection of Torah, Prophets and Writings with commentaries, Talmud with commentaries, books of Jewish law, philosophy and ethics easily amounts to over 200 volumes. Many homes have more extensive libraries containing a thousand or more books. A more complete library of Torah works, such as one found at a rabbinical school, may contain over 30,000 volumes.[52] The very presence of a Torah library in the home has a significant impact on the children, showing them where the family's priorities lie, as well as providing an opportunity for study at any time.

Elementary and High School Education

The ideal system of education, according to the Bible, is one in which parents themselves educate their children.[53] Nevertheless, in 81 B.C.E.

Rabbi Yehoshua ben Gamla[54] instituted compulsory public schooling. The Talmud explains that this occurred during a period of war and widespread poverty and many parents were unable to educate their children properly. The Sage therefore established schools for Torah education in every city and town.[55]

Further legislation regulated the new system: The entire community was financially responsible for the education of all children, and no one could object to the construction of a school on their street. Class size was limited to 25 students per teacher. Preference was given to a teacher who was accurate, but slow, over a teacher who covered more material, but was less accurate. The Sages outlined a model system of public schooling that has lasted for over 2,000 years.

Today, children attend a wide variety of Jewish schools. The majority of day schools offer a full curriculum of Torah studies, including the Five Books of Moses, selections from the books of the Prophets and Writings, the Mishnah and Talmud, Jewish law, Hebrew language and Jewish history. In addition, the schools teach all the required courses in general studies. In cities where the Jewish population is too small to support a full day school, synagogues usually arrange after-school programs of Jewish studies.

In some communities, primarily in Israel, secular studies are kept to a minimum (usually math, science and geography) while the bulk of the day is spent on Torah study. A school of this type is called a *cheder* or *Talmud Torah*. The word *cheder* means "room" and derives from the fact that in most Jewish villages in Europe the school consisted of one room, usually attached to the synagogue. A beautiful Yiddish lullaby that my father used to sing to me when I was a child describes such a *cheder* in which the first letters of the Hebrew alphabet are being lovingly taught:

> *Oyf'n pripitchuk brent a fire oys* — *In the fireplace burns a fire,*
> *In der shtib iz heis* — *In the room it's warm.*
> *Zitz a rebbenyu* — *A young teacher sits,*
> *Mit kleine kinderlach* — *With small children,*
> *Un lernt dem Alef Beis* — *Teaching them Alef Beis.*

The Yeshivah

Yeshivah literally means "a dwelling place." The origins of modern *yeshivot* (plural of *yeshivah*) lie in Babylon in about 200 C.E., in the academies where Jews studied the text of the Mishnah, and recorded their discussions and conclusions in the Talmud.[56] Jewish communities around the world have always had places where people would spend most of their waking hours in the study of Torah. This is the reason for the term "a dwelling place"; for the scholar, the place of study is virtually his home.

Yeshivot are often incorrectly described as "rabbinical schools," but the majority of students do not intend to become rabbis. They are pursuing the ideal of *"Torah lishmah,"* i.e., the study of Torah for its own sake. They study in order to know and understand the Torah, not for financial gain or career advancement. It is becoming increasingly common for students, both men and women, to spend a year or two after high school studying in a yeshivah in order to become a more complete, knowledgeable Jew. These students do not necessarily plan to continue with intensive Torah study and they expect to go on to college or enter the business world after their time in a yeshivah. They have decided that if they are going to spend four to six years at college studying in order to "make a living," they would like to devote at least a year of two to studying *how* to live.

The world of the *yeshivah* today encompasses a broad spectrum of learning styles, academic levels and student populations.[57] Some *yeshivot* cater to people who know very little or nothing about Judaism, others accept only those who already have advanced knowledge of Jewish texts. There are Chassidic *yeshivot*, Sephardic *yeshivot*, *yeshivot* that combine Torah study with Israeli army service (known as Hesder *yeshivot*), and *yeshivot* that specialize in training rabbis, educators and judges for rabbinical courts (*beit din*). One type of *yeshivah*, the *kollel,* accommodates advanced married students who live off campus and often receive a stipend from the institution in which they study. Some *kollels* are operated within a larger *yeshivah*; others exist as independent institutions. They often serve as an educational resource for the community.

Study Style

For most of the day, students study together with a partner in the classic *chavruta* (literally, comrade)[58] style, discussing and analyzing their particular Talmud tractate. *Chavruta* study is ideally suited in many ways to understanding complex subject matter.[59] Explaining an idea to another person forces one to clarify it in his own mind. The debate between the study partners will refine it even further. As one of the greatest Talmudic scholars of the last century, Rabbi Chaim Soloveitchik, said, "The degree to which one is able to explain something is directly proportional to the degree to which one understands it."[60] In addition, studying with a partner provides an opportunity to see ideas from someone else's perspective.

An environment of study, an exchange of ideas, interaction with teachers, students and one's *chavruta* are so vital for the study of Torah that Maimonides considers it tantamount to a death sentence to isolate someone from such a setting. He discusses the case of an individual who is exiled to a place where he has no one with whom to study or teach, and maintains that such a punishment would be unfair since "he was sentenced to exile, not death — and for a wise person and one who seeks wisdom, life without the study of Torah is like death."[61]

Students at the yeshivah also attend daily classes but these are very different from standard college lectures. The students are expected to analyze and question what the teachers say; they are free to ask questions, point out contradictions and argue with the instructor. An atmosphere of inquiry and intellectual honesty is created, in which students and teachers attempt to discover the truth together. A Talmudic Sage once stated, "I learned much Torah from my teachers, even more from my friends, and from my students most of all."[62]

Study, Study Everywhere

Torah learning goes on in many settings outside the yeshivah as well, often in the local synagogue. One of the primary purposes of the synagogue is to serve as a place of study, not just of prayer, and a major part of the rabbi's job is to teach Torah to his community. Classes are held at the synagogue, and people go there to study with their *chavruta*. Many synagogues also organize extracurricular programs for children, invite guest lecturers and arrange weekend seminars and specialized study groups. One of the Hebrew names for a synagogue, *beit midrash,* means house of study.

For the committed Jew, Torah learning is a lifelong occupation and goes on in the workplace as well. Numerous law firms, hospitals and accounting firms in the United States, Israel, the United Kingdom, Canada and Australia arrange lunchtime learning sessions, popularly known as "lunch and learn." I know of a medical laboratory, a health club and a law office that all have rooms designated as a *beit midrash*. Many individuals designate time for study at home, on the subway and even over the phone. EL AL Israel Airlines has a Torah class on its audio entertainment system. The People of the Book take very seriously the verses in the Book:

> *And these matters that I command you today shall be upon your heart. You shall teach them thoroughly to your children, and you shall speak of them when you sit in your home, while you walk on the way, when you retire and when you arise.*[63]

The Levys Learn a Thing or Two

At 5:45 a.m. the alarm rings, rousing Mr. Levy from a deep sleep. He quickly washes up, dresses, drains a cup of strong, black coffee (after the appropriate blessing, of course) and recites the blessings on Torah study,[64] before rushing to his 6:15 Daf Yomi Talmud class.[65] He and 15 other men in the community meet at the synagogue every morning to attend a class in Talmud given by the rabbi. They cover one folio (two pages) of Talmud every day, and complete the entire Babylonian Talmud in seven and a half years. (For Talmud study, this is considered a fast pace.)

Mr. Levy always takes along a miniature volume of the tractate he is studying, so that he can review the class on the subway. Even when he travels for business, or when the family goes on vacation, he never misses a day of "the daf"; he either studies the section by himself or finds a local class. The study of Daf Yomi is a coordinated, worldwide effort; people all around the world study the same folio every day.

There is a beautiful feeling of unity, knowing that one can find a synagogue virtually anywhere in the world, from Sao Paulo to Glasgow, where people will be studying the same subject, and the same page as the visitor. "Dial-a-Daf" is available on the phone,[66] and Daf Yomi can be accessed on the Internet.[67] One can even "do the daf" on the Long Island Railroad.[68] (The most popular English translation of the Babylonian Talmud is ArtScroll's Schottenstein elucidated edition.)

Mr. Levy's class finishes by 7:15 a.m. The participants recite the morning service together, have a light breakfast (sponsored by a different member of the Daf Yomi group each month) and then rush off to work.

Shlomo, the eldest of the Levy children, spends most of his day studying Talmud (Gemara). He is enrolled at a post-high school yeshivah, where he lives in the dormitory and comes home twice a month for Shabbat. Instead of a folio a day, Shlomo studies the Talmud in much greater depth, and his class may cover only 20 pages in the space of four or five months. Every word, every phrase and every argument is examined in the light of many commentaries. The purpose of this type of study is not only to expand the student's base of information, but to enable him to absorb the analytical Talmudic method.[69]

Shlomo finds the in-depth study of Talmud the most exciting part of his curriculum. The intellectual challenge of finding the thread of logic that lies behind every topic, or sugya, tests his abilities to the maximum; his joy in discovering that logic exceeds even the pleasure of sinking a shot from midcourt. He also studies Jewish law, the weekly Torah portion and texts on ethics and character improvement, known as mussar.

A typical day for Shlomo begins with Shacharit, morning prayers, at 7:30 a.m., followed by half an hour of Jewish law, and then breakfast. At 9 o'clock, he and his chavruta begin preparing for the daily Talmud lecture, which takes place at noon and goes for one hour. This is followed by Minchah, the afternoon service, lunch, and a break. Shlomo either plays basketball during the break or catches up on some sleep. He has another chavruta with whom he studies a different tractate at a faster pace (two daf a week), from 3:00 p.m. until 6:30 p.m. After that, he studies a classic text on ethics and character improvement, called Mesilat Yesharim, Path of the Just, by Rabbi Moshe Chaim Luzzatto. The evening service, Maariv, comes next, then supper, and the night study session, during which he reviews the midday Talmud class and does further research until 10:30 p.m. Shlomo has an interest in Jewish philosophy, so he usually researches specific topics until about midnight.

The younger Levy children attend the Jewish day school in their community. Their school day always begins with morning prayers in the classroom followed by classes in Torah studies. This includes the Five Books of Moses with some commentaries, portions of the Prophets, Mishnah and Talmud (for the older boys), Jewish law, Hebrew language and classes about the upcoming events in the Jewish calendar. After lunch, the children have secular studies (English, math, history geography, etc.),[70] sports, art and music. Boys and girls attend separate schools.[71] The curricula are similar in the lower grades, except that the boys are prepared for concentration on the Mishnah and Talmud, while the girls concentrate on Torah, Prophets and law.

Mrs. Levy attends a women's study group on the Torah reading of the week (Parshat Hashavuah) two mornings a week, which is led by the rabbi's wife, and she independently studies one of the commentaries on the Torah whenever she has some spare time. Mrs. Levy also teaches a course on Jewish philosophy at a post-high school seminary for women.

On the surface, the Levys seem to be an average, suburban, middle-class family. Esther loves her nursery school teacher and spends hours with her friends on the swings in the backyard; Eli goes to judo classes two nights a week and plays ball with his friends; Tova studies guitar and enjoys ice-skating; Shlomo loves basketball; and Mr. and Mrs. Levy relish listening to music. Their *interests are diverse. Yet every week, the Levys all get together at the Shabbat table where they discuss interpretations of the weekly Torah reading. They discover insights in the same Torah that their ancestors studied and that Jews all over the world study today.*

Mrs. Levy's parents regularly visit on Shabbat and their greatest joy is hearing their grandchildren repeat the same words of Torah that they learned as children in cheder in Europe. The medieval thinker, Rabbi Sa'adiah Gaon, once commented: "Our nation is a nation only by virtue of its Torah."[72] The family is a microcosm of a nation, and it too becomes more of a family by virtue of its Torah.

Supplemental Material

The Talmudic Method

From *Crescas' Critique of Aristotle; Problems of Aristotle's Physics in Jewish and Arabic Philosophy* by Harry Austryn Wolfson: Harvard University Press [1971, c1929]

Confronted with a statement on any subject, the Talmudic student will proceed to raise a series of questions before he satisfies himself of having understood its full meaning. If the statement is not clear enough, he will ask, "What does the author intend to say here?" If it is too obvious, he will ask, "It is too plain, why then expressly say it?" If it is a statement of fact or of a concrete instance, he will then ask, "What underlying principle does it involve?" If it is a broad generalization, he will want to know exactly how much it is to include: and if it is an exception to a general rule, he will want to know how much it is to exclude. He will furthermore want to know all the circumstances under which a certain statement is true, and what qualifications are permissible.

Statements apparently contradictory to each other will be reconciled by the discovery of some subtle distinction, and statements apparently irrelevant to each other will be subtly analyzed into their ultimate elements and shown to contain some common underlying principle. The harmonization of apparent contradictions and the interlinking of apparent irrelevancies are two characteristic features of the Talmudic method of text study. And similarly every other phenomenon about the text becomes a matter of investigation. Why does the author use one word rather than the other? What need was there for the mentioning of a specific instance as an illustration? Do certain authorities differ or not? If they do, why do they differ? All these are legitimate questions for the Talmudic student of texts. And any attempt to answer these questions calls for ingenuity and skill, the power of analysis and association, and the ability to set up hypotheses, and all these must be bolstered by a wealth of accurate information and the use of good judgment. No limitation is set upon any subject; problems run into one another; they become intricate and interwoven, one throwing light upon the other.

And there is a logic underlying this method of reasoning. It is the very same kind of logic which underlies any sort of scientific research, and by which one is enabled to form hypotheses, to test them and to formulate general laws. The Talmudic student approaches the study of texts in the same manner as the scientist approaches the study of nature. Just as the scientist proceeds on the assumption that there is a uniformity and continuity in nature so the Talmud student proceeds on the assumption that there is a uniformity and continuity in human reasoning. Now, this method of text interpretation is sometimes derogatorily referred to as Talmudic quibbling or *pilpul*. In truth, it is nothing but the application of the scientific method to the study of texts.

NOTES

References to books of the Talmud refer to the Babylonian Talmud unless otherwise noted.

1. "*Um al kitab*" — *Q'uran*, Sura 2:99, uses the term to refer to Jews and Christians; however it has become almost exclusively associated with the Jews.

2. *Mishneh Torah*, Laws of Torah Study, 1:9.

3. Circa 65 B.C.E. *Gittin* 57b; *Sanhedrin* 97b. (The commonly used term A.D. when referring to calendar years is not used because of its Christian origin and meaning. Jews refer to this era as the Common Era. For example, this book was written in 2005 of the Common Era. B.C.E. refers to Before the Common Era.)

4. Circa 80 C.E. *Megillah* 3a; *Gittin* 56b.

5. Circa 170 C.E.

6. The central text recording the Jewish Oral Tradition, redacted in Israel in about 170 C.E.

7. *Avodah Zarah* 11a.

8. Circa 65 B.C.E. *Yoma* 35b.

9. Jewish "supreme court."

10. 1040-1105 C.E.

11. Circa 1075 -1141 C.E.

12. 1135-1204 C.E.

13. 1194-1270 C.E.

14. Deuteronomy 33:4.

15. *Braita*, quoted in Talmud *Shabbat* 127a — "And the study of Torah is equivalent to them all."

16. *Mishneh Torah*, ibid. 1:8.

17. *Sifri, Parshat Eikev,* Piska 10; *Kiddushin* 29b.

18. *Code of Jewish Law, Yoreh Deah,* 246:6, Ramah.

19. Rabbi Yisrael Meir Kagan, *Likutei Halachot*, Sotah Ch. 3, *"venireh."*

20. Cited in Telushkin and Prager, *Why the Jews?,* Simon and Shuster, NY, 1983, p. 49.

21. Beryl Smalley, *Study of the Bible in the Middle Ages*, University of Notre Dame Press, Notre Dame, Indiana, 1970, p.

78. As cited in Haim Hillel Ben-Sasson, *Trial and Achievement: Currents in Jewish History,* Keter Publishing House, Jerusalem, 1974, p. 42.

22. *Mishneh Torah*, ibid. 1:10.

23. *Ethics of the Fathers* 2:6.

24. *Sefer Hachinuch*, 419; Rabbi Menachem Recanati, *Sefer Ta'amei Hamitzvot*, Positive Commandment 176.

25. Rabbi Moshe Chaim Luzzatto, *Mesilat Yesharim*, Chap. 1; *Derech Hashem*, section 1, 2:1.

26. Mishnah *Sofrim* 3:13; *Mechilta, Beshalach,* 3 "*zeh Eli ve'anveihu*"; Maimonides, *Mishneh Torah*, Laws of the Intellect, 1:5-7.

27. Raymond Chandler and Robert B. Parker, *Poodle Springs*, Berkeley Publishing Group, 1998.

28. *Shabbat* 10a, 119b; Rashi, Commentary on Exodus, 18:13.

29. Rabbi Chaim of Volozhin, *Nefesh Hachaim*, Sha'ar 4, Chap. 6 — *He should intend to connect, through his studies, to the Torah and to God. That is, to cling with all his strength to the word of God, which is halachah. And through this, he is united with God Himself (so to speak), as He and His Will are one, as is explained in the Zohar.*

30. Rabbi Joseph B. Soloveitchik, *Halakhic Man*, The Jewish Publication Society of America, Philadelphia, 1983, p. 19.

31. Leonard Zusne and Warren H. Jones, *Anomalistic Psychology: A Study of Magical Thinking*, Second Edition, Lawrence Erlbaum Associates, Publishers, NJ, 1989, pp. 84-85.

32. Analogy heard from Rabbi Mendel Weinbach.

33. The Talmud is the edited version of the discussions and commentaries on Jewish law of the academies of

Babylon, from about 170 C.E. until about 500 C.E.

34. Rabbi Moshe Chaim Luzzatto, *Derech Tevunos*, Chap. 1.

35. Jeremiah 33:25.

36. *Midrash Rabbah* Exodus, 47:4; *Midrash Tanchuma, Ha'azinu* 3; *Pesachim* 68b; *Sanhedrin* 99b.

37. Genesis 1:27.

38. Rabbi Chaim of Volozhin, *Nefesh Hachaim*, Sha'ar Alef, Chaps. 1-2.

39. *Midrash Kohelles Rabbah*, 7.

40. Isaiah 51:16.

41. *Nefesh Hachaim*, ibid. Chap. 3.

42. Ibid. Sha'ar Dalet.

43. Quoted by William James, *The Will to Believe, Essays in Popular Philosophy,* The Sentiment of Rationality, Dover Publications, Inc., NY, 1956. p. 72.

44. *Berachot* 11b; *Code of Jewish Law, Orach Chaim*, 47:1-2. The blessings for Torah study are a Biblical obligation. *Responsa Shaagas Aryeh* 24; see also *Mishnah Berurah* and *Biur Halachah, Orach Chaim*, ibid. ad loc.

45. *Code of Jewish Law*, ibid.; *The Complete Artscroll Siddur, Ashkenaz,* NY, 1992, pp. 16-17.

46. Rabbi Avraham of Sochatchov, Introduction to *Eglei Tal.*

47. *Kiddushin* 40b; Jerusalem Talmud *Berachot* 1:1; *Midrash Rabbah,* Deuteronomy 7:4; *Masechet Kallah Rabbati*, 8.

48. Exodus 24:7. Some translate as "we will do and we will obey."

49. Rabbi S. R. Hirsch, *The Hirsch Siddur*, Feldheim Publishers, Jerusalem – NY, 1978, pp. 6-7.

50. Education only begins when the child is able to speak — *Sifri, Parshat Eikev*, Piska 10; *Tosefta, Chagigah*, 1:3.

51. *Teshuvot Mabit* 1:165; Rabbeinu Yerucham, *Toldot Adam V'Chavah* 23:3; *Teshuvot Rabbi Yoseph ibn Migash*, 71.

52. The library of the Harry Fishel Institute in Jerusalem, a rabbinic college, has more than 30,000 volumes.

53. Deuteronomy 4:9, 6:7, 11:19; *Bava Batra* 21a; *Mishneh Torah*, ibid., 1:2,3.

54. A Talmudic Sage and a High Priest during the Second Temple era — Rashi, *Bava Batra*, ibid., ad loc.

55. Ibid. 21a.

56. Written down and edited by Ravina and Rav Ashi from 475 C.E. to 500 C.E.

57. See Appendix at the end of the book for a list of study resources.

58. Talmud in *Yevamot* 62b refers to Rabbi Akiva's 12,000 *pairs* of students.

59. *Berachot* 63a.

60. Heard from my teachers as an oral tradition from Rabbi Soloveitchik.

61. Maimonides, *Mishneh Torah*, Laws of Homicide, 7:1.

62. *Makkot* 10a.

63. Deuteronomy 6:6-7.

64. *The Complete Artscroll Siddur, Ashkenaz*, NY 1992, pp. 16-17.

65. This system was established in 1923 by Rabbi Meir Shapiro of Lublin. The Babylonian Talmud contains 2,711 folios (each folio is two sides of a page), so studying one folio per day takes approximately seven and a half years to complete.

66. In New York, the phone number for Dial-A-Daf is: (718) 436-4999.

67. http://www.dafyomi.co.il/, http://www.ohr.org.il/web/yomi.htm

68. 7:53 a.m. Long Island Railroad train from Far Rockaway to Penn Station, NY (except for Saturday and Sunday).

69. See Appendix of this chapter on Talmudic method.

70. Rabbi Moshe Feinstein, *Igrot Moshe, Yoreh Deah* 3:83.

71. Ibid. 3:78,79.

72. Rabbi Sa'adiah Gaon, *Haemunot Vehadeot*, 3:7.

Getting Up on the Right Side of the Bed: Prayer

The philosophy, history and meaning of prayers

The Need for Prayer

*A*ccording to a recent survey, approximately 86 percent of Americans say they believe in God,[1] while 9 out of 10 Americans claimed to "engage in prayer regularly."[2] Judaism maintains that human beings have a natural desire to seek a relationship with God and to connect with a reality beyond the purely physical. The statistics indicate that this is true even in a nation where wealth and comfort abound. We are drawn to prayer, explains the 13th-century poet and philosopher, Rabbi Yehudah Halevy, because, "Prayer benefits the soul just as food benefits the body."[3]

The Book of Psalms (*Tehillim*) reflects our longing to connect with God through prayer. The fact that millions of people of many cultures and backgrounds have turned to Psalms for inspiration attests to the universality of that longing. *Tehillim* are the prophetically composed prayers written by several authors, but primarily by King David, of ancient Israel.[4] Prophecy is usually defined as God speaking to people. *Tehillim,* on the other hand, consists entirely of people speaking to God.

This "reverse prophecy" is nonetheless considered prophecy, and teaches us a fundamental idea about prayer. Just as prophecy is necessary in order to know what God is saying to us, we also need prophecy to know what we really want to say to God. On one level, it is clear that we want to ask God for health, wealth, dignity and other human requirements. *Tehillim* allows us to access the deepest desires of our soul and to convey its needs to God.

The natural inclination to pray must be encouraged and nurtured. If an individual is never able to communicate his true feelings, he will become depressed and unable to function well. Similarly, the soul needs to express itself and speak with God, and if it is prevented from doing so through prayer, it too will experience depression and become dysfunctional. Rabbi Abraham Isaac Kook[5] explains that by allowing the soul to articulate its desire for contact with God, prayer removes a burden from the soul and gives it a feeling of relief and freedom.

The Talmud[6] criticizes a person who looks upon the act of prayer as a burden, because he fails to understand that it is beneficial to him. Prayer relieves his soul of a burden that otherwise rests on it. The Bible describes prayer as the "pouring out of the soul before God."[7] In times of need and distress, calling out to God is an expression of our deep-seated belief in Him and in His capacity to help us. That God listens when we call out to Him is a kindness on His part,[8] but it is also something that we expect as His children. The Bible tells us on numerous occasions, "You are children to the Lord, your God."[9] Just as nothing is more natural for a child than to call to his parents when he is in trouble, so too human beings instinctively cry out to God in times of distress.[10]

The Obligation to Pray

How does one respond to difficulty and disappointment in life? If an individual turns to God in prayer, it becomes clear that God is his ultimate source of hope and the one in whom he places his trust.[11] For this reason, all of mankind is obligated to pray in times of suffering, as a fulfillment of the universal obligation to believe in God. According to Rabbi Moshe Feinstein, one of the leading 20th-century Torah luminaries:

> *The essence of belief in God is that only He can ultimately guarantee our livelihood or cure our sicknesses. And when a person does not trust in God and does not pray to Him, it is as if he is denying belief in God.*[12]

In addition to praying in times of need, an independent Biblical commandment obligates every Jew to pray every day, as Maimonides writes:[13]

There is a commandment to pray every day, as it is written, "You shall serve the Lord Your God with all your heart." … This "service" refers to prayer, as it says "And to serve Him with all your heart." Our Sages said, "What type of service takes place in the heart? Prayer."[14]

To fulfill this obligation, prayer must contain three distinct elements: praise of God, requests for needs, and the acknowledgment of God as the Source of everything by expressing thanks to Him.[15] All of our prayers are included under one of these three categories, while the central prayer of the daily liturgy contains all three.[16]

Why does God require us to pray every day, rather than just when the feeling moves us to do so? Prayer is clearly not for God's benefit. He does not need our praise, because He has no ego. He does not need us to inform Him of our needs, because He is omniscient. He does not need our thanks, because He is completely altruistic. The Bible makes it very clear that our sins do not hurt God, and neither do our good deeds help Him. The Book of Job (35:6-7) states this rather clearly:

If you have sinned, how have you affected Him? If your transgressions multiply, what have you done to Him? If you were righteous, what have you given Him, or what has He taken from your hand?

In simple terms, God wants us to enjoy the world He created for us and wants to bestow only goodness upon us. He requires us to pray because prayer benefits the human being.

The Benefits of Prayer – Self-Evaluation

Prayer helps us realize that God is the Source of life and existence. Asking for health, wealth and dignity forces a person to contemplate how he will use these gifts.

A teenage girl knocked on our door one Sunday morning, offering a free copy of a local newspaper. I declined, since I did not like that particular newspaper. She then asked if I would like to buy a subscription. (Obviously she was not a student of logic — if I did not want a free copy, I was certainly not going to pay for a subscription!) Not deterred by my refusal, she then begged me to reconsider. I asked her why she was so desperate to sell the paper, and she replied, "If I sell two more subscriptions I will win a Diskman®, and I *really* need one!" Now, had she said that she was saving up for college, or helping to support her family because her father was unemployed, I would have been more sympathetic — but fulfilling her "need" for a portable CD player was not something that I felt required my contribution.

When we pray, we should ask ourselves, "Is this a frivolous request? Will I use God's gift for a positive purpose? How have I used the gifts He has given me until now?" Prayer, therefore, involves an appraisal of one's life, a reality-check. This idea is reflected in the Hebrew word *lehitpallel* to pray. The verb *"pallel"* actually means "judge,"[17] while the prefix *lehit* makes the word reflexive.[18] The correct translation of *"lehitpallel,"* therefore is "to judge oneself." Rabbi Samson Raphael Hirsch describes prayer:

> *[It is the means]… to step out of active life in order to attempt to gain a true judgment of oneself, that is, about one's ego, about one's relationship to God and the world, and of God and the world to oneself. It strives to infuse mind and heart with the power of such judgment as will direct both anew to active life — purified, sublimated, strengthened.*[19]

Stillness, Tranquility and Prayer

Prayer instills a state of rest and tranquility,[20] because as the individual prays he increases his awareness that everything is in the hands of God. It is for this reason that our central prayer, the *Amidah*, is recited while standing with our feet together: This stance is identified as being similar to the angels,[21] whom the prophet Ezekiel describes as having "one straight foot."[22] It is a posture that denotes immobility and demonstrates our belief that without God we are completely powerless and unable to move.[23] Jewish law requires that we take responsibility for our life in this world, that we work,[24] take care of our health[25] and even buy life insurance.[26] Nevertheless, we believe that the success or failure of our endeavors is dependent upon the will of God.[27] Since God is benevolent, and everything is in His hands, it follows that all events that befall us are ultimately for our good. The Talmud states, "Everything that the All-Merciful does is for the good."[28]

Internalizing this concept enables a person to feel less anxious, more secure and tranquil, no matter what challenges are encountered. Clearly, we should not be jellyfish, flowing with the tides of life without exerting effort or trying to change direction. Nor is the positive aspect of every circumstance always obvious to us. On the other hand, we should realize that whatever may happen, we are in good hands.[29]

The principal technique for acquiring this attitude is regular, focused, meaningful prayer. The very fact that we stand with our feet together, as if immobilized, is a form of prayer through body language. We are saying that all we are really capable of doing is asking God for life, health, sustenance and everything that we need. Our efforts alone, without God's blessing, will accomplish nothing.[30]

Prayer, therefore, is not a way of nagging God until He changes His mind about our fate. Rather, it is a means of changing ourselves.[31] The order of the prayers serves to reinforce this idea even before we begin. The Sages directed people to first engage in praise of God and only afterwards to request help from Him.[32] When we begin by praising God, we remind ourselves of Whom exactly we are praying to and what prayer is meant to achieve. We then continue with our requests, understanding that prayer is more than an eloquent *kvetch*.[33]

In addition to the benefits already discussed, prayer also helps us to achieve the primary purpose of our existence, namely, to forge a relationship with God.[34] One of the ways of strengthening this relationship is by standing before God, expressing one's innermost thoughts and placing oneself in His hands.

Authors of the Prayers

In the early years of Jewish history, every person would pray once a day using his or her own words. Prayer had no specified time or form. During the Babylonian Exile (circa 423 B.C.E.), however, the Jewish people began speaking Aramaic, Persian, Greek and other foreign languages. Their ability to express themselves in pure Hebrew with all the beauty and depth of the Bible began to diminish. In approximately 335 B.C.E., the Jewish leader, Ezra, and the court over which he presided[35] — which included a number of prophets[36] — composed the daily prayers, the blessings and the order of the services. They also decreed that one should pray three times a day — in the evening, morning and afternoon.[37]

The Sages established the times of prayer using two models — the prayers of the Patriarchs Abraham, Isaac and Jacob, and the services in the Temple of Jerusalem.[38] The morning prayer, *Shacharit*, corresponds to Abraham's prayer to God which was said in the morning,[39] as well as the service in the Temple.[40] The afternoon prayer, *Minchah*, corresponds to the afternoon prayer instituted by Isaac,[41] as well as the afternoon service in the Temple.[42] Jacob prayed in the evening.[43] Although there was no regular service in the Temple in the evening, the evening prayer, *Maariv*, corresponds to the activities that completed the previous day's services.[44] Sephardim refer to the evening prayer by a variation on this word, *Arvit.*

A Prayer in Time ...

Praying at the beginning of the day serves several purposes. The most appropriate time to thank God for the gifts of life and existence is at the first moment of perception, when a person wakes up and appreciates his own existence and that of the world around him.[45] This is also the time to set our spiritual and moral compass for the day, and to focus on the purpose of life before becoming immersed in the minutiae of daily activity.[46] Ideally, the morning service should be recited at dawn or shortly afterward, but it may be recited up until one quarter of the day has passed.[47] Most synagogues begin the weekday morning service at around 7 a.m., and Sabbath services somewhat later.

The afternoon service, which is said in the middle of the day, helps us step out of the rat race for a moment and remind ourselves of where we should be headed and why. It creates a brief sanctuary of spirituality, calm and contemplation, no matter how busy we may be. *Minchah* acts as a spiritual check, much like verifying our course with navigation equipment to see if we have stayed on the path that we set for ourselves at the beginning of the journey.[48] The afternoon service is recited from a half-hour after midday until sundown.[49] (In some communities, *Minchah* is still recited for a short period after sundown.)

The evening service, said at the end of the day's activities, is like the captain's log at the completion of one portion of the journey. We take stock of what we have done and see how far we have progressed. As we are about to relinquish our active involvement in life, to sleep and give our souls over to God, from Whom we received them as a loan, we contemplate whether we are worthy of a further loan. Finally, we dedicate our rest to gaining energy for a productive, purposeful life the following day.[50] The evening service should be said after nightfall, but before midnight.[51] (If one did not have the opportunity before midnight, however, the service may be said during the remainder of the night.)

The Minyan

The essence of prayer is internal. It develops the personal and private relationship between God and His creations. Some of the greatest examples of prayer took place in complete privacy. Moses prayed to God to forgive the Jewish people for the sin of the Golden Calf, as he stood alone on Mount Sinai. In Biblical times, a woman named Hannah prayed in solitude for a child that she desperately wanted. She later became the mother of the prophet Samuel. In fact, many of the laws of prayer are derived from her heartfelt, private prayer.[52]

Both men and women are obligated to pray to God every day, as explained earlier. Women are not obligated, however, to participate in the public, external manifestations of communal prayer, rather in the ideal form of individual prayer.[53] In fact, even a brief personal prayer would fulfill the obligation to communicate daily with God. Men, who by nature are less private and internal, are obligated to pray with a community in the synagogue.[54]

The Jewish legal definition of the minimum unit for such a community is 10 adult males.[55] Since women are not obligated in the communal form of prayer, they cannot form the quorum for the fulfillment of that obligation.[56] This communal prayer is a public declaration of belief in God.[57] It is also a way of making the individual aware of the needs of the community, so that when he prays, he will include the needs of others along with his own.[58]

Prayer retains some of its individual character, even in the synagogue. A *chazzan*, (cantor) facilitates the service by pacing the prayers and by leading the recitation of the prayers that are to be said in unison. Most of the prayers are recited in an undertone by each individual as the *chazzan* says the first and last few words aloud.

Good Morning!

The first words that a Jew says upon waking are: "*Modeh ani lefanecha* — I give thanks before You, living and eternal King, that You have returned my soul within me with compassion — great is Your faithfulness."[59]

Our first word in the morning is "thanks," because gratitude is a fundamental element in our obligation to obey God[60] and in our ethical behavior toward other human beings.[61] In fact, the Hebrew word for thanks, *modeh*, is the same as the word for "admit" and has the same root as the word for Jew, *Yehudi*.[62] The essence of being Jewish is to proclaim the existence of God, and to recognize that He is our Creator and we are His creatures. Saying these words as we wake up helps us to appreciate the gift of life that God gives us every morning. With our first thoughts of the day, *Modeh Ani* reminds us that our purpose in the world is to be representatives of God and to reveal His presence in every facet of existence.

Washing the Hands

While we sleep, our hands may wander instinctively to any place on the body. Therefore, they are considered impure. In order to purify and rededicate ourselves to the service of God, we wash our hands in the morning as soon as we wake up. The washing is done by pouring water from a cup over the hands — three times on each hand — alternating right and left. Washing three times and alternating hands are both based on Kabbalistic ideas associated with the impurity of the hands as a result of sleep.[63]

The Amazing Body

The proper functioning of the body is highly complex and delicately balanced. It is a system that we usually take for granted. The Torah wants us to appreciate every aspect of life, even the routine. The Sages composed a blessing that celebrates and gives thanks to God for the proper, regular functioning of the digestive and waste systems of the human body. The blessing is recited after relieving oneself any time during the day, but is first recited after the blessing for washing the hands in the morning.[64]

Morning Blessings

"Thank God for the rooster!" is hardly what most people think when they are woken at dawn by its crowing. "Where's the axe?" is a more likely reaction. Nevertheless, the first of a series of morning blessings, *Birchot Hashachar,* thanks God for giving the rooster wisdom to distinguish between day and night.[65] In actuality, the rooster is used symbolically in this blessing which praises God for creating the intricately connected eco-system that is our world. Flora and fauna, animal and human, each element is connected to every other.[66] The rooster's crowing at the beginning of the day is of no benefit to himself, but acts as a natural alarm clock for human beings. Each day, it is the first manifestation of this interconnection and of the many ways in which the entire natural world is meant for our benefit. Even if you live in the city and you're woken daily by your alarm clock or the sweet sound of garbage trucks, this blessing is a pleasant reminder of the perfection happening out there beyond the city limits.

A series of blessings follow that expresses our gratitude for the broad range of kindnesses that God has granted us. We offer our thanks to Him for clothing, shelter, vision, freedom, mobility and all the essential requirements of life. By stopping each day to appreciate every aspect of our existence, we are able to achieve greater happiness, and to be more content in life. It is also easier to remain humble when we recognize that we are the recipients of so many undeserved gifts.

Preparations for Prayer

Prayer is an activity that requires preparation. A person must be physically clean, dignified in appearance,[67] free of all distractions and in an appropriate mood.[68] The Talmud states: "One should not stand up to pray from the midst of sorrow, inactivity, laughter, light talk, frivolity or idle matters — rather from a state of happiness in the performance of a *mitzvah.*"[69]

Most of the first half of the morning service consists of Psalms, known as *P'sukei D'zimrah,* meaning "verses of song." The afternoon service is also preceded by a selection from Psalms. Through their recitation we try to attain the state of being that the Talmud describes as the "happiness of a *mitzvah*." The beautiful poetry of the Psalms, the expressions of appreciation for life and for the Torah, and the praises of God combine to create the desired mood for prayer.

The chapters of Psalms that we recite also increase our awareness of God's connection to the world through nature and through Divine providence. The Psalms explore almost every aspect of God's interaction with the world: As we read them, we come to the realization that we too have a personal connection to God and are able to address Him through prayer. Only when we see God as the One Who sustains, orders and runs the world can we honestly approach Him in prayer.

Shema – The Pledge of Allegiance

A central part of the morning and evening prayers is the recitation of three sections of the Torah, known as *Kriat Shema*. Technically, this is not a prayer, because there is no praise, supplication or thanks. The Sages included it in the daily liturgy, however, because the principles found in *Shema* are so important, and because there is an obligation to recite it twice daily. Since reciting them is fulfilling a Biblical commandment, the recitation is preceded and followed by a series of blessings.[70] *Shema* itself begins with the sentence that is the ultimate declaration of belief in monotheism and God's special relationship to the Jewish people. Throughout history, and today, Jews recite this sentence with their final breath because it encapsulates Jewish faith so completely in this one short phrase. This verse is recited aloud while covering the eyes with the right hand, in a state of total concentration:[71] "Hear, O Israel: The Lord is our God, the Lord, is One."[72]

The short blessing that follows, "Blessed is the Name of His glorious kingdom for ever,"[73] is said quietly, because it is not of Biblical origin.[74] We then continue with the following three Biblical passages, referred to collectively as *Shema*:

> You shall love the Lord your God with all your heart, and with all your soul, and with all your might. And these words that I command you today shall be upon your heart. You shall teach them thoroughly to your children, and shall speak of them while you sit in your home, while you walk on the way, when you retire and when you arise. Bind them as a sign upon your arm and let them be ornaments between your eyes. [The reference is to tefillin.] And write them on the doorposts of your house [mezuzah], and upon your gates.[75]
>
> It will be, that if you hearken to My commandments that I command you today, to love God, your God, and to serve Him

with all your heart and with all your soul. Then I shall provide rain for your Land in its proper time, the early and the late rains, that you may gather in your grain, your wine and your oil. I shall provide grass in your field for your cattle, and you will eat and you will be satisfied. Beware for yourselves, lest your heart be seduced, and you turn astray, and serve gods of others and prostrate yourselves to them. Then the wrath of God will blaze against you; He will restrain the heaven so there be no rain, and the ground will not yield its produce; and you will be swiftly banished from the goodly Land that God gives you. You shall place these words of Mine upon your heart and upon your soul; you shall bind them for a sign upon your arm, and let them be an ornament between your eyes. You shall teach them to your children to discuss them, when you sit in your home, while you walk on the way, and when you retire and when you arise. And you shall write them on the doorposts of your house and upon your gates. In order to prolong your days and the days of your children upon the Land that God has sworn to your forefathers to give them, like the days of the heavens over the earth.[76]

God said to Moses, saying, "Speak to the Children of Israel and say to them that they shall make themselves fringes [tzitzit] on the corners of their garments, throughout their generations. And they shall place upon the fringes of each corner a thread of turquoise wool. It shall constitute fringes for you, that you may see it, and remember all the commandments of God and perform them; and do not follow your heart and your eyes after which you stray. So that you may remember and perform all My commandments and be holy to your God. I am God your God, Who has removed you from the land of Egypt to be a God unto you; I am the Lord your God.[77]

These three short paragraphs contain many of the basic principles of Judaism. They constitute a succinct declaration of our beliefs, our obligations and the nature of our relationship with God.

The first paragraph speaks of the obligation to love God, to teach and study the Torah and to transmit it to the next generation. It continues with the obligation to inscribe the Torah on our actions, thoughts and environment, as symbolized by binding *tefillin* on the arm and head, and affixing the words of *Shema* to the doorposts of our dwellings, as a *mezuzah*.

The next paragraph teaches us the obligation of obedience to God's commandments, the concept of reward and punishment and Divine providence, and the promise that the Land of Israel will belong to the Patriarchs and to us, their descendants. The final paragraph contains the prohibition against blindly following our senses and desires, and the obligation to keep the commandments at the forefront of our consciousness.

The wearing of fringes, *tzitzit*, on our garments helps us keep these responsibilities in mind and is the central commandment of the last paragraph. The *Shema* ends with a mention of the Exodus, thus enabling us to fulfill the Biblical command "that you may remember the day of your departure from Egypt all the days of your life."[78]

The Prayer of Prayers

The central prayer of all services is called the *Amidah*, the standing prayer, also known as the *Shemoneh Esreh*, "The Eighteen," after the eighteen blessings included in it. It is recited while standing up, with the feet together as if at attention, as explained above. It consists of three parts: The first three blessings praise God, the middle blessings are requests and the last three express gratitude.[79] This prayer is the climax of the service because it encapsulates all three components of the commandment to pray. It also involves a higher degree of concentration than other prayers and includes all the major categories of human desires, hopes and needs.[80] It is the one prayer in which we are actually standing face-to-face, so to speak, with the Divine Presence.[81]

The main points of each of the eighteen blessings:

1. *Avot,* Patriarchs, identifies God as the God of Abraham, Isaac and Jacob, Who guided, protected and made a Covenant with them. It impresses on our minds the idea that God is involved in the world, cares about it and has a personal relationship with His creatures.[82] This section also reminds us that we are praying to the eternal God, the same God Who spoke to our forefathers and guided them as the Jewish nation took form.

2. This blessing describes God as the source of life, Who will someday resurrect the dead, but even now infuses life into what would otherwise be a lifeless world. This teaches us that existence itself cannot be taken for granted and that without God's continuous input of creative energy into the world, it would cease to be.[83]

3. The third blessing describes God as elevated above this world of space, time and physicality. God is described as *Kadosh,* meaning holy, separate or transcendent.[84] Since the first two blessings emphasize God's involvement in the world, the third blessing is a necessary counterbalance to teach us that although He is involved, He is not *part* of this world. God is holy and exalted beyond any possibility of description or comparison. He is not affected by time,

space or anything material.[85] All we can do is use human words to attempt to describe God, but we know that it is impossible to do so adequately.[86]

4. This is the first blessing of request, a prayer for wisdom, perception and understanding. It begins with the acknowledgement that these capacities are gifts of God, as the verse in Psalms states, "the beginning of wisdom is the fear of God."[87] We ask first for understanding because it is the primary tool in our quest for morality, spirituality and happiness. Without wisdom, all other achievements are impossible.[88]

5. We ask for God's help in returning to the Torah, to God's service and in achieving complete repentance, *teshuvah*. Repentance means regretting the wrong that we have done, confessing the sin to God and resolving never to repeat it.[89] It is impossible to succeed in this process of self-improvement and repentance without the help of God.[90]

6. In this blessing, we actually begin the process of repentance by acknowledging that we have done wrong — sometimes deliberately, sometimes through negligence and occasionally even in rebellion against God. We ask God for forgiveness for all of our sins and recognize that He is the only source of forgiveness. The request for forgiveness can only come after the blessing of repentance, because the sinner's first obligation is to make amends to the greatest degree possible; only then can he be forgiven.[91]

7. We ask God to deliver and redeem us from hardship, even if we are not deserving of this. This redemption will be a tangible sign that we have been forgiven for our sins.

8. This is the prayer for health and for healing, and recognizes God as the only true Healer and source of life. Even though we are obligated to take responsibility for our health, we must realize that the state of our health is in God's hands. The physician, drugs and medical procedure are merely agents of God's will. We should also appreciate that human knowledge and the human ability to develop cures is also a gift from Him.[92]

9. Although the Torah requires us to make reasonable efforts to earn a living, nonetheless we recognize that our financial success or failure is totally in the hands of God. Part of our effort for sustenance is prayer.[93] We pray for our own livelihood, but also for blessing and livelihood in the Land of Israel. In this way we remind ourselves that we are inextricably bound to the Land of Israel and that it is the conduit for bringing all blessing to the world.[94]

10. We ask God to bring the Jewish people back to our homeland, Israel, from wherever they are scattered around the world. This ingathering will be heralded by the blast of a great *shofar* as predicted by Isaiah, "And it will be on that day, that He will blow a great *shofar,* and those who are lost in the land of Assyria will come, and those who are scattered in the land of Egypt, and they will bow to God at the Holy mountain in Jerusalem."[95]

11. We ask that another of Isaiah's prophecies be fulfilled. In the days of the Redemption, law courts and judges of the Jewish people will be restored to their former power and glory. Justice will be administered by the *Sanhedrin* — the Jewish court — according to the laws of the Torah.[96] The blessing ends with a reminder that God loves righteousness and justice. The message is clear: If we are asking for justice, we should certainly behave justly ourselves.[97]

11A. One of the great tragedies of the Exile is that evildoers appear to go unpunished; too often, they seem to get away with it. This situation creates a desecration of God's Name, because it seems to indicate an absence of the Divine Presence. We ask that those who are enemies of God and the Jewish people be punished. We pray that they should lose their power and that they be totally vanquished by good and justice.

    This blessing was not one of the original eighteen (which is why we have listed this point as 11A) but was added later,[98] during a period of heavy persecution that was made even more tragic by acts of disloyalty and collaboration with the enemy on the part of Jewish sectarians.[99]

12. The flip side of punishing the evildoers is rewarding the righteous. We now pray for reward and compensation for the righteous, the leaders of the Jewish people, the Sages, the sincere converts and all those who trust in God.

13. All of the prophets predicted the return of the Jewish people to Jerusalem and the rebuilding of the city and the Temple. "Therefore thus says God, 'I will return to Jerusalem in mercy, My house will be built there ...'"[100] We face Jerusalem every time we say the *Amidah*, and we pray for the restoration of Jerusalem to its former glory and sanctity.

14. The prophet Nathan told King David, "Your dynasty and your kingdom will remain steadfast before you for all time; your throne will remain firm forever."[101] Belief in the coming of the Messiah and the restoration of the monarchy by a descendant of King David is central to Judaism. It is the hope that has sustained the Jewish people throughout the

best and worst times of our history.[102] We pray to see the Redemption arrive quickly and declare that we wait in daily expectation of that moment.

15. We do not assume that our prayers are automatically answered in the way we would like. We recognize that the ability to pray to God is a privilege and kindness, not a right.[103] In this blessing we ask God to receive our prayers, to answer them favorably, with compassion and mercy. We acknowledge that God listens to and answers all of our prayers in a way that is ultimately for the best.[104] This prayer provides the opportunity to insert our own words (in any language) to make personal requests.[105]

16. Our prayers stand in place of the Temple service in Jerusalem, as the prophet Hosea taught, "Take words with you and return to God; say to Him, 'May You forgive all iniquity and accept good [intentions], and let our lips substitute for animal offerings.'"[106] During the Temple eras, the primary means of coming closer to God was through animal offerings. After the Temple's destruction, Hosea tells the Jewish people that we now approach God primarily with the "words of our lips." In this paragraph, we ask God to accept us, and our prayer service; to return the Temple service to its central place in Jewish life; and to view us, our prayers and our devotion with approval. We end with a blessing that we should witness the complete return of the Divine Presence to Zion.

17. We now begin the third section of the *Amidah* prayer: gratitude.[107] We bow in appreciation that we have received, and continue to receive God's blessings. We recognize that our entire lives are in His hands, that His miracles are with us always and that everything in existence owes its creation and continued existence to God. All, therefore, are obligated to acknowledge and thank Him.

18. The last sentence in the Mishnah[108] states: "The Holy One, Blessed be He, did not find a receptacle to hold the blessings for the Jewish people other than peace, as it says,[109] 'God will give might to His nation, God will bless His nation with peace.'"[110] Thus we end all the prayers of praise, request and thanks with the final, all-inclusive blessing of peace. The blessing of peace certainly refers to the physical state of peace as opposed to war, but its fuller meaning refers to peace between one person and another, between the body and the soul, and between the human being and God. We ask to be blessed with peace, life, kindness and mercy, for us and for the entire Jewish people. We also pray that we merit to be inspired by God and His Torah, and to fulfill the potential that God placed within each of us for love, kindness, charity and mercy.

The Talmud[111] relates that different rabbis had specific prayers that they would recite after the *Amidah*. The universal custom today is to recite the prayer of the Sage, Mar son of Ravina.[112] In this prayer, we ask God's help to always speak kindly and in an ethically correct manner, and not to become jealous or angry. We ask Him to open our hearts to the words of Torah and to give us a desire to pursue the commandments. We pray that all who plot against us be confounded and that all evil planned against us be thwarted. Finally, we ask again that our prayers be accepted. At this point, it is customary to add individual requests, using our own words in any language.[113] The prayer concludes with the plea that God grant peace to us and to all of Israel, and that the Temple be rebuilt. "He Who makes peace in His heights [the heavens],[114] may He make peace upon us and upon all Israel."[115]

It's Déjà Vu All Over Again

During the morning and afternoon services, after the congregation completes the silent prayer, the cantor (also known as a *shliach tzibur*, emissary of the community) repeats the *Amidah* aloud. This repetition is for the benefit of those who are unable to say the prayers themselves (though all are required to listen). By listening to and concentrating on what the cantor is saying, and by answering amen to his blessings, it is considered as though one had said the prayer himself.[116] During the repetition, the cantor adds the *Kedushah,* the sanctification of God's Name, which expresses our very purpose as a people — to provide testimony to God's existence through our behavior as beings created in His image.[117] This is what is meant by "sanctifying His Name."[118] *Kedushah* is recited communally and responsively while standing.

Winding Down

The Talmud tells us that the "pious ones would wait one hour before prayer, pray for one hour and wait one hour after prayer."[119] The hour before was for preparation, just as we say blessings, Psalms and *Shema* before the silent prayer. The silent prayer itself would take an hour (this works out to about seven seconds concentration on each word!). They would wait one hour after prayers to fulfill the verse, "Only the righteous will give thanks to Your Name; the upright will dwell in Your Presence."[120] One who has tasted the pleasure of the Divine Presence and the uplifting of the soul in prayer will not be in a hurry to escape or run away. On the contrary, he will linger to "dwell" in the Presence of God. In this spirit, the

Sages decreed that we too stay a bit longer and recite several prayers after the *Amidah.*

The first post-*Amidah* prayer is *Tachanun,* "supplication." *Tachanun* is recited only at the morning and afternoon service. It is a prayer in which we confess our sins to God, ask for forgiveness and declare our shame for our misdeeds. Part of this prayer is recited sitting down, covering one's face with one's arm.[121] This position reflects our feelings of shame, and encourages us to feel regret for our sins. It is also a sign of subjugation to God and His law and therefore is done only when a Torah scroll is present in the room.[122] It symbolizes as well our ability to control our senses (covering the eyes) and to use our strength in appropriate ways (covering the arm).[123] Due to the poignant nature of *Tachanun,* it is not recited on happy occasions, such as the Sabbath and festivals, nor on the day of a circumcision in the synagogue, or in the presence of a groom.[124]

Back to the Mountain

At this point in the morning service, a designated section of the Torah is read aloud from a scroll. This is done on Mondays and Thursdays, as well as on Sabbaths, festivals and fast days.[125] The practice of publicly reading from the Torah every Monday, Thursday and on every Sabbath and festival dates back to Moses. With his decree of readings on Monday, Thursday and the Sabbath, no Jew would ever be more than three days away from hearing the words of the Torah.[126] Later in history, Ezra the Scribe[127] decreed that the Torah also should be read at afternoon services on the Sabbath, in order to engage even the idle and ignorant in some Torah study. Ezra also specified the minimum number of verses that should be read each time.[128]

The Torah portion is always connected in some way to the events that occurred on that day in history. The Torah states, "And Moses declared the appointed festivals of God to the Children of Israel."[129] The Talmud understands this passage to mean that Moses was teaching the Jewish people to read, study and engage in relevant Torah portions at their appropriate times.[130]

A Biblical commandment obligates us to study the Torah every single day,[131] so even without the decree of Moses, a Jew should never be even a day away from Torah study. Evidently, Moses must have had an additional goal in mind when he decreed the public Torah reading. The true nature and deeper purpose of this ceremony are revealed by a closer examination of the laws of the Torah reading. The public reading may be performed only in the presence of a community; representatives of all elements of the Jewish people participate (*Kohen, Levi, Israelite*[132]); it is read from the *bimah,* a lectern in the middle of the synagogue; at one point the scroll is lifted high, and the congregations declares that "This is the Torah that Moses placed before the Children of Israel,[133] upon the command of Hashem [God], through Moses' hand."[134]

These characteristics of the reading suggest that what is taking place is not merely reading from a Torah scroll, but actually a reenactment of the Revelation of the Torah on Mount Sinai and a reacceptance of the Torah every time that it is read.[135] The *bimah*, like the mountain, is surrounded by the people; a *gabbai* [a synagogue functionary] acts as an intermediary, like Moses, to call the Jews to the Torah;[136] and the community proclaims together their acceptance of the Torah as they did at Mount Sinai. With the fulfillment of this practice, there is never a period when the Jewish people are more than three days' journey from the Revelation at Mount Sinai and from their voluntary acceptance of the Torah.

The most widespread practice is to read through the entire Torah — all of the Five Books of Moses — over the course of a year. In this way, one actually hears the entire Torah sung in the traditional tune and pronounced with care every year.[137] The weekly portion, known as the *parshah*, is studied (usually with translations and commentaries) during the week preceding its reading.[138] When these laws and practices are properly observed, the result is a Biblically literate, well-versed people that rightfully deserves the appellation "The People of the Book."

One of my most enduring childhood memories is of my father[139] reviewing the portion of the week with the commentary of Rashi[140] while waiting for customers in his store. The entry of a customer for most store-owners is a moment of joy in anticipation of making a sale. I always felt that for my father, it was a bit of an annoyance to have to stop his learning for business. When I was first introduced to my wife's grandmother[141] it was a Friday afternoon, and I saw an elderly lady holding a piece of paper the size of a builder's blueprints. The paper was an enlarged copy of the *parshah* made for her by her grandchildren, so that even with her failing eyesight she would be able to read all the commentaries.

Aside from the regular portion of the week, a designated section of the Torah is read on each festival and fast day. These selections usually consist of the parts of the Torah dealing with the observance or origin of that festival and the verses detailing the Temple service for that occasion. On Sabbaths and festivals, additional readings, known as the *Haftarah*,[142] are recited from the books of the prophets. The practice of reading the words of the prophets dates to a time of persecution when Jews were forbidden to read publicly from the Torah. The rabbis decreed that the community should substitute a section of the prophets relevant to the Torah portion of that week, or to the festival or fast day.[143] We retain this practice today, even though the cause of the decree is long gone, to gain inspiration from the timeless words of the prophets. In many congregations, a boy who has just reached the age of Bar Mitzvah will mark this occasion by chanting the *Haftarah*, as he is now qualified as a full-fledged adult to do so.

On a regular weekday, three men are called by the *gabbai* to participate in the Torah reading; a *Kohen*, a *Levi* and an *Israelite*.[144] In earlier times, each would read a section of the Torah and recite the blessings that precede and follow it. Nowadays, an expert reader (*ba'al koreh*) usually reads the Torah portion and the men who are called up only recite the Torah blessings.[145] (This "calling up" is known as an *aliyah* to the Torah, which means literally to go up. One ascends the *bimah* in order to approach the Torah and recite the blessings.) On Sabbaths, seven men are called up as well as one additional (*maftir*) person who will say the blessings for the *Haftarah*. On festivals, five men are called up, with one addition for the *Haftarah*.[146] The reading of the Torah is also a time when prayers are said for those who are ill, when babies are named, people make pledges to charity and milestones in life are marked (e.g., Bar Mitzvah, *yahrzeit*, etc.).

Concluding Prayers

One of the psalms recited in the *P'sukei D'zimrah* is Psalm 145, known as *Ashrei*. This psalm, written so that the first letter of each verse forms an acrostic of the Hebrew alphabet, praises God's sustenance of the world from *aleph* to *tav*, "from A to Z," so to speak. It also includes a verse that encapsulates the theme of the entire *P'sukei D'zimrah* and much of prayer in general: "You open Your hand and satisfy the desire of every living thing."[147] For both of these reasons, the Sages consider *Ashrei* to be one of the most important prayers, to the extent that they say, "One who recites *Ashrei* three times a day is a member of the World to Come."[148] In addition to the *Ashrei* recited earlier in the morning service, we say this Psalm again after *Tachanun,* or after the reading of the Torah (depending on the day of the week). *Ashrei* is recited for the third time just prior to the *Amidah* of the afternoon service.

Ashrei is followed by Psalm 20 in the morning service. This prayer pleads with God to save the Jewish people from our troubles and exile. Because of its sad tone, this psalm is omitted on happy occasions. The next prayer is a compilation of numerous verses, some of which were said earlier in the service. Some commentaries maintain that the purpose of this unusual prayer is to let even the latecomers participate in some way in the sanctification of the Name of God, as the rest of the congregation did earlier.[149] The Sages designated a specific psalm to be said on each day of the week,[150] because every moment in time has a unique spiritual character. The daily psalm is recited to remind us that our task is to try to capture the sparks of Godliness in every moment of our lives.

We conclude all service with the prayer, *Aleinu*.[151] *Aleinu* is also central in the Rosh Hashanah (New Year) and Yom Kippur (Day of Atonement) services. According to tradition, Joshua, the disciple of Moses who succeeded Moses as the leader of the Jewish people (circa 1270 B.C.E.), composed this prayer upon his entry into the Land of Israel.[152] It expresses our joy at having been given the Torah, and our gratitude that we are not pagans. We pray for the time when the whole world will come to recognize the truth and be able to clearly perceive the presence of one God.

Kaddish

Kaddish, literally, "the sanctification," is a prayer that dates back to the Mishnaic period, at least 1,900 years ago.[153] It expresses our conviction that no matter what happens, and despite all the tragedies and sorrows of this world, ultimately there will come a time when God's existence will be apparent, and His Name will be on everyone's lips.[154] The *chazzan* recites this declaration at the end of every major segment of the prayers along with a request that God should accept our service and our prayers. Mourners also recite *Kaddish* several times during the service. By saying *Kaddish* they reaffirm their belief that despite the loss of an individual, God's purpose will be fulfilled through the Jewish people as a whole. For this reason, *Kaddish* is recited only in the presence of a community (a *minyan*), never privately. Although individuals die, the community will never perish. Throughout the generations, the Jew has been sustained by this conviction; for even when an individual experiences a difficult loss, he is reminded that he is part of an eternal unit,[155] that every single part of that unit was created for a purpose, and that ultimately the purpose will be realized.[156]

Ashkenaz, Sephard and Everything In Between

Because the prayers are essentially the same from one Jewish community to another, one can enter an Orthodox synagogue anywhere in the world and be able to follow the service. However, some differences in text and the order of prayers can be found in various Jewish communities. Each set of customs is called a *nusach*. Originally, each of the Twelve Tribes of Israel had its own prayer *nusach* to correspond to its individual spiritual needs and characteristics.[157]

The common forms of prayer used today are the remnants of these 12 distinct customs, filtered through the Diaspora experience. *Ashkenaz*, meaning "Germany," is the *nusach* of most Jews of European origin (though Jews of German/Jewish descent have customs of their own!)

Sephardi, "Spanish," is the *nusach* of most Jews of Middle Eastern or North African origin, and *Sephard,* or *Nusach Ha'AriZal* (modified version of the *Sephardi nusach),* is used by all elements of the Chassidic movement. There are strong differences between them in tune and pronunciation. Nevertheless, the essential features of the prayers and blessings that are described in this chapter remain constant in each *nusach.* Throughout the centuries, and around the world, Jews have used the same words and forms of prayer, but each approaches God in his own unique way.

For Further Reading

Recommended prayer books:

▶ *ArtScroll Transliterated Linear Siddur* (if you don't read Hebrew) in weekday and Sabbath editions (ArtScroll/Mesorah)

▶ *The Complete ArtScroll Siddur* (with English translation — also published in Russian and Spanish) (ArtScroll/Mesorah, 1989)

▶ Schottenstein Edition Interlinear Series: Weekday Siddur, Sabbath and Festival Siddur, Birchon (ArtScroll/Mesorah)

About prayer:

▶ *Growth Through Tehillim: Exploring Psalms for Life Transforming Thoughts* by Rabbi Zelig Pliskin (ArtScroll/Mesorah, 2004)

▶ *Kaddish* by Rabbi Nosson Scherman (ArtScroll/Mesorah, 1980)

▶ *Twerski on Prayer* (originally: *Prayfully Yours*) by Rabbi Abraham J. Twersky, M.D. (Shaar Press, 2001)

▶ *Shema Yisrael* by Rabbi Meir Zlotowitz (ArtScroll/Mesorah, 1982)

▶ *The Art of Jewish Prayer* by Rabbi Yitzchak Kirzner and Lisa Aiken (Jason Aaronson, 1993)

▶ *The World of Prayer* by Rabbi Elie Munk (Feldheim, 1963)

NOTES

References to books of the Talmud refer to the Babylonian Talmud unless otherwise noted.

1. Gallup Poll survey, December 1999.
2. Ibid. May 1999.
3. Rabbi Yehudah Halevy, *Kuzari*, 3:5.
4. *Pesachim* 117a; *Zohar* 1:179b, 2:67b.
5. Rabbi Abraham Isaac Kook, *Siddur Olat Reiyah*, Mossad Harav Kook, Jerusalem, 1983, vol. I, p. 15.
6. *Berachot* 29b.
7. I Samuel 1:15; Rashi, *Berachot* 5b, "*toref nafsho.*"
8. Nachmanides, Critique of Maimonides' *Sefer Hamitzvot*, Mitzvah 5.
9. Deuteronomy 14:1; see also Psalms 103:13.
10. Psalms 107:13,19; Exodus 14:10; Rashi ad loc.
11. *Orchot Tzadikim*, Sha'ar 9, *Simchah*, "*Habitachon harevii*"; Maharal of Prague, *Netivot Olam, Netiv Ha'avodah,* Chaps. 1-2.
12. Rabbi Moshe Feinstein, *Igrot Moshe, Orach Chaim* 2:24, Moriah, NY, 1959.
13. Maimonides, *Mishneh Torah*, Laws of Prayer 1:1,4; *Sefer Hamitzvot*, Mitzvah 5.
14. Maimonides is quoting Exodus 23:25, Deuteronomy 11:13 and *Ta'anit* 2a respectively.
15. Maimonides, *Mishneh Torah,* ibid., 1:2.
16. Ibid. 1:4.
17. See Deuteronomy 32:31; Genesis 11:7; Psalms 32:6; Commentary of Rabbi Samson Raphael Hirsch ad loc.
18. The Hebrew *Hitpael* grammatical form. The prefix "*le*" means "to."
19. Rabbi Samson Raphael Hirsch, *Horeb*, para. 618.
20. *Talmidei Rabbeinu Yonah* on *Rif*, Tractate *Berachot, Dapei HaRif* 3b, "*Hayotzei.*"
21. *Code of Jewish Law, Orach Chaim,* 95:1.
22. Ezekiel 1:7.
23. *Code of Jewish Law,* ibid. — The reason given in the *Code* is "to be similar to the angels"; however, the idea of immobility as the meaning of "imitating the angels" is offered by Rabbi Moshe Shapiro.
24. *Mishnah Kiddushin* 82a.
25. Maimonides, *Mishneh Torah*, Laws of Character 4:1.
26. Rabbi Moshe Feinstein, *Igrot Moshe, Orach Chaim* 2:111; 4:48.
27. *Berachot* 33b.
28. Ibid. 60b.
29. Rabbi Isaiah Karelitz, *Chazon Ish, Emunah Ubitachon*, Chap. 2:1.
30. Rabbi Moshe Shapiro provided this elaboration on the concept of praying in this stance.
31. Rabbi Eliyahu Dessler, *Michtav Me'Eliyahu.*
32. *Berachot* 32a.
33. Rabbi Kook, ibid. p. 14. *Kvetch* is a Yiddish word meaning to carp or whine.
34. Rabbi Moshe Chaim Luzzatto, *The Way of God; The Knowing Heart; The Path of the Just* 1:1.
35. Also known as Malachi, leader of the Jewish people during the Babylonian Exile, and head of the Jewish "Supreme Court," the Sanhedrin. He was the author of the Biblical Books of Ezra and Malachi and also of most of the Book of Chronicles, *Divrei Hayamim* according to *Bava Batra* 15a and *Megillah* 15a. The particular court of Ezra was known as the "Men of the Great Assembly" according to *Ethics of the Fathers* 1:1.
36. *Megillah* 17b.
37. *Mishneh Torah*, ibid. 1:3-6; *Berachot* 26b, 33a-b.
38. *Berachot* 26b; *Mishneh Torah*, ibid. 1:5-6; The Talmud cites the two sources of prayers as a dispute,

however, Maimonides quotes both as legitimate sources.

39. Genesis 19:27.
40. The first daily communal offering, called the *Korban Tamid shel Shacharit.*
41. Genesis 24:63.
42. The last daily communal offering, called the *Korban Tamid shel Bein Ha'arbayim.*
43. Ibid. 28:11.
44. The left over parts of the two communal offerings (*eivarei hatamid*) were left burning on the altar overnight.
45. Rabbi Kook, ibid. p. 1, Commentary on "*Modeh Ani.*"
46. Ibid. *Horeb,* para. 628.
47. *Code of Jewish Law*, ibid. 58:1-2; 89:1.
48. *Horeb,* para. 643.
49. *Code of Jewish Law*, ibid. 233:1.
50. *Horeb,* para. 646.
51. *Code of Jewish Law,* ibid. 235:1,3.
52. *Berachot* 31a.
53. For a thorough discussion of women and prayer see Rabbi Menachem Nissel, *Rigshei Lev: Women and Tefillah*, Targum Press, Jerusalem, 2001.
54. *Code of Jewish Law,* ibid. 90:9.
55. *Megillah* 23b; *Code of Jewish Law*, ibid. 55, *Mishnah Berurah* 3.
56. Rabbi Reuven Margalit, *Margaliyot Hayam*, Sanhedrin 74b, para. 27.
57. Nachmanides, *Commentary on the Torah*, Exodus 13:15.
58. Rabbi Yehudah Halevy, *Kuzari*, 3:19.
59. *The Complete ArtScroll Siddur*, Ashkenaz, Ashkenaz, NY, 1984, pp. 2-3.
60. Rabbi Bachya ibn Pakuda, *Duties of the Heart*, Sha'ar Ha'avodah, Introduction and Chap. 6.
61. Rabbi Yitzchak Hutner, *Pachad Yitzchak*, Rosh Hashanah, Ma'amar 3.
62. Genesis 29:35; See also *Megillah* 12b.
63. Ibid. *The Complete ArtScroll Siddur*, Ashkenaz, pp. 14-15.
64. Ibid.
65. Shabbat 118b; ibid. *The Complete ArtScroll Siddur, Ashkenaz,* pp. 18-19.
66. Rabbi Kook, ibid. Commentary on Morning Blessings.
67. Ibid. 92:4, and 91.
68. *Code of Jewish Law*, ibid. 96:1 and 93:2-3.
69. *Berachot* 31a.
70. Ibid. *The Complete ArtScroll Siddur, Ashkenaz,* pp. 84-97.
71. *Code of Jewish Law*, ibid. 61:4; 61:5; 61:1.
72. Deuteronomy 6:4.
73. *Code of Jewish Law*, ibid. 61:13; *Midrash Tanchuma*, Lech Lecha, chap. 1; *Pesachim* 56a; Nachmanides, *Commentary on Deuteronomy*, ibid.; *The Complete ArtScroll Siddur, Ashkenaz,* pp. 90-91.
74. *Code of Jewish Law*; ibid. *Mishnah Berurah* 30.
75. Deuteronomy 6:5-9.
76. Ibid. 11:13-21.
77. Numbers 15:37-41.
78. Deuteronomy 16:3; *Berachot* 12b.
79. Maimonides, *Mishneh Torah*, Laws of Prayer 1:4.
80. Ibid.
81. Ibid. 4:16; *Code of Jewish Law*, ibid., 97:2 Ramah.
82. Rabbi Yehudah Halevy, *Kuzari*, 3:19.
83. Ibid.
84. *Siddur Otzar Hatefillot*, Iyun Tefillah on "*Kadosh, kadosh, kadosh*" citing Avudraham and Rabbi David Kimchi.
85. Ibid.
86. *Kuzari*, 2:3.
87. Psalms 111:10.
88. *Kuzari*, 3:19.
89. Maimonides, *Mishneh Torah*, Laws of Repentance, 1:1.
90. *Kiddushin* 30b.
91. *The Hirsch Siddur*, Feldheim Publishers, NY, 1978, p. 137.
92. *Code of Jewish Law*, ibid. 230:4, *Mishnah Berurah* ad loc., 6.

93. *Niddah* 70b.

94. *Siddur Otzar Hatefillot,* Iyun Tefillah ad loc., citing the *Sifri* in Deuteronomy, para. 40.

95. Isaiah 27:13.

96. Ibid. 1:26.

97. *Siddur Otzar Hatefillot,* Eitz Yosef ad loc.

98. *Berachot* 28b.

99. E.g. Early Christians and Sadducees — *Siddur Otzar Hatefillot,* Iyun Tefilah ad loc.

100. Zechariah 1:16.

101. II Samuel 7:16.

102. See chapter on "Belief, Knowledge and Faith," 12th Principle of Faith.

103. Nachmanides, Critique of Maimonides' *Sefer Hamitzvot,* Positive Mitzvah 5.

104. *Berachot* 60b.

105. *Code of Jewish Law,* ibid.119:1.

106. Hosea 14:3.

107. Maimonides, *Mishneh Torah,* Laws of Prayer, 1:4.

108. Second century compilation of the Oral Tradition by Rabbi Judah the Prince.

109. Psalms 29:11.

110. *Mishnah Uktzin* 3:12.

111. *Berachot* 16b.

112. Ibid.17a.

113. *Code of Jewish Law,* ibid. 122:1-2, *Mishnah Berurah* 119:12.

114. Job 25:2.

115. Liturgy.

116. *Rosh Hashanah* 34b; *Code of Jewish Law,* ibid. 122:1.

117. *The Hirsch Siddur,* ibid. p. 134.

118. Maimonides, *Sefer Hamitzvot,* Positive Mitzvah 9.

119. *Berachot* 32b.

120. Psalms 140:14.

121. *Code of Jewish Law,* ibid. 131:1.

122. Ibid. 131:2.

123. Rabbeinu Bachay, *Commentary on Numbers* 15:22.

124. *Code of Jewish Law,* ibid. 131:5-7.

125. *Mishnah Megillah* 3:3-6.

126. *Bava Kamma* 82a; Maimonides, *Mishneh Torah,* Laws of Prayer 12:1.

127. Circa 350 B.C.E.

128. *Bava Kamma* ibid.; Maimonides, ibid.

129. Leviticus 23:44.

130. *Megillah* 32a; *Aruch Hashulchan, Orach Chaim* 135:2.

131. See chapter on Torah Study.

132. *Kohen* — descendant of Aaron, High Priest and brother of Moses. Levi — descendant of *Levi,* son of Jacob. Israel — all other tribes of the Jewish people.

133. Deuteronomy 4:44.

134. Numbers 9:23.

135. Rabbi Moshe Shapiro.

136. Jerusalem Talmud *Megillah* 27b; *Code of Jewish Law,* ibid. 141:4.

137. Maimonides, *Mishneh Torah,* Laws of Prayer 13:1.

138. *Berachot* 8a; *Code of Jewish Law,* ibid. 285:1-7.

139. Mr. Solomon Becher of Melbourne, Australia.

140. Rabbi Shlomo Yitzchaki (acronym Rashi) One of the greatest of Biblical commentators. He lived in France, 11th century.

141. Mrs. Miriam Devorah Wiener, of blessed memory.

142. Meaning "exemption," because through this we are "exempted" from reading the Torah.

143. *Levush Haorah, Orach Chaim,* 284.

144. *Code of Jewish Law,* ibid. 135:1.

145. *Code of Jewish Law,* ibid. 141:2; *Mishnah Berurah* ad loc. 8; Blessing can be found in *The Complete ArtScroll Siddur, Ashkenaz,* ibid., pp. 142-143.

146. *Code of Jewish Law,* ibid. 282:1-4 and 488:3 respectively.

147. *Berachot* 4b; Rashi ad loc.

148. Ibid.

149. *Avudraham,* Weekday Prayers.

150. *Mishnah Tamid,* 7:4; *Code of Jewish Law,* ibid. 132:2, Ramah.

151. *Code of Jewish Law,* ibid. 132:2, Ramah.

152. *Teshuvot HaGeonim,* Shaarei Teshuvah 43; *Sefer Kol Bo,* 15.

153. *Mishnah Sofrim,* 10:7.

154. *The Hirsch Siddur,* ibid. pp. 104-105.

155. *Horayot* 6a.

156. *The Hirsch Siddur,* ibid.

157. *Code of Jewish Law, Orach Chaim* 68, *Be'er Heitev* 2 and *Mishnah Berurah* 2.

Blessings and Appreciation

Laws and significance of blessings

"Life's a Bore!"

Many people seem to be bored with their lives. They look for diversion in activities such as swimming with sharks, bungee jumping and extreme sports. Others obsessively pursue whatever is new — fashion, music, or high-tech gadgets. This boredom really stems not from a lack of novelty, but from a lack of appreciation of life itself and all the blessings of life. A person who takes pleasure in his very existence, who savors the beauty of the natural world and the richness of human relationships is unlikely to be bored, or to take anything for granted. A young child finds the world endlessly fascinating; but too often the sense of wonder erodes in adulthood. Through the recitation of blessings, Judaism tries to help us retain this unspoiled perspective and increases our appreciation of the pleasure and wonder of life.

Rabbi Yehudah Halevy, a 12th-century philosopher and poet, taught,[1] "God wants us to rejoice in the good that He has given us, as the verse states, 'You shall rejoice in all the good that the Lord your God has given you.'"[2]

A crucial technique in achieving this goal is enhancing our awareness of what we really have. This is done by saying a prayer of appreciation to God before we benefit from His world and by thanking Him after we enjoy His blessings. These prayers are called *berachot,* blessings.[3] If we go through each day, understanding the blessings that we recite, we can become happier, more generous people, grateful to God for all His goodness.[4]

Some of these blessings are recited before partaking of a pleasure, others praise God for the wonders of the natural world or beautiful sights and some are recited before the performance of a *mitzvah.*[5] All of these prayers enable us to pause, reflect and to appreciate what we are about to do, what we have just done, or what we are experiencing.

Rather than a generic "thank you, God," Jewish law specifies a different blessing for every category of food and enjoyment. In this way, Judaism impresses upon us the abundance of good, the diversity of pleasures and the rich complexity of God's gifts to us. Even though we could survive without things like cinnamon, chocolate, kiwi, roses and magnificent sunsets (OK, not chocolate), God chose to create a world that is abundant in pleasurable foods, fragrances, sights and experiences. In our blessings, we acknowledge this diversity by saying specific prayers for each pleasure, thereby enhancing our gratitude for every one.[6]

Please and Thank You

The Talmud[7] points out an apparent contradiction. One verse in Psalms states that, "the world, and everything in it, is God's."[8] Yet another verse states, "the heavens are God's heaven, but the world He gave to man."[9] The Sages explain that the first verse refers to the world before one has said a blessing, and the second verse applies after one has said a blessing. The Talmud[10] deduces from this that one may not derive benefit from this world without saying a blessing. It is essential to our understanding of our relationship with God that we acknowledge Him as Creator and Sustainer of the world. The fact that God created the world *ex nihilo,* from nothing, and continues to sustain it, confers upon Him absolute rights of ownership. We acknowledge this ownership and our indebtedness to God by saying a blessing before we eat or derive any benefit from His world. Only when we have done this, we have earned the right to partake of the world and enjoy it. Thus, in addition to the psychological benefits that it confers, saying *berachot* is a moral imperative as well. It is the way we request permission to use God's world and show our awareness of the existence of the Benefactor.

Highs and Lows

In moments of happiness, whether at the birth of a child, upon hearing good news, or even when putting on a new suit, we say,[11] "Blessed are You, God, our God, King of the universe, Who has kept us alive, sustained us, and brought us to this time."

When a person hears sad news, such as the death of a relative or friend, he must recite a blessing as well:[12] "Blessed are You, God, our God, King of the universe, the true judge." The *Code of Jewish Law*[13] writes that the blessing over bad news should, ideally, be said with the same feelings of love for God as the blessing for good news. A believer recognizes that everything that happens, whether it seems good or bad from the limited human perspective, is for the ultimate good. Such a person serves God with joy even when misfortune befalls him, because he understands that a parent's love can be manifested when the parent punishes the child, or says "no," just as much as when the parent rewards the child, or says "yes."

Judaism specifies *berachot* for all occasions because we believe that every event in an individual's life provides an opportunity to grow spiritually and ethically. The blessings express both our gratitude to God for the good things that come our way, and our recognition that even that what appears to be bad is ultimately for our good as well.[14] Reciting these prayers enables us to channel the emotions from the highs and the lows toward a closer connection with God. Times of happiness and confidence or sadness and confusion can equally strengthen our relationship with the Creator.

The Patriarch Jacob exemplified this approach to life in the most extreme circumstances. The Book of Genesis tells us that Jacob did not see his son Joseph for 22 years, nor did he know what had happened to him during all that time. When Jacob finally met Joseph in Egypt, they embraced and, as one would expect, they cried. When the Torah[15] describes the meeting, however, the word "cry" is written in singular form, indicating that only one of the two was crying. The great Biblical commentator Rashi[16] explains that, in fact, only Joseph embraced and cried. His father Jacob did not do so because he was reciting *Shema*[17] at the time. This seems a strange time to pray. Jacob sees his beloved son after a 22-year separation, and he chooses that precise moment to recite *Shema*? The Maharal of Prague offers the following explanation:[18]

> When Jacob saw his son Joseph as a king, the love and awe of the Holy One, Blessed be He, filled his heart. [He realized that] everything that God does is good and perfect, and that He rewards those who fear Him. This is a characteristic of a pious individual; when a good event occurs he draws closer to God as a result of the good … that God has bestowed upon him.

Although it may be difficult to imagine ourselves acting as Jacob did, we attempt to emulate this ideal by reciting blessings on every significant occasion. In this way we direct all our emotions toward the love of God.

Impulse or Intellect?

When I was growing up in Australia, I had a pet dog — a lovable cocker spaniel-Labrador cross. I used to give him his dinner on the patio at the back of our house, around the same time that our family had supper. The contrast between the two suppers was profound. When the dog's bowl came to within about a foot of the ground, he would bury his face in it and not take it out until the bowl was cleaned on a molecular level. He would not wait, pause, smell the aroma, or even take a breath until every particle of dog food was consumed. In contrast, we would wash our hands in a specific way and say a blessing, then start the meal with bread, over which we would say another blessing. We ate our food slowly, course by course, and ended with another, longer prayer, Grace After Meals. Finally, we thanked my mother before helping to clear the table.

Thankfully, very few people eat in the same way as my dog. Many people, however, do eat without thinking, without appreciation and without thanking anyone (neither God, their mother nor their spouse). My father often uses the evil Esau as a model of how one should not eat. The verse in Genesis[19] states: "Jacob gave Esau bread and lentil stew — he ate and drank, got up and left; thus Esau scorned the birthright."

My father would always say, "Look at Esau, 'he ate and drank' without washing and saying a blessing, 'he got up' without saying Grace After Meals, and 'he left' without saying 'Thank you'!"

Eating is a very instinctive act, but it can be transformed into something meaningful, involving the brain as well as the stomach, by saying blessings before and after eating. The *berachot* remind us that human beings have needs beyond the purely physical. As psychologist Victor Frankl pointed out, more than food, clothing, or even pleasure, man's greatest need is for meaning in life.[20] The *berachot* are powerful tools that inject meaning into even the most mundane and physical actions of human existence.

Washing Away Routine

Another way the Sages raised our consciousness about how we can access spirituality when eating is by obligating us to wash our hands before we eat bread.[21] In the days of the Temple in Jerusalem, the Priests (*Kohanim*) always purified themselves completely before eating tithes and other sanctified foods. King Solomon's[22] court legislated that all Jews imitate this priestly behavior[23] by washing their hands and reciting a blessing before eating bread. An additional motivation for this decree was hygiene, a revolutionary concept in general society until about 150 years ago.[24] *Netilat yadayim*, washing the hands, is performed by pouring water from a cup[25] twice over the right hand then twice over the left.[26] Using a cup to pour the water makes the washing more of a conscious process and distinguishes it from washing purely for the sake of cleanliness. Rabbi Samson Raphael Hirsch notes that *netilat yadayim* also helps refine the way a person eats:

Washing hands before eating bread, using a traditional "washing cup."

> *If you consecrate your hands for the meal ... [and understand] that even your lower physical functions should be Divine service ... will you then allow yourself to be taken captive by allurements of pleasure ...? [If you] realize that your eating should only be a strengthening for life, will you then be able to eat more than is necessary for this? ... Be temperate ... remain master over the animal instincts in you and ultimately ennoble them ... By thus harmonizing the conflicting forces within you, you will achieve that unity and holiness which are reflections of the Unity and Holiness of your Father in heaven.*[27]

Not By Bread Alone ...

Kabbalists[28] explain the profound significance of *berachot* in dimensions that are less evident to human intellect. Everything in the world contains sparks of spirituality, the creative energy of God that sustains all existence. The *berachot* serve to capture the sparks of spirituality in the food we eat and in everything we experience. It is this spiritual element of the food that is really essential. The connection between the body and the soul necessitates both physical nourishment for the body and spiritual nourishment for the soul. When we eat and fulfill the attendant commandments, such as the laws of *Kashrut*[29] and the blessings, we provide for both the body and the soul. With this seemingly mundane act, we cement the connection between the physical world and the spiritual world.[30] This insight also offers a key to understanding the famous verse in Deuteronomy:

> ... He fed you the manna[31] that you did not know, nor did your forefathers know, in order to make you know that not by bread alone does man live, rather by everything that emanates from the mouth of God does man live.[32]

An individual will not survive "by bread alone" because that sustains only the physical aspects of the human being. The spiritual dimension thrives on "everything that emanates from the mouth of God," namely, our connection to God. One of the ways we can nurture that connection and capture the Divine light that exists in everything is by acknowledging God and connecting to Him every time we eat, by saying *berachot*.

What Does "Bless" Really Mean?

What do we actually mean when we say, "Blessed are You," to God? When someone sneezes and we say, "Bless you," we are really praying to God to heal the person who may be sick.[33] Clearly this cannot be the intent when we say, "Bless You," to God. The Hebrew word for blessing, *berachah*, is related to the word *"bereichah,"* which means "pool," or more specifically, the pool into which the waters of a spring collect. When we describe God as "blessed" we mean that He is the ultimate "pool" of all that is good. He is the spring from which all of existence emanates. We acknowledge this reality by saying a *berachah*.[34] We ask God to continue to pour forth His influence and His good upon us, and upon the whole world, because we want God's presence and influence to be felt by every being in the world.[35] Beyond acknowledging God as the source of all existence, a *berachah* is the means by which we reveal God to others and make His presence known in the world.[36]

The word *berachah* is also related to the word *berech*, knee.[37] Some commentators understand the word "blessing" as an expression of praise and subservience. When we say, "Blessed are You, God," we are engaging in a verbal "bending of the knee" in humility, praise and acknowledgment of our dependence on God.[38]

Format of the Blessings

The structure and content of our blessings were composed at the beginning of the Second Temple era by Sages known as the Men of the

Great Assembly.[39] These scholars took great pains to reflect the beauty and grandeur of the spiritual world in the words of the blessings. The basic format of all blessings begins with the following phrase:

> *Blessed are You, God, our God, King of the universe, Who has* ...[40]

The continuation is determined by the specific focus of that blessing, such as:

> ... *created the fruit of the tree*
> ... *created the fruit of the ground*
> ... *given pleasant smells to herbs*
> ... *created everything with His word*
> ... *sanctified us in His commandments.*

Let's look at the deeper implications of each word.

Blessed

This word, as we explained, acknowledges God as the source of all blessings.

Are You

— teaches us that we have a personal and direct relationship with God because His presence permeates all of time and place. We can therefore address Him as "You."[41]

God

We use the specific Hebrew name of God that indicates that He was, is and always will be. It also means that He created and sustains all of existence.[42]

Our

This teaches us that we, the Jewish people, have a special relationship with God because He took us out of Egypt, and gave us the Torah and His commandments. Therefore we can say "our God."[43]

God

— Who is powerful and the source of all powers.[44]

King of the Universe

A king is concerned with, involved in and directs His kingdom. God is not just a distant Creator: He is our Lawgiver, our Commander and our King.

The pleasure that is about to be enjoyed is then identified specifically, as noted above. Just as the pleasures of the world are unique and varied, so too, a proper thanks to God must be unique and varied.[45] After enjoying a delicious meal, a guest may express a general "Thanks." One who feels real gratitude however, will acknowledge specific aspects of the host's kindness. ("The stale bread crumbs in water were delicious; I must have the recipe.")

Before and After

Some of the *berachot* that we say are explicitly mandated in the Bible. The obligation to bless God after eating a meal is stated explicitly in the Torah:

> *You shall eat, and you shall be satisfied and you shall bless the Lord, your God, for the good land that He gave you.*[46]

We fulfill this commandment by reciting the Grace After Meals[47] (called *Birkat Hamazon* in Hebrew, *bentching*, meaning "blessing," in Yiddish) after eating a meal that included bread. A shorter version is said after eating other foods. The blessings before eating or performing a *mitzvah*, or on special occasions, however were composed and ordained by the Sanhedrin, circa 400 B.C.E.[48]

The practice of saying blessings *before* eating raises an interesting question. If the reasons detailed above for it are indeed valid, why is that from a Biblical perspective we are only obligated to say a blessing *after* eating, and not before? A scholar of the last century answered that a person who is feeling quite full and content may tend to forget God, and is in danger of becoming self-centered and egotistical, as the verse states, "And you will eat and be satiated... and forget the Lord, your God."[49] The scholar explains:

> *Therefore God commanded us that when we eat and are satisfied we should mention the name of God in gratitude, and bless Him and remember that He is the One Who gave us the strength to accomplish what we have done, and that we are eating from His hand to fill ourselves when hungry.*[50]

The Torah only obligates those who are at greatest spiritual risk (of forgetting God when satiated) to counteract that danger with a blessing. One who is hungry or in need is less vulnerable, therefore his obligation to bless God before eating is Rabbinic and not Biblical.

Although the Biblical obligation to bless God after eating only applies to a meal that includes a minimum amount of bread, the Sages legislated in the spirit of the law that a blessing be said after anything that we eat.[51] Since the obligation in these cases is not of Biblical origin, the after-blessings are much shorter — consisting of either one long,[52] or one short blessing.[53] The full Grace After Meals consists of four lengthy blessings with some additional prayers.

Due to the importance of the Grace After Meals, the Sages formulated a communal recitation of this prayer, known as *zimun*,[54] in which one individual formally invites the others to participate in the blessing. They respond with a short blessing and continue the Grace After Meals together, with certain parts said aloud and responsively.[55]

Blessings for Mitzvot

The Sages also instituted blessings to be said before[56] the performance of a *mitzvah*.[57] The format of these blessings is, *Blessed are You, God, our God, King of the universe, Who has sanctified us in His commandments and ... commanded us to ...*

Two principal ideas underlie the blessings before commandments. One is much like the reason we say blessings over food. We are thanking God for the opportunity to do His commandments and achieve closeness to Him. We do not look at the commandments as a burden, but as incredible gifts. Therefore we say "thank you" before we fulfill them. Although we know that the *mitzvot* are obligations, we appreciate that God gives us these opportunities to build a relationship with Him. Therefore we thank Him for his love and kindness.[58]

Another reason for saying these blessings is based on a legal concept regarding the *mitzvot*. The fulfillment of a *mitzvah* is only complete if a person also thinks about the action that he is doing. In the words of the Talmud:[59] "*Mitzvot* require intent (*kavanah*)." The performance of a *mitzvah* should be an expression of the person's inner self, not merely a physical motion. The Rabbis wanted us to focus on the fact that we are doing a commandment of God, to think about what we are doing, rather than going through rote actions. Therefore, they decreed that we stop and recite a blessing before doing a *mitzvah*.[60] (Regarding the blessings before Torah study, see Chapter 23 on Torah Study, subheading "It's a Mitzvah!")

Sights, Sounds and Smells

Blessings are not limited to eating and doing *mitzvot*. There are also blessings relating to sight, sound and smell.[61] When we see manifestations of God's power, wisdom or providence in the world, we also say a blessing. When, for example, one sees lightning and hears thunder, two blessings are recited, one that mentions God's power and strength filling the universe, and another other that reminds us of the fact that God created the world.[62] When we see a beautiful and majestic natural phenomenon, such as Niagara Falls or exceptionally beautiful creatures, we also bless God that "such is in His world."[63] In spring, when the first blossoms appear on fruit trees, we declare that "nothing is lacking in His universe, and He created in it beautiful [good] creatures and beautiful [good] trees, to give humanity pleasure in them."[64] Upon smelling fragrant spices, we praise God for "creating all manner of fragrant spices."[65]

Saying *berachot* on such a variety of experiences helps us appreciate the beauty and grandeur of the world around us. As we recite the blessings with awareness and understanding we can begin to learn, in the words of a contemporary Jewish philosopher, "the art of living in amazement."[66]

Berachot, Briefly

Blessings included in the daily prayers are discussed in Chapter 24, Getting Up on the Right Side of Bed. For a complete list of blessings see *The Complete ArtScroll Siddur* pp. 182 – 231.

Some laws pertaining to the most frequent blessings:

1. Before eating or drinking any food or smelling a fragrant herb or plant, one first recites a blessing.[67]

2. A blessing is recited *before* eating or drinking, no matter how little is consumed.[68] A blessing is recited *after* eating or drinking, only if one has eaten about 1 fl. oz. (28 cc.) of food, or has drunk about 3 fl. oz.(86 cc.) of liquid.[69]

3. If one is eating or drinking a nonfood for therapeutic purposes (such as medication), one does not say a blessing.[70]

4. The blessings should be said slowly and clearly,[71] keeping in mind the meaning of the words, especially God's Name.[72]

5. The blessings should ideally be said in Hebrew, but may be recited in any language that one understands.[73]

6. The blessings begin with "Blessed are You, God, Our God, King of the Universe ..."[74]

   ▸ **For vegetables**
   continue, "Who created the fruit of the ground."

   ▸ **For fruit**
   continue, "Who created the fruit of the tree."

   ▸ **After washing one's hands before bread**
   continue, "Who has sanctified us with His commandments, and commanded us regarding washing the hands." One should not speak after this blessing until he has eaten bread.[75]

   ▸ **For bread**
   continue, "Who brings bread forth from the ground."

   ▸ **For anything else** (aside from bread) **made of wheat, barley, rye, spelt or oats,** and also on **rice**
   continue, "Who creates species of nourishment."

- ▸ **For wine or grape juice**
  continue, "Who creates the fruit of the vine."

- ▸ **For any other foods or drinks**
  (meat, cheese, milk, water, etc.) or when one is unsure of the appropriate blessing, continue, "through Whose word, everything came to be."[76]

6. There are a variety of blessings for fragrances, but the most common blessing (and the one recited if one is uncertain of which blessing to say) is "Who creates species of fragrance."[77]

7. After eating bread, one recites the *Birkat Hamazon,* Grace After Meals (ibid. pp. 184 – 195).

8. After eating anything else (aside from bread) made from flour of wheat, barley, rye, spelt or oats, or after eating one of the species of fruits with which Israel is blessed (grapes and grape products, figs, pomegranates, dates and olives), one recites the blessing of *Me'ein Shalosh* (ibid. pp. 200 – 201).[78]

9. After eating anything else, one recites *Borei Nefashot,* "Who creates living things" (ibid. top of page 202 – 203).[79]

10. Before performing (most) *mitzvot,* one recites the appropriate blessing.[80]

11. One who hears someone else say a blessing should say "*Amen*" afterward, to show his agreement and belief in the blessing.[81]

12. If one forgot to say a *berachah* before eating or drinking, he may still say it as long as he is still eating or drinking.[82]

13. If one forgot to say *Birkat Hamazon,* one may still say it as long as he is still satiated from the meal,[83] even if he has moved from the place where he ate.[84]

For Further Reading

- ▸ *A Guide to Blessings* (food) by Rabbi Naftali Hoffner (OU/NCSY)

- ▸ *Birchon* — Schottenstein Interlinear Edition (ArtScroll/Mesorah)

- ▸ *The NCSY Bencher* by David Olivestone (OU/NCSY)

NOTES

References to books of the Talmud refer to the Babylonian Talmud unless otherwise noted.

1. Rabbi Yehudah Halevy, *Kuzari,* 3:11.
2. Deuteronomy 26:11.
3. Ibid., *Kuzari.*
4. Heard from Rabbi Nathan T. Lopez-Cardozo.
5. Maimonides, *Mishneh Torah,* Laws of Blessings, 1:4.
6. *Berachot* 40a.
7. Ibid., 35a-b.
8. Psalms 24:1.
9. Ibid. 115:16.
10. Ibid. *Berachot.*
11. *Code of Jewish Law, Orach Chaim* 222.
12. Ibid., 222:2.
13. Ibid.
14. *Berachot* 48b.
15. Genesis 46:29.
16. Genesis ibid. ad loc.
17. See chapter on Prayer.
18. Maharal, *Gur Aryeh,* Genesis ibid., ad loc.
19. Genesis 25:34.
20. Viktor E. Frankl, *Man's Search for Meaning,* pp. 119-122. Washington Square Press, NY, 1959.
21. *Code of Jewish Law, Orach Chaim,* 158:1.
22. Ibid. *Eruvin* 21b.
23. *Chullin* 106a.
24. Ibid. *Chullin, Tosafot* ad loc., "*mitzvah lishmoa.*"
25. Ibid. 159:1.
26. *Code of Jewish Law,* ibid. 162:2 Ramah.
27. Rabbi Samson Raphael Hirsch, *Horeb,* The Soncino Press, NY, 1962, par. 464.
28. Scholars of Jewish mysticism.
29. See chapter on Soul Food: The Kosher Dietary Laws.
30. Rabbi Yishayahu Halevi Horowitz, *Shnei Luchot Habrit,* Sha'ar

Ha'otiyot, Emek Brachah, par. 2; *Parshat Vayikra,* Torah Ohr, par. 4.
31. The food that miraculously fell from heaven while the Jews were in the Sinai Desert.
32. Deuteronomy 8:3.
33. *Mishnah Berurah,* 230:7.
34. *Responsa Rashba,* vol. 5, 50-52.
35. Rabbi Chaim of Volozhin, *Nefesh HaChaim,* 2:2.
36. Rabbeinu Bachya, *Commentary on the Torah,* Deuteronomy 8:10.
37. Matityahu Clark, *Etymological Dictionary of Biblical Hebrew,* p. 31, *barech,* Feldheim Publishers, Jerusalem, 1999.
38. Rabbi David Kimchi, *Sefer Hashorashim, Berach.*
39. Maimonides, *Mishneh Torah,* Laws of Blessings 1:5. See chapter on Prayer.
40. *Berachot* 12a, 40b.
41. Rabbi Chaim of Volozhin, *Nefesh Hachaim,* 2:4.
42. There are numerous names of God, each with its own significance. *Code of Jewish Law, Orach Chaim* 5:1.
43. Nachmanides, *Commentary on the Torah, Exodus* 20:2.
44. Ibid.
45. *Berachot* 40a.
46. Deuteronomy 8:10.
47. *The Complete ArtScroll Siddur, Ashkenaz,* pp. 182-195.
48. Maimonides, *Mishneh Torah,* Laws of Blessings 1:2.
49. Deuteronomy 8:11-14.
50. Rabbi Meir Simchah of Dvinsk, *Meshech Chochmah,* Deuteronomy 8:10.
51. Maimonides, *Mishneh Torah,* Laws of Blessings, 1:1.
52. *The Complete ArtScroll Siddur, Ashkenaz,* pp. 200-201.
53. Ibid. pp. 202-203 (top paragraph).
54. Mishnah *Berachot* 7:1.

55. *The Complete ArtScroll Siddur, Ashkenaz,* pp. 184-185.

56. *Pesachim* 7b.

57. *Berachot* 11b; *Code of Jewish Law, Orach Chaim,* 47:1-2.

58. Maharal, *Netivot Olam,* Netiv HaTorah, Chap. 7.

59. *Berachot* 13a; *Code of Jewish Law, Orach Chaim,* 60:4.

60. Rabbi Yechezkel Landau, *Responsa Noda BiYehudah, Yoreh Deah* 1:93.

61. For a complete list of these blessings, see *The Complete ArtScroll Siddur, Ashkenaz,* pp. 224-231.

62. *Code of Jewish Law, Orach Chaim,* 227:1-3.

63. *Berachot* 58b; *Code of Jewish Law,* ibid., 225:10.

64. *Berachot* 43b; *Code of Jewish Law,* ibid., 226:1.

65. Ibid. 43a; Ibid. 215:2.

66. From a lecture of Rabbi Dr. Nathan T. Lopez-Cardozo: "Halachah: The Art of Living in Amazement."

67. *Berachot* 35a-b; *Code of Jewish Law, Orach Chaim* 210:1, 215:1.

68. Ibid. 210:1.

69. Ibid.

70. Ibid. 204:8.

71. *Berachot* 47a, Rashi ad loc.

72. *Code of Jewish Law,* ibid. 5:1.

73. Ibid. 62:2, *Mishnah Berurah* 3; *Biur Halachah,* 62:2 and 101:4; *Teshuvot Vehanhagot* 1:355 rules that if one prays in a language other than Hebrew, the Name of God should be said in Hebrew.

74. Ibid. 214:1.

75. Ibid. 167:6.

76. Paragraphs 6-12, Mishnah *Berachot,* chap. 6.

77. *Code of Jewish Law, Orach Chaim,* 216.

78. Ibid. 208:1.

79. Ibid. 207:1.

80. *Pesachim* 7b.

81. *Code of Jewish Law,* ibid. 215:1-2.

82. Ibid. 172:2-3.

83. Ibid. 184:5.

84. *Mishnah Berurah* 5.

Who Are the Jews, and Where Do They Come From?

A brief Jewish family history

Origin of the Species

The Jewish people originated in Sumer[1] when Abraham was born in 1812 B.C.E.,[2] or 1948 years after the creation of Adam. Sumer was the cultural center of its age; it boasted the pyramid temples known as the Ziggurats of Ur. The Epic of Gilgamesh[3] and the Code of Hammurabi[4] were both written there.[5] At the time of Abraham, Sumer and the entire world were focused on idolatry as a way of life and belief. Some worshiped two or three gods; to many, every natural phenomenon represented another god or force to worship.[6] Human sacrifice was a common method of appeasing the gods, and kings claimed that they were gods or descended from them.[7]

Abraham, The Revolutionary

Abraham was the world's first religious revolutionary; he questioned, debated and challenged pagan beliefs and stood alone against the whole world.[8] This is one reason that he was called *"Avraham HaIvri,"* Abraham the Hebrew. The word "Hebrew (*Ivri*)" is related to the word "*ever*," meaning "the other side" — because the whole word stood on "one side" and Abraham stood on the "other side"[9] — which has been true of his descendants for much of history.

With his brilliant intellect and spiritual sensitivity, Abraham discovered that the true nature of the world was one of unity, harmony and design. He came to the conclusion that there is one God Who created and sustained all of existence and from Whom everything emanates, both light and darkness, water and fire, good and bad.[10]

This God demanded of mankind moral behavior, not blood offerings. Abraham understood God as a giver, and as the ultimate "philanthropist," so Abraham and his wife Sarah emulated God by extending hospitality and kindness to all.[11]

Abraham and Sarah wanted the entire world to know God as well.[12] They taught others and succeeded in bringing people to belief in ethical monotheism.[13] After Abraham had developed to a high spiritual level, God gave him his first commandment. "Go from your land, your birthplace and your father's house to the land that I shall show you."[14] By sending Abraham to this specially designated land — what today is Israel — God gave Abraham an environment for spiritual development;[15] in promising the land to Abraham's descendants, He also gave him one of the primary hallmarks of nationhood — a homeland.[16]

Because Sarah was infertile and Abraham needed offspring to whom he would pass his spiritual mission, she urged Abraham to marry her maidservant, Hagar. Their son was Ishmael, who became the father of the Arab nations.[17] At the age of 99, Abraham was commanded by God to circumcise himself. (The Arabs today practice circumcision and are monotheistic, both remnants of Abraham's legacy.) After his circumcision, God promised Abraham and Sarah that they would have a child who would continue their heritage.[18] A year later Isaac was born, though Abraham and Sarah were both at an advanced age. When Isaac was 8 days old, God commanded Abraham to circumcise him and all males in his household as a sign of the eternal covenant between God and the people of Abraham.[19]

Monotheism: The Next Generation

Isaac married Rebecca, a relative of Abraham from Sumer, and they had twin sons, Jacob and Esau.[20] Jacob is described as a "wholesome man who dwelt in the tents"[21] [i.e., a man who sought to perfect his spirituality]. The spark that Abraham and Sarah had kindled was now passed down to Jacob, who also married Abraham's relatives. He married two sisters, Rachel and Leah, and their half sisters, Bilhah and Zilpah. These four mothers bore the children who became the 12 tribes of Israel. Jacob's name was changed by God to Israel, a name meaning "he who becomes great before God" or "he who will struggle with the Divine."[22]

The Family Becomes a Nation

As Jacob's family grew, his focus turned toward building a nation that would have an impact on the world.[23] The focus of the Children of Israel was now inward, but the purpose of this inward focus was for the sake of perfecting themselves in order to create a moral, monotheistic example for the world to follow.

There was, however, discord among the brothers. Joseph's vision of the Jewish people included himself as monarch, and the other brothers were suspicious of his ambitions. In their experience, kings were despotic dictators and their subjects merely bricks to build the fame and ambition of a single dynasty, lowering the status of the individual. The brothers envisioned the future of their nation as a society based on freedom and equality, where the value and nobility of every human being is recognized, and God alone is the ultimate Sovereign over all people.[24]

As a result of their differences, the brothers sold Joseph as a slave to nomadic traders who eventually sold him in Egypt. Through a series of providential incidents, Joseph became, in effect, prime minister of Egypt. Eventually, to escape famine in Canaan (Israel) the rest of his family came to settle in Egypt. The family was once again united, reconciled and complete, but was now in a state of exile in a foreign land.[25]

The enslavement, servitude and oppression of the Children of Israel began in Egypt once Joseph and all his brothers died.[26] A new pharaoh arose who enslaved them through trickery, propaganda and force.[27] The exile lasted for 210 years and the people suffered both physically and spiritually.[28]

Go Down, Moses!

Pharaoh's astrologers told him that an Israelite boy would be born who would lead his people out of Egypt, so he immediately decreed that all Israelite newborn boys should be killed. The mother of Moses saved her son by putting him in a floating crib on the Nile. Ironically, he was found by the daughter of Pharaoh, who had compassion on the child, saved him and adopted him as her own. She named him Moshe (Moses) which means, "drawn from the water."[29] Moses was raised in the royal court of Egypt. However she hired an Israelite nurse to care for him, who "happened" to be Moses' mother, who imbued him with a deep sense of his identity. As

Moses matured, the Torah tells us that "he went out to his brothers,"[30] identifying with his Israelite brothers and sisters in their slavery.

Moses: Justice and Compassion

Moses was also prepared to take action to defend his people, and when he witnessed an Egyptian beating an Israelite, he killed the Egyptian.[31] His concern was not merely ethnic; Moses could not tolerate injustice even within his own people, and the next episode in his life describes his preventing one Israelite from hitting another.[32] His killing of the Egyptian taskmaster became known, and Moses fled from Egypt to Midian to escape capture and prosecution. In Midian, he came upon another test of his passion for justice.[33] He arrived at a well in Midian and encountered local shepherds who were accosting some shepherd-girls. Here again, Moses intervened and saved the girls, who were daughters of the one monotheist in Midian, Jethro.[34]

Moses married one of Jethro's daughters, Ziporah, and they had two sons, Gershom and Eliezer. Moses, like his ancestors, chose the quiet, contemplative life of a shepherd, and worked for his father-in-law, caring for his flocks. One day a lamb ran away from the flock in search of water and Moses found it bleating in distress. He carried the lamb to a source of water. While he was engaged in this act of compassion he noticed an amazing phenomenon: a bush that was burning but was not being consumed by the flames. The Sages of the Midrash explain that although Moses was clearly a seeker of justice, God also wanted to test his compassion and quality of mercy before speaking with him.[35] Moses approached the bush, and there received his first prophecy from God: He gave him the task of taking the Children of Israel out of Egypt and bringing them back to the mountain of the bush, Mount Sinai,[36] so that the entire nation would hear the word of God.

The Exodus

Moses joined his older siblings, Aaron and Miriam, in Egypt as leaders of the Children of Israel. He and Aaron commanded Pharaoh, in the name of God, to free their people. Pharaoh refused to recognize God and His authority and ignored the demands of Moses.[37] God now brought the Ten Plagues as punishment for Egypt's past sins and as a warning for the future. The plagues culminated in the death of the Egyptians' firstborn sons, and the departure of the Israelite nation from Egypt. Even after all this, however, Pharaoh assembled his loyal troops to pursue them as they left. The Children of Israel came to the Sea of Reeds[38] where God split the waters for them, and engulfed the pursuing Egyptians in the returning waves.[39]

The Sinai Desert

Although they were miraculously saved from Egyptian slavery and witnessed the Ten Plagues, the Children of Israel still had their doubts about the validity of Moses' leadership and his mission.[40] When they saw the Egyptian army in pursuit, they taunted Moses with classic Jewish ironic humor:[41] *"Were there no graves in Egypt? Is that why you took us out to die in the desert?"*[42]

In the barren Sinai Desert, their stubborn streak came to the fore. Whenever food and water shortages were feared, the people complained to Moses and challenged the wisdom of leaving Egypt.[43] Despite all these complaints, God saw good qualities in this people. True, they were cynical, stubborn and "stiff necked,"[44] but all of these qualities were survival skills necessary for their future life as a nation. History has borne this out. Had we not been cynical, we would have followed the influence of every "prophet" or "miracle-worker" that came along. Had we not been stubborn, we would have given in long ago to the pressures of anti-Semitism, assimilation and missionary activities and would have disappeared as a nation. A nation that is stiff necked is a nation that is passionate about the truth and is not easily swayed.[45]

Mount Sinai

Six weeks after leaving Egypt, the Children of Israel camped at the base of Mount Sinai.[46] The Biblical census of the Israelite army at that time indicates that there were "about 600,000 men on foot"[47] over the age of 20. The estimate of the total population, including women and those under 20, comes to about two or three million.[48] At Mount Sinai the entire nation prepared themselves to enter into an eternal covenant with God by accepting His law, the Torah, unconditionally.[49]

The Torah describes this dramatic and seminal event in Jewish and world history in great detail.[50] It must have been terrifying: The Torah relates that the people trembled as they saw fire and smoke coming from the mountain and heard increasingly louder blasts of a *shofar,* a ram's horn. They heard God speak to Moses and declare him to be His prophet and the one who would bring the message of God to the Children of Israel.[51] They entered into an eternal covenant with God at Mount Sinai.[52] God then communicated the first two of the Ten Statements directly to His people. (The Biblical Hebrew term, *Aseret Hadibrot*, is usually mistranslated as the Ten Commandments.) As the intensity of this experience was more than they could stand, the people asked that God transmit the rest of the Torah to them through Moses.[53]

The revelation of the full contents of the Torah continued throughout the 40 years in the desert. They received the written text of the Torah, the Five Books of Moses,[54] as well as the explanations of the text in oral form, known as the Oral Torah.[55] During those 40 years, they experienced the ultimate educational seminar: Their food and water were miraculously supplied by God; for most of the time they had no economic, political or military problems and they had the world's greatest teachers instructing them in the Torah.[56]

Entry to the Land of Israel

Moses and Aaron passed away before the nation entered the Land of Israel and are buried east of the Jordan River in the mountains of Moab. (The demise of Miriam had occurred somewhat earlier.) Moses' primary disciple and most dedicated student was Joshua; and before Moses died, God told him to bestow his authority on Joshua. He was appointed as the leader who would take the Israelites into the Land of Israel.[57]

The conquest of the Land took seven years of battles and then seven years of settlement and division of the land among the Twelve Tribes of Israel. The events of the conquest and settlement, as well as the external and internal borders of the Land, are recorded in the Book of Joshua.

Prophets and Kings

After the death of Joshua, the Children of Israel were ruled by "Judges" who were great scholars, and in some cases prophets, who acted in place of a monarch. Some of the most famous of these leaders were Eli, Samson and Deborah, whose lives and teachings are recorded in the Book of Judges. The period of the Judges lasted approximately 400 years, until the prophet Samuel anointed the first king, Saul. Saul was a pious king, but he made a grievous error during his reign, eventually losing the monarchy. He died a tragic death, together with his sons, in battle against the Philistines.[58]

King David, King Solomon and the First Holy Temple

At God's direction, Samuel anointed David, son of Jesse[59] and great-grandson of Ruth, the famous Moabite woman who had converted to Judaism.[60] King David succeeded in uniting his people and also fought many successful wars to ensure the territorial integrity and safety of the state. Though a warrior, King David is well known for his composition of the Book of Psalms.[61] The Messiah will be descended from the "House of David."[62]

King David established Jerusalem as the capital and moved the Holy Ark there. After King David's death, his son Solomon became king and the nation experienced peace and prosperity during his reign. He built the First Temple in Jerusalem, which stood for 420 years, until its destruction by the Babylonians.

King Solomon was famous for his wisdom and the Talmud attributes to him authorship of The Song of Songs, Proverbs and Ecclesiastes.[63] Solomon's kingdom had treaties with the countries surrounding it, engaged in a great deal of foreign trade and was a world spiritual center for many people in addition to the Israelites.[64]

After the death of King Solomon, internecine strife divided the kingdom into two separate countries — Israel in the north, home of 10 of the tribes, with its capital in Shechem (today, Nablus); and Judea in the south, home of the tribes of Judah, Benjamin, and most *Kohanim* ("Priests") and Levites, with its capital in Jerusalem.[65]

The Northern Kingdom was eventually invaded and destroyed by the Assyrian king, Sennacherib, who was responsible for the exile of the 10 tribes who lived there. What became of the 10 tribes is somewhat of a mystery. Some returned to Israel, some remained true to their heritage in isolated locations (the Jews of Ethiopia, for example, are believed by some to be from the tribe of Dan) and most of them probably assimilated into the host countries where they were exiled, and disappeared.[66]

The remaining tribes, Judah (the largest), Benjamin, the Levites and the *Kohanim* are the ancestors of today's Jewish people, though there probably were members of other tribes mixed among them at the time. The Children of Israel now became associated primarily with the tribe of Judah and the land of Judea, and they became known henceforth as Jews.[67]

Judea was subsequently invaded by the Babylonians army under the rule of King Nebuchadnezzar. He destroyed the Temple and exiled most of the Jews to Babylon (modern Iraq and Iran).[68] It was during the exile in Babylon that the events of the Purim story occurred, facilitating the return of the Jews to the Land of Israel.[69]

Most of the Jews in Babylon stayed there or migrated to other parts of the Middle East. However, after a 70-year exile, some returned to their homeland under the leadership of Ezra and Nehemiah. The returnees resettled the land, rebuilt the walls around Jerusalem and rebuilt the Holy Temple.[70]

The Second Temple lasted for 420 years, survived the attacks of the Syrian-Greeks and was rededicated by the Maccabees at the time of the revolt against Greek rule (140 B.C.E.), marked by the Chanukah celebration. The Holy Temple was renovated by the Maccabees, and later by King Herod (60 B.C.E.).[71] Eventually the Roman Empire ruled Judea, and after a series of Jewish revolts against Roman rule, the Holy Temple was destroyed by the Roman Legions and the Jews were exiled all over the Roman Empire (70 C.E.).[72] Egypt, North Africa, Spain, France, Germany and Italy (as they are known now) all became home to communities of Jewish exiles who are the ancestors of most of today's Jews.

NOTES

References to books of the Talmud refer to the Babylonian Talmud unless otherwise noted.

1. Genesis 11:28, see footnote ad loc., *The Living Torah*, Aryeh Kaplan, Moznaim Publishers, NY, 1981. Also known as Mesopotamia, see *Midrash Rabbah,* Genesis 30:10.
2. *Avodah Zarah* 9a.
3. Sumerian creation epic.
4. Sumerian code of civil law, written during the reign of King Hammurabi.
5. Leah Bronner, *Biblical Personalities and Archaeology*, Chap. 2, Keter Publishing, Jerusalem, 1974; James B. Pritchard, *The Ancient Near East*, Section II, Princeton University Press, 1958.
6. Maimonides, *Mishneh Torah,* Laws of Idolatry, 1:1-2; Bronner ibid. Pritchard ibid.
7. *Avodah Zarah* 54b; Mishnah *"sha'alu"* and Gemara ad loc.
8. Maimonides, ibid. 1:3.
9. *Midrash Rabbah*, Genesis 42:8 "Rabbi Yehudah."
10. Ibid. 39:1.
11. Genesis 17:1, 18:19; *Midrash Rabbah,* Genesis 49:5; *Yevamot* 79a, *Sanhedrin* 57b; Maimonides, *Mishneh Torah*, Laws of the Intellect 1:7, Laws of Gifts to the Poor 10:1.
12. Rabbi Moshe Sofer, *Responsa Chatam Sofer*, Introduction to *Yoreh Deah, Pituchei Chotam*.
13. *Midrash Rabbah*, Genesis 39:14; Nachmanides, *Commentary on the Torah*, Genesis 2:3; Maimonides, ibid.
14. Genesis 12:1.
15. Rabbi Yehudah Halevy, *Kuzari* 2:14.
16. Maimonides, *Book of the Commandments*, Positive Commandment 153.
17. Genesis 21:33, Rashi ad loc.; Maharal of Prague, *Gur Aryeh* ad loc.
18. Genesis 21:12.
19. Ibid. 21:1-5.
20. Genesis 25:20.
21. Ibid. 25:27, Rashi ad loc.
22. Genesis 32:29, commentaries ad loc.
23. Nachmanides, *Commentary on the Torah*, Genesis 12:8.
24. Rabbi Samson Raphael Hirsch on Genesis 37:11-12.
25. Genesis Chaps. 39-47.
26. Exodus 1:6; Commentaries, ad loc.
27. Ibid. 1:8-14; Commentaries, ad loc.
28. Rashi on Exodus 12:40.
29. Exodus 2:1-10.
30. Ibid. 2:11.
31. Ibid. 2:12.
32. Ibid. 2:13.
33. The idea of the tests of justice was heard from Rabbi Dr. Dovid Gottlieb.
34. Exodus 2:16-18.
35. *Midrash Rabbah,* Exodus 2:2.
36. Exodus 3:12. Sinai is related to the word *"sneh,"* which means bush. See Nachmanides' *Commentary on the Torah*, Deuteronomy 33:15.
37. Exodus 5:2.
38. The Hebrew *"Yam Suf"* actually means "Sea of Reeds."
39. Exodus, Chap. 14.
40. Maimonides, *Mishneh Torah,* Laws of Foundations of the Torah, 8:3-5.
41. Rabbi Samson Raphael Hirsch, Commentary to Exodus 14:11.
42. Exodus 14:11.
43. Ibid. 16:3 and 17:2-3.
44. Ibid. 32:9, 33:3-5, 34:9, Deuteronomy 9:6.
45. Maharal, *Netzach Yisrael*, Chaps. 14 and 25.
46. Also known as *Horeb*. Exodus 33:6.
47. Exodus 12:37.
48. *Mechilta* and *Targum Yonatan* on Exodus 12:37.
49. Exodus 19:9-11.
50. Ibid. 19:16-20.
51. Ibid.

52. Exodus 19:8, 24:7; Deuteronomy 5:2-4.

53. The grammatical form of the first two statements is first person, indicating that God Himself was speaking directly; the form of the other statements refers to God in the third person, indicating that Moses was speaking. *Kli Yakar*, Commentary on Exodus, 20:2. According to Nachmanides, *Commentary on the Torah*, ibid. 20:7, they heard all ten statements, but only understood the first two directly from God's communication, and needed Moses to interpret the other eight.

54. Exodus 24:7, Deuteronomy 31:24.

55. *Gittin* 60a-b.

56. Maimonides, Introduction to Commentary on the Mishnah.

57. Deuteronomy 3:28.

58. I Samuel, Chap. 31.

59. II Samuel, Chap. 2.

60. Book of Ruth 4:21-22.

61. Written primarily by King David, but with contribution from another 10 authors as well.

62. See chapter on Belief, Knowledge and Faith.

63. *Megillah* 7a.

64. I Kings, Chaps. 5,10.

65. I Kings, Chaps. 11-14.

66. II Kings 15:29, II Kings 17:1-6; Mishnah, *Sanhedrin* 10:3; *Yevamot* 16b-17a, Meiri ad loc.

67. The English word *Jew* is from the Old French *giu*, earlier *juieu*, deriving from the Latin and the Greek *iudeus*. The Latin means *Judaean*, i.e. from the land of Judaea [commonly spelled Judea today].

68. II Kings, Chap. 24.

69. See chapter on Purim.

70. Book of Ezra and Book of Nehemiah.

71. See chapter on Chanukah.

72. See chapter on Fast Days — Tishah B'Av.

The Books of the People, for the People of the Book

A basic outline of key works in Jewish tradition

Scripture

The Five Books of Moses (Torah, Chumash) [choo-MASH]

1. Genesis (Bereishit) [be-ray-SHEET]

This Book's Hebrew name is *Bereishit,* which means "In the beginning." It deals with the Creation; Adam and Eve; the Flood; the Patriarchs and the Matriarchs of the Jewish people, and ends with the descent of Jacob and his family to Egypt. It also contains the commandment of circumcision, and God's promise to Abraham that he would receive the Land of Israel and that his descendants would be a major, positive influence on the entire world.

2. Exodus (Shmot) [sh-MOTE]

The title of this Book, *Shmot,* meaning "Names," refers to the names of the Jews who entered Egypt with Jacob. It deals with their exile, slavery and suffering; the life of Moses, and his initial prophecies;

the Ten Plagues and the Exodus. It also describes the Revelation at Mt. Sinai, where the Jewish people received the Ten Commandments, and the Written and Oral Torah. Exodus closes with the building of the Tabernacle *(Mishkan),* a portable Temple that housed the Holy Ark containing the Tablets of the Law.

3. Leviticus (Vayikra) [va-yikRA]

Vayikra, meaning, "He called," is the first word of this Book. God calls to Moses and informs him in detail of the laws regarding the festivals, Priests *(Kohanim)* and the Temple service. Much of the Jewish code of morality, ethics and charity appears in *Vayikra*, including the famous commandment "Love your neighbor as yourself" (Leviticus 19:18).

4. Numbers (Bamidbar) [ba-midBAR]

Bamidbar, "In the desert," details the travels, battles and struggles of the Jews during their 40-year sojourn in the desert after the Exodus. It records a census of the tribes, the positioning of each tribe when they camped and traveled, Korach's rebellion and the events surrounding sending the spies to Israel. *Bamidbar* ends with the capture of the East Bank of the Jordan River and the subsequent settlement there of the tribes of Reuben and Gad.

5. Deuteronomy (Devarim) [d'vaREEM]

Devarim, "Words," refers to Moses' address to the Jewish people before his death. This prophetic farewell includes rebuke, encouragement, warnings and prophecies. In it, many commandments that would only apply in the Land of Israel and that govern interaction with other nations are explained and new commandments are given, many of which concern the courts and justice system. After his farewell, Moses wrote 13 complete copies of the Torah, gave one to each tribe and placed one in the Holy Ark. The Five Books close with the death of "the greatest of all prophets" and "the most humble of all men," Moses.

The Prophets (Nevi'im) [ne-vee-YIM]

EARLY PROPHETS

6. Joshua (Yehoshua) [yeho-SHUa]

This first Book of the Prophets continues from the death of Moses, with the appointment of Joshua as the new leader of the nation. It recounts the battle of Jericho, the further conquest and subsequent division of the Land of Israel and gives detailed accounts of the wars with the Canaanites. It closes with Joshua's exhortation to the people to remain unified in their service of God.

7. Judges (Shoftim) [shau-fe-TEEM]

The Book of Judges details Jewish history following the era of Joshua up to the first kings. The Judges ruled the people in matters of civil and criminal law, Jewish practice, and military and political affairs. The Theme of the book is that when the Jewish people were loyal to God, they enjoyed tranquility. When they lapsed, they were oppressed by invaders until they repented, and a Judge chosen by God would drive out the enemy. Among the numerous Judges in the book are Gideon, Samson and Deborah.

8. Samuel (Shmuel) [shmu-EL]

There are two Books of Samuel: I Samuel and II Samuel.

Samuel was born in answer to the prayers of his childless mother, Chanah, and served from his youth in the Tabernacle under the High Priest, Eli (who was also the last of the Judges). One of the greatest of all prophets, at God's behest he anointed Saul to be the first king of Israel, and chose David as Saul's replacement when the latter failed to destroy the Amalekite enemies of the Jewish people. The life of King David, certainly one of the most renowned of Israel's monarchs, is recounted, including his slaying of Goliath, the Philistine; his flight from King Saul; and the rebellion of his son, Absalom, against him. Both a warrior and a poet, David became known as "The Sweet Singer of Israel." David's Psalms, written over his lifetime of ordeals and tribulations, have given hope and inspiration to millions of people the world over. A descendant of King David is destined to be the Messiah.

9. Kings (Melachim) [m'la-CHEEM] I and II

King David's son, Solomon, ruled over Israel at a time of peace and prosperity and built the First Holy Temple. At the end of his reign, Jeroboam and Rehoboam (Solomon's son) split the country into the kingdoms of Judah and Israel. The Book of Kings describes the history of the nation, and those who reigned until the destruction of the Temple and the exile of the Jews to Babylon. The kingdom of Judah was led most of the time by righteous kings; but the kingdom of Israel (comprised of ten tribes) was led almost exclusively by notorious sinners. As a result, the kingdom of Israel was exiled several generations before Judah (hence the mystery of the Ten Lost Tribes). Other main topics include the prophecies of Elijah and Elisha, and Elijah's discrediting of the worshippers of the idol Baal on Mt. Carmel.

LATER PROPHETS

10. Isaiah (Yeshayahu) [yesha-YAHU]

Isaiah predicted the destruction of the First Temple in vivid detail. He is best known for his prophecies of consolation and redemption, which are read as Haftarot on the Sabbaths following the Ninth of Av. Isaiah's prophecy includes the well-known verse, "They will beat their swords into plowshares ... nation shall not raise sword against nation, and they will no longer study war."

11. Jeremiah (Yirmiyahu) [yeer-mee-YAHU]

The Book of Jeremiah warns of the Holy Temple's coming destruction and records the history of the period leading up to that tragedy. Jeremiah witnessed the destruction and describes the terrible suffering that ensued. His later prophecies comfort the Jewish people in their exile, counsels them to put down roots in Babylon, but at the same time to prepare for their return to Israel. Jeremiah's uplifting prophecy that "the sound of joy and the sound of gladness, the voices of a bride and groom" will again be heard "in the cities of Judah and in the streets of Jerusalem" is part of the Jewish wedding ceremony.

12. Ezekiel (Yechezkel) [yeh-chez-KAIL)

Ezekiel rebuked the Jewish people for their failings and warned that if they do not change, the Temple would be destroyed. He saw the destruction of the Temple and joined the people in their exile to Babylon. He offered them hope of the return to Zion and the future Messianic age. Ezekiel's vision of the "Divine Chariot" is a primary source for many Jewish mystical writings. His book closes with his description of the Third Holy Temple, which will be built in the Messianic era.

13. The Twelve Shorter Books of the Prophets (TREI ASAR) [tray aSAR]

These 12 Books of Prophets are grouped because of their brevity. One of the most famous is Jonah, in which the prophet warns the city of Nineveh of its impending destruction. The people of Nineveh repent, and the decree is rescinded. Malachi closes the Books of the Prophets with an exhortation to follow the Torah and a prophecy of Messianic times, when "the hearts of parents will return to their children, and the hearts of children to their parents." The 12 Books are:

1. Hosea (Hoshea) [ho-SHAY-a]
2. Joel (Yoel) [yo-EL]
3. Amos [ah-MAUS]
4. Obadiah (Ovadiah) [oh-vad-YAH]

5. Jonah (Yonah) [yo-NAH]
6. Micah (Michah) [mee-CHAH]
7. Nahum (Nachum) [na-CHOOM]
8. Habakkuk (Chavakuk) [cha-va-KOOK]
9. Zephaniah (Tzephaniah) [tzeh-phan-YAH]
10. Haggai (Chaggai) [chah-GUY]
11. Zechariah [ze-char-YAH]
12. Malachi [mal-a-CHEE]

Writings (Ketuvim) [ke-too-VIM]

14. Psalms (Tehillim) [te-hee-LEEM]

The Hebrew name of Psalms — *Tehillim* — means "praises." It refers both to the content and purpose of this book. Here, King David, along with nine authors who contributed individual psalms, gives expression to the whole range of human emotion and thought as it relates to God. Through poetry and song, the Psalms capture the soul's praise for God in all situations, favorable and unfavorable. Much of Jewish liturgy, music and poetry are based on Psalms. Individual psalms were sung by the Levites in the First and Second Holy Temples and today they form a central part of the Jewish prayer book (*siddur*).

15. Proverbs (Mishlei) [mish-LAY]

Proverbs was written by King Solomon and contains his ethical and practical teachings in the form of proverbs. This book forms the basis of many later works of ethics and character improvement.

16. Job (Iyov) [EeYAUV]

The Book of Job recounts the story of the sufferings of a righteous man, Job, and various responses to his suffering. Throughout the centuries, this Book has been a source of insight into some of the foremost philosophical problems in religious thought: the suffering of the righteous; the existence of evil; Divine Providence and free will; and the workings of Divine Justice.

The next five Books of Writings are The Five Scrolls (*Chamesh Megillot*):

17. Songs of Songs (Shir Hashirim) [sheer ha-shee-REEM]

The Sages describe the Song of Songs as the most holy of all prophetic literature. Its author, King Solomon, portrays the love between the Jewish people and God in the form of a poetic dialogue between a man and a woman. Extensive Midrashic and Rabbinic commentaries elucidate this beautiful work and explain the depth of the allegories used by King Solomon. The work is read in synagogues on Passover, when God designated the Jewish people as his own.

18. Ruth (Rut) (root)

This Book tells about a Moabite woman, Ruth, and her Jewish mother-in-law, Naomi, who lived during the period of the Judges. Because of a severe famine, Naomi and her family left the Land of Israel and settled in Moab. When both her husband and sons died, Naomi decided to return to her homeland, bidding her Moabite daughters-in-law to return to their families. Instead, Ruth insisted on accompanying Naomi back to the Land of Israel. A righteous convert to Judaism, Ruth later married Boaz, the leader of that generation. She gave birth to a son, who was to be King David's grandfather. She is therefore the mother of the royal line of David. Ruth embraced Judaism with the famous phrase: "Wherever you go, I will go ... your nation is my nation, and your God is my God." The Book is read in the synagogue on the holiday of Shavuot, the anniversary of David's death.

19. Lamentations (Eichah) [ay-CHAH]

The prophet Jeremiah predicted and witnessed the destruction of the First Temple by the Babylonians. In this Book, he mourns the destruction of the Temple and Jerusalem, the desolation of Israel, and the exile of the Jewish people. *Eichah*, meaning "How" is the tragic lament that begins this Book and is often repreated: "How does the city sit solitary, [the city] that was full of people? How has she become like a widow? She that was great among the nations, and princess among the provinces, how has she become a vassal?" The Book of Lamentations is read annually in the synagogue on Tishah B'Av, when the destruction is mourned.

20. Ecclesiastes (Kohelet) [kau-HELet]

Ecclesiastes was written by King Solomon, who refers to himself here as Kohelet, son of David. In this book, King Solomon analyzes the futility of a totally materialistic life, and points out the frustrations and the cynicism of one who lives without a spiritual dimension. The often quoted-passage, "To everything there is a season, and there is a time for everything under heaven ..." is from Ecclesiastes. It closes with a verse that proclaims the essential holy message of the Book: "The sum of the matter, when all has been considered: Fear God and keep His commandments, for that is man's whole duty." Ecclesiastes is read in the synagogue on the holiday of Sukkot.

21. Esther [eh-STARE]

The Scroll of Esther, named for Queen Esther, relates the story behind the celebration of Purim. Set in the capital city of Persia,

Shushan, c. 360 B.C.E., it describes Haman's plan to annihilate the Jews and the miraculous turn of events through which they were saved. It shows how a seemingly unrelated string of "coincidences" was orchestrated by God to achieve His goals, teaching us to recognize the Hand of God in seemingly mundane events. This Book is read publicly on Purim, and tells us to celebrate the festival through charity and joy.

22. Daniel [danee-YALE]

Daniel, a Judean youth, of great wisdom and beauty, was captured and taken to Babylon shortly before the destruction of the First Temple. He was trained to be a servant to the king, Nebuchadnezzar. There, he laid the foundation for the continuity of Torah study and Judaism for which Babylonian Jewry later became famous. The Book of Daniel is written in Aramaic, the language of Babylon. It contains the famous message of the "handwriting on the wall," and portrays the various enemies of the Jewish people using the famous metaphor of the four beasts.

23. Ezra and Nehemiah (Nechemiah) [ne-chem-YAH]

The Books of Ezra and Nehemiah are regarded as one Book, because of their common author, Ezra, and common subject matter, the return to Israel from captivity in Babylon. The resettlement of the Jewish people in Israel and the building of the Second Temple are described in detail. Ezra instituted public reading of the Torah on Mondays and Thursdays, in addition to the usual reading on Shabbat (which had been introduced by Moses).

24. Chronicles I and II (Divrei Hayamim) [div-RAY ha-ya-MIM]

Divrei Hayamim means "the events of the days." It details the genealogy of all the major figures in the Bible, from Adam to Ezra the Scribe. Chronicles is also a summary of Jewish history from the beginning of time until the building of the Second Temple.

The Oral Tradition

Six Orders of the Mishnah (Shishah Sidrei Mishnah, acronym – Shas)

This is the first codification of the Oral Law. It was redacted by Rabbi Yehudah "The Prince." He was known simply as "Rabbi," because he was the paramount teacher and leader of the nation. The

Mishnah was redacted during the second century C.E. Following are the six sections, known as tractates.

1. Seeds (*Zeraim*)

The first tractate (*masechta*) of this order is *Berachot* — "Blessings" — that teaches the laws of blessings, prayers and the synagogue service. The other ten tractates discuss the agricultural laws that apply in the Land of Israel as well as those that apply outside of Israel.

2. Times (*Moed*)

This order deals with the sanctity of time. It contains 12 tractates that discuss the Sabbath, festivals, the High Holidays, the calendar and the fast days.

3. Women (*Nashim*)

This order deals with the sanctity of the male-female relationship. Its seven tractates discuss the laws of marriage and divorce, the marriage contract (*ketubah*), incest and adultery, vows and their annulment, and levirate marriages (*yibum* and *chalitzah*).

4. Damages (*Nezikim*)

This order deals with the laws governing a person's possessions. Its nine tractates discuss: damages and torts; lost and abandoned objects; business ethics and laws of trade; property and inheritance; jurisprudence, government and the monarchy; laws of evidence, punishment and oaths; the prohibition of idol worship and relationships with pagans; and the laws of erroneous rulings by a court.

5. Holiness (*Kodashim*)

Kodashim contains 11 tractates. It discusses the laws of the offerings in the Holy Temple; the laws of redemption of the firstborn; donations to the Temple treasury; and the laws of *Kashrut*, the Jewish dietary code.

6. Purity (*Taharot*)

Taharot deals with the laws of spiritual purity and impurity (*tumah v'taharah*). Its 12 tractates discuss the laws of family purity, impurity caused by death and disease and the various methods of purifying people and objects. The laws, structure and purpose of the *mikveh* are also detailed.

The Talmud

The Talmud compiles the discussions and explanations of the Mishnah. This voluminous work is the basis of Jewish religious law and civil law, ethics, morality and Scriptural interpretation. Because Roman oppression made it impossible for the centers of scholarship in Israel and Babylon to work together, each country produced its own edition of the Talmud.

Jerusalem Talmud (Talmud *Yerushalmi*, also called Gemara *Yerushalmi*)

The Jerusalem Talmud was redacted in 350 C.E. by Rav Muna and Rav Yossi in the Land of Israel. It contains explanations of the Mishnah, legislation, customs, case histories and moral exhortations. The Gemara is a synopsis of the discussions, questions and decisions of the academies in Israel. The agricultural laws of the Land of Israel are discussed in great detail. It is written in the Hebrew-Aramaic dialect of the time.

Babylonian Talmud (Talmud *Bavli*, also called Gemara *Bavli*)

The Babylonian Talmud was redacted in 500 C.E. by Ravina and Rav Ashi, two leaders of the Babylonian Jewish community. Like the Jerusalem Talmud, it is written in Hebrew-Aramaic. It contains explanations of the Mishnah, legislation, customs, case histories and moral exhortations. The Gemara is a synopsis of the discussions, questions and decisions of the Babylonian academies in which the Mishnah was studied for more than 300 years. Of the two, Talmud *Bavli* is studied more commonly than the Talmud Yerushalmi. When one speaks of "learning Gemara," one is generally referring to Talmud *Bavli*.

Midrash

Midrash is a generic term for a group of approximately 60 collections of rabbinic commentaries, stories, metaphors and ethical essays organized according to the Books of the Torah, Prophets and Writings. It also includes various commentaries on the letters of the Hebrew alphabet. Most *midrashim* date back to the time of the Mishnah and Gemara. Many authors of the *Midrash* appear in the Mishnah and vice versa. Many of the central concepts and commentaries of the *Midrash* are part of the Oral tradition from Sinai. The most famous collections of *midrashim* are the Midrash Rabbah, the Midrash Tanchuma, Sifri, Sifra, Mechilta and Yalkut Shimoni. Regarding *Midrash*, the Maharal of Prague wrote that, "most of the words of the Sages were in the form of metaphor and the analogies of the wise ... *unless they state that a particular story is not a metaphor, it should be assumed that it is a metaphor.* Therefore one should not be surprised to find matters in the words of the Sages that appear to be illogical and distant from the mind" (*Be'er Hagolah*, Fourth Be'er p. 51).

Zohar

The Zohar was written by the students of Rabbi Shimon bar Yochai, who transcribed his teachings circa 170 C.E. in the Land of Israel. It discusses the concepts of Creation *ex nihilo;* Divine Providence and its mechanisms; the metaphysical meaning of the commandments of the Torah; and the connection between the physical and the spiritual. Written in Aramaic, it follows the order of the Five Books of Moses. The Zohar is the primary text of the Kabbalah, the Torah's mystical teachings.

Scholars and Their Works

"Exalted Ones" (Geonim)

The Geonic period extends from c. 690 C.E. until the 11th century. The first Geonim were the heads of the Babylonian academies. Most of the Geonim lived in Babylon, Egypt or North Africa. They wrote responsa (responses of Torah scholars to questions of Jewish law posed to them by both laymen and experts), as well as brief commentaries on the Talmud. Among the most famous Geonim were Rav Saadya Gaon, Rav Hai Gaon and Rav Sherira Gaon.

Early Scholars (Rishonim)

The period of the *Rishonim* starts from approximately the 11th century C.E. and extends to the 15th century. Among the most famous *Rishonim* are:

Rashi: "Rashi" [RAH-she] is an acronym for Rabbi Shlomo Yitzchaki, a French scholar born in 1040. He is the most popular and prolific of the medieval commentators. Rashi wrote commentaries on the Five Books of Moses, the Prophets,the Writings, the Mishnah, the Gemara and the Midrash. His works are such an essential part of Jewish literature, that the *Code of Jewish Law* considers it mandatory for every Jew to study the Torah with Rashi's commentary weekly.

Tosafot: Tosafot literally means "additions" and refers to commentaries on the Talmud written by a number of schools of scholars from approximately the 13th century to the 15th century. The scholars lived mostly in France, Germany and England and the four major teachers and leaders of these schools were grandchildren of Rashi. These commentaries are found on the page of all standard editions of the Talmud.

Rif: Rif is an acronym for Rav Yitzchak Alfasi, i.e., Rabbi Isaac of Fez (Morocco). The Rif lived from 1013 to 1103 and wrote one of the earliest Jewish legal tracts after the Talmud. He condensed the Talmud, leaving out parts that were not accepted as law (*halachah*) and much of the discussion and debate. His condensation is therefore the basis for much of the codification of Jewish Law.

Rosh: Rosh is an acronym for Rabbeinu Asher, i.e., Our Teacher Asher, who lived from 1250 to 1327. He lived most of his life in Germany and eventually became a leader of the Jewish community in Spain. He is best known for his codification of the legal parts of the Talmud in a style that combines the discussions of the Tosafos and the codification of the Rif.

Maimonides: Rabbi Moshe ben Maimon, acronym Rambam [RAHM-bahm], was one of the first codifiers of Jewish law. His fourteen-volume *Mishneh Torah* covers all of Jewish law, belief and practice. He was born in Spain in 1135, lived most of his life in Egypt and died there in 1204. His works include the *Book of Mitzvot*, enumerating and explaining all 613 commandments; the *Guide for the Perplexed*, a complete philosophy of Judaism; many letters and responsa. He was also a famous physician who wrote numerous medical treatises.

Nachmanides: Rabbi Moshe ben Nachman is also known by his acronym Ramban [rahm-BAHN]. He was born in Spain in 1195, where he lived for most of his life, and died in the Land of Israel in 1270, after immigrating there in his later years. Nachmanides wrote commentaries on the Five Books of Moses, the Talmud and on a number of books of the Tanach. He is considered one of the greatest of the Kabbalists and his commentary on the Torah contains many mystical insights.

Rashba: Rashba is an acronym for Rav Shlomo ben Avraham ibn Aderet, i.e., Rabbi Solomon son of Abraham son of Aderet. The Rashba lived from 1235 to 1310, and was a student of the Ramban. He wrote a commentary on the Talmud, various works on Jewish law and authored thousands of answers to Jews on virtually every subject in Judaism. He lived in Barcelona, and was the leader of all Spanish Jewry.

Later Scholars (Acharonim)

The period of the *Acharonim* starts from approximately the 15th century C.E. and extends to contemporary times. Among the most famous of the *Acharonim* are: Rabbis Yosef Karo and Moshe Isserles, the authors of the *Code of Jewish Law*; Rabbi Eliyahu, the Gaon of Vilna; and the Chassidic masters "the Baal Shem Tov," Rabbi Levi Yitzchak of Berditchev and Rabbi Shneur Zalman of Liadi. In the last 150 years, Torah study and halachic rulings have been enriched by Rabbi Chaim Soloveichik; Rabbi Yisrael Meir Kagan, known as the Chafetz Chaim; and Rabbi Moshe Feinstein, to name just a few. These scholars wrote commentaries on the Talmud and the Written Law, works of philosophy and ethics, and responsa. You will often hear the use of the Hebrew word *Rav* (meaning Rabbi) in regard to their titles.

Code of Jewish Law (Shulchan Aruch)

Shulchan Aruch means the "Set Table" because it arranges Jewish law systematically. It contains four sections:

1. *Orach Chaim* — the laws of daily practice, Sabbaths and festivals.

2. *Yoreh Deah* — the laws of *Kashrut*, mourning, family purity, vows, circumcision, Torah scrolls and conversion.

3. *Choshen Mishpat* — the laws of business, finance, contracts, jurisprudence, torts and damages.

4. *Even HaEzer* — the laws of marriage and divorce.

The *Shulchan Aruch* was written in Safed in approximately 1560 C.E. by Rabbi Yosef Karo, a Sephardic scholar. Current editions also contain the concurrent rulings and comments of Rabbi Moshe Isserles of Cracow regarding European Jewish customs (Ashkenazic).

Responsa Literature (She'elot U-Teshuvot)

Responsa are the responses of Torah scholars to questions of Jewish law posed to them by both laymen and experts. These scholars apply the law and philosophy of Judaism to the changing circumstances of Jewish life; to technological and social innovations; to medical issues; and to other aspects of contemporary living. Responsa literature provides insight into the workings of Jewish law and reveals the concerns of Jews around the world and throughout the ages.

Thank you to Rabbi Moshe Newman, with whom I wrote this for the Ohr Somayach website.

Recommended Reading

$\mathcal{S}$pecific recommendations for books pertaining to subject matter in each chapter are listed at the end of each chapter.

Many of those titles, and selected others, appear here, arranged by area of interest.

This list is by no means comprehensive. Visit your local Hebrew bookstore — or go to one of the many online Jewish bookstores — to purchase these books and to see additional titles.

Classics

▶ *Stone Edition Tanach* (the Bible with English translation, explanations, charts and maps) (ArtScroll/Mesorah, 1996)

▶ *Stone Edition Chumash* (Five Books of Moses, with translation and commentaries) (ArtScroll/Mesorah, 1993)

▶ *The Living Torah,* Aryeh Kaplan (Moznaim Publishing, 1981)

▶ Schottenstein Edition of Talmud Bavli (The Talmud, translated and elucidated in English) (73 volumes, ArtScroll/Mesorah, 1990-2005)

Jewish Thought and Belief

▶ *Biblical Questions, Spiritual Journeys*, Rabbi Emanuel Feldman (Shaar Press, 2004)

▶ *Fingerprints on the Universe,* Louis Pollack (ArtScroll/Mesorah, 1994)

▶ *Fundamentals and Faith: Insights into the Rambam's 13 Principles,* Rabbi Yaakov Weinberg (Feldheim, 1991)

▶ *Horeb,* Rabbi Samson Raphael Hirsch (Soncino Press 1962)

▶ *Letters to a Buddhist Jew*, Rabbi Akiva Tatz and David Gottlieb (Targum, 2005)

▶ *Maimonides' Principles,* Rabbi Aryeh Kaplan (OU/NCSY, 1984)

▶ *My Father, My King,* Rabbi Zelig Pliskin (ArtScroll/Mesorah, 1996)

▶ *On Judaism: Conversations on being Jewish in today's world,* Rabbi Emanuel Feldman (Shaar Press, 1994)

▶ *Our Amazing World*, Rabbi Avrohom Katz (ArtScroll/Mesorah, 1996)

▶ *Our Wondrous World*, Rabbi Avrohom Katz (ArtScroll/Mesorah, 1999)

▶ *Permission to Believe,* Rabbi Lawrence Keleman (Feldheim, 1990)

▶ *Permission to Receive,* Rabbi Lawrence Keleman (Targum/Feldheim, 1996)

▶ *Rabbi Freifeld Speaks*, adapted by Rabbi Yaakov Yosef Reinman (ArtScroll/Mesorah, 2004)

▶ *The Aryeh Kaplan Anthology* (OU/NCSY, 1991)

▶ *The Aryeh Kaplan Reader* (ArtScroll/Mesorah, 1983)

▶ *The Informed Soul,* Rabbi Dovid Gottlieb (ArtScroll/Mesorah, 1990)

▶ *The Jewish Self,* Rabbi Jeremy Kagan (Feldheim, 1998)

▶ *The Jewish Theory of Everything: A behind-the-scenes look at the universe*, Max Anteby (Shaar Press, 2002)

▶ *The Real Messiah*, Rabbi Aryeh Kaplan (OU/NCSY, 1976)

▶ *Twerski on Spirituality*, Rabbi Abraham J. Twerski, M.D. (Shaar Press, 1998)

▶ *Understanding Judaism: A basic guide to Jewish faith, history and practice*, Rabbi Mordechai Katz (ArtScroll/Mesorah, 2000)

▶ *What the Angel Taught You: Seven Keys to Life Fulfillment*, Rabbi Noah Weinberg and Yaakov Salomon (Shaar Press, 2003)

▶ *With Hearts Full of Faith: Insights into faith and trust in Jewish life*, Rabbi Mattisyahu Salomon/ Rabbi Yaakov Yosef Reinman (ArtScroll/ Mesorah, 2002)

Ethics

▶ *Chofetz Chaim: A Daily Companion* (daily lessons on appropriate speech), Michoel Rothschild with Rabbi Shimon Finkelman (ArtScroll/ Mesorah, 1999)

▶ *Chofetz Chaim: A Lesson a Day* (concepts and laws of proper speech), Rabbis Shimon Finkelman and Yitzchak Berkowitz (ArtScroll/ Mesorah, 1995)

▶ *Chofetz Chaim: Lesson in Truth* (daily studies in honesty and fundamentals of Jewish faith), Rabbi Shimon Finkelman (ArtScroll/ Mesorah, 2001)

▶ *Chofetz Chaim: Loving Kindness — Daily lessons in the power of giving*, Rabbi Fischel Schachter and Chana Nestlebaum (ArtScroll/ Mesorah, 2003)

▶ *Guard Your Tongue*, Rabbi Zelig Pliskin (Pliskin, 1975)

▶ *Journey to Virtue: The laws of interpersonal relationships in business, home and society*, Rabbi Avrohom Ehrman (ArtScroll/Mesorah, 2002)

▶ *Love Your Neighbor*, Zelig Pliskin (Aish HaTorah Publications, 1977)

▶ *Pirkei Avos: Teachings for Our Times*, Rabbi Berel Wein (Shaar Press, 1003)

▶ *Successful Relationships — at Home, at Work and with Friends*, Rabbi Abraham J. Twerski (ArtScroll/Mesorah, 2003)

▶ *The Challenge of Wealth*, Meir Tamari (Jason Aaronson, 1995)

Jewish Law and Ritual

▶ *Kashruth*, Rabbi Yacov Lipschutz (ArtScroll/Mesorah, 1988)

▶ *Kosher By Design*, Susie Fishbein [cookbook including information on *and recipes for the Sabbath and Festivals*] (Shaar Press, 2003)

▶ *Living Jewish: Values, Practices and Traditions*, Rabbi Berel Wein (Shaar Press, 2002)

▶ *Outside/Inside: A Fresh Look at Tzniut*, Gila Manolson (Targum, 1997)

- *Sefer Hachinuch: The Book of Mitzvah Education* (Feldheim, 1989)
- *Tefillin,* Rabbi Aryeh Kaplan (OU/NCSY, 1973)
- *The Fifth Commandment: Honoring Parents* (ArtScroll/Mesorah, 1998)
- *The Jewish Dietary Laws,* Rabbi Isidore Grunfield (Soncino Press, 1975)
- *The Laws of Tzedakah and Maaser,* Rabbi Shimon Taub (ArtScroll/ Mesorah, 2001)
- *The Mitzvot,* Rabbi Abraham Chill (Urim Publications, 2000)
- *The Tzedakah Treasury,* Rabbi Avraham Chaim Feuer (ArtScroll/ Mesorah, 2000)
- *Tzitzith: A Thread of Light,* Rabbi Aryeh Kaplan (OU/NCSY, 1984)

Sabbath

- *Muktzeh,* Rabbi Simcha Bunim Cohen (ArtScroll/Mesorah, 1999)
- *Shabbat: Day of Eternity,* Rabbi Aryeh Kaplan (OU/NCSY, 1983)
- *Shemirath Shabbath* (English edition), Rabbi Yehoshua Neuwirth (Feldheim, 1989)
- *The 39 Melochos*, Rabbi Dovid Ribiat (Feldheim, 1999)
- *The Magic of Shabbos,* Rabbi Mordechai Rhine (Judaica Press, 1998)
- *The Radiance of Shabbos,* Rabbi Simcha Bunim Cohen (ArtScroll/ Mesorah, 1986)
- *The Sabbath,* Rabbi Isadore Grunfield (Feldheim, 1959)
- *The Sanctity of Shabbos,* Rabbi Simcha Bunim Cohen (ArtScroll/ Mesorah, 1988)
- *The Shabbos Home,* Rabbi Simcha Bunim Cohen (ArtScroll/Mesorah, 1992)
- *The Shabbos Kitchen,* Rabbi Simcha Bunim Cohen (ArtScroll/ Mesorah, 1991)

Festivals

- *A Time to Weep,* Rabbi Leibel Reznick (CIS Publishers, 1993) (Tishah B'av)
- *Chanukah: Its History, Observance, and Significance* (ArtScroll/Mesorah, 1986)

▸ *Days of Awe — Sfas Emes,* Rabbi Yosef Stern (ArtScroll/Mesorah, 1996)

▸ *Eichah/Lamentations* (ArtScroll/Mesorah, 1976) (Tishah B'Av)

▸ *From Bondage to Freedom* Haggadah, Rabbi Abraham J. Twerski, M.D. (Shaar Press, 1995)

▸ *In Every Generation* Haggadah, Rabbi Moshe Grylak (ArtScroll/ Mesorah, 2003)

▸ *Kinnos/Tishah B'Av Service* (ArtScroll/Mesorah, 1991)

▸ *Living Jewish,* Rabbi Berel Wein (ArtScroll/Mesorah, 2002)

▸ *Passover Survival Kit,* Shimon Apisdorf (Leviathan Press, 1997)

▸ *Purim: Its Observance and Significance* (ArtScroll/Mesorah, 1991)

▸ *Rosh Hashanah/Yom Kippur Survival Kit,* Shimon Apisdorf (Leviathan Press, 1993)

▸ *Rosh Hashanah: Its Significance, Laws, and Prayers* (ArtScroll/Mesorah, 1989)

▸ *Shavuos: Its Observance, Laws, and Significance* (ArtScroll/Mesorah, 1995)

▸ *Succos: Its Significance, Laws, and Prayers* (ArtScroll/Mesorah, 1982)

▸ *Tashlich,* Rabbi Avrohom Chaim Feuer (ArtScroll/Mesorah, 1979)

▸ *The ArtScroll Children's Megillah* (ArtScroll/Mesorah, 2005)

▸ *The ArtScroll Family Haggadah* (ArtScroll/Mesorah, 1981)

▸ *The ArtScroll Youth Megillah* (ArtScroll/Mesorah, 1988) (Purim)

▸ *The Book of Our Heritage,* Rabbi Eliyahu Kitov (Feldheim, 1979)

▸ *The Book of Ruth* (ArtScroll/Mesorah, 1976) (Shavuot)

▸ *The Haggadah with Answers,* Rabbi Yaakov Wehl (ArtScroll/ Mesorah, 1997)

▸ *The Jewish Calendar: Its Structure and Laws,* Rabbi David Feinstein (ArtScroll/Mesorah, 2004)

▸ *The Megillah/Esther* (ArtScroll/Mesorah, 1976) (Purim)

▸ *The Pesach Haggadah,* Rabbi Berel Wein (Shaar Press, 2004)

▸ *Tishah B'Av: Texts, Readings, and Insights* (ArtScroll/Mesorah, 1992)

▸ *Turnabout,* Rabbi Mendel Weinbach (Feldheim, 1976) (Purim)

▸ *Viduy/Confession* for Yom Kippur, Rabbi Nosson Scherman (ArtScroll/ Mesorah, 1986)

- ▶ *Yom Kippur: Its Significance, Laws, and Prayers* (ArtScroll/Mesorah, 1989)
- ▶ *Yonah/The Book of Jonah,* Rabbi Meir Zlotowitz (ArtScroll/Mesorah, 1978) (Yom Kippur)

Prayer

Prayer books:

- ▶ *The ArtScroll Transliterated Siddur* (if you don't read Hebrew) in weekday and Sabbath editions and *Machzor* for Rosh Hashanah and Yom Kippur (ArtScroll/Mesorah)
- ▶ *The Complete ArtScroll Siddur* (with English translation — also published in Russian and Spanish) and Machzorim for Rosh Hashanah, Yom Kippur, and Festivals (ArtScroll/Mesorah)
- ▶ Schottenstein Edition Interlinear Series (with the English translation beneath each Hebrew word): Weekday Siddur, Sabbath and Festival Siddur, Rosh Hashanah Machzor, Yom Kippur Machzor, Birchon (ArtScroll/Mesorah)

Books on prayer:

- ▶ *A Guide to Blessings* (over foods), Rabbi Naftali Hoffner (OU/NCSY)
- ▶ *Birchon/Grace After Meals* — Schottenstein Interlinear Edition (ArtScroll/Mesorah)
- ▶ *Growth Through Tehillim: Exploring Psalms for life-transforming thoughts,* Rabbi Zelig Pliskin (ArtScroll/Mesorah, 2004)
- ▶ *Kaddish,* Rabbi Nosson Scherman (ArtScroll/Mesorah, 1980)
- ▶ *Shema Yisrael,* Rabbi Meir Zlotowitz (ArtScroll/Mesorah, 1982)
- ▶ *The Art of Jewish Prayer,* Rabbi Yitzchak Kirzner and Lisa Aiken (Jason Aaronson, 1993)
- ▶ *The NCSY Bencher,* David Olivestone (OU/NCSY)
- ▶ *The World of Prayer,* Rabbi Elie Munk (Feldheim, 1963)
- ▶ *Twerski on Prayer* (originally: *Prayfully Yours*), Rabbi Abraham J. Twerski, M.D. (Shaar Press, 2001)

Marriage and Relationships

- ▶ *A Hedge of Roses,* Rabbi Norman Lamm (Feldheim, 1987)

▶ *A Woman's Guide to the Laws of Niddah,* Rabbi Binyomin Forst (ArtScroll/Mesorah, 1999)

▶ *Doesn't Anyone Blush Anymore?,* Rabbi Manis Friedman (Harper Collins, 1990)

▶ *Made in Heaven,* Rabbi Aryeh Kaplan (Moznaim, 1983)

▶ *The Jewish Way in Love and Marriage,* Rabbi Maurice Lamm (Jonathan David, 1991)

▶ *The Magic Touch: A Jewish Approach to Relationships,* Gila Manolson (Feldheim, 1992)

▶ *The Sacred Trust: Love, Dating and Marriage — The Jewish View,* Rabbi Pinchas Stolper (OU/NCSY, 1999)

▶ *Waters of Eden* (about mikveh), Rabbi Aryeh Kaplan (OU/NCSY, 1993)

Parenting

▶ *Bris Milah,* Rabbi Paysach J. Krohn (ArtScroll/Mesorah, 1986)

▶ *Positive Parenting: Developing Your Child's Potential,* Rabbi Abraham J. Twerski, M.D. and Ursula Schwartz, Ph.D. (ArtScroll/ Mesorah, 1999)

▶ *The Bat Mitzvah Treasury,* Rabbi Yonah Weinrib (Judaica Illuminations/ Mesorah, 2004)

▶ *To Kindle a Soul,* Rabbi Lawrence Keleman (Targum/Feldheim, 2001)

▶ *To Raise a Jewish Child,* Haim Halevy Donin (Basic Books, 1991)

Death and Mourning

▶ *If You Were God,* Rabbi Aryeh Kaplan (OU/NCSY, 1993)

▶ *Kaddish,* Rabbi Nosson Scherman (ArtScroll/Mesorah, 1980)

▶ *Making Sense of Suffering,* Yonason Rosenblum and Jeremy Kagan (ArtScroll/Mesorah, 2002)

▶ *Mourning in Halachah: The Laws and Customs of the Year of Mourning,* Rabbi Chaim Binyamin Goldberg (ArtScroll/Mesorah, 1991)

▶ *Out of the Whirlwind,* Rabbi Joseph Soloveitchik (Ktav, 2003)

▶ *The Jewish Way in Death and Mourning,* Rabbi Maurice Lamm (Jonathan David, 2000)

General

▸ *Jerusalem: Eye of the Universe* (also, in an edition with pictures with added subtitle *A Pictorial Tour of the Holy City*), Rabbi Aryeh Kaplan (OU/NCSY, 1993)

▸ *Perek Shirah: The Song of The Universe* (attributed to King David, with magnificent photography of nature's beauty) (ArtScroll/Mesorah, 2004)

▸ *The Land of Our Heritage,* David Rossoff (Feldheim, 1987)

▸ *Reading the Talmud:* Developing Independence in Gemara Learning, Dr. Henry Abramson, (Feldheim, NY, 2006)

▸ *After the Return:* A Practical Halachic Guide for the Newly Observant, Mordechai Becher and Moshe Newman, (Targum/Feldheim, Jerusalem, 1994)

Jewish History

▸ Rabbi Berel Wein's trilogy on Jewish History (Shaar Press):
Triumph of Survival The story of the Jews in the modern era — 1650-1990 (1990)
Echoes of Glory The story of the Jews in the Classica Era — 350 BCE-750 CE, (1995)
Herald of Destiny The story of the Jews in the medieval era — 750-1650 (1993)

▸ *The Jewish Time Line Encyclopedia*, Rabbi Mattis Kantor (Jason Aronson, 1992)

▸ The World That Was Series — Jewish life in pre-Holocaust Europe (The Living Memorial, Hebrew Academy of Cleveland):
The World That Was: Lithuania (1997)
The World That Was: Poland (1997)
The World That Was: Hungary/Romania (1999)

Biography

▸ *Between My Father and the Old Fool* (a Holocaust memoir), Maeir Cahan (ArtScroll/Mesorah, 2004)

▸ *Lieutenant Birnbaum* (U.S. Army in World War II), Meyer Birnbaum and Yonason Rosenblum (ArtScroll/Mesorah, 1993)

▸ *Rabbi Dessler,* Yonasan Rosenblum (ArtScroll/Mesorah, 2000)

▸ *Reb Moshe* (Feinstein), Rabbi Shimon Finkelman (ArtScroll/Mesorah, 1986)

▶ *Reb Yaakov* (Kaminetzky), Yonasan Rosenblum (ArtScroll/Mesorah, 1993)

▶ *Rebbetzin Grunfeld* (Dr. Judith Grunfeld, who spiritually saved hundreds of children in WWII England), Miram Dansky (ArtScroll/Mesorah, 1994)

▶ *Silent Revolution* (Eliyahu Essas, leader of *baal teshuvah* movement in Russia), Miriam Stark Zakon (ArtScroll/Mesorah, 1992)

▶ *The Youngest Partisan* (a Holocuast memoir), A. Romi Cohen and Dr. Leonard Ciaccio (ArtScroll/Mesorah, 2001)

For Children

▶ *ArtScroll Children' Siddur* (ArtScroll/Mesorah, 2001)

▶ *The 39 Avoth Melacha of Shabbath,,* Rabbi Baruch Chait, (Feldheim, 1991)

▶ *The ArtScroll Children's Haggadah* (ArtScroll/Mesorah, 2000)

▶ *The ArtScroll Children's Megillah* (ArtScroll/Mesorah, 2003)

Young Children

▶ *Alef to Tav,* Yaffa Ganz (ArtScroll/Mesorah, 1989)

▶ *Bedtime Stories to Make You Smile,* Shmuel Blitz (ArtScroll/Mesorah, 2003)

▶ *Dovy and the Surprise Guests*, Goldie Golding (ArtScroll/Mesorah, 1993)

▶ *Eli and His Little White Lie*, Goldie Golding (ArtScroll/Mesorah, 1990)

▶ *Hurry, Friday's a Short Day*, Yeshara Gold (ArtScroll/Mesorah, 2000)

▶ *Is it Shabbos Yet?,* Ellen Emerman (Hachai, 1990)

▶ *Labels for Laibel,* Dina Rosenfeld (Hachai, 1990)

▶ *Mitzvos You Can Do*, Yaffa Rosenthal (ArtScroll/Mesorah, 1986)

▶ *My First Book of Jewish Holidays,* Shmuel Blitz (ArtScroll/Mesorah, 2004)

▶ *My Hebrew Picture Dictionary: The Alef-Bet Word Book*, Shmuel Blitz (ArtScroll/Mesorah, 1995)

▶ The ArtScroll Children's Holiday Series, Yaffa Ganz (ArtScroll/Mesorah)

▶ *The Children's Book of Jewish Holidays,* David A. Adler (ArtScroll/ Mesorah, 1987)

▶ *The Little Old Lady Who Couldn't Fall Asleep*, Yaffa Ganz (ArtScroll/ Mesorah, 1982)

▶ The Savta Simcha Series, Yaffa Ganz (Feldhiem)

▶ *Where are You, Hashem?*, Yaffa Ganz (ArtScroll/Mesorah, 1991)

Older Children

▶ *ArtScroll Youth Pirkei Avos*, Rabbi Avie Gold (ArtScroll/Mesorah, 1990)

▶ *Sand and Stars: A Jewish Journey Through Time*, Yaffa Ganz and Rabbi Berel Wein (Shaar Press, 1994-1995)

▶ *Take Me to the Holy Land* (a youngster's tour of Eretz Yisrael), Tsivia Yanofsky (ArtScroll/Mesorah, 2000)

▶ *Take Me to the Zoo* (lions, elephants and snakes in the midrash and nature), Tsivia Yanofsky (ArtScroll/Mesorah, 2003)

▶ *The Jewish Experience: 2,000 Years* — A collection of significant events, Rabbi Nachman Zakon (Shaar Press, 2002)

Where Do I Go From Here?

An insider's list of websites and contact information

At this point, I hope that you are interested in exploring Judaism in greater depth. To help you in your journey, I have included brief descriptions of several national and international organizations (in alphabetical order) that I have worked with personally. Many additional resources are also easily accessible.

Aish Hatorah

▸ **www.aish.com**
▸ **Jerusalem World Center: (from US) 011-972-2-628-5666**
▸ **See website for local US branches**

Aish HaTorah is a network of educational centers where Jews from all backgrounds can explore their heritage in an open, nonjudgmental atmosphere. Aish operates programs in over 100 cities on five continents, with its World Center located in Jerusalem, directly opposite the Western Wall. Aish offers lectures, family programs, singles events and tours to Israel. The Aish.com website features insightful and practical wisdom on spirituality, relationships, work and current events, weekly Torah portion, holidays and a live Western Wall camera. Its flagship **Discovery** seminar (**www.discoveryproduction.com**) is a dynamic one-day program that explores the rational basis for Jewish belief and practice. Aish instructors conduct Discovery and related seminars in the US and around the world. Another project of Discovery is a national placement service where Jews can experience an authentic Shabbat or find home hospitality when traveling. Simply call **1-800-SHABBAT** for Shabbat placement nationwide. Discovery can also be reached by calling 212-921-9090.

Chabad/Lubavitch

▶ **www.Chabad.org**

Chabad-Lubavitch maintains over 3,300 institutions, such as Chabad Houses, literally around the world. They are located on college campuses, cities and towns, and in isolated parts of the globe where they are virtually the only Jews for miles around. These outposts are directed by more than 4,000 emissary families who consider it a privilege to dedicate themselves to the religious and personal welfare of the Jewish people worldwide. Inspired by the principles and teachings of the centuries-old Chabad chassidic movement, today's Chabad/Lubavitch continues the programs set in motion and guided by Rabbi Menachem Mendel Schneerson o.b.m., the seventh Lubavitcher Rebbe. Its institutions and emissaries are non-judgmental and open to every Jew, whatever his or her level of knowledge and observance, offering a wide array of programs, including classes, prayer services, hospitality and information.

Gateways Organization

▶ **www.gatewaysonline.com**
▶ **1-800-722-3191**

Gateways provides the information on Judaism that thinking Jews need to make informed decisions about life. Classes, seminars and home-study groups in numerous locations are attended by thousands of Jewish people of every background and level of observance. The Gateways flagship programs are its weekend and holiday seminars held at luxurious hotels in New York, New Jersey and Connecticut, and in communities across the country. At the seminars, you can hear a wide range of fascinating lectures (perhaps by Rabbi Becher himself!), enjoy sumptuous kosher cuisine, experience a traditional Shabbat, have your children entertained at the Gateways day camp, attend a campus networking group or a singles program. The Gateways website also provides an "Ask the Rabbi" service, as well as updates on lecture schedules and upcoming seminars and programs. Gateways presenters lecture and serve as scholars-in-residence across the country and internationally at community centers, synagogues, schools, educational programs and college campuses.

Isralight

▶ **www.isralight.org**

Isralight empowers Jews to experience Jewish wisdom by sharing a Judaism that is relevant, profound, spiritual and joyful. The inclusive, multidimensional approach offers a warm, welcoming atmosphere where participants from all backgrounds feel comfortable and spiritually nourished. The Isralight curricula and method address the needs of all Jews — from those with little or no formal Jewish education, to affiliated and observant Jews — who yearn for the spiritual spark that can ignite their souls. It offers spiritual retreats, online Jewish information and inspiration, as well as study and touring in Israel.

Jewish Learning Exchange

▶ **(44)-020 8458 4588**
▶ **www.jle.org.uk**

A London branch of Ohr Somayach in Jerusalem (see below), the Jewish Learning Exchange (JLE), is an educational and social center for young Jews (17 to 35 years old). It offers an extensive program of weekly classes in the JLE center, as well as in home groups; young professionals groups, schools, international guest-speaker tours across the UK, young couples groups (including premarriage courses) and social events. In addition, the JLE runs several highly successful educational tours to Eastern Europe each year and short and long-term programs in Israel.

Jews for Judaism

▶ **www.jewsforjudaism.com**

Jews for Judaism is an international organization that provides a wide variety of counseling services, along with education and outreach programs that enable Jews of all ages to rediscover and strengthen their Jewish heritage. Jews for Judaism is a positive resource, utilized and endorsed by all denominations of Judaism. Its warm and open-minded approach successfully reaches out to individuals who have been lured away from Judaism by other belief systems or through assimilation.

Jews for Judaism was established in 1985. It has become the Jewish community's leading response to the multimillion dollar efforts of cults and evangelical Christians who target Jews for conversion. In addition to the website, it has branches in New York, Los Angeles, Baltimore/Washington DC, Toronto and Johannesburg.

Neve Yerushalayim Educational Network

- ▶ **www.nevey.org**
- ▶ **Israel (from US): 011-972-2-654-4555**
- ▶ **New York: 212-422-1110**

Neve Yerushalayim College, established in Israel in 1970, offers women a high-quality Jewish studies curriculum relevant to contemporary Jewish life. Students are accepted into the college with prior backgrounds in Jewish studies that range from the most rudimentary to the highly advanced. Every student, however, finds a course of study suitable to her level that is both challenging and stimulating. The college has three schools, each teaching in a different language, but all with a parallel educational program. The Neve School of General Jewish Studies (SGJS), the largest and oldest of the schools, has an English-speaking student body that originates from the United States, Canada, Great Britain, South Africa and Australia. In addition, Neve Yerushalayim has seminary programs for recent graduates of secular and religious high schools, academic programs that provide a dual curriculum of advanced Jewish and secular studies that lead to a bachelor's degree, a master's program in Family Counseling, and other professional training for careers that serve the Jewish community.

Ohr Somayach

- ▶ **www.ohr.edu**

"Educating Jews whom no synagogue or movement will ever find."

Ohr Somayach, based in Jerusalem, gives Diaspora youth coming to Israel in search of their roots a chance to experience Jewish learning in their own language, at their own pace and at an intellectual level that rivals and surpasses that of the Ivy League universities from which many have come. Ohr Somayach caters to outstanding college students and graduates — who are accomplished in secular studies, but have never found a comparable level of excellence in Jewish studies. Ohr Somayach's exceptional staff includes scholars who are former professors at leading universities in the United States and who are as conversant in Kant and Hegel as they are in Maimonides. They teach basic Talmud skills to small groups, offer individual counseling to young people at a crossroads in their lives and address the "big picture" issues that so preoccupy college students in their quest for meaning. The main center is in Jerusalem, with branches in the USA, Canada, South Africa, UK and Australia.

Outreach Judaism

▶ **www.outreachjudaism.org**
▶ **1-800-315-5397**

Outreach Judaism is an international organization that responds directly to the issues raised by missionaries and cults, by exploring Judaism in contradistinction to fundamentalist Christianity. The organization's goal is to generate a lasting connection between Jewish families and Judaism through building immediate awareness of the current Hebrew-Christian movement worldwide.

Partners in Torah

▶ **www.partnersintorah.org**
▶ **1-800-STUDY-4-2**

Partners in Torah matches Jewish adults who want to learn more about their heritage with a friendly, personal Torah trainer or "mentor" for up to an hour a week of Jewish study and discussion. Meetings are either in person ("Partners in Person") or over the phone ("TelePartners"). It is self-directed and is driven by the personal, often varied interests, of each student. With your personal Torah trainer, your mind will enjoy an incredible workout. In just one hour a week you can learn about Judaism from a starting point that works for you. Among other possibilities, you can learn to read Hebrew, discuss Jewish philosophy, or take a dip in the vast and brilliant ocean of the Talmud. The program is strictly one on one and is offered free of charge. Free phone cards are provided when necessary to accommodate long-distance study.

Project Genesis – The Judaism Site

▶ **www.torah.org**
▶ **1-888-WWW-TORA or 410-602-1350**

Project Genesis is a pioneer in the use of the Internet for Jewish outreach and education. It has developed a successful network of "on-line classes" — a program of ongoing Jewish studies executed entirely by email — that provides the rich content archives on their website, Torah.org. Project Genesis also launched the Internet's largest archive of Torah audio, **www.torahmedia.com**, and provides information and access to a wide range of Torah programs, speakers and special events. Their latest innovation is **www.jewishanswers.org** — Answers for Your Jewish Questions. They've assembled a team of nearly 50 rabbis around the world to field questions in a variety of topic areas. You can send your question to a rabbi via email, and expect a helpful reply. You also will find easy access to a searchable archive of past questions, and information on further learning opportunities.

The Jerusalem Fellowships

- **www.jerusalemfellowships.org**
- **1-800-FELLOWS (355-5697)**

Thousands of qualified young adults from the United States, Canada, England, South Africa, South America and Australia have received scholarships for Jerusalem Fellowships, the most popular college-age short-term study trip to Israel. Many of the programs are sponsored by "Birthright." The Jerusalem Fellowships combine touring Israel, studying the richness and relevance of Judaism, and meeting Israel's top leadership. Jerusalem Fellows have met with Israeli prime ministers, mayors and other prominent leaders from across the political spectrum.

Meor: College Program

- **admin@meor.org**
- **1-800-284-4110**

Meor is a collegiate educational organization in the USA. It offers sophisticated, relevant and personal campus programs and has attracted thousands of students to its Israel trips, learning opportunities, and Shabbat experiences. A staff of dynamic scholars are available on over 25 campuses to connect with students. The Maimonides Leadership Fellowship program creates Jewish literacy, communal bonding and develops student leaders through a 10 week classroom and experiential learning curriculum. Meor offers exciting international trips that enable students to broaden their Jewish horizons and knowledge around the globe. Summer study retreats and Capitol Hill internships allow students to learn concepts of leadership and apply what they have learned. Meor seeks to create Jewish lives of meaning and develop a new generation of leaders.

Glossary

A

Adar (I and II) Sixth month of the Hebrew calendar. Jewish leap years add a second month of Adar, making 13 months in that year.

Aleph Beit First two letters of the Hebrew alphabet and the term for the Hebrew alphabet.

Aleinu Prayer that concludes all services, traditionally attributed to Joshua.

Al Hanissim Prayer included in the Silent Prayer and Grace After Meals on Chanukah and Purim.

aliyah Literally, "ascent." Referring to the act of immigration to the Land of Israel as well as calling someone to "go up" to say a blessing on the Torah during a synagogue service.

Amidah Literally, "the standing," referring to the Silent Prayer, the central prayer of all services that is recited while standing.

amud The lectern from which the *chazzan* (cantor) or leader of prayers leads the service.

Aneinu A prayer inserted in the Silent Prayer on Fast days, asking God to answer our prayers in the merit of our fasting.

Arachin A tractate which discusses the dedication of a person's financial value to the Temple.

aravot Willow branches that are used on the festival of Sukkot as one of "the four species."

Arba Minim The "four species" of plants — willow, palm branch, citron and myrtle — that are held during prayers on the festival of Sukkot.

Aron Kodesh The Holy Ark, the cabinet which contains the Torah scrolls in the synagogue.

Ashrei First word of Psalm 84, verse 5; the introduction to Psalm 145, recited in prayers three times every day. Many prayers, such as *Ashrei*, are named for the first word of the prayer.

Aseret Yemei Teshuvah The Ten Days of Repentance, from Rosh Hashanah (the New Year) to Yom Kippur (the Day of Atonement) inclusive.

Ashkenazim Jews of European origin.

Av 11th month of the Hebrew calendar.

Avinu Malkeinu "Our Father, Our King," a moving prayer of supplication recited on fast days and during the Ten Days of Repentance.

Avodah Zarah Idol worship. Also the name of a tractate dealing with the laws pertaining to idol worship.

B

ba'al koreh Reader of the Torah scroll in the synagogue.

Babylonian Talmud Vast compendium of laws, explanations, discussions and application of Jewish law, written in Babylonia and completed in about 500 C.E. Also known as Gemara. Like the Mishnah, it is divided into tractates.

Bar Mitzvah (celebration) Celebration of a boy turning 13 years old and becoming obligated in the privileges and commandments of Jewish law.

bat Daughter, or daughter of.

bar/bat mitzvah (person) A boy who has just turned 13 or a girl who has just turned 12 who now has the privileges and obligations of an adult in Jewish law.

Bava Batra Tractate dealing with property and inheritance laws.

Bava Kamma Tractate dealing with torts and damages.

Bava Metzia Tractate dealing with property, contracts and employment laws, as well as business ethics.

B.C.E. and C.E. Before the Common Era and Common Era. Rather than using B.C. and A.D. (to designate calendar years), both of which explicitly refer to Jesus as a reference for the era, many non-Christians use these terms to refer to the more neutral "common era."

bedekin Veiling of the bride by the groom just before the *chuppah* ceremony.

bein hametzarim "Between the tragedies" referring to the period between the fast of the 17th of Tamuz (a fast day commemorating the breaching of the walls of Jerusalem by the Babylonians c. 500 B.C.E.) and the fast of the 9th of Av (commemorating the destruction of the First Temple by the Babylonians and the Second Temple by the Romans in 70 C.E.).

beit din Jewish court, usually consisting of a panel of three judges.

beit midrash House of study, usually referring to a synagogue that is used mainly for study of Torah.

Beitzah Tractate dealing with the laws of the festivals.

ben Son, or son of.

Bentching Yiddish for "blessing" referring specifically to Grace After Meals.

berachah (sing.), **berachot** (pl.) A blessing, blessings.

Biblical law A law that is either explicit in the Five Books of Moses, is based on an Oral Tradition received by Moses at Mt. Sinai, or was derived from the text using the rules of exegesis of the Oral Tradition.

bikur cholim Visiting the sick and taking care of their needs.

Bikurim The first fruits of a harvest, brought as an offering in the Temple.

bimah Platform in the center of a synagogue from which the Torah is read; lectern.

Birchot Hashachar Morning blessings of gratitude to God recited before the Morning Service every day.

Birkat Hamazon Grace After Meals.

Book of Jonah Book of the Bible about the prophet Jonah that is read in synagogue on Yom Kippur.

Borei Nefashot Blessing recited after eating food that is not made from grains, and is also not grapes, wine, figs, dates or olives.

Braita Section of the Mishnah containing ideas alluded to in the Mishnah, but not considered the main body of Mishnah.

Brit (or Bris) Milah The covenant of circumcision, also the ritual of circumcision itself.

C

Chadash New grain harvested after Passover before Shavuot, which may not be eaten.

Chag HeAsif Festival of the Gathering, Biblical name for the festival of Sukkot.

Chag Habikurim Festival of the First Fruits, Biblical name for the festival of Shavuot.

Chagigah Festive offering brought to the altar in the Temple. Also the name of a tractate.

chalakim Talmudic time measure. There are 1080 *chalakim* in an hour, so each *chelek* (sing.) is about 3⅓ seconds.

challah The small piece of dough that is taken and burned before baking bread. The term also refers to the braided bread that is prepared for Sabbath meals.

chanukiah Candelabra of eight branches that is lit on the festival of Chanukah.

Chashmonaim Hasmoneans (standard transliteration) were the Jews who fought against Greek oppression and rule in Israel c.140 B.C.E. It is the family name of the priestly family of Matityahu and of Judah the Maccabee.

Chassid (Chassidim, pl.) Various groups of Ashkenazic Jews who follow the ideology and practices of Rabbi Israel Baal Shem Tov and his disciples. The Chassidic movement originated in the Ukraine and Podolia in the beginning of the 18th century. Male Chassidim are usually identifiable by their distinctive clothing of long, black suits, fur hats called *shtreimels* (worn on Sabbaths and festivals) and *peot*, long earlocks. They emphasize joy, sincerity and spontaneity in the service of God, as well as the need to attach oneself to a great person, a Rebbe, for inspiration and guidance.

chavruta Aramaic term for a Torah-study partner.

chazakah Presumptive title to something.

chazzan Cantor, a singer who leads services in the synagogue.

Cheshvan 2nd month of the Jewish calendar.

chessed Kindness.

chessed shel emet Literally, "Kindness of truth," referring to kindnesses performed for the deceased.

Chevra Kadisha Holy Society, referring to the group of people who take care of the deceased and prepare them for burial.

chillul Hashem Desecration of the Name of God. Usually referring to an improper action done by one who represents a Torah-observant lifestyle.

cholent Stew traditionally eaten on Shabbat at lunchtime.

Chol Hamoed Intermediate days of the festivals of Sukkot and Passover.

chukim Statutes, usually referring to laws of the Bible that have no apparent explanation.

Chullin Tractate dealing with the kosher dietary laws.

chuppah Wedding canopy under which the Jewish wedding ceremony is held.

Clouds of Glory The clouds that surrounded the Jewish people during their sojourn in the Sinai Desert after the Exodus from Egypt. The clouds indicated God's presence and providence.

Code of Jewish Law Sixteenth-century work of Jewish law by Rabbi Joseph Caro of Safed, Israel.

D

da'at Knowledge or perception.

daven or davening (Yiddish) pray, praying.

Day of Judgment A term for Rosh Hashanah, the festival of the New Year.

Days of Awe The period of Rosh Hashanah and Yom Kippur.

Diaspora Dispersion of the Jews throughout the world.

divrei Torah Words of Torah, a Torah thought delivered orally.

drashah Sermon.

dreidel Four-sided toy top, used by children on Chanukah.

E

Elul 12th month of the Hebrew calendar. The month preceding Rosh Hashanah and Yom Kippur and hence heavily focused on introspection and repentance.

Emor One of the Torah portions: Leviticus, Chapters 21 to 24.

Emunah Belief or faith.

Eretz Yisrael The Land of Israel.

Eruvin Tractate dealing with the laws of property definitions and the prohibition of carrying on the Shabbat.

etrog Citron. A citrus fruit used on Sukkot as one of the "four species."

Exile A reference to either the current worldwide dispersion of the Jews, or to the Babylonian Exile.

ex nihilo (Latin) "from nothing," referring to God's creation of the world from a total void; something from nothing.

Exodus The Exodus of the Jewish people from Egypt after 210 years of slavery and oppression. Also, the second book of the Five Books of Moses.

ezrat nashim Women's section of the synagogue.

F

fleishig (Yiddish) adj. Referring to food made of meat, or meat by-product.

G

gadol Literally, big. Sometimes used to mean an adult or a great rabbi.

Gemara The part of the Talmud that expounds on the Mishnah.

Gemilut Chassadim Bestowing kindness.

Gittin Tractate of the Mishnah dealing with the laws of divorce.

golah, galut Exile.

Golden Calf A statue created as a substitute for Moses, taken to be a god by some, at Mount Sinai soon after the Revelation. The sin of worshipping the Golden Calf was a grievous development with long-lasting repercussions. Described in Exodus, Chapter 32.

Grace After Meals A series of blessing recited after eating a meal that includes bread.

grogger Noisemaker used by children on Purim to make noise and obscure the name of the evil villain Haman when it is read in *Megillas Esther*.

H

Hachnassat Kallah Helping a bride obtain her wedding needs.

hadas, hadassim Myrtle, a plant used on Sukkot as one of the "four species."

Haftarah Section of the Prophets read in synagogues on Sabbaths and festivals after the reading of the Torah.

Hakafot Literally, circuits, referring to the custom of circling the *bimah* with the Torah scrolls on Simchat Torah.

Hakotel Hama'aravi The Western Wall of the Temple Mount in Jerusalem.

Halachah Jewish law.

Hallel Selections from Psalms recited during prayers on festivals; Psalms 113 to 118 with added blessings.

hamantashen Triangular dough cakes with a filling (usually of poppy seed), eaten on the festival of Purim.

"Hanerot Hallalu" "These candles..." a prayer recited while lighting the Chanukah candles.

Hashem Literally "the Name." Out of respect for God and His Name, He is often referred to as "the Name."

Hatarat Nedarim Release from vows, customarily performed before Rosh Hashanah.

Havdalah Ceremony marking the end of Shabbat.

Hebron City in central Israel where Adam and Eve, and the Jewish Patriarchs and Matriarchs, Abraham and Sarah, Isaac and Rebeccah, Jacob and Leah, are all buried.

Holy Ark The box of gold and wood that contained the Tablets of Law and was kept in the Holy of Holies, the innermost, most sanctified chamber of the Temple.

Holy Temple The Temple in Jerusalem in ancient times. The first was built by King Solomon and destroyed by the Babylonians. The second was built after the Jews returned to Jerusalem from Babylonia. It was later destroyed by the Romans.

I

ikarim Principles of belief.

Iyar 8th month of the Hebrew calendar.

K

Kabbalah Jewish mysticism.

Kabbalat Shabbat Prayer service for the beginning of Shabbat.

Kabbalist Scholar of the *Kabbalah* (mysticism).

Kaddish Prayer recited in public by mourners and/or by the leader of a prayer service.

Kashrut The Jewish dietary code.

kallah Bride

katan Small, sometimes used to mean a minor.

kavanah Intention, also concentration during prayer.

kedushah Holiness.

Keritut Name of tractate dealing with prohibitions that carry Divine punishment.

ketubah Marriage contract.

Ketubot Tractate dealing with the laws of the marriage contract.

Kiddush Hachodesh Sanctification of the New Moon (new month) by the Jewish court, the Sanhedrin.

Kiddush Levanah The blessing recited over the reappearance of new moon each month.

Kiddushin The act of sanctifying a marriage; also the name of a tractate dealing with the laws of marriage.

kilayim Prohibited mixtures of seeds.

Kinot Elegies. Liturgical poems mourning the destruction of the Temple and the exile recited on the fast of the 9th of Av.

Kislev Third month of the Hebrew calendar. Chanukah occurs on the 25th of Kislev.

kittel Plain, white robe worn by men on Yom Kippur, at the Passover Seder and by the groom at his wedding.

klaf Parchment on which are written Torah scrolls, *tefillin* and *mezuzot*.

Kohen (sing.), **Kohanim** (pl.) Male descendant(s) of Aaron the High Priest, brother of Moses.

Kol Nidrei First prayer recited in the synagogue on the night of Yom Kippur, the Day of Atonement.

kollel Post-graduate Torah study program for married men.

kosher Complying with the Jewish dietary laws.

Kotel The Wall, referring to the Western Wall of the Temple Mount.

Ktav Ashurit An ancient Hebrew script used for Torah scrolls, *tefillin* and *mezuzot*.

L

Lag B'Omer 33rd day of the Omer, the time between the festivals of Passover and Shavuot.

Lashon Hara Lit."evil tongue," slander, libel, gossip and unethical speech.

L'chaim "To life!" Customary Jewish toast.

"Lecha Dodi" Song in the Friday night service welcoming the Shabbat. Composed by Rabbi Shlomo Alkabetz in Safed, Israel, in the 16th century.

Levi (sing.) **Leviim** (pl.) Male descendant(s) of the Tribe of Levi, known as a Levite.

lulav Palm branch, one of the "four species" used on Sukkot.

M

Maariv Evening service, known by *Sephardim* as *Arvit*.

ma'aser Tithes. Percentages of the agricultural produce of the Land of Israel that were given to Priests, Levites and the poor. Some tithes were also eaten in Jerusalem by the owner of the produce. Also refers to the custom of separating a tenth of one's income for charity.

Machpelah Literally double, the name of the double cave Abraham purchased in Hebron in which to bury his wife, Sarah.

machzor (sing.), **machzorim** (pl.) Prayerbook(s) for the festivals.

Maftir Final section of the weekly Torah portion read in synagogues on Shabbat and festivals.

Maggid The section of the Passover Seder when the story of the Exodus is told.

Makkot Plagues, specifically referring to the Ten Plagues in Egypt. Also the name of a tractate.

manna Food that miraculously fell from heaven to feed the Jewish people while in the Sinai desert, as detailed in Exodus, chapter 16.

Maot Chittim Lit. "money [to purchase] wheat." Money collected for the poor before Passover to help them celebrate the festival.

"Maoz Tzur" Poem sung after lighting the Chanukah candles.

marror Bitter herbs eaten at the Passover Seder.

Matanot La'evyonim Gifts to the poor given on the festival of Purim.

matzah Unleavened bread eaten at the Seder and throughout Passover.

Mazal Tov! Two Hebrew words, "Mazal" — meaning "Divinely decreed conditions of life," or "fortune;" and "tov" — meaning "good". This is a greeting or blessing usually said to people on happy occasions. Commonly mistranslated as "Good luck."

mechitzah The screen which separates men and women in the synagogue.

megillah Lit. scroll, usually referring to one of the books of the Bible known as scrolls — Esther, Ruth, Song of Songs, Lamentations and Ecclesiastes.

melachah Prohibited activity on Shabbat.

Melaveh Malkah Festive meal eaten after Shabbat.

Menorah The seven-branched candelabra in the Holy Temple in Jerusalem.

mezuzah, mezuzot (pl.) Parchment with sections of the Bible inscribed, rolled up in a case and placed on the doorpost of a home.

mikveh Ritual pool.

milchig Adj. referring to foods that are dairy.

Minchah Afternoon service.

minhag Custom. A practice that is not in the Torah, and was not legislated, but is commonly practiced by Jewish communities.

minyan Quorum of ten adult men necessary for certain communal prayers.

Mishloach Manot Presents of food sent to friends on Purim.

Mishnah Central, primary text of Jewish law. Edited by Rabbi Judah the Prince in Israel c. 200 C.E.

mitzvah (sing.), **mitzvot** (pl.) The 613 commandments of the Torah. They are divided into 248 imperatives (you shall), sometimes known as "positive commandments" and 365 prohibitions (you shall not), sometimes known as "negative commandments."

"Modeh Ani" "I give thanks." First words of the first prayer recited upon waking up in the morning.

mo'ed festival.

muktzeh Things which may not be moved (or handled) on Shabbat or festivals.

Musaf Additional service after the morning service recited on Shabbat, festivals and other special occasions.

mussar The study of ethics and personality development.

N

Nedarim Tractate dealing with the laws of vows.

ne'eman Faithful or reliable.

nefesh Soul or life force.

Ne'ilah The "closing of the gates," the last prayer on Yom Kippur.

neshamah Soul.

netilat yadayim Ritual washing of hands before eating bread and upon waking in the morning.

Nissan Seventh month of the Hebrew calendar, during which Passover occurs.

nusach Format of prayers.

O

Olam Haba The World to Come, the afterlife.

Omer The period of time between Passover and Shavuot.

Oral Torah, Oral Law or Oral Tradition The laws, rules and information transmitted by God to Moses on Mt. Sinai and transmitted verbally, person to person, until it was recorded in the Mishnah, Zohar and Midrash c. 170 - 200 C.E.

orlah Fruit produced by a tree during its first three years of growth, which may not be eaten.

P

parochet Curtain in front of the Ark in the synagogue.

parshah A section of the Five Books of Moses. The entire Five Books are read publicly in the synagogue each year.

The section read on a particular week is called a *parshah*.

Parshat Hashavua The portion of the week, as explained above.

parve Neutral; a food that is neither meat nor dairy, such as eggs, fruit, or vegetables.

paschal lamb Offering brought to the Temple in Jerusalem on the eve of Passover.

payah, payot, (pl.) Sidelocks.

Peah The corner of a field (in the Land of Israel) which is supposed to be left uncut, for the poor to harvest. Also the name of the tractate dealing with the laws of *Peah*.

Pesachim Tractate dealing with the laws of Passover.

pikuach nefesh A life-threatening predicatment.

Pirkei Avot Ethics of the Fathers, a tractate of the Mishnah dealing with ethics and virtues.

P'sukei D'zimrah Aramaic, "Verses of Song," the introductory part of the morning service, consisting primarily of Psalms.

R

Rabbinic law A law that was legislated by the Sanhedrin, the Jewish supreme court. The earliest Sanhedrin existed at the time of Moses (c. 1300 B.C.E.) and the last Sanhedrin was convened c. 350 C.E.

Rebbe Rabbi who is the leader of a Chassidic group.

Revelation Referring to God's giving of the Torah to the Jewish people in a public revelation on Mount Sinai, as detailed in Exodus Chapters 19, 20, 24, 32, 33 and 34.

Rosh Chodesh New month, the minor festive day or days at the beginning of each Hebrew calendar month.

Rosh Hashanah The two-day festival marking the beginning of the New Year, also known as the Day of Judgment. Also the name of a tractate dealing with the laws of the Hebrew calendar.

S

Sanhedrin   The Jewish supreme court, consisting of 71 sages, which existed from the time of Moses, c. 1300 B.C.E., until c. 350 C.E. Also the name of the tractate dealing with the laws of the Sanhedrin, jurisprudence, punishment and evidence.

Seder   The meal and service mandated on the first two nights of Passover, during which the story of the Exodus is told, and *matzah*, bitter herbs and four cups of wine are consumed.

sefer   Book.

Sefer Torah   Torah Scroll.

Sefirot   Ten manifestations of God's Will.

Selichot   Prayers of repentance recited from just before Rosh Hashanah until Yom Kippur, and on fast days.

semichah   Rabbinic ordination (certification).

Sephardim   Hebrew for "Spaniards," refers to Jews of Spanish, Portuguese, Middle Eastern and African origin.

Seudat Havraah   The first meal fed to mourners as they begin the mourning period. This meal should be provided by others.

seudat mitzvah   A meal that is eaten to celebrate the fulfillment of a *mitzvah* (commandment).

shaatnez   A garment in which wool and linen are combined.

Shabbat   Sabbath, the day of rest, starting just before sundown on Friday and ending after nightfall on Saturday.

Shacharit   Morning service.

shamash   Sexton, religious functionary in the synagogues, responsible for the functioning of prayer services.

"Shanah tovah"   "[Have a] good year!" Greeting on Rosh Hashanah, the Jewish new year.

Shas   The entire Mishnah or Talmud.

Shechinah   Divine Presence.

shechitah   Kosher slaughter of an animal.

Shehecheyanu   Blessing recited at moments of great joy.

Shema   The section of the Bible which contains the declaration of Jewish faith, "Hear O Israel: The Lord is our God, the Lord is One" (Deuteronomy 6:4), and the three paragraphs which are recited every day during prayers (Deuteronomy 6:4 to 6:9, Deuteronomy 11:13 – 21 and Numbers 15:37 – 41).

Shemoneh Esreh   Lit., Eighteen blessings, the term for the silent prayer or *Amidah*, the central prayer of all services.

Sheva Berachot   Seven blessings recited at weddings and during the celebratory meals in the following week.

shiur, shiurim (pl.)   Class or lecture.

shivah   Lit. seven, referring to the 7-day period of mourning for a close relative.

shliach tzibur   Leader of the prayer service.

Shma Koleinu   Blessing in the *Amidah*.

Shmittah   Sabbatical year for the land (in Israel), occurring every seven years.

shofar   Hollowed out ram's horn, blown on Rosh Hashanah.

shteitl (sing.), *shtetlach* (pl.).   Yiddish term for a small town or towns.

shul   Yiddish, literally "school"; refers to a synagogue.

Shulchan Aruch   Code of Jewish Law.

Shvat   Fifth month of the Jewish calendar.

Siddur   Prayer book.

simanim   Special foods eaten on the night of Rosh Hashanah symbolizing prayers, hopes and blessing for the new year.

Simchat Beis Hashoeivah   The water-drawing ceremony in the Temple and the accompanying festivities. This ceremony was held on the intermediate days of Sukkot, and many communities commemorate the festivities today.

Simchat Torah   Celebration of the completion of the yearly cycle of reading the Torah.

sinat chinam   Baseless hatred.

Sivan Ninth month of the Hebrew calendar, during which the festival of Shavuot occurs.

siyum Celebration on the completion of study of a Talmudic tractate.

sofer Scribe.

Sofrim Tractate dealing with the laws of the Torah scroll.

sufganiyot Donuts, traditionally eaten on Chanukah.

sugya Section of Talmud dealing with a particular subject.

sukkah A temporary dwelling in which Jews eat, sleep and live in during the festival of Sukkot.

Sukkot "Festival of Booths."

T

Ta'anit Fast day.

Ta'anit Esther The Fast of Esther, immediately preceding Purim.

Tachanun Prayer of penitence and repentance recited on most weekdays during the morning and afternoon services.

tahor Ritually pure.

tallit Prayer shawl. A large four-cornered garment with *tzitzit* (fringes), worn by men during morning service.

tallit katan Small *tallit*. A four-cornered, fringed garment worn by Jewish males.

talmid Student.

talmid chacham Lit., wise student, a Torah scholar.

Talmud The edited discussions, explanations, applications and legislation of laws in the Mishnah. The Talmud also contains explanations of verses in the Bible, ethical instruction, mysticism and practical advice. The two versions are the Jerusalem Talmud, edited in Israel in 350 C.E. and the Babylonian Talmud, edited in Babylon in 500 C.E. Both are written in Aramaic and form the primary text for all Jewish law.

Tashlich Custom of symbolically casting sins into the depths of the water, usually performed on the afternoon of Rosh Hashanah.

tamei Ritually impure.

Tamuz Tenth month of the Hebrew calendar.

Tanach Acronym for *Torah* (Five Books of Moses), *Nevi'im* (Prophets), *Ketuvim* (Writings).

tcheilet Blue-colored dye that was used in the production of wool *tzitzit* fringes on garments.

tefillah Prayer.

tefillin Phylacteries: two black, square, leather boxes with straps, containing parchments with sections of the Torah inscribed on them. *Tefillin* are worn by men every weekday during the morning service. The commandment is found in Deuteronomy, Chapters 6 and 11.

Tehillim Psalms. Book of the Bible written principally by King David consisting of prayers to God. Much of the prayer service is based on the Psalms.

Ten Plagues The ten plagues that God visited upon the Egyptians before the Exodus, described in Exodus Chapters 7 to 12.

tenaim Lit., conditions, referring to a contract signed by the parents of the bride and groom delineating obligations regarding the wedding.

teshuvah Repentance.

Tevet Fourth month of the Hebrew calendar.

Tishah B'Av The Fast of the Ninth (*tishah*) of (*b'*) Av, mourning the destruction of the First and Second Temples and all the tragedies of the Jewish exile that ensued.

Tishrei First month of the Hebrew calendar. The festivals of Rosh Hashanah, Yom Kippur and Sukkot all occur in Tishrei.

Torah Usually refers to the Five Books of Moses, also known as the Pentateuch or in Hebrew as *Chumash*. However, it is sometimes used as a generic term for the whole body of Jewish literature, including the whole Tanach, the entire Oral Tradition and all the commentaries.

treifah, treifot (pl.) In common parlance, means not kosher in general; specifically refers to an animal with a fatal injury or disease, which is not permitted to be eaten.

T'rumah Donation, referring to one of the agricultural taxes in Israel that was given to a Kohen.

Twelve Tribes of Israel The descendants of the 12 sons of Jacob: Reuven, Shimon, Levi, Judah, Issachar, Zebulun, Gad, Asher, Dan, Naphtali, Joseph (later divided into Manasseh and Ephraim) and Benjamin.

tzedakah Charity.

tzitzit Fringes worn on the corners of four-cornered garments in accordance with the commandment in Numbers 15:37- 41.

tzniut Modesty.

U

Ushpizin Literally, guests, referring to the seven spiritual "guests" — Abraham, Isaac, Jacob. Moses, Aaron, Joeph, and David — who join us in the sukkah.

V

Viduy Confession, referring to the confession recited during prayers on Yom Kippur and the confession recited by those near death.

W

World to Come Life after death, or the existence of the soul in a purely spiritual world after leaving the body.

Written Law Another term for the books of the Bible.

Y

Yaaleh veyavo Prayer added to Silent Prayer on festivals and on the New Moon (new month).

Yahrzeit Anniversary of a death.

yarmulka Skullcap.

yeshivah, yeshivot (pl.) Academies of Torah study.

Yiddish Middle-German adopted and adapted by Ashkenazic Jews as a Jewish language. Written in Hebrew letters and incorporates many Hebrew and Aramaic words.

Yom Kippur Day of Atonement, a day of fasting and prayer.

Yoma Tractate dealing with the laws of Yom Kippur.

Yom Tov, Yamim Tovim (pl.) Lit., "A Good Day," reference to a festival.

Z

Zemirot Traditional songs sung at the Shabbat meals.

Zman Time. Often refers to a specific time a *mitzvah* must be performed.

Zman Matan Torateinu "The time of the giving of our Torah." The festival of Shavuot as referred to in the prayers.

Zohar Central books of the Jewish Kabbalistic tradition, written by the students of Rabbi Shimon bar Yochai in the Land of Israel in about 200 C.E.

Index

The Table of Contents lists additional topics that may not be included in this index.

Lashon Hara 340, 341

Leah 260, 466

Levites 46, 177, 274, 393, 442, 444, 471, 479

Levy family 9, 11, 52-55, 74-76, 102-106, 123-125, 155-158, 170, 171, 183, 184, 202-206, 226, 227, 307, 308, 366, 367, 420-422

Luria, Yitzchak 182, 261

Ma'aser kesafim 274, 363

Maccabees 91, 167, 169, 170, 261, 306, 471, 472

Maharal of Prague 218, 453, 483

Maimonides 16, 44, 117, 136, 147, 150, 168, 208, 234, 263, 273, 316, 323, 338, 339, 341, 345, 356, 360-362, 374, 376, 377, 380, 394, 409, 410, 419, 428, 485

Marital intimacy 21, 26, 27, 43, 133, 140, 243, 283, 284

Marriage contract (ketubah) 21, 32, 482

Mechitzah 24, 253

Melaveh Malkah 107

Messiah 40, 90, 118, 119, 224, 237, 376 386, 439, 471, 477

Mezuzah 21, 123, 314-317, 326, 327, 387, 403, 436

Midrash 405, 483

Mikvah 27-29, 126, 132, 179, 229, 363, 482

Miriam 468, 470

Mishloach Manot 183, 184, 186

Mishneh Torah 10, 356, 360, 377, 483

Mitzvah, mitzvot 17, 19, 26, 37, 38, 43, 44, 46-50, 60, 66-68, 71, 73, 125, 135, 141, 146-148, 151, 156, 158, 160, 172, 173, 181, 185, 199, 208, 223-225, 248, 270, 273, 276, 319, 321, 324-326, 329, 330, 337-339, 349, 356, 359, 363-365, 393, 395-398, 402-404, 406, 410, 414, 434, 435, 459

Modesty 281-284, 289, 318

Mohel 44, 45

Monotheism 168, 195, 377, 380, 386, 466, 467

Moral relativism 372

Morality 43, 49, 86, 116, 166, 168, 241, 285, 286, 295, 303, 316, 318, 336, 344, 346, 362, 372, 375-377, 380, 385, 394, 395, 397, 399, 404, 412, 413, 467

Mordechai 178, 181

Moses 32, 46, 67, 83, 88, 89, 91, 106, 115, 132, 135, 138, 157, 169, 191, 197, 221, 222, 238, 247, 251, 268, 317, 321, 340, 380-385, 387, 432, 442, 443, 445, 467-470, 475, 476

Mount Meron 219, 220

Mount Sinai 49, 89, 90, 106, 119, 132, 148, 155, 168, 189, 192, 217, 218, 221-225, 227, 238, 248-252, 321, 342, 382, 384, 402, 415, 432, 443, 468, 469, 476

Nachmanides 26, 60, 86-88, 167, 198, 251, 261, 267, 273, 283, 317, 337, 372, 410, 485

Nebuchadnezzar 177, 178, 238, 240, 471, 481

Nehemiah 122, 260, 471, 481

Oral tradition, Oral Torah, Oral Law 82, 97, 100, 105, 148, 169, 321, 322, 325, 383, 476, 481

Paganism, idolatry 85, 87, 89, 197-199, 238, 241, 286, 298, 378-380, 477, 482

Parkes, James 270

Passover Seder 191, 199-202, 204-206, 209, 211, 212

Pidyon haben 46, 47

Pluralism 371

Rabbi Akivah 90, 121, 132, 218, 219, 236, 237, 365, 394, 395

Rachel 466

Rashi 67, 267, 335, 345, 410, 443, 453, 484

Rebecca 22, 260, 466

Recanati, Menachem 37

Revelation of the Torah 90, 132, 192, 217, 220-224, 238, 249, 252, 376, 382, 384, 415, 443, 469, 476

Rosh Chodesh 83, 84, 88, 89

Ruth 224, 230, 470, 480

Sa'adiah Gaon 237, 248, 422, 484

Sabbath (Shabbat) 40, 41, 43, 44, 59, 69, 82, 88, 95-102, 104-108, 110, 131, 140, 154, 166, 174, 207, 208, 229, 243, 273, 325, 329, 343, 363, 375, 393, 403, 442-444, 482, 486

Sabbatical year, Shmittah 274, 357

Sacks, Jonathan 373

Sanhedrin 83, 84, 167, 271, 410, 439, 458

Sarah 42, 259, 260, 466

About the Author

*R*abbi Mordechai Becher, originally from Australia, is a Senior Lecturer for the Gateways Organization, one of the fastest growing and most successful adult education providers in North America. He lectured at Ohr Somayach College in Jerusalem for 15 years, served in the Israel Defense Forces and taught in training programs for rabbis and educators. Rabbi Becher received his rabbinic ordination from the Chief Rabbinate of Israel and the Chief Rabbi of Jerusalem. He has co-authored two books on contemporary issues in Jewish law and has responded to thousands of legal, ethical and philosophical questions on the "Ask the Rabbi" website on the Internet. His expertise in applying classic Jewish concepts to contemporary life has made him a sought-after lecturer around the world. A student of comparative religion, archaeology and history, he is on the speakers list of the Israeli Consulate in New York. He lives with his wife, Chavy, and their six children in Passaic, New Jersey.

Rabbi Becher is available to speak on the following topics, among many others:

1. The Shabbat: Who Invented the Weekend Anyway?
2. Too Many Mitzvot? Or Why Is Judaism so Nitpicking?
3. Do You Have to Be Religious to Be Spiritual?
4. Getting Up on the Right Side of Bed, or Why Do We Pray?
5. Ten Commandments of Jewish Parenting
6. Judaism, Love and Intimacy

7. Seeds of Conflict: Spiritual and Religious Roots of the Arab-Israel Conflict
8. Free Will and Conditioning: A Delicate Balance.
9. In Pursuit of Pleasure
10. What Is Kabbalah? (Audio-visual presentation)
11. Occupied or Liberated: Whose Land Is It Anyway?
12. The Rabbi Made Me Do It! Accuracy of the Oral Law
13. Where on Earth Is the World to Come? The Concept of Life After Life
14. Why Do Good Things Happen to Bad People and Bad Things to Good People?
15. The Miracle of Jewish Survival (Audio-visual presentation)
16. Unearthing Ancient Mysteries: Archaeology and the Bible (Audio-visual presentation)
17. Jerusalem, Eye of the Universe (Audio-visual presentation)
18. Simon the Just and Alexander the Great: The Meaning of Chanukah
19. Ancient Hatred, Modern Passion: Judaism, Christianity and "The Passion" (Audio-visual presentation)
20. No Fear: Living Without Fear in an Age of Terror

Rabbi Becher can be reached at rabbibecher@yahoo.com.